THE EMILY DICKINSON HANDBOOK

The EMILY DICKINSON HANDBOOK

EDITED BY

Gudrun Grabher
Roland Hagenbüchle
Cristanne Miller

UNIVERSITY OF MASSACHUSETTS PRESS *Amherst*

Copyright © 1998 by
The University of Massachusetts Press
All rights reserved
Printed in the United States of America
LC 98-29853
ISBN 1-55849-169-4
Designed by Dennis Anderson
Set in Janson Text with Poetica display by Keystone Typesetting, Inc.
Printed and bound by BookCrafters

Library of Congress Cataloging-in-Publication Data

The Emily Dickinson handbook / edited by Gudrun Grabher, Roland Hagenbüchle, Cristanne Miller.
    p. cm.
    Includes bibliographical references and index.
    ISBN 1-55849-169-4
    1. Dickinson, Emily, 1830–1886—Handbooks, manuals, etc.   2. Women and literature—Massachusetts—History—19th century—Handbooks, manuals, etc.   3. Women poets, American—19th century—Biography—Handbooks, manuals, etc.   I. Grabher, Gudrun.   II. Hagenbüchle, Roland.   III. Miller, Cristanne.
PS1541.Z5E396   1999
811'.4—dc21
[b]   98-29853
                                                                                 CIP

British Library Cataloguing in Publication data are available.

Contents

Editors' Preface

*S*tudents of Emily Dickinson have often regretted the fact that there is no one source for quick reference containing basic and up-to-date information on the poet's life, her art, the manuscripts, and the current state of Dickinson scholarship in general. The essays collected here are meant to fill this gap. They reflect the many facets of Dickinson's œuvre as well as the principal trends in current Dickinson studies. The editors have been fortunate to persuade a number of internationally known critics from both the United States and overseas to write essays expressly for this *Handbook*, scholars who represent their several fields with authority and expertise. Their contributions to this volume reflect the fact that the field of Emily Dickinson studies has been thoroughly internationalized at the same time that the poet's œuvre has gained an international readership. Translation of Dickinson's poems into other languages and discussion of her works are now truly global and intercultural phenomena.

The overall organization of the *Handbook* is self-explanatory. For ease of use, individual essays have been structured as follows:

Each essay provides a historical overview of the relevant issues under scrutiny.

The essays offer detailed discussions of important aspects pertaining to the fields in question.

Unlike encyclopedic entries, each of the several essays reflects the author's own perspective, presenting a distinct point of view, at times a controversial one.

The *Handbook* has not adopted a standard convention of reference to Dickinson's texts since this is an area fiercely debated at present. To simplify reference for our readers, however, we have asked all contributors to include reference to Thomas H. Johnson's numbering, even if they use Franklin's facsimile edition of the *Manuscript Books* in citing Dickinson's texts. Where there is no specific mention of a text source, reference is to the Johnson editions of the *Poems* (cited as P) and the *Letters* (cited as L). Franklin's edition of the poems is cited with fascicle or set number as F, followed by the page number(s). Prose fragments are cited with PF, following Johnson's numbering in the *Letters*. References to Johnson's introductory remarks to the *Poems* appear as *P*, followed by the roman numeral page number(s).

The bibliography at the end of the volume does not aim at completeness. It provides bibliographical information for the primary and secondary works cited in this volume and hence may serve as a guide to both earlier and current studies of Dickinson without being comprehensive. Our index, primarily of names but also including a few repeated topics, will guide readers to some of the multiple connections between the essays and within the fields of Dickinson study.

We intend this collection of essays to provide a useful source of information for both undergraduate and graduate students needing an introduction to the various aspects of Dickinson scholarship. At the same time, we hope that the essays included in this *Handbook* will also prove useful to scholars who are looking for a quick review of, or entry into, areas of Dickinson studies with which they are less familiar. While the *Handbook* cannot represent all aspects of Dickinson study, it should give general and scholarly readers a solid introduction to a number of aspects of the field that have proved most crucial and enduring. The reader will emerge with a clear grasp of how critical thinking on Emily Dickinson has evolved in recent times.

ACKNOWLEDGMENTS

The editors want to express their gratitude to the University of Massachusetts Press, to its director, Bruce Wilcox, for his confidence in this venture, and to Pamela Wilkinson for her editorial assistance. Additionally, we are grateful for the support provided by our institutions, the University of Innsbruck, Austria, the Catholic University of Eichstätt, Germany, and Pomona College in Claremont, California. Barbara Clonts and Maria Meth deserve special thanks, as does Martina Antretter for setting up the index.

Gudrun Grabher,
Roland Hagenbüchle,
Cristanne Miller

INTRODUCTION

Richard Sewall

The Continuing Presence of Emily Dickinson

I am glad to welcome this *Handbook* into the world. It is another answer to the question proposed by a prominent American banker (and a man of literary inclinations) in 1891 when Dickinson's poems were first seeing the light of day. In October of that year, the banker, Samuel G. Ward, wrote a letter about Dickinson to Thomas Wentworth Higginson, who promptly sent it to Mabel Loomis Todd, whose daughter, Millicent Todd Bingham, in turn included it in her *Ancestors' Brocades* of 1945 (169–70). In a covering note to Mrs. Todd, Higginson began: "This is the most remarkable criticism yet made on E.D." It strikes me, a century later, as still remarkable (if only for its prophetic third sentence), and, as a reminder of certain essentials about Emily Dickinson, an apt introduction to the special studies of this book.

Leaving Narragansett Pier
Oct 11, '91

My dear Mr. Higginson:

I am, with all the world, intensely interested in Emily Dickinson. No wonder six editions have been sold, every copy, I should think, to a New Englander. She may become world famous, or she may never get out of New England. She is the quintessence of that element we all have who are of Puritan descent *pur sang*. We came to this country to think our own thoughts with nobody to hinder. Ascetics, of course, & this our Thebaid. We conversed with our own souls till we lost the art of communicating with other people. The typical family grew up strangers to each other, as in this case. It was *awfully* high, but awfully lonesome. Such prodigies of shyness do not exist elsewhere. We got it from the English, but the English were not alone in a corner of the world for a hundred and fifty years with no outside interest. I sat next to Jones Very for three years [in a Boston school] & he was an absolute enigma till he flashed on me with the Barberry Bush. [?] Afterwards he sought me at my office one day with his heart in his hands & said he had come to lay axe at my root, to bring to me the Spiritual Life. I was deeply touched to find that he had all the time thought me good enough for the axe! Did you know Ellen Hooper (born Sturgis) & do you know her poems? If the gift of articulateness was not denied, you had Channing, Emerson, Hawthorne[,] a stupendous example, and so many others. Mostly it was denied, and became a

3

family fate. This is where Emily Dickinson comes in. She was the articulate inarticulate. This is why she appeals to so many New England women.

You were fortunate and skillful in drawing her out.

> Believe me
> Sincerely yours
> Sam'l G. Ward
> 1608 K St., N.W.

1608 K. St., N.W.
Washington, D.C.

P.S. Was it one of your family or mine that came up from Salem one day and said to a "mutual" friend, "John is dead. He died yesterday. He didn't want much said about it."

In his note to Mabel Todd, Higginson added a few words about Ward: " . . . an early transcendentalist & writer in *Dial* but for many years a N.Y. banker & agent of Barings — a rich man with a wife." He might have added that Ward was an old-line New Englander (grandson of the colonial General Artemas Ward), that he had grown up in Boston with Jones Very and Ellery Channing (namesake and nephew of the great Unitarian), that he lived with his wife near Concord and was a close friend of Emerson and Thoreau (whom he helped financially). Ward's ranking Channing as first among the great New England "articulates" is, of course, a sheer anomaly, to be explained possibly by Ward's desire to please Higginson, whose first wife was Channing's sister. As a poet, Channing was honored in Concord mostly for his "promise" and his sociability. (He was near brother to Thoreau after the real one died.) Emily Dickinson wrote at least five letters, one of them accompanied by a copy of Emerson's essays, to Mary Channing Higginson.[1]

It is not by chance that Ward's interest in Dickinson's poetry should lead him at once into a little essay on New England Puritanism. Being *"pur sang"* himself, he understood the New England brand of "asceticism" (from Gr. *askein,* "to exercise" — in this case, one's talents); its tendency toward discipline and self-denial; its particular inwardness ("we conversed with our own souls," as Dickinson did in well over a hundred poems); its "shyness," which Ward equates with the lost art of communicating with others; and what it means to be "articulate" (born with a gift for words) in a community of "inarticulates" — all qualities, I suggest, essential to an understanding of Dickinson. Ward applies them to Dickinson long before they could be documented by her letters, which were not to appear in print until 1894 — for instance, Emily's relations with members of her family ("The typical family grew up strangers to each other"). Emily confirms this in letter after letter: "My father seems to me the oldest and oddest sort of a foreigner. Sometimes I say something and he stares in a curious sort of bewilderment though I speak a thought quite as old as his daughter. . . . And so it is, for in the morning I hear his voice and methinks it comes from afar & has a sea tone & there is a hum of hoarseness about [it] & a suggestion of remoteness as far as the Isle of Juan Fernandez" — which is about as far from Amherst, Massachusetts, as you can get. Sister Lavinia fares no better:

> Vinnie, Joseph, it is so weird and so vastly mysterious, she sleeps by my side, her care is in some sense motherly, for you may not remember that our amiable mother never taught us tailoring, and I am amused to remember those clothes, or rather those apologies made up from dry goods with which she covered us in nursery times; so Vinnie is in the matter of raiment necessary to me; and the tie is quite vital; yet if we had come up for the first time from two wells where we had hitherto been bred her astonishment would not be greater at some things I say. (R. Sewall, *Lyman Letters* 70–71)

Her mother may have been "amiable," but, as Emily told Higginson, "I never had a mother. I suppose a mother is some one to whom you hurry when you are troubled."[2] Brother Austin seems to have been closer to her than the others, but one picture of him still clings: standing over his father's coffin, he kissed him on the brow, saying: "There, father, I never dared do that while you were living" (Sewall, *Life* 1: 61). Cousin Clara Newman (Turner), who, with her sister Anna, lived with the Austin Dickinsons for ten years after she and her sister had been orphaned, said that she had never seen any outward sign of affection between members of the Dickinson family (cf. Sewall, *Life* 2: 324). As Ward says, "It was *awfully* high, but awfully lonesome."

For all his perception into the realities of Dickinson's family life and even her reclusiveness (surely there was more to it than "shyness"), it is still remarkable that he should have been interested in her poetry to the extent of associating her with the New England "Thebaists" and predicting its ultimate worldwide fame. (I take the "may" of the third sentence to be a banker's hedge.) But why he could think well enough of Channing's poetry to rank him, too, with the greatest (even if he did it partly to please Higginson) is hard to explain. Channing wrote a great deal, published mostly in *The Dial*, was devastated by one of the severest reviews Poe ever wrote, and never got beyond utter conventionality. And this was at the same time (1891) when most of the reviews were critical of Dickinson's "barbarisms," her faulty rhymes, skewed syntax, and bumpy rhythms — that is, her *un*conventionality — all of which bothered Higginson's conventional taste, too, and explain why he urged her not to publish. He was even reluctant to help in the editing. So his delight at this letter from Ward, a man of standing, is predictable. As if those "six editions" weren't enough — there were five more within a year — Higginson seems to be assuring Mable Todd that the current was going their way. Emily Dickinson was becoming a "presence."

It is good to have Ward's hearty, nonprofessional, on-the-spot response to the poems as they first became known to the world. His interest was "intense" — and he a banker. There was something prophetic, in view of to-day's developments, in his sense that Dickinson, as an "articulate inarticulate," was providing a voice for women. But his great distinction was that he saw her as a *popular* poet not only for New England, and for New England women, but for the world, a "presence" here to stay.

That her presence is continuing — and growing — hardly needs document-ing. The evidence is on every hand as book after book and essay after essay roll off the presses. In my small Massachusetts college (Williams) in the late 1920s, only a range of hills from Amherst, she wasn't even mentioned — and I ma-jored in American literature. As time went on, a few of her lyrics appeared in anthologies and from there in survey courses. Then, in the 1950s, after several decades of piecemeal publication, the complete poems and letters made it possible to see her work steadily and see it whole. It was as if America (and now the world) had discovered a new treasure. As a colleague of mine, a specialist in American poetry, said, "I never knew what was there." Two major studies in recent years, Alfred Kazin's *An American Procession* (1984) and Harold Bloom's *The Western Canon* (1994), contain chapters on Dickinson (a phenomenon unheard of in the 1920s) that give what could be called official sanction to her continuing presence — Kazin in America, Bloom in the world. Kazin: "She was the first modern writer to come out of New England." Bloom: "Except for Shakespeare, Dickinson manifests more cognitive originality than any other Western poet since Dante."

The few poets who speak a New Word, who re-create and refresh the lan-guage, are often difficult, "strange" (Bloom's word).[3] It takes time to accom-modate ourselves to the shock of their new idiom, new rhythm, the "inner music" that, for instance, Mabel Todd was the first to hear in Dickinson's poems. Such poets, in a sense, have to be domesticated, given shape and form and meaning before we take them to ourselves; before teachers feel confident enough to present them to their classes and parents don't think twice before giving their collected works as graduation gifts; before, that is, they become a presence in our lives. In the 1920s we wrestled with T. S. Eliot for longer than I like to admit; even our teachers didn't know what to say about him, or about Faulkner, whose convoluted, sometimes page-long, sentences seemed outra-geous. Now we talk with (relative) assurance among their pages — and among Dickinson's poems.

But, as with the greatest, the strangeness never wears off. Shakespeare is still a mystery, and so is Dickinson. We still argue about *Hamlet*, and those poems will never let us rest. But we have, at least, a sense of direction. In play after play, Shakespeare challenges a mystery, Dickinson in poem after poem;

and from each we learn a little more about *what it means to be alive*. The purport of Kazin's "modern" and the dynamic of Bloom's "cognitive originality" are embedded in a quatrain of Dickinson's maturity that has become, for me, a continuing presence:

> Experiment escorts us last —
> His pungent company
> Will not allow an Axiom
> An Opportunity (P1770, late 1870)

Notes

1. Frederick T. McGill, Jr.'s *Channing of Concord* (1967) gives a lively picture of Channing's life in Concord and his friendship with Thoreau and Emerson. It is frank about his failure as a poet. Ward's relationship with the Concordians is amply documented.

2. From Higginson's report to his wife about a conversation with ED (see L342b).

3. "Strangeness, as I keep discovering, is one of the prime requirements for entrance into the Canon" (Bloom 292).

BIOGRAPHY

MARTHA ACKMANN

Biographical Studies of Dickinson

$\mathcal{I}$n 1996 the town of Amherst, Massachusetts, installed a public sculpture in honor of its two most celebrated literary residents. Just east of Sweetser Park near the town common two silhouetted steel figures face each other as if engaged in conversation. Robert Frost, looking settled and professorial, sits casually on a low flat rock. His hand rests on his knee as he appears to listen to the words of his opaque partner. Emily Dickinson perches with less certainty atop a second, more sizable, boulder. Her legs do not touch the ground, and she sits erect, starched, impatient — a bit of a schoolgirl ready with the next answer or question. Based on an 1845 rendering of the poet, the Dickinson likeness presents her as have some of our twentieth-century perceptions. She is more a girl than a woman, more precocious than profound, more two-dimensional than fully formed. Yet at dusk the sculpture prompts an altered impression, as it casts a shadow much taller, much bolder, and with edges more ambiguous than its more corporeal likeness. It is as though in escaping the confines of the sculpture Dickinson is reminding us that even a substance as formidable as steel cannot wholly capture her. "Biography first convinces us of the fleeing of the Biographied — ," Dickinson wrote near the end of her life (L972). She may be right. Part of our interest in Emily Dickinson is our unremitting desire to track down answers to questions about the poet's life that continue to elude scholars. Although we clearly have learned much over the past century about the life of Emily Dickinson, we also recognize that much remains to be fully understood. As every biographer of the poet knows, Dickinson always remains a bit on the loose.

Thomas Wentworth Higginson was among the first who sought to know more about Dickinson by actually "see"[ing] her and the way she lived her life. Writing in 1869, Higginson confessed, "Sometimes I take out your letters & verses, dear friend, and when I feel their strange power, it is not strange that I find it hard to write & that long months pass. I have the greatest desire to see you, always feeling that perhaps if I could once take you by the hand I might be something to you; but till then you only enshroud yourself in this fiery mist & I cannot reach you, but only rejoice in the rare sparkles of light. . . . I think if I could once see you & know that you are real, I might fare better" (L330a).

Turning to the poet's biography as a means for understanding her literary work has long been a valuable approach in Dickinson scholarship. Biographical studies have been central in correcting one of the most far-reaching myths associated with Dickinson, namely, that the poet lived apart from the cultural forces of her time. Especially in the last twenty-five years, Dickinson biographies increasingly have concentrated on the context in which Dickinson created her poetry — the historical, religious, economic, familial environment — in order to show that the poet lived with the door more than a little ajar.

Biographical studies of Dickinson also have been pivotal in demonstrating the creative interplay between the poet's life and her poetry. Ideas expressed through Dickinson's actions or in her letters to family and friends often are similarly articulated by the personae of her poems, illuminating overarching tenets of her thought and the ways in which she transformed the quotidian into poetry. Moreover, comparisons between Dickinson's biography and ideas expressed in her poetry also have been essential in highlighting the poet's incongruities, reminding us that to understand the Dickinson life and art most fully we must recognize her paradox.

Inasmuch as biographical studies have provided valuable ways for understanding the context in which Dickinson created and the substance and arc of her thought, over the last century they occasionally have run too recklessly with speculation, arguing that individual lines of poetry chronicle specific events or relationships in Dickinson's life. Williams H. Shurr's *Marriage of Emily Dickinson: A Study of the Fascicles* (1983) is a case in point. And yet, just as Higginson would find — and perhaps always knew — biographical details of the poet's life provide no single key for unlocking the enigmatic genius of the literature. Studies such as Shurr's that offer a quintessential biographical clue for decoding the poetry may temporarily dazzle but ultimately fade in intrinsic reductiveness. Certainly Dickinson was unequivocal when it came to the question of her work's autobiographical intent. "When I state myself, as the Representative of the Verse — it does not mean — me — but a supposed person" (L268), she proclaimed to Higginson three months after their correspondence began. Biographies of Emily Dickinson have contributed significantly to our understanding of the poet when they have acknowledged the power of her imagination and resisted reducing her poetry to autobiographical notations.

In contemplating the circumstances and design of her own life, Emily Dickinson plainly observed, "My life has been too simple and stern to embarrass any" (L330). Although in 1869 Dickinson could not have anticipated the number of scholars who would offer interpretations of her life, her single sentence nevertheless has served as a kind of comforting reassurance to any biographer who has set out to confront the considerable challenges posed in capturing a life of Emily Dickinson. Surveying biographical studies of the poet from the earliest reflections of her contemporaries through the most recent works of the 1990s proves that the poet was right, in a way. Few biographers have been chagrined by their efforts as a wealth of portraits have contributed to our ever-emerging perceptions of the poet.

The depictions of the poet offered in the 1890s provided an essential beginning for an analysis of Dickinson biographical study since these views present insights into personal relationships with the poet and firsthand, although certainly subjective, accounts of interacting with her. (Mabel Loomis Todd's recollections, of course, are the exception since Todd never actually saw Dickinson.) The two most useful of these personal accounts are Susan Dickinson's perceptive obituary of the poet published in the *Springfield Daily Republican* and Higginson's entire correspondence with Dickinson, especially his August 1870 letter detailing their first meeting in Amherst. His 1891 *Atlantic Monthly* article recounting the history of their relationship also is instructive. Susan Dickinson's essay is prescient in addressing many of the questions that have become the focus of biographical research over the last 100 years: questions regarding the poet's artistic taste, audience, and creative impetus. Her perceptiveness regarding Dickinson's work and the intimate tone of the obituary also underscore the importance of Susan Dickinson's relationship with the poet, a subject currently gaining much deserved attention. Higginson's correspondence, of course, provides considerable biographical information since he often assumed an interviewer's role and asked questions of Dickinson to which family either knew the answer or felt too presumptive to ask. More than most of Dickinson's correspondents, Higginson sensed that what he was coming to understand about Dickinson had historical importance and so posed questions and recorded her responses as though he were gathering information for posterity. Dickinson answered many of his queries, and even her evasiveness toward other questions is revealing for what it seeks to skirt. Higginson's 1870 recollection of their first visit presents perhaps the most quoted primary source in Dickinson biography, the record of an afternoon when "she talked soon & thenceforward continuously — & deferentially — sometimes stopping to ask me to talk instead of her — but readily recommencing" (L342a). Mabel Loomis Todd's prefaces to the first editions of the poems and letters offer another valuable initial glance at Dickinson biography as one can see the myth begin to take shape through Todd's emphasis on the poet's seclusion and what she views as Dickinson's fragile nature.

Conrad Aiken in writing about the second period of Dickinson's biographical research lambasted the efforts of Genevieve Taggard and Josephine Pollitt for their use of conjecture and their interest in identifying a suspected object of Dickinson's love. Although it would appear that Aiken would find nearly any biographical portrait of the poet useless, his point regarding a blurring between the subject of the poetry and the life is well taken. What Aiken misses in Taggard's and Pollitt's studies, and what we have yet to see fully developed in Dickinson biography, is their attempt to render a sense of the life actually being lived. There is an immediacy and freshness to their narratives that make the academic literary biographies of the late twentieth century seem almost torpid. The 1930s were marked by two other important biographical contributions, one that advanced our understanding of the poet and one that obscured it considerably. George Frisbie Whicher's *This Was a Poet* (1938) was the first biographical study to examine in reliable detail the intellectual and social culture that influenced Dickinson's life, focusing on the poet's reading, her friends, and New England culture. Martha Dickinson Bianchi's *Emily Dickinson Face to Face* (1932), however, spins a tale of "a romantic figure" (38) flitting in the garden, dressing only in white, with hardly a word about writing poetry.

The three most important biographical studies of the 1950s were Rebecca Patterson's *The Riddle of Emily Dickinson* (1951), whose lasting significance rests in its assertion that women in the poet's life need to be taken seriously because the poet regarded them that way; Thomas Johnson's *Emily Dickinson: An Interpretive Biography* (1955), which serves as a companion piece to his variorum editions of the letters and poems; and Jay Leyda's indispensable *The Years and Hours of Emily Dickinson* (1960), a two-volume compilation of events, observations, and records related to Dickinson, which are arranged chronologically and gleaned from an exhaustive list of sources from newspapers to sermons to personal correspondence of acquaintances in the poet's life. Although not explicitly analytical, the weight of Leyda's raw biographical data argues that the lasting significance of a life can be best understood by examining dailiness, proving the poet's point (which Leyda cites in his introduction) that "Forever — is composed of Nows — " (P624). Although the information presented in *Years and Hours* has been mined by every Dickinson biographer since 1960, the enduring legacy of the book is its insistence that the continuing recovery of historical documents is at the heart of every biographical enterprise and that the need to tell the story of the poet's commonplace life, what Leyda calls "the tinier scale of the immediate, the intimate, the day-by-day — the 'Now,' " is where Dickinson biography should always begin (xix).

Without question the paramount achievement in Dickinson biography during the last century is Richard B. Sewall's *The Life of Emily Dickinson* (1974), the most comprehensive biography of the poet yet written. Continuing to emphasize the importance of the "recovery effort" of factual material that Leyda advocated, Sewall presents an impressive mass of new biographical information, most notably the revelation of the romantic relationship between Austin Dickinson and Mabel Loomis Todd. That Sewall relies much on the point of view of Millicent Todd Bingham, the daughter of Mabel Loomis

Todd, is undeniable, and his analysis of Susan Dickinson's role in the poet's life, for example, reflects Bingham's allegiance to her mother. Nonetheless, the biography is a generous, no-nonsense view of the poet, whom Sewall saw more as her father's daughter (the Norcross influence is not fully developed) than as an adult woman making independent choices regarding her work and relationships. Sewall's biography also demonstrates a reluctance to peer too deeply into what is termed the mystery of Dickinson's life, presenting itself as a kind of factual antidote to speculative studies that preceded it, John Cody's psychoanalytic *After Great Pain: The Inner Life of Emily Dickinson* (1971) chief among them. In terms of the biography's style, while highly readable, Sewall's work does not offer a narrative of the poet's life but instead presents the poet as seen through her relationships with individuals and ideas. Sewall describes this style as one that uses "Jamesian 'reflectors,' [in which] each relationship gives back a phase, or facet, of her character, her personality, and her literary purpose" (12). In Sewall's *Life of Emily Dickinson* we see the poet brilliantly revealed as we never have before. What we miss, however, is a sense of her life's movement and dailiness: a depiction of the life being lived.

Whereas Sewall's biography emphasizes the establishment of a factual record, Cynthia Griffin Wolff's *Emily Dickinson* (1986) offers a provocative interpretation of Dickinson's life that focuses on her struggle with religious faith and against the gender expectations of the time. Wolff's portrait of Dickinson paints a far more conflicted and lonely poet who was deeply affected by her emotionally distant parents and by the oppressive evangelical fervor of the time. Analyzing Dickinson's interior life as it relates to her poetry is Wolff's primary objective; once the poet begins writing verse in the 1850s, Wolff's study shifts into literary criticism and leaves biography behind.

During the last quarter century, the most significant development in Dickinson biography has been the evolution of feminist scholarship. The publication of Elsa Green's "Emily Dickinson Was a Poetess" (1972), Suzanne Juhasz's "'A Privilege So Awful': The Poetry of Emily Dickinson" (1976), and Adrienne Rich's especially arresting "'Vesuvius at Home': The Power of Emily Dickinson" (1976) all charged that the poet's identity as a woman informed her poetry, that her gender was a source of power, and that questions of gender be incorporated into our analyses of the poet. These essays were followed by critical studies by scholars such as Paula Bennett, Joanne Dobson, Jane Eberwein, Betsy Erkkila, Lillian Faderman, Sandra Gilbert and Susan Gubar, Margaret Homans, Wendy Martin, Adalaide Morris, Barbara Mossberg, Vivian Pollak, Dorothy Oberhaus, and many others who have blended contextual biographical interpretations with literary criticism to offer new feminist readings of Dickinson's work. While feminist scholarship has had its greatest impact on literary analyses of Dickinson's work, it has affected biographical studies in two significant ways: it has established the importance of Dickinson's relationships with women and female culture, and it has interjected new questions related to gender into our investigations of the poet. An example of these new queries is Aífe Murray's current work on Dickinson family domestic Margaret Maher, which examines the poet's use of Hiberno-English and Gaelic linguistic constructions. Not only does Murray's work present a new analysis of Dickinson's poetic syntax, it also posits intriguing questions about how the poet's interactions through housekeeping with "Maid Maggie" affected both Dickinson's attitudes toward ethnicity and her literary production.

In considering the direction of Dickinson biography during the last twenty-five years, one also is struck not so much by what has developed as by what has slowed down. The essential work of expanding the factual record related to Dickinson's life and excavating and analyzing relevant biographical document has noticeably lagged since the publication of Sewall's *Life of Emily Dickinson*. It is as if scholars assumed that all that can be recovered has been recovered and that what remains is the task of reinterpretation, not discovery. There are notable exceptions, the most important of these revelations being Karen Dandurand's 1984 discovery of additional poems published in the poet's lifetime, which has led scholars to reconsider a range of assumptions connected to the poet's seeming reluctance to publish. Barton Levi St. Armand's *Emily Dickinson and Her Culture: The Soul's Society* (1984) also is especially useful in its examination of the ways in which the poet was influenced by American Victorian culture. Polly Longsworth's *Austin and Mabel: The Amherst Affair and Love Letters of Austin Dickinson and Mabel Loomis Todd* (1984) and Vivian Pollak's *A Poet's Parents: The Courtship Letters of Emily Norcross and Edward Dickinson* (1988) both made available intriguing documents that broaden our knowledge of the poet's family and in particular their attitudes toward romance, love, and societal expectations. A second work by Longsworth, *The World of Emily Dickinson* (1990), substantially increased the photographic record on the poet's environment.

The essential work of recovery and analysis that Leyda called for in 1960 and that Sewall continued in 1974 is in a sense even more important to current biographical studies than it was a generation before. The further removed we are historically from the years during which Emily Dickinson lived, the more documents are in danger of being destroyed or vanishing entirely. Three recent biographical discoveries I have uncovered underscore that primary material indeed remains to be found just as it is threatened by extinction. The first of these discoveries are educational records of Emily Norcross Dickinson that alter our perception of her intellectual sophistication and prompt a new reading of the poet's indelible judgment, "My Mother does not care for thought — " (L261).

Recently I recovered in a basement boiler room of Wilbraham-Monson Academy in Massachusetts documents from the early years of Monson Academy which were salvaged after a fire at the Academy in 1953 and then forgotten after Monson and Wilbraham merged in 1971. The records verify that for over ten years Dickinson's mother attended the Academy, which was founded by her father, Joel Norcross, among others, and which served as a model for other progressive coeducational schools in the Commonwealth, including Amherst Academy, which was founded ten years later in 1814. In attending Monson Academy Emily Norcross received an impressive education that very few young women were permitted to obtain. Among the courses open to Emily Norcross at Monson were classes in Latin, natural philosophy, astronomy, chemistry, botany, physiology, geography, algebra, logic, history, and rhetoric.[1] At a time when many people considered educating girls an unnecessary expense or a threat to females' reproductive capacity, the Norcross family and Emily Norcross herself clearly were nonconformists. Diantha Blodgett, who attended Monson Academy during the same period as Emily Norcross, reported that she "would tramp down and up that long hill to get all [she] could at the Academy." Blodgett's daughter explained that she "told me how they used to laugh at her for taking so much Latin and mathematics and wondered what she thought she was going to do with them, she a girl."[2] Mary Dickinson, writing to her brother Edward in 1822, expressed the sentiment of many who felt providing an intellectual experience for girls was a waste of time. She observed, "They have so little business to do in this town they are about undertaking to build a *Female Seminary*" (Edward Dickinson Papers). That Emily Norcross engaged in such an unconventional education at Monson and then continued her studies at Mr. Herrick's school in New Haven, Connecticut, is testimony to the value both she and her family placed on education. The poet, in this light, should be seen as following a tradition begun by her mother a generation before of young women exploring their minds within a culture that offered scant encouragement or validation for educating women.

Throughout her years at Monson, Emily Norcross received particularly fine training in the sciences. Joel Norcross was so interested in scientific education that he appealed to the Academy Board of Trustees to purchase scientific instruments from London in order further to enhance students' educational experiences. Monson had a close link to Yale University; many alumni came to teach at the academy and brought with them the innovative approach to natural and physical science that Benjamin Silliman pioneered at

Yale. Arguing that science could reveal truths about both the natural *and* the metaphysical worlds, Silliman trained a generation of scholars, including Edward Hitchcock. In 1848, when the poet enthused about "studying 'Silliman's Chemistry'" (L20) at Mount Holyoke Female Seminary, Dickinson quite possibly was recalling her mother's scientific education at Monson and the knowledge and appreciation of the natural world which she and other members of the Norcross family were likely to have shared with the poet.[3]

Science was not the only discipline in which Emily Norcross received an exceptional education. Monson Academy also required her to prepare weekly compositions and occasional declamations. Literary studies and oral renditions especially seemed to engage Monson students. While Emily Norcross attended the Academy, female students formed the Philomathean Society devoted to poetry readings, debates, and presentation of original compositions. An Emily Norcross manuscript at Harvard University's Houghton Library — in light of these recent discoveries — now bears special significance regarding her literary education. The manuscript is the only known example of Norcross's imaginative writing and was written while she was a student at Monson. Entitled "On Amusements: A Dialogue," the work is a moralistic, energetic debate between two confident young women arguing that time should not be wasted on follies and amusement and that spiritual reflection is essential. The dialogue is notable for one character's pronouncement that a life of retirement focused on the solitary contemplation of spiritual questions was worth pursuing, although apt to be misunderstood. The character Julia professes, "Do cherish these serious thoughts and I can assure you that you will find that peace which this world can neither give nor take away" (Norcross Family Papers). Emily Norcross's education at Monson Academy taught her that addressing "serious thoughts" was an appropriate and indeed obligatory responsibility for women. Moreover, she also demonstrated that those thoughts could find expression in imaginative writing.

Recognizing that Emily Norcross Dickinson did receive a superior education for her time and for her sex prompts us to reconsider Dickinson's seemingly disparaging comment about her mother's intelligence. Biographical interpretation up to this time had suggested that the poet was indicating that Emily Norcross Dickinson was a simple woman, not capable of intellectual pursuits, and clearly someone who could not comprehend her daughter's literary endeavors. The recent work in textual editing that Ellen Louise Hart has conducted, when placed alongside this recovery of biographical material, provides an intriguing new insight into the poet's statement "My Mother does not care for thought —" (L261). It is Hart's contention that Thomas Johnson did not correctly transcribe the capital "T" in the word "Thought," a proper noun Dickinson frequently used when referring to her poetry, not contemplation in general.[4] Rather than implying that Dickinson regarded her mother as an intellectual nonentity, the statement could mean that Emily Norcross Dickinson simply did not take a personal interest in poetry.

A second recent biographical discovery concerns Louise and Frances Norcross, the poet's "little cousins," and their associations with the literary elite of Concord, Massachusetts. Although Emily Dickinson certainly regarded the Norcross cousins with respect and fondness (her seventy-seven extant letters to them are among the most candid in her entire correspondence), early biographers have either denigrated or dismissed the women as unimportant. Mabel Loomis Todd initiated condemnation of them with her remark, "They adored her (Dickinson) like a god. . . . They were such geese" (Bingham, *Ancestors'* 238). Johnson, for example, in his 1955 *Biography* claimed "the girls" helped Emily with life's trivialities, lending support for "such minor realities as . . . relatives who came and went, spring housecleaning, or Vinnie's cats" (59). More recent studies have indicated that the Norcrosses deserve a second look which these new discoveries help to provide. Records and documents uncovered in archives in Concord reveal that Louise and Frances Norcross were actively involved in a range of political and cultural activities that brought them into frequent contact with influential figures such as Ralph Waldo Emerson. The discoveries are important for two reasons: first, they suggest that Dickinson had access to the professional world of literature through the Norcrosses, and second, a fuller understanding of the cousins more accurately reveals what they represented to the poet.

From 1874 when they moved to Concord until their deaths, the Norcrosses immersed themselves in a variety of activities including suffrage organizing, Bronson Alcott's Concord School of Philosophy, and fund raising to build schools for minorities in the South and West. In addition, Frances was particularly involved with a women's theater troupe which in 1888 produced an original play accompanied by an all-woman's orchestra that drew enthusiastic audiences from Boston and was reviewed favorably in the *New York Theatre Magazine*. Frances's obituary noted that she was "always actively interested in anything of a literary nature" (*Concord Enterprise*). Louise in describing herself underscored that she was "an ardent crusader for women, a whole-souled suffragist, and a lover of every progressive 'ism'" (Scharnhorst 484).

Of all the Norcrosses' many activities, none was more important to their relationship with Dickinson than their involvement with the Concord Saturday Club. Founded by Abbie May Alcott in 1876, the club was composed of fifty elected members including Bronson and Louisa May Alcott, William Ellery Channing, II, Ednah Dow Cheney, Ellen Emerson, Lydia and Ralph Waldo Emerson, Daniel Chester French, Robertson James, Frank Sanborn, and James Whitney. Both Louise and Frances Norcross were voted into membership in 1877 and remained members until their respective deaths. The purpose of the club was to pursue the study of literature, the arts, and general culture in bimonthly meetings at members' homes. The first meeting Frances attended on November 3, 1877, was representative of the group's intimacy and purpose. Meeting at the home of Lydia and Ralph Waldo Emerson, who lived two miles from the Norcrosses, nine members gathered to take part in a program organized by the hosts. The Emersons chose to read unpublished manuscripts that friends of theirs had shared with them, including a manuscript given to them by Henry David Thoreau (Saturday Club Files). Reading an unpublished literary manuscript was a common practice of the Saturday Club which acknowledged an author's right to privacy by asking no outsiders to be present at the reading and referring to the writer as anonymous if so desired. In describing the work of the club, the *Concord Freeman* in 1884 paid special attention to this practice of reading unpublished manuscripts, noting that "Many papers well known to fame have had their first reading before this club, and several articles by well-known writers of too personal a character for general publication have found their audience in it" (11 Jan. 1894).

Archival records do not indicate whether Louise and Frances Norcross shared any of Emily Dickinson's poems or letters with the Saturday Club. The topics of the meetings they hosted, unfortunately, are not noted. What can be determined, however, and what is of utmost importance is that through the Norcross cousins' involvement with the Saturday Club, Dickinson had before her an opportunity for circulating her manuscripts among a larger audience, for receiving literary critique, and possibly for eventual publication. The poet could have sought through Louise and Frances an influential liaison with the professional world of literature as she was aware of their Concord involvement. That no evidence exists indicating Dickinson sought her cousins' help in presenting her poems to the Alcotts, Emerson, and others suggests that she preferred another audience for her work — an audience composed of selected family and friends — and that she did not view publication as the overriding objective for her poetry.

A final biographical discovery concerns striking new evidence of Dickinson declaiming her poetry. Two independent recollections are now on record of the poet reciting her verse for family members. The first source to be recovered was Gary Scharnhorst's find of a 1904 letter to the *Woman's Journal* in which Louise Norcross observed: "I know that Emily Dickinson wrote most emphatic things in the pantry, so cool and quiet, while she skimmed the milk; because I sat on the footstool behind the door, in delight, as she read them to me. The blinds were closed, but through the green slats she saw all those fascinating ups and down going on outside that she wrote about" (Scharnhorst 485). The second record came from Sylvia Swett Viano, Dickinson's oldest living relative, in an oral history I conducted with her. Viano, who died in 1995, was the granddaughter of Anna Jones Norcross Swett, first cousin of Emily Dickinson. Swett's father was the poet's uncle Joel Warren Norcross, youngest brother of Emily Norcross Dickinson. As the only grandchild of Swett, Viano heard many recollections of her grandmother's frequent visits to the Dickinson Homestead. Dickinson was someone who would "capture you," Viano remembers her grandmother saying. But Swett's most vivid memory was of the poet declaiming her work. Reported Viano, "My grandmother said Dickinson would open the window or curtains and say poetically what she saw outdoors in the garden or a bird or whatever it was. My grandmother stood in awe . . . to hear this going on." Viano remembered her grandmother described the experience as observing Dickinson "talk poetry" (Ackmann 123). These two recollections reveal a Dickinson who — in an exceptionally demonstrative way — identified herself as a poet and selected members of her family as her audience. In declaiming, Dickinson was hardly the modest and reticent artist that we often have considered her to be. Certainly Dickinson at times assumed a diminutive pose; one has only to think of her initial letter to Higginson to recall the way she cast herself as Higginson's unschooled pupil. These new revelations regarding declamation suggest, however, that she also could adopt a proud and confident posture that unequivocally laid claim to her poetry. In addition, through declaiming her poetry, Dickinson could exert nearly total control over the way in which her verse was presented, regulating inflection, intonation, pace, and pause in precisely the manner she desired — control which she by necessity would have had to relinquish had she published her poetry.

The most unsuspecting remark Emily Dickinson ever made may have been her response to Thomas Wentworth Higginson when he asked to know more about her life. "But I fear my story fatigues you — ," she replied (L261). Nearly 140 years after her response, our interest in the life of Emily Dickinson remains as animated as Higginson's as we seek to know more about the woman whose startling poetry "captures" us just as it did Anna Norcross Swett. There are many areas of Dickinson biography that deserve more research. A fuller portrait of Lavinia Dickinson is necessary in order to convey the qualities that sustained the sisters' relationship for fifty-three years. Examining the periods in Dickinson's life that she spent outside the family home and away from Amherst would provide additional insights into the poet's independence and seclusion. More needs to be known about Elizabeth Holland, one of the poet's most intimate friends. Useful work could be contributed that builds on the research of Wand and Sewall, Bernhard, Guthrie, and Hirschhorn and Longsworth that considers the effects of the poet's eye problems. Dandurand's ongoing investigation into editors who solicited Dickinson's poetry is especially promising, as is the analysis of the poet's relationship with Susan Dickinson that is currently being produced by Ellen Louise Hart and Martha Nell Smith.

Biographical inquiries prompted by feminist scholarship and continuing excavation and recovery of primary material undeniably must inform biographical studies of Emily Dickinson in the next century. Moreover, biography needs to provide what other critical studies of the poet cannot, namely, a sense of her life as it was lived. Photographers have a term for the technique of capturing an image in which all distances from close-up to infinity remain in focus. Called "deep focus," the technique enables both the nearest and the most distant perspective to be clearly perceived.[5] Biographical studies of Emily Dickinson will be enriched by an approach that evokes both the intimate immediacy of her nineteenth-century life and our most current critical perspectives. Park Honan, author of *Jane Austen: Her Life*, refers to this biographical approach as creating the "historical present," presenting a dynamic portrait of the life as it was lived viewed through the lens of history.

Lastly, biographers also must work to represent Dickinson in her entirety, not as a poet only. Contemporary literary biographers, in their understandable urgency to delineate the ways in which writers' lives may have affected their writings, often present their subjects in almost disembodied ways as if head, hand, and pen constituted the whole human being and as though a linear narrative focusing on the pivotal steps the writer took to become a literary figure rendered a writer's life most realistically. Yet literary biography must explore those areas of a writer's life that may not be directly linked to an author's production of literature in order to demonstrate that lives are complex, often lacking in coherence, largely unpredictable, and richly unraveled. Future full-scale biographical studies of Emily Dickinson must strive for this more expansive consideration of the woman, bringing into focus both the writer and the depth of her world beyond the upstairs window.

Notes

1. Recovered records of Monson Academy do not indicate exactly which courses Emily Norcross took. The courses cited are some that were available to her at the Academy (Monson Academy Catalogue, 1819).

2. The source of this quotation is taken from a torn newspaper clipping found among the papers I recovered at Wilbraham-Monson Academy. The only identification on the clipping is a running headline, reading *The Springfield*.

3. Lavinia Norcross studied at Mr. Herrick's school in New Haven after her older sister studied there. In a letter Lavinia reported that she was attending Professor Silliman's lectures on the Deluge and was "being very interested" (Lavinia Norcross to Emily Norcross Dickinson, 22 July 1830, Norcross Family Papers).

4. I am grateful to Ellen Louise Hart for sharing her insight with me. Conversation, 23 June 1996.

5. Elizabeth Lambert kindly pointed out to me the concept of deep focus. Conversation, 11 July 1996.

FURTHER READING

Benfey, Christopher. *Emily Dickinson: Lives of a Poet.* New York: Braziller, 1986.

Morse, Jonathan. "Memory, Desire, and the Need for Biography: The Case of Emily Dickinson." *Georgia Review* 35.2 (1981): 259–97.

Sewall, Richard B. "In Search of Emily Dickinson." *Michigan Quarterly Review* 23 (1984): 514–28.

Van Dyke, Joyce. "Inventing Emily Dickinson." *Virginia Quarterly Review* 60 (1984): 276–96.

Wolff, Cynthia Griffin. "The Women in My Life." *Massachusetts Review* 24 (1983): 438–52.

Historical Context

Jane Donahue Eberwein

Dickinson's Local, Global, and Cosmic Perspectives

*I*t was probably to counteract readers' anticipated tendencies to caricature Emily Dickinson as some fragile, otherworldly creature that Mabel Loomis Todd and Thomas Wentworth Higginson introduced their editions of her poems with an opening group labeled "Life." Verses gathered under that rubric supposedly differed from those in the Love, Nature, and Time and Eternity groups by reflecting the poet's awareness of the world beyond her home and garden. Mrs. Todd had herself fallen under the spell of the mythic Emily back in 1881 when she first picked up from Amherst folklore an impression of this "*character* of Amherst," "the climax of all the family oddity," a spectral storybook figure blessed with a mind said to be "perfectly wonderful" (R. Sewall, *Life* 216). Finding, however, that many poems created by that mind bespoke a broad and disciplined education along with sharp observation of the local scene, these first editors attempted to foreground those that related their poetess to a familiar world.

In the process, they skipped over this minor example of her talent:

> What is — "Paradise" —
> Who live there —
> Are they "Farmers" —
> Do they "hoe" —
> Do they know that this is "Amherst" —
> And that I — am coming — too —
> Do they wear "new shoes" — in "Eden" —
> Is it always pleasant — there —
> Wont they scold us — when we're hungry —
> Or tell God — how cross we are —
>
> You are sure there's such a person
> As "a Father" — in the sky —
> So if I get lost — there — ever —
> Or do what the Nurse calls "die" —
> I shant walk the "Jasper" — barefoot —
> Ransomed folks — wont laugh at me —

> Maybe — "Eden" a'nt so lonesome
> As New England used to be! (P215)

Here is one of those poems that — on the surface, anyway — reinforce the image of Emily Dickinson against which most of her editors, biographers, and critics have contended since 1890. Spoken by a pitiful waif, it reflects a child's narrow perspective that constricts attention to home, town, region, and some materially conceived heaven. The speaker is limited by immaturity, anxiety, provinciality, and a reductive imagination. What comes across most strongly here is fear born of deprivation. The child's social class is ambiguous, though reference to "the Nurse" suggests that the speaker comes from a household with servants — more than the hired girls and gardeners known to comfortable Amherst families like the Dickinsons. That she or he classifies potential acquaintances either as farmers or not-farmers, however, suggests experience restricted to an agricultural economy. Perhaps the nurse enters the picture because our speaker is one of those pathetic little invalids so familiar in sentimental fictions of the time. Perhaps, on the other hand, there is a nurse because there are no parents, a conjecture aroused by doubts about the heavenly "Father." In the 1945 *Bolts of Melody* edition of this poem, Todd and her daughter introduced one change in line 9, substituting "homesick" for "hungry" to suggest that the speaker is already lost in the narrow confines of her or his local environment and dreads being similarly outcast for eternity. Poverty and insecurity come to mind in references to hunger as well as to the presence or absence of new shoes. It seems that this speaker has been laughed at by more fortunate children to the point of fearing continued scorn in heaven even though paradise otherwise proffers a welcome escape from New England's humiliations and isolation. If we are to imagine Emily Dickinson as the speaker of this poem, we can find bountiful evidence supporting her mythic self-image as lonely, childlike, timid, and too fragile to withstand the pressures of a world she never understood. This is not the kind of responsive and even controlling intelligence we expect of an artist, even supposing that the reading I have so far provided for this poem is complete and adequate.

Scholars, however, have convincingly dismantled this distorted image of Emily Dickinson as a fugitive in time and space by amassing detailed information about her life's circumstances. Convinced that "what is presently most needed in the study of the life and works of this enigmatic poet, who has been the subject of so much distorting gossip and legend, is the most factual treatment possible," Jay Leyda compiled his chronologically ordered documentary record of her likely range of awareness, listing year by year events in the Dickinson households, Amherst, the United States, and the world as experienced by her family's numerous associates or represented in publications the poet was known to read (the *Springfield Republican, Atlantic Monthly, Harper's,* and *Scribner's* among others) to demonstrate conclusively through *The Years and Hours of Emily Dickinson* that "she wrote more *in time,* that she was much more involved in the conflicts and tensions of her nation and community, than we have thought" (xix–xx). Leyda's documentary record provides abundant factual grounding for biographical, cultural, and critical studies along with inspiration to fill gaps remaining in our knowledge; lately, it has inspired Daniel Lombardo to sketch out in *A Hedge Away: The* Other *Side of Emily Dickinson's Amherst* a host of brief, entertaining, and sometimes scandalous narratives opening insight on local events as they impinged on the poet's consciousness.

Both of Dickinson's major biographers, Richard Sewall and Cynthia Griffin Wolff, build upon Leyda's example of coming to know this intensely private poet by gathering information about the many very public figures in her world even while acknowledging that available information about the woman herself makes a less enthralling story than the rumor-enhanced narratives biographers attempt to refute; nor do the facts go far to explain the poems. Sewall responds to this biographical challenge by accepting that, as an artist, Dickinson lived her life metaphorically in ways that call for interpretation. In developing his detailed *Life of Emily Dickinson,* he builds a context for her mystery by focusing attention on whatever can be known: chiefly her Dickinson family background and the distinctive familial rhetoric characteristic of her generation, the "War between the Houses" fomented by her brother's affair with Mabel Todd, information about the poet's childhood and schooling, her reading, and her many friendships. By demonstrating how much she meant in declaring "My friends are my 'estate,' " Sewall assaults impressions of her New England provinciality (9). By heeding the intellectual atmosphere of her home and town, he traces the origins of her metaphors. "She was not reared in a household of lawyers and treasurers for nothing," he observes; "she did not live in a college town for nothing" (10). Also recognizing how much more there is to tell about Emily Dickinson's companions than herself, about her poems' editing history than the circumstances of their creation, Wolff concentrates on placing the poet in an informative social-historical context, finding in her a subtle register of a time of crisis: "She lived in a time and place when God's grandeur still glimmered in the panorama of New England. Yet she never knew the dawning or even the noon of America's heroic age, but only the long shadows of its twilight; and later, she knew the darkness of the merely commercial, instrumental society that was to follow hard upon heroism's end" (*Dickinson* 9). Tracing her central metaphor of Dickinson as "pugilist poet" combating God, Wolff interprets the poetry in terms of her era's intellectual and spiritual currents. More amply than Sewall, she also places the poet within a world of nineteenth-century women, observing the rhythms and pressures of lives spent managing households, nurturing children, and tending the sick — often in the shadows of prominent men.

Other recent studies confirm these biographers' discoveries of Emily Dickinson's alert responsiveness to particular circumstances and ambient culture. In *Emily Dickinson's Readings of Men and Books*, Benjamin Lease demonstrates her "passionate involvement with family, with friends, with a cultural legacy of rebellion against orthodox answers to the religious questions of her time" by foregrounding her friendships with her spiritual counselor, Charles Wadsworth, and literary mentor, Higginson (xii). Paula Bennett, by contrast or complement, shows in *Emily Dickinson: Woman Poet* how "the poet not only lived her entire life 'at home,' but spent her life largely in a circle of women" (14). Like Lease, she focuses on Dickinson's reading — contemporary British women writers, in this case, rather than Shakespeare, the Bible, Watts's hymns, and seventeenth-century devotional writings. This context of an international nineteenth-century feminine culture leads Bennett to discovery of a distinctively gender-grounded poetic (19). Martha Nell Smith's focus in *Rowing in Eden* on the poet's intense relationship with her sister-in-law, Sue, represents another attempt to balance already well-documented discussions of Wadsworth, Higginson, Samuel Bowles, and Josiah Gilbert Holland as influences on Dickinson.

Paying close attention to the poet's relationships both with Sue and with their mutual friend Bowles, Judith Farr moves beyond biography in *The Passion of Emily Dickinson* and reads the poetry in its cultural context to reveal Dickinson's "passion to lead a life in and through art — her own and that of others" (viii), specifically art understood in the Ruskinian sense of Victorian high culture. Barton St. Armand shares that concern in *Emily Dickinson and Her Culture*, where he draws analogies between what Higginson identified as his friend's "Poetry of the Portfolio" and popular arts like quilting and scrapbook assemblage practiced by middle-class nineteenth-century American women as well as American folk art and Ruskin's aesthetics (considered in relation to Austin Dickinson's choice of paintings for The Evergreens). Like Karl Keller, whose *The Only Kangaroo among the Beauty* cleverly links Dickinson to her Puritan literary predecessors and to Robert Frost as well as to authors of her own period (Stowe, Hawthorne, Emerson, Whitman, Boston Bluestockings, and her own literarily ambitious circle of friends), St. Armand finds revealing affinities between Dickinson and the sentimental, aesthetic, and nature writers of her time.

Investigation of Emily Dickinson's environment, then, opens fruitful insight into her poetry's response to specific circumstances of place and time. From the first appearance of her poems, it has been recognized that her

rootedness in Amherst, Massachusetts, and particularly in the family household profoundly shaped her imagination. Martha Dickinson Bianchi, her
niece, stimulated public curiosity with books that blended family tradition,
personal reminiscence, and snatches of correspondence. *Emily Dickinson Face
to Face* and *The Life and Letters of Emily Dickinson* provided an idyllic image of
Homestead life that tended to generate myths in an attempt to deflect negative
attention from Austin and Susan Dickinson's marital discord. Millicent Todd
Bingham offered a slightly less self-interested perspective — though necessarily a more distant one — in *Emily Dickinson's Home*, her answer to Bianchi.
Among recent scholarly studies, Jean McClure Mudge's *Emily Dickinson and
the Image of Home* most fully relates the poet's inner space to the physical
designs and contrasting ambiences of her two houses: the Homestead, a brick
mansion built by her grandfather, where she was born and spent her first ten
years and to which she returned in 1855 to pass her remaining three decades,
and the Pleasant Street house of her adolescence and young womanhood — the
one Mudge says she associated with "the idyllic possibilities of home" (4).
Except for two terms at Mount Holyoke, two extended periods spent in Cambridge to get care for her eyes, a few weeks spent visiting her father in Washington, and some minor youthful excursions, Dickinson lived entirely within
the protective confines of "my Father's ground" (L330). By secluding herself
in late years and seeing virtually nobody beyond her immediate circle, she
freed space and time for creativity while fostering gossip about whatever may
have gone on within the Homestead and her brother's home next door.

Grasping for explanations of Emily Dickinson's strange reserve, Higginson
was the first to identify her father as key to her psychic formation. He wrote to
his wife about his 1870 visit to the Homestead, noting "I saw Mr. Dickinson
this morning a little — thin dry & speechless — I saw what her life has been"
(L342b). Certainly, her father dominated their patriarchal household, where
lofty moral, intellectual, and spiritual standards were imposed on all, habits of
stern self-discipline fostered yet a parodic form of merriment generally encouraged, but where gender roles were clearly defined in ways that put pressure on the one son for public success and both daughters for domestic submission.[1] Other studies, notably John Cody's psychobiography, *After Great
Pain*, Wolff's *Emily Dickinson*, and Barbara Mossberg's *Emily Dickinson: When a
Writer Is a Daughter*, redirect attention to Emily Norcross Dickinson's influence on her daughter, one generally regarded as negative. Mary Elizabeth
Kromer Bernhard, however, rebuts this judgment in "Portrait of a Family" by
tracing to the poet's maternal family heritage intellectual and civic values
generally associated with the Dickinsons and finding the major distinction
between the two families to be the Norcrosses' stronger tradition of female
education. Other aspects of home life merit study also as stimuli to the poet's

imagination. Home obviously provided a wealth of domestic diction as well as the legal and economic vocabularies on which Dickinson drew in her poems — for comic effect sometimes as in "Alone and in a Circumstance" (P1167), linked to religious hope in the manner of Puritan covenant theology in "Mine — by the Right of the White Election!" (P528), or applied to romantic passion as in the poems Joan Burbick examines in "Emily Dickinson and the Economics of Desire."

Given the Dickinsons' intense involvement with their town and its institutions, Amherst may be recognized as a communal extension of household values. Biographical studies necessarily foreground the influence on this poet of growing up in a college town with her father and brother among its most prominent men. Polly Longsworth's pictorial compilation of *The World of Emily Dickinson* now provides a graphic record of the changing local environment that strongly contributed to the world view of this citizen who occasionally even signed herself "Amherst." The town's architectural and spatial features can be documented: its grand homes and mill housing; its churches, college buildings, hat factories, and business blocks; its graveyard behind both the Pleasant Street house and the Homestead meadow; its Common — undeveloped until Austin Dickinson took on the challenge of landscaping; its surrounding hills — Berkshires to the west and Pelhams to the east; and the Connecticut River. So can its sharing in the conservative Congregational culture of New England's historic Connecticut Valley. More important for the formation of Emily Dickinson's mind was the interconnectedness of its domestic, religious, and educational institutions — all of which reinforced a traditional Christian perspective.

A child raised in the habit of family prayer presided over by her father and probably nurtured by her mother in the *New England Primer* (from which Dickinson later snipped engravings for comic messages to Sue) soon came under the church's influence, and Emily Dickinson grew up in a time of special religious excitement. The Second Awakening stretched far beyond Amherst, of course, and is best known for frontier camp meetings and Charles Grandison Finney's spirited revivals. But it was also an occasion of more decorous revivalism in New England's evangelical churches. Among many converts joining Amherst's First Church in 1831, just after the poet's birth, was Emily Norcross Dickinson. Edward Dickinson, although not officially joining the church by proclamation of faith for another twenty years, managed the First Church's business affairs.[2] The whole family attended Sunday worship; and, even though Emily eventually chose to remain home, it is worth noting that the church and the manse were about the last places she ceased to visit as her anxieties about public exposure gradually confined her. She heard a vast amount of preaching over her first thirty years, from guest clergy as well as her

own pastors — scripturally centered and often elaborating on doctrines summarized in the *Westminster Catechism*. She also sang hymns at the First Church,
with well-known effects on her poetic style and less widely recognized impact
on her sense of personal involvement in salvation history. A look at hymnals
available to her, *The Sabbath Hymn Book* and *Village Hymns*, demonstrates their
systematic theological design and evangelical purpose.[3]

Waves of revivalism touched her town frequently, affecting its Congregational churches, the college, and nearby Mount Holyoke Female Seminary. As
an adult, Dickinson came to take a laughing attitude toward these phenomena,
but they touched her deeply as a girl. Letters to Abiah Root, the most pious
among her early friends, reveal that Emily Dickinson experienced a false
conversion as a child that left her with memories "as of a delightful dream, out
of which the Evil one bid me wake" (L11). This betrayal of hope also left her
skeptical, self-protective, and resistant both to the emotional excitement and
social pressure of awakenings. Although expressing hope for her eventual
conversion, her letters to Abiah report that she stayed away from revival
meetings while watching with fascination how others responded to apparent
outpourings of grace. After withstanding still more pressure at Mount Holyoke, however, and witnessing her father's and sister's 1850 conversions, she
declared to Jane Humphrey that "I am standing alone in rebellion" (L35). As
an adult, she pursued an independent religious quest that has been the subject
of considerable scholarly attention.[4] Virginia H. Oliver concludes in *Apocalypse of Green* that Amherst's religious institutions failed to answer Dickinson's
persistent questions, leaving her "to make her weary way alone, taking what
she could from tradition, science, nature, philosophy, and especially from the
Bible, until she outdistanced them all" (45). If the First Church failed to
answer Dickinson's questions, it was not because of any conflict with Amherst's
educational institutions, all of which strongly supported Congregational orthodoxy. In "The Preparation of a Poet," Rowena Revis Jones shows how the
region's elementary textbooks reinforced domestic and ecclesiastical teachings. Benjamin Dudley Emerson's *National Spelling Book*, for example, included biblical passages and exhortations to piety among its lessons, while
Noah Webster's *American Spelling Book* featured a Moral Catechism. Webster's
other contribution to Emily Dickinson's lifelong education, his *American Dictionary*, provided abundant snatches of poetry to awaken her to nuances of
literary language but no doubt also reached her with its painstaking elabora-
tions on words with theological import. Defining one of her favorite nouns,
"Glory," for instance, Webster provides three synonyms, a line of natural
description from Pope, and an example from 2 Peter with the comment that
"in this passage of Peter, the latter word *glory* refers to the visible splendor or
bright cloud that overshadowed Christ at his transfiguration. The former

word *glory*, though the same in the original, is to be understood in a figurative sense."[5] A temporary resident of Amherst and grandfather of Dickinson's friend Emily Fowler, Webster exerted major force on the community's intellectual life.

Even more influential was Edward Hitchcock, the geologist-theologian who presided over Amherst College during the period Emily Dickinson studied at its affiliated institution, Amherst Academy. Hitchcock's contribution, carefully studied in Wolff's and Sewall's biographies, was to demonstrate how natural revelation discovered through rigorous pursuit of modern science supported scriptural revelation as transmitted through the church. This confident pursuit of scientific knowledge, matched with religious orthodoxy and philosophical conservatism, suffused the curricula by which the poet was educated at Mount Holyoke as well as the Academy. Carlton Lowenberg's bibliography, *Emily Dickinson's Textbooks*, documents the systematic intellectual formation that prepared her to use various kinds of technical language in apt, imaginative ways. Dickinson's education, which she saluted merrily in a valentine cheer, "Hurrah for Peter Parley!" (P3), opened her eyes to the intricate drama of nature while inspiring her to seek — and question — correspondences between science and God.[6] Growing up in a town known for its collection of prehistoric fossils also nurtured the metonymic tendencies evident in "A science — so the Savans say" (P100); although, as her punctuated reference to "Savans" suggests, her academic background prepared her to doubt authority. Even after leaving Mount Holyoke, Dickinson continued to profit from Amherst's lyceum, reading clubs, bookstore, and private libraries as Jack Capps's inventory of *Emily Dickinson's Reading* demonstrates.

Yet it would be a mistake to assume that Dickinson's experience was limited to her hometown or that Amherst itself was culturally isolated. As a college community, it drew a constant influx of students from other rural New England towns, of faculty educated elsewhere, and of alumni returning from exotic places. Since Amherst College prepared its graduates for foreign missions, there was a strong global impetus. When Abbie Wood Bliss and her husband left for Syria, where they founded the American College, Dickinson wrote cheerily that "Mr Bliss' *Coronation* takes place tomorrow, at the College church. Charge to the Heathen, by the Pastor! Front seats reserved for Foreign Lands!" but then immediately warned Jane Humphrey, "dont let your duty call you 'far hence'" (L180). Teaching eventually took Jane to Ohio, anyway, and Sue Gilbert to Maryland. Staying in Amherst, Dickinson fretted over friends' departures — whether economically necessitated moves or pleasure trips. Those friends, however, became her envoys to the world, bringing back news of distant states, Europe, and Asia.

Proud of the geographic knowledge she absorbed in school and played with in her poems, Dickinson smiled at local provincials who confused Vermont with Asia (L473, L685) but commented to her often-migrant Norcross cousins that "moving to Cambridge seems to me like moving to Westminster Abbey, as hallowed and as unbelieved, or moving to Ephesus with Paul for a next-door neighbor" (L962).[7]

Nonetheless, she lived during the heyday of westward expansion. Even though their father deflected Austin's thoughts of pursuing a career in Michigan or Illinois, other acquaintances made drastic breaks with the East—most notably Charles Wadsworth when he accepted a call from Calvary Church in San Francisco and Helen Hunt Jackson—or "Helen of Colorado" as Dickinson learned to call her. It was also a period when many Americans of Dickinson's social class traveled for prolonged periods in Europe, enriching their historical and cultural perspectives while learning to cope with alien traditions of an aristocratic and still largely Catholic continent. Rather than asking Samuel Bowles about his European observations in the summer of 1862, however, she wrote: "We wish we knew how Amherst looked, in your memory. Smaller than it did, maybe—and yet things swell, by leaving—if big in themselves" (L266). Her apprehensions about travel may be traceable to the loss of her grandfather, Samuel Fowler Dickinson, who died in Ohio exile after ruining himself financially in founding Amherst College. She seems to be thinking of him in "I noticed People disappeared" (P1149), a badly fragmented draft that equates settlement of "Regions wild" with dying, itself for her always "a new Road" (L332). Professor Nathan Fiske, Helen Jackson's father, had departed the Holy Land directly for heaven when both Helen and Emily were young girls, yet Dickinson never forgot President Humphrey's elegy: "From Mount Zion below to Mount Zion above" (L1042). Clinging herself to the security of home, Dickinson availed herself of cultural opportunities from Europe—Jenny Lind's singing and the touring Germania Orchestra as well as English literature—and remained alert to news about freedom fighting in Hungary, British military actions in the Sudan, and the escape of an Egyptian rebel.

She followed public events in her own country also, despite her claim that "The Only News I know / Is Bulletins all Day / From Immortality" (P827), and current scholarship grounds Dickinson almost as strongly in time as in place—if a fruitful distinction can be made, given that the Amherst of her youth clearly reflected the intellectual, moral, and social climate of a particular era. Betsy Erkkila's "Emily Dickinson and Class" stresses the generally ignored fact that Dickinson's formative years came in the Jacksonian era, a time of ferment characterized by a revisionist historian as "an age of materialism and opportunism, reckless speculation and erratic growth, unabashed vulgarity, surprising inequality, whether of condition, opportunity, or status, and a politic, *seeming* deference to the common man by the uncommon men who

actually ran things" (Pessen 327). One of those uncommon men was Amherst's
Squire Dickinson, who expounded on his ambitions and values in courtship
letters to Emily Norcross. Convinced that "we live in a country & in an age
when all offices & honors are held out to the deserving, and where the man of
merit — the man of untiring energy & perseverance can hardly fail of promo-
tion — & where a man of decision & determination & resolution & energy of
character, seldom fails of success," the poet's father tied his personal hopes to
community advancement in his resolute quest for power and wealth (Pollak,
Parents 8). He pursued public service in the electoral realm as a state legislator
and Massachusetts representative to the United States Congress while functioning as treasurer to Amherst College, promoting public works from temperance societies to railroad access, and maintaining a prosperous law practice.
Erkkila's argument is that, although women were pointedly excluded from the
public realm, Emily Dickinson nonetheless profited from her family's social
privilege and shared her father's Whig ideology. Seeking "the historical and
specifically class formations of Dickinson's life and work" ("Class" 2), Erkkila
concludes that the poet "sought to secure the declining status of both her
gender and her class through the accumulation of cultural and spiritual capital,
what she called 'My Soul's *entire income*'" (17).

Pointing to collegian Emily's nightmare that Amherst's Locofoco postmas-
ter had acquired a lien on the Dickinson rye field (L16) as well as to her
dismissive comments about servants, Austin's Irish pupils, and other social
inferiors as evidence of the poet's anxiety about aspirant social groups, Erkkila
pays less attention to counterevidence of republican spirit. Rather than accepting her father's equation of success with virtue, Dickinson wrote scathingly of
someone with "A face devoid of love or grace, / A hateful, hard, successful
face" (P1711) and seemed to identify with the cheery robin whose "Dress
denotes him socially, / Of Transport's Working Classes" (P1483). Looking at
her world from perspectives either of nature or of eternity provided a corrective to Whig ideology while demonstrating her keen-eyed, satiric awareness
of her contemporaries' deluded ambitions. "'Tis sweet to know that stocks
will stand / When we with Daisies lie," she mocked, "That Commerce will
continue — / And Trades as briskly fly — " (P54). From the celestial perspective, status roles had no importance: "Color — Caste — Denomination — /
These — are Time's Affair — / Death's diviner Classifying / Does not know
they are — " (P970).

There were a number of destabilizing factors in Jacksonian America that
prompted anxieties in conservative Connecticut Valley families tracing their
ancestry back to the Pilgrim Fathers. Foremost among these was the wave of
internal and external immigration that drew small-town New Englanders to
the industrial cities, rural youth to western territories, free blacks to the

North, and masses of Irish and German immigrants to America. Amherst felt these changes, and so did the Dickinson household. Edward Dickinson's stance was a conservative one, and the few political views his daughter expressed tended to echo his — if only because they often arose in letters to Austin, whose ambitions depended to a great extent on their father's. Despite her personal reclusiveness, Dickinson apparently took some pleasure in acquaintance with the powerful men to whom Edward Dickinson connected her, boasting in a childish letter of knowing Governor Briggs (L18) and threatening in a witty poem to retain Lemuel Shaw, chief justice of the Massachusetts Supreme Judicial Court, in a lawsuit against God himself (P116). On the other hand, she worried about the burdens public service placed on men she admired and resisted threats to pull her father away from Amherst. When the new Constitutional-Union party proposed to nominate the Squire for state office in 1860, she objected to her cousins, "I hear they wish to make me Lieutenant-Governor's daughter. Were they cats I would pull their tails, but as they are only patriots, I must forego the bliss" (L225). The very name of that party, along with its ephemeral nature as one of many fragments spun off by the exploded Whigs, points to the threat of secession that Edward Dickinson, like Daniel Webster, attempted to stave off by acquiescence to southern demands.[8] Later, freed from her father's aspirations, the poet expressed indifference to public affairs in a letter to Mrs. Holland: " 'George Washington was the Father of his Country' — 'George Who?' / That sums all Politics to me" (L950). Still, she checked the morning newspapers each day to learn of President Garfield's condition after his shooting (L721), apparently responding to this public figure in a humane if not a patriotic way, and referred occasionally to economic scandals and political agitation. Amused by the posturing of political orators she likened to frogs (P1379), Dickinson again shifted perspective in a way that both linked the women's sphere of domestic service to her father's and brother's male sphere of power and cast both into a kind of comic-cosmic relief when she remarked of her sister's prodigious energy that "Vinnie is far more hurried than Presidential Candidates — I trust in more distinguished ways, for *they* have only the care of the Union, but Vinnie the Universe — " (L667).

Lavinia's formidable industriousness prompted her sister to claim for her the "patent action" admired in an industrialized, mechanical age (L194). Dickinson's letters, more than her poems, demonstrate alert awareness of those technological advances that swelled her countrymen's pride, although her responses to the arrival of the Amherst-Belchertown railroad reflect a mix of filial delight and discomfort. Letters to Austin adopt a celebratory tone with respect to their father's achievement in securing the railroad for the town — wishing her brother home to join in the jubilation and claiming that "I verily believe we shall fall down and worship the first 'Son of Erin' that comes, and the first sod he turns will be preserved as an emblem of the struggles and victory of our heroic fathers" (L72). Yet among the first loads to arrive was an excursion group of 325 New London visitors, placing heavy burdens of hospitality on Amherst's more realistic if less heroic sisters and mothers (L127). Machinery proved destructive, too, resulting in calamities she read about in newspapers "where railroads meet each other unexpectedly, and gentlemen in factories get their heads cut off quite informally" (L133). Railroads, moreover, promoted westward expansion that threatened her region. It was mainly in an ironic spirit, obviously, that Emily Dickinson claimed enthusiasm for what her contemporaries hailed as progress. In her 1850 prose valentine, she parodied familiar rhetoric:

> But the world is sleeping in ignorance and error, sir, and we must be crowing cocks, and singing larks, and a rising sun to awake her; or else we'll pull society up to the roots, and plant it in a different place. We'll build Alms-houses, and transcendental State prisons, and scaffolds — we will blow out the sun, and the moon, and encourage invention. Alpha shall kiss Omega — we will ride up the hill of glory — Hallelujah, all hail! (L34)

That skeptical attitude held for reformism in general and for social causes enlisting women in particular. Though declaring admiration for Elizabeth Fry and Florence Nightingale in an apology to Bowles for mocking at women (L223), she remarked drolly to Jane Humphrey a decade earlier about the sewing society she avoided in their hometown, noting wryly that "all the poor will be helped — the cold warmed — the warm cooled — the hungry fed — the thirsty attended to — the ragged clothed — and this suffering — tumbled down world will be helped to it's feet again — which will be quite pleasant to all" (L30). When solicited for a literary contribution to help some charitable cause, she claimed to have burned the letter "requesting me to aid the world by my chirrup more" (L380).

Dickinson's spirited contempt for "Soft — Cherubic Creatures" among the "Gentlewomen" she observed (P401) should not blind us, however, to ways in which she drew strength from a network of female friends and the sentimental women's culture of her time. Paula Bennett argues persuasively that the poet willingly submerged herself in the feminine sphere of home and garden and that "her presentation of herself as 'poetess' (a *woman* poet) was, therefore, a good deal more than simply a role she played in order to keep from playing others" (*Woman Poet* 13). She found intellectual, artistic, and psychological support in women's writings also. Dickinson's relationship to the distinctively female literary culture of her time, chiefly British, is the subject of Sandra Gilbert and Susan Gubar's groundbreaking *Madwoman in the Attic;* while

Joanne Dobson examines in *Dickinson and the Strategies of Reticence* how this poet carried to an extreme the restrictions placed by Jacksonian-Victorian culture on American poetesses. In " 'One Unbroken Company': Religion and Emily Dickinson," Joan Burbick discloses a Dickinson whose spiritual pilgrimage "is more relational than individualistic" by placing her within the context of a sentimental religious culture that significantly altered the emphasis and tone of evangelical Calvinism (63). Beth Maclay Doriani, in *Emily Dickinson, Daughter of Prophecy*, links Dickinson to a deeply rooted New England tradition of female prophecy that combined in antebellum America with transcendentalist oratory, evangelical preaching, and the Bible's wisdom literature to provide the poet with both a culturally sanctioned rhetoric and the courage to employ that rhetoric in her unorthodox expression of spiritual searching.

Countering the hoary supposition that Dickinson's seclusion in the 1860s and intensive engagement with both her poems and her eyes precluded her taking an interest in the Civil War, Shira Wolosky demonstrates in *Emily Dickinson: A Voice of War* that she shared in the national political and moral crisis in a way that severely challenged her faith. Arguing that Dickinson's poetry "can be seen as profoundly engaged in problems of the external world and aggressively so," Wolosky places her at "a point of intersection of literary, cultural, and metaphysical concerns" exacerbated by national conflict that found expression in the "disjunctions and discontinuities" of her writing (xiii, xviii). Particularly compelling questions brought to the forefront were those prompted by massive, incomprehensible human suffering that challenged belief in God's providential justice. St. Armand brings the war's theological impact home to Amherst in analyzing that community's response to the 1863 battle death of Frazar Stearn, the valiant, spiritually searching, but unconverted son of Amherst College's president and friend of Austin Dickinson. How could Amherst—or evangelical Christians more generally—rationalize "the loss of an entire generation of young men who in sacrificing their lives on the altar of their country, simultaneously condemned themselves to eternal hellfire and damnation, all for the lack of a public profession of religion" (*Culture* 103)? St. Armand traces to that quandary the triumph of the Brother-Christ of a sentimental love religion like Dickinson's over the Father-God of traditional Calvinism. Lease (*Readings*) shows how the Civil War affected Dickinson through her vicarious sharing in transformations it brought to lives of her two mentors, Wadsworth and Higginson, prompting her lament to the latter (then colonel of a black regiment) that "I did not deem that Planetary forces annulled—but suffered an Exchange of Territory, or World—" (L280).

Such evidence of complexity and contradiction in Dickinson's experience compels a rereading of "What is—'Paradise'—" (P215). It should be obvious by now that the speaker is a persona, perhaps voicing some latent child within this sophisticated and knowledgeable poet but hardly articulating her full mind. Like many poems in which Dickinson adopts a child's persona, this one should be read ironically as her means of raising subversive thoughts. This speaker naively grasps at literal interpretations of promises held out by teachers, pastors, and the Bible, much as the speaker of poem 460 construes the scriptural promise that saints will "thirst no more" in heaven to mean that "The Wells have Buckets to them there." Dickinson often travestied such literalism, seeing how it entrapped imaginations in images introduced at the earliest stages of religious formation. "Is Heaven a Place—a Sky—a Tree?" she demanded, then answered her own question: "Location's narrow way is for Ourselves— / Unto the Dead / There's no Geography— // But State— Endowal—Focus—" (P489). What we realize in following the trail of her child-persona's anxious inquiries in poem 215 is how *un*heavenly he or she finds pious Amherst and how negative a view of eternity New England Calvinism projects. Moreover, quotation marks around key words communicate the writer's doubts about language's ability to represent truth, not just about "Paradise" and "Eden" that might be considered examples of religious myth but even about here-and-now seeming realities like "Amherst" and its economy. The poem offers nothing but questions—perhaps fortunately, since answers might prove so devastating to the faith society was attempting to transmit to its children, including Emily Dickinson.

On the other hand, that Amherst culture also educated her to ask questions and to settle for nothing less than experiential knowledge of both science and the soul, and the question to which she devoted her energies was the same one we recognize behind the little waif's queries. "Is immortality true?" That was what Dickinson apparently asked the Reverend Washington Gladden when staggered by deaths and alarmed about Judge Lord's stroke (L752a). In writing to a Congregational minister, locally educated at Williams College but known for receptivity to newer kinds of biblical criticism, she turned to someone who might help her resolve doubts exacerbated by intellectual currents of her day that threatened the science-religion bond she had been educated to search out. By this last decade of her life, she wondered who could provide authoritative solace: "Are you certain there is another life?" she asked Charles Clark after his brother's death. "When overwhelmed to know, I fear that few are sure" (L827). Dickinson's response to the crumbling religious and scientific orthodoxies of her youth is the subject of Oliver's *Apocalypse of Green*, which examines how intra- and intersectarian strife disrupted New England churches while "scientific discoveries, which at first seemed benign and often supportive of religion, quietly became treacherous and life-threatening to cherished theological beliefs" (17). Chief among these threats, obviously, were Darwin's findings about evolutionary natural selection that challenged the familiar Genesis narrative. Equally alarming was the Higher Criticism of the Bible, which employed historical methods to display the mythic aspects of Scripture. Dickinson, who confessed once that "sermons on unbelief ever did attract me" (L176), confronted many challenges to her faith—challenges that reached her from her reading, certainly, but also from directly observed changes in Amherst.

When Emily Dickinson was born in 1830, Amherst had two churches, both Congregational. When she died in 1886, it claimed a third Congregational church, an Episcopal one, and even a Roman Catholic parish. While successive statements of communal belief from the 1834 *Articles of Faith and Government* through the 1880 *Manual of the First Congregational Church* showed Amherst's First Church maintaining its basic doctrinal core, they revealed heightened awareness of community with other churches and gradual softening of requirements for admission so that, had she desired full membership, Dickinson might easily have qualified for admission to the Lord's Supper even without experiential evidence of conversion.[9] Although the Dickinsons' church remained solidly Trinitarian, their Norcross cousins in the Boston area were Unitarians.[10] Dickinson chose a Presbyterian minister as her spiritual confidant and a Unitarian one as her literary guide. Amherst College, founded to prepare Congregational clergymen, numbered among its most distinguished alumni Austin's friend Bishop Frederick Dan Huntington. Another Episcopalian leader among the town's summer residents was E. Winchester Donald, rector of Boston's Trinity Church. The new Massachusetts Agricultural College had no connection to any church.

An 1859 Christmas letter reflects the diversity of spiritual influences bearing down on Emily Dickinson (L213). Thanking Mary Bowles for Theodore Parker's *The Two Christmas Celebrations*, she writes, "I never read before what Mr Parker wrote. I heard that he was 'poison.' Then I like poison very well." But her apparent openness to transcendentalist assaults on New England orthodoxy clashes with her next statement, which is an amused report about Austin's staying home from church to read and Sue's asking how to spell "Puseyite." Evidently the younger Dickinsons were somehow balancing Congregationalism, transcendentalism, and the Oxford movement—and finding the play of mind invigorating. Other influences to which she was exposed through Wadsworth, Higginson, and even Hitchcock included the Christian spiritualism to which Lease devotes a chapter. Choices in the religious realm seemed as various—and even more life-threatening—than medical options that befuddled her neighbor: "'Mrs Skeeter' is very feeble," Emily told Austin, "'cant bear Allopathic treatment, cant have Homeopathic'—dont want Hydropathic—Oh what a pickle she is in—should'nt think she would deign to *live* — it is so decidedly vulgar!" (L82). Yet she laughed as wryly at "The Fop — the Carp — the Atheist," all those who refused to credit evidence for immortality she discovered everywhere (P1380). Dickinson's typical stance in her letters was a brave one, holding herself open to Charles Darwin, George Eliot, and similar influences that her cautious mother dismissed as "very improper" (L650). Nonetheless, she held to the central promises of Scripture, even if — in sophisticated society — "no one credits Noah" and "No Moses there can be" (P403, P597). "Better an ignis fatuus / Than no illume at all," she reasoned, in a world left unprotected by scholarship's amputation of God's right hand (P1551).

Finally, what Dickinson most derived from her culture was a searching mind — and the resilience not to be overcome by mysteries that eluded religion, science, and the law. "Why the Thief ingredient accompanies all Sweetness Darwin does not tell us," she remarked to Mrs. Holland; "Each expiring Secret leaves an Heir, distracting still" (L359). Living in an era of expiring secrets, the period Wolff describes as that of "the fading of transcendence from the world" (*Dickinson* 10), Dickinson exposed herself courageously to conflicting, disruptive currents of thought and responded with a mind firmly educated to demand experiential evidence in all areas and an imagination that found metonymic suggestiveness in fragmentary observations and metaphoric illuminations even in darkening light. And, for all her awareness of local and global environments, her truest perspective remained more vertical than horizontal, more attuned to speculations on immortality (experienced even now and promised hereafter) than on Amherst, America, or the wider world opened by friendships and reading.

NOTES

1. Vivian Pollak's edition of their courtship letters in *A Poet's Parents* revealingly discloses assumptions both Edward Dickinson and Emily Norcross brought to their marriage. Pollak expands upon implications of this "family romance" in *Dickinson: The Anxiety of Gender.*

2. The Reverend Aaron M. Colton reminisced in *The Old Meeting House* about being interviewed by Edward Dickinson (and meeting his young family) while a candidate to fill the Amherst pulpit. As Colton served the First Church from 1840 to 1853, his memoirs offer valuable insight into the solid doctrinal substance but genial tone that apparently characterized Emily Dickinson's acculturation into the church.

3. Although not focused on Dickinson, Mary De Jong's " 'With my burden I begin' " provides rich insight into the effect of hymn singing on the spiritual development of nineteenth-century women churchgoers.

4. In the concluding chapters of *Dickinson: Strategies of Limitation* and in several articles, I have attempted to do more justice to this topic than is possible here.

5. I rely here on Dickinson's beloved lexicon, the 1844 two-volume edition she used

as an adult, while recognizing that she probably also had access at school, in college, and in friends' homes to other versions of this widely used reference that was first published in 1828.

6. See Fred D. White's essay, " 'Sweet Skepticism of the Heart': Science in the Poetry of Emily Dickinson," for a listing of major scientific and technical developments of the 1830s and 1840s.

7. The best discussion of Dickinson's geographic vocabulary is Rebecca Patterson's essay, "Emily Dickinson's Geography" (chap. 6 in *Imagery*).

8. In *Touching Liberty*, Karen Sanchez-Eppler explores Dickinson's antipolitical response to contemporary agitations for freedom, considering "what has happened when a concern with the corporeality of identity that appears political and public in the writings of feminist-abolitionists, Whitman, and Jacobs is fashioned by Dickinson into a poetic, ahistorical and ontological dilemma" (106).

9. Sister Regina Siegfried draws upon dissertation research on the doctrinal odyssey of the First Church in her "Bibliographic Essay."

10. See Jones, "A Taste for 'Poison,' " for illuminating insights into the denominational interplay in the poet's environment.

FURTHER READING

Conforti, Joseph A. *Jonathan Edwards, Religious Tradition, and American Culture*. Chapel Hill: University of North Carolina Press, 1995.

Douglas, Ann. *The Feminization of American Culture*. New York: Knopf, 1977.

Epstein, Barbara Leslie. *The Politics of Domesticity: Women, Evangelism, and Temperance in Nineteenth-Century America*. Middletown, Conn.: Wesleyan University Press, 1981.

McLoughlin, William G. *Revivals, Awakenings, and Reform: An Essay on Religion and Social Change in America, 1607–1977*. Chicago: University of Chicago Press, 1978.

Smith-Rosenberg, Carroll. *Disorderly Conduct: Visions of Gender in Victorian America*. New York: Knopf, 1985.

Welter, Barbara. *Dimity Convictions: The American Woman in the Nineteenth Century*. Athens: Ohio University Press, 1976.

GARY LEE STONUM

Dickinson's Literary Background

*A*t the center of any serious investigation of Emily Dickinson's poetry, as Cynthia Griffin Wolff has noted, is the problem of context. Not only do we know relatively little about the intentions, inspirations, and constraints shaping Dickinson's literary career, but the poems regularly challenge us to imagine backgrounds they conspicuously fail to specify. Poem after poem seems to avoid some "circumstance too well known to be repeated to the initiate," so we the uninitiated keep trying to invent or reconstruct contexts that will remedy the omission (Leyda 1: xxi).

The question of context most often gets raised biographically, in the hope that recovering the private circumstances of the poet's life will anchor the poetry in referentiality. Context is a cultural and historical problem as well, for like any body of writing Dickinson's emerges from a network of symbolic practices and takes many of its possibilities of meaning from this array. The hope here is that if only we could properly identify and describe the cultural milieu we could more securely understand the poetry and better appreciate Dickinson's achievement. Unfortunately, biographical criticism has more often amplified disagreements about Dickinson's writing than dissipated them, and research into the cultural contexts of her work has likewise reproduced rather than resolved disputes about how best to read it. At its best, rather than answering interpretive questions, historical study typically reconfigures the stage on which they get posed.

CHALLENGES

The biographical critic's difficulties stem in part from a lack of documentation: Lavinia Dickinson burned Emily's papers after her sister died; only a small portion of the poet's apparently voluminous correspondence has survived and been located; and we have relatively little testimony from those who knew her, especially by contrast to writers of the time who led more public lives. The difficulties of specifically cultural contextualization begin with the same lack. We would certainly like to glean more information about the literary roles Dickinson imagined for herself, about the books she and her circle of friends admired or scorned, and about the references, allusions, and sayings they might have taken as starting points. Actually we do know more about these matters than about, say, the poet's erotic life. The further difficulty stems from her poetry's careful singularity, which both coaxes and frustrates a search for explanatory contexts.

The same singularity defines the boundaries of our search. Consider Dickinson's insistence on uniqueness in an 1862 letter to Thomas Wentworth Higginson. Apparently fearful he would suspect her of plagiarism, she wrote that "I marked a line in One Verse — because I met it after I made it — and never consciously touch a paint, mixed by another person — I do not let go it, because it is mine" (L271). The remark indicates a determination to avoid all literary indebtedness, especially stylistic, and it thus specifically disavows one familiar kind of context.

True to her word, with the exception of a few openly allusive poems, Dickinson does successfully conceal whatever immediate textual sources and inspirations her poetry might have. Her "Lay this Laurel on the One" (P1393), a four-line redaction of the seven stanzas composing Higginson's "Decoration," would be unrecognizable as such if we did not know from their letters that his elegy was a source. We would be equally in the dark about the quatrain's origin in Dickinson's grief over her father's death, which had happened three years before. How many other poems arise from comparable but now unrecoverable contexts? We do not know and for the most part can only mark our ignorance as one boundary of the determinable backgrounds for her work. Dickinson's 1862 letter also implicitly indicates the other boundary, namely, the broad literary values and ideals shaping her work. By claiming the marked line as inalienable property and in assuming that originality is requisite, Dickinson pledges allegiance to a pair of romanticism's central tenets (Woodmansee 35–55). That is, at the very moment Dickinson insists upon the singularity of her poetry and hence its distance from all contexts, she allies herself to an established, historically specific definition of poetry as the creation of singular genius. On the other hand, romanticism can be such a broad concept, not to mention a disputed one, as to be of limited use in establishing a context for Dickinson's writing. Even the insistence upon originality presupposes a historicism otherwise strikingly absent from her writing.

Books and reading were Dickinson's primary access to a world beyond Amherst. We can thus at least be reasonably confident that the cultural contexts of Dickinson's writing are primarily literary, particularly if that term is defined inclusively. Her surviving letters are filled with references to favorite authors, and some of the poems allude in one way or another to recognizable elements of her reading (Pollak, "Allusions"). To be sure, she is by no means a learned poet in the vein of Milton or Pope, writers who can hardly be appreciated without understanding their allusions and allegiances. Yet she is also surely not the unlettered author Richard Chase once unguardedly deemed her, uninfluenced by literary sources in either style or thought.

A few cautions need to be kept in mind as we examine various claims about Dickinson's literary milieu. First, we know very little about how or even whether Dickinson imagined her work as participating in any public enterprise. By contrast to a Keats, who dreamed of being among the English poets after his death, or a James Joyce, who schemed tirelessly to shape his own reputation, Dickinson hardly trafficked in any cultural arena. We do possess information about the books she read or admired, and we know from the persistent testimony of her letters and poems that she regarded poetry as an exalted calling. Yet, although we can reasonably infer from this a certain broad ambition, we simply do not know if Dickinson regarded her vocation as entailing some sense of a role in literary history or as obliging her to bargain in the cultural marketplace. We do not, for example, know whether or in what respect she regarded herself as a woman poet, in spite of a number of lively arguments supposing that she did.

Indeed, because Dickinson showed so little interest in the cultural position her work might occupy, even the most credible claims about her filiations usually testify as much to the critic's context as to the poet's. Forty years ago, for example, when New Criticism held the fort and T. S. Eliot's praise of the metaphysical poets heavily influenced Anglo-American literary taste, scholars regularly identified Donne, Herbert, and Vaughan as her important predecessors. By 1980, however, the ascendancy of poststructuralist theory in the United States had brought with it a keener appreciation of the major English romantics, and for a brief time Wordsworth and Keats were regarded as exemplars of the tradition from which Dickinson sprang. More recently and resoundingly, as feminist theory has called attention to a distinctively women's literature, critics have looked to nineteenth-century American and English women writers as Dickinson's sources and inspirations.

Evidence can be found to support all these claims. Two stanzas copied from George Herbert's "Matins" were found among Dickinson's papers and even mistaken for a time as her own composition (Bingham, *Home* 571–73). Likewise, Dickinson's letters make it clear that she eagerly followed the careers of several female contemporaries, particularly Charlotte Brontë, George Eliot, and Elizabeth Barrett Browning. Yet evidence that Dickinson had some familiarity with another writer's work should not be confused with confirmation that the work is a significant context for her own. Indeed, we should probably distinguish two sorts of context, the writerly and the readerly. To reconstruct a writerly or compositional context would be to delineate the origins of particular texts and the circumstances in which they were written. As with "Lay this

Laurel on the One," historical evidence is crucial to such a task. To construct a readerly or interpretive context, on the other hand, would be to set the work in telling relation to literary or cultural tradition. Historical evidence can be suggestive, but it is rarely conclusive or even obligatory. A similarity to Christina Rossetti, say, can thus be mildly illuminating, even though Dickinson seems to have had no acquaintance whatsoever with the English poet (Leder and Abbott).

At the writerly end of the spectrum lie the sources Dickinson drew upon or referred to as she wrote, which are of varying importance. Dickinson's regard for Elizabeth Barrett Browning makes it likely that her "Vision of Poets" is a source of "I died for Beauty" (P449), as well as or even rather than Keats's now more famous "Ode on a Grecian Urn." On the other hand, the identification is by no means crucial to an understanding of the poem.

The more interesting cases are those in which the source is disputed and identification would make some difference to our reading. Dickinson was notably fond of exotic place-names, most of which she must have come upon in her reading and some of which may carry thematic associations. The reference to "Chimborazo" in "Love — thou are high" (P453) may well derive incidentally from Edward Hitchcock's *Elementary Geology*, where it stands among a list of the world's tallest mountains, or it may originate from similarly casual uses in Barrett Browning and Emerson. On the other hand, if we heed Judith Farr's investigations into the influence of contemporary painting, then we might recall that Frederic Church's mammoth painting of Chimborazo was one of the most celebrated luminist canvases of the day ("Disclosing" 73–74). If the poem is read in the latter context, then the "Love" addressed by the poem as like the mountain would function more insistently as a figure of sublime theophany. (The poem also clearly alludes to Exodus 33, the chief biblical commonplace for such an event.)

Likewise, two equally recherché possibilities have been identified for the source of "The Malay took the Pearl" (P452), each linking the poem to different parts of Dickinson's work. Theodora Ward proposes Robert Browning's *Paracelsus* and along with Jack Capps associates the poem with others using the image of diving for pearls (Ward 61–63; Capps, *Reading* 89–90). Farr nominates De Quincey's *Confessions of an English Opium Eater*, which would corroborate her reading of the poem as representing Emily's rivalry with Austin over the affections of Susan (*Passion* 148). Farr's case is helped by our knowledge that Dickinson tried to obtain a copy of *Confessions* in 1858 and that the book may be found in the family library (Capps 81–82).

In addition to supporting this or that interpretation of a poem, writerly contexts can themselves become a starting point for interpretation. According to Martha Dickinson Bianchi, three portraits hung in her Aunt Emily's room

(*Life* 83). Two are of writers we know from other sources that she admired greatly: Elizabeth Barrett Browning and George Eliot. That the other is Thomas Carlyle, whom she never mentions, may suggest that he, too, helped shape her literary imagination. On the relatively slender basis of this clue, my own work has stressed an affinity between Carlyle's *Heroes and Hero-Worship* and Dickinson's "This was a Poet" (P448). The claim is highly speculative, and its value no doubt depends less on the historical evidence (itself from a some-what unreliable source) than on the explanatory power gained from linking Dickinson and Carlyle.

On the other end of the spectrum are readerly or interpretive contexts, which must be judged entirely on explanatory power. Consider as an extreme example George Whicher's otherwise admirable biography from 1938. Whicher is one of the few early critics to notice Dickinson's comic writing, which he links to the raucous, largely populist strand of American humor championed in the thirties by Constance Roarke. We may smile today at the thought of placing Dickinson next to her contemporary Mark Twain (both clad in white, of course), but the very unlikeliness calls attention to the grounds of comparison. The association does serve an interest, even an ideo-logical program. Seeing Dickinson as a Yankee humorist distances her poetry from the conservative and patrician social milieu in which she lived her en-tire life, and it gives her a place of some pride in the Popular Front vision of American literary history. Yet unbuttoned humor seems alien to the pre-ponderantly psychological and metaphysical orientation of many Dickinson poems, so Whicher's argument ultimately calls more attention to differences than to resemblances.

Although Whicher has not persuaded many readers, his proposal is also neither illegitimate nor different in kind from more winning claims. It is an act of assimilation, and the test of such acts is whether they help us understand and evaluate the appropriated material. As Dickinson herself affirms, we see com-paratively, and the very visibility of Dickinson's work partly depends upon our seeing it in comparison to some context. Moreover, such comparisons are almost always a form of judgment. Whicher clearly values the thought that Dickinson's poetry participates in the progressive social and intellectual fer-ment of her day, and his commentary singles out for attention and admiration those aspects of her work that do so participate.

SOURCES

Our information about Emily Dickinson's reading comes from a finite body of documents, and most of it can now be found conveniently in a handful of collections and studies. The vast majority of the references in her own poetry are helpfully annotated and indexed in Thomas Johnson's 1955 edition of the *Poems*. Although Johnson's edition has come under criticism for its typographic representation of her manuscripts and for its confident separation of poems from correspondence, these complaints do not apply to his identification of the names, places, tags, and quotations in her verse. The letters are a richer source of information about Dickinson's reading, and here too Johnson's edition is essential, although not as fully annotated as the *Poems*. Of the handful of documents by and about Dickinson that have turned up in subsequent years, the most important for conveying a sense of her cultural milieu are the *Lyman Letters*, which Richard Sewall has edited.

Many of the references in Dickinson's writings are discussed in Jack Capps's indispensable *Emily Dickinson's Reading*, which includes a detailed index of the books and authors she mentions in poems or letters. Capps also surveys the contents of the family library, much of which is now at Harvard. Unfortunately, the usefulness of the library "is limited by the fact that books from the Austin Dickinson and Edward Dickinson household have been mixed and, in most cases, dates of acquisition and individual ownership are uncertain" (8). Likewise, although these volumes include inscriptions, marginalia, and other evidence of use, few of the markings can be confidently traced to the poet herself.

Capps describes a number of suggestive facts about the library, noting for example that of a three-volume *Works of Thomas Browne* belonging to Susan the only cut pages are those containing "Religio Medici" and "Christian Morals." This casts doubt on Emily's avowal to Higginson that Browne was one of her favorites. In one of her earliest letters to him she had written that "For Poets — I have Keats — and Mr and Mrs Browning. For Prose — Mr Ruskin — Sir Thomas Browne — and the Revelations" (L271). The account may be more polite than accurate. Several of the writers she names were singled out for praise in Higginson's *Atlantic Monthly* essay, "Letter to a Young Contributor," the occasion of her writing to him in the first place.

Capps's account of the Dickinson library is not meant to be exhaustive, but one can find various additional remarks about marked passages and well-thumbed pages in the writings of others who have used the Harvard archive. In addition to Capps, the richest accounts are Sewall's biography and the books written by Ruth Miller and Judith Farr.

A brief but tantalizing account of the periodical literature Dickinson read is available from Joan Kirkby. In "Dickinson Reading," a preliminary report out of her ambitious project of identifying and reading all the books, newspapers, and magazines that the poet would have encountered, Kirkby concentrates on the contents of the two newspapers received at the Dickinson household, the *Springfield Republican* and the *Hampshire and Franklin Express*.

Capps also briefly lists the textbooks in use at Mount Holyoke during Dickinson's time there. The list is substantially amplified by Carlton Lowenberg's *Emily Dickinson's Textbooks*, which interprets its subject broadly, including hymnals and devotional writings in the family library as well as the authors and texts Emily may have encountered at Amherst Academy and Mount Holyoke Seminary. Lowenberg also describes the markings in books belonging to the Dickinsons, including those in a number of volumes not retained in the Harvard collection.

The other most important record of primary sources is Jay Leyda's remarkable *Years and Hours of Emily Dickinson*, which excerpts in chronological order an impressive array of letters and diaries of the Dickinsons, newspapers and magazines available to the family, and various public and private writings by those in and around their world. In some respects his book is a more useful introduction to the poet's life than either of the two best biographies. Whereas Sewall and Wolff both properly give organized interpretations of her world, Leyda offers something more like raw materials.

A number of anecdotes and recollections have been preserved by Dickinson's family, friends, and early editors. Such reports, which may be found scattered throughout the works of Martha Dickinson Bianchi and Millicent Todd Bingham, need to be used with some care. However, no one has actually challenged Bianchi's account of the three portraits or questioned Susan's attribution to Emily of this remark about Emerson: "It was as if he had come from where dreams are born" (Leyda 2: 351–52). Of special although uncertain significance for Dickinson's literary milieu is an essay by Bianchi, which provides our only listing of books said to have been kept on the mantel of Emily's room: *Ranthorpe, The Mill on the Floss, The Imitation of Christ, Abelard and Heloise, The Life of Jean Paul,* and *The Last Days of Byron and Shelley.* Bianchi's essay is included as an appendix to Barton Levi St. Armand's *Emily Dickinson and Her Culture.*

One additional source deserves special mention. Dickinson seems to have made frequent and extensive use of Noah Webster's *American Dictionary of the English Language* in writing her poems, harkening not only to definitions but to etymologies (sometimes dubious ones) and illustrative quotations. It therefore matters considerably which of the considerably different versions she consulted. The scholarly consensus is for (an 1844 reprint of) the 1841 edition, rather than the 1828 edition (also in the Dickinson library), and for any of the ones dated 1847 or later (Buckingham). Although reprinted several times, the 1841 edition is relatively rare. Students of Dickinson are thus likely to welcome the annotated reconstruction of her lexicon being prepared under the direction of Cynthia Hallen.

CONTEXTS

The extant claims about Dickinson's readerly and writerly filiations divide roughly but conveniently into three areas: Jacobean literature, including Shakespeare, the King James Bible, and some of the metaphysical poets; New England culture from the Puritans up through such contemporaries as Emerson; and nineteenth-century English literature from Wordsworth to the Brownings. Overlapping the last two but also possibly a distinct category for Dickinson were the English and American women who were Dickinson's immediate predecessors and peers. Dickinson herself might not have recognized any of the categories, we should keep in mind. Unlike most other writers of the time, Dickinson did not hold a historicist view of literature, or at least left no record of doing so.

Jack Capps has proposed that Dickinson showed little interest in literature not written in English and also that she did not pay much attention even to English literature prior to Shakespeare. The observation needs some qualification. Dickinson studied both French and Latin in school, and as Vivian Pollak notes, classical mythology contributes the second-largest group of fictive characters mentioned in her writings. Likewise, George Monteiro has argued for the influence of the sixteenth-century Portuguese poet Luis Vaz de Camoes, whom Dickinson would have encountered from reading Elizabeth Barrett Browning. In addition, it is possible that Dickinson shared somewhat in the romantic medievalism of her day and so may have cared more about earlier literature than Capps suspects. Farr and St. Armand both make cases for an affinity with Pre-Raphaelitism, for example.

Nevertheless, Capps's view largely holds. The Greek and Latin references are almost all proverbial, and Dickinson was surely far less interested in foreign or historically remote cultures than most of her peers. One further omission is notable. Although morally respectable authors from the Restoration and afterward were staples of her school curriculum, Dickinson makes conspicuously few references to Milton, Cowper, Pope, Johnson, Young, Thomson, or Goldsmith (R. Sewall, *Life* 349–53). The only eighteenth-century writer arguably to have influenced her is Isaac Watts, whose hymns have often been seen as the main source of her prosody. However, besides a fondness for odd rhymes and numerous examples of common meter and its kin, Watts seems at most to have contributed an occasional point of rhetorical departure or a target for parody. For a recent, measured view on this subject, consult Judy Jo Small's *Positive as Sound*, which qualifies the influential claims of Martha Winburn England.

The difference between readerly and writerly looms largest in discussions of Dickinson's seventeenth-century predecessors. A prime example of readerly claims, the once commonplace link with the metaphysicals, is based chiefly on similarities of style and subject. Following the lead of numerous earlier reviewers and critics, Judith Farr (writing then as Judith Banzer) has concluded that Dickinson resembles Donne, Herbert, and their successors in favoring abrupt or startling opening lines, epigrammatic forms, and unusually concise or elliptical expressions. Her "Before I got my eye put out" can thus be compared with Herbert's "I struck the board, and cried, No more," and her "To disappear enhances" with Donne's frequently paradoxical and riddling conceits. The resemblance appears the stronger when Dickinson is set against her contemporaries, and indeed the similarity is often emphasized as a way of advocating the superiority of Dickinson's style to Victorian lushness and fluency.

The intense and highly personal religious concerns in much of Dickinson's poetry have also been seen as a link to the seventeenth century, regarded as the font of English devotional and meditative verse (Martz). In this, however, she differs less from her American contemporaries, especially the Victorian writers of England and America most likely to be scorned by advocates of the seventeenth century. One issue in the relative importance of these two contexts is the stress on intellectual and pointedly antisentimental meditations; to like a look of agony or to declare that the admirations and contempts of time show justest through an open tomb is thus arguably to exhibit a metaphysical sensibility. On the other hand, much of Dickinson's religious verse resembles the sentimental consolation verse of her day in emphasizing the pathos of death and the pain of separation from loved ones.

Although Dickinson clearly had some acquaintance with Herbert and Vaughan and probably also knew a bit about Donne and others, the evidence suggests that her awareness would have come too late and been too casual to have actively influenced her own art. Such at least is the conclusion of Ruth Miller, based on examining dates and markings in the Dickinson family library and investigating references to seventeenth-century poetry in the newspapers and periodicals read by Emily. Most of the sources date from the 1860s, by which time her mature style was fully formed and her characteristic themes and attitudes well established.

By contrast, the evidence is considerable for the writerly impact of the King James Bible and of Shakespeare on Dickinson's writing. The Bible is by far the text most frequently quoted or referred to in her poetry, albeit not quite as a literary source. (Fordyce Bennett's *Reference Guide* provides a poem-by-poem list of scriptural echoes and allusions.)

The Bible is also the main source for what Ruth Miller calls Dickinson's reply poems, texts staged as a rejoinder to some other text. Sewall cites the following example in his biography:

"And with what body do they come?" —
Then they do come — Rejoice!
What Door — What Hour — Run — run — My Soul!
Illuminate the House!

"Body!" Then real — a Face and Eyes —
To know that it is them! —
Paul knew the Man that knew the News —
He passed through Bethlehem — (P1492)

Like most reply poems, this one quotes the source text conspicuously. Oddly, but also typical of her reply poems in this respect, this poem is known to us only for having been sent in a letter; it is not to be found among the fascicles. In quite different ways, both features suggest Dickinson's care that her reader recognize the staging. She both supplies the reference and addresses the poem to a known audience, upon whose understanding she can presumably rely.

Although only a handful of poems can unmistakably be identified as replies, others may also originate more covertly as responses to a particular source. Noting the playful allusiveness in much of Dickinson's correspondence, for example, Richard Sewall has suggested that parts of a favorite text and even single words regularly served as a stimulus to her imagination. His suggestion exemplifies the frequent suspicion that many of Dickinson's poems stem from sources we are unable to identify, sources as likely to be textual as biographical and possibly to be both at once.

Like reply poems, the many references in Dickinson's letters to Dickens, George Eliot, and most of all Shakespeare presuppose a shared and often also what is obviously a mutually cherished context. Early on they seem a badge of group identity. The regular recourse to Donald G. Mitchell's *Reveries of a Bachelor* in letters to girlhood friends suggests, for example, that Ik Marvel (Mitchell's pen name) served her circle as a source of erotic and probably also parentally disreputable pleasures of the imagination. Well beyond adolescence, in addition, literary references proliferate in letters to many of Dickinson's correspondents, and they also have been taken as signs of a special relation to her audience.

The most fully argued case concerns the Shakespearean tags and allusions that proliferate in letters between the poet and her sister-in-law and also in the poems that Emily sent to Susan. In line with similar observations by Rebecca Patterson and Paula Bennett, Judith Farr has proposed that references to the plays, particularly *Antony and Cleopatra*, served Emily and Susan as a code language (Patterson, *Imagery*; Bennett, "Orient"). The single word "Egypt," as in Antony's "Egypt, thou knew'st too well," could thus invoke the entire passion of the play's principals, and it could call up an identification of Emily as Antony and Susan as Cleopatra.

Shakespeare is not the only candidate for such a private lexicon. Farr makes a similar claim about *Jane Eyre* as a source for the Master letters and as a code used in writing to Samuel Bowles (whom Farr identifies as the addressee of the Master letters). Likewise, St. Armand proposes in "Veiled Ladies" that Bettina von Arnim's *Die Günderode* (in Margaret Fuller's 1842 translation) played a comparable role in correspondence with Susan and that Dickens and Shakespeare both served that function in letters to Bowles and later to Judge Lord.

Another aspect of the Shakespearean references, second in number only to the Bible but confined mainly to letters, points to a different kind of literary model. Dickinson never refers to the sonnets, though in their lyric and seemingly confessional mode and their frequent recourse to a shadowy but coherent erotic narrative those poems might seem to resemble many of Dickinson's. Likewise, she refers sparingly to the histories, comedies, and romances, although the last two genres might be thought to have the same kind of appeal and also to attract Dickinson's attention by their wit and wordplay, activities at which Dickinson also excels. Dickinson's evident bardolatry — "While Shakespeare remains Literature is firm" (L368) — is of another sort, however. She attends overwhelmingly to the tragedies, referring primarily to characters and dramatic speeches rather than to theme or style. Dickinson may thus have admired Shakespeare most for what Keats called his negative capability, the art coming from the embodiment of character more than sheer verbal skill or a capacity to express the poet's own thoughts and feelings. When Dickinson protests to Higginson that it is not she but a representative of the verse who speaks in the poems, we may suspect her of staking out some privacy from what otherwise are revealingly personal poems. But Dickinson's admiration for Shakespeare suggests the appeal of role playing and hence a fondness for representing characters other than her own.

Whereas the seventeenth century is a context Dickinson would have had to search out or select, New England is one she would have had difficulty avoiding, so the task for her readers and critics is to specify which aspects are most important or illuminating. Except for a common and often unspoken assumption that Dickinson is a quintessentially American writer, by which is usually meant a quintessentially New England writer, opinions differ about what her countrymen meant to her and which of them loomed the largest. Earlier cultural historians stressed the importance of a Puritan intellectual and religious heritage but were usually unable to locate particular influences. More recently critics have paid attention to the popular literature of the times, especially by women. Dickinson knew this literature quite well, as her letters make clear. In addition, from the beginning a debate has raged about the importance to Dickinson of Emerson and Emersonianism.

Emily Dickinson lived all her life in the Connecticut Valley, a stronghold of uncompromising Calvinism and the site during her formative years of the last great religious revivals in New England. Although she ultimately resisted conversion and although she showed no special interest in reading devotional texts, she seems nevertheless to have been well schooled in the New England mind by the sermons she heard and by the influence of family, friends, and teachers. Questions of faith get explored in Dickinson's poetry against a background of three divergent sources: the older Puritanism lingering in conservative Amherst, the liberalizing and rationalizing trends of Enlightenment thought that culminated in Emersonian transcendentalism, and a sentimental or domestic religiosity that arose during Dickinson's own lifetime.

I find that the surest guide to the first two sources is Karl Keller, who offers separate, detailed comparisons with Anne Bradstreet, Edward Taylor, and Jonathan Edwards and a canny critique of the frequent emphasis on Emerson's importance. Keller argues that as a whole Puritanism chiefly supplied to Dickinson a mythic framework within which poetic and existential dramas could be staged. The most important plank in the scaffolding is that value and meaning are to be discovered by scrutinizing the soul; real life is within. The importance of introspection is, of course, a cliché about New England culture, in that it supposedly links together everyone from Cotton Mather to Wallace Stevens. The cliché takes on considerable force in Dickinson's writing, however, since she arguably privileges interiority to a greater and more exclusive degree than any American poet. Moreover, her corresponding inattention to social and historical externalities distinguishes her from another important line of American writing that also descends from Puritanism. Unlike the New England writing that Sacvan Bercovitch has recently much emphasized, Dickinson does not identify the soul's fate with a national destiny. She writes no jeremiads.

Instead, Dickinson couples introspection with a more specifically religious doctrine, namely, the ontological gap between man and God and the absolute importance of this divide. In numerous poems the difference between time and eternity or earth and heaven is precisely what makes a difference, that is, makes meaning and makes the concerns of her poetry meaningful. According to Calvinism, one more feature of the same scene is that God is above all the source of judgment, however much divinity may also be associated with charity, grace, wisdom, and so forth. Dickinson, too, never abjures this possibility, although she also entertains other opinions about divine justice and sovereignty.

Although she evinces a keen respect for human intellect, especially her own, Dickinson seems true to her Connecticut Valley roots in resisting the confidence in human reason that gave rise to Unitarianism and other liberalizing trends. However, many of her poems about nature take seriously the collateral Emersonian belief that one can and should read the landscape for signs of transcendental truth. Not only are there sermons in stones, but we are equipped to hear them, at least some of the time. As the Wordsworthian tag indicates, Emerson is not the only source of this romantic tenet, but he was certainly the dominant voice in the United States and he is clearly the father in this respect of the nature writings of Thoreau and Higginson, which Dickinson seems to have read appreciatively.

In a great many Dickinson poems rehearsing a number of different views, the most urgent religious and existential issues are reasonably well defined by the distance between Connecticut Valley dread and Concord enthusiasm. That Dickinson at least knew of the latter is undeniable. She was given a copy of Emerson's *Poems* in 1853, and she writes approvingly of *Representative Men*. On the other hand, she neglected meeting him in 1857 when he lectured in Amherst and then spent the night next door at Austin and Susan's house. More strikingly, none of their several mutual literary acquaintants seemed to have shown any of her poems to him.

Emerson and Dickinson both care a great deal about the soul's access to supernal power and to a transcendent state of being, and she often joins him in demanding such a boon. On the other hand, for every poem in which she imagines herself as a debauchee of dew, there is another in which she represents such rapture as an earthly paradise that too competes with heaven. In other words, she regularly imagines rivalry and conflicting motives in the soul's traffic with the divine, whereas Emerson is prone to emphasize continuity and harmony.

The relation with Emerson and the Puritan past is one emphasized in American studies by what must now be regarded as the old consensus. That school of thinking has been challenged in converging ways by feminist critics and by historical scholars such as St. Armand. Both newer approaches stress Dickinson's immersion in the popular culture of her time and her fondness for at least some of its once scorned motifs. Next to the highbrow tradition running from Edwards to Emerson, for example, St. Armand juxtaposes the literature of what he calls a Sentimental Love Religion, which is primarily a construct of the women of Victorian America. He thus notes that a number of Dickinson's lyrics presuppose as background some version of the widely popular narratives in which "death, love, the afterlife, nature and art are all bound in fealty to the great idea of romance" (*Culture* 80). Such narratives are both literally and metaphorically operatic, serving commonly as the plots for actual libretti and finding a place in numerous popular novels of the day.

Several aspects of this literature obviously resonate with a number of Dickinson's poems. One key motif is that of separated, banned, or otherwise star-crossed lovers, who often can hope only for reunion after death. Another is the centrality of deathbed scenes and of a sentimental rhetoric of consolation, which is especially important to the verse of the time. It has long been obvious that many of Dickinson's poems both draw upon such mortuary verse and also importantly depart from it. Now that such poetry is again being read with some respect for its historical valences, it should become possible to sort out Dickinson's relation to this work and compare the influence more judiciously to sterner Puritan notions about death and dying.

A third aspect of such literature stresses religion's material comforts, imagining heaven as a well-furnished house in which the self can feel at home. This is the aspect that most diverges from Puritanism, with its more disembodied theology and its emphasis on the perils of damnation over the promises of salvation. It is also the most significantly gendered aspect, Puritanism representing a harsh, masculine tradition against the feminized religion of the heart. Dickinson's relation to the materialist aspect of sentimentality remains a subject open to investigation. A comparison between home and heaven is clearly crucial to Dickinson, but it is less likely that she shares the Biedermeier sensibility of an Elizabeth Stuart Phelps, St. Armand's chief exemplar of material domesticity.

Joining St. Armand in decrying the tendency to dwell too exclusively on highbrow culture are both David Reynolds, who links Dickinson to the themes of the sensation fiction of the 1840s and 1850s, and a number of feminist scholars who stress Dickinson's kinship with the once much-lamented women poets of the century. The important claims here go beyond similarities of theme and imagery to the possibility that women's poetry differed in kind and genre from nineteenth-century poetry by men. Cheryl Walker offers the richest discussion so far of this claim, singling out such categories as verse fantasies of power, poems that on the other side identify with powerlessness and abjection, and poems that imagine some sanctuary for the sensitive or threatened soul. Above all, she notes, women's poetry stresses feeling and sensibility over thought or fact, largely exemplifying in this respect the culture's separation between men's and women's spheres.

American literature seems more a source of intellectual and thematic contexts for Dickinson than of specifically literary inspirations and challenges. Dickinson's gnomic style sufficiently resembles Emerson's that when published anonymously one of her poems was misidentified as his. Yet, except for one redaction of William Ellery Channing (P1234), and early references to Bryant (P131) and Longfellow (P284), Dickinson does not invoke American authors in her verse. The case for the specifically literary influence of American literature comes more from the models it may have provided for her imaginative and artistic life. Richard Sewall, for example, explores in some detail the possible influence on Dickinson's imagination of Longfellow's *Kavanagh* and Mitchell's *Reveries*.

Pursuing a similar topic in a different fashion, Joanne Dobson examines how Dickinson's ardent but invisible literary identity figures against both the careers of other women writers of the time and the models of female selfhood available in their writing. Partly stressing the code of reticence to which women were expected to adhere, Dobson also makes it clear that many women either transgressed it or found ways to mitigate it. The result is to modify the picture of Dickinson as rebel and nonconformist that is usually derived from her obvious stylistic and intellectual daring. Dobson portrays Dickinson, in her reluctance about publication and publicity, as largely acquiescing to an orthodoxy against which others often struggled.

In *New England Literary Culture* Lawrence Buell also portrays Dickinson's literary identity as more conventional than others have seen. He first acknowledges her stylistic and rhetorical obliqueness, then notes that it can and has been equally well explained as resulting from two different forms of ambivalence on her part, one about Puritan theology and the other about the ideology of true womanhood in Victorian America. In either case the result is that Dickinson is torn between private passion and established morality, and in this she is said importantly to resemble Longfellow, Lowell, and other middlebrow poets of her region. Buell accordingly portrays her as an especially telling representative of New England culture rather than an idiosyncratic exception to its main patterns.

One drawback of Buell's argument is that it would apply equally well to most English writers of the time, and indeed he acknowledges at one point that a regional focus risks blinding the critic to larger patterns. More generally, the silently nationalist bias of much Dickinson criticism may similarly limit the visibility of larger contexts. Dickinson herself was no respecter of frontiers. Perhaps conspicuously, she never echoes one of the resounding commonplaces of antebellum culture, namely, the importance of establishing a distinctively American literature. Although recent scholarship has stressed the forgotten American writers, particularly women, whom Dickinson would have learned from, thereby correcting an undue stress on Emerson, Whitman, and other male standards, Dickinson herself expressed the greatest enthusiasm for English writers, many of them female contemporaries, and seemed otherwise wholly indifferent to the cultural nationalism prevalent in her day.

More specifically, she admired the writers of her day (the Brownings, the Brontës) who most clearly carried forward the idealistic program of English romanticism. I have elsewhere argued that Dickinson felt an allegiance to the poetry of sensation, which begins with Keats and Shelley and continues with such "spasmodics" as Elizabeth Barrett Browning and the early Tennyson. This is a school contrasted in Victorian England with the poetry of reflection, deriving from Wordsworth and perhaps finding its culmination in Arnold's criticism. More generally, Sewall observes that at a fundamental level "her sense of self had Romantic origins, rebellious at first, developing into a kind of heroic individualism," and that she had a "Romantic sensitivity to Nature" (*Life* 714).

On the other hand, she makes few references to the major romantic poets, and the one full-scale study of her relation to English romanticism, Joanne Feit Diehl's, is obliged to posit rather than demonstrate the connection. Indeed, Diehl's work depends upon the notably ahistorical and context-indifferent poetics developed by Harold Bloom. It is, in other words, another readerly appropriation, in which the detailed comparison of "Frost at Midnight" and "The Frost was never seen" depends for its value on mutually illuminating the two poems and not on the hunch that Dickinson's poem is a reply to Coleridge's.

Furthermore, in her own references to nineteenth-century English literature Dickinson more often expressed enthusiasm about novels and novelists than about poetry, the more so if we regard Browning's *Aurora Leigh* as essentially a novel in verse. Dickinson refers usually to the characters rather than to phrasings, plot, settings, and so on. Gilbert and Gubar accordingly argue that these characters offer broad models for the personae in her poems. Moreover, Dickinson's references to the characters are of a piece with her abundant interest in the writers' biographies. As Margaret Homans observes, Dickinson seems to have grouped both real and fictional characters under the category of "exemplary lives" (*Women Writers* 164). The pattern may thus further confirm Dickinson's greater interest in imagining character than in expressing the self. On the other hand, exemplary lives may chiefly be models for oneself; Homans's point is that Dickinson looked especially to other women writers for examples of literary identity.

Except for one telling phrase commemorating Elizabeth Barrett Browning (P312) and another that praises Helen Hunt Jackson, perhaps dutifully and politely (L368), Dickinson does not actually single out women writers as a category, nor does she ever explicitly identify her own situation as that of a woman writer. On the other hand, the issue of female authorship was so widely debated in her day that Dickinson could hardly have been unaware of it. Moreover, even if the issue plays an uncertain role as a compositional context, it emphatically dominates recent interpretive contexts. Much contemporary criticism reads Dickinson symptomatically, as inevitably expressing the situation of the woman writer although not necessarily thematizing it.

In addition to the otherwise separable contexts that can briefly be designated as poetry by American women and novels by English women, two cases can be made for gender as a context that crosses borders and genres. Paula Bennett makes the most forceful claim for the first: "Dickinson's definition of herself as woman poet was . . . rooted in her positive feelings for women. If, with the exception of Jackson, Dickinson never mentions American women poets by name, she nevertheless saw herself as part of a female literary tradition which she and they shared. British in origin, this tradition had found its richest, most complicated, expression in the work of Elizabeth Barrett Browning, the Bronte sisters, and George Eliot" (*Woman Poet* 1415). According to this view the American divide between a sentimental religion of the heart and a Puritan religion of the head is for Dickinson chiefly a dispute between gynocentric and androcentric notions of selfhood. As such, it links up with the social and erotic issues faced by such as Aurora Leigh and Jane Eyre.

The other case, which I find more suggestive, depends on contemporary theories about the gendering of language and meaning. According to such a perspective, which is best represented by the work of Diehl, Homans, and Loeffelholz, Dickinson draws her "unique power from her particular way of understanding her femininity" (Homans, *Women Writers* 171). However, both this argument and the more specific one that she adheres to a nonreferential language, one which she and her culture would have regarded as female, stand at some distance from historically verifiable claims about Dickinson's sources and background.

JUDITH FARR

Dickinson and the Visual Arts

$\mathcal{P}$raising Emily Dickinson's poem about a hummingbird, "A Route of Evanescence / With a revolving wheel" (P1463)[1] in the *Atlantic Monthly* of October 1891, Thomas Wentworth Higginson remarked that it was "an exquisite little . . . strain, every word a picture" (Buckingham, *Reception* 191). Having helped to edit the first, best-selling collection of Dickinson's poems published in 1890, Higginson was eager to continue an astute promotional effort that he had begun by commending her as a painter. Probably in order to disarm criticism of what he conceded was the "rugged frame" of Dickinson's verse, he always insisted on its "vividly objective" pictorial qualities. Indeed, he wrote in the *Christian Union* just before *Poems* appeared that Dickinson's readers were about to see "sea picture[s]" better than those sketched in the poems of Celia Thaxter, done by a hand that moved with "vigor" as the author "draws the [even] mightier storms and shipwrecks of the soul" (Buckingham 4). Linking Dickinson's poetic accounts of natural scenes like "This — is the land — the Sunset washes — " (P266) with her visions of the mysteries of death, Higginson presented them all as distinctive kinds of painting that exhibited "an extraordinary vividness of descriptive and imaginative power" (Buckingham 14).

By joining the word "strain," used by the Victorians as synonymous with verse measure or line, with "picture" in his account of her hummingbird poem, Higginson evoked the Roman poet Horace's concept *ut pictura poesis* ("it [should be] in poetry as in painting"). This concept, relating the arts in a single sisterhood and directing that each be judged in its successful relation to the other, had enjoyed exceptional prominence during the romantic and Victorian periods.[2] Although the friend whom she loyally called her dear "Preceptor" (L265) failed to grasp the innovative genius of Emily Dickinson, here he did *not* fail her. With his considerable knowledge as a cultivated social historian, he called upon the assumptions and tastes of the age. Painters in nineteenth-century America were accorded great prestige; they also enjoyed a popularity matched by few American writers. Thus Higginson cleverly directed her public to judge Emily Dickinson not as a verse writer alone but as a type of that hero of long magazine articles and crowded showrooms, the visual artist.[3]

This essay seeks to provide an overview of the relation of Emily Dickinson's poetry to the visual arts and briefly to summarize scholarship, past and present, on this topic. The essay's chief theme is Dickinson's knowledge and employment of the subject matter and techniques of mid-Victorian painting; but it will also attempt to indicate the presence in her poetry of imagistic and stylistic attributes common to graphic and decorative arts such as engraving, collage, and needlework. To judge from internal evidence provided by her poems and letters and by her own acknowledgment, Emily Dickinson was sensitive to most visual arts of her day, including sculpture. But it was painting and the related art, drawing, that seem most significantly to have affected her choice of subject and language while shaping her aesthetic — her conception of the function of poetry.

That aesthetic was influenced by the painter-critic John Ruskin (1819–1900), who held that art's purpose is to see and then project in clear *pictures* the relation between mortal nature and the enduring universe. Art was transcendent, greater even than science for Ruskin and his followers; but it had the moral purpose of explaining the Creator to the created. (Or, as Dickinson's less theocentric phrase puts it, art must depict "Eternity in Time" [L688]). Ruskin's influence on painters *and* writers in the United States was profound. Dickinson herself admired *Modern Painters* and was apparently drawn to painterly "texts" by such masters as Frederic Edwin Church (1826–1900), thought of as the best American exemplar of Ruskin's ideas. She behaved like many artists of her time in experimenting with Ruskin's program for composition, recommended topics, and preferred techniques. Indeed, her lineation in the fascicles may, I propose, have been affected by Ruskin's theories about creative sketching. Emily Dickinson's sophistication as a poet, her lively participation in the culture of her day, and even the deeper meaning of poems that "quote" works of art she knew become clearer when she is studied as a visual artist.

THE CONNECTION between Dickinson's art and other forms of visual art — I say "other" because as soon as one puts a line on a blank page or a stitch in a piece of fabric one has a kind of "visual art" — began to attract intense, systematic scholarly scrutiny in 1984 with the publication of Barton Levi St. Armand's rich and important study, *Emily Dickinson and Her Culture*. St. Armand conceives Dickinson as a poet nourished by the mid-Victorian folk and high arts and crafts. He associates the fascicle poems with the portfolio and sketchbook traditions; lists and describes the painting collections of the Austin Dickinsons, known to Emily; demonstrates some shaping influences on Dickinson's verse of Ruskin, Emerson, and such artistic commentaries as Asher B. Durand's "Letters on Landscape Painting" (1855); hypothesizes the relation of Dickinson's subject matter to that of contemporary folk art; and shows that

Dickinson participated in the "cultural maelstrom" of her own time, though always "on her own terms" (221). St. Armand's invaluable chapter "Lone Landscapes: Dickinson, Ruskin, and Victorian Aesthetics" reconstructs the imagination of Emily Dickinson in terms of nineteenth-century aesthetic theory and discriminates the distinctions between her poetic evocations and those of a painter like Durand, showing that "her palette, if not her specific subject or interpretation, was . . . Ruskinian" (287).

To this palette, Rebecca Patterson also paid attention in *Emily Dickinson's Imagery* (1979). She declared that Dickinson "knew that a poet handled color words as a painter handled colors, and when she decided to become a poet she set about acquiring a serviceable selection of color words as one more element in the vocabulary appropriate to her craft" (115). Both Patterson and St. Armand comment on Dickinson's characteristic fondness for purple, red, and yellow, associating it with the mid-Victorian palette. Earlier twentieth-century critics, to be sure, had alluded to Dickinson's knowledge of Ruskin without considering its deeper implications for her subject matter or technique. Many commentators offered generalized observations about her reading in art theory or her visual/visionary imagination (a topic about which Roland Hagenbüchle has more recently offered refined distinctions). George Whicher observed that "her browsings in Ruskin" may have given her a "moral view" of the 'Martyr Painters' that she expressed in one poem" while "suppl[ying] her with allusions to Guido, Titian, Domenichino . . . and Van Dyke" (212–13). Charles R. Anderson, speaking of Dickinson's use in "Because I could not stop for Death" of "progressively fewer visible objects" (*Stairway* 245), argued that hers was an imagination that often sought to illustrate by strategic placement of forms in space, an artist's method. Recent linguistic critics like E. Miller Budick, even, resort to a diction bordering on the art-aesthetic in calling the poems a "hesitating collection of independent perceptual moments" which "picture reality . . . in discontinuous and disparate frames of sense information" (26).

Before Patterson and St. Armand, however, those who specifically compared Emily Dickinson's poetry to the works of painters were themselves nineteenth-century writers. Indeed, Dickinson's work was immediately compared to the visual arts when the 1890 *Poems* appeared. The first to associate Dickinson with visual artists were her early reviewers. In a magazine devoted to painting and belles lettres called the *Art Amateur* (May 1891), one critic compared Dickinson's poetry to three other artistic expressions: the painting of the German Lucas Cranach (1472–1553), "the early wood-cuts of the emblem writers" who had vogue chiefly in the sixteenth and seventeenth centuries, and finally to "impressionist pictures" — probably French impressionism, which originates in the 1860s and to which Mabel Loomis Todd would also compare Emily Dickinson's verse (Buckingham, *Reception* 135, 237). The *Christian Register* (December 1890) likened Dickinson's elegiac subject matter to that of Michelangelo, the great sculptor-painter whose skill she envies in one of her Master letters (Buckingham, *Reception* 63).[4]

To erect such a wide frame of comparison may seem feckless. But her readers were struggling to find suitable analogues in the visual arts to qualities they perceived in Dickinson's poetry and were unused to meeting in popular late-Victorian verse. Their comparisons were not insensitive. For example, Cranach is famous for exquisitely refined, somewhat cerebral landscapes and for boldly executed scenes of death and resurrection, all to be found in *Poems* (1890). (He is also famed for eroticism; but despite "Wild Nights," the 1890 reviewers probably did not intend that comparison.) The emblem writer/engravers — whose art influenced that of Thomas Cole (1801–48), founder of American landscape painting and a vital influence on Emily Dickinson — were noteworthy for giving symbolic expression to moral proverbs, adages, ideas, or beliefs. They would print a quatrain about hope, for example, illustrating it with the picture of a woman holding aloft an anchor. Such a poem as "Exultation is the going / Of an inland soul to sea" (P76) with its boat, headlands, and symbolic traveler could be similarly seen to define by illustration. Indeed, Dickinson's many poems of definition — "Faith is . . . ," "Hope is . . . ," "Love is . . . " — bear precise relation to the emblem tradition in British art, transmitted by the Puritans to the New England of her day. Her poetry also exhibits a graphic specificity — she speaks of a splinter's swerve or a smitten rock — that is considered advantageous in the emblem tradition, wherein objects are presented explicitly and conceptually as ideas. Finally, "impressionism," a word formally established in 1874[5] but casually used in Dickinson's lifetime, was thought to characterize the rapid-sketch staccato quality of some of her verses. It seemed to describe her fascination with the play of light on forms which appears in many poems like "There's a certain Slant of light" (P258).

Since Victorian literary critics were usually cultivated in the arts, they moved among them freely, comparing architecture to music, music to painting, dance to poetry, with a wide referentiality. Moreover, artists themselves enjoyed borrowing nomenclature and insights across artistic boundaries: Whistler painted "nocturnes"; Schumann composed "scenes"; Dickinson imagined her poems as canvases one could carry in the hand (P308). The rival art form an artist chose was also revealing: thus, for example, Whistler's choice of music as descriptive of the content and form of his paintings sprang from an effort to deny that they had narrative content, to insist that they presented design and color alone, to emphasize their innovative lyricism and liquidity of brushstroke. As I seek to demonstrate in *The Passion of Emily Dickinson*, painting was the primary symbolic "language" of Emily Dickinson's aesthetic discourse and practice. The degree of her absorption in the process (actual and symbolic) of perception and its practical, critical, and historic lore in the fine arts is therefore as essential to an understanding of her work in general as to successful reading of individual poems.

Although they compared her poems to paintings, her early critics could not have known that she herself described her poetic acts as "painting" and asked that her writing be judged as painting: "Do I paint it *natural?*" (L85). She customarily associates good writing with an imperishable painting, one that can bear being read/seen by the light of day (reality) without losing its power: "Some phrases are too fine to fade" (L277). Her loneliness for Susan Gilbert makes her long to be able to describe it — in paint, not words: "I would paint a portrait which would bring the tears, had I canvass for it, and the scene should be — *solitude*, and the figures — solitude — and the lights and shades, each a solitude. I could fill a chamber with landscapes so lone, men should pause and weep there" (L176). (Here Dickinson's choice of the two genres, portraiture and landscape painting, that were most popular in American painting during her lifetime, and her mention of the solitary figures conceived in light and shade that immediately suggest the characteristic themes of Thomas Cole and his preference for chiaroscuro scenes make her knowledge of contemporary painting obvious.) In several poems and letters Emily Dickinson joined "Martyr Poet" and "Martyr Painter" in the mutual, costly, elevating, and reassuring enterprise of seeing and recording whereby one seeks "in Art — the Art of Peace — " (P544). As in "I would not paint — a picture — " (P505), she often precedes a discussion of the process, experience, and effects of writing poetry by imagining what it would be like to have a painter's "celestial fingers" that can provoke "Torment" and "Despair." Her conception in poem 505 of the painter's skill as heavenly and of what he stimulates in the viewer as suffering accords with classic late-eighteenth- and early-nineteenth-century views of the artistic sublime (see Novak, *Nature* 34–44).

Throughout her artistic life, Dickinson painted portraits and meditated on images made by others: sculptured "Men of Ivory" or the colorful "Boys and Girls, in Canvas" (P499) whose mortal faces invited her to imagine them as immortal. Studying the world framed by her window or garden, she fashioned various landscapes, describing day as it advanced from dawn to sunset or the seasons as they supplanted one another. Their "Splendors" were to her like a "Menagerie" (P290) or a circus or a theater, and God a royal "Showman" (P628), whose art she sought to imitate. Such painters as Cole and Church, exhibiting their smoldering canvases of sunrise and sunset to wide audiences, were often described as showmen in competition with the Lord; and they, too, saw both nature and art as rival forms of "theater." For all their idiosyncracy, the style, motifs, and symbolic content of Dickinson's landscapes often evoke those of the Hudson River, luminist, or Pre-Raphaelite painters.[6] In addition, American art historians like Barbara Novak and John Wilmerding predicate general connections between the incisive detail of Dickinson's landscapes and that common to miniature painting in her day.[7] Wilmerding compares certain poems to the canvases of the still-life painter William M. Harnett (1848–92), remarking that "like Harnett, [Dickinson] shaped her art with refined concentration and shadowy closure, employing repeated rhythms . . . , economy of form, and concern for the transience of life" (154). Meditation on mutability is deeply intrinsic to still-life painting. So such poems as Dickinson's "His Bill is clasped—his Eye forsook—" (P1102), wherein she laments the bird "Gored through and through with Death," justify a comparison to still life, another synonym for which is *nature morte*. From almost all the American painting of her time, however, Emily Dickinson would have learned that "the true purpose of art . . . was 'impressing the mind through the visible forms of material beauty, with a deep sense of the invisible and immaterial'" (Ferber 248). Still life, landscape, portrait and history painting: all conspired, like so much of her own poetry, to provide that revelation.

Remarkably, moreover, Emily Dickinson's art shows similarities even to contemporary art works she might never have seen. Working within the *zeitgeist* of her time, she reflects it, often anticipating directions taken by some visual artists in a later period. So, in her meditative explorations of the Soul and Mind, Dickinson shows the kind of surrealistic fascination that preoccupied the American orientalist painter Elihu Vedder (1836–1923), a friend of Dickinson's friend Dr. Josiah Holland, whose drawings appeared in Holland's *Century* magazine. The surreal iconography of her visions of death — as in her fantasy about a dead woman in a "Sod Gown" riding to meet her doom with "Horses of Blonde" in a "Coach of Silver," a ghastly scene in *grisaille* (P665) — points to the work of American artists like Albert Pinkham Ryder (1847– 1917). Dickinson would not have known Ryder's paintings, but she illustrates the spirit of several.[8] David T. Porter, in "Assembling a Poet and Her Poems," has linked her oeuvre to visual modernism and her writing techniques to those of the dada assemblagist Joseph Cornell, but one need not go further from the mid-Victorian period than her near contemporary Winslow Homer (1836– 1910) to meet a painter whose dark meditations on mortality and specifically on empty space — what she called "Miles of Stare" (P243) — court shapes resembling Emily Dickinson's.[9]

What one consistently observes in her own art is evidence of sympathy with the ideas and techniques of painters. Sometimes, as St. Armand indicates, that sympathy resulted from Dickinson's participation in the cultural enterprises of her time. But in my view there were also singular personal reasons for Dickinson's uses of, and allusions to, the works of painters. Emily Dickinson seems to have been so conversant with the high art in particular of her own day that one may confidently hypothesize that she specifically cites famous mid-Victorian paintings by Church and others in order to fashion a personal language for such readers as Susan Dickinson or Samuel Bowles, who shared her tastes. Her awareness of the visual arts may be explained in part by her education and in part by the great prestige, particularly of painting, both in mid-Victorian culture and in her own family circle. Austin and Susan Dickinson were passionate collectors of Hudson River and Barbizon paintings.[10] Samuel Bowles's unpublished correspondence with the Dickinsons enthusiastically describes his own paintings and makes arrangements for the display of Austin's at Springfield charity events.[11] Despite the fact that she did not travel after her early thirties and probably did not visit the popular shows of Hudson River and Pre-Raphaelite art in Boston in the late 1850s, Emily Dickinson could meet the art of her day in magazines. Her favorite magazines—*Harper's Monthly*, the *Century*, the *Atlantic Monthly*, and *Scribner's*—not only published articles about America's painters but occasionally provided descriptions and reproductions of their work. (So did some newspapers like the *Christian Register*, read by the Dickinsons.) The Austin Dickinsons, whose library Emily used, subscribed to the *Art Journal*. The verbal and visual sophistication of these magazines made it possible for her to see the work of such painters as Church through strikingly clear reproductions that rendered an accurate impression of the painters' subject matter and techniques. The wood engravings executed by Winslow Homer for *Harper's*, for example, would have met Dickinson's eye with an etched precision that makes some museum-worthy today. A habitual reader of *Harper's*, Dickinson would have encountered Homer's eloquent genre and war scenes so crisply rendered that she could become instructed in the manner and modes of contemporary visual art without visiting galleries and exhibitions.

Her interest, and her family's interest, in art, however, cannot explain the prominence of the idea of art and the artist in her work or, to be sure, the highly visual content of Emily Dickinson's poetry. For all her fascination with abstraction, she possessed a "visual" "sensibility" (St. Armand, *Culture* 221). That she herself drew, that she had taken lessons in linear and perspective drawing at Mary Lyon's Seminary, that she was "apt with a pencil" (Leyda 2: 284) and frequently illustrated her writing with pictures, underscores her personal attraction to the visual arts. This attraction, so variously manifested in the letters and poems, must be the underlying premise of such a topic as this one. Those closest to Dickinson were well aware of her proclivity to associate poems and pictures. It is significant that Susan Dickinson's original if discarded plan was to bring out an "article" on Dickinson's poems accompanied by her "witty" drawings (Bingham, *Ancestors'* 118).

Hundreds of Dickinson's poems make her visual imagination abundantly clear. Many present her as a painter, first studying what she sees, then rendering the scene. Since the idea of eternity is, of all her metaphysical themes, the one that most preoccupies Emily Dickinson, she often discriminates what will last from what fades; and so even her domestic scenes often seek revelations. In "The Angle of a Landscape —," she describes herself measuring the small area of ground that meets her eye when she wakes: it holds the "Pattern of a Chimney," a hilltop, a steeple. The ground of her "Picture" shifts with the seasons, filling with emerald leaves in spring and snow-diamonds in winter. But the architecture of her landscape remains, like an essential self, and "never stir[s] at all — " (P375). Though she gazes, as a painter might, at a fixed picture in poem 375, Dickinson immediately invests it with motion: a property foreign to painting. She prefers to describe nature in movement or change. When she captures a sunrise or "finishe[s]" a sunset, as she says in poem 308, hers is usually an account of the progress of the event: "I'll tell you how the Sun rose — / A Ribbon at a time — " (P318). Her concentration is on what I have called *transitus* or movement from one state to another (*Passion* 7, 36, 83, 84, 329). This movement may be from life to death or from one to another context or stage of being. Thus one of her metaphors of *transitus* is a flower, seen first as a bulb, next as a bud, and last in bloom. Observing "Mornings," she says they "blossom into Noon — / And split their Pods of Flame — " (P620); watching sunset, she calls it "Bloom upon the Mountain — stated — / Blameless of a Name — " (P667). Her many descriptions of birds in flight, a frequent subject for artists, were also ways to describe natural motion. Sometimes she suggested a relation between flight and supernatural life: "Curve by Curve," "Out of sight? What of that? / See the Bird — reach it!" (P703). Higginson's favorite among her bird paintings, "A route of evanescence," studies the quick iridescent rush of the hummingbird among flowers with a verbal speed that is mimetic. Martin Johnson Heade (1819–1904) was famous for his studies of hummingbirds in the 1860s; but his canvases do not render the experience of actual flight so persuasively as Dickinson's words.

For painting, after all — as distinguished from painted assemblages like Alexander Calder's, for example — does not easily convey the phenomena of change or movement; painting is static. Serial paintings like Thomas Cole's *Course of Empire* (1834–36), which Dickinson's poems suggest that she knew,[12] triumph over this fixity by juxtaposing scenes that describe beginning, development, and end, the telescoping of processes which poetry may establish and complete in the span of one lyric. Their material stillness is the singular disadvantage of painting and other graphic arts when compared to literature or music, and, indeed, Emily Dickinson makes this disadvantage one of her more salient subjects. Despite her respect for painting, Dickinson likes to acknowledge its deficiencies in describing animation. And, as I have said, she makes her own "paintings" *move*. In her poem "The Trees like Tassels — hit — and swung —," for example, everything is in motion — not only the wind-tossed tree but the sun, the growing orchards, the busily gossiping birds, a snake "winding round a Stone —," and even the flowers slitting their calyxes. Compared to this scene, either in nature or her poem, she calls the seventeenth-century British painter Anthony van Dyck's "Delineation" of summer days "mean" (P606).

Nevertheless, Emily Dickinson seems always to recognize the cardinal advantage painting does have over literature: its immediacy of illustrative effect. That Dickinson, the writer, acknowledged and possibly envied this advantage is suggested by the fact that she sometimes drew a picture upon a page that contained a poem in order, she said, to convey her meaning more directly than words would permit. Possibly she did this because "All men say 'What' to me" (L271). Forced to accept the difficulty some found in deciphering her verbal pictures, she might accompany them with crayoned cartoons whose occasional crudeness could mock both her addressee's obtuseness and her own fervor — as if to say "You don't understand? Then let me *show* you."[13] Her habit suggests that she often associated drawing with *telling*, with narrative. So she says in poem 291 that, for all his eloquence, the great sixteenth-century Venetian painter Titian "never told" completely how beautiful nature is.

In the initial quatrains of her poem "It will be Summer — eventually —," telling and drawing fuse, as the poet describes the change of seasons as the making of a painting:

> It will be Summer — eventually —
> Ladies — with parasols —
> Sauntering Gentlemen — with Canes —
> And little Girls — with Dolls —
>
> Will tint the pallid landscape —
> As 'twere a bright Bouquet —
> Tho' drifted deep in Parian —
> The Village lies — today — (P342)

Here Emily Dickinson envisions a village buried in snow that, by a characteristic association of marble or sculptured forms with lifelessness or inanition, she compares to the porcelain Parian ware in use around 1850 and after for statuettes. During winter the village is as still and colorless as "Parian," she says, or, we may infer, a white canvas. But Summer will soon arrive. Then the landscape will be colored and populated by ladies carrying parasols, gentlemen with canes, and little girls with dolls. (Strikingly, Dickinson's poem anticipates the scene in Georges Seurat's *Un Dimanche à la Grande Jatte* by about thirty years.) Her conceit of color transforming a white canvas need not suggest impressionism; but the "pallid" landscape juxtaposed with "bright Bouquet" evokes the startling effects many impressionists sought with light. Though Summer tints Dickinson's landscape — her use of the word "tint" in association with "pallid" makes this seem like a scene done in watercolor, not oils — her poem ends with the word "done" and with the awareness that summer always ends. Nevertheless, she reminds us, too, that "Lilacs — bending many a year / Will sway" again. Despite that voluptuous line, Dickinson's picture achieves the fixity of a Parian piece. It is a still life, composed of real and symbolic flowers: frilled gentians and a sunset like a red aster. Significantly, Dickinson provides us in poem 342 with a verbal "painting" based on the conceit of painting, in which the very word "landscape" conveys her interest in art. In the nineteenth century, *landscape* could mean either a portion of land ("Village") or a picture of it.[14] In poem 342, both meanings are relevant. Moreover, in the Dickinson family, *landscape* also seems to have been a metaphor for harmony and happiness. In "I reckon — when I count at all — " (P569), Emily Dickinson lists summer as among her four most cherished experiences. Therefore, it was perhaps inevitable that "It will be Summer — eventually — " describes summer as a living picture whose stillness implies rebirth, not death.

FEW DICKINSONIANS are unaware that, when T. W. Higginson asked her to tell him what she liked to read, Emily Dickinson listed "Mr. Ruskin" first among her favorite prose writers. Volume 1 of *Modern Painters* had appeared in the United States when she was a schoolgirl in 1847. It electrified the American painter-editor William Stillman, friend of the Pre-Raphaelite poet-painter Dante Gabriel Rossetti, who took Ruskin as a "spiritual mentor" (Gerdts 55) in his art magazine *The Crayon*. By 1862 when Dickinson was writing Higginson, volume 5 had appeared and been highly praised. *Modern Painters* was to change the public conception of what art is or should be. An extravagant, learned, compellingly written celebration of the art of Joseph Mallord William Turner (1775–1851), Ruskin's book sought to explain Turner's revolutionary absorption in luminosity, romantic subject matter and movement in nature, as well as his liberated brushwork and composition — so free that it seemed to the nineteenth century almost abstract. Turner's forms appeared to dissolve in a brilliant haze of color. His art was to Ruskin prophetic; and it led Ruskin to revise his estimate of the relative importance of painting and literature. An ardent student of medieval and Renaissance art, periods in which painting was frequently regarded as a form of decoration related to furniture building while writing poetry was considered a semidivine act, Ruskin was moved by the art of Turner to glorify painting as an equal, even superior art. Having thought that "in representing human emotion words surpass painting, but in representing natural scenery painting surpasses words," Ruskin began to hand the palm to painters altogether: "the painter will become of more importance, the poet of less" (*Works* 5:330, 331). This had been the classic view; for while Horace's injunction joined literature and painting in a single mission of seeing and recording, Cicero's remark "Quam multa vident pictores in umbris et eminentia, quae nos non videmus" represented painters as mysteriously, semimystically, "seeing in light and shadow what we [others, even poets] do not" (see Hagstrum 3–29).

Ruskin, therefore, restored painting to a critical eminence it had not maintained for many hundreds of years; and his criticism was having its full effect just as Emily Dickinson began to read, think, draw, and write. Probably due to Ruskin—and before him, to the criticism of Emerson and Thomas Cole (who often composed poetic accounts of his series paintings like the seminal *Voyage of Life* [1840])—nineteenth-century writers frequently attempted to draw while painters sought to illustrate their portraits or landscapes in sonnets as well as on canvases. There came to be, then, a "privileging of the act of vision" (Freedman 388) in Dickinson's culture. Ruskin specifically encouraged it when he wrote in the third book of *Modern Painters* that "The greatest thing a human soul ever does in this world is to *see* something, and tell what it *saw* in a plain way. Hundreds of people can talk for one who can think, but thousands can think for one who can see" (5:333). Ruskin had not known the work of Emerson until 1856, when one of his students remarked on the congeniality of their aesthetic commentary; and so he was astonished to confront Emerson's similar words in *Nature* (1836), an essay that Emily Dickinson certainly knew and that greatly influenced the Hudson River painters: "Standing on the bare ground,—my head bathed by the blithe air and uplifted into infinite space,—all mean egotism vanishes. I become a transparent eyeball; I am nothing; I see all; the currents of the Universal Being circulate through me; I am part or parcel of God."[15]

Emerson's words have limited application for the work of Dickinson, whose speaker (despite her pose in "I'm Nobody!" [P288]) never disappears into "nothing" but retains a shrewdly measuring, idiosyncratic gaze. Even when assumed into the elements in "Behind Me—dips Eternity—" (P721), she does not become part of a personal God but is set adrift in a menacing landscape. Nevertheless, the Dickinson reader—confronted with her incessant use of forms of the verb "see," her emphasis on the analytic eye of the "I" or speaker, her frequent conception of the poetic act as requiring insight and an illustrative imagination—knows how important such statements as Emerson's or Ruskin's must have been to her. Dickinson's own aesthetic observations in "This was a Poet" (P448) make clear that her poet is akin to Emerson's transcendental poet-seer and Ruskin's artist-hero: she/he is "Of Pictures, the Discloser" and, like Ruskin's Pre-Raphaelites with their respect for definition and detail, "distills amazing sense" from the "ordinary Meanings" — truths/facts/scenes — that nature and life present. For Dickinson, moreover, art's transformative powers over the psyche could often be playfully described in terms of painting (though music also gave her the "fascinating chill" [P1480] she identified with rapture). "Make me a picture of the / sun —," she jests, "So I can hang it in my / room — / And make believe I'm getting / warm / When others call it 'Day' " (P188).

The topic of what *Modern Painters* might have offered Emily Dickinson in the way of an artistic rationale, points of view (about composition, the uses of space, important subjects, etc.), is, quite simply, vast. *Modern Painters* literally falls open to passages that find analogues in her own writing. Just one example: Ruskin muses, "Whatever beauty there may result from effects of light on foreground objects . . . there is yet a light which the eye invariably seeks with a deeper feeling of the beautiful, — the light of the declining or breaking day, and the flakes of scarlet cloud burning like watch-fires in the green sky of the horizon; a deeper feeling . . . having more of spiritual hope and longing." And he continues, moving toward a word, a concept, that is central to Dickinson's work: "There is one thing that [distant space] has . . . which no other object of sight suggests in equal degree, and that is — Infinity" (2:200, 201).

St. Armand (*Culture* 261–77) has discussed Dickinson's affection for portraying sunset and sunrise scenes that are akin to Ruskin's, in both his prose and his drawings, though she does not always take spiritual hope but sometimes "Despair" (P258) from their light. The extremes of day she found mystically meaningful. Her intense preoccupation with light — all painters share this preoccupation, but it manifested itself quasi-scientifically in luminist and impressionist painting — is sometimes characterized by seeing visions in the sunset. Ruskin had encouraged this practice of finding shapes in the sky, which the earlier painter John Constable, influenced by Leonardo, called "skying." Doing some skying herself, Dickinson describes that "Juggler of Day," the sun,

> Blazing in Gold and quenching in Purple
> Leaping like Leopards to the Sky
> Then at the feet of the old Horizon
> Laying her spotted Face to die (P228)

In some poems she sees ships in the sky, perhaps remembering the many volatile Turner seascapes described by Ruskin and reproduced in thousands of steel engravings in the United States in the 1850s and 1860s. (Turner's art was so well known, especially in New York and Boston, by 1859 that the *New York Times* praised Church's *Heart of the Andes* by comparing it to one of Turner's "noblest works" [Roque 44]). Dickinson's sunset poems, "Where ships of purple" (P265) and "This — is the Land — the / Sunset washes — " (P266), regard the sunset as a colorful scene of sailors, wharves, ships, and bales in the "Western Mystery" of the dying of the day: just the subject Turner continually essayed, either in vaporous yellow or in reds that resembled Dickinson's own "Fleets" of fire (P658).

When Ruskin spoke of "distant space" in Turner's art, moreover, and linked it to "Infinity," he reflected upon the "Stupendous Vision" (P802) on which Dickinson continually meditates, appealing to the conceits of broad vistas and terrifying spaces. Her poem "Behind Me — dips Eternity" (P721) conceptualizes the infinite in a manner akin to Turner's on one hand and to surrealism's (a movement Turner's fantasias helped kindle) on the other. Thus actual and eternal landscapes blend terrifyingly for Dickinson's disembodied speaker. Natural regions like East and West and natural bodies like the moon are placed on the canvas of poem 721 in unnatural, chaotic, and hence awful and threatening positions. Here, Dickinson moves beyond the later melancholy of Turner and toward a more nihilistic, modernist vision. Moreover, in some poems like "Because I could not stop for Death," she anticipates the metaphysical obsession with death manifest in the last canvases of a few important nineteenth-century American painters: not only Ryder, in such works as *With Shaping Mast and Dipping Prow* (n.d.) but Winslow Homer — for Homer's *Cape Trinity, Saguenay River* (1904–9), in which he avowedly equated the giant empty blackness of the Cape with a problematic Eternity, might serve as an illustration of the mood of Dickinson's speaker in poem 712, where she associates Eternity with continual placelessness.

At the same time, if Dickinson sees no comfort in sunsets or vistas in such poems as 721, she also writes more tranquil lyrics such as "The Lilac is an ancient shrub" (P1241) in which her poetic sunset *does* evoke that spiritual longing and those intimations of immortality that Ruskin associated with the death of day. In reading Ruskin, moreover, Dickinson probably took seriously not only his ideas about making an artwork but his praise of two faculties in the art of Turner and the Pre-Raphaelites. Ruskin insisted that these faculties were not contradictory but related. One was Turner's apocalyptic brilliance, evident in such paintings as *The "Fighting Téméraire" tugged to her Last Berth to be broken up* (1838) and *Snowstorm: Steamboat off a Harbour's Mouth* (1842), wherein ships either float within veils of cloud and water or toss indistinctly in whirls of vaporous white. This romantic apprehension Ruskin described as "completeness of the expression of ideas," "fineness of finish" (3: 155, 154). The other — highly influential, one feels, for Emily Dickinson — was Turner's distinctness of line.

For Ruskin judged Turner to be rightly committed to drawing the hard, bright, settled scenes with sharp outlines and specific detail that the Pre-Raphaelite Brotherhood associated with Giotto and all European art before Raphael. Turner provided "downright facts" "in all respects like Nature as possible" (Ruskin 3: 174). Emily Dickinson, to be sure, achieves visual representations of downright fact. For them, she is well known. And, as Ruskin claimed of Turner's, her factual scenes possess an underlying poetical truth. Thus she observes that "A Light exists in Spring / Not present on the Year / At any other period —." It is a kind of color standing abroad on "Solitary Fields." Such light is very real; indeed, Monet painted outdoors to catch its precise, somewhat withdrawn intensity. At the same time, like Turner's scenes that project desolation or exultation, Dickinson's poem about light in spring conveys an emotional response, the recognition of "A quality of loss" (P812).

Though hers is an affinity primarily with the subject matter of the high art of her day, Dickinson's poetry sometimes recalls American Naïve painting in its manner of presenting "facts." Sometimes she renders a scene reminiscent of those of the American limners[16] and Naïve painters like Thomas Doughty (1793–1856), who drew a series of objects together to make a primitive but illustrative picture. So, in a different approach to the theme of sunset, she describes the "Lady of the Occident," whose "Candle so expire / The flickering be seen / On Ball of Mast in Foreign Port— / And Spire — and Window Pane —" (P716). Even when she attempts the unsophistication of limning, Dickinson records beauty as fleeting. Her still lifes of mountains, flowers, and noon skies that become a "well" before a storm breaks (P1649) are, as I have remarked earlier, never really "still"; for she prefers the energy and glamor of nature in movement. When "a lane of Yellow led the eye / Unto a Purple Wood" (P1650) in her imagination, it was usually to find that a bird or a flower "contradict[ed]" the "silence" — the stillness — there. These poems, like the rest, are keenly observant, often exhibiting a detachment that fulfills the precepts of Ruskin. Ruskin's precepts had been espoused by the American Pre-Raphaelites in particular, many of whom worked in New England and, in 1863, formed what they called the Association for the Advancement of Truth in Art.

ON ONE PAINTER, the British expatriate who gave its direction to serious American landscape painting, such works by Turner as the grandly eloquent *Dido Building Carthage* (1815) had been an immense influence. Thomas Cole's epic series *The Course of Empire* (1834–36) everywhere shows the influence of Turner. The importance of Cole's art and aesthetic for Emily Dickinson is equal to Ruskin's and Turner's, and even more specific. Cole was a painter of American scenes, among them such seminal landscapes as *View from Mount Holyoke . . . after a Thunderstorm (The Oxbow)* (1836) in which a panoramic view not far from Dickinson's home was bifurcated in two "visual and symbolic oppositions" — "storm and sunshine, wilderness and pastorale" (Truettner and Wallach 77). These categories and such a bifurcation appear in some of her own landscapes. Cole's scenic paintings, largely done in the Catskills or New England, seem to have exerted a direct hold on Dickinson's imagination, and she probably had seen Cole's paintings and either read or heard about his widely influential "Essay on American Scenery" (1835) even before she encountered Ruskin's glorification of Turner in *Modern Painters.*

It was Cole's name—a painter's, not a poet's, or more precisely a painter-poet's, since Cole also published poetry—that Dickinson chose as a pseudonym for herself as artist. Joking with Susan Dickinson about her skill as a draftsman in a note scribbled on a page from the *New England Primer* in 1859,[17] she wrote:

> My "position"!
>   Cole.
>
> P.S. Lest you misapprehend, the unfortunate insect upon the left is Myself, while the Reptile upon the *right* is my more immediate friends, and connections.
>
>   As ever,
>   Cole (L214)

Dickinson's jest is an acknowledgment that Cole's name was, for her, synonymous with nature painting. Since her scene includes a snake, she may have been recalling Cole's famous painting *Expulsion from the Garden of Eden* (ca. 1827–28). (Indeed, as I will suggest here, Dickinson's frequent use of "Eden" as a symbol together with her vision of herself as "Eve" may come as much from Cole as from her knowledge of Genesis and *Paradise Lost.*) When Dickinson adopted his name, Cole was the best-known landscape painter in the United States during an era when landscape had begun to surpass portrait painting in popular appeal. After Cole's death in 1848, there followed a huge wave of new reproductions of his scenes of the American wilderness and countryside. With their blasted tree trunks, sharp contrasts between light and dark, cascading rivers and angry skies, the wilderness scenes were to portray the glory of nature and the power of the Almighty. Dickinson's allusions to "Maelstrom" (P414), "Gale" (P1327), and "Thunder" (P1172) describe this power and glory as great but alarming. "Nature's Temper" (P1172) often suggests to her the vengefulness of a jealous deity.

Cole's synthesizing image for both the violence implicit in nature and its endurance—a proof of the benevolence of God—was the blasted or quartered tree. In well-known landscapes like *The Clove, Catskills* (ca. 1827), and *The Ox-Bow* (1836), this devastated tree appears at the left margin of the canvas. It was adopted by Cole's followers as a metaphor of conquered suffering. If trees could survive lightning and storm, so human beings could transcend pain and civil disorder. In her poem "The Wind begun to knead the Grass—," Emily Dickinson paints a landscape that could be Amherst in a storm: farm wagons, birds, and cattle hurry for shelter as lightning streaks across the sky. But she concludes her poem with the emblem that was Cole's trademark, saying "The Waters Wrecked the Sky," "Just Quartering a Tree —" (P824). She makes Cole's associations between storms and psychic storm in such poems as 362, in which lightning and storm are not external but metaphors of emotional distress.

Cole's verdant fields and pleasant valleys were meant to emphasize the providence of God, in which Emily Dickinson tried hard to believe. He found God's providence most evident in the American landscape. Although "American scenery is destitute of many of those circumstances that give value to the European," Cole wrote, "still it has features, and glorious ones, unknown to Europe." He urged Americans, who could not boast of the elegant palaces and ancient ruins so charming in Europe and European art, to "cultivate a taste for . . . scene[s] of external nature" (100, 101). Cole's "Essay on American Scenery," which, like Emerson's *Nature* (1836), became fundamental reading for American writers, painters, and connoisseurs, established a kind of program for looking, writing, and painting. The subject matter he prescribed may be found throughout Emily Dickinson's poems although, as in the case of poem 824, she frequently regards nature with a more suspicious or ironic eye than he.

I believe that Cole's famous series of four paintings *The Voyage of Life* (1840) was probably known to Emily Dickinson even as a girl at Mary Lyon's Female Seminary. These radiantly devout, delicately triumphal paintings about a traveler and his guardian angel voyaging through life to eternity were so popular in the 1840s that, after *The Voyage* toured Boston and Philadelphia in 1843–44, they were turned out in subscription steel engravings and color reproductions by the "tens of thousands" (D. Sewell 226) and sold not only to families but to schools, hotels, churches, and hospitals all over the United States. In New England especially, *The Voyage* adorned schoolroom walls. Cole had painted it for the father of Julia Ward Howe, who intended it as a formative religious "text" for his motherless daughter. The famous engravings done by James Smillie (1848) were accompanied not by Cole's poems for *The Voyage* but by anonymous sentimental quatrains demonstrating the series' hold on the popular imagination. Certain of these quatrains bear substantive though not stylistic resemblance to a few of Dickinson's lines about the voyage to Eternity.[18]

Despite her religious skepticism, Dickinson appears to allude to Cole's iconography as to a traditional and appealing paradigm of salvation. Many of her poems employ the imagery of *The Voyage*; so, for example, the lines "Never to pass the / Angel / With a glance and / a Bow / Till I am firm in / Heaven / Is my intention now" (P895) evokes the second panel in which Cole's imprudent youth, intent on an imaginary palace in the sky, turns his back on the Guardian Angel and thus nearly loses his soul on the dangerous river's current. In the third Master letter (L248), Dickinson entreats the Master's love in a picture evoking Cole's last panels, *Manhood* and *Old Age*. She writes, "Oh how the dying tug, till the angel comes. Master — open your life wide, and take me in forever." Cole had represented the voyager struggling on the sea, his angel's reappearance; and the wide sky opening to receive him with the ascending and descending angels that Dickinson also pictures — "to and fro, the angels go, with their sweet postillions" — in Master letter l (L187).

There are other instances in Dickinson's writing wherein she seems to "quote" Cole's *Voyage* (see Farr, *Passion* 74–82). Thus Dickinson follows a custom intrinsic to the history of art and especially to painting whereby the newer artist cites the work of an older one in order to achieve a variety of effects from justification to satire to ironic comparison, lyrical emphasis, or more. "In nineteenth century aesthetics," moreover, it was "assumed that new compositions would often include references to earlier works" (Bolger and Bennewitz 110). Thus it was expected that Cole might quote Salvator Rosa or Claude and that Cole's student Frederic Church would certainly quote Cole — as indeed Church *did*, incorporating rivers and a cross in his landscapes, like Cole himself. Dickinson's poetic allusions to other texts, both verbal and visual, have notoriously caused one critic to call her a plagiarist (Walsh, *Hidden Life*, passim). But in Emily Dickinson's unique art, allusions work as metaphors.

Cole's assertion that America was a new "Eden" was instinctive to a painter-poet for whom Genesis was favorite reading and who had been impressed by the mezzotints about the Fall and the lost Eden done by John Martin (1789–1854). In 1828 Cole had represented *The Garden of Eden* as a pastoral landscape lightened by morning with tiny naked figures bathed in the radiant light of their own innocence. "I sow sweet flower from garden bed — " (P104), Dickinson writes in one of her early, sprightly poems that picture "Lawn[s]" and gardens dotted by spicy . . . "Carnations" (P81) as in Cole's Eden, a "still . . . Landscape" (P73) of "loving forests" (P50) and sweet serenity. But Cole's first Eden canvas was followed by another that is relevant to the more mature poems of Emily Dickinson. In these poems, nature is not always comforting but "troubles" (P956) the viewer with portents of death, suffering, and loss. Summer gives way to frost, and "when the sun reveal, / The Garden keep[s] the Gash — " (P951). Cole's second view of Eden was the momentous

Expulsion from the Garden of Eden (1827–28). There, tiny wraithlike figures of Adam and Eve are portrayed, cringing and fearful, as they leave the sunny, fruitful landscape of paradise behind and are sent forth in terror to a shadowy, storm-ridden place of shattered tree stumps and barren mountains. The *Expulsion*, as it came to be called, was Cole's symbolic portrayal of the anguish of living, with the Beautiful represented by the closed Eden and the awful Sublime by the endless, dark road into pain.

In a letter written in 1878 Emily Dickinson acknowledged a gift of flowers by using the same words as Cole's title: "Expulsion from Eden grows indistinct in the presence of flowers so blissful, and with no disrespect to Genesis, Paradise remains" (L552). Dickinson's sentence reveals her perfect understanding of Cole's premise that the beauty of nature in America recalled what was lost — "We are still in Eden" (P109) — and that Americans might cope with the afflictions of life by turning to nature for solace. Several of Dickinson's letters, together with a remarkable group of love poems that use the word "Eden" as a metaphor of sexual joy, envision paradise regained. The experience is so transporting as nearly to intimidate: "Come slowly — Eden! / Lips unused to Thee — / Bashful — sip thy Jessamines — " (P211). Dickinson's Eden, like Cole's, is full of Persian flowers such as the jasmine. (Indeed, Cape jasmines — known today as gardenias — grew in her conservatory.) Cole's South American voyages and Italian journeys provided him with exotic flora that he placed in his North American scenes. Emily Dickinson's magically far-off *Peru, Zanzibar, Domingo,* or *Potosi* are so personally realized as to become New England neighborhoods.

The poet who wrote "A loss of something ever felt I — " and "A Mourner walked among the children" (P959) was probably describing a tendency to depression (as many psychologically investigative critics show);[19] "loss" and "lost" are frequent words with her. Since the loss of Eden was the primary human loss, it was therefore easy for Dickinson to see herself as "Eve." The conceit, humorously conceived, had amused her at age sixteen, when she was feeling a "stiff-necked" backslider in religion: "why," she asks pious Abiah Root, "am I not Eve?" (L9). The tiny figure of Cole's Eve, and indeed all the miniature figures of men and women that inhabit the landscapes of the Hudson River painters, recall Dickinson's minimizing vision of herself as the "Least Figure — on the Road — ." She says she is "A single Ragged Child" in "Nature['s] monstrous House," both all day and at midnight, amid "Hills" and "Heavens" (P400). Cole, Church, Jaspar Cropsey, Asher Durand, Bowles's favorite painter Sanford R. Gifford, and other members of the Hudson River school typically depicted men and women in this way as insignificant amid nature's impressive grandeur. Thus Church's boy in *Morning* (1849) watches with awe as the vast red bowl of the sky fills up with light. His is certainly a *"little life,"* even as Dickinson says of her own, compared to eclipses, sunrise, midnights, and *"Dawn"* (P236). Her lines "The Sun went down — no Man looked on — / The Earth and I, alone, / Were present at the Majesty" (P1079) describe that wonder which the American painters made an implicit subject in canvases that set a single human being amid nature's profound stillness. In *The Ox-Bow*, Cole represents himself with his canvas and easel, solitary—like Dickinson in poem 1079—before the landscape he paints.

Mountains, emblems of permanence, aspiration, and antiquity, were among Cole's favorite subjects. Again and again, he pictured them crowned by clouds, stalwart in lightning, waiting in massive splendor for dawn. Emily Dickinson's poem 975 is the portrait of the ancestral potentate familiarly met in Cole's canvases:

> The Mountain sat
> upon the Plain
> In his tremendous Chair —
> His observation omnifold,
> His inquest, everywhere —
>
> The Seasons played
> around his knees
> Like Children round a sire —
> Grandfather of the Days
> is He
> Of Dawn, the Ancestor — (F7, 1187; P975)

Here Dickinson imagines the mountain as an omniscient, ageless natural presence—her alternative for "tremendous" was "eternal"—such as broods at the heart of Cole's canvases. Her conceit of the childlike seasons at play below and her allusion to the mountain's primordial significance evoke many of Cole's works, but in particular the first panels of his seminal *The Course of Empire*, "The Savage State" and "The Pastoral or Arcadian State" (1834), which concern themselves with the passage of time. The former painting establishes a mountain just to right center, Turneresque clouds swirling round it as if to suggest its emergence from the dawn of Creation. The latter painting (see fig. 1) shows the mountain bathed in benign light, a temple (suggesting Dickinson's wisdom, or "observation omnifold") below it and children, like her "Seasons," at play in the grass beneath. While Dickinson's poem 975, like the others, may have arisen from personal experience—the sight of Mount Tom, so near her home?—Cole's many mountain studies, disseminated in the 1850s in mechanically reproduced images, might also have inspired her. It is

1. Thomas Cole, *The Course of Empire: The Pastoral or Arcadian Scene* (1834). Oil. Collection of the New-York Historical Society.

useful to recall that, as Nicolai Cikovsky, Jr., observes, "the products of the [American] image industry [at this time] were so ubiquitously available that they became a mode of experience nearly equivalent to reality itself" (65).

Though Dickinson chose "Cole" as a playful pseudonym, she was probably equally familiar with the famous art of Frederic Church, as her symbols "Cordillera" and "Chimborazo" — a mountain range and a volcano much associated for Americans with Church's art — indicate. An elegant, sophisticated painter, Church's superb *Twilight in the Wilderness* (1860), like his many Niagaras, his South American volcano and landscape scenes, and, in particular, his visions of Chimborazo, made him wealthy, famous, and the subject of adulation in magazines like Dickinson's avidly read *Harper's*. The public showing of Church's *Heart of the Andes* (1859), with its river, volcano, Edenic trees, and blend of tropical with northeastern flowers (as if to imply, as Dickinson does, that Eden is at hand) was a national event.

During the early 1860s, Church spent his summers in East Eden, Maine, when Samuel Bowles was also vacationing there. Two famous men in a small town, they probably knew each other. In a letter dated May 21, 1863, Bowles wrote the Austin Dickinsons that he was learning to "row" off the "wild" coast of Eden. With her vitally symbolic fancy, Dickinson once observed of Bowles that "he was himself Eden" (L567), using the metaphoric Eden symbolism established by Cole and Church. (One recalls, as well, her poem "Wild Nights — Wild Nights!" [P249], with its line "Rowing in Eden.") For all its peculiarly Dickinsonian brilliance, "Wild Nights" shares in the tradition Cole and Church established of equating the American Wilderness with the New Eden. Another Dickinson love poem, "Love — thou art high — " (P453), moreover, describes a pacific scene in which a rower attempts to cross a lake toward a volcano, the same scene struck off by Church in *Chimborazo* (1863–64). Church began many sketches for *Chimborazo* in Eden, Maine, and it is possible that Bowles described them to the Dickinsons. In poem 453, Dickinson describes love as "the Chimborazo" — a mountain concealing fiery lava that, as it did for Church, signified passion yet was ringed round with the ice of repression. Dickinson's own poems about volcanoes, and even her association of Susan Dickinson's fiery temperament with volcanoes, argue her familiarity with their topicality in her culture: one that Church had distinctly stimulated.[20]

Frederic Church was a poet in paint, often more dynamic and symbolic in his vision and methods than Cole. His flower studies like *Cardamum* (1865; see fig. 2) remind us that Dickinson's flower studies do not only invite comparison or contrast with those of women artists, poets, and painters on china, though of course she would have been familiar with such efforts. In *Emily Dickinson, Woman Poet*, Paula Bennett associates Dickinson's floral poems with "the literature of flowers and sentiments," "books of poems and pictures too" (94) done

2. *Cardamom (Ginger) in Blossom.* June 1865, Frederic E. Church, 1826–1900. Oil on thin cream board. 10¹⁵⁄₁₆ x 8⁷⁄₁₆ (27.8 x 21.4 mm). Courtesy of the Cooper-Hewitt, National Design Museum, Smithsonian Institution/Art Resource, New York. Gift of Louis P. Church, 1917-4-676B.

by such as Henrietta Dumont in *The Floral Offering: A Token of Affection and Esteem; Comprising the Language and Poetry of Flowers* (1851) or Mrs. C. M. Badger, whose *Wild Flowers Drawn and Colored from Nature* was given to Emily by Edward Dickinson in 1859. Bennett reasons that "for Dickinson, as for most women poets in this period, the poem was "the verbal . . . representation of its subject — a 'painting' of another kind" (100) and hypothesizes that Dickinson's frequent choice of small flowers and small rather than grand natural subjects results from her feminine experience of nature.

Perhaps it may be seen as evidence of the androgynous character of true art, however, that while Mrs. Badger's "Fringed Gentian" print does present some of the qualities of careful arrangement of parts notable in Dickinson's herbarium pressings, Church's *Cardamum* even more successfully evokes the character of Dickinson's floral poems and of such pressed flowers as her "Coreopsis" (see fig. 3). Floral drawings were part of a wide artistic enterprise in which great painters like Church himself regularly shared. A topic intrinsic to this subject was the nineteenth-century study of botany, done both by schoolgirls who made herbariums like Dickinson and by artists who collected leaves and read botany handbooks. Dickinson's flower pressings in her herbarium in the Harvard Collection reveal a romantic sensibility with a fondness for lilies in particular, as well as a taste for symmetrical arrangement. Her "Coreopsis" is arranged to show its appealing "face" and delicate leaves at their most sprightly and therefore ultimate moment. Church's *Cardamum* (blossoming ginger, more exotic than her coreopsis or tickseed, yet similarly viewed with plain seriousness) is also shown at a moment of vibrant transcendency which Mrs. Badger's literal-minded "Gentian" does not attain. Church, Martin Johnson Heade, Jaspar Cropsey, and American flower painters like Fidelia Bridges — a mid-Victorian woman artist whose minute observation of detail is often comparable with Emily Dickinson's — might closely observe a flower; but they usually tried to imply its ephemeral delicacy, the beauty that resulted from imminent decay. Dickinson worked similarly: she liked to think of herself and her friends as "Roses of a steadfast summer" in a "steadfast land" (P163). But her flower studies almost always acknowledge the *transitus*, the "fading" of the flower "unto Divinity — " (P682). Such acknowledgment had been traditional, ever since the Dutch Renaissance floral studies that were foundational to this genre and in which a wilting or dead flower is usually depicted alongside bud and bloom.

Church's subjects, like Emily Dickinson's poems, include daily events. His painting *The Meteor of 1860* memorialized a double meteor that had occurred in July of that year. It was executed and shown around 1863, at the time when Emily Dickinson was writing a poem imagining meteors that described martyrs (for love?) convulsed by their light (P792). Like Dickinson's, too, Church's paintings suggest portents of the extraordinary in the events of everyday. In lambent works like *The After Glow* (1867) or *Twilight (Catskill Mountain)* (1856–58), Church painted the aurora borealis in 1864 as if it were a scene from his — and Emily Dickinson's — favorite Revelations. Its brilliantly apocalyptic rays predicted the glory of everlasting life. Around 1865, Dickinson wrote:

3. Pressed Coreopsis (*upper left*) in Dickinson's Herbarium, c. 1845 (?). By permission of The Houghton Library, Harvard University. (bMS AM 1118.11). © The President and Fellows of Harvard College.

Aurora is the effort
Of the Celestial Face

Unconsciousness of Perfectness
To simulate, to Us (P1002).

Emily Dickinson's lineation in the poems is, and will probably remain, a topic of singular importance. Is it possible that principles of design may shed light on it? Are there any inherent connections between Ruskin's hypotheses in *Modern Painters* about freedom of form and Dickinson's idiosyncratic linear arrangements in the later manuscript books? Ruskin composed as a writer-draftsman. From first to last, he associated the methods of poetry with those of painting. *Modern Painters* (its subtitle *Their Superiority in the Art of Landscape Painting to All the Ancient Masters*) began as a defense of the progressive art of Turner against its detractors, who had viciously mocked his filmy atmospheric effects and the strange "bursts of light and color" (Gordon 119) in *Rockets and Blue Lights* (1840). Arguing for Turner's innovations, Ruskin proposed several rules for the poet-painter. One might be simplified thus: "artists should look for and abide by the laws of nature rather than seek to apply an artificial scheme of beauty to their compositions" (Newall 86). Another proposed that great art must be inventive and penetrate nature's meaning by eschewing arbitrary encasement in inherited forms. For Ruskin, "Line," in its "constant variety and unpredictability," "represented the infinity of nature" (Newall 113). Ruskin compared architecture and drawing to bookmaking and to literature on the page, likening the building process to the breadth of margins and the lengths of sentences. He composed his *Elements of Drawing* with a firm desire to teach pupils how faithfully and simply to "render nature" (*Works* 3: 196). But although he began his career by praising classical composition as the "type . . . of the Providential government of the world" (15: 162), his feelings toward government, as toward religion, altered; and in the art criticism Dickinson met in *Modern Painters* he demonstrated respect for recording detail but chiefly for improvisation, looseness of brushstroke, freedom of form. The "fully Ruskinian style of drawing [was] a style almost of absence of style." For example, "there is never any attempt to fill up the paper" (Hilton 17). Finally, Ruskin announced that "a sketch might give a more truthful account of a subject" (Newall 114) than either an oil or a photograph. And he compared the daguerreotype he had taken of the fanciful town of Fribourg with his drawing of it, claiming that the "sketch . . . conveys . . . a truer idea" (6: 46).

Dickinsonians may recall that Emily Dickinson disliked her 1847 daguerreotype and preferred to give T. W. Higginson a verbal sketch of herself instead. "I . . . am small, like the Wren, and my Hair is bold, like the Chestnut Bur — and my eyes, like the Sherry in the Glass, that the Guest leaves — "

(L268). The photographic "truth" was that she was slight, with auburn hair and hazel eyes; but Dickinson offers Higginson a sketch made to charm, like one of D. G. Rossetti's tremulously lyrical drawings of women. Taken by itself, this gesture of Dickinson's is not so significant; but if it is associated with much in her writing that has the bright celerity of a sketch, it implies a truth about her art that recalls Ruskin's precepts. Like him, she valued, and her art is celebrated for, poetic concretion, what she called "the peculiar form — the Mold of the Bird" (L671). Nevertheless, her telegraphic messages with their abrupt, acute insights and the dashes that remind one of brushstrokes present the objective *and* emotional "truth" of the Ruskinian sketch. Suggestions of incompleteness Ruskin found "excit[ing to] the imagination" (3: 354). Dickinson's poems sometimes suggest, rather than define.

Recently, Dickinson scholars have been increasingly engaged in studying her unconventional lineation in many fascicle poems.[21] It is an issue charged with uncertainties, for Dickinson may write the same poem in a regular metric form like the quatrain or triplet in a letter but copy it in an improvised "form" in the manuscript books. Her fascicle lineations were regularized by Thomas H. Johnson, who assumed that, if Dickinson isolated a word or phrase like "the Dark" from poem 419 ("We grow accustomed to / the Dark") at the left margin of the page, she was observing the nineteenth-century custom of the turnover line for lack of space. Susan Howe, Jerome McGann, and other critics, however, have challenged Johnson's assumption, regarding Dickinson's lineation as intrinsic to her design and often metaphoric of her meaning.

We cannot know Dickinson's intentions in this matter; David Porter conjectures, even, that Dickinson's eccentric "scriptural forms" may result from "impaired peripheral vision" that caused an inability to "reliably ascertain a sheet's edges" (Review 127). But it is true that faithful reading of the visual "statements" made by her departures from traditional form often yields riches. In poem 419, for example, she contrasts ignorance with knowledge, and her symbolic opposition of the two (darkness with light / "Lamp") is emphasized by her lineation:

> We grow accustomed to
> the Dark
> When Light is put away
> As when the Neighbor holds
> the Lamp
> To witness her Goodbye (F15, 317, P419)

Emily Dickinson was a worker in words. For all the associations that may be made between her writing and the visual arts, drawing for her was secondary to writing (and her drawings were cartoons, inferior by far to her verse).[22] It was with words that she "painted." I do not mean to suggest here that Ruskin's prescriptions for drawing, rather than verbally inspired conceptions, directed her improvised lineations, which do sometimes seem crypto-modern: premonitions of modern poems in form. True it is, however, that Dickinson always regarded words as "symbols traced upon paper" (L15). It is also true that freed-up lineation in the fascicles seems to begin around 1861 (with fascicle 10) during the period when she told Higginson she was reading Ruskin. Did the free-form fascicle poems seem to her more like a Ruskinian sketch as opposed to the shapely cage of the quatrain — itself analogous to Ruskin's classical picture or daguerreotype? "What Liberty / A loosened spirit brings — " (P1587) was a theme of hers.

St. Armand associates John F. Kensett's painting *Sunset with Cows* with the imagery of poem 628, which, he says, "transfers Kensett's cows to the realm of cloud" (*Culture* 282) in a poignant verse-sunset. As we have seen above, Dickinson sometimes chose famous paintings as pointed subtexts for poems and letters. Since many of her love poems, in particular, were intended for and sent to Susan Dickinson, and since Susan's fondness for painting — like Austin's or Bowles's — was well known, the poet's practice in this style was witty. It cleverly enabled her to say a great deal swiftly and strikingly with the borrowed, implicit picture lending her poem resonance. An important instance of this strategy is provided by poem 317, "Just so — Christ — raps," which Dickinson sent to Sue. The subtext of this poem (as I hypothesize in the texts listed in "Works Cited") is almost certainly the Pre-Raphaelite painter William Holman Hunt's *Light of the World* (1853–56), the most famous of all mid-Victorian religious paintings, analyzed by Ruskin in Dickinson's well-read third book of *Modern Painters* and featured in the Boston press in winter of 1857 and spring of 1858 as the painting was being shown in New York. The iconography of this painting eloquently fits Emily Dickinson's purpose in poem 317. Hunt's Christ is red-haired like Dickinson and wears a white robe even as, by 1862, she wore white. On his head is a jeweled crown, surrounded by the halo or "disc" with which her passionate speakers often imagine themselves adorned. Like the speaker of this poem and others (e.g., P248) in which Dickinson dramatizes the fidelity of love in the presence of reluctance or rejection, he knocks at a door that will not open to him. Dickinson's script in 317 is inscribed by a bold hand that makes loose letters akin to brushstrokes while, emphasizing the poem's nature as a sketch, the independent entries "standing," "hiding soul," "for me," and "low" demonstrate the loneliness of the speaker. "Just so — Christ — raps" conveys its meaning through visual as well as verbal means.

THE RELATION OF Emily Dickinson's poetry to arts other than painting also offers insights fruitful to understanding it. Sandra Gilbert and Susan Gubar refer to the verse as her "Yarn of Pearl" and reflect that "she must have been . . . proficient with needle and thread," a proficiency asserted finally in the sewing of the fascicle books (*Madwoman* 639). To consider the needlework tradition from the 1740s to the 1850s in New England yields even more than this essential premise, which Gilbert and Gubar develop as an illustration of the poet's posture toward patriarchy in art and politics. Even for such a girl as Emily, who would attend a formal secondary school with education in languages, mathematics, and science, needlework was a traditional subject. St. Armand (*Culture* 154) observes that Dickinson "expresse[d] pride in her provinciality" by writing "I cannot tint in Carbon nor embroider Brass, but send you a homespun rustic picture I . . . saw in the terrific storm. Please excuse my needlework" (PF28). The "needlework" was her poem "Forever honored be the Tree" (P1570) about two angelic robins feeding on apples. (The robin nourished by new apples was a frequent sampler image, probably suggestive of the New Eden promised by Christ's Redemption.) As a girl of fifteen, Dickinson herself embroidered a sampler with a verse rather more infantine than was usual for girls her age.[23] Its purpose was apparently twofold: instruction in the useful art of embroidery and, as Puritan New England conceived it, in the more crucial reflexes of Christian devotion.

Four characteristics of the American needlework tradition are relevant to the growth of Emily Dickinson's mind. First, needlework had as its "frequently sounded theme" the "acceptance of death, including that of the sampler-maker herself." Thus a typical sampler, worked by Lydia Cogswell in Dover, New Hampshire, in 1804, reads: "When my short glass its latest sand shall run / And death approach to fright the lookers on / Softly may I sigh out my soul in air / Stand thou my pitying guardian angel there / Guide and conduct me through the milky way / To the bright region of eternal day / Then shall I joy to leave this clay behind and peace in happier mansion find."[24] Second, children were set to incorporating verses, like the above, within their samplers, most meditating on mortality. In addition, composition of the samplers was frequently inspired by prints or paintings, often European and often sophisticated, which broadened the scope of the girls' learning. A sampler wrought by Evelina Hull of Charlestown Academy in Massachusetts in 1812 was inspired by a Bartolozzi engraving after Angelica Kauffmann's painting *The Shepherdess of the Alps* (1785). That the iconography of famous paintings passed into the sampler tradition complicated and enriched the latter visually and technically. Finally, the sampler tradition encouraged the depiction of remarkably exotic scenes of faraway lands, one famous Connecticut sampler colorfully showing "a Grecian Lady visiting the Harem in the Bay of Bengal, India" with a (probably unintended) comical caricature effect accomplished by harem women ranged in rows. For Dickinson, with her mortality and mutability themes and her metaphoric susceptibility to the allure of "The Habit of a Foreign Sky" and "Ports and Peoples" "fairer — for the farness — / And for the foreignhood" (P821, P719), this tradition could only have been another formative element.[25]

Martha Nell Smith's rewarding study of "The Poet as Cartoonist" explores Dickinson's performance not only as a caricaturist but as an artist in collage, for her cutouts from the Bible, the *New England Primer* (the cartoon accompanying her letter about Cole above derives from this source), and Edward Dickinson's copies of such works of Dickens as *The Old Curiosity Shop* reveal, as Smith asserts, the poet's "manipulations of texts" as "transformations" (71), new works — as is always the case with collage. The fact that Dickinson was willing to employ sacred or otherwise hierarchical texts for such purposes (which St. Armand calls her "art of assemblage" ["Garden" 9]) suggests to Smith that she made an intense transformative use of popular art. Dickinson's "collages" are often humorous, ironic, or satiric, providing new insights upon what Smith, Suzanne Juhasz, and Cristanne Miller call her "comic power"; yet at the same time, her jaunty stick figures bear an uncanny resemblance to the often tragically conceived small figures of Thomas Cole, suggesting once again the complicity of Dickinson's artistic stratagems in one poetic design.

Thomas Cole spoke of lifting his *pencil* (108) as the metaphor for painting. Emerson, praising Tennyson, said that "color . . . flows over the horizon from his pencil" (199). Once again, poet and painter become one in the imagery of the nineteenth century. Whether Dickinson is speaking of herself writing or sketching is sometimes ambiguous: "I took a pencil / To note the rebels down" (P36), she says of snowflakes. Which did she mean, drawing or writing? The fact is, the two were in a way one for her. The painters to whom Dickinson alludes — Michelangelo, Guido Reni (much loved by the Victorians), "Domenichino" or Domenico Zampieri, Van Dyke, and Titian — were seen by her as types of the universal creator. Although when she "count[s]" what matters most in poem 569 it is "First — Poets — " whom Emily Dickinson names, not painters, her subject matter, her Ruskinian aesthetic, her sensitivity to the look of her text on the page, and her frequent address in poetry to the idea of *seeing* make the connections between her art and the visual arts conclusive.

Dickinson's short poem "Image of Light, Adieu" (P1556) is an apostrophe to light itself, which for the luminist and impressionist painters was like a "character with a role to play" (Huntington 172) in the universe. A farewell to daylight, this deeply Platonic and mimetic poem salutes the idea of light as a metaphor of the transcendent. Imitating the rays, her dashes between "So long" and "so short" acting as defining brushstrokes, Dickinson declares light the universal "Preceptor" that "impart[s]" the truth about the "whole" of experience. If it may be said of Emily Dickinson's art that it is a "celebration of the act of perception" (Huntington 162), then "Image of Light" is her tribute to the natural power that enables it. For perception — light — is essential to both poet and painter, but it is especially associated with the visual arts.

NOTES

1. References to Emily Dickinson's poems and letters are to Thomas H. Johnson's numbering. In quoting the poems, I have used the arrangements in R. W. Franklin's *Manuscript Books of Emily Dickinson* when different from Johnson's.

2. Jean H. Hagstrum in the course of *The Sister Arts* usefully reconstructs the history of "pictorialism" (*enargeia*), a complex aesthetic phenomenon founded on belief in the "power that verbal visual imagery possesse[s]" and on Plutarch's conception that painting, because it has a superior "moral force," must be poetry's mentor in all matters of representation (11, 10). From about 1790 to 1890, the period of Dickinson's education and her own life, pictorialism became intensely suasive, resulting in an "exchange of imagery between painters and writers. . . . The painters raided literature, while the writers were endlessly describing and transliterating the paintings they had seen" (Dijkstra 150).

3. In *The Art-Idea* (1864), one of several critical studies owned by the Austin Dickinsons and possibly borrowed by Emily, the influential James Jackson Jarves complained that Benjamin Franklin's empiricism still ruled the American mind, choking incipient American art. But this was untrue. By 1864 the romantic Hudson River painters were celebrities. Frederic E. Church wrote a friend, "I cannot avoid creating a sensation wherever I go; I can't even walk Broadway without the street being crowded . . . on my account" (see Kelly 199). The painters' lives and works were continually remarked upon by the press, not only in professional journals like *The Crayon* but in those intended for general circulation: *Home Journal, Century, Knickerbocker,* and *Harper's Monthly.* All were read by the Dickinsons. Traveling shows of American art rival circuses as major public attractions (see Avery for a description of a typical show).

4. Using the mid-Victorian spelling of the painter's name, she writes in Master letter l (L187), "I wish that I were great, like Mr. Michael Angelo, and could paint for you."

5. A critic, Louis Leroy, mocked Monet's *Impression: Sunrise* in 1874 as "impressionism," and the disparaging term stuck. See Boyle 17.

6. "Hudson River School" was a disparaging term applied by the *New York Tribune* (1879) to the American landscape tradition of 1840–80. "Luminism," with its preference for restrained brushstroke, smooth surface, white light, has been considered either a spontaneous alternative tradition to Hudson River painting or its culminating phase. For thorough discussion of these movements, see the essays in Roque, *American Paradise;* Wilmerding, *American Light;* and Novak, *American Painting.* For a discussion of British Pre-Raphaelite art, see Hilton, and for Ruskin and the American Pre-Raphaelites, see Ferber and Gerdts.

7. Impressionistically, Novak compares Dickinson to the "still small voice" of miniature and Whitman to "grand opera" (*Nature* 33).

8. Ryder, a visionary painter, chose themes of voyage to fuse this life with the next. His paintings, especially of riders and carriages, have an uncanny similarity to Dickinson's more surreal landscapes. See, e.g., *Pegasus Departing* (1901).

9. Specific analogies between Dickinson's poetry and nineteenth/twentieth-century painting pointed out here have been discussed at the greater length the subject requires in Farr, *Passion*.

10. Barbizon, a French school (1840s–1870s) recommending *plein air* painting, took its name from a village near the forest of Fontainebleau, home of Théodore Rousseau. Barbizon painters like Corot and Millet were deeply absorbed in nature study; but their works do not present subject matter or imagery so directly analogous, like Cole's or Church's, to the work of Emily Dickinson.

11. The Bowles Papers (Houghton Library, Harvard University) show that the Austin Dickinsons' interest in collecting and showing paintings was shared by their — and Emily's — intimate friend, additional evidence of the family's exposure to the contemporary art scene. Pointedly informing Austin (in a letter of 14 Dec. 1863) that "specimens of Church come from . . . Northampton," Bowles urges him to send his "pictures" to "The Soldiers' Rest Fair" in Springfield, where "all Springfield [gathers] its gems for the occasion." Bowles adds in this letter that he has called on "[James Jackson] Jarves and talk[ed] about art and artists." The casual use of Jarves's surname suggests that Austin may have known him too (cf. n. 3 above).

12. See, e.g., "The Mountain sat / upon the Plain" (P975), quoted later in this essay.

13. As if he might fail (or try not) to perceive the deep feeling in her letter, Dickinson tells Bowles, "I must do my Goodnight, in *crayon* — I *meant* to — in Red" (L259).

14. Lavinia Dickinson's "There is no landscape since Austin died" suggests this. Bingham, *Home* 477.

15. Wilmerding briefly indicates a relationship between luminism and Emerson's ideas (97–98). Emerson's relation to American painting is curiously indirect; he was not fond of painting, but "it is clearly Emerson's parallel sentiments that make him the spokesman for painters" (Novak, *Nature* 300, 86ff.). To Dickinson's art, of course, Emerson's essays are foundational.

16. "Limner" is the antique word for painter. (When Dickinson writes Kate Scott Anthon, "you do not yet 'dislimn' " [L222] with *dislimn* in quotes, she is probably taking the word from her favorite play by Shakespeare, *Antony and Cleopatra* [4.14.10].) In the seventeenth/eighteenth-century United States, limners were often anonymous, crude portraitists with literal-minded, childlike techniques. "Sophisticated artists may deliberately affect a naive style" (Chilvers 323). So sometimes does Dickinson.

17. Reproduced in Smith, "Poet" 83.

18. For example, Smillie's engraving of Cole's "Old Age," depicting the old voyager on the brink of heaven, carried this inscription below: "This world recedes, it disappears! / Heaven opens on my eyes, my ears / With sounds seraphic ring!" Dickinson's poem 160 declares: "Just lost, when I was saved! / Just felt the world go by! / Just girt me for the onset / with Eternity, / When breath blew back, / And on the other side / I heard recede the disappointed / tide!"

19. See, e.g., the studies of Cody, Pollak, and Wolff.

20. Volcanoes, like other geological phenomena, were represented in landscape painting to describe Darwin's idea of struggle in nature. See Gould 94–107; Novak, *Nature* 47–77. Dickinson writes six poems about volcanoes; in 1677 she sees herself as a volcano to image her efforts to repress emotion.

21. See Martha Nell Smith's account of the editing controversy in this volume.

22. For example, the cartoon of her stick-figure father's arrival in Washington to serve in Congress is, as Smith says ("Poet" 74), both clever and satiric; but like

Susan Dickinson's doodlings of houses on scraps in the Harvard Collection, it is also rudimentary.

23. The sampler: "Jesus Permit Thy Gracious Name to stand / As the First efforts of an infants hand / And while her fingers oer this canvas move / Engage her tender heart to seek thy love / With thy dear children let her share a Part / And write thy name thyself upon her heart." Note use of the word "canvas" as for a painting to allude to the fabric.

24. Quoted in Rita F. Conant, "Schoolgirl Samplers of Dover, New Hampshire," *Antiques* Aug. 1997: 201.

25. Works (other than Cogswell's) cited in this paragraph appeared in "American Schoolgirl Needlework," Eugenie Prendergast Exhibition of American Art, Metropolitan Museum of New York, Dec. 1995, and quotations are from its curatorial texts.

FURTHER READING

Flexner, James Thomas. *That Wilder Image: The Painting of America's Native School from Thomas Cole to Winslow Homer.* Boston: Little, Brown, 1962.

Nash, Roderick. *Wilderness and the American Mind.* New Haven: Yale University Press, 1967.

Rosenblum, Robert. *The Natural Paradise: Painting in America, 1800–1950.* New York: Museum of Modern Art, 1976.

Wilmerding, John. *The Genius of American Painting.* New York: Morrow, 1973.

PAUL CRUMBLEY

Dickinson's Dialogic Voice

*D*ialogic criticism, which draws heavily on the key concepts of "polyvocality" and "heteroglossia" to describe poetic utterance, begins in earnest with the Caryl Emerson and Michael Holquist translation of Bakhtin, *The Dialogic Imagination: Four Essays by M. M. Bakhtin*, published in 1981. Previous to this date Bakhtin's work was already well known in Europe; the availability of this English edition significantly sped his introduction to Americanists around the world and for that reason acts as a watershed moment after which voice acquires new focus and direction within discussions of Dickinson's poetics.

Despite the fact that Bakhtin-inspired criticism of Emily Dickinson's poetry is a relatively new development, its antecedents can be traced back to her earliest readers' concerns with poetic voice. The initial emphasis on voice that began with the first edition of her poems in 1890 continued until the publication of Thomas H. Johnson's variorum edition in 1955 sparked a newly sophisticated approach to Dickinson's voice in what I term the first stage of dialogic criticism. Though innocent of the specialized vocabulary of Bakhtinian theory, the work of these critics provided a foundation upon which subsequent dialogic approaches would build. A second stage of criticism is more obviously indebted to theories of the dialogic voice, but it tends to incorporate such analysis incidentally: instead of being a focus for critical inquiry, dialogism in the writings of these critics becomes a way of answering questions raised by such approaches as historical influence studies, genre study, gender analysis, and the investigation of manuscript material. A third, most recent stage of critical concern with Dickinson's voice overlaps in many areas with second-stage criticism, distinguishing itself by its concentration on the dialogic voice as the primary starting point for inquiry into other aspects of Dickinson's poetics.

In the late nineteenth century, "voice" tended to be analyzed and appreciated simply as the poetic fingerprint of a poet — the "sound" which distinguished one poetic genius from all others. In his preface to the 1890 first edition of her poems, for instance, Thomas Wentworth Higginson concludes that while readers may "catch glimpses of a lyric strain, . . . the main quality of these poems is that of extraordinary grasp and insight, uttered with an uneven vigor" (Preface 14). He marvels that this quality is achieved by a poet "indifferent to all conventional rules" but nonetheless possessed of "an ear which had its own tenacious fastidiousness" (13). The predominant tendency during the first half century of Dickinson criticism was to see the poems the way Higginson did — as replicating speech patterns and intonations characteristic of a unique person, Emily Dickinson of Amherst. It is no wonder, given the subjective responses such stress on Dickinson's unconventional individuality encouraged, that during the decade following the first edition Dickinson was "compared or contrasted to no fewer than ninety-five other writers," according to Willis J. Buckingham (*Reception* xvii). As this observation suggests, the "alien force of her voice" (xii) has from the outset thwarted reader efforts to reach agreement about the nature and identity of this elusive poet.

It was not until 1938, with the publication of George Frisbie Whicher's biography of Dickinson, that the scholarly community embraced the *possibility* that Dickinson's "I" is not necessarily the same "I" as that of the woman who wrote the poems. Whicher was the first to attend seriously to the artistic implications of the representative "I" Dickinson outlined in her July 1862 letter to Higginson: "When I state myself, as the Representative of the Verse — it does not mean — me — but a supposed person" (L268: Woodress 193–94). Despite Whicher's reasoned effort to establish Dickinson and her voice within a larger and less personal cultural context, however, his study ultimately sharpened rather than closed the division between readers who understand Dickinson's voice as biographical and those who hear in her poems speakers addressing social, political, and literary issues that exceed the boundaries of a particular individual's immediate personal experience. Hence, Archibald MacLeish could write in 1961 that her poems possess "not only a *voice* . . . but . . . a particular voice — Emily's voice" (154). And Elizabeth Phillips could express her amazement that in 1988 "the view that she wrote almost exclusively about herself . . . pervades Dickinson studies" (81).

After the publication of Johnson's 1955 variorum edition of the poems, critics began to raise questions about Dickinson's poetic voice that would usher in the first phase of dialogic criticism. The issue of voice emerges now because for the first time the variorum relies on the chirographic nuances of her holograph manuscripts as authoritative guides to print translation. Consequently, this edition made available to the public poems that not only looked different but required a radical reconsideration of the way Dickinson constructed speakers and their voices. Perhaps the feature of the poems that most directly influenced thinking about voice was the now famous "dash"; the category of marks referred to as dashes suddenly introduced to the reading public a primary form of punctuation that opened rather than closed the poet's syntax. As Richard B. Sewall states in the introduction to his 1963 volume, *Emily Dickinson: A Collection of Critical Essays*, "her ubiquitous and eccentric form of punctuation — the dash . . . has been a matter of concern to almost all post-1955 commentators" (3). This new dimension of the poems greatly magnified textual uncertainties about inflection and tone, thereby significantly complicating efforts to codify the way speakers' voices sound and what they mean.

Many critics responded to the challenge that such uncertainty posed by making two related assumptions: first, that Dickinson inscribed her voice in coded language; second, that the critical task at hand was to break that code and impose order on her otherwise chaotic practice. Embedded in this approach is a deep-seated belief in the power of a unified poetic voice to authorize accurate readings of texts. Johnson's remarks in the introduction to his variorum point to the extent that he and others believed identification of this voice would grant readers the authority to modify poems once the code was broken and the mind's ear attuned to Dickinson's predictable modulations. Commenting directly on the dashes, Johnson observes that, while in the variorum a "literal rendering [of manuscript punctuation] is demanded," he can imagine future editions in which "such 'punctuation' can be omitted" (P lxiii). Presumably, the aim of critics seeking to make sense of variorum poems by "correcting" the punctuation was to rescue Dickinson from the unfortunate circumstances of her manuscripts and by this means secure her the recognition they believed she deserved.

Edith Wylder's *The Last Face: Emily Dickinson's Manuscripts* and Brita Lindberg-Seyersted's *The Voice of the Poet: Aspects of Style in the Poetry of Emily Dickinson* represent the way holding fast to traditional belief in an authoritative unified voice created problems for even the most sensitive and imaginative scholars. For the sake of future discussions of voice, the precise terms of their arguments have proven less significant than the attention drawn to difficulties attendant upon any effort to establish a unified voice on the basis of manuscript evidence.

Wylder's 1971 book defended the position she first presented in a March 30, 1963, article in the *Saturday Review*, where she argued that Dickinson drew her punctuation from Ebenezer Porter's system of elocutionary marks. When Wylder presents Dickinson as instructing readers in voice qualities, she links voice to punctuation, demonstrating that the class of marks represented as dashes in the variorum may signify far more than the en dash suggests. For Wylder, Dickinson's "unique punctuation system became one of her means for bridging the communications gap, of lending to the written language much of that precision of tone, that 'breath' of meaning, otherwise possible only in speech" (4–5). The "system" Wylder applies to Dickinson uses four of Porter's primary elocutionary marks in combination with her own detailed descriptions of the length, position, and angle of Dickinson's "irregular" notations (8–12).

Lindberg-Seyersted's 1968 book builds on her monograph, *Emily Dickinson's Punctuation*, originally published in *Studia Neophilologica* in 1965. In both works, she disputes Wylder's theory that elocutionary marks form the basis for punctuation in Dickinson's poems. Lindberg-Seyersted also makes two observations about punctuation that remain important to any discussion of voice. She notes that in taking a poem through multiple drafts Dickinson "did not discard the dashes as belonging only to an experimental initial stage, but retained them as essential to the poem" (*Voice* 196); and she concludes that punctuation is "an inherent feature both of her style and her personality" (*Punctuation* 2). Against the assertion that Dickinson was schooled in Porter's *Rhetorical Reader*, she offers an alternative rhetoric, a copy of which was part of the Dickinson family library, underlined, and signed "with her father's name and the year 1839" (*Punctuation* 24). This work, Richard Whately's 1834 *Elements of Rhetoric*, is described as "radically opposed to the kind of elocutionary principles . . . exemplified by Porter's *Reader*"; more precisely, Whately emphatically rejects as artificial the notion that "it is requisite to study analytically the emphases, tones, pauses, degrees of loudness, &c . . . and then, in practice . . . conform the utterance to these rules" (*Punctuation* 25). Lindberg-Seyersted then backs up her preference for Whately's more flexible approach to rhetorical rules by showing how difficult it is to apply Porter's method to manuscript poems without violating rhythm and meaning (*Voice* 192–95).

Despite their differing conclusions about the function of punctuation, Lindberg-Seyersted and Wylder both seek to excavate a consistent voice from Dickinson's stylistic innovations. Wylder opens her book with the declaration that Dickinson used Porter's notations to ensure that her poems

> communicated her meaning as fully and precisely and with the same sense of immediacy *as if* she had spoken them. That is the point. Her punctuation system is an integral part of her attempt to create in written form the precision of meaning inherent in the tone of the human voice. (4)

In seeming contradiction, Wylder later admits that "Dickinson's capitalization may either coincide with or alter the rhythms of her hymnal meters, depending on whether the particular meaning demand a conscious alteration of the logical base" (42). The suggestion here that prior meaning determines tone and inflection runs counter to her original claim that meaning is dependent on sound qualities determined by elocutionary marks. Two pages later, writing of the horizontal or monotone notation (flat dash) that "prevails in most of the poetry," she concludes, "surely the monotone is a guarded tone (and therefore often ambiguous)" (44). Both of these comments indicate the difficulty of achieving a precise sense of the "meaning inherent in the tone of the human voice," no matter how elaborate the notational system.

Like Wylder, Lindberg-Seyersted's determination to discover a single voice in Dickinson's poems inadvertently reveals the difficulty of achieving that objective. She states her underlying conviction in the clearest imaginable terms: "In the bulk of Dickinson's poetry there is clearly a single voice speaking directly to a second person" (*Voice* 57). Yet just nine pages earlier she observed of the " 'spoken' character of the poems": "Sometimes it is a childish voice; often we hear a woman speak; at other times, we cannot identify the voice precisely" (48). Are the child, woman, and unknown the same voice, or do we hear a single speaker with multiple voices? In her preface, Lindberg-Seyersted declares her allegiance to the traditional view of voice: "By the *voice* of the poet I understand her style" (10). According to this statement, the voice of style must accommodate all manifestations of voice in the poet's work, leaving the clear implication that poems not attributable to this voice are either flawed, anomalous, or evidence that the critic has yet to provide a sufficiently comprehensive description of voice.

As we begin to explore the second stage of criticism related to Dickinson's dialogic voice, we see a much closer resemblance of Bakhtinian concepts to increasingly complex ideas about voice. Bakhtin proceeds on the assumption that all living language is social, consisting of utterances with specific speech properties, including voice. Within this framework, voice expresses the unique perspective of a speaker whose utterances generate experience through dialogue with the historical meanings of words. "Heteroglossia" is Bakhtin's term for the point where conservative, centripetal histories of words meet the centrifugal forces of the present. "The processes of centralization and decentralization . . . intersect in the utterance; the utterance not only answers the requirements of its own language . . . but it answers the requirements of heteroglossia as well" (*Dialogic* 272). Words like "revolution" and "free market" that are quickly implicated in specific ideologies readily express the tensions Bakhtin describes between the centripetal histories of words and the centrifugal expansion of meanings possible in present utterances. The voice that emerges through such a dialogue with prior discourse implicitly or explicitly comments on that discourse; this commentary can then be read as the "socioideological position of the author amid the heteroglossia of his epoch" (300).

Writers interested in examining the way Dickinson engages the Bahktinian cultural dialogue have used the concept of polyvocality to explore problems posed by the search for a unified voice. The work of critics like Lindberg-Seyersted and Wylder, which makes clear the impossibility of discovering a totalizing poetic voice in Dickinson's writing, becomes the starting point for later studies that define the speaking self as capable of multiple voices. For example, Lindberg-Seyersted's search for a univocal speaking self gets her into trouble when attempting to account for Dickinson's girl-persona: "a great many of her poems maintain a girl's or child's speech and outlook without the necessary distance to an outgrown state" (*Voice* 38). "Often," she writes, there is a notable "discrepancy between the childish language and attitudes and the grown-up situations in which the persona is involved — for instance, a love relationship with a man." The problem a "discrepancy" posed for Lindberg-Seyersted ceases to be a problem, however, when the voice possibilities available to the speaking self are no longer bound by a demand for uniformity. Cynthia Griffin Wolff has no trouble acknowledging more than one voice in her 1986 discussion of the child's presence in love poems: "love is an awakening from childhood into maturity, and the most elegant use of the child's Voice in Dickinson's love poetry can be found in an intricately wrought 'Anniversary' poem" (*Dickinson* 372). Even though Wolff holds to the belief that no matter how "disparate these many Voices are, somehow they all appear to issue from the same 'self' " (178), she does resolve the conflict evident in Lindberg-Seyersted's writing and by this means demonstrates how early contributors to the second stage of voice criticism moved away from belief in a univocal authorial voice consistent in all its manifestations.

The "dialogic voice," which assumes that texts are polyphonic and therefore contain within them complex voice relationships, provides the theoretical background most applicable to the social and cultural commentary that Wolff and other critics of the second stage present as issuing from Dickinson's voice. As Gary Lee Stonum has demonstrated in his 1990 work, *The Dickinson Sublime*, situating Dickinson in the midst of social discourse rather than on its margins affects our understanding of her role as a leading American poet. Dickinson, he observes, has rejected the "dominant myth of American literary culture," according to which "the great writer is an isolato, who retreats from the uncaring or impure realm of public discourse in order to create a world elsewhere, the artistic sanctuary in which [she] is the lord of meaning and form" (192). This new view of Dickinson as polyvocal artist speaking from the heart of her culture reflects the extent to which the analysis of voice promoted within this group begins to overlap with key Bakhtinian concepts.

Though Wolff makes no reference to Bakhtin in *Emily Dickinson*, she joins a number of prominent critics whose work in the 1970s and 1980s discusses specific voices in the poems with the clear aim of compelling fresh thought about Dickinson's involvement with central social and cultural issues. John Emerson Todd's 1973 *Emily Dickinson's Use of the Persona* identifies four categories of speakers: the little girl, the "lover-wife-queen" (xv), the experiencer of death and eternity, and "Personae Involving Psychology and the Divided

Personality" (72). In 1975 Robert Weisbuch's *Emily Dickinson's Poetry* describes Dickinson as a "tripartite poet" whose writing reflects "the awed child of perception, the suffering heroine of experience, the contemplative queen of connective thought" (77). Seven years prior to Wolff's 1986 book on Dickinson, Sandra M. Gilbert and Susan Gubar's *Madwoman in the Attic: The Woman Writer and the Nineteenth-Century Literary Imagination* delineates a broad array of personae that can be thought of as masks for a composite self made up of the child, the woman/wife and the queen: "is not the little girl really, covertly an adult, one of the Elect, even an unacknowledged queen or empress?" (608). Wolff's "Voice" chapter in her *Emily Dickinson* presents three subheadings that identify "The Voice of the Child," "The 'Wife's' Voice," and "The Proleptic Voice" as providing distinct perspectives from which Dickinson launches her critique. All four of these approaches acknowledge the importance multiple voices play in a poetic project that seeks both to expand the range of perspectives available to speakers and to use divergent points of view to critique American culture.

The perception that Dickinson uses multiple speakers, each one of which is capable of possessing more than one voice, helps explain why the process of establishing her position in literary history has been so contentious. Scholars who hear a single clear voice in Dickinson's poetry are countered by others who identify multiple voice qualities that may simultaneously affirm and depart from established traditions. Feminist critics represent this divergence of views with special vividness because of their interest in the socioideological implications of Dickinson's voice. Joanne Feit Diehl's 1981 analysis of Dickinson's relationship to Anglo-American romanticism, *Dickinson and the Romantic Imagination*, for instance, presents Dickinson as a woman poet whose "radical experimentation" reflects her "estrangement" from this "patriarchal tradition" (11). Diehl's ultimate assessment of Dickinson's importance emphasizes her creation of a voice that speaks in opposition to this dominant male line of influence: confronting a "canon formed by voices whose experiences she could only partially share," Dickinson creates "a deeply original voice" that places her "at the center of a newly emerging tradition of women poets" (186). In seeming opposition to this view, Cheryl Walker's 1982 study, *The Nightingale's Burden: Women Poets and American Culture before 1900*, places Dickinson in a tradition of American women writers whose concern with patriarchal oppression deemphasizes originality of voice in favor of covert communication: women poets "have constituted themselves as '*femmes sages*,' wise women, midwives of a sort, whose knowledge as it is passed on to others carries a female burden of dark and sometimes secret truths" (19). This voice, concealed as "a sort of palimpsest" (31), arises from a "self that has been violated, almost rubbed out, but that speaks nevertheless" (32). Along similar lines,

Gilbert and Gubar present Dickinson as responding to the anxiety of authorship characteristic of nineteenth-century women writers by literally becoming the madwoman written about by other authors, most notably Emily Brontë (*Madwoman* 583). Doing so, they argue, allows Dickinson to sustain a multitude of public and private voices, leading them to conclude that Dickinson's "is a fiction of multiplicity which artistically adopts numerous roles and, even more artfully, settles for none" (636). Cristanne Miller seizes on the linguistic multiplicity alluded to by Gilbert and Gubar in her 1987 *Emily Dickinson: A Poet's Grammar* and adds to it "a negative stance, indirection, and subversion" (162) to suggest that Dickinson's language "could almost have been designed as a model for several twentieth-century theories of what a woman's language might be" (161). For Miller, Dickinson's indirection comes through a combination of women's speech and men's language (159) that keeps "audible both her love of the world and of language and her rejection of its attempts to keep her 'still'" (184). By acknowledging the language of men, Dickinson frees herself to confidently create "a new poetic language" through which she reveals "a whole spectrum" of "speaker's roles" (185).

Such a wide range of arguments, all sensitive and compelling readings, indicate the difficulty in categorizing Dickinson's multifaceted poetic voice. As if in response to such a dizzying array of possibilities, Mary Loeffelholz's 1991 *Dickinson and the Boundaries of Feminist Theory* and Betsy Erkkila's 1992 *The Wicked Sisters: Women Poets, Literary History, and Discord* focus on the difficulty of establishing clear lines of influence leading up to and away from Dickinson. Loeffelholz writes of "Dickinson's first-person plural" that distances "one consciousness from the next" but does not constitute "an erasure of other existences" (38). This "inflected presence of another's voice" reflects the self's suspicious embrace of the other that Loeffelholz sees as indicative of a "nonidealizing 'countertradition' of women's writing" (38, 170). Erkkila similarly argues that, rather than imputing to Dickinson an "essentializing . . . desire" for "a univocal female psychology" (44), it would be more productive to view the entire "category 'woman poet' as itself the subject of historical struggle" (8). According to her, Dickinson transforms culture and literature by realizing "that it is on the level of language that she can resist subjection to the systems of masculine power — religious, social, and linguistic — by questioning and destabilizing its terms" (24). In this context, Dickinson becomes part of an antitradition that makes difficult either the identification of roots in the nineteenth century or speculation about her contribution to a future feminine language.

This array of differing and often conflicting perspectives betrays the dialogic character of Dickinson's voice, particularly its evocation of divergent discourses, none of which it totalizes or masters. The syntactic ruptures and sudden shifts of perspective that give rise to such a diversity of responses have quite understandably provoked speculation about her stature as a lyric poet. Investigations into Dickinson's use of the lyric form have sparked debate about the interrelationship of voice and self, as lyric is generally considered the literary genre best suited to single-voiced speakers. Sharon Cameron introduces the way Dickinson expands the repertoire of options available to lyric poets in her 1979 study *Lyric Time: Dickinson and the Limits of Genre*. There she describes lyric speech as arising from a "choral voice . . . disguised under the cloak of a customary first-person speaker" (207). In making her point, Cameron refers to J. Hillis Miller's observation that in narrative voice " 'there is always . . . something left over or something missing' " so that " 'one way or another the monological becomes dialogical' " (208). Cameron concludes that despite Dickinson's use of what Wallace Stevens "would have called 'flawed words and stubborn sounds,' " her poetry addresses conventional lyric aims by throwing "into relief the shape of the lyric struggle itself" (260). Margaret Dickie significantly extends the implications for the speaking self hinted at by Cameron when she argues in her 1991 *Lyric Contingencies: Emily Dickinson and Wallace Stevens* that Dickinson's poetry "may offer not only a new model for reading the lyric but a new and perhaps persuasively feminist model of self-presentation." Dickie sees the imposing of master narratives by feminists as part of a long line of critical maneuvers designed to tame "an individuality that resists final representation" (29).

The persistence of efforts like Cameron's and Dickie's to define Dickinson's writing as part of a literary genre or school of thought points to the dialogic complexity of a poetic project that resists containment in established literary categories. Stonum has this resistance in mind when he writes that she "shows very little concern with form as such, and she manifests a positive dislike for achieved stability" (66). The generic "indeterminacy" and "semantic open-endedness" implicit in these analyses of Dickinson's practice suggest a link to what Bakhtin describes as the "novelization of other genres" (*Dialogic* 6–7). Bakhtin argues that through this novelization all genres become

> more free and flexible, their language renews itself by incorporating extraliterary heteroglossia . . . they become dialogized . . . and finally . . . the novel inserts into these other genres . . . a living contact with unfinished, still-evolving contemporary reality (the openended present). (7)

Barton Levi St. Armand speaks directly to this novelized quality of Dickinson's work in his 1984 *Emily Dickinson and Her Culture: The Soul's Society* where he describes her creation of a new and paradoxical female genre that distinguishes itself by its mix and hence defiance of codes that would fix genre identity: "an art of assemblage, a 'quilting' of elite and popular ideas onto a sturdy underlying folk form, frame, of fabric" (9). St. Armand's admission that "it is still far too early in the history of Dickinson criticism to declare that there is no other design at all, no mega-motif that makes the whole comprehensible" (10), both reflects the openendedness of novelization and accurately sums up the way Dickinson's voices defy any easy categorization according to genre.

Respecting the visual representations of speakers who can wield such potent voices has posed a special challenge for critics who work directly with Dickinson's holograph manuscripts. Once Dickinson scholars began to read her manuscripts and letters as a literary artist's explorations into cultural definitions of self and not the eccentric outpourings of a "partially cracked poetess" (qtd. in note to L481), interest naturally gravitated to possible linkages between her textual innovations and polyvocality. Examination of manuscript materials has been especially influential in directing scholarly attention to the multitude of chirographic markers Dickinson uses to show readers that speech resists monologic containment. Bakhtin's observation that "there are not voiceless words" but, rather, that "each word contains voices that are sometimes infinitely distant . . . and voices resounding nearby and simultaneously" (*Speech Genres* 124) has special implications for Dickinson's highly disruptive style. Her punctuation, line breaks, and capitalization appear designed to isolate words and release voice possibilities that challenge the view of self as unified and single-voiced.

If speakers in the letters, poems, and fascicle books are continuously transforming the immediate present in ways no master narrative accounts for, how can we make sense of these materials? Cameron takes up these issues in her 1992 study of the fascicle manuscripts, *Choosing Not Choosing: Dickinson's Fascicles*, where she argues that concerns like these come down to "a question of the in(ter)determinacy of meaning, whether with respect to the relation *among* poems in a fascicle or with respect to variants *in* poems" (159). According to Cameron, a distinctive feature of Dickinson's writing is the way she brings indeterminacy to the foreground, denying monologic exclusivity at every turn: "the presumption that choosing is necessary is contested by the representation of not choosing, for in the poems the choice of particular words implied by the lyric frame to be imperative is rather shown to be impossible" (23). The lyric promise of the poems is in this way deliberately frustrated precisely because the voice is always plural, the speakers polyvocal. Cameron concludes that "Dickinson herself was uncertain about how her poems should be read, an uncertainty demonstrated by the fact that she both sent her poems to friends as individual lyrics and also copied them in the fascicles in sequences" (40).

In her 1992 *Rowing in Eden: Rereading Emily Dickinson*, Martha Nell Smith reverses the question of Dickinson's relation to genre by asking not whether she fits into or defies the lyric mold but rather how critics might best characterize her intentional creation of new genre possibilities. A more complete knowledge of this project will contribute to what Smith calls a "hermeneutics of 'Possibility'": "a story of reading lending itself to a thousand and more interpretations, all of which may be faithful to Dickinson's poetic project" (58). Referring specifically to Bakhtin, Smith states that readers' sensitivity to "the 'heteroglossia' of all forms of communication" is an indispensable feature of the hermeneutics she has in mind. Acknowledging heteroglossia will increase reader appreciation for "the poet with a 'Vice for Voices'" who always creates "multivoiced" representations that "tell stories they do not intend as well as those the author and editors mean to convey" (48).

Cast in this light, the concept of the dialogic voice not only offers a methodology for reading Dickinson's many stylistic innovations but aids in the formulation of a rationale for her reluctance to publish her poems. As recent studies like Smith's and Cameron's testify, Dickinson may have chosen not to publish because she knew that doing so would have meant either bowing to established editorial practice or failing to reach an audience. Publishing conventions would have demanded that she regularize her punctuation, capitalization, and line breaks, thereby sacrificing innovations clearly linked to voice in a bid to win public approval.

The most frequently cited evidence of Dickinson's refusal to conform to the demands of publication comes from her March 17, 1866, letter to Higginson in which she objects to the *Springfield Republican*'s having altered punctuation in "A narrow Fellow in the Grass" (P986, including the editor's note; L316). Critics increasingly agree that the basis for Dickinson's objection lies in the way regularized punctuation monologizes meaning and unifies voice. Martha Nell Smith sees Dickinson's dissatisfaction with the editorial insertion of a question mark at the end of the third line as demonstrating her sensitivity to the imposition of unity where multiplicity was intended:

> By emphasizing the break between the lines, the punctuation practically insists on a particular reading, whereas its omission makes the relationship between the two lines more indeterminate, hence encouraging more interaction by the reader and more possibilities to create meaning. (*Rowing* 12)

Commenting on this same question, Stonum similarly concludes that Dickinson's version conveys "the more striking, more Dickinsonian note" by "allowing two different possibilities (in this case vocally incompatible ones)" (28).

As these remarks demonstrate, sensitivity to the dialogic voice in Dickinson comes from the willingness of readers to embrace the uncertainty provoked by her introduction of heteroglossia, that opening of the text to what Bakhtin calls "the Tower-of-Babel mixing of languages that goes on around any object" (*Dialogic* 278). When this occurs, readers are called upon to thread the maze of languages actively according to their individual perceptual horizons. Reader participation of this kind corresponds to a growing interest in the performance features of Dickinson's poems. Citing Stonum's recognition of the affective dimension of reading Dickinson, particularly his observation that she was "programmatically unwilling to dictate how her work was to be taken" (106), Suzanne Juhasz, Cristanne Miller, and Martha Nell Smith argue in their 1993 book, *Comic Power in Emily Dickinson*, that audience involvement is crucial to the way Dickinson's poems perform. These authors make the case that "Dickinson's writings are directed toward their futures with readers' responses, which are technically 'outside' the originary work" (14). More specifically, performance of "feminist comedy" demands that readers share a dissatisfaction with the cultural norms being subverted by the speaker, which is to say that performing this sort of poem is possible only when the hold of dominant discourse is sufficiently loosened to allow activation of heteroglossia.

Martha Nell Smith sums up the expressly dialogic nature of Dickinson's demands on readers in *Rowing in Eden:* "Her manuscripts, with multiple variants and variant punctuation and line breaks, will not let us forget that reading is a dialogic drama, always a matter of editing, of choosing what to privilege, what to subordinate" (53). Perhaps more than anything else, Smith's emphasis on the active role of the reader as decision maker who sorts through dialogic language shows how much critical thought about reading has changed since the publication of the variorum. Wylder and Lindberg-Seyersted both responded to textual uncertainties but tended to view them as lapses in an otherwise coherent narrative voice. Today, the choices they wrestled with are celebrated as evidence of Dickinson's stylistic achievement. As poet-critic Susan Howe makes clear in her 1985 *My Emily Dickinson*, Dickinson teaches readers the joys of choice: "I feel my own freedom . . . the Liberty in wavering. Compression of possibility tensing to spring. Might and might . . . mystic illumination of analogies . . . instinctive human supposition that any word may mean its opposite" (22). The title of Sharon Cameron's *Choosing Not Choosing* is itself evidence that current criticism has come full circle; critics now take pleasure in the proliferation of voices that a few decades ago threatened standards of artistic accomplishment.

The third stage of criticism foregrounds the theoretical work of Bakhtin as the place to begin analysis of Dickinson's writing. Lynn J. Shakinovsky's 1990 essay, "Hidden Listeners: Dialogism in Emily Dickinson," initiates this stage through her use of Bakhtinian thought to establish her conclusion that in many of Dickinson's poems meaning cannot be found "in the simple monologic utterances or claims of speakers"; rather, "the essentially dialogic nature . . . is indicated by the suppressed, hovering presences and voices, which haunt the poems and which refuse to disappear" (212). This direct acknowledgment of polyvocality in Dickinson's writing, together with the assertion that Bakhtin provides the appropriate theoretical context for future readings of Dickinson's voice, marks a significant new development in the analysis of voice in Dickinson studies.

My own 1992 essay, "Dickinson's Dashes and the Limits of Discourse," uses Bakhtinian theory to explain the way Dickinson associated voice properties with poetry from an early stage in her development as a poet. In that essay I propose that for Dickinson the dash is an especially significant form of punctuation precisely because it "is the least accommodating to conventional readings that stress linear progression and logical coherence" (8). In a footnote, I explain that the family edition of Webster's 1828 *An American Dictionary of the English Language* describes the dash "in a manner that would strike the young poet's eye as highly suggestive":

> "A mark of line in writing or printing, noting a break or stop in the sentence; as in Virgil, quos ego —: or a pause; or the division of the sentence" (55a verso). The words of Virgil, "quos ego —," which mean "what I am" or "that which I am," suggest an inconclusive assertion of identity; Virgil asserts that he is something but does not further define what this something is. (27)

The definition's use of Virgil's "quos ego —," then, associates the syntactic rupture represented by the dash with the creation of not just any identity but the identity of a great poet. The dash in this way both challenges the linear progression of sentences and emphasizes the uncertainty of poetic identity.

I argue that Bakhtin helps readers understand that Dickinson's disruptive style requires hearing "a speaking subject whose utterances reflect . . . a mix of personal and social discourses not containable within a unified voice" ("Dashes" 10). As a result, readers must be sensitive to syntactic ruptures that bring heteroglossia into the text, activating the voices Bakhtin locates in "each word" (*Speech Genres* 124). Kamilla Denman also writes of the way the dash directs reader attention to specific words in her 1993 essay, "Emily Dickinson's Volcanic Punctuation": "through her unconventional use of punctuation, particularly the dash, Dickinson creates a poetry whose interpretation becomes a process of decoding the way each fragment signals meaning" (33).

Erika Scheurer's important 1995 essay, " 'Near, but remote': Emily Dickinson's Epistolary Voice," speaks to the current status of scholarship that begins with Bakhtin in dealing with Dickinson's dialogic voice. Scheurer provides an informative review of past criticism related to voice, all of which undergirds her conclusion that current scholarship has reversed the "traditional image of the singular, private, unified voice" (88). Treating the application of Bakhtinian theory as an established critical practice, Scheurer concerns herself with the problems critics face once "the *voice* . . . becomes *voices*" (89). As a corrective to excessive critical emphasis on the centrifugal component of hetero-glossia that would distort Bakhtin by overlooking the equally powerful socially conservative counterforce of discourse, she urges a highly nuanced treatment of voice that takes into account monologic utterances and resists the tendency to value writing over speech. Cautioning against any easy binarism, she proposes, first, that writing can "present a fixed self" as easily as speech and, second, that polyvocality plays a role in any reading of either speech or writing: "while Dickinson did not value writing over speech, she did value dialogic writing and speech over monologic writing and speech" (93). Her comments on Dickinson's letters suggest an intriguing addition to past discussions of voice by introducing the enchanting concept of "dialogic silences" that "blend with the voices Dickinson treasures to create her dialogic voice" (97). Thus even the gaps in language resonate with voices in dialogue.

I will conclude this overview with a dialogic analysis of the poem Higginson selected as "Prelude" to the 1890 first edition of Dickinson's poems. The poem, "This is my letter to the World" (P441), has become synonymous with the entire body of Dickinson's writing. For this reason it provides an appropriate locus for examining the ways print translations of her poems encouraged interpretations of voice and meaning that differ dramatically from those arrived at through readings based on holograph manuscripts. The following is drawn from my 1992 essay, in which I worked exclusively with the variorum version of the poem, and the opening chapter of my 1997 book, *Inflections of the Pen: Dash and Voice in Emily Dickinson*, where I base my reading on the holograph manuscript contained in R. W. Franklin's *Manuscript Books of Emily Dickinson*.

The first published version of "This is my letter to the World" demonstrates the influence editorial normalization of punctuation and lineation of the sort practiced up until 1955 has had on reader perceptions of univocality. The poem in Todd and Higginson's 1890 first edition of *Poems* contains only one dash, and that is softened by a preceding comma. In this way the disjunctive power of the dash is diminished, and each of the two stanzas becomes a complete sentence.

> This is my letter to the world,
>   That never wrote to me, —
> The simple news that Nature told,
>   With tender majesty.
>
> Her message is committed
>   To hands I cannot see;
> For love of her, sweet countrymen,
>   Judge tenderly of me!

According to this representation of the poem, the "simple news that Nature told" is conveyed in the speaker's "letter to the world" with the hope that future readers will, out of love for Nature, "judge" the letter writer "tenderly." The speaker presents herself as communicating Nature's words and therefore trading on the authority of Nature to win the approval of unknown readers.

Read in juxtaposition to this early version, the fascicle manuscript clearly shows how the disjunctions signaled by the dashes and lineation encourage readers to discover meaning through dialogue with a polyvocal text. The hierarchical distribution of power from "Nature" through the poet to the audience is altered significantly; suddenly, the speaker seems to be saying not that she is communicating news transmitted to her by Nature but that Nature is part of a "World" that never wrote to her:

> This is my letter to the World
> That never wrote to Me —
> The simple News that Nature told —
> With tender Majesty
>
> Her Message is committed
> To Hands I cannot see —
> For love of Her — Sweet — country-
> men —
> Judge tenderly — of Me (F24, 548)

Read with an eye to the dashes, the poem suggests the possibility that the speaker never received the "simple News that Nature told" and that Nature's "Message" was sent to others, whose "hands I cannot see." The very possibility that there could exist such things as "simple News" and "tender Majesty" is placed in question. By means of dashes, these clichéd depictions of nature and nature's sympathetic bearing on human life are held at arm's length, suggesting the speaker's rejection of the discourses to which they are attached. As Cameron has noted, this "is not necessarily a poem about a benign telling of nature's secret"; rather, "the secret being told is ominous" (*Choosing* 33). And here, in this recognition of ominous possibilities, lies the key to the text's multiple voices: as the speaker questions the validity of culturally determined voices, she distances herself from these voices, so that through her we hear voices that no longer confine her.

Dickinson's multiplication of discourse possibilities through the dash also magnifies the importance of reader assent in attaching meaning to language. As readers who become aware of the speaker's ambivalent relation to prevailing thought, we do not "Judge tenderly," precisely because we detect the speaker's anger at an indifferent Nature that counters the rhetoric of "simple

News" and "tender Majesty." The manuscript lineation that separates "country" from "men" increases our sense of the speaker's detachment from communal values, particularly those articulated by the male voices of patriarchal culture. Cameron effectively captures this element of the poem, describing the voice qualities refracted through the speaker's reproachful delivery: "the letter to the world . . . is inescapably to be read as analogous to those stern communications the speaker has herself received" (*Choosing* 33). The reader's response to this poem now grows from an appreciation of the speaker's disappointment, a disappointment directed to a "World" that never wrote.

In addition to presenting Nature as uncertain and antagonistic, the speaker also undermines the authority of her audience. The insertion of a dash between "Sweet" and "country- / men" separates the terms of an otherwise positive salutation, suggesting that the speaker is once again distancing herself from conventional discourse and, in this case, twisting the meaning ordinarily attributed to a congenial epistolary form of address. As previously indicated, the maleness of addressees is here singled out as a potentially damning attribute. Yet as we hear the speaker's tone become ironic, instead of sincere, we do not entirely reject her sincerity and replace it with something more akin to sarcasm. Rather, we observe the speaker's moving through the network of discourses that constitutes the socioideologic domain of language, interrogating and manipulating culturally determined voices. By this means the speaker admits to complicity with her audience in assenting to the very voices she finds most offensive.

At the same time, we can see that the speaker's participation in this process acknowledges the power of the larger culture without accepting that power as determinant; we hear voices that are not the speaker's and yet contribute to a discussion in which the speaker is a party. In this way, the poem traces the speaker's movement away from conformity without excluding the influence conventional discourse has on the self—a self that both includes and exceeds the voices that permeate it. Like many Dickinson poems, this one alerts readers to the importance of not becoming settled in any particular linguistic locale. As she indicates in her 1883 letter-poem to Maria Whitney, creative minds are never fully at home in language: "Fashioning" and Fathoming" "dissolves the days / through which existence strays / Homeless at home" (L815; P1573).

While the dashes, in particular, point to the open and unresolved character of Dickinson's poem, this very openendedness militates against any exclusionary tactic that would deny the possibility of a poem's achieving closure. The poem emphasizes resistance to closure by respecting but not submitting to its appeal. A truly dialogic reading of "This is my letter to the World," for example, would respect this quality of being "Homeless at home" by not dismissing the interpretation made available through the regularization of punctuation; rather, the dialogic approach builds on interpretations that assert unifying movement in the poems. In fact, the voices in the poem acquire distinction as they depart from unified discourses, making such discourses a necessary part of readings that acknowledge the dialogizing influence of the dashes. Consequently, the regularization practiced by Dickinson's editors usefully clarifies impulses toward univocality and closure while unfortunately muffling the very forces that urge polyvocality and the multiplication of meanings so crucial to Emily Dickinson's dialogic voice.

FURTHER READING

Wardrop, Daneen. *Emily Dickinson's Gothic: Goblin with a Gauge*. Iowa City: University of Iowa Press, 1996.

THE MANUSCRIPTS

Martha Nell Smith

Dickinson's Manuscripts

"The Poems" will ever be to me marvellous whether in ms. or type.

Susan Dickinson to Thomas Higginson, Christmas 1890

I have a little article in mind, with illustrations of her [Emily's] own, showing her witty humorous side, which has all been left out of her [Lavinia's] vol. [as Sue chose to call *Poems* (1890)].

Susan Dickinson to William Hayes Ward, *Independent*, 23 March 1891

*L*ike Susan Dickinson, who had been intimately familiar with Emily Dickinson's handwritten creative works for nearly four decades, the earliest editors who worked to produce posthumous volumes of her poetry noticed the significant difference between reading the poems in her chirography and reading them in print. At least one of them, Thomas Wentworth Higginson, was for decades fascinated by her scriptures — or so her handwritten copies of poems, letters, and letter-poems might be called if readers invoke the full range of definitions recorded in her beloved *Webster's* to distinguish her holographs from their typographic translations.[1] Of his first letter from her and its material embodiment, Higginson remarked that "it was in a handwriting so peculiar that it seemed as if the writer might have taken her first lessons by studying the famous fossil bird-tracks in the museum of that college town. Yet it was not in the slightest degree illiterate, but cultivated, quaint, and wholly unique"; and of its enclosures' content, "the impression of a wholly new and original poetic genius was as distinct on my mind at the first reading of these four poems as it is now, after half a century of further knowledge" ("Letters," 1891). Not surprisingly, then, the second series of poems he edited features "There came a day – / at Summer's full –" (P322); "Fac-simile of 'Renunciation,'" *Poems* [1891]).

Yet Millicent Todd Bingham, Mabel Loomis Todd's daughter, claimed the facsimile production in *Poems by Emily Dickinson* (1891) was "*solely*" to correct a supposed misreading of "There came a day – / at Summer's full –" by Susan, who had placed a copy in *Scribner's* (1890) that featured a key word change from the version Higginson and Loomis Todd had printed in the 1890 *Poems* as "Renunciation" (58–59; *Ancestors'* 149). Bingham argued that the facsimile was an attempt to fix the identity of the poem. Yet Dickinson herself made at least three different copies of this poem, each variant from the other—one she sent to Higginson; another, with numerous cancellations and alternative wordings, she bound into a manuscript book (F13, 275–77, P322); and there is a copy in the Amherst College library that may be the "lost" copy she sent to Susan or that may be yet a fourth copy; and there may be or have been others. Whatever Loomis Todd's reasons for including the facsimile, Higginson was clearly very taken with Dickinson's handwriting: his inclusion of her work in *A Reader's History of American Literature* (1903) again featured a facsimile, of "Safe in their Alabaster Chambers" (P216), of which there are also several holograph copies. His reason for doing so was not to fix the poem's identity but to illustrate the contrast between Dickinson's poetic endeavors and those of her frequently printed contemporary Helen Hunt Jackson (also an Amherst native). Higginson's judgment that Dickinson's handwriting is "cultivated" is one with which almost every editor who has worked with the manuscripts would concur; the significance of that stylizing for her poetics is debatable. The dispute over wording in "There came a Day – at / Summer's full – (F13, 275–77)—between "soul" and "sail" in the printed line of "Renunciation," "As if no soul / sail the solstice passed"—and the Todd–Bingham claim of correcting a misreading highlight other editorial concerns.[2] From the beginning and indeed throughout much of the first century of producing books of her poems, editors have labored to establish the identities of particular poems and to make *author*itative—most faithful to the poet's original or final intentions and/or most aesthetically, sensibly pleasing—printed translations of Emily Dickinson's holographs, though question after question has been raised about what constitutes "most authoritative."

As these examples show, Dickinson often left poems in what to book-trained eyes appear to be "unfinished" states, with variant stanzas or lines or, most frequently, variant words marked with a "+" and placed above or beside lines or below the poem's last line; in many holographs of Dickinson poems, then, no final choice is made among alternatives to "finish" the poem by choosing a particular variant. In the early stages of bookmaking Dickinson left variants only once or twice[3] and lineated her poems according to the (usually tetrameter) meter. But after gaining some experience making a few manuscript books, she began to distribute metrical units (tetrameter, trimeter, pentameter) over more than one line[4] and to leave more and more variants. In fascicle 10 Dickinson records three alternative stanzas for a coupling with a first stanza beginning "Safe in their Alabaster Chambers" (a version of which is also recorded in fascicle 6 and which was sent not only to Higginson but, in several iterations, to Susan; see F6, 103, P216, and F10, 193–94, P216). The first poem in fascicle 11 features an alternative word and line choice, as do all her subsequent poetic groupings. In these products of her middle and later book-making — thirty fascicles and fifteen "sets" (what R. W. Franklin calls groups of poems gathered together but not sewn into books by Dickinson), or the vast majority of "books" she left to posterity — Dickinson routinely left variants from which readers might pick and choose. By itself, this practice might appear to signal that the fascicles were her private workbooks, yet the fact that her highly stylized script begins to emerge so dramatically in the ninth fascicle, concomitantly with the variants, argues for both as components of her conscious poetic strategies.

For the first half century of printing Dickinson's writings, choosing among variants to finish poems for readers' editions was regarded as necessary. Once such choices had been made, variants were rarely mentioned by editors until, sixty-five years after the first printed volume, Thomas H. Johnson produced a scholarly edition of *The Poems of Emily Dickinson* (1955), "Including variant readings critically compared with all known manuscripts." For the first time since their publication to the world, Johnson represented her variant word choices by printing them at the end of the lyric, numbering them according to a line in which they fit. This was a radical and welcome departure from previous editorial praxes. What Johnson shared with his predecessors, however, was the opinion that for all of her poetic career Dickinson conceived of corporealized poems as existing on the printed poetic page.

This stating-the-obvious about editorial assumptions is important to examine, for Dickinson never saw more than a few of her poems in print. The brief history of her use of variants and evolutions in her handwriting shows ways in which she began to alter her writing practices as she copied more and more poems into manuscript books and into letters. In the first eight fascicles, Dickinson was obviously writing bibliographically, or with the book and the printed page in mind — her poetic forms in these are regularized variations on the tercet and quatrain, predictably lineated. Paul Fussell's critical insight into the age of printing transforming the sense of stanzaic forms from the exclusively "aural" to include the "visual" poignantly pertains to the specific case of Dickinson — "the joint work of eye and inner ear necessitated by the reader's new encounter with the printed page . . . reveal[ed] to both poets and readers the new world of metrical delight based on an aesthetic of pattern-and-variation" (135–36). By the ninth and in all subsequent fascicles, Dickinson writes as if "the joint work of eye and inner ear" is being shaped by her persistent encounters with the manuscript page, a striking visual contrast to print, and with patterns guided entirely by her hand. The material record suggests that she began to focus more and more on the possibilities afforded by the manuscript page, and experimented with lineation, calligraphic orthography, angled marks of punctuation, and with leaving alternative word choices from which readers can choose. In other words, she began to render her poetic embodiments in terms of her holograph and cottage industry rather than in terms of typography and the publishing industry. Only with Franklin's publication of *The Manuscript Books of Emily Dickinson* (1981) has a multitude of readers been able to learn from new encounters with Dickinson's manuscript pages, hundreds of which are featured in facsimile.

Over the first century of making her work available to the public, editors worked to translate Dickinson's holograph into easily legible typeface. Not surprisingly, how poems are conventionally typeset has framed perceptions of her lyrics and thus dictated conceptions of accurate representations of Dickinson's poems, of what does and does not count as a constitutive part of the poem and as the techniques and forms of its expression. Thus, following routine procedures, editors have debated which variant is preferable and have chosen one to make a reader's edition instead of imagining that presenting all variants and leaving the choice up to readers' improvisations might make Dickinson's poetic project more fully available to her readers. Though Johnson displays all variants, his method of marking them with a numeral corresponding to a particular line is more directive than Dickinson's method of marking words within the body of the poem and their alternatives with a "+" so that specific exchanges are ambiguous: in Dickinson's holograph an alternative word may fit into more than one line in a poem.

The standard editorial procedure of choosing the "best," most authoritative variant was probably necessary during this first century of reading her in order to create and cultivate a receptive climate for Dickinson's creative work. Popularizing editors Higginson and Loomis Todd, who produced three volumes of poems in 1890, 1891, and 1896, and Martha Dickinson Bianchi, who produced *The Single Hound* in 1914, and, with the "invaluable assistance" (xi) of Alfred Leete Hampson, *The Complete Poems of Emily Dickinson* in 1924, then with Hampson produced four more volumes of her aunt's poetry between 1929 and 1937, as well as scholarly editor Johnson all translated her holograph into print by interpreting her marks as if Dickinson was writing with the printed page in mind. The collective opinion was that holographic anomalies like angled dashes and arresting line breaks are manuscript accidentals, not poetic experimentation, and that editorial reconstructions to conform to print conventions are necessary improvements to render most intelligibly all the meaningful aspects of Dickinson's creative work. Anything eliminated by these typographical reconstructions was therefore deemed negligible, and readers, unfamiliar with the manuscripts, did not ask questions about elements

Dickinson inscribed but that they did not even know had been erased from print iterations.

Now, however, with so much more information about the manuscripts so widely circulated by facsimile reproductions in *The Manuscript Books*, and at a time when movements in literary theory and developments in popular and scholarly reading and writing practices highlight process, dynamics, and interactions between and among authors and audiences, standard editorial procedures do not necessarily seem the "best" means of representing Dickinson's writings. In the wake of *The Manuscript Books*, many readers have begun to ask, as has Susan Howe, whether "in her carefully handwritten manuscripts," the poet was "demonstrating her conscious and unconscious separation from a mainstream literary orthodoxy in letters" (*Birth-mark* 1) and whether what had been eliminated by print reproductions was in fact meaningful. In short, readers such as myself have concluded that Dickinson "published" her work via circulation in letters and in her manuscript books (*Rowing* 11–16). In the words of Jerome McGann, Emily Dickinson rejected a "market-model of publishing, with its medium of print, because she came to see how restrictive and conventional that medium had become" and opted instead for a "scriptural and epistolary" medium for dissemination of her ambitious poetic project rather than a "publishing and bibliographical one" ("Visible" 43, 45). Computer technologies that will enable distribution of facsimiles across the World Wide Web and on CD-ROM as well as in books create even more possibilities for thorough critical interrogations of the material evidence left by the poet at work. Hence the present need for evolving editorial procedures, procedures which recognize, as did Franklin three decades ago, that Dickinson's work pushes editorial inquiry "to the limits of ontology and epistemology" (*Editing* 143).

The following sections first recount the transmission of the Dickinson manuscripts and their translations into print: how they came to be divided in the 1890s and the subsequent competing editing endeavors of the houses of Todd–Bingham (1890–96, 1945–55) and Bianchi–Hampson (1914–37); Johnson finally bringing all the documents together in scholarly Harvard University Press editions of poems (1955) and letters (1958); and the perceptual changes initiated by Franklin's facsimile edition. Each of these three sections will analyze how editors have seen Dickinson's scene of writing and thus sought to reproduce her poetic page for print. Also, in order to examine benefits and limitations of taxonomies used to understand her literary project these analyses will interrogate the categories of genre used to organize the Dickinson documents for study.

When Emily Dickinson distributed or "published" her poems to her contemporaries, she did not do so through the conventions of the printed book but made her own "books" by binding poems together into hand-sewn fascicles and into correspondences to particular addressees. Her production and distribution practices are thus both analogous to and in strong, telling contrast to the mechanized, highly regulated procedures of the "Auction" (P709), or publishing world. Each of the subsequent major editorial translations of her unique literary productions might be seen as an attempt to reconsolidate and restabilize the commodity The Book, to tame work that otherwise sometimes seems wildly unmanageable so that it conforms to conventional publishing standards. Ironically, the authority engendered by the purview of the book imposes and finalizes generic distinctions, organizational strategies, lineation and punctuation techniques not evident in Dickinson's fluid writing practices. Dickinson's medium of handwriting modified her "aural and visual" poetic sensibilities, and the print medium has similarly shaped readers' interpretive sensibilities; she increasingly wrote for her manuscript page, a territory unfamiliar to most of readers; and thus that her generic and technical standards may have been other than those tailored for print has not usually been imagined.

The conclusion will analyze how every attempt to stabilize Dickinson's texts into books has revealed more of the multitude of challenges the documents themselves make to print representation. Every effort to consolidate and fix Dickinson's writings for books has raised the questions with which her first editors began: What counts as a poem? What counts as a letter? What counts as a Dickinson poem? What counts as a Dickinson letter? What counts as writing by Emily Dickinson? What counts as a poetic mark? What counts as an accidental? What elements of marks are poetic? What characteristics are habitual and accidental, or meaningless for critical inquiry? In his anthology of American letters, Higginson could have been speaking for her first (and many of her subsequent) editors and perhaps most of her readers:

> Emily Dickinson never quite succeeded in grasping the notion of the importance of poetic form. The crudeness which an Emerson could mourn over, she could only acknowledge. With all its irregularity, however, her poetry preserves a lyrical power almost unequaled in her generation. (Higginson and Boynton 131)

This is a logical conclusion by one whose sensibilities were cultivated by the medium of print. Yet a century later, other media afford other opportunities for appreciating scriptural poetic forms.

DISCOVERY AND EARLY EDITIONS

"The Bustle" (P1078) in Emily Dickinson's room after her death in 1886 uncovered the correspondence that she had treasured and hundreds of poems in what appear to be various states of completion — the forty bound fascicles, or handmade books, and fifteen unbound "sets" of fascicle sheets published in facsimile edition by Franklin, as well as numerous drafts and fragments, some of which have been published in facsimile edition in *Emily Dickinson's Open Folios: Scenes of Reading, Surfaces of Writing* (1995) by Marta Werner. Dickinson's sister Lavinia burned the correspondence from others but kept the poems, indeed all of Emily's writings, about which she had a " 'Joan of Arc' feeling" (Bingham, *Ancestors'* 87), and set about finding an editor to publish a printed volume. Not surprisingly, she first sought the help of Susan Dickinson, Emily's dear friend, most frequently addressed correspondent, and most constant literary advisor. For reasons that have never been and will probably always remain insufficiently explained, Susan, though she successfully placed poems in publications like the *Independent* (P160, P792), *Scribner's* (P322), *Youth's Companion* (P1391) and approached editors of magazines like the *Century* (Bingham, *Ancestors'* 88, 115; Smith, *Rowing* 15, 214), did not edit the hundreds of poems Lavinia brought to her, though she did make extensive notes for her "Book of Emily" (notes her daughter Martha followed to produce *The Single Hound* the year after Susan's death) and corresponded with editors (including Higginson) as an authority about Dickinson's intentions, their mistranscriptions, and titles.[5]

After two years, Lavinia retrieved the manuscripts from Susan and asked Loomis Todd to copy out the poems in order to send them to Higginson, who, having told Susan during an 1886 stay in her home that Dickinson's poems were "un-presentable" for publication, had, by 1888, had a change of heart. Higginson asked Loomis Todd to group the poems before passing them along to him, and her work led to her name appearing on the title page of the 1890 *Poems by Emily Dickinson*, though Lavinia had specifically requested that Loomis Todd's involvement be "sub rosa" (Bingham, *Ancestors'* 60). Though reviewers frequently reviled that first posthumous volume of Dickinson's poetry for its formal eccentricities, the earliest criticisms might best be characterized as ambivalent, for many, perhaps even most, remarked a fascination for this extraordinary poetic vision, however crudely expressed. Whatever the critical reception, the *Poems* sold well, and in 1891 Higginson and Loomis Todd brought out *Poems by Emily Dickinson*, Second Series, and in 1894 Loomis Todd published *Letters of Emily Dickinson* and in 1896 *Poems by Emily Dickinson*, Third Series.

Eighteen ninety-six was also the year in which Loomis Todd had a bitter falling-out with the Dickinson family. Having been Austin Dickinson's (Emily and Lavinia's brother, Susan's husband) mistress since weeks after his and Susan's youngest son Gib died in 1883 (at the tender age of eight) to Austin's death in 1895, Loomis Todd's relationships with the Dickinsons were far from simple. Though Austin flirted with the fancy, he never left the home he had made with Susan for Mabel but probably did ask Lavinia to sign over a deed of property adjoining the house he had built for Mabel and her husband David. After his death, at Mabel's behest, Lavinia did this, thought better of it, was sued by Mabel, who lost, both in District Court and on appeal. Needless to say, the parties parted acrimoniously, each retaining the manuscripts in their possession (Lavinia the packets Loomis Todd numbered 1–38, 40; Mabel, packets 80–95, as well as many loose poems).[6]

Susan inherited Lavinia's manuscripts in 1899. Then her daughter Martha gained custody of both hers and Lavinia's after Susan died in 1913 and published *The Single Hound*, a volume of her aunt's poems, letters, and letter-poems to her mother, in 1914. With Hampson, she produced *The Complete Poems of Emily Dickinson* (1924), *Further Poems of Emily Dickinson* (1929), *The Poems of Emily Dickinson* (1930), *Unpublished Poems of Emily Dickinson* (1935), *Poems by Emily Dickinson* (1937), as well as lives of the poet and her family in *The Life and Letters of Emily Dickinson* (1924) and *Emily Dickinson Face to Face: Unpublished Letters with Notes and Reminiscences* (1932) (in 1924, Hampson assisted Bianchi on her epistolary biography; eight years later he wrote a foreword for *Face to Face*). Hence the Bianchi–Hampson house of Emily Dickinson, producing Dickinson–Bianchi–Hampson poems and biographical data.

Mabel locked her manuscripts in a box and did not publish anything until the "New and enlarged edition" of *Letters of Emily Dickinson* in 1931. After her mother's death in 1932 and Bianchi's more than a decade later in 1943, Millicent Todd Bingham began mining the box of Dickinson writings withheld since the 1896 lawsuit and published *Bolts of Melody: New Poems of Emily Dickinson* (1945; Loomis Todd, thirteen years deceased, is listed as coeditor), as well as narratives of Dickinson lives in *Ancestors' Brocades: The Literary Debut of Emily Dickinson* (1945), *Emily Dickinson: A Revelation* (1954), *Emily Dickinson's Home: Letters of Edward Dickinson and His Family* (1955). Hence the Todd–Bingham house of Emily Dickinson, producing Dickinson–Todd–Higginson or Dickinson–Todd–Bingham poems (Franklin, *Editing* 141).

A cursory glance at the subtitles of some of these volumes reveals the war between these houses over the most authoritative presentation of Dickinson's work and life. The 1890 *Poems* is edited "by two of her Friends"; *Further Poems* (1929) are poems "withheld from publication by her sister Lavinia" and "edited by her niece"; the letters, notes, and reminiscences of *Emily Dickinson Face to Face* (1932) are again edited "by her niece"; *Ancestors' Brocades* purports to tell the "literary debut of Emily Dickinson" as it tells the story of the productions by Dickinson–Todd–Higginson. The subtitle *Letters of Edward Dickinson and His Family* for *Emily Dickinson's Home* invokes patriarchal authority even as it attempts to establish familial proximity to Dickinson herself. The

Todd–Bingham clamor for authority via a kind of "gnosis" regarding the Dickinson family is apparently to counteract the familial authority asserted by Bianchi–Hampson repeatedly emphasizing the niece yoked to her aunt via bloodline and daily face-to-face contact.

Through its various publications, each of these houses producing Emily Dickinson and her creative works tries to consolidate and stabilize the story of her writing and then the rescue of her poems from oblivion. Each set of stories is riddled with inconsistencies and manipulative half truths, and reproductions of poems and letters by each are disappointing editorial reconstructions. Dickinson–Todd poems sometimes alter Dickinsons' writing enough to excise stanzas (P712 n.), sometimes as much as half of a four-stanza poem (P271 n.; Smith, *Rowing* 30–33; Maun 72–73 n.1), and Dickinson–Bianchi–Hampson producers sometimes mismatch stanzas (Franklin, *Editing* 44–45) and excise sentences from letters (L73; Faderman, "Letters" 211–17). There are many critical stories to tell about the motives for willful changes and inadvertent mistakes that these editors made, and there are many kinds of fruitful critical inquiries that might be made of these alterations; however, for our purposes, it is enough to know that, in general and in keeping with their respective generations, the houses of Todd–Bingham and Bianchi–Hampson strove to produce what they considered to be *user-friendly* works by Emily Dickinson. Johnson's observation nearly a half century ago still holds: Todd–Higginson altered words to "smooth rhymes, regularize the meter, delete localisms, and substitute sensible metaphors" and, I will add, organized the poems according to the conventional themes of "Life," "Love," "Nature," and "Time and Eternity," all to conform to late-nineteenth-century readers' expectations and maintain a "maximum of decorum"; twenty years later, Dickinson's "verbal and metric irregularities were recognized as essential to the form and meaning of her poetry," and thus Bianchi did not feel pressured to smooth rhyme and meter, and by 1929, when she was editing with Hampson, irregularities in form and content were widely accepted and even inspired them to accentuate and perhaps exaggerate what had previously been regarded as mandating editorial correction (Johnson, "Editing the Poems: 1890–1945," P xlv, xlvii–xlviii).

Important for today's readers, then, are the following facts: Both Todd–Bingham and Bianchi–Hampson sought to make Dickinson's writings more palatable to the general reader and, translating her holographs to print, changed them accordingly; neither source is entirely reliable, and some of the errors are, regrettably, in bad faith, though most can be justly received as well intentioned; for a variety of reasons the Todd–Bingham house has gained precedence, but both houses served equally important, indeed vital, functions for creating a readership for Emily Dickinson, and readers need not take sides in their war, need not hold one in high regard at the expense of prejudice against the other; hearsay from either party in stories of analyzing Dickinson's creative practices is not fact. Last and most importantly, Lavinia, Dickinson's beloved sister, deserves credit for Emily's manuscripts being preserved and transmitted for posterity's scrutiny. In the words of Johnson, "be it to Lavinia Dickinson's everlasting credit that her singleminded persistence won through" (P xliii).

"CREATING THE POEMS" FOR JOHNSON'S VARIORUM

In contrast to Todd–Higginson–Bingham and Bianchi–Hampson, who sought to render Dickinson's poems presentable to conventional tastes, Thomas Johnson aimed "to establish an accurate text of the poems and to give them as far as possible a chronology" (P lxi) when he published his variorum in 1955. Similarly, in contrast to the fact that a "very large number of letters were subject to extensive deletion when they were previously published," Johnson sought to present "all autograph letters . . . in their verbatim form" (L xxv). His primary goal, then, was to present Dickinson's poems and letters as they were written, to translate her holograph to print accurately, precisely, and in ways that placed Dickinson's intentions before all other arbiters and did not privilege prevailing literary appetites and critical fashions as had Todd–Higginson–Bingham and Bianchi–Hampson.

For bringing all Dickinson's writings together and publishing them in the three-volume variorum *The Poems of Emily Dickinson* and the three-volume *The Letters of Emily Dickinson*, scholars, critics, and readers are ever indebted to Johnson's tireless, painstaking efforts that, as Adrienne Rich remarks, foreground "the unquestionable power and importance of the mind revealed" ("Vesuvius" 59–60). Ironically, then, the first section in his Introduction to the variorum, "Creating the Poems," just as aptly describes Johnson's reproductions as Dickinson's original productions. Working when the tenets of New Criticism held sway in the profession of literature, Johnson saw bibliographic not scriptural poems, isolated lyrics that were perfect as objects of New Critical inquiry, and so the 1,775 Dickinson–Johnson poems fit rather neatly into this paradigm. This is not a fault but a way in which Johnson's critical opinions are marked by their situation in time, as the conclusions of this essay are marked by possibilities made imaginable by technological advances at this fin-de-siècle.

Johnson isolated poems and letters from their larger contexts and exalted the single lyric and/or epistolary unit as the primary, most significant source of meaning. Scrupulous in his production of a scholarly edition, Johnson then numbered poems, marking particular units for study, each lyric discrete from every other and from its appearance in Dickinson's "books" of poetry and/or from its presentation in her "books" of correspondence to specific addressees. Letters are likewise numbered, each discrete from every other missive and from its place in Dickinson's "book" of other letters, letter-poems, and poems to the same addressee. The prevailing criterion for ordering in Johnson's scheme for both letters and poems is chronology, consideration of which supersedes that of either audience or occasion for presentation (in a correspondence or manuscript book).

Because he saw the poems bibliographically, Johnson categorizes as if they were prepared for conventional publication and thus concludes that a poem may be one of three types: (1) a *fair copy*; (2) a *semifinal draft*; or (3) a *worksheet draft* (P xxxiii). Seeing each poem in the context of its encounter with the printed page, he reasonably assumed that Dickinson believed a text could be completed and that she never changed her mind toward this idea of completion. In other words, throughout her decades-long poetic career Johnson's Dickinson always saw poems as *finished, still in process but very nearly finished*, or *still very much in process*. This vision is shaped by what might be called the ideology of the book, and the printing apparatuses that produce books, and is, as we have seen, what shaped Dickinson's early bookmaking (F1–8), though she appears never to have titled any of the hand-sewn volumes. To produce printed pages, choices must be made among variants and finalized, and Johnson's Dickinson was writing with this in mind throughout her career, not only in its earlier stages.

What Johnson did not entertain was the possibility that what he was labeling "semifinal" or "worksheet" may at least in some instances have referred to works with which Dickinson was in one sense finished, works in which she was consciously forestalling limits imposed on her writing and her audience; what he did not entertain was the possibility that, by leaving variants among which readers may pick and choose, Dickinson may have been extending her work toward her audience, demanding a kind of performance or what Cristanne Miller calls "actively expectant reading," requiring "the reader's participation in establishing the text of a poem" (*Grammar* 49). The Emily Dickinson whom Johnson imagined would never have invited a reader to coauthor in quite this way, for she was writing with print ideology's notions of fixity and finishing in mind. For Johnson, Dickinson's leaving variants meant that she had not decided how to complete a poem rather than that she was decidedly refusing closure (see Smith, *Rowing* 70–75; Cameron, *Choosing* 13–14). This is understandable, for his formidable challenge was to bring together, organize, and translate into print original documents housed primarily at the Houghton Library, Harvard (Bianchi–Hampson),[7] and the Frost Library, Amherst College (Todd–Bingham), and dispersed throughout other collections. Johnson's main objective was to make sense of these myriad texts for scholarly publica-

I reason -
        Earth is short -
And Anguish - absolute -
And many - hurt -
But, what of that?
        I reason -
                We should
die -
the best - Vitality -
Could not excel Decay -
But - What of that?
        I reason -
                that in Heaven -
Somehow - it will be even -
Some new Equation - given -
But - What of that!

Copy of "I reason –" sent to Sue. (H274; P301). By permission of The Houghton Library, Harvard University. © The President and Fellows of Harvard College.

tion, and his methods of perceiving, collating, organizing, and redistributing were bibliographic.

Operating on the assumption that Dickinson was writing for the world of print dictates not only how he sees the poem as a lyric whole to be completed by accepting or rejecting possible parts but also how he understands the identity of each part and its relationship to the lyric whole. Fixity and finality govern his sense not only of where parts belong but also of how they belong. For Dickinson–Johnson poems, variants belong to particular lines and only to those lines and are numbered accordingly; the same variant cannot be placed in different lines. Similarly, lines have singular identities; they are always metrical units, never visual components. Lines are the tetrameter or trimeter or near approximations thereof common to the hymnal stanza and are determined by meter, not by any meaning their visual presentation may make or that may be generated by profound, conscious breaking of metrical form via visual arrangement (for examples of Dickinson's visual punning in lineation, see Smith, *Rowing* 19, and Hart, "New Strategies" 71). Stanzas, too, are quatrains or other conventionally printed forms.

Thus, when he reproduces the version of "I reason – / Earth is short –" (H274; P301) that Dickinson sent to Susan (see illustration), Johnson does not see that a radical scheme for lineation supplants stanzaic division to punctuate and accentuate the poem's bold ironies. Instead of transposing a sixteen-line, single-stanza poem, Johnson imposes spaces where there are none and produces a three-stanza poem of five-line stanzas (P301 n.).

Using the staggered placement of words on sixteen lines arrests the reader's attention and slows the process of perusal to a halting pace, encouraging unpredictable, exploratory strategies for reading beyond conventionally formulated receptions of poetic technique. The thrice-repeated clause "I reason" and the query "But, what of that?" redirect the reader and recast her understanding to underscore the *un*reasonableness and irrationality of the Christian assurances Dickinson's poem calls into question. This version, with its underlinings and dramatic placement of the solitary syllable "die" on a line by itself, seems bitingly sarcastic, contributing to the lyric's gist, "What does it matter that I reason about divine justice? What does it matter if I rationalize earthly plights as the price paid for heavenly reward?" Its material embodiment demands that readers and thus editors see the poem, its lines, its spacings, all its constitutive parts in dramatically fresh fashion. Indeed, the cessations and emphases urged by linear arrangement and underlinings encourage a sensual as well as sensible interpretation, thus reminding one that both Dickinson and her most constant reader, Susan, proclaimed poetry's affective powers physical as well as mental; Higginson reported that Dickinson remarked, "If I read a book [and] it makes my whole body so cold no fire ever can warm me I know *that* is poetry" (L342a), a commentary closely allied with Susan's response to "Safe in their Alabaster Chambers": "I always go to the fire and get warm after thinking of it, but I never *can* again" (L238). These provocative experimentations with a poet's contract with readers' expectations are not reproduced in Johnson's print translation of this version of "I reason –." In fact, he does not see that vertical spacing carefully indicates only line but not stanza division, nor does he see the indented, abbreviated, beginning-in-the-middle or beginning-with-the-presumed-end (*"die"*) line arrangements as meaningful (Smith, *Rowing* 67–69). Conventional expectations govern his field of vision, and he assumes that Dickinson must have intended three stanzas, each beginning "I reason."

Johnson's variorum of the poems and edition of the letters had, until Franklin's *Manuscript Books*, the highest status as textual representations of Dickinson's writings. His editions mediate, at least somewhat, the possessiveness of the houses Todd–Bingham and Bianchi–Hampson of the author Emily Dickinson. Yet the Johnson editions have produced some unanticipated effects that are crucial for anyone editing the manuscripts to consider. His numbers have become part of the identity of the Dickinson–Johnson poems, in effect "titling" them. As often as not, critics will refer to poems not by the words of their first lines but by Johnson's numbers, so that a discussion of "I reason –" becomes one of "poem #310." Naming poems by their cataloging information, by Johnson's numbers instead of by Dickinson's words, in effect possesses the unit he has identified as a poem or letter. Thus the Dickinson materials have been imbued with a possessiveness of definitude that Johnson himself never intended to convey about their genres, having observed that "the letters both in style and rhythm begin to take on qualities that are so nearly the quality of her poems as on occasion to leave the reader in doubt where the letter leaves off and the poem begins" (L xv). Johnson thereby substantiates that Susan Dickinson's identification of some of Emily Dickinson's writings as "letter-poems" in a February 8, 1891, letter to William Hayes Ward is reasonable (H Lowell Autograph; Smith, *Rowing* 110) and that identities of many of these writings are debatable. Nevertheless, Johnson's print translations have been received as if they are practically identical with Dickinson's holographs, so much so that some confuse the print translations and holographs as one and the same.

For example, in 1993, to produce poems he deems "permanent addition[s] to the Dickinson canon," William H. Shurr takes lines "from Thomas H. Johnson's three-volume work, *The Letters of Emily Dickinson*" (*New Poems* ix). He did not consult the manuscripts for this project. Thus, when he says that "Johnson did not include the following lines in his edition of Dickinson's poems, although she formatted them as poetry" (9), Shurr refers to lines that

Johnson indented and set apart, poemlike, when in 1958 he printed an 1880s letter to Susan (L912). If Shurr had consulted the manuscript to learn how Dickinson formatted lines, he would know that she did not indent the lines as did Johnson but in fact structured all the lines in this letter-poem "as poetry," as Hart pointed out in her 1990 article, "The Encoding of Homoerotic Desire" (251). Shurr's "Dickinson" poems are most accurately described as "Shurr–Johnson poems based on the letters of Emily Dickinson," for unlike Todd, Higginson, Bianchi, Hampson, Bingham, and Johnson, Shurr did not make his poems from the Dickinson holographs but took them from Johnson's print translations.[8] Shurr's belief that Dickinson indented poems in her letters comes from Johnson's having done so and evinces his confusion of print translations with the manuscripts themselves. Lewis Turco more accurately describes this enterprise of making poems from Johnson's edition of Dickinson's letters when he calls his 1993 poetic castings of her epistolary words "Centos," or literary works made up of parts from other works.

Two textual facts are worth keeping in mind, for readers and editors alike. First is recognition of the ontological questions raised by Dickinson's writings, many of which cannot be clearly identified as either letters or poems. Again, Susan Dickinson, her most frequent contemporary reader, descried these writings "letter-poems," a label Johnson sometimes used. Second is recognition that the sharp generic distinction purveyed by Johnson's three-volume *Poems* and three-volume *Letters* is not to be found in much of Dickinson's writing. Franklin, at work on a new comprehensive collection of her poems, has said that he will be more conservative than was Johnson about what counts as a poem in the Dickinson canon, so the number of poems identified by scholarly editors working with the manuscripts is not stable.

FRANKLIN'S FACSIMILES AND FASCICLES

Rejuvenating critical thinking about the corporealizations of her literary project, Franklin's facsimile reproductions of the holographs in *The Manuscript Books of Emily Dickinson* and *The Master Letters of Emily Dickinson* have made visible lineation, unusual punctuation marks (labeled "dashes," they are frequently slanted up and down, sometimes curviform, usually short, occasionally long), calligraphic orthography, spacing, revising strategies, and technical developments that had been occluded by print translations, even though Todd–Higginson–Bingham, Bianchi–Hampson, and Johnson all featured a few facsimiles. A Dickinson–Franklin fascicle poem is a halftone photographic image, not the manuscript itself. Features are, therefore, obscured or highlighted by the lens but not the eye. Mutilations to texts, so obvious in the cancelation of "One Sister have I in the house" (F2, 28–29, P14), are in other instances difficult to evaluate via photographs. Erasures on "The face I carry with / me – last –" (F19, 431–32, P336) and on " 'tis true–They shut me / in the Cold –" (F30, 717, P538) are impossible to discern in photograph, and Franklin's note is necessary for readers even to notice the tamperings (*Manuscript Books* 701, 1383). In photographs, pen and pencil are often not distinguishable, everything is flattened into black and shades of grey, so that pinholes are the same color as ink, the embossed Queen's head or letters or double-headed eagle are blurred marks in the corner of the page, and the gilded edges of much of Dickinson's stationery are not visible. On the other hand, the photographs plainly portray the lineation, diacritical marks, calligraphic orthography, variants, and at least one of the most hysterical mutilations, as well as the fact that, in holograph, Dickinson's poems visually control the page, while in print the white space of the page practically consumes the poems, miniaturizing them in ways the handwritten documents will not allow (Smith, *Rowing* 80). All of these characteristics are beginning to be interrogated as elements vital to Dickinson's vastly complex and wide-ranging poetics, and there is much more work to do (see Hart, Holland, Howe, Cameron, Crumbley, Werner, Wylder, McGann).

Editing is always interpretation, and one of the primary values of facsimile reproductions is that, as editions, they leave more decisions — about the poet's intentions and what counts as poetic technique — up to individual readers than do print translations. Franklin's facsimiles have already inspired interpretations that depart from his own in complementary contrast. In 1967 Franklin declared that the "capitals and dashes were merely a habit of handwriting" and used a recipe that Dickinson had copied to demonstrate his point (*Editing* 120–22), saying that since these were evident in the recipe they could not be regarded as poetic techniques elsewhere. Yet the opposite conclusion might just as well be drawn: in my copies of recipes, I somewhat haphazardly use commas and periods and semicolons and lower- and upper-case letters, but that does not invalidate my using them with grammatical and stylistic intent in other writings. As is made clear in a 1985 letter to Howe, Franklin also does not regard Dickinson's line breaks as conscious poetic strategies, for he believes the primary form she had in mind was the stanza (*Birth-mark* 134). In his introduction to *Manuscript Books*, he proclaims that Dickinson's primary unit for poetic production "had always been the sheet" and that one of her primary motives "in constructing these little books was to reduce disorder in the manuscripts" (x–xiii), and in a 1983 article he concludes that the fact that sheets within the same fascicle were copied in different years is a sign that "no fascicle-level order governed their preparation" ("Fascicles" 17). Again, the opposite conclusion might just as feasibly be drawn: that she was arranging poems after copying them suggests consciousness of intertextualities varying according to organization; time-consuming, deliberate assembly of poems arranged other than chronologically could spell premeditation and argue just as well for their functioning more than merely to reduce disorder.

Analyzing the fact that "Franklin would preserve the idea of the sequence" and is in fact "responsible for reestablishing it" but "would contest any sense of its significance," Sharon Cameron posits an interpretation quite different from Franklin's regarding the fascicles and sets (*Choosing* 12). The sets are the fifteen groups of poems that Dickinson placed together but did not bind into a particular sequence. Of the sets, Franklin says that the "physical evidence is insufficient to arrange them in a specific order" and that the "lack of binding would suggest that none was intended" ("Fascicles" 10). Cameron notes that "such a distinction correctly implies the importance of a different understanding of those poems intended to be bound than of those for which no binding appears to have been intended," and then astutely points out that Franklin attributes the same "motive for deciding *not* to bind" as he did to Dickinson's binding poems into fascicles: both facilitated her "browsing" among poems so that she could locate specific ones. In sharp contrast to Franklin, Cameron concludes that "something was differently intended for the fascicles than for the sets" (13). As have Howe, Hart, McGann, Oberhaus, myself, and others, Cameron employs evidence that Franklin's facsimile edition provides to draw a conclusion very different from his. The fact that such conscientiously produced facsimile editions do not impose an editor's formal assumptions marks an astounding advancement in editorial achievement: producing facsimiles, an editor can state and argue for her interpretations of formal strategies but is not forced to seal nearly so many of them into representation as producing print translations requires. Thus, departing from Franklin's own opinions about the fascicle arrangements and their sequences' meanings, Cameron and others can reasonably conclude that "in the Johnson edition the unit of sense is the individual poem" but "in the Franklin edition the unit of sense is not the individual poem but rather the fascicle book" (15).

So Franklin's reassembly of Dickinson's sequences, torn asunder by Loomis Todd, enables critical perceptions of developments in style and technique previously occluded by regularizing print translation and dispersion into single units of meaning. Thus readers can determine for themselves whether Dickinson's directing her dashes up or down was, as Edith Wylder argued, an intentional appropriation of rhetorical notation learned at the Amherst Academy, or was, as Johnson and his assistant Theodora Ward had claimed, an "especially capricious" (P lxiii) accident of emotional "stress." In *The Last Face: Emily Dickinson's Manuscripts*, Wylder argues that Dickinson absorbed rhetorical notation into her literary practices to make her punctuation more poetically suggestive (2–7, 12–13). The dramatic evolutions in Dickinson's lineation style after the first eight fascicles is concomitant with the dramatic changes in the holograph itself, in which the crossings of *t*'s, for example, routinely appear with much more flare. Individual letters become larger and more stylized so that in unbound set 8 there are more and more spaces between them and by set 13 spaces between letters and between words are more and more difficult to distinguish. Instead of interpreting these as mere changes in habits of handwriting, they might just as reasonably be viewed as poetic innovations. What Hart observes about Dickinson's lineation might just as well be said about her angled punctuation marks, vertical and horizontal spacing, placement of variants — that she uses them "to direct emphasis, create meaning, control pace, and guide her readers" ("New Strategies" 50). Yet without Franklin's facsimiles and the encouraging generosity of his own critical views, these insights would be obscured. True to Dickinson herself, Franklin's editorial performance enables readers to "dwell in Possibility" (F22, 495, P657) and to judge for themselves to what extent photographic displays of her writings and the critical observations about them lay the foundation for altering aesthetic norms and creating opportunities for new aesthetic pleasures.

The Screen and The Book

Franklin realized early on that "if we want the poems in a finished state, we must apply other principles of selection [than authorial intention] and must take responsibility for doing so" (*Editing* 131). Whatever the intentions of editors, inherent in editorial endeavors, however sophisticated, are dissolutions of fixed, stable representations of the Dickinson codex. As his perplexed remark about being uncertain where a letter leaves off and a poem begins shows, Johnson was not as sure of generic distinctions as his division of printings into volumes of *Poems* and *Letters* implies. As is clear from his treatment of the letter he numbered 912 (discussed above), the varied margins and indentations he used to mark lines of poetry were not consistently applied to embody Dickinson's own technical variations. He also does not clearly distinguish between letter-poems headed with the addressee's name — "Dear Sue" or "Sue," for example — and those with the addressee's name written on the verso but with no direct address heading the poem. Johnson will describe a letter-poem addressed only on the verso as "addressed 'Sue' and signed 'Emily'" (P316 n.), while describing a letter-poem with direct address heading the poem only subtly differently, "It is headed, 'Dear Sue'" (P299 n.). Since all this information is described in notes but not visually represented in the printed forms, the distinctions may easily elude readers and become conflated with one another. Hence print translation mutes the sense of distinction he attempts to draw.

Photographic representations like Franklin's facsimiles are more stable representations of the Dickinson codex yielding vastly different, equally credible interpretations regarding designs and purposes of her writings in both textual details like punctuation marks and whole textual bodies like whether the manuscript books are artistic groupings. Of those in the Dickinson canon, none have created more fictions than the "Master" letters. Franklin's facsimile edition *The Master Letters of Emily Dickinson* appears to stabilize them as epistolary, "real-life" transactions, packaged as the little book is with an envelope slipped inside the front cover with the facsimile sheets folded into leaves, easy to hold in hand just as Dickinson or their supposed addressee might have held them (the facsimiles also appear on pages of the book, with printed line-for-line transcriptions on facing pages). The packaging thus emphasizes Franklin's position that "Dickinson did not write letters as a fictional genre" (5) and that these are autobiographical. Yet close scrutiny of the facsimile representations, which reveals extensive revision and careful construction of a heartbroken, plaintive speaker, as reasonably suggests that Dickinson was in fact writing epistolary fiction. Thus a welcome advantage of the facsimile book is that it contains within itself and prominently displays evidence that challenges its own substantiation of these three writings as definitively nonfiction and as addressed to the same real person.

Technological advances which have made possible a hypermedia archive of the Dickinson documents (distributed via World Wide Web and CD-ROM) could also enable editors and readers to peruse and theorize beyond the scope of the book. Such basic but crucial questions as M. L. Rosenthal's "What, for us, is the real bearing of Dickinson's abjuring publication even while she wrote so intensely and tried her best to organize her poems in richly interactive groupings?" (Rosenthal and Gall) could be elaborated, and questions such as "What for us is the real bearing of Dickinson's works having been presented as if they can be definitively divided into discrete genres — poems and letters — and as if the techniques of her marks are only typographic?" could be more thoroughly explored. Similarly, Franklin's observation that "if we want the poems [and other writings] in a [definitive,] finished state, we must apply other principles of selection [than authorial preference] and must take responsibility for doing so" (*Editing* 131) might be fruitfully extended into a question, "What for us are the implications if this inherent tendency toward destabilization was an important point of Dickinson's poetic project?"

The Dickinson Editing Collective was formed at the first Emily Dickinson International Society Conference (in 1992) in order to discuss the production of new Dickinson books — Franklin's forthcoming edition of the poems, Smith and Hart's *Open Me Carefully: Emily Dickinson's Intimate Letters to Susan Huntington Gilbert* and Marta Werner's two editions of late scraps, *Emily Dickinson's Open Folios: Scenes of Reading, Surfaces of Writing* and *Radical Scatters: An Electronic Archive of Emily Dickinson's Late Fragments* — and to facilitate the development of a hypermedia archive of all of Dickinson's writings, beginning with her correspondences and late scraps, since only bits and pieces of these "books" have been featured in facsimile (whereas the fascicle "books" have been featured in full). Smith has developed several samplers (including "Emily Dickinson Writing a Poem," "Dickinson, Cartoonist," "The Letter-Poem, a Dickinson Genre") for the Collective's Web site, which also features "Writings by Susan Dickinson," many of which allude directly to writings by Emily or comment directly on print representations of Emily's poems (*http://jefferson. village.virginia.edu/dickinson/*). For the first time, all her drawings, cutouts, and visual manipulations of paper shape and type and assembly (from stationery to shopping bags, to affixed stamps and illustrations scissored from other books; see Holland, Werner, Smith) will be available in one venue for critique by those unable to go to the special collections in which the original documents are housed. In such an archive, photographic reproductions and publication histories of all Dickinson documents are being made available to scholars, who can in turn directly engage and more thoroughly analyze problems of translating her texts into print (both macro problems of organization and genre and micro problems of accurately reproducing her marks on the page and correcting scholarly mistranscriptions) and into electronic forms (again, macro problems organizing documents in networks and micro problems evaluating the critical significance of advantages and limitations of computer enhancement of documents). Thus the *Dickinson Electronic Archives* is not an ultimately "authoritative" edition but serves as a valuable resource for exploring theoretical implications of the material structures of Dickinson's texts (both individual documents and the organization of their relationships to one another) which will contribute to understanding her project and its reception in particular and textual studies and the construction of American literary history in general.

To imagine how the archive works, consider examining the writing and transmission of "Safe in their Alabaster Chambers" (P216), featured in "Emily Dickinson Writing a Poem." A reader can call this poem up onto the screen in various forms and open several windows on the screen to compare those forms simultaneously. Of the choices to be examined are: its appearance in two different fascicles (F6 and F10), and those are presented in facsimile; its appearance during an exchange between Emily and Sue concerning variations of the second verse, and those are also presented in facsimile (H B74a, 74b [Sue's response], 74c); typographical transcriptions of these presentations; Johnson's transcriptions of this exchange in facsimile (P216; L238); its first printing as "The Sleeping" in the *Springfield Daily Republican* (1 Mar. 1862) in facsimile; its printings in Bianchi's *Life and Letters of Emily Dickinson* and *Emily Dickinson Face to Face* in facsimile. The facsimile reproduction of the holograph to Higginson and surrounding commentary in his and H. W. Boynton's *A Reader's History of American Literature* is also available to anyone browsing in the archive, as are facsimile reproductions of his discussion of the poem in an 1890 article in the *Christian Union* and his and Loomis Todd's reproduction of the poem as a three-stanza entity in the 1890 *Poems*. The many print and facsimile reproductions of "Safe in their Alabaster Chambers" are therefore for the first time accessible in a single place for readers' comparative perusals.

When examining the exchange over the poem with Sue, readers are enabled to see "Safe in their Alabaster Chambers" not simply as part of an individual letter but also as part of the "book" comprising all Dickinson's correspondence to Susan. The same sort of contextualizing is enabled when the reader examines the fascicle presentations. Readers are invited to distinguish the contexts created by editors, including those of the electronic archives, from the contexts created by Dickinson in order to formulate analysis of a particular document for scholarly inquiry. Notes arguing for this exchange as documentation of Susan's (sometimes coauthoring) entanglement in Emily Dickinson's poetic project are readily accessible and situated amidst facsimiles on which these interpretive positions need not be imposed. The bias of the archive's overall organization is to present materials in the groups in which they were left at Dickinson's death — "individual correspondences, the manuscript volumes, and ungathered poems and drafts" (Hart, "New Strategies" 45). The electronic medium encourages pliant and accommodating principles of judgment regarding manuscript characteristics "as we contemplate what counts as the scene of writing, as the poetic mark on the page, as the most productive method of organizing Dickinson's writings for study" (Smith, "Hypermedia" 84).

Dickinson's writings, both in content and in form and both in holograph and in print, encourage readers' free play, as the editorial free play of a reader like Shurr makes so clear. From the archive, which will include facsimile reproductions of all Dickinson's letters and letter-poems, every reader can, if she desires, make her own "new poems of Emily Dickinson," "own an Emily of her own" (P1401; L531), as it were. Dickinson's sets, groups of poems which she gathered as if for a fascicle but refused to bind, invite each reader to make a new pattern for every reading and in that sense anticipate hypermedia reproduction, *un*bound and liberated from the fixed patternings that books cannot eschew.

Though the Dickinson literary project will always prove impossible to contain in a book (or for that matter in hypermedia display), its significant aspects can and have been, as Susan Dickinson's remark upon the first volume of *Poems by Emily Dickinson* reminds us, successfully conveyed in a variety of printed forms, for the "spirit" of Dickinson's poetry is fiercely resilient, even when inadequately embodied. Hypermedia representations do not aim to replace books, for the mobilities of each are different and valuable. Hypermedia enables readers to consider documents in a wider variety of contexts, to examine contrasting representations simultaneously on the same screen, to study research materials from numerous books and special collections on the same screen and without damaging the original documents via more direct handling. A broad range of scholarly and cultural information can be transported from original sources into the hypermedia archive. Books, on the other hand, can be transported from place to place, carried in hand, and are usable without an electronic support system. The editing of Dickinson's manuscripts will continue, for both book and electronic forms. The one medium will enhance appreciation of the other, not compete against and diminish the other's value. These proliferations of textual embodiments seem much more in the spirit of the poet whose variants and various presentations to audiences encourage possibilities and living texts rather than the closure and possessiveness of definitude.

APPENDIX: EDITIONS OF EMILY DICKINSON'S WRITINGS

Bianchi, Martha Dickinson. *Emily Dickinson Face to Face: Unpublished Letters with Notes and Reminiscences.* Boston: Houghton Mifflin, 1932.

——, ed. *The Life and Letters of Emily Dickinson.* Boston: Houghton Mifflin, 1924.

——, ed. *The Single Hound: Poems of a Lifetime by Emily Dickinson.* Boston: Little, Brown, and Company, 1914.

——, ed. *The Complete Poems of Emily Dickinson.* Boston: Little, Brown, 1924.

Bianchi, Martha Dickinson, and Alfred Leete Hampson, eds. *Further Poems of Emily Dickinson.* Boston: Little, Brown, 1929.

——, eds. *Poems by Emily Dickinson.* Boston: Little, Brown, 1937.

——, eds. *The Poems of Emily Dickinson.* Centenary Edition. Boston: Little, Brown, 1930.

——, eds. *Unpublished Poems of Emily Dickinson.* Boston: Little, Brown, 1935.

Bingham, Millicent Todd. *Ancestors' Brocades: The Literary Debut of Emily Dickinson.* New York: Harper, 1945.

Bingham, Millicent Todd, and Mable Loomis Todd, eds. *Bolts of Melody: New Poems of Emily Dickinson.* New York: Harper, 1945.

Dickinson Editing Collective (Martha Nell Smith, Ellen Louise Hart, Marta Werner, general eds.). *Dickinson Electronic Archives.* http://jefferson.village.virginia.edu/dickinson/.

Franklin, R. W., ed. *The Manuscript Books of Emily Dickinson.* Cambridge: Belknap Press of Harvard University Press, 1981.

——, ed. *The Master Letters of Emily Dickinson*. Amherst: Amherst College Press, 1986.

——, ed. *Poems of Emily Dickinson*. Cambridge: Belknap Press of Harvard University Press, 1998.

Higginson, Thomas Wentworth, and Henry Walcott Boynton, eds. "New England Period." *A Reader's History of American Literature*. Boston: Houghton Mifflin, 1903. 108–33.

Higginson, Thomas Wentworth, and Mabel Loomis Todd, eds. *Poems by Emily Dickinson*. Second Series. Boston: Roberts Brothers, 1891.

Johnson, Thomas H., ed. *The Poems of Emily Dickinson*. 3 vols. Including variant readings critically compared with all known manuscripts. Cambridge: Belknap Press of Harvard University Press, 1955.

Johnson, Thomas H., and Theodora Ward, eds. *The Letters of Emily Dickinson*. 3 vols. Cambridge: The Belknap Press of Harvard University Press, 1958.

Shurr, William H., ed., with Anna Dunlap and Emily Grey Shurr. *New Poems of Emily Dickinson*. Chapel Hill: University of North Carolina Press, 1993.

Smith, Martha Nell, and Ellen Louise Hart. *Open Me Carefully: Emily Dickinson's Intimate Letters to Susan Huntington Gilbert*. Ashfield, Mass.: Paris, 1998.

Todd, Mabel Loomis, ed. *Letters of Emily Dickinson*. 2 vols. Boston: Roberts Brothers, 1894; new and enlarged ed., New York: Harper, 1931.

——, ed. *Poems by Emily Dickinson*. Third Series. Boston: Roberts Brothers, 1896.

Todd, Mabel Loomis, and Thomas W. Higginson, eds. *Poems by Emily Dickinson*. Boston: Roberts Brothers, 1890.

Turco, Lewis, ed. *Emily Dickinson, Woman of Letters: Poems and Centos from Lines in Emily Dickinson's Letters Selected, Arranged, and Augmented by Lewis Turco; Together with Essays on the Subject by Various Hands*. Albany: State University of New York Press, 1993.

Ward, Theodora Van Wagenen, ed. *Emily Dickinson's Letters to Dr. and Mrs. Josiah Gilbert Holland*. Cambridge: Belknap Press of Harvard University Press, 1951.

Werner, Marta. *Emily Dickinson's Open Folios: Scenes of Reading, Surfaces of Writing*. Ann Arbor: University of Michigan Press, 1995.

——, ed. *Radical Scatters: An Electronic Archive of Emily Dickinson's Late Fragments*. Ann Arbor: University of Michigan Press, 1998.

NOTES

1. Most manuscript scholars use this term to distinguish between Dickinson's holographic originals and print translations. In "Emily Dickinson's Visible Language," Jerome McGann uses "scriptural" to refer to Dickinson's handwritten copies, concurring with Susan Howe and others that the *Manuscript Books* reveal a dramatic shift in style; in earlier texts "linear metrical units correspond to their scriptural presentation," but then, starting in fascicle 9, "metrical units are distributed over two scriptural lines."

2. Susan Dickinson first printed this poem as "Renunciation" in *Scribner's Magazine* 8 (August 1890): 240. *Scribner's* editor E. L. Burlingame then gave his permission for the poem to be reprinted in *Poems* (1890). Editorial handlings of this poem are discussed in Sands.

3. A variant appears in the fifth fascicle in "Her breast is fit for pearls" (F5, 86, P84), where "home" is a variant for "rest," and variants are perhaps rendered in the first

fascicle, if the two stanzas of "So has a Daisy vanished" are alternatives for the last two of "Morns — like these — we parted — " (F1, 13–14, P27, P28), as Bingham thought.

4. Unexpected line breaks occur earlier than the ninth fascicle, as both Howe and McGann remark; e.g., the pentameter line "Have you got a Brook in your / little heart" in the fourth (F4, 58, P136). Readers might consult Franklin's *Manuscript Books.*

5. No simple explanation for Susan's not having produced her own "Book of Emily" will suffice. Readers should be aware that in the decade preceding the discovery and printing of poems from her beloved Emily's manuscript books, Susan had suffered a number of devastating losses: the deaths of her youngest son Gib, her close friend Samuel Bowles, her mother-in-law, and Emily; within weeks of Gib's death, her husband embarked on his (publicly flaunted) affair with Loomis Todd. Unlike Loomis Todd, who lost a fascinating literary acquaintance whom she never met face-to-face, Susan lost her most faithful and intimate companion and correspondent of four decades when Emily died (see Smith, *Rowing* 213 ff.). New information from the Evergreens papers is coming to light regarding Susan and Emily's mutual withdrawal after the death of Gib in 1883 and regarding Susan's extensive editing and writing activities in the years following Emily's death (she worked closely with her daughter Martha, who considered Susan the ultimate authority on what to include and how to arrange *The Single Hound*), and this information will undoubtedly recast long-held confusions about Susan's relationships to Emily's writings and her handling of them after Emily's death. Readers might consult *Open Me Carefully*, edited by Ellen Louise Hart and myself.

6. There are no packets numbered 41–79. The mysterious gap in numbering has never been adequately explained (Franklin, *Editing* 3–17).

7. Manuscripts at the Houghton Library will be cited as H with the library catalog letter and/or number.

8. Occasionally Bianchi reprinted a Todd–Higginson poem without consulting the manuscript, but she never made a "Dickinson" poem from a Todd print translation of a letter; she reprinted poems after the copyright on the 1890 editions expired, as did Robert Linscott decades later for his *Selected Poems and Letters of Emily Dickinson* (Garden City, N.Y.: Doubleday/Anchor, 1959) and as have numerous others who have produced gift books or greeting cards in the name of Dickinson without copyright restrictions. The Bartleby hypermedia project (Columbia University) has published the out-of-copyright 1896 edition of *Poems* (http://www.cc.columbia.edu/acis/bartleby/dickinson/), and the Humanities Text Initiative (University of Michigan) has published the out-of-copyright 1890 edition of *Poems* (http://www.hti.umich.edu/english/amverse/; this volume is mistakenly identified as the 1891 edition, but it is an 1891 printing of the 1890 edition).

Further Reading

Dickie, Margaret. "Dickinson in Context." *American Literary History* 7.2 (1995): 320–33.

Franklin, R. W. "Three Additional Manuscripts." *American Literature* 50 (1978): 113–16.

Hart, Ellen Louise. "Poetic License." *Women's Review of Books* Jan. 1994: 24.

Horan, Elizabeth. "Mabel Loomis Todd, Martha Dickinson Bianchi, and the Spoils of the Dickinson Legacy." *A Living of Words: American Women in Print Culture.* Ed. Susan Albertine. Knoxville: University of Tennessee Press, 1995.

Howe, Susan. "Women and Their Effect in the Distance." *Ironwood* 28 (1986): 58–91.

Johnson, Thomas H. "Establishing a Text: The Emily Dickinson Papers." *Studies in Bibliography* 5 (1952–53): 31–32.

Longsworth, Polly. *Emily Dickinson: A Letter.* Amherst: Friends of the Amherst College Library, 1992.

———. " 'Upon Concluded Lives': New Letters of Emily Dickinson." *Emily Dickinson International Society Bulletin* 7.1 (1995): 2–4.

McGann, Jerome. "Composition as Explanation (of Modern and Postmodern Poetries)." *Cultural Artifacts and the Production of Meaning.* Ed. Margaret J. M. Ezell and Katherine O'Brien O'Keefe. Ann Arbor: University of Michigan Press, 1994. 101–38.

Smith, Martha Nell. "A Hypermedia Archive of Dickinson's Creative Work, Part II: Musings on The Screen and The Book." *EDJ* 5.2 (1996): 18–25.

———. "Corporealizations of Dickinson and Interpretive Machines." *The Iconic Page in Manuscript, Print, and Digital Culture.* Ed. George Bornstein and Theresa Tinkle. Ann Arbor: University of Michigan Press, 1998. 195–221.

Smith, Martha Nell, Ellen Louise Hart, and Marta Werner, eds. "Emily Dickinson Writing a Poem," "Dickinson, Cartoonist," "The Letter-Poem, a Dickinson Genre," and "Writings by Susan Dickinson." *Dickinson Electronic Archives. http://jefferson.village.virginia.edu/dickinson/.*

Werner, Marta. *Radical Scatters: An Electronic Archive of Emily Dickinson's Late Fragments* (a CD-ROM). Ann Arbor: University of Michigan Press, 1998.

Sharon Cameron

Dickinson's Fascicles

The Subject of Context

*T*o look at the history of Dickinson criticism is to see that what is memorialized are her ellipses, her canceled connections, the "revoked . . . referentiality" of the poetry. The phrase is from Geoffrey Hartman's *Criticism in the Wilderness* (129), but one thinks also of Jay Leyda's description of Dickinson as writing "riddle[s]," poems of the "omitted center" (1: xxi); of Robert Weisbuch's characterization of this poetry as "sceneless," producing "analogical language which exists in parallel to a world of experience, as its definition" (*Poetry* 19); of David Porter's assessment that "here is the verbal equivalent of *sfumato*, the technique in expressionistic painting whereby information . . . on a canvas is given only piecemeal and thereby necessarily stimulates the imaginative projection of the viewer, who, out of his own experience, supplies the missing . . . context" (*Early Poetry* 99) of an earlier claim of my own that the poems "excavate the territory that lies past the range of all phenomenal sense" (*Lyric Time* 9). Or, to allow Hartman to make the point one more time: Dickinson, the "dangerous" purifier, italicizes "leanness," more than leanness even—the "zero" meaning of the hyphen that punctuates the poetry (130–31). In Hartman's discussion, the hyphen becomes emblematic. "Perhaps because it both joins and divides, [it is like] a hymen. . . . That hyphen-hymen persephonates Emily" (126).

But does it?[1] What if this way of reading her poetry belies the way it was written or, once written, put together (both internally structured and also made contiguous)? What if these poems are less alien than we had supposed? Or not alien in the way we had supposed? What if they are not quite as sceneless or cryptic (even apparently subjectless) as the characterizations insist? Or what if the scenes and subjects can be said to unfold between and among the poems as well as within them?

To consider poems as individual lyrics is to suppose boundedness. To consider poems as related—as, say, a sequence would relate them—is differently to suppose boundedness, in that poems which are seen to be connected must first be seen to be discrete. To consider poems as not discrete but also as not related is to complicate the negotiations between interior and exterior. This Dickinson does by raising questions about the identity of the text. With respect to Dickinson's fascicles — to anticipate my argument — the variant is a way of getting at what the text "is." That is, in Dickinson's poems, variant words (and poems which we come to see as variants of each other) raise the question of what counts as the identity of the text in question. The question raised is: if this word — or this second poem — conventionally understood to be *outside* the poem is rather *integral* to the poem, how is the poem delimited? What is the poem? I shall argue that words that are variants are part of the poem outside of which they ostensibly lie, as poems in the same fascicle may sometimes be seen as variants of each other. In Dickinson's fascicles — where "variants" are more than the editorial term for discrete delimited choices — variants indicate both the desire for limit and the difficulty in enforcing it. The difficulty in enforcing a limit to the poems turns into a kind of limitlessness, for, as I shall demonstrate, it is impossible to say where the text ends because the variants extend the text's identity in ways that make it seem potentially limitless.[2]

Initially, however, my aim is to ask how the situation for understanding Dickinson's poems changes when we consider that they are at once isolated lyrics, as Thomas H. Johnson presented them in *The Complete Poems* (and in the variorum text), and poems that have the appearance of a sequence, as R. W. Franklin presented them when he published *The Manuscript Books of Emily Dickinson*, a volume crucial for our reassessment of this poetry, about which I shall therefore say a few words before proceeding.[3] First, the assertion that Franklin presents Dickinson's poems in sequences is one he would not accept. Dickinson organized most of her nearly 1,800 poems into her own form of bookmaking: selected poems copied in ink onto bifolia "sheets of letter paper already folded by the manufacturer to produce two leaves" (Franklin 1: xi). Then she stabbed them and bound them with string. Franklin has argued that no aesthetic principle governs their binding. It was, nevertheless, Franklin's goal to reproduce in facsimile the manuscripts that Dickinson bound with string into forty fascicles from about 1858 to 1864 and the fifteen "sets" — poems which, primarily after 1864, she copied but never bound.[4]

Second, Franklin claims the binding was a means of keeping order among her poems. But an alternative speculation is that the fascicles were a form of private publication.[5] Franklin's assumption that they were a means of keeping order among her poems begs the question of what such an order would be. The alternative, that the fascicles were a form of private publication — halfheartedly endorsed by Franklin in the introduction to the facsimile, and (as I shall explain) contested by him elsewhere — has its plausibility heightened by reference to "New Poetry," an essay of Emerson's printed in *The Dial* in

1840, in which he advised authors, in distinction to the dominant strain of poetic tradition, to collect album poetry, for, Emerson writes, a "revolution in literature is now giving importance to the portfolio over the book." (Porte 169). In making her lyrics into manuscript books — in effect, constituting manuscripts as if they were books — Dickinson may have been responding to a revolution like the one predicated by Emerson. Indeed, once Dickinson had copied poems into fascicles she usually destroyed her worksheets. Such a practice invites us to regard the poems copied in the fascicles in the same way that her manner of collecting them suggests she might herself have regarded them: as definitive, if privately published, texts. The copying and binding, and the destruction of the worksheets, insist that this is the fascicles' status, despite the fact that Dickinson subsequently adopted variants from the fascicle sheets in the "text" she sent to friends, and despite the fact that it is one of the characteristics of the fascicle texts, especially after 1861, that variants to words also exist in fair copy, indeed exist as *part* of the text of the last thirty fascicles.[6]

When Franklin writes that the fascicles were a means of keeping order among Dickinson's poems, he means that they literally helped her to tidy up: "The disorder that fascicle sheets forestalled may be seen in the 'scraps' of the later years. When she did not copy such sheets and destroy the previous versions, her poems are found on hundreds of odds and ends — brown paper bags, magazine clippings, discarded envelopes and letters, the backs of recipes" ("Fascicles" 16). Thus Franklin imagines Dickinson's keeping order as her means of making the poems consistent with respect to their physical appearance, rather than as her means of organizing them. According to his explanation, the poems are not "artistic gatherings" at all but rather "private documents with practical uses, gatherings of convenience for poems finished or unfinished" (17).

When Franklin speculates that the fascicles are meant to order (tidy up) rather than to arrange (make significant), as evidence of this he cites the fact that Dickinson may have had a backlog of poems written before they were copied and bound. This was probably the case in 1862 when, Franklin writes, "Emily Dickinson could have had a significant number of poems in her pool and, in that year, perhaps spurred on by the correspondence with Higginson, set in vigorously to organizing them, now letting poems enter the fascicles trailing many alternates" ("Fascicles" 15). An opposite assumption is that Dickinson was saving these poems to see *how* they would go together, allowing single lyrics, or several lyrics copied onto one bifolium, to remain temporarily separate or piecemeal so that she could ultimately stitch them into the different comprehensive entity that the fascicle gathering made of them. And if it is more probable to suppose (as Franklin also does; see "Fascicles" 13) that the poems in twenty of Dickinson's forty fascicles were *copied* rather than all (necessarily) written in 1862, then whether Dickinson saved her poems with the idea of eventually organizing them or whether in 1862 she came to group and identify poems previously seen as discrete—identifications marked by the copying and the fascicle binding—is in a sense less significant than that we consider what the gatherings made of these poems. It is important that we consider, as the copying most dramatically in that year instructs us to do, whether structures are being created out of ostensibly discrete entities. Sometimes sheets were copied in different years and only subsequently bound. Of these Franklin writes: "Binding followed copying, sometimes years later mixing sheets from different years. That such sheets were copied in different years suggests that no fascicle-level order governed their preparation" (17). Yet sheets copied in different years and only subsequently bound rather suggest to me sheets over which a high degree of order has been exercised, suggest that, in the delay between the copying and the binding, what is precisely being governed, made visible, and materially determined is the preparation of an entity.

Whatever his suppositions about Dickinson's texts, Ralph Franklin's reestablishment of the order in which the sheets in each fascicle were bound is of inestimable value to all readers of Dickinson, and in fact to all readers of poetry. Indeed, Franklin's restoration of the internal sequence of the fascicles—no internal order could be established for the sets since they were never bound—in *The Manuscript Books of Emily Dickinson* has immediate practical consequences for Dickinson's reader, for reading Franklin's text of the poems is different from reading Johnson's text of the poems. This is the case even when Franklin and Johnson ascribe identical dates to the poems so that there is the same consecutive relation among several poems in both editions. In the Johnson edition the unit of sense is the individual poem; beyond that, it is whatever arbitrary place the reader decides to close the book. In fact, although Johnson arranges the poems chronologically, that arrangement of poems gives the reader the impression of no arrangement at all, because in a year like 1862 there are over 300 poems. In the facsimile, these poems do not follow on the page as they do in the Johnson variorum. Rather, as I hope to show, in Franklin they exist in groups with internal sequences.[7] Thus, in the Franklin edition the unit of sense is not the individual poem but rather the fascicle book, and one wonders about the relation among the fascicles as well as about the relation between the fascicles and the sets—or at least the question of such relations is raised by the contiguity of these units.[8]

That Dickinson ordered her poems is argued by other evidence of the manuscripts: by the fact that, for example, on the first leaf of fascicle 9 (dated by Franklin and Johnson as copied in 1860) Dickinson added "Bound — a trouble —" (P269, dated as added about 1861), although there would have been room to add this poem elsewhere in the same fascicle (on the second side of the next leaf), and by the fact that in fascicles 12 and 14 poems from different years — from 1860 and 1861, in the case of 12, and from 1861, 1858, and 1862, in the case of 14 — are bound together, although in each of these years Dickinson wrote numerous poems and in other fascicles she characteristically bound poems from the same year together. It is further argued by the example of fascicle 8, in which a poem is copied twice in different places in the fascicle with variant first lines ("Portraits are to daily faces" [P 170] becomes in the second instance of copying "Pictures are to daily faces"), as if each were a separate poem. Since the repeated poems are separated by several leaves and by nine intervening poems, and since there is space earlier in the fascicle to have copied "Pictures are to daily faces," Dickinson may have been structuring the fascicle by her disparate placements of the so-called same poem. This arrangement of poems — perceptible in Dickinson's copying practices; in her adding to a "completed" fascicle, in her repeating a poem within a fascicle, in her copying on matching leaves poems she then placed in separate fascicles, in her composing a fascicle with poems from different years — suggests a conceptual scheme, although fascicle 9, the same fascicle that suggests that scheme by virtue of the added poem, also leaves the reader uncertain how the scheme is to be understood, because it is not clear to what the poem is "added" (the immediate sequence of poems? the specific poem preceding it? the whole fascicle?).

Here one could equivocate about questions of order by saying that whether Dickinson produced the order or whether the reader produces the order of the fascicles by registering the poems' juxtaposition there is immaterial, since the question of the author's intention is always undecidable. But the question of intention, at least at one level, is not undecidable — because we know that Dickinson intended something. After all, she copied the poems into the fascicles. The question then is: in doing so, what did she intend? Looking at the fascicles it might even appear that Dickinson's intention was to be indeterminate with respect to the relation among these poems, since lyric structures whose boundaries are conventionally left intact are in the fascicles characteristically punctured by the "outside" (which I shall argue is not an "outside") composed of variants and other poems. Or, to explain the situation in positive terms, it seems that given such violations of boundaries it might differently appear that Dickinson intended to redetermine our very understanding of how the identity of a poetic structure is to be construed. With respect to the binding, we do know, however minimal this knowledge may initially be deemed to be, that Dickinson intended to associate these poems with each other. Thus the question is not whether intentions are relevant. The question is rather how to understand the extraordinarily complex, perhaps even conflicted, set of intentions, beliefs, desires that are registered when Dickinson's poems are read in the fascicles in which she copied them. For to read the poems in the fascicles is to see that the contextual sense of Dickinson is not the canonical sense of Dickinson.

The point, then, is to examine what kinds of connections among poems are apparent when they are read in the fascicles, and perhaps even on what principle the "apparent" will be produced. Connections, while not possible to illustrate in all of the poems in a given fascicle, are demonstrable in a sufficient number of the poems to give the fascicle as a whole the appearance of a structure. This apparent structure consequently affects our understanding of the subjects of the poems. Specifically, as I shall explain, it affects our understanding of what subjects are. By "subjects" I do not here mean the first-person speaker, but I also do not mean the conventionally defined headings that Johnson produces in his "Subject Index," which designate rhetorical and wholly unproblematic topics or themes. In fact, while the poem I shall consider at the beginning of the next section of this essay confirms the standard notion that a lyric of Dickinson's is devoid of a subject; when one returns that lyric to the fascicle context the question of the subject comes back in a different way as a question about the nature of poetic subjects.

To sum up, then, I mean to ask how reading a lyric in a sequence is different from reading the lyric as independent, for to do the latter is to suppress the context and the relations that govern the lyric in context — a suppression generating that understanding of Dickinson's poems as enigmatic, isolated, culturally incomprehensible phenomena which has dominated most Dickinson criticism, including my own. At issue in the following examination is the question of what happens when context — when the sequence — is not suppressed.

THE FASCICLES INVITE us to read Dickinson's poems in the context of other sequences — Herbert's *The Temple*, Barrett Browning's sonnets, Tennyson's *In Memoriam*, Shakespeare's sonnets — which we can presume Dickinson had read.[9] Yet to place Dickinson's poems in the context of other lyric sequences does not imply that we should read her poems only in sequence, or even mainly in sequence, rather than as isolated lyrics. Therefore, demonstrating that the poems can be read in sequence, and demonstrating the multiple ways in which sequences can be read (as I shall in fascicle 15), does not clarify whether the poems are to be read in sequence or isolation. But the reason it does not illuminate this, I shall argue, is that Dickinson herself was uncertain about how her poems should be read, an uncertainty demonstrated by the fact that she both sent her poems to friends as individual lyrics and copied them in the fascicles in sequences. Or, to formulate the point more strongly, it is not merely that Dickinson was uncertain, but that she refused to make up her mind about how her poems should be read. This refusal—another aspect of what I have called choosing not to choose—is crucial to the problematic of reading her poetry.

Multiple ways of reading Dickinson's poems are consonant with the multiple variants in those poems; I have touched on this topic earlier. Interestingly, the variants have characteristically been understood as a nuisance by her readers. In 1890 Dickinson's first editors, T. W. Higginson and Mabel Loomis Todd, eliminated all variants when they made other substantive textual changes. In 1960 Thomas Johnson did the equivalent, as he chose among the variants he had recorded to make a reader's edition. But what if we are to see the variants interlineated in a poem as posing alternatives to given words, which—this is crucial—are part of the poem? What if what Dickinson has to teach us is the multiplicity of meanings that, properly understood, resist exclusion? In other words, Dickinson appears to be understanding variants as non-exclusive alternatives—a phenomenon that would have analogues in Christopher Ricks's description of the antipun in which a poet "creates meanings which take into account those absent senses of a word which his verse is aware of fending off" (99). In Ricks's discussion of antipuns, though, these senses are absent in the sense of being implied while also being precluded. They are incorporated, for instance, in the second sense of a word which is implicitly ruled out. In Dickinson's poems alternative senses are displaced but not decisively so because they remain ambiguously counterpointed to the word to which they stand in explicit juxtaposition, and to which they often stand in direct proximity on the manuscript page. Thus, whereas in Ricks's notion of the antipun a second sense is entertained and then dismissed, in Dickinson's poems alternative words collide without particular words being clearly made secondary or subordinate. For alternatives to various words are not treated in Dickinson's text as *other* than those words.

One way of understanding variants is that a reader is required to choose between them and there is even evidence for both choices. Preliminary dilemmas aside, one is supposed to choose, and, indeed, if one had the right evidence, one could make the right choice. There is nothing ontologically tricky about such a situation.

A second way of understanding the problem of two entities that look like variants is that while they look as if they require to be chosen between, they do not so require because both are clearly part of the poem or of the single entity, as the following from Whitman's and Yeats's poetry clarify. Thus, for instance, in section 4 of *Song of Myself* where we are told of the grass, "I guess it must be the flag of my disposition . . . / Or I guess it is the handkerchief of the Lord / Or I guess the grass is itself a child . . . " we are not meant to choose among these possibilities. Similarly, in the last stanza of Yeats's "Among the School

Children," where "nor" in effect means "or," when we are told that "Labour is blossoming or dancing where / The body is not bruised to pleasure soul, / Nor beauty born out of its own despair / Nor blear-eyed wisdom out of midnight oil" we are not meant to choose among the possibilities. Not only is no choice required, but a choice would in fact be a mistake.

A third way of understanding variants — a way of understanding them necessitated by reading Dickinson's fascicles — is that they are meant to be experienced *as* variants, and so one is also meant to be experiencing the necessity of choosing between them. Thus the situation exemplified by Dickinson's variants is more like the first case than it is like the second. But it is different from the first case because there are no possible criteria that could enable one to choose. So, in this third case, the reader experiences the necessity for choosing, without access to the criteria by which she could make a choice. In other words, the problem is not solved by having more evidence, because the problem is not raised as a question of evidence. And in fact, as I have argued elsewhere, there is no way that the problem posed by the imperative to choose countered by the prohibition against choosing could be simplified or solved.[10]

One implication of not being able to choose among the variants is that we would have only one adequate text of Dickinson's poems — that of the facsimile — an unsatisfactory solution because in effect no one reads this text. That problem would seem to be solved if the decision were made to print a transcript of the fascicle texts, for then people would read them. Yet even if a transcript of the fascicle texts were printed, such publication would not address what I take to be the real problem: the nature of the relation between poem and text. That is, there is the "text" that is the document; there is the "text" that is the poem as the published or, in Dickinson's case, publishable entity; and there is the more contemporary sense of "text," which is what the poem becomes as "read." In Dickinson's case the contemporary or semiotic nature of "text" depends on the text as document. It specifically depends on the felt ladenness of the document's *alternatives* in some exacerbated way.

What is central here is the question of form. What the fascicles raise is precisely a question about the relation between text and poem (about the nonidentity of text and poem), a relation shown to be problematic by the fact that our difficulty of reading is not solved once one has chosen which text (Johnson's or Franklin's) one is going to read. For once a text has been chosen, if there are variants to that text, one has still not cleared up the question of how to read the variants. The metrics of the poem insist we choose only one of the variants. But the presence of the variants insists on the impossibility of doing so. Another way to describe the dilemma is that, since Dickinson refuses to choose among the variants, she disallows us from doing so. The conventional interpretation of this situation is that there are as many poems as there are variants. This is precisely the wrong way to understand how words work in poems. The variants exert pressure against each other in a *particular* poem and at particular places *within* that poem.

DICKINSON'S NOT CHOOSING among the variants opens onto other aspects of not choosing in her poetry. I enumerate, albeit briefly, other aspects of doubleness — of choosing not to choose — in Dickinson's poetry that the examination of the textual situation helps to enlarge.

   1. First, it is a commonplace that at the level of syntax Dickinson is characteristically choosing not to choose. It is not, for instance, clear whether "Slow Gold — but Everlasting — " in "Some Work for Immortality — / The Chiefer part, for Time — " (P406) refers to the compensations of "Time" or those of "Immortality." By association with the previous line the tenor of the metaphor would be "Immortality," not "Time," but in light of the following line it would be "Time" rather than "Immortality." Nothing will produce a resolution to the question about reference, since the syntax is unresolved, and definitively so, for according to the indeterminacy conveyed by the dashes the line cannot but be read in opposite directions and this simultaneously. Such doubleness, both syntactical and semantical, is less complicated in "At least — to pray — is left — is left —" (P502). But it is quite complicated in the last stanza of "Rehearsal to Ourselves" (P379): "We will not drop the Dirk — / Because We love the Wound / The Dirk Commemorate — Itself / Remind Us that we died." In these lines there is a choice between reading "Itself" as allied with "Dirk," with the reflexivity applied to the instrument, and reading "Itself" as applied to the wound inflicted by the dirk. In the second interpretation of the syntax the recollection is still fatal, but it is not, as in the first, futile. Since the fatality is caused by the loss — rather than by the recollection of the loss — it is compensated by being also caused by the "Bliss" associated with the loss, and inevitably recollected at the same time. And this choice is unresolvable since no amount of parsing will convert the syntax into conventionally punctuated lines that indicate which noun is underscored as object of the self-reflexive action. The dashes permit, even insist on, these overlapping, disparate meanings, suggesting both the futility of recollection and its compensations.

   2. But if Dickinson characteristically does not choose syntactically, she also characteristically does not choose between the story ostensibly being told and the story actually being told. In "I cannot live with You —" (P640), for instance, choosing not to be with a lover rather means choosing the grounds on which to meet him: it means equating him with the God for whom he has ostensibly been given up. Often apparent in the difficulty of this poetry is the fact that two conflicting stories are told simultaneously (see Cameron, *Lyric Time* chap. 2). While the disruption caused by the doubleness punctuates the

experience of reading the poems, it is also a characteristic of these poems not to acknowledge the existence of double stories, hence not to establish alliances with one or the other of the stories, and thus to predicate a seamlessness belied by what is being voiced. So voice is at odds with itself in these poems, so much so that the proper term for the disagreement is in fact heteroglossia.

3. Dickinson is also choosing not to choose between the suggestion that certain experiences can be mapped — can be made comprehensible in terms of geographies and exteriors — and the suggestion made by the same poems that such experiences cannot be. Thus, for example, in a poem like "Bereaved of all, I went abroad — " (P784) a speaker attempts to reside elsewhere than where the loss is, literally to place herself at a geographic distance from loss, although the speaker is more explicit about the futility of such efforts than elsewhere. Such poems, in search of correlatives for interior experience, often resort to the language of measurement in order to insist on the impossibility of it (as in "A nearness to Tremendousness — " [P963]). Or they raise questions about what it means to define experience in terms of categories without content ("I stepped from Plank to Plank" [P875]). These poems might be described as sceneless, but in fact they avail themselves of quite elaborate maps, geographies, scenes, and coordinates ("Behind Me — dips Eternity — / Before Me — Immortality — / Myself — the Term between — " [P721]), even if the claim made by the elaborate representations is countered by the categorical emptiness of the same representations, by the fact that what is being mapped is only technically or terminologically coherent. In the poems Dickinson is choosing not to choose whether certain experiences *can* be mapped — whether something that is only categorically comprehensible is comprehensible or not. She is choosing not to choose what the coordinates of an experience are, choosing not to choose whether internal scenes can have external coordinates. And she is choosing not to choose whether certain exteriorizations ("a Funeral, in my Brain" [P280]) fulfill the task assigned to them — here to make a conceit of repression — or whether, in not forestalling the repression, the exteriorization fails to fulfill the task assigned to it. In fact, this exteriorization is itself equivocal; it gives literal, external form to an inner event but immediately relocates it within ("in my Brain").

4. Dickinson is also not choosing how particular words are to be read. Consider "None may teach it — Any — " in "There's a certain Slant of light" (P258) where what is implied is "None may teach it — [not] Any[one else] — "; "None may teach it — Any[thing]" (it is not subject to alteration); and "None may teach it — [to] Any[one else] — ." In "I felt a Funeral, in my Brain," consider the poem's last line: "And Finished knowing — then —," where it is ambiguous whether knowing is finished or whether the experience which prevents knowing is finished. And consider the last line of "After great pain, a

formal feeling comes — " (P341), "First — Chill — then Stupor — then the letting go — " with its ambiguity about whether what "letting go" implies is the ability to feel, which would reverse the "Chill" and "Stupor" that have preceded it, or whether what is oppositely implied by the whole series of nouns are the final stages of the inability to feel that terminate in death.

5. The refusal to choose — choosing not to choose — how syntax is to be read, how double voices and sometimes contradictory stories are related to each other, how lines which *can* be read in antithetical ways *should* in fact be read, is reiterated in the question mark with which so many of Dickinson's poems conclude: "Which Anguish was the utterest — then / To perish, or to live?" (P414), "Could it be Madness — this?" (P410), "And could I, further, 'No'?" (P446), "Say, Jesus Christ of Nazareth — / Hast thou no Arm for Me?" (P502), " 'My Husband — women say / Stroking the Melody — / Is *this* — the way?" (P1072), and so on.

6. Finally, Dickinson's choosing not to choose is dramatically reiterated in the questions raised by the discrepancy between the boundedness implied by the quatrain form and the apparent boundlessness implied by the variant. Not choosing in Dickinson's poetry thus results in a heteroglossia whose manifestations inform every aspect of the poetry.

Excess

In an atypical but logically first example of what we might expect from consideration of a poem in its fascicle placement, recourse to the fascicle context can prove simply clarifying. Consider the following poem (P378) as an isolated lyric:

> I saw no Way — The Heavens were stitched —
> I felt the Columns close —
> The Earth reversed her Hemispheres —
> I touched the Universe —
>
> And back it slid — and I alone —
> A Speck upon a Ball —
> Went out upon Circumference —
> Beyond the Dip of Bell —

Read thus — as an isolated lyric — the poem seems like an exercise in solecism, as well as solipsism, having not only no referent but also no context: barely comprehensible.

But to read the poem differently in the context of the poem that precedes it on the same bifolium in fascicle 31 is to see that there could be a referent for the experience. For the first line of the previous poem, copied on the other side of the page of "I saw no Way" is "To lose one's faith — surpass / The loss of an Estate —" (P377), and this proximity, however loosely, establishes the poems in a relation to each other, suggesting that the cause of the disorientation might not be mysterious at all, but rather loss of faith. Moreover, to read "I saw no Way" in relation to yet a different poem, the first in the same bifolium, "The Soul's Superior instants" (P306), is to see that it too represents a geography in which recognizable features of a scene are abolished, the speaker in "The Soul's Superior instants" being said to have "ascended / To too remote a Hight / For lower Recognition" — to have ascended, in other words, to a sphere in which what occurs is called "Mortal Abolition," the abolition of the mortal world which is then replaced by an apparitional world not dissimilar to that in "I saw no Way."

Yet to establish a relation between and among poems is not yet to clarify it. Would, for instance, the epithet "Superior," which characterizes the moments of dissociation from the earthly world in "The Soul's Superior instants," equally apply to similar moments in "I saw no Way"? Or would it rather be the case that the exaltation and the despair of such alien moments were, in the two poems, being counterpointed to each other? Ultimately, in the second of the poems in the same bifolium ("Me prove it now — Whoever doubt" [P537]) what is represented simultaneously is the imminence of a *speaker's* death and the recollection of her lover's death. As "Me prove it now" precedes "To lose one's faith — surpass / The loss of an Estate," would the lover's death in one poem be the cause of the loss of faith in the next, a loss of faith whose *consequences*, one could say, are demonstrated in the apocalyptic imagery of the poem "I saw no Way — the Heavens were stitched —" with which we began? To ask these questions, as the poem read in the fascicle context makes it inevitable that we do, is not to arrive at a more stable interpretive situation, but it is to arrive at a different interpretive situation than that in which the poem is read elliptically as a decontextualized utterance. It is to be confronted by a different interpretive situation just to the extent that there are relations among poems that we cannot disregard and, as much to the point, that we do not precisely know how to comprehend.

To see a poem contextualized by a fascicle is sometimes to see that it has an altogether different, rather than only a relationally more complex, meaning when it is read in sequence rather than as an isolated lyric. For example, to read "Because I could not stop for Death —" (P712) with reference to other fascicles and to other poems in fascicle 23 is to see that the speaker's journey may not be solitary, not because she is accompanied by the abstract figures of death and immortality but perhaps rather because she is accompanied by a lost lover here personified as death. This way of understanding the poem would be consonant with the many poems in the other fascicles and some of the poems in this one, poems in which a lover has died, and it would explain why in "Because I could not stop for Death —" death is figured as a lover or in any case as a suitor. Such a contextualization changes the sense of the poem. It changes it since the speaker's inability to imagine an end to the journey because death cannot be imagined (the conventional reading of the poem) is different from her inability to imagine death's end because she is not in fact dead. Reread in the context of the fascicles, "Because I could not stop for Death —" proposes a haunted relation to a death, which, though always there in memory, *cannot* deliver passage to eternity since, though death is always present, it is never, in fact, one's own.[11]

Yet if to read a poem in the fascicle context is potentially to domesticate it — to make it less uncanny than the conventional interpretation does — in other instances poems read in the fascicle context call such a domestication into question. Thus, in fascicle 24, "This is my letter to the World / That never wrote to Me — / The simple News that Nature told — / With tender Majesty" (P441) — that poem anthologized in high-school textbooks to epitomize Dickinson at her most saccharine — is not necessarily a poem about a benign telling of nature's secret. Rather, at least with reference to surrounding poems in the fascicle, the secret being told is ominous. One poem in the same fascicle, for example, describes the earth as "A Pit — but Heaven over it —" (P1712); in others, life extends without significance or value, one speaker explaining: "Therefore — we do life's labor — / Though life's Reward — be done — / With scrupulous exactness — / To hold our Senses — on —" (P443). In still another poem, "It sifts from Leaden Sieves —" (P311), nature in the form of a snowstorm obfuscates the visible, making it unrecognizable, as negation makes things unrecognizable. In "This is my letter to the World," the telling of nature's story is not benign but rather informed by sinister aspects of the fascicle's other poems. For the letter to the world, its delivery to our "Hands," to hands the speaker "cannot see," is inescapably to be read as analogous to those stern communications the speaker has herself received.

But if reading poems in the fascicle context specifies subjects for poems and even in some cases their antecedents, it also raises problems about how the very groupings that contextualize poems are related to each other within the fascicles. I want now to sketch out these problems with respect to two issues raised in fascicle 15: the way in which the pairings of poems within a fascicle govern lyrics not implicated in the pairing; and conversely, the way in which a central poem in a fascicle can be seen to govern poems that appear paired or clustered.

By "paired" I mean the following: In several of the fascicles the first and last poems are either complementary or antithetical, or the poems are complementary *and* antithetical. In fascicle 28, for instance, the first poem ("My period had come for Prayer — " [P564]) and the last ("I prayed, at first, a little Girl" [P576]) refute each other, in that while one suggests that prayer is transcended by worship the other suggests that prayer is deflected by the impossibility of worship. In fascicle 34 the first poem ("Bereavement in their death to feel" [P645]) represents a speaker's experience of a death for which there is no recompense, while the last poem "Essential Oils — are wrung — " [P675]) represents consolation for death in the essence that survives it: "this" ("The Attar from the Rose") "Make Summer — When the Lady lie / In Ceaseless Rosemary — ." In fascicle 40, the last of the fascicles, the first and last poems ("The Only News I know / Is Bulletins all Day / From Immortality" [P827] and "Unfulfilled to Observation — " [P972]) represent speakers who perceive immortality and who, oppositely, are unable to do so. Thus the first and last poems of many of the fascicles, while differently related to each other, are undeniably linked, often by the reversal or countering of the idea in the initial poem. While outside of the fascicle context to see the same theme treated differently in disparate poems can seem an accident resulting from arbitrarily placing these poems in proximity, within a fascicle context, in the instances I have described, it is impossible to see such conjunctions as arbitrary, since, placed by Dickinson at the beginning and end, they in effect frame what lies between them.

Fascicle 15 exemplifies the terms in which the phenomenon of pairing — and the heteroglossia made manifest in the pairing — is significant. Fascicle 15 contains paired poems governed by three sets of antithetical assertions: first, that madness can't be stopped ("The first Day's Night had come — " [P410]) and that it *can* be ("We grow accustomed to the Dark — " [P419]); second, that losing a lover — and therefore only having him speculatively — is unbearable ("It is dead — Find it — " [P417]) and, conversely, that having him only speculatively is entirely bearable ("Not in this World to see his face — " [P418] and "If I may have it, when it's dead" [P577]); third, that direct knowledge is desired ("You'll know it — as you know 'tis Noon — " [P420]) and, conversely, that oblique knowledge is superior ("A Charm invests a face / Imperfectly beheld — " [P421]). Moreover, these three apparently unrelated topics may be seen to be connected because, in the fascicle context, through the proximity of the poems, antithetical attitudes toward madness and toward knowing are generated by the specific subjects of not knowing — and of not having — the lover. Therefore a narrative not suggested by any of the poems read singly is suggested by the poems read in relation, though not in chronological relation.

In fascicle 15, as noted, the connections among paired poems also affect a reader's understanding of poems not implicated in the pairing. More, poems that are not part of a pair, and not apparently implicated in the concerns of any of the pairs, may seem to govern all of the pairs by applying, if only indeterminately, to even one of the three concerns they manifest. This is the case with "I found the words to every thought / I ever had — but One —" (P581), because which *one*—which thought—seems to refer to one of the fascicle's three central topics (not having the lover, not knowing [the lover], madness [because of not knowing or not having the lover]) without being definitively identified with any one of these. The indeterminacy has the effect of retaining the ambiguity of the one subject for which words cannot be found. Indeed, it has the effect of heightening the tension around the poem's ambiguity since the possibilities are narrowed to three without being reduced to one. Similarly, "I had been hungry, all the Years —" (P579), that poem which, even read singly, presents hunger as a conventional metaphor for desire, addresses, by changing the terms of, the three topics that dominate the fascicle. It does so because, as this is the last poem in the fascicle, "I had been hungry, all the Years —" would seem to advocate *not* having, *not* knowing, *not wanting*, except speculatively, the lover of whose presence the speaker had—in the paired antitheses—earlier been *deprived*. Thus the final poem in the fascicle, which in effect specifies a complicated connection between having and desiring, itself exists in opposition to the attitude toward desire expressed by the poems that have preceded it. They adopt various stances toward what the speaker desires but does not have. The final poem oppositely defines having as itself antithetical to desire.

That a fascicle's various paired antitheses should, by proximity or contiguity, be associated with each other; that poems unimplicated in any of the fascicle's antithetically paired poems should nevertheless seem to refer to them (as "I found the words to every thought / I ever had — but One —" does); that a single poem should come into definitive antithetical relation to the series of paired opposites against which that single poem chronologically positions itself (as "I had been hungry, all the Years —" does)—in other words, that patterns discernible in some of the poems should inevitably affect a reader's perception of other poems ostensibly outside of that pattern—reveals yet another order a fascicle imposes on the poems within it. The order not of a narrative, and not of a single structure, it is, in the case of fascicle 15, the order of antithetical perspectives that come to seem complementary, come even to seem unified when they are read in opposition to a poem—the last in the fascicle—whose assertions assault the supposition on which the oppositions are founded. It is the order of poems whose allegiances shift, and can be seen to do so.

To exemplify, one last time, the differences between reading in the fascicles and reading lyrics singly, consider the relationship between two celebrated poems, "Of Bronze — and Blaze —" (P290) and "There's a certain Slant of light" (P258), that follow each other in fascicle 13, a juxtaposition which is

1. Fascicle 13, "Of bronze and blaze." By permission of The Houghton Library, Harvard University. (Ms Am 1118, 3 [74]). © The President and Fellows of Harvard College.

2. Fascicle 13, "There's a certain slant of light." By permission of The Houghton Library, Harvard University. (Ms Am 1118, 3 [74]). © The President and Fellows of Harvard College.

fascinating for the disparate stances it offers toward the attempt to take loss impersonally, to reconstrue nature's manifestations of indifference to persons as benign. In "Of Bronze — and Blaze —" nature's indifference to us is what we are to cultivate in relation to ourselves. But if "Of Bronze — and Blaze —" records the indifference to the self that the self should and does adopt, "There's a certain Slant of light" cannot do this, the speaker there rather internalizing indifference as the difference that is betrayal — as a sign of despair and death. Fascicle 13 records a series of connected attempts to understand loss as natural, as a mere conversion, say, of day into night. To the extent that the speakers accept the impersonality of such a metaphor (as "Of Bronze — and Blaze —" does), loss is inconsequential; to the extent that loss seems only alien, the speaker is afflicted by the difference that registers as internal ("Where the Meanings, are"). For with respect to the shifting light that "comes," that "goes," this shifting, when internalized, when taken in or taken personally, turns to despair. "Of Bronze — and Blaze —" does not, then, simply contextualize "There's a certain Slant of light"; it also changes its meaning, for when the two poems are read as retorts to each other, the second becomes a denial of the neutral perspective advanced as natural in the poem that precedes it. Or rather the second poem makes clear that the *natural* perspective is not the *person's* perspective and cannot be made so.

In my discussion of Dickinson's fascicles in general and of fascicle 15 in particular, I have raised questions rather than answering them: What is the difference between reading a poem in a fascicle context and reading it as an isolated lyric? What are the distinct ways in which poems are related in a fascicle? How do poems which seem grouped in clusters or pairs affect poems not ostensibly implicated in that grouping? How do single poems become central poems in the fascicle context? Finally, I would want to ask why these are not merely formal questions. Or in what way do formal questions have theoretical implications for rethinking the very nature and limits of form? I conclude this essay by briefly taking up the last of these questions.

BLAKE SYSTEMATIZED MEANING. Spenser allegorized it. Whitman eroticized it. More than any other poet Dickinson economizes it: makes the question of its economy (how much or little) and the question of its relativity, its in(ter)determinacy (how much and how little in relation to what), central to the poetry. For while a first, cursory understanding of economy would endorse the ideology of leanness as an absolute condition of Dickinson's poems and of their meaning, in fact what Dickinson is ultimately always questioning is the economy according to which poems are written, as she is also always questioning the economies within them, endlessly raising questions of relation and magnitude. It is as if sense for Dickinson were defined in the tension between too little and too much — specifically the tension occasioned by how subjects are construed, given delimited boundaries and related — that imperfectly regulates the experience of her poems. This too little or too much is easily recognizable in the thematics of her poetry, as in the disequilibrium of the "one Draught of Life" paid for by "existence — " (P1725) or the temporal disequilibrium of "Transporting must the moment be — / Brewed from decades of Agony!" (P207). And there are other examples: "Because You saturated Sight — / And I had no more Eyes / For sordid excellence / As Paradise" (P640); "Why Floods be served to Us — in Bowls — / I speculate no more — " (P756); "I had not minded — Walls — / Were Universe — one Rock . . . But 'tis a single Hair — / A filament — a law — / A Cobweb — wove in Adamant — / A Battlement — of Straw — " (P398). But this too little or too much is also recognizable in the disequilibrium of excess — words crowding each other out in the displacements of variants that don't in fact displace each other, in alternative ways of reading that are not really alternative.

As this description implies, if Dickinson's poems economize meaning, in so doing they make it problematically relational, illuminating what could be described as a central discovery of Dickinson's poems, perhaps even the thing they most have to teach us: how relations specify subjects by obliquity and juxtaposition, and indeed specify subjects in the process of either evolving or shifting. I have now indicated preliminarily how this works in a fascicle context where poems are paired in ways that are both antithetical and fluid. In conclusion I touch on how meaning is made relational in a single instance. For although one manifestation of Dickinson's presumed intention may be seen to confine the reading of poems to the fascicle, when lyrics are nevertheless read outside this context the poems may newly be seen to reveal, perhaps by virtue of the fascicle reading, what the boundaries of their subjects are and how those boundaries must be seen to shift. Or perhaps it is the case that the multiple shifts that we see in the fascicles suddenly make sense of — even actually make visible — shifts that have always, albeit unaccountably, marked aspects of our reading of the poems considered singly.

At the end of "Because I could not stop for Death — " (P712), the "Horses Heads" loom over the edge of the poem, claiming our attention, for these heads, which are regarded from the vantage of the carriage, block or obstruct. The "Horses Heads" are not, then, only a synecdoche for the horses; they are also, more precisely, a way of delineating that impediment to the speaker's vision: they are all she can see, or what she cannot see beyond. What I mean to emphasize in this familiar instance is the way in which the subject is made to change as the part subsumes the whole, or potentially does so — synecdoche being a governing as well as a topical issue — even while its unspecified relation to that whole remains insisted on, in the vision of the "Horses Heads" that replaces the vision of "Death." The formal concerns raised by the fascicles duplicate the formal concerns raised by single lyrics, occasioning, not incidentally, questions that are not formal.

What is a subject? How is it bounded? What are the boundaries around what something is? Dickinson raises these questions because she writes into being subjects (in the sense of topics) that are conventionally written out of it. But she also raises these questions by reconstructing the subject as something that is at once economized and relational; by insistently treating the subject as something not given and also not single (one specific relation in question being that of part to whole); by amplifying the idea of a subject to include its variants as well as variant ways of conceiving it. Finally, Dickinson raises these questions by producing utterances that are extrageneric, even unclassifiable, and (for that reason, in a way that it seems to me no one yet has quite explained) untitled.

NOTES

1. Certainly the history of Dickinson criticism from the 1890s to the present, as the quotations above indicate, has preserved a consistent account of the poet. It has stressed the separations in the poems (among grammatical and syntactical units), as well as the separation of any given utterance from a decipherable situation that it could be said to represent; and it has stressed vexed connections among them. Specifically, as the chronology of the poems is not seen to signal development, critics are deprived of one conventional way of discussing the poetry, and this deprivation is often countered by certain primitive groupings of the poems, according to thematic similarities, formal properties, evaluative assessments that discriminate poems that are successful from those that are not—with the constant implication that there is no inherent way of understanding relations among the poems. The taxonomies advanced for Dickinson's poems are different from those advanced for other poets, because when the poems are sorted it is precisely to emphasize idiosyncrasies and repetitions (of traits, themes, syntactic features), as if what Dickinson had to teach us were that there is no way to comprehend the alien except by the most critically reductive strategies of categorizing and comparison.

2. In this essay I primarily exemplify the ways in which poems are associated, rather than also the ways in which variants to words in lines are associated. However, as variants to words in the line and variant poems are central features of the fascicle text, both are discussed. For an amplified discussion of the two subjects, see Cameron, *Choosing.*

3. When in my discussion I consider a single line that includes variants, I enclose the variants in brackets, with slash marks separating the alternative words. When I discuss variants without quoting a whole line, brackets are omitted, and a slash mark alone indicates the presence of alternatives.

4. The sets have many of the characteristics of the fascicles except that they were not stab-bound and tied. According to Franklin, Dickinson stopped *binding* fascicle sheets around 1864, though there are a few unbound sheets as early as 1862 (set 1 is dated 1862 by Franklin; sets 2–4, 1864). In the late 1860s Dickinson stopped *copying*

fascicle sheets. In the 1870s she began copying fascicle sheets again (sets 5–7 are dated between 1864 and 1866, though, as noted, the majority of the poems in the remaining sets [8–15] are from the 1870s), but she never again bound them (see *Manuscript Books* 1: xii–xiii). For a concise discussion of the differences among the bound fascicles, the unbound fascicle sheets, the worksheets, and the miscellaneous fair copies, as well as for Franklin's speculations about the ways Dickinson variously used the bound fascicles, and for a detailed description of how Franklin reassembled them, see the introduction to *Manuscript Books*.

5. It is important to reiterate that this and the following assertions about Dickinson's intentions with respect to the fascicles are speculative. While the following pages produce an empirical argument about how the fascicles work, and about what the fascicles are, the basis of that argument is, and could only be, speculative.

6. The earliest fascicles have no variants; the first occurrence of a variant is in fascicle 5, and there are only five other variants for poems through fascicle 10. These variants, often multiple and not uniformly positioned at the end of the poem, as in the Johnson edition, are sometimes signaled in the facsimile text by the little "+" signs that Dickinson used near a word to indicate variants to that word. In the facsimile text the variants appear in the following diverse positions: at the end of the poem, to the side of the poem, and underneath or above a particular stanza, word, or line. Sometimes the variants to words are virtually inseparable from the text, as in the second stanza of "I think the Hemlock" (P525). Frequently a variant appears above the word: "The [maddest/nearest] dream — recedes — unrealized —" (P319). Or to the side of the line: "The Cordiality of Death — / Who [drills/nails] his Welcome in —" (P286). Or to the side of and at right angles to the poem, as in "There is a pain — so utter —" (P599) and "Like Some Old fashioned Miracle —" (P302). Or underneath the word: "An Island in dishonored Grass — Whom none but [Daisies / Beetles —] know" (P290). In the same poem another variant ("manners") is also noted below the word ("attitudes") that is on the line. But a third variant appears at the end of the poem, "An/Some — Island," making it seem that different ways of noting variants indicate different ways of understanding alternatives in relation to each other. Only in the later years of the copying are the variants positioned characteristically at the poem's end, Dickinson having apparently standardized her placement of them.

Infrequently Dickinson drew a line through words to signal their replacement by alternatives. See, e.g., P241, "I like a look of Agony," in which in the first line of the second stanza, "Death comes," is decisively crossed out and replaced by "The Eyes glaze once — and that is Death —," and P322, "There came a Day — at Summer's full —," where substantive decisions against word choices are marked by lines through those words, with the preferred alternatives unambiguously chosen. I say "unambiguously chosen," but even here the choice unambiguously made may subsequently have been *un*made. A second fair copy, for which no manuscript is extant presumably written after the fascicle copying, is reproduced in facsimile on four pages preceding the title page of *Poems by Emily Dickinson*, Second Series, ed. T. W. Higginson and Mabel Loomis Todd (1891). That fair copy adopts some of the canceled fascicle readings which had appeared (erroneously) to have been definitively deleted. There Dickinson restores words in the second, third, and penultimate stanzas.

However exceptional, these excisions insist, by distinction, that Dickinson's typical way of *noting* variants is not random but indicates her way of *understanding* variants. I elaborate in the body of the text.

7. In the fascicles Dickinson often, though not always, drew a line after the variants that concluded a poem, thereby indicating an end to the unit of sense. But because the poems are ordered and bound and because there are sometimes several poems to the bifolium, the collocation oppositely implies a potential relation among poems. (In fascicle 14, where poems from 1861, 1858, 1862 are bound in that sequence, the implications of "order" are differently unmistakable.)

Moreover, within the bifolium, the method of copying is varied. It is varied because, as indicated, a line is frequently but not always drawn after a poem, and because, although the bifolia are customarily filled, there are instances of blank half rectos and versos. This is particularly the case in fascicle 11, where whole sheets and half sheets are left blank. But there is also a three-quarters blank first verso in fascicle 15; nine blank lines and a blank verso conclude fascicle 18, while in fascicle 13 the first bifolium contains a three-quarters blank second recto. Such variations indicate that Dickinson may be regulating *which*, as well as *how many*, poems belong in a particular bifolium. The method of copying is also varied because, while the fascicles are ordinarily composed of single, folded sheets — with a disjunct leaf or slip added rarely, where necessary, to continue a poem — fascicle 11 contains as many as four disjunct leaves (see Franklin's tables for Dickinson's manner of accommodating overflow of poems and for the locations of disjunct leaves within particular fascicles, in *Manuscript Books* 2: 1413 and 2: 1414, respectively).

Further, while Dickinson characteristically tries to complete a poem on a single page, and if it runs over, it characteristically does so by as many as four lines, in fascicle 11 there are only two lines on the verso of the fourth sheet. Finally, although Franklin is right to say that the sheet or bifolium is the unit of *manuscript* integrity (an assumption borne out by Dickinson's manner of accommodating overflow from the sheet), the sheet or bifolium is not the unit of *thematic* integrity.

8. The relation "among" the fascicles is itself problematic because, in Franklin's words, Dickinson "did not number or otherwise label" or index them (*Manuscript Books* 1: x). Thus, though in the facsimile they are now arranged according to a presumed chronology, it is only arbitrarily that fascicle 13 precedes fascicle 14. This is the case because, while one can determine that certain fascicles were copied in the same year, it is now impossible to determine the particular order in which they were copied within that year. Fascicle 13 would seem to precede fascicle 14 in that the former dates from 1861 while the latter has poems which Franklin dates from 1862, as well as from 1858 and 1861. But fascicle 11, too, has poems from 1861, and fascicle 12 has poems from 1861 as well as 1860. Moreover, by virtue of these different dates, it would appear that in binding the sheets Dickinson worked from a pool of manuscripts, and therefore the exact relation of fascicle 13 to fascicle 14, if Dickinson intended one, cannot be surmised. Fascicles 11 through 14 are the most problematic of the fascicles, since in them the binding practices are inconsistent. Specifically, Dickinson there deviates from her practice of binding poems presumably copied in the same year.

9. Herbert was anthologized in Chambers's *Cyclopaedia of English Literature*, as he also was in Griswold's *Sacred Poets of England and America* (New York: Appleton; dated 1849 on the title page and 1848 on the copyright page). Susan Gilbert Dickinson owned the 1844 edition of the *Cyclopaedia* published in Edinburgh by William and Robert Chambers; Edward Dickinson's copy was printed in Boston in 1847 by Gould, Kendall, and Lincoln. A separate edition of *The Temple* was owned by Susan Gilbert Dickinson. Finally, although there is no proof that Dickinson read Shakespeare's son-

nets, since her letters do not allude to them in particular, Edward Dickinson had a copy of the sonnets in his eight-volume 1853 edition of Shakespeare's *Comedies, Histories, Tragedies, and Poems*, which we know Dickinson had read, and which Richard Sewall tells us Edward Dickinson purchased in 1857. See Capps, *Reading* 12, 68–69, and *Life* 2: 467. See, too, Sewall's list of books in the Dickinson Collection at Houghton Library, some of them, as indicated by the library's register, containing markings "probably" or "perhaps" by Dickinson (*Life* 2: 678–79). Dickinson mentions Tennyson and Barrett Browning in her letters, and the collections of their poems owned by the Dickinson family are in the Houghton Library.

10. See, e.g., the discussion of P319, "The [maddest/nearest] dream recedes unrealized," in which I argue that the variants must be considered in relation to each other rather than as alternative possibilities: "maddest" and "nearest"; "maddest" because "nearest" — the intoxication being caused by the proximity, not simply conjunctive but perhaps more, strongly, consequent (in *Choosing* 63–66). With respect to variants like these Dickinson sets up a situation that seems exclusionary, and, in letting both alternatives stand she refuses choices she presents as inevitable.

11. Other poems in fascicle 23 about the apprehension of death ("The Whole of it came not at once — / 'Twas Murder by degrees —" [P762], "Presentiment — is that long Shadow — on the Lawn —" [P764], "He fought like those Who've nought to lose —" [P759]) and about apprehension of another's death ("You constituted Time — / I deemed Eternity / A Revelation of Yourself —" [P765]) substantiate that possible reading.

THE LETTERS

AGNIESZKA SALSKA

Dickinson's Letters

FROM CORRESPONDENCE TO POETRY

*E*mily Dickinson's letters constitute as large a part of her writings as the poems, yet they cover a greater span of her life. No other prose by Dickinson survived,[1] no journals or notebooks, which in the case of such near contemporaries as Emerson, Whitman, Hawthorne, or Thoreau provide important insights into the writers' workshops, inspirations, and intellectual concerns. What is more, since the better part of the poems can be only tentatively dated, the burden of providing a surer structure for our sense of the artist's psychic and stylistic growth rests on her correspondence. Letters, too, supply contexts for the poems' often cryptic messages and, especially later in the poet's career, tend to become integrated with her verse beyond any possibility of painless separation.[2] The importance of Dickinson's correspondence for any appreciation or study of her work cannot be overestimated; her epistolary output constitutes an intrinsic part of her literary achievement.

The first known piece of her writing is a letter to her brother Austin composed when Emily was less than twelve years old. Her last writings are also letters, brief farewell notes sent to Thomas Wentworth Higginson, her literary friend and correspondent of nearly a quarter of a century, and to her cousins Louise and Frances Norcross, with whom she had been exchanging messages of affection and concern since the elder of the two, Louise (born in 1842), was a girl in her teens. The addressees of those last missives symbolically represent the two overriding concerns of the poet's whole epistolarium: the cultivation of intimacy with her "select society" and the care and growth of her writing talent. In the most literal sense, Dickinson's letters contain the fullest record that we have of the poet's conscious life: from its budding adolescent state to the very threshold of the terminal coma.

The letters' literary merit and link with the poems were recognized from the very beginning of the history of Dickinson's publishing. Encouraged by the success of the first (1890) volume of poems, Thomas Wentworth Higginson presented, in the *Atlantic Monthly* for October 1891, some of the letters and poems sent to himself, adding appreciative comments and an account of his acquaintance with the author. In 1894 Mabel Loomis Todd edited a selection of *Letters of Emily Dickinson*, and before Thomas Johnson and Theodora Ward produced the three-volume edition of 1958, there appeared several selections by different editors, either as separate volumes or as parts of miscellaneous collections.[3]

In Johnson's 1958 edition, there are 1,037 letters addressed to over ninety known correspondents plus twelve more to unidentified recipients; altogether 1,049 letters as compared with 1,775 poems collected in the variorum edition. Still, Dickinson's biographers agree that what we have is only a fraction of the correspondence she maintained. Whole sequences of letters to important addressees are missing, among them those she must have written to Benjamin Newton after he left her father's office or those she certainly wrote to the Reverend Charles Wadsworth, one of the candidates for the "Master." To complicate the matter further, many letters, as, for example, her correspondence with the Norcross cousins, are known only in transcripts made by the addressees. Other manuscripts had been excised and mutilated before publication.[4] Gaps in the correspondence stimulate countless questions which Dickinson scholarship untiringly attempts to answer. Scholarly and critical interest in Dickinson's letters has grown considerably over the past two decades. Both Richard Sewall and Cynthia Griffin Wolff made extensive use of the letters in their biographies of the poet, with Wolff especially pointing to the recurrent patterns of imagery and phrasing between letters and poems.

Scholars who have written on Dickinson's correspondence often aim at providing their own profile of the poet. However, the crucial fact emerging from the research is a growing recognition of the fluidity of borders between the writer's poetry and prose. Already in 1958 Thomas Johnson observed that since the early 1860s "the letters both in style and rhythm begin to take on qualities that are so nearly the quality of her poems as on occasion to leave the reader in doubt where the letter leaves off and the poem begins" (L xv). Especially in their emotionally heightened sections, Dickinson's later letters scan easily and often rhyme too.[5] This permeability of the generic borders within the writer's oeuvre prompted the radical assertion that "writing letters that scan, enclosing poems in letters, composing poems that are letters, revising and rerevising both, Dickinson did not always sharply distinguish between the uses of her art" (Farr, *Passion* 16).

> Categories such as prose, poetry, letter, and verse should not deceive her readers: Emily Dickinson neglected, denied, or defied these pigeonholes; and readers of her poetry who fail to recognize this risk losing sight of the confidence she had in her most intimate correspondents and their abilities to appreciate the games she played with words and genres. For it is easy to miss poems and verses masquerading as prose in the letters addressed to those three friends she regarded as her

most sensitive and intelligent correspondents, Sue, Bowles, and Higginson. (Lambert 187)

Dickinson's refusal to differentiate between the functions of her poetry and her correspondence points in turn to the convergence of the principles of poetics for all her writing. In a study of the letters, Suzanne Juhasz showed how Dickinson adopted carefully personalized stances vis-à-vis her different correspondents in order to "seduce" each of them into an intimate relationship answering her special affection and need ("Reading" 171–72). The "seducing" attitude is also the practice of her poems, with the once notorious "I'm Nobody! Who are you?" instantly coming to mind. The intimate impersonality of Dickinson's letter-poems was noted by Cristanne Miller, while, pointing to the eroticism inherent in Dickinson's response to correspondence, Margaret Dickie argued that the poet envisioned an analogously erotic response to her poems on the part of her readers (*Lyric* 55–74). In a 1993 article, William Decker views Dickinson's letter writing as essentially based on the elegiac impulse. His argument that letters explore loss and absence in a powerful compensatory effort has been long familiar in relation to the poems. What is more, it really focuses on, so to say, the flip side of the love coin. Thus Dickinson's scholarship seems ready today not only to accept but to investigate in depth the postulate that generic and stylistic affinities between poems and letters result from the fact that "the two are from the same source," as Mark Van Doren suggested long ago. Recent studies of Dickinson's letters seek to demonstrate that, nourished by a culture of intimacy of which the letter was a primary vehicle, the poet formulated principles of her poetics in the course of her intense and extended correspondence (Salska, "Letters"). Her poetry and her correspondence are founded on the epistemological resistance to "closure in all its forms" (Bennett, "Mouth") and on the primacy of the intimate but dialogic, not monologic, voice (Wider; Scheurer), a base from which other stylistic affinities between her poetry and prose derive.

In relying on correspondence as a means not only of interpersonal communication but also of self-expression, Dickinson follows the practice of her epoch. Collected works of almost any of her contemporaries, such as Emerson or Whitman, Hawthorne or Longfellow, Carlyle or Hopkins, contain volumes of letters. Apart from its practical, communicative function, such prolific epistolary production must be recognized as part of a larger Victorian cultural and literary phenomenon. As George Levine and William Madden observed,

it was in the Victorian age that non-fiction became a central and dominant literary genre. . . . non-fiction was increasingly invading areas conventionally thought to belong to poetry. . . . We are close here to an expressionist aesthetic in which all language is self-expression, that is art. (xiii–xiv)

From the very beginning, cultivation of emotional intensity seems to constitute the common ground of Dickinson's letter writing and poetry. In this
respect, too, famous instances of Victorian correspondence provide enlightening context where intimate emotional and literary experience comes together
with spectacular dramatic and romantic force. Dickinson was certainly thrilled
by both the poetry and biography of the Brownings, whose love-elopement-
marriage story began with an exchange of letters. Although she could have had
no knowledge of Mrs. Gilchrist's letters sent to Walt Whitman in the 1870s,
those attempts to "touch" with letters the man whose book the reader admired
provide another background for Dickinson's own correspondential practice.
And, pointing to the affinities in language and imagery between Dickinson's
Master letters and passages in *Jane Eyre*, Judith Farr assumes that the stimulus
behind the novel was Charlotte Brontë's own, largely correspondential, involvement with her Brussels "Maître," Constantin Hagger: "This was an instance in which life and art, art in life, came together" (*Passion* 204). It is
precisely against such confusion of life and art that Henry James reacted
toward the end of the century and against which today's readers have been
warned by practically every modernist and postmodernist critic. Still, the
premise that an intimate, person-to-person contact was of supreme value and
that an author's work provided a measure of familiarity with him or her as a
human being underlay not only Dickinson's interest in collecting photographic portraits of her favorite authors but also her important decision to
write to Thomas Wentworth Higginson, whose writings she knew. She lived
in a culture that persistently encouraged the fusion of literary[6] and personal
experience beyond the need and, really, the possibility of separating the two.
The epoch's intense correspondence implemented both the cultivation of intimacy and the pervasive literariness of the culture. Dickinson's epistolarium
must be viewed within such a context. The argument that the genre of personal letter constituted a characteristically female form of publication seems
too reductive when applied to Dickinson's work. Bearing in mind the prolific
correspondence conducted in the nineteenth century by both male and female
writers and remembering the contemporary convention that extended the
intimacy of private epistolary writing onto the relationship between the author and the literary reader, it seems that in the course of her wide correspondence Dickinson not only worked out the principles of her poetics but also
arrived at a concept of her ideal relationship with the reader. Writing letters,
the artist Dickinson was not so much making a virtue out of necessity as, quite
radically and experimentally, putting to her own use a pervasive cultural habit.
The essence of her attitude in letting the genre of the private letter color all
her writings and pattern her relationship with the reader should be seen as

analogous to the innovative use she made in the sphere of prosody of popular ballad and hymn meters.

AMONG THE MANY recipients of Dickinson's letters are members of her immediate and extended family, her schoolmates, friends, and friends of friends. She wrote systematically to her brother when Austin was away from home, at school or teaching. She corresponded with the friends of her girlhood until they married and became absorbed by a different way of life. In 1850 she started writing to Susan Gilbert, who in the summer of 1856 became Austin's wife. The exchange continued with varying intensity throughout the poet's life, despite or perhaps because of the fact that the Austin Dickinsons lived next door. In 1853 she opened another lifelong exchange with Dr. and Mrs. Josiah Gilbert Holland and in the late fifties (1858) began sending letters to Samuel Bowles and his wife, an exchange she would maintain beyond Bowles's death by writing to his son, Samuel, Jr., and Bowles's friend, Maria Whitney. While, except for Susan Gilbert, contacts with friends of her adolescence and early youth waned, in 1859 the poet started another long-lasting and intimate exchange with her Norcross cousins, to whom her final message, "Little Cousins, Called Back," would be addressed. As Jerome Loving observed (84–85), the circle of Dickinson's correspondents widens after 1862 to include persons outside the immediate family relations. The single, most significant gesture marking that opening must be recognized in the famous letter she wrote to Thomas Wentworth Higginson, having read his "Letter to a Young Contributor" in the *Atlantic* for April 1862. Her correspondence with Higginson led in turn to the professional exchanges with the poet-novelist Helen Hunt Jackson and with Thomas Niles of Roberts Brothers publishers in Boston. In the center of the mystery of Dickinson's life stand three drafts of letters that may never have been sent, written, to the best of our knowledge, between 1858 and 1861 to someone she called "Master." We do not know and most probably will never know with a satisfactory degree of certainty who the Master was. Yet the three drafts continue to tantalize because, when compared with her earlier letters, they seem to offer a glimpse of the poet forging, presumably under extreme stress, in broken syntax and cryptic metaphors, her characteristic, powerfully intense style.

Even this cursory glance at the range of Dickinson's correspondents shows that at least one of the important functions of her letter writing was very practical. Letters maintained her connection to the intellectual and literary circles of the New England of her time. At first she utilized for the purpose the opportunities that her father's and brother's social position provided. Very early in her poetic development she began including poems in letters not only to Sue but to the Hollands and to Bowles. They, too, served as her intellectual partners and were, moreover, visible figures in the New England literary establishment. Her next step was to take the initiative herself and to write Higginson, a personally unknown but very prominent man of letters. Whether she wrote him because neither Dr. Holland nor Samuel Bowles responded adequately to the poems she kept sending must remain a matter of conjecture. Still, the contact with Higginson led to further connections and resulted in something like a network of Dickinson's literary friends. She did let it be known in the competent and influential literary circles outside her immediate family and friends that she was seriously a poet. Apart from the ordinary communicative function, this was the central practical aspect of her letter writing. Letters prepared and created an audience for her poetry.

On a deeper though more elusive level, letters became the territory where she could work out her own style, create her poetic voice, and crystallize the principles of her poetics. We seem to glimpse the final stages of this process in the well-known and much-written-about exchange with Susan Dickinson concerning one of Emily's most famous poems "Safe in their Alabaster Chambers" (P216). Throughout the 1850s, Dickinson's formative decade, Sue served as the catalyst for Emily's intense emotional explorations, as her responsive model reader, and as her first critic.[7] Letters to Sue written over that period, like no other exchange within the Dickinson epistolarium, link her young exercises in expressing emotional urgency with the beginnings of her poetic creation.

Whatever emotional intensities their correspondence achieved, its initial stimulus was undoubtedly intellectual companionship and a shared interest in literature. Dickinson's first surviving letter to Sue (L38) contains a reference to Longfellow's *Kavanagh*, which the writer elaborates into a conceit fitting the situation. She expects Sue not only to decode the allusion but also to appreciate the cleverness of its appropriative use. Almost a year later, a long letter (Oct. 9, 1851) opens with a conceit taking as its starting point the moon "sailing around the sky in a little silver gondola with stars for gondoliers" (L56). Will she, please, give Emily a ride as far as Baltimore where Sue resides? Then there are extended allusions to the shared fondness for "Ik Marvel" and news of the expected sequel to his "reveries" as well as information about the appearance in the local bookshop of Longfellow's *Golden Legend*. In another letter of that period (Apr. 5, 1852) Dickinson comments on her reading in an often quoted passage:

> I have just read three little books, not great, not thrilling — but sweet and true. "The Light of the Valley," "Only" and "A House upon a Rock" — I know you would love them all — yet they don't bewitch me any. There are no walks in the

wood — no low and earnest voices, no moonlight, no stolen love, but pure little lives, loving God, and their parents, and obeying the laws of the land; yet read, if you meet them, Susie, for they will do one good. (L85)

Apart from the early recognition here of an important temperamental difference between herself and Sue, and, perhaps, of Sue's inclination to conformity, the passage points beyond Dickinson's liking of the Gothic and the sensational to the fact that she missed in those books what she must have missed in her life. And so she set out to supply the missing factor by reading, by exerting her imagination, and by straining her sensibility almost to the breaking point. Letters to Sue expatiate on the states of lovelorn longing, mounting them somewhat ostentatiously to expressions of affected rather than uncontrollable intensities:

So sweet and still and Thee, Oh Susie, what need I more, to make my heaven whole? Sweet Hour, blessed Hour, to carry me to you, and to bring you back to me, long enough to snatch one kiss, and whisper Good bye, again. (L88)

The longevity of Dickinson's emotional claims on Susan Gilbert may have been helped at the early stage by Sue's dependence on Emily for a desired social advantage. In the economy of their relations, the social imbalance in favor of Emily may have been mirrored in the emotional imbalance in favor of Sue, from which, however, it would have been difficult for Sue to extricate herself until she became Dickinson's social equal. But after she married Austin in 1856, relations between the young women turned into a family connection and acquired the family resilience to irreconcilable breach.

Except for two verse valentines of 1850 and 1852 and a short poem enclosed in a letter to Austin on October 17, 1851, Dickinson's earliest surviving poems were all sent to Sue. What is more, the first two seem to indicate a sense on the poet's part that she was losing Susan as an emotional partner. In her letters, then, the experience of loss is, even this early, tied to the influx of poetic creativity.[8] Though Emily Dickinson continued throughout her life to send letters and poems to her sister-in-law, there is no indication anywhere that she ever asked for Sue's criticism after the loaded exchange over "Safe in their Alabaster Chambers." In its course, it seems, Dickinson lost confidence, if not in Sue's judgment, then perhaps in her goodwill, since she later did send Higginson a version of the second stanza beginning "Grand go the Years — ," which Susan had dismissed with the somewhat supercilious remark, "You never made a peer for that verse [i.e., the first stanza], and I *guess* your kingdom doesn't hold one" (L238). In response to Sue's verdict, Dickinson sent yet another (third!) version of the stanza "Spring — shake the sills — " together with a guarded confession of confidence in her own work: "Could I make you

and Austin proud—sometime—a great way off—'t would give me taller
feet—" (L238). The exchange demonstrates Sue's readerly and critical partnership in the development of Dickinson's talent. But by the summer of 1861,
when it took place, Emily feels ready to assert herself as a poet against or
regardless of Sue's opinion. Anyway, several months later it was precisely the
stanza disqualified by Sue that the poet incorporated in a version of "Safe in
their Alabaster Chambers" sent with the first letter to Higginson, in which she
certainly wanted to appear at her strongest. Sue's role as Emily's literary authority seems here to have come to an end, most of all, perhaps, because the
poet had by then gained enough confidence in her own judgment and talent.

Looking through Dickinson's early correspondence, the reader is struck
not by unusual subjects or deep perceptions but by the fact that a girl of twelve,
fifteen, or seventeen was willing to write so much. She wrote even more after
1850, when Austin went away to teach and then entered Harvard. Obviously
she was doing the better part of family writing to Austin, informing him from
time to time that Vinnie, too, meant to enclose a note but "has commenced
snoring" (L42, 47) or "is busy getting her lesson" (L65). Letters to Austin
survey the home scene, give him local gossip, and express not just the family's
but, first of all, her own love and longing for his companionship at home.
There are, perhaps, two characteristics in these letters which become intensified in her later correspondence. Even this early, she begins to consider and
evaluate her homebound position. She may at times sound envious or even
rebellious, realizing Austin's advantage in getting formal education and an
experience of the world. Yet she is quite ready, too, to assert the emotional
benefits of her own domestic existence. "Home is a holy thing," she writes
Austin toward the end of October 1851,

> nothing of doubt or distrust can enter its blessed portal. I feel it more and more
> as the great world goes on and one and another forsake, in whom you place your
> trust—here seems indeed to be a bit of Eden which not the sin of any can utterly
> destroy—smaller it is indeed, and it may be less fair, but fairer it is and brighter
> than all the world beside. (L59)

The other feature is her need to establish and cultivate the illusion of an
exclusive bond with her correspondent, allowing for a sense of alliance between them against "the others." In the case of Austin, the others are parents
and, more generally, other members of the family with whom mutual understanding may never be so full and who are often, however whimsically or
subtly, satirized.

The same, though emotionally much more intense, exclusiveness of the
relationship is postulated in correspondence with the female friends of her
youth,[9] and especially with Susan Gilbert. Letters to Sue are so emotionally

loaded that some critics have felt the relationship must have been homoerotic in essence if not in fact.[10] Leaving judgment in this matter to Dickinson's biographers and to her readers, I would like to suggest that letters to the female friends of Emily's youth, to Susan Gilbert, and the drafts to "Master" form a continuum, whose importance for the purposes of Dickinson's art resides in the opportunities provided, on one hand, for cultivation of intense sensibility through enlarging the writer's emotional experience and, on the other, for practicing the craft and skill of its expression. As a vehicle of intimacy, the genre of personal correspondence constituted a perfect form for such a "creative writing" program. And the safety and leisure of her home-anchored position provided conditions of implementing it. I do not want to imply that Dickinson was from the beginning conscious of what she was doing, but she intuited early enough what the available ways and means of developing her talent were and she made efficient use of them.

The general characteristic of the early letters is that they are overwritten. The writer takes her time to paint the scene and develop a thought. Young Dickinson extends her conceits somewhat ostentatiously, delighting in their cleverness, as for instance her early valentines or the cold-catching episode in a letter to Abiah Root (L31) show. To her girlfriends, she expatiates on the state of her emotions with a marked tendency toward the melodramatic. And she borrows, perhaps quite consciously at this stage, conceits and devices from her readings. A long letter to Jane Humphrey (L86) written according to Johnson around April 1852, seems very instructive in this respect. As the editors point out, "the opening echoes that moment in *David Copperfield* when David sits in church and imagines the preacher talking about Dora (chapter 26)": "And what will dear Jennie say, if I tell her that selfsame minister preached about her again *today*, text and sermon and all." The author then goes on to consider her friend's orphaned condition vis-à-vis her own safety at home. The reflection, however, does not lead, as expected, to expressions of sympathy for Jane but to fantasies of Emily's own possible orphanhood and loss of home: "if God choose, Jennie, he could take my father, too, and my dear Vinnie, and put them in his sky to live with him forever." Perhaps frightened by what she imagines, the writer immediately takes her words back, promising to pray to God every day "not to take them." Yet she cannot refrain for long from evoking for herself, rather than for her reader, situations stimulating intense emotions. In the very next paragraph Emily imagines herself dead,

with my eyes shut, and a little white gown on, and a snow-drop on my breast; and I fancied I heard the neighbors stealing in so softly to look down in my face — so fast asleep — so still — Oh Jennie, will you and I really become like this. Don't mind Darling, I'm a naughty, bad girl to say sad things, and make you cry.

It is a strange and illustrative letter, not only for the way it mixes emotional and literary concerns but also for the insight it offers into the mechanisms and problems of such exercises in "imaginative emotionality." Straining for intensity, it is clearly a practice letter calculated to "make you cry" with borrowings from Dickens and popular "death-of-the-young-virgin" iconography. On the other hand, persisting with such an exercise, the future poet experiences at every turn inhibitive scruples of conscience. She checks herself at the impropriety of imagining her father and her sister dead; she also realizes that she is hurting her friend because she composes a letter that, in fact, has very little to do with solicitude for the addressee and everything to do with the writer's own interests and pursuits. Her retreats and apologies indicate that she feels guilty writing such a letter, yet she is also compulsive about its intensities. Her sense of guilt here, though she does not know it yet, is really akin to Hawthorne's qualms over violation, through the writer's probings, of the sanctity of the human heart. One could go on pointing to passages in the early letters, where the sense of guilt Dickinson experiences while pursuing her exercises in expanding sensibility results not only from the fact that they entail transgression of the socially accepted behavior (like not helping enough with the housework or skipping church or writing intense love letters to a friend of the same sex)[11] but also from the intuition that she is drawing her correspondent into an at least potentially transgressive situation for reasons that are basically egotistic and manipulative. The daring of such experiments on the human heart could be recompensed and possibly justified by the strength and exclusiveness of the emotional tie with the correspondent. Thus her youthful female friends like Jane Humphrey, Abiah Root, then Susan Gilbert, and most probably also "Master" become drawn into the double role of the catalysts intensifying her emotional reactions and the readers of their ever more skillful presentations.

Unlike a diary or journal but centrally for Dickinson's artistic purposes, correspondence enforced the double perspective: subjective — that is, her own as experiencer's — and external, because she had to consider her addressee's response. The letter to Jane Humphrey quoted above presents the early, unsophisticated stage of the interplay between the two perspectives. The backing away from emotional fantasies when they seem to become too radical and their compulsive returns in modified forms enact the dance of her imaginative needs with anticipations of the more conventional response of her reader. If she could find a willing coplayer in this game of and for her life, she might be able to monitor the effectiveness of her attempts at making her intensities real to her reader in the course of an extended exchange. Ideally, the relationship should be simultaneously intimate and aesthetically and critically competent, with her correspondent capable of informed response. That something like the pattern outlined above could have been her early intuitive model seems confirmed by the fact that when she started writing poems she treated them from the very beginning like letters; that is, she enclosed them when writing to her closest friends: Susan Gilbert, the Hollands, Samuel Bowles. This practice more than suggests that she had formed her notion of the writer-reader bond on the paradigm of the relation between intimate correspondents.[12]

It is no wonder that school friendships with Abiah Root, Jane Humphrey, or Emily Fowler could not sustain the emotional and intellectual burden Dickinson was eager to place on them. Neither was her friendship with Austin sufficiently receptive to such intensity. The final stages of Dickinson's correspondence with Abiah Root illustrate the process in which, as the relationship disintegrated, a growing sense of loss and tension resulting from efforts to accommodate it furnished the characteristic stimuli of Dickinson's best writing (Salska, "Letters" 10–11). It is possible to trace a similar development in the climactic moments of the exchange with Sue.

Read in the context of letters to her youthful female friends and then to Susan Gilbert Dickinson, the three Master letters may be viewed as a continued manifestation of Dickinson's hunger for intensity. The fact that they survive only as fragments of an unidentified but certainly larger exchange keeps challenging the curiosity of Dickinson's biographers and readers. Not even their dating is reliable. Thomas Johnson places the three drafts between 1858 and early 1862; Ralph Franklin, between 1858 and 1861. Yet, more than the unknown addressee, more than the approximate dating, it is the language and style of the letters and their but roughly decodable content that endow them with the aura of crucial mystery. Their salutations vary from the calm "Dear Master" in the first letter, through "Master," to no salutation at all in the most pained of the three beginning "Oh — did I offend it — ." She had tried the effect of removing the adjective from the conventional opening phrase in an earlier tense moment with Sue: "Sue — you can go or stay — ." And she sometimes began her letters to Mrs. Holland with the simple "Sister" (L204) or addressed Samuel Bowles and the Norcross cousins as "Dear Friend(s)" (L229, 230). But she has never before denied her addressee both the individuality of the personal name and, if that were missing, the compensating stress on the affectionate nature of their relationship. Neither has she ever before tried to reduce her correspondent's identity to status alone, an attempt standing in sharp contrast to the body of the letter, which is surcharged with emotion.

In all three messages the writer refers to the addressee as "Master." The unusual form of address wants to schematize a relationship overburdened with intensity, and the fact that in the two later, much more intense letters she calls herself "Daisy" brings the effort into sharper focus. The relationship between herself and the addressee is thus turned into a confrontation of roles, into an encounter between his status and power and her commonness and humility.

Whatever that technique may be telling us about the nature of the personal relationship between them, it first of all points to a need for distancing experience, for controlling intensity through a stylized formalization of expression. We can feel the language struggle to suppress and pattern the content of experience. That is a new need, a new development in Dickinson's correspondence. The feature has never entered even the most intense exchanges with Sue. On the contrary, lengthy epistles to Sue tend to indulge in descriptions of uncontrolled, semihysterical behavior:

> I ran to the door, dear Susie — I ran out in the rain, with nothing but my slippers on, I called "Susie, Susie," but you didn't look at me; then I ran to the dining room window and rapped with all my might upon the pane, but you rode right on and never heeded me. It made me feel so lonely that I couldn't help the tears, when I came back to the table, to think that I was eating breakfast, and you were riding away — . (Feb. 1853; L102)

Compared with such effusions, the language of the Master letters seems radically pared. In the reminiscence of their parting in the letter beginning "Oh — did I offend it — " the language works truly poetically, aiming simultaneously at metaphoric generalization of meaning and at metonymic economy of expression: "Daisy — who never flinched thro' that awful parting, but held her life so tight he should not see the wound — who would have sheltered him in her childish bosom (Heart) — only it wasn't big eno' for a guest so large — " (L248). Circumstantial facts are disregarded, and we are offered instead a metaphorical paradigm of any intensely painful parting. As in the fragment to Sue, emotion is rendered through physical action. However, unlike in the earlier letter, the intensity of feelings does not directly translate into multiplicity of actions. On the contrary, in this passage the action indexes of psychic experience are few, with the verbs put mostly in the negative or conditional form: never flinched, held tight, should not see, would have sheltered, wasn't big eno'. Not only the vocabulary but grammar as well becomes emotionally meaningful as it echoes the speaker's efforts to deny or hide her emotions. The psychic content of experience, the struggle to remain in control of pain, becomes thus effectively foregrounded. It is instructive to read this parting scene against the parting in the letter to Sue where proliferation of detail and frantic activity obscure rather than clarify the essence of psychic experience, the absurd contrast between petty daily routine and the emotional catastrophe of separation.

Both of the 1861 (Franklin's dating) Master letters rely heavily on metonymy. "Master" is substituted for the beloved's identity, the new coat for his body, his beard for his masculinity, knee for the whole person, it for you. This last substitution is a striking reductive device not only for distancing but for depersonalizing him. No part of Dickinson's correspondence up to that time shows a similarly concentrated struggle for distance and control, though her letters to Samuel Bowles, to the Norcross sisters, and to Mrs. Holland evidence the growth of her preference for metaphorical and somewhat cryptic expression. It seems as if in the Master letters all her earlier exercises in intensity brought her to some edge beyond which the realization or intuition came that language does not render intensity by expansiveness and description but through concentration and suppression. What is implied in negations and omissions may be imaginatively and emotionally more powerful than what is enumerated and described in detail. Thus it seems only natural that her most creative time as a poet should coincide with and immediately follow developments in style traceable in the Master letters.[13] It also makes sense that by the summer of 1861 she felt ready to leave Sue behind as her critic.

Instead, in April 1862 the poet turned to Thomas Wentworth Higginson. She had read his lead article in the *Atlantic Monthly* for that month, and she was certainly familiar with his earlier work. It is not at all clear what kind of response she expected. If she wanted publication of the four poems enclosed[14] and possibly others in the future, she did not say so. If she wanted criticism and advice, she couched her request in the language of metaphors, leaving her correspondent all the freedom of interpretation. Perhaps she only wanted an appreciative reader or was not very clear herself about exactly what it was that she needed from him. She had just gone through the Master experience; Samuel Bowles, with whom she used to share her poems and her secrets, left for Europe on April 9, 1862; and there is a conspicuous two-year gap during 1862–63 in the correspondence with Susan. She must have felt quite desperate for intellectual partnership. Whatever her motives, however, in writing Higginson, she made a crucial move for herself as a poet. Here, for the first time in her life, Dickinson separates her artistic concerns from her emotional involvements and attempts to test the response to her poetry of a reader who was personally unknown to her but professionally well established. Writing to Higginson seems a "coming-of-age" gesture of a "homegrown" artist. It is a gesture in which she divorces her personal entanglements in experience and the poet's concern for the effectiveness of her art:

April 15 1862

Mr Higginson,

Are you too deeply occupied to say if my Verse is alive? The Mind is so near itself — it cannot see, distinctly — and I have none to ask —
Should you think it breathed — and had you the leisure to tell me, I should feel quick gratitude —
If I make the mistake — that you dared to tell me — would give me sincerer honor — toward you —

I enclosed my name — asking you, if you please — Sir — to tell me what is true?
That you will not betray me — it is needless to ask — since Honor is its own
pawn — (L260)

While the Master letter quoted above eventually trails off into incoherence,
this text self-consciously exhibits its discipline as a means of bringing out its
tone of urgency. The feature suggests affinities with the Master letter.[15] The
direct salutation, reminiscent of the charged "Master" used to open one of the
drafts, boldly dispenses with rules of conventional epistolary politeness in a
letter addressed to a personally unknown member of the cultural establishment. It is worth noticing, too, how the urgency of the appeal would have
suffered, had she begun with the usual "Dear Mr. Higginson" instead of the
forceful two-stress opening she used. The whole letter scans easily, its sentences broken with dashes into units of meaning which may be written out as
verse lines of predominantly three or four beats. Obviously, here is a writer
who can play the rhythms of her prose by the true poet's ear, who can match
the rhythmical effects of directness and urgency with images presupposing the
actual physical life, not of abstract language but of the Word made Flesh.[16]
    She wants to know "if her verses breathed" because "the Mind is so near
itself — it cannot see, distinctly — ." This central question of her letter stems
from the realization that she needs distance to her art, the way she earlier
needed distance to her experience. Just as in the Master letters we see her
struggling to distance intensity, so in this first letter to Higginson she expects
to be helped with acquiring distance to her poetry, whose roots she knows to
be deeply intimate. Without distance she can evaluate neither her art nor her
own position as an artist in her time. The new need to reflect on her art
constitutes the essence of the leap to artistic maturity that she made between
the Master letters and her letter to Higginson. The five letters she wrote to
him between April and November 1862,[17] when the eminent man of letters
became a soldier in the Union army, contain, apart from her metapoetic verse,
most of Dickinson's reflection on the roots of her poetry and the nature of her
art. She did not really aim at anything as programmatic and formal as a definition of her aesthetic stance or a statement of the principles of her poetics, but
she did give him (or herself) some idea of both. She never asked directly for an
opportunity to publish, and he never offered one. Rather, their exchange
revolves (apart from her stylized responses to his inquiries about her person,
background, and readings) around the issue of power through language and of
artistic control of experience in poetry. She consistently points out that the
sources of her verse lie in emotional intensity: "I had a terror — since September — . . . and so I sing, . . . — because I am afraid — " (L261), and on another
occasion: "I felt a palsy, here — the Verses just relieve — " (L265).

Even if she is artfully posing as an artistic innocent, there is no need to assume that she is at the same time falsifying the truth about her creative experience. On the other hand, more confidently than she did to Sue the previous year, she reaffirms her belief in her talent and her commitment to her art: "If fame belonged to me, I could not escape her — " (L265). With quiet dignity, she thanks Higginson for his appreciation of the poems she had sent: "Your letter gave no Drunkenness, because I tasted Rum before — . . . yet I have few pleasures so deep as your opinion." However, as their correspondence continues, she becomes increasingly impatient with his inability to see what she is trying to do and with his helplessness before the freedom her poems leave him as reader: "Beyond your knowledge. You would not jest with me, because I believe you — but Preceptor — you cannot mean it?" The crux of their misunderstanding seems to reside in her recognition, which he is unable to share, that what "many exercise" is "fraud" (L271). Her art will not regulate experience to make it feel "sweet," and "smooth," and "cherubic." It aims, instead, at rendering it in all its "breathing" violence and complexity. Hence her "gait" must feel "spasmodic" and "uncontrolled" in reception, which does not mean that her craft is deficient. It is only more true to the contradictory nature of experience. Until this is recognized, she must, heroically, remain "the only Kangaroo among the Beauty" (L268). Yet she keeps asking his advice, expects his criticism, and insists on maintaining the contact. She needs to talk about her art, about other writers' books, and, perhaps most importantly, provide herself with an intellectual stimulus, which her more and more sequestered life would not give — a stimulus that at the present stage of her self-conscious poetic maturity could do for her art what the intensely emotional exchanges of her younger years did, that is, feed it and keep the creative impulse vital. This much seems clear from the way she transferred to Higginson some of the authority of the Master and, to the professional correspondence with him, some of the urgency of her love letters.

In her very first letter to him, Dickinson places the nationally famous writer and critic in the position of her confidant: "That you will not betray me — it is needless to ask — ." Strategies developed in personal correspondence to control but also convey intensity are utilized here to "seduce" her professional reader into intimacy. A de facto business letter enforces, from the very start of their exchange, a personal relationship. She had used the same phrase before to conclude a note to Samuel Bowles (L250; early 1862) in which, apparently by way of confession, she enclosed poem 1072, "Title divine — is mine!" Her use of the same phrase in two very different messages, one in which a poem substitutes for a confidential personal disclosure and the other in which emotionally neutral, professional content is couched in the language of urgent intimacy, illustrates the completion of the process through which the poetics of intimate letter came to underlie all Dickinson's writings. In effect her poetry and her prose increasingly became not only exchangeable in their functions but formally permeable to each other.

Dickinson's contact with Higginson settled after the war into a sort of friendship, with him visiting her in Amherst twice and her extending gestures of solicitude also to his family. When she accepted and even actively sought such a personal relationship, perhaps as a substitute for wholehearted critical acclaim, Dickinson must have felt that she had won this reader precisely on the terms her poetry offered. She had made an intimate, person-to-person contact. It is hardly surprising that, within a similar conceptual but also pragmatic frame of her writing, the generic lines between letters and poems became increasingly unstable after 1860. Her poetic creativity clearly decreased after 1866, and letters took over as the dominant form of her writing. Occasionally, the same poem was incorporated into two or even three different letters, its meaning changed by the new context or adjusted to suit it. Thus Dickinson herself seems to teach us as readers that her letters are unique creations in which the formality of a poem and the informality of a personal communication reflect on each other. Poems become connected to the immediacy of the moment while letters participate in the impersonality of the finished artifact.

Scholars have often commented on the fact that Dickinson's poetry, always aware of the conventional norm, challenges its authority and transforms it to suit her own needs.[18] Reading the poems in the context of her correspondence makes us see Dickinson's need for innovative freedom[19] as much more radical. Eventually, the impulse led her to a mode of writing that altogether destabilized divisions between poetry and prose and yoked the two by the force of emotion underlying all her written expression. For, as she repeated[20] to her Norcross cousins as late as 1881,

> The beautiful words for which Loo asked were that genius is the ignition of affection — not intellect, as is supposed, — the exaltation of devotion, and in proportion to our capacity for that, is our experience of genius. (L691)

APPENDIX: HISTORY OF THE PUBLICATION OF DICKINSON'S CORRESPONDENCE

Letters of Emily Dickinson. Ed. Mabel Loomis Todd. 2 vols. Boston: Roberts Brothers, 1894.

The Life and Letters of Emily Dickinson. Ed. Martha Dickinson Bianchi. Boston: Houghton Mifflin, 1924.

Emily Dickinson: Friend and Neighbor. By MacGregor Jenkins. Boston: Little, Brown, 1930.

Letters of Emily Dickinson. New and enlarged edition. Ed. Mabel Loomis Todd. New York: Harper, 1931.

Emily Dickinson Face to Face: Unpublished Letters with Notes and Reminiscences. By Martha Dickinson Bianchi. Boston: Houghton Mifflin, 1932.

Ancestors' Brocades: The Literary Debut of Emily Dickinson. By Millicent Todd Bingham. New York: Harper, 1945.

Emily Dickinson's Letters to Dr. and Mrs. Josiah Gilbert Holland. Ed. Theodora Van Wagenen Ward. Cambridge: Harvard University Press, 1951.

Emily Dickinson: A Revelation. Ed. Millicent Todd Bingham. New York: Harper, 1954.

Emily Dickinson's Home: Letters of Edward Dickinson and His Family with Documentation and Comment. Ed. Millicent Todd Bingham. New York: Harper, 1955.

The Letters of Emily Dickinson. Ed. Thomas H. Johnson and Theodora Ward. Cambridge: Belknap Press of Harvard University Press, 1958.

Emily Dickinson: Selected Letters. Ed. Thomas H. Johnson. Cambridge: Belknap Press of Harvard University Press, 1971.

The Master Letters of Emily Dickinson. Ed. Ralph W. Franklin. Amherst: Amherst College Press, 1986.

Notes

1. Analyzing Dickinson's prose, David Higgins suggested in 1967 that the poet must have kept some kind of a workbook or scrap basket that later she or someone else destroyed.

2. Robert Graham Lambert, Jr., extensively demonstrated this aspect of Dickinson's letter writing in chapters 3 and 4 of his 1968 dissertation published in 1996 as *A Critical Study of Emily Dickinson's Letters: The Prose of a Poet.*

3. For details of the history of publication of Dickinson's correspondence, see Myerson.

4. Most probably, Austin and Lavinia Dickinson censored their sister's letters before they went into print, but Mrs. Todd also cut the manuscripts, with the result that it is difficult or impossible to return some of the separated fragments to their proper context.

5. William Shurr, in *New Poems by Emily Dickinson*, presents selected fragments of Dickinson's letters as poems. His criterion of selection, though unambiguous (the lines should scan as fourteeners), is much too mechanical for the modern sense of the nature of poetry. Investigating in depth the metrical patterns of Dickinson's prose, Lambert finds that her letters, especially those written in the decade of 1860–70, and especially those written to Higginson, largely fall into the rhythms of the common meter (175–205). See also my article "The Place of Letters."

6. The dependence of Dickinson's letters on models culled from the author's reading becomes clearer through the work of recent researchers. Martha Nell Smith (*Rowing*) explores an earlier suggestion of Susan Howe's (*My Emily*) that there is a relationship between drafts of the Master letters and the letters little Em'ly writes home after her elopement with Steerford in *David Copperfield*. Also, Judith Farr (*Passion*) studies patterns of imagery in Jane Eyre's thoughts about Rochester in relation to the Master letters.

7. At least two books of Dickinson scholarship ascribe central importance to the poet's relationship with Susan Gilbert Dickinson: Smith's *Rowing in Eden* and Farr's *Passion of Emily Dickinson.*

8. See, e.g., the context Johnson supplies for the first poem sent to Sue about March 1853, which he interprets as "a note asking for a letter" (P4). The second poem was sent in a letter beginning "Sue — you can go or stay — There is but one alternative — We often differ lately, and this must be the last" (L173; ca. 1854). And the writer went on: "You need not fear to leave me lest I should be alone, for I often part with things I fancy I had loved —." She echoes thus what she had told Abiah Root in 1850 about letting fancies blossom " — perchance to bear no fruit, or if plucked, I may find it bitter" (L39). By 1853 Dickinson seems to realize that her craving for personal bonds so intense that they demanded unconditional intellectual and emotional communion only led to enter-taining "fancies" that bore little relation to the daily practice of the human intercourse.

9. On the difference between Dickinson's attitudes in love poetry for men and women, see Morris, "Love of Thee." In a substantial part, Morris's observations may be extended to the letters as well.

10. The earliest suggestion of Dickinson's lesbianism came in 1955 from Rebecca Patterson, though its object was identified not as Sue but as Kate Scott Anthon. Since then a number of critics have emphasized Dickinson's homosexual identity, among others Lillian Faderman in her well-known essay of 1977, Vivian Pollak, Judy Grahn, Paula Bennett, Martha Nell Smith, and Judith Farr.

11. See, e.g., L36, 88, or 93.

12. Intimacy with the reader was also a more general ideal of the literary culture of Dickinson's times. One need only to think about Jane Eyre's direct addresses to the reader ("Reader, I married him") or of Hawthorne's theorizing about his ideal reader in "The Custom House."

13. See also Cynthia Griffin Wolff's discussion of the letter beginning "Master, If you saw a bullet hit a Bird" (*Dickinson* 407–10). In its conclusion, Wolff writes: "The force with which the Voice of the poet dominates this letter suggests that at some level Dickinson had already made her choice — preferring the safety of mediating language" (410).

14. They were "Safe in their Alabaster Chambers" (P216), "The nearest Dream recedes unrealized" (P319), "We play at Paste" (P320), and "I'll tell you how the Sun rose" (P318).

15. Some letters to Higginson do, indeed, address him as "Master" (see L381, 413) or even refer to him with the pronoun "it" (L323). Dickinson seems to have transferred to Higginson some of the authority of the Master and some of the intensity of that relationship.

16. Lambert points out that "it was Thomas Wentworth Higginson with whom she played her most brilliant game of 'hiding' verses. Whole sections of her earliest letters to Higginson scan so perfectly — especially when she 'doubts' her poetic abilities — that several of the letters can virtually be regarded as practical jokes, challenging him to hear the rhythm as well as read the prose sense of her words" (193).

17. There is one more brief note of October 6 asking him if she had "displeased" him, presumably because he did not respond to her previous communication.

18. For example, see Porter (*Early Poetry* 136) or Hagenbüchle, "Precision."

19. In the preface to *The Manuscript Books of Emily Dickinson*, Ralph Franklin com-ments on the growth of freedom evident in the poet's treatment of the manuscripts of her poems as the fascicles yield to loose "sets" of sheets and collections of drafts (x).

20. Dickinson here quotes from memory words that "were in a letter that I do not find," but the context shows that she wholly approves of "thoughts so magical" (L691).

DICKINSON'S POETICS

David Porter

Searching for Dickinson's Themes

$\mathcal{B}$y mapping the themes in a poet's oeuvre we seek in a standard way to classify and thereby broadly comprehend the writer. Contextual descriptions that include historical, cultural, and gender analyses also contribute to comprehension but tend to obscure the artist's individuality and the art. Confronting Dickinson's 1,775 brief poems, we want to know what besides the book binding and the author's name holds the poems together. The question is, in fact, both daunting and uniquely illuminating in her case. Because the theme search encounters major obstacles to finding clear ideational linkages between hundreds upon hundreds of compacted poems, it is the interpretive approach that, surprisingly, is most revealing of the singular nature of Dickinson's poetics.

In the unruly body of her poetry there may be found a theme to fulfill every critic's predisposition. For example, the lines on a worksheet that strikingly dramatize an Amherst sunset — "Soft as the massacre of Suns / By Evening's Sabres slain" (P1127) — have been said to depict a female evening slaughtering the male solar power, a sort of massacre of sons. What, then, intrinsically holds the poetry together? Even more simply, what did this poet, the foremost woman poet in the American canon, write about? The associated question in the case of Dickinson, then, is inescapable: How many poems make a theme in the Dickinson oeuvre, 17 (1 out of 100) or 170 (1 out of 10)? If repetition is at the heart of theme perspective, what is the requisite number?

Other major American poets of Dickinson's time induce full and coherent thematic understanding in their persistent readers. With Ralph Waldo Emerson and with Walt Whitman a half generation later, in the transparent eyeball and the autochthonous poet-hero, we have comparable and discernible figures scanning an intelligible and exhilarating world. Emerson is intent upon depicting the noble potential in every countryman, exhorting each to stand on his own feet and to think his own thoughts. Whitman celebrates the stimulating fullness of both individual and community experience. With Dickinson, our impassioned search for a similar thematic preoccupation leads to a formidable array of mysteries concerning her intellectual focus and her intentions. The centerless display of her brief and brilliant stanzas explains why biographical interpretations are so numerous. Yet the privacy of her life creates a tempting but unreliable explanatory circle whereby apparent events in individual poems are adduced to be her actual experiences, which are then employed to interpret other poems as biographical.

What is required of earnest Dickinson readers, then, is patience of mind, the ability to live with indefiniteness and indeterminacy, more so than with any other major American poet before the postmodern onset of pastiche as a form and the deliberate evasion of linguistic closure as communication. Like Georges Poulet, who has commented brilliantly on Dickinson, we must attend to both the implications and the withholdings of indeterminacy in literary practices (345–50). Even so, we may also be elated when messages are clear, as Charles Anderson and I were when, after we had been discussing indeterminacy at length with Poulet on one occasion in Nice, Madame Poulet appeared from an adjoining room in the apartment to say "Yes, Georges spends all his time with indeterminacy, but sometimes I like to be *determinate!*"

Yet enigmatic expression in linguistic art, by its nature unique in each occurrence, as in every art form no matter the medium, captivates us as readers even as we cherish order and the familiarity that repetition and worldly reference provide. What is to be discovered, I propose, in the vexing search for thematic pattern in Dickinson, is the sharp disjunction in her poetry between the interiors of poems, that is, the poetics, and the exteriors where one seeks the actual referents. Which poems refer to real lovers, to the Civil War that touched every household in her most creative years, to the death of loved ones, to the lives of women, to her family, to her poetic aspirations, to her religious faith, to her own psychic breakdown? Much more significant, by contrast, are the *interiors* where syntactical mysteries, untraceable references, and stunning lexical creations prompt an intellectual, emotional, and sign-tracing agility in the reader that is quite remarkable because of the extremely limited space of the poem in which all the promptings take place.

Preparing a study guide to Emily Dickinson's poetry canon is both the teacher's and the student's daunting challenge. This is because of what is in the canon and what is not in the canon. What is there is more than 1,700 poems, almost all of them brief compositions. In addition to sheer numbers, there are difficulties of pronominal and other references, ungrammatical novelties and ellipses, syntactical compressions and disconnections, and irregular punctuation that conceals sentence structure. Then there are the elements that are *not* in the canon: selection and grouping of poems by the poet herself (I refer to the fascicles below), a chronology of composition, a clear pattern of development in the poet's skills, publication that would have required revision and finish on the poet's part, titles for the poems, and a sustained explanation of her intentions and, comparable to what exists in brilliant clarity in the work of Emerson and Whitman, her conception of her own poetics. Robert Frost distilled Dickinson's evident mode in a single zany remark: "When she started a poem, it was 'Here I come!' and she came plunging through" (qtd. in Keller 313). Poetry and love, Dickinson wrote with the vexing brevity of a plunge, "We both and neither prove — / Experience either and consume — / For None see God and live —" (P1247).

She did in fact copy more than 800 of her poems, many with variant words appended, into forty small booklets made of folded letter paper and tied each with string that she passed through two holes pierced at the left edge of each gathering. She assembled these fascicles quite deliberately for seven years beginning when she was twenty-seven. The worksheets, which would have provided a detailed chronology and insight into her compositional practices, were evidently destroyed as the fair copies were made. What was her intention in making these booklets? Are there thematic threads that bind the fascicle groupings together? I return to these core questions later when I survey some major commentaries on the poet's topical preoccupations. Her own pronouncement on her aim is as baffling as it is brief: "My business is Circumference" (L268). It is yet another dimension of the thoroughly engaging enigma of central themes in this poet's work.

Teachers' efforts at organizing the canon for classroom instruction are revealing. Two master teachers, over many years, attest to the challenges. Richard Sewall pinpoints the difficulties in a concise essay entitled "Teaching Dickinson: Testimony of a Veteran." He begins with the basic observation, "As with Shakespeare, there are many routes to the center; only, with Dickinson, the country is curiously uncharted, quite unlike the fine familiar territories of the great ones." He then names poets from Chaucer and Milton to Keats, the Brownings, Whitman, Eliot, Frost, Stevens, and Yeats, asserting: "None of these poets presents the problems of those 1,775 short, tense, disparate pieces . . . that Emily Dickinson left in her bureau drawer." In short, he says, "she left us her workshop." Set a class to reading *The Complete Poems*, writes Sewall, "and almost everyone will find something that rings a bell." And this:

> She defies easy classification. At first, one is struck by the *dis*unity of the canon, the disparity of the parts. We hear many voices — joy, sorrow; pleasure, pain; faith, doubt; the voice of innocence, the voice of experience; and many more. Which is Emily Dickinson's? . . . As to theme, the first editors in the 1890s divided the poems into four categories — Life, Love, Nature, Time and Eternity, — but ever since then those distinctions have been breaking down as we become more sensitive to the implications of her metaphoric way of thinking. (In a single poem, she may be directing her thought to all four). (30–32)

Charles Anderson published the first book-length study of Dickinson's poetry in 1960, having available at long last the complete poems in the variorum edition edited by Thomas H. Johnson and published in 1955. Anderson describes the difficulties of organization that the critic must confront and proposes his own thematic groupings.

> There are no marked periods in her career, no significant curve of development in her artistic powers, no progressive concern with different genres, such as might furnish the central plan for a book on Milton or Yeats. Continuing the search for an order and a suitable body of poetry to interpret, one happily remembered her tendency to return again and again to a few fundamental themes or areas. This was recognized by her earlier editors, but since their groupings are quite unsatisfactory the critic must make his own by re-searching the entire canon. Thus the approach that suggested itself was a thematic one, and it remained to find some really meaningful sequence for the groups. (*Stairway* xii)

Anderson chose a thematic sequence beginning with "her theory of art," followed by "her theory of perception, what use the poet can make of the external world," with nature as her subject. He then followed with "the inner world" that included "her treatment of the dramatic poles of human existence, Ecstasy and Despair." Finally, he perceived a thematic concern with "man's knowledge of Death and his dream of Immortality." The categories then are, in Anderson's summary, "art, nature, the self, death and its sequel." He then observes that these categories "are in no sense hard and fast or mutually exclusive."

> Some of the poems on the inner world are essential to her esthetic by defining her concept of reality. Some of her finest nature metaphors occur in poems dealing with despair or immortality. The only possible place for the fulfillment of love came to be heaven, reached through the grave.

These groupings, Anderson asserts, "clearly define the major areas of her achievement and provide a climactic order in terms of excellence" (xii–xiii).

My own tactics in the classroom run to polar extremes. I have tried the random-chaotic approach in first classes on the poet. That is, I say simply, "As your first assignment in the book of complete poems — always complete, to be sure — read for two hours." When the class next meets my questions are these: Where did you begin reading — at the beginning, the middle, the end? Or did you open the book as it lay on the floor where you deliberately dropped it for fate to open? Did you leave some poems unfinished because of their difficulty? How many poems did you read? How much time did you spend on each poem? Can you characterize the cluster of poems that you read? What were the themes? What, in fact, did she write about? Please answer this last question in a paragraph or two.

At other times I have begun with groupings of the poems according to a list of themes: the soul's society, psychic distress involving pain, terror, and breakdown, death, poets and poetry itself, nature and the Amherst region, God and faith, problem poems in which the subject is unclear, suicide poems. When Masako Takeda published her book of Dickinson's love poems translated into Japanese, I took her index of over 180 poems and began study and discussion in the class with these poems (77). The love theme, concentrated in this way, makes a whole new beginning identity for this poet and for the students' perception of her.

Thematic groupings that readers identify among the poems far exceed the few I have named so far. Albert Gelpi, for example, in an early critical study of Dickinson, subtitled *The Mind of the Poet*, lists in his index at least thirty-eight "Themes of Poems" (199–200). The list ranges from awe and beggary, bride and caterpillars, Eden and other faraway places, to royalty, lightning, freckles, and wife, and this number, at a glance, does not include the Bible, immortality, love, or poetry and the role of poets. By contrast, a statement on what she sees as the three most significant themes in Dickinson and an underlying central theme has been made recently and concisely by Fatima Falih Ahmed Al-Bedrani of the University of Baghdad:

> Emily Dickinson wrote on various themes, and one can say that no other poet has written on such a variety of themes as Emily Dickinson did. Yet beneath all, truth is the motif.
>
> Although Emily Dickinson's poetry is almost personal, she explores themes on her own account, yet she expresses the deepest feelings of the soul of man. Her various themes are those of humanity, and her poems are notable for their nakedness, for the fearless presentation of experiences which are deeply and painfully personal. In this personal, spiritual experience Emily Dickinson recognizes two moments in life as being crucial, or, as she defines them, "sacramental": the moment of love and the moment of death. Love and death are the most significant themes, both are the experiences of the spirit, each of which annuls the past "tract" of life but opens another and better life as immortality, which is her third significant theme.

Fatima Ahmed indicates the merging of these three themes as well:

> Death assumes the form of love, which is, paradoxically, a form of creativity. Emily Dickinson's life without love is death, and her death in love is life. Love becomes life, life love, and death dies into life (P491). In the end, love surpasses both life and death to catch the blessing of immortality (P769).

"Truth is not hidden from man but man is ignorant," this scholar adds. "It is the dazzling light, and it is associated with beauty."

Despite such evocative clarity and assurance of interpretation, however, a seeker after themes discovers that poem after poem, perhaps as many as half of the entire canon, resists a fixed interpretation, evades a definite thematic expression, instead activating unbridled reader-response free play. A notable example is the poem beginning "My Life had stood — a Loaded Gun —" (P754). Joseph Duchac's indispensable *Guide to Commentary* on the poem lists seventy-five readings of the poem that range from helpless awe at the interpretive challenge to impatient dismissal of the poem to confident articulation of its thematic statement. Here, with necessary brevity, the commentator's quotations within the editor's distilled paraphrases, are examples from Duchac's survey dating back to 1939 (1: 327–31, 2: 257–62):

> The poem defies analysis, but its "reverberations are infinite." (Louise Bogan)

> An example of a type of poem by Dickinson in which conceits are "almost hounded to death, pursued as they are beyond the realm of reason into an intellectual vacuum." (D. G. van der Vat)

> The poem's conceit conveys "the amorous potential of a human being who remains dormant until 'identified' into ecstatic awareness by the owner taking possession of her." The poem's central paradox is that of "finding oneself through losing oneself in love." (Charles Anderson)

> The poem is cited as evidence of Dickinson's "unconscious phantasies of possessing the attributes of masculinity, including the anatomical ones." (John Cody)

> The poem is "a powerful symbolic enactment of the psychological dilemma facing the intelligent and aware woman, and particularly the woman artist, in patriarchal America." (Albert Gelpi)

> Extended exploration of poem's images, language, and significance. Relates to Shakespeare, Elizabeth Barrett Browning, Emily Bronte, Cooper. "This austere poem is the aggressive exploration by a single Yankee woman, of the unsaid words — slavery, emancipation, and eroticism." (Susan Howe)

> "The poem is hysterical in certain ways and that hysteria must be understood in the historical context of a continent and a century in which women were invited to assume certain sorts of power while at the same time subtly tortured for their desires to do so." (C. Walker)

My own entry must be included here. Not surprisingly, it finds Dickinson concerned, as she consistently was, with the power of language.

> "Three related functions create the signification of the poem: the poem's voice is language itself, the language gun has the power to kill, and language to be purposeful and not randomly destructive must be under some mature authority." (David Porter)

A final example of interpretive commentary on the poem specifically identifies the speaker and the "Master," neither of them Dickinson, so that the poem takes its place as one of the riddles of her poetry that "are intimately related to Biblical paradoxes and pertain to the enigmatic promise that we shall be deliv-

ered from death into the eternal life of Heaven" (Wolff, *Dickinson* 442). One
literary scholar expressed his most appreciative relief that the poem at long last
is finally understood! Here is the Duchac entry:

> "Who am 'I,' and who is 'He'? To an Amherst audience . . . the answers would
> probably have been patent: death and Christ." (Cynthia Wolff)

In the search for thematic patterns in the Dickinson canon a reader encounters distraction after distraction as poems of trite concern and indifferent
artistry stand side by side, significantly in the fascicles arranged by the poet
herself, with poems of authentic power and stunning insight. For example, in
fascicle 23, which begins with "Because I could not stop for Death," one finds
the next poems to be "He fought like those Who've nought to lose" (P759)
and "Fame of Myself, to justify" (P713). This unevenness reflects, it seems, the
poet's own lack of concern, for whatever reason, for sustained patterning of
her attention. Critical readings of the poetry, then, and not surprisingly, range
the entire gamut from visions of sharp and thorough coherence in the canon
to pleasures of indeterminacy to at least one that charts a canon with no fixed
aim outside its poems' interior brilliance and audacity.

My own conclusions as to her preoccupations reflect, in the same instant,
my earnest desire to find dominant themes and to acknowledge that the absence of such themes — apart from the unavoidable subjects of life and love and
death — is instead the central perception. In one commentary, I quoted the
remarkable prose fragment of Dickinson's that echoed earlier passages in
some letters:

> Death being the first form of Life which we have had the power to Contemplate,
> our entrance here being an Exclusion from comprehension, it is amazing that the
> fascination of our predicament does not entice us more. With such sentences as
> these over our Heads we are as exempt from Exultation as the Stones — (Prose
> fragment 70)

My conclusion then was this: "Exclusion from comprehension: this is the stark
vacancy at the center. The disabling, decohering ignorance streams through
the entire canon and forms time after time the significance of her allegories. . . . Nature thus was indeed a haunted house" (*Idiom* 149). Elsewhere in
the same study, I linked that vacancy directly to characteristics of her poetic
expression itself. "When we confront the actual character of her composition
and the ways the hymn form and the allegorical abstraction distorted her
syntax and obscured her referents, we come upon the phenomenon most basic
of all in her technique: the absence of connective webbing in her work" (137).
My overall conclusion — that Dickinson is the only major American poet without a clearly discernible project, that is, an inhering and evolving axis of

thought—continues to set critics' teeth on edge, prompting their outspoken delineations of central theme after central theme!

Sharon Cameron's fresh and provocative perspective is intended to expand readers' frames of comprehension beyond fixed themes in these poems of irregular sequence with variant words appended, to suggest the power and "wholeness" that uncertainty promotes and how rich indeterminacy can be. She finds herself at the outset depicting that most evasive of all activities: Dickinson's state of mind. "[D]emonstrating that the poems can be read in sequence," Cameron asserts, "and demonstrating the multiple ways in which sequences can be read (as in Fascicles 15 and 16), does not clarify whether the poems are to be read in sequence or isolation. But the reason it does not illuminate this," she argues, "is that Dickinson herself was uncertain about how her poems should be read." Formulating the point more strongly, Cameron writes: "it is not merely that Dickinson was uncertain, but that she refused to make up her mind about how her poems should be read. This refusal—another aspect of what I have called choosing not to choose—is crucial to the problematic of her poetry" (*Choosing* 40).

The poet's choosing precise meanings and identities could have been "empowering," to use Cameron's term, but *not* choosing, she argues, "empowers in an entirely different way. For if everything is inconclusive, if nothing is absolute, then, also, nothing is excluded" (153). Seekers of thematic charts have their work cut out for them! Dickinson's indecision is said to shift the interpreter's task, then, from finding meanings to finding whether there are boundaries to the meanings. The poet, writes Cameron,

> regulates the relation between part and whole so that the question What is a subject? becomes What are its parameters? including What are its textual parameters? This is really a question of the in(ter)determinacy of meaning, whether with respect to the relation *among* poems in a fascicle or with respect to variants *in* poems. Meaning in Dickinson's poems is thus understood as relational. Moreover, it is produced by relations that evolve and shift (159).

One is not surprised to find that at a still further pole from Cameron's view of indeterminate wholeness and my own focus upon the absence of a clear project on the poet's part is the view that a coherent single theme structures the entire expression of the forty bound fascicles, which hold almost half of the poems in the canon. Abundant references to the biblical language and figures in Dickinson's poetry, as well as forceful pronouncements of both religious faith and skepticism, have been noted by many interpreters, most notably Richard Sewall and Jay Leyda, Martha O'Keefe in private publications, and extending back to Thomas Wentworth Higginson and Susan Gilbert Dickinson in her obituary for the poet.

The most concentrated study to date is a recent one by Dorothy Huff Oberhaus, who sees fascicle 40 as "the key to comprehending the fascicles' long lyric cycle." Dickinson's forms and figures place the poet in the tradition of Christian devotion, writes Oberhaus, adding, "The Bible pervades her mind and art, as it does the mind and art of all Christian devotional poets and writers. And the Bible was not, as many have supposed, merely a source of imagery for her. Rather, the Bible is essential to her structure and meaning, the very sum and substance of her art" (*Fascicles* 185). The "singularly cryptic" poems of fascicle 40, says Oberhaus, require the reader to "enact the role of sleuth." This done, what she sees is "F-40 as an architectural tour de force, a three-part meditation, a letter addressed to the reader, a garland of praise, and a conversion narrative, as well as the triumphant conclusion of the protagonist's account of her poetic and spiritual pilgrimage from renunciation to illumination to union and finally, after many conflicts, to contentment with this union" (168).

Many other studies could be cited if further evidence were needed to demonstrate how fluid and expansive and, indeed, how manipulable, in many cases, the listing of thematic glimpses in Dickinson's poetic canon is. I shall touch on a few more before concluding. Only passing reference to feminist studies that isolate feminist themes is required here. Perhaps all that is necessary is a caveat directed to earnest feminist investigators whose theses often tend to be not only predetermined, stereotypical, and based on narrow readings of highly selective bits of the canon but, sometimes most egregious of all, unacceptably reductive of both the poet's intellect and her art.

Harold Bloom's assessment of the poet stands in useful contrast to the simplifications. His claims for the poet's status in the Western canon are major indeed: "Except for Shakespeare, Dickinson manifests more cognitive originality than any other Western poet since Dante" (291). In her nation, he writes, "she had the best mind of all our poets, early and late, and she illuminates the American religion as no other writer does. The aesthetic equivalent of our national blend of Orphism, Enthusiasm, and Gnosticism is originality, and not even Emerson thought through originality as subtly as Dickinson did" (300). As for the religious theme in Dickinson, Bloom asserts that her "anguish is intellectual but not religious, and all attempts to read her as a devotional poet have crashed badly. The entity named 'God' has a very rough career in her poetry and is treated with considerably less respect and understanding than the rival entity she names 'Death'" (295). How might Bloom, we ask, read the poem "My Life had stood — a Loaded Gun — "?

Her major position in the tradition, he implies, has little to do with possible themes. "Her canonicity," he writes, "results from her achieved strangeness, her uncanny relation to the tradition. Even more, it ensues from her cognitive

strength and rhetorical agility, not from her gender or from any gender-
derived ideology. Her unique transport, her Sublime, is founded upon her
unnaming of all our certitudes into so many blanks; it gives her, and her
authentic readers, another way to see, almost into the dark" (308–9).

Bloom's central perception is entirely agreeable to my conclusion that Dickinson practiced no thematic preoccupation or project but rather a brilliant, repeated rendering of what I have called "the menacing ascendance of consciousness" (*Idiom* 6). Here is Bloom on the poem beginning "The Tint I cannot take
— is best —": The "poem knows, as no other poem in her century knows, that
we are always besieged by perspectives. Dickinson's entire art at its outer limits,
as in this poem, is to think and write her way out of that siege" (305).

Her historical circumstance, of course, provided thematic conventions that
were too pervasive to escape. We noted earlier her enigmatic statement that
"My business is Circumference," and historical context may yet confirm the
probability that she meant by this the outermost capacity of mind. But she also
asserted that "My business is to Love," a theme for women in her time and
prominent in her poetry. A further declaration on her part, in a letter to her
Norcross cousins during the Civil War, displays her own awareness of her
perspectives again and again on the matter of death. "Sorrow seems more
general than it did," she writes, "and not the estate of a few persons, since the
war began." And then, in a rare instance of self-description and reference to
her poetry, she added: "I noticed that Robert Browning had made another
poem, and was astonished — til I remembered that I, myself, in my smaller way,
sang off charnel steps" (L298).

Her earliest editors placed her poems in conventional categories of her
time, thereby suggesting, misleadingly to be sure, the comfortable and graspable themes her readers would expect: Life, Love, Nature, and Time and
Eternity. In contrast, Thomas H. Johnson's subject index to the variorum
edition is thirteen pages long, beginning with the subjects "Achievement" and
"Action" and ending with "Worm," "Wren," "Probing the Wound," "Death
of the Year," "Yesterday," and "Immortal Youth." At the outset of this eye-
catching display — in part of one column the list reads Faith, Fame, Famine,
Fancy, Fate, Fear, Feather, February, Fence, Fire, Firefly, Fitness, Flowers,
Fly — Johnson is careful to advise readers that the subject index should not "be
regarded as an attempt at interpretation of the poems" (1213).

Space does not permit a full survey of commentary on Dickinson's thematic
concerns as seen by other comprehensive and discerning American readers
as well as analysts from outside the United States. Such a survey would include the probing or impressively broad studies by Richard Wilbur, Jane
Donahue Eberwein, and others, Brita Lindberg-Seyersted of Sweden, Sirkka
Heiskanen-Mäkelä of Finland, Françoise Delphy of France, and the group of

Japanese scholars represented in *After a Hundred Years,* edited by Tamaaki Yamakawa.

An exciting challenge is in order for theme seekers who are forcefully caught up in current end-of-century postmodern and postaesthetic theoretical approaches. That challenge is to attempt to envision a poetic practice that is comprehended best apart from the ready-to-hand thematic conventions both of today and of the era in which Dickinson wrote. Her poem beginning "Dare you see a Soul *at the White Heat?*" (P365) together with Helen Vendler's pointed remarks provide the conception.

> Dare you see a Soul *at the White Heat?*
> Then crouch within the door —
> Red — is the Fire's common tint —
> But when the vivid Ore
> Has vanquished Flame's conditions,
> It quivers from the Forge
> Without a color, but the light
> Of unanointed Blaze.
> Least Village has its Blacksmith
> Whose Anvil's even ring
> Stands symbol for the finer Forge
> That soundless tugs — within —
> Refining these impatient Ores
> With Hammer, and with Blaze,
> Until the Designated Light
> Repudiate the Forge —

Other poets, Vendler reminds us, have employed the image of the blacksmith's forge.

> It seems to be an image that transcends history and biology. Insofar as questions of race, class, creed, gender, nation, and historical moment cannot be answered by inspection of the poem, and insofar as the text speaks to us without answering them, we must acknowledge a plane of selfhood and speech, accessible to everyone, in which the usual social categories are irrelevant. If Dickinson's greatest work validates that plane, as indeed it does, might it not serve our own critical inquiry best to ask whether we are acquainted with that plane of language and thought, and what Dickinson can tell us about what it is like to live there and attempt to become, ourselves, that Designated Light?

Contextualizing critics, Vendler goes on, "do not believe that we can 'repudiate the Forge.' Dickinson knew the effort it took to do so, and embedded that knowledge in her poem." She concludes: "It is the poem of the private mind. It aims to shed, not to embody, quotidian conditions" (37).

What persists in Dickinson, then, as we see when we search for her themes, is the brilliant activity of her language apart from the mute universe outside it. I turn my attention then to her words. "The Brain is just the weight of God —," Dickinson wrote in poem 632:

> For — Heft them — Pound for Pound
> And they will differ — if they do —
> As Syllable from Sound —

The triumph of language is in the articulation that the material world, full of sounds as it is, like the invisible spiritual world, cannot enunciate. Yet, without thematic continuities, Dickinson's syllables create a discontinuous body of work, the whole made up of particles and attitudes of more or less equal weight and never arranged by the poet herself for a public readership. The incoherence is a modern dilemma, and it explains in part why her pages of poems speak more directly to the twentieth century than the titled but forgotten works of her contemporaries.

Dickinson made individual consciousness in the poems the nexus of attention, unmediated by a philosophical theme. Unlike Emerson and Whitman, she brought into view with her audacious and critical metaphors the opaque being of humans, the "mysterious peninsula" as she called it, the unmanageable but excruciatingly sensitive and needful portion that we might describe as her preoccupation. She had, as William Carlos Williams once said, a distaste for lingering, and the resulting compression and fragmentation in her brief poems defeat our efforts to summarize her. A crucial affair does stand out, however, as I have said elsewhere. It is "living after things happen. It is a preoccupation with afterknowledge, with living in the aftermath. The perspective of poem after poem is from afterward, from behind the 'soft Eclipse' " (*Idiom* 9). A single phrase of Dickinson's embraces it all: "these problems of the dust." She recorded it in a letter that concerned her mother's disabling illness. "I often wish I was a grass," she wrote with characteristically willful grammar to a longtime correspondent, "or a toddling daisy, whom all these problems of the dust might not terrify" (L148). Yet she departed from the revered themes of her time that one would expect.

> Her colloquial and irreverently casual heresy at times ("It's easy to invent a Life"), her deliberate inelegance in a primitive offbeat diction ("It is simple to ache in the Bone or the Rind"), and the seemingly sophisticated skepticism in offhand phrases ("Our Savior, by a Hair") combine to give a considerable portion of the poetry a discordant tone that undercuts the poetry of unquestioned assent with which her contemporaries filled the verse books of the day. (Porter, *Idiom* 230).

Dickinson's daring language, startling in its quick probes and disclosures, is less suited to sustained description, argument, and thematic continuities.

Spare in a Poundian sense, dry and hard often, her surgical language constitutes an analytical instrument of brilliant but momentary accuracy. Emerson's language, as I have asserted elsewhere, "clarifies and liberates, sweeps particulars in and absorbs, makes large synthetic designs, but Dickinson's . . . resists clarity, excludes rather than accumulates, carves out instead of combining. With an aesthetics of its own, her language became both an instrument and a form for atomizing reality, the idiom a cutting tool, a separator, a dispersal instrument rather than one of broad inclusiveness" (*Idiom* 260).

Are sunsets a vehicle for one of Dickinson's themes? She courted visual excitement, movement, and mystery, and so the motif associated with her poems of the western sky is distinctive. Beneath the painterly affection, her language does not rehearse the thematic conventions of the association of sunset with death and funeral solemnity of her times but startles with its novelty. Her language, I have asserted before, "together with the snapshot brevity of her hymn form, courted instability and change and spotted the vulnerability of settled states. This is why sunsets evoked some of her best imagistic effort. The spectacle of day's end was intensely, exaggeratedly visual, it was naturally associated with death, and it was recurrent novelty, change taking place before the eyes. The sunset was thus a visual allegory for what most centrally engaged this poet" (*Idiom* 226–27).

Excluded from comprehension, she characteristically combined in one poem the idioms of the tale-teller, the philosopher, and the farm wagon repairman to put Ideals — shall we say the Great Themes? — into proper relationship not only with human hope and invention but also with the opposing natures of wagon wheels and friction. It all takes place, including the rhymes and sound repetitions and the essential but unelaborated terms, in twenty-two words.

> Ideals are the Fairy Oil
> With which we help the Wheel
> But when the Vital Axle turns
> The Eye rejects the Oil. (P983)

The persistence of the metrically compact hymn form in Dickinson's poetry canon bears significantly on a reader's search for themes and continuities. Everything takes place in those hymnal stanzas, from questions of immortality to June bugs dropping from the ceiling. In other words, the form persists without regard, as in Whitman as an example, to the scope of subjects and themes that exist outside the poems. The linguistic audacity with which Dickinson invests this traditional form highlights the artful interior of the poems and its dominance over exterior reference, including thematic coherence.

The poems are thus patently literary texts, proseless, engagingly riddled by the silences that written language always embodies, absorbing the reader with their enigmas. Spatial travel by a reader within the poems is also insistent, as in the art of collage, where juxtaposition of objects characteristically occurs without syntactic connection. Much as we cherish the order that provides themes, we are captivated by enigma. In Dickinson the reader's absorption in enigma extends from novel words, isolated phrases, and individual poems to the profusion of themes without a center. The centerlessness, in turn, prompts the biographical readings that rush to fill the void.

Our search for themes, then, daunting as it is in the case of Dickinson, leads to the essential revelation of her genius and uniqueness. As I have asserted, "She disengaged poetry from the complicated network of exterior existence, making the art self-conscious, private, momentary" (*Idiom* 254). It was a stunning turn in the language of American literature. And in the extraordinary omissions that I have highlighted and that are the most telling aspect of Dickinson's work, we find the marvelous mysteries that cannot be explained away. For theme-seeking readers especially, Dickinson is not forbiddingly but, rather, *triumphantly* unmanageable.

FURTHER READING

Benfey, Christopher E. G. *Emily Dickinson and the Problem of Others.* Amherst: University of Massachusetts Press, 1984.

Delphy, Françoise. *Emily Dickinson.* Paris: Didier Erudition, 1984.

Johnson, Thomas H. "The Vision and Veto of Emily Dickinson." *Final Harvest: Emily Dickinson's Poems.* Ed. Thomas H. Johnson. Boston: Little, Brown, 1961. vii–xiv.

Wilbur, Richard. "Sumptuous Destitution." *Emily Dickinson: Three Views.* By Richard Wilbur, Louise Bogan, and Archibald MacLeish. Amherst: Amherst College Press, 1960.

Yamakawa, Tamaaki, ed. *After a Hundred Years: Essays on Emily Dickinson.* Kyoto: Apollon-sha, 1988.

Robert Weisbuch

Prisming Dickinson; or, Gathering Paradise by Letting Go

*B*egin with this idea, that each memorable poet teaches you a new way of thinking. Granted, the logics of language and the history of literary conventions set some bounds; but within that huge space, your thought becomes as not before. What Dickinson teaches is a kind of poetic Bauhaus, a less-is-more in which what is required is not added cognitive activities but a letting-go, a releasing of interpretive habits and idiot-questioner demands. Unclench a mental fist and you can do what Dickinson says she does: "The spreading wide my narrow Hands — / To gather Paradise —" (P657).

To get there, we must become prohibitive in shutting down some of the mind's demands for certainty. Though Dickinson despised "shalt nots," I always give myself three dogmatic orders to reach this radically undogmatic poet: Don't point; don't pry; don't settle for one truth. Not pointing, you will be embraced by multitudes of meaning. Not prying, you will discover intimacies. Not settling for one truth, you can rush toward revelations. Each of these renunciations provides, lets you "gather," something of that freed bounty by which Dickinson makes poetry and makes over your thought.

"Don't point" gets explained by one of those joking sayings Dickinson employed to state her most serious commitments. "Subjects hinder talk," she wrote to Susan Gilbert (L397), and her best poems refuse to be confined to a single subject. It is perfectly natural for us to ask as a first question of any poem what it is about, and yet this is exactly the wrong question to pose to almost any Dickinson lyric. The brevity of the poems enhances the effect that they are speaking of everything at once. The smaller the hands, the more capacious the paradise; and Dickinson's hand-spreading, translated into terms of poetic logic, is the making of analogies that become inclusive graspings of how all things appear from a certain vantage. Dickinson draws a pattern in one, then many carpets, to use James's phrase. The carpets are mundane, not magical; it is the pattern that is magical, for it lays carpet upon carpet until all the carpets vanish, making the pattern starkly plain and yet filling it with their hues. That is, once we see that the same law applies to any number of "subjects," then it applies to innumerable unnamed experiences as well, perhaps to all experience as viewed in this moment. Dickinson's poems are not about a subject matter but enact a way of seeing everything at once. It is a little sad that critics spent the 1950s and 1960s dividing her poems into balky subjects — nature, art, god, love, whatever — when each of the most important poems is about all of those subjects simultaneously; and it is similarly inapt that a more recent generation of critics has sometimes tended to posit one-dimensional Dickinsons — the religious Dickinson, the feminist Dickinson — when, spiritual and feminist as she very individually is, no poet ever so fiercely refused such confinements. Dickinson's ideal is the "stopless" life (P463), and she seems to have spent some of the summer of 1862 tallying what she could not stop for. She worries that her would-be mentor Thomas Wentworth Higginson, editor of the *Atlantic Monthly* to whom Dickinson wrote for advice she received in abundance and took not at all, will "smile at me" mockingly, then goes on, "I could not stop for that — My Business is Circumference —" (L268). "Perhaps the whole United States are laughing at me too!" she tells her friends the Hollands in a next letter. "I can't stop for that. My business is to love," and then, comparing herself to a bird no one hears, "My business is to sing" (L269). Circumference, which generally in Dickinson connotes both the mind's capacities and an admission of its limits, she here associates with the utmost of mind, or at least the attempt to enlarge its bounds. It contains but will not stop for subjects, just as the bird's song transcends topics.

Let me say this one more way. Most poems refer to an occasion. Even the metaphysical poets to whom Dickinson is often compared fix a scene. Donne keeps one arm of his compass on the situation of a lovers' parting while the other arm circles in search of a best simile that will not merely express but hope to modify the situation. But there is a situation to be modified, and that is exactly what is strikingly, almost gaudily absent from Dickinson's most interesting poems. There may seem to be one such, but it won't abide:

> Did the Harebell loose her girdle
> To the lover Bee
> Would the Bee the Harebell *hallow*
> Much as formerly?
>
> Did the "Paradise" — persuaded —
> Yield her moat of pearl —
> Would the Eden *be* an Eden,
> Or the Earl — an *Earl?* (P213)

We move from the backyard garden of the first stanza via a medieval moat, which is also a feminine yielding to the Garden, Eden, at the poem's conclusion. There are two full scenes posited, a third — a feudal castle — implied for two instants (first by "moat," then by "Earl"), and, if one reads the castle's yielding of the moat and the harebell's loosing of the girdle as sexual compliance, a metaphorized fourth scene, which is the female body.

I now dare you to point, that is, to tell me where we are, what is the occasion, and what the subject of the poem. The poem begins with a worry that the consummation of love might consume the love altogether, be the end of it. Harebell is to bee as maiden is to lover, with the pun on "girdle" pulling the poem toward a sexual reference. One is reminded of the warnings of mothers to daughters not to "yield" to the desires of boys, lest respect be lost. But in the second stanza the bee is replaced by the Earl of Eden, which may be to say God, the yielding flower is now a castled paradise, and almost suddenly the sexual questioning becomes theological. The poem has raised its bet to ask whether, if we achieved Heaven and could be with God, It and He might not lose their capitalized letters, their supernal stature. But then we notice that Dickinson is not talking merely about Paradise but "paradise" in quotes, which is to say anything that we feel would be heavenly to us in the more colloquial sense. If that which is most desired is by definition something we do not possess — whether it is intimacy with a romantic object of desire or the actual presence of a deity or for that matter the possession of a longed-for consumer item — then will not whatever becomes ours, or known, lower itself in our esteem rather than elevating the seeker? Is not longing, or deprivation, then, a precondition for desire and worship? Will not any Eden, not just the sexual or the biblical paradises, cease to be an Eden? As another poem has it,

> "Heaven" — is what I cannot reach!
> The Apple on the Tree —
> Provided it do hopeless — hang —
> That "Heaven" is to me (P239, ll. 1–4)

Heaven is not just what but *whatever* I cannot reach, just as in the "Harebell" poem. Thus the apparently trivial act of a harebell and a bee becomes an illustration of personal, sexual doubt concerning whether desire can outlast consummation; that fear in turn becomes a cosmological doubt, both an illustration of the dreary thought that only by a failure to achieve the thing sought can the thing remain worthy of the seeking and, in a more cheerful aspect, a justification for the nonappearance of God in our daily lives and the absence of heaven on earth. In either case, the analogical examples collect toward a general denial of that fond hope that we can have our cake and eat it; and finally, this is no more a poem about a bee and a flower than it is about adolescent romance, than it is about medieval warfare, than it is about God's absence and availability, than it is for that matter about finally affording the

Porsche only to find it a routine drive after 1,000 miles. The pattern can absorb all of those subjects.

But this is not to say that the specific imagery is unimportant. It does pull the poem toward references — with romance and religion shockingly analogized (and all the more impressive in its capacity to shock, given that comparisons of carnal and spiritual love are so historically frequent in poetry as to be stale news unless brilliantly refigured, as here) — even while, by the very distance between the two prime references, we can fit much else inside. But the sexual fears vitalize the abstract fear they example. They provide an urgency for the otherwise abstruse questioning of God's ways, and the carnal and the spiritual are connected by the almost anatomical implication of a Paradise that might "yield her moat" (with Paradise and its castle made female). Conversely, within the "sexual" first stanza, the theologically tinged verb "hallow" anticipates the later development of the analogy and gives to the sexual an idealized spiritual dimension. That is why I said earlier that, while the carpets (or subject areas) finally disappear, they have lent their hues to a law of life that now seems not at all cold and impersonal but earned by an implied sense of suffered experience. By the time we derive the law I stated above, its imaged life has hit upon so many areas of our consciousness — social, libidinal, natural, botanical, mythic, cosmological — that whatever areas have not been hit feel the shot nonetheless. This is and is not, then, a poem about sex, about religion, about consumer culture for that matter, because the divisions of consciousness are acknowledged to be kidded into oblivion.

Don't point then, because assigning the poem to one aspect of experience will rob it of its vital versatility. This versatility depends upon what we can call scenelessness, as each apparently mimetic scene in the poem is revealed to be a choice from an infinitude of potential examplings of the poem's unifying proposition. The scenes are not concrete but mentalized, illustratory, chosen, temporary, analogous. There is nothing quite like this scenelessness in any other poet, and by it lyric does gain something of the purity of motive of a birdsong while retaining a determinate quality of meaning that no bird achieves. Most poetry is occasional, even if the occasion is a made-up one. Usually a certain circumstance serves as a goad to speech, but Dickinson speaks unbidden, or bidden by nothing less than the "Bomb upon the Ceiling" (P1128), which is her own notion of life as constant peril. Why do we require anything more to encourage response? Subjects hinder talk.

This scenelessness holds even when in a poem structured as a series of analogies the final one is more clearly the destination of the foregoing images. In this poem, for instance, the final analogy not only takes in the earlier ones but reverses their meaning — and yet it too fails to provide a defining subject:

As the Starved Maelstrom laps the Navies
As the Vulture teased
Forces the Broods in lonely Valleys
As the Tiger eased

By but a Crumb of Blood, fasts Scarlet
Till he meet a Man
Dainty adorned with Veins and Tissues
And partakes — his Tongue

Cooled by the Morsel for a moment
Grows a fiercer thing
Till he esteem his Dates and Cocoa
A Nutrition mean

I of a finer Famine
Deem my Supper dry
For but a berry of Domingo
And a torrid Eye. (P872)

From the very first line, in which a whirlpool becomes a demonic and huge kitty that "laps" whole battalions of ships like cream in a bowl, the first three stanzas reduce animal and human victims to mere petits fours, appetizers, and dainty dinners, served up to the hungers of the savage forces of nature, which in turn are made into social diners. They develop a law, that the ghastly hors d'ouevre does not exhaust digestive desire but whets the appetite to become more demanding than starvation might; and this law holds but gets spiritualized in the final stanza where now it is a human being, the speaker of this poem, who is intensely appetitive. The speaker's "Famine" is "finer" than the vulture's or the tiger's, of course, because the hunger is metaphorical rather than bodily. There is just enough liturgical meaning in the phrases "berry of Domingo" and "torrid Eye" to imply a creative desire rather than a destructive need, an epistemological completion or an intimate consummation rather than blood sport. Earlier, by making people into food and animals of prey into gourmets, one reversal had taken place; now in turn it gets reversed by a pun on the notion of appetite. But the earlier images, as in the "Harebell" poem, establish an immediacy, here even a ferocity, for the speaker's frustrated desire. They even provide that desire with something of a history, as each of the preliminary analogies presents a more complete appetitive history than the last; and finally, with the Tiger, drawing out the full implication that the greater one's past satisfaction, the greater the longing for a sustenance no longer available. The speaker then once did achieve fulfillment, and the hunger now is dependent upon her knowledge of what is not present. The poem is something of a wild and unconsoled rewriting of Wordsworth's "Intimations Ode," a dirge in which mere intimations of the thing itself torture more than console. But what is that missing thing? Is it God, as the vaguely eucharistic imagery of the berry might suggest? (The "torrid Eye" clearly is not part of the food, despite the witty syntactical linking, but the speaker's own intense gaze at an absence.) Or is this the wine of libidinal romance? Or—granted, a bit facetiously—is the missing sustenance that Porsche which the speaker once rented but cannot purchase for keeps? In truth, that anachronistic reading is not of equal validity because the images do pull toward the sacramental one way and the sexual another, just as in the "Harebell" poem; and yet here again, by refusing a single sure subject, Dickinson allows for an extraordinary absorption of varied concerns. Thus, if the poem is about anything, it is not about desiring x or y but about the psychology, almost the politics, of desire itself—a perfectly appropriate emphasis for a poet who argues that what matters most is "internal difference / Where the Meanings, are — " (P258).

But what of those poems in which there is only one analogy rather than many? We return to the bee and flower for this short lyric:

> Come slowly — Eden!
> Lips unused to Thee —
> Bashful — sip thy Jessamines —
> As the fainting Bee —
>
> Reaching late his flower,
> Round her chamber hums —
> Counts his nectars —
> Enters — and is lost in Balms. (P211)

As soon as Eden is made portable, once again quote marks appear around any allusion to paradise, and both it and the flower which is its analogue lose their literal plainness. The poem transforms "Eden" from a place in the Christian lost past to whatever any individual seeker deems most desirable, and Paradise here as before is by definition what is not easily available, though in this bee-and-flower poem availability with desire is late rather than logically impossible. As in other poems like, most famously, "Tho' I get home — how late — how late" where "Better will be the Extacy / That they have done expecting me —" (P207), delay here increases the pleasure of the ultimate fulfillment, which in this happier poem does not cancel desire but rewards its postponement. The bee–flower analogy is comical here, vividly describing the bee's delighted sense of luxury: now that he finally has found his bliss, he provides himself with a deliciously intellectual further delay, counting his nectars, reckoning his anticipated delight, before diving into it. Death itself is invoked to be reversed in this act of sacrifice — "lost in Balms" — that is no sacrifice at all, unless it is the sacrifice of unfulfilled solitude for the balm of ecstatic union.

But here again, with just one analogy and one garden, bee and flower can be identified in a multitude of ways; and again too we have not a statement about botany, religion, sex, or commerce but a dramatization of a philosophy of desire, which gains the dignity of serious thought Dickinson clearly feels it deserves.

But if we are still seeking for a subject, perhaps we will have better luck by looking to those poems in which Dickinson appears to tell a story. She is, in fact, a superb teller of tales, embracing of the most vivid of details, and yet here again, every potential scene gets troped!

> I started Early — Took my Dog —
> And visited the Sea —
> The Mermaids in the Basement
> Came out to look at me —
>
> And Frigates — in the Upper Floor
> Extended Hempen Hands —
> Presuming Me to be a Mouse —
> Aground — upon the Sands —
>
> But no Man moved me — till the Tide
> Went past my simple Shoe —
> And past my Apron — and my Belt
> And past my Bodice — too —
>
> And made as He would eat me up —
> As wholly as a Dew
> Upon a Dandelion's Sleeve —
> And then — I started — too —
>
> And He — He followed — close behind —
> I felt His Silver Heel
> Upon my Ankle — Then my Shoes
> Would overflow with Pearl —
>
> Until We met the Solid Town —
> No One He seemed to know —
> And bowing — with a Mighty look —
> At me — The Sea withdrew — (P520)

One of my colleagues, frustrated with my refusal to allow for a literalizing Dickinson, asked why we couldn't simply read this as a poem about a little girl who visits the seashore with her dog and gets scared when the tide comes in; to which the fast answer is, because, sir, mermaids don't really exist. They are part of that wildly creative and yet potentially destructive imaginative desire that helps to define the human and that is represented here by the sea, compellingly attractive yet potentially fatal, like its mermaid creatures. Yet many published interpretations of this poem, while affording it some scope, simply read the sea as death. It is something like that, of course, but it is also the transformative if destructive sea of Shakespeare's *Tempest* — Dickinson's shoes hypothetically overflowing "with Pearl" recalls Ariel's "Those are pearls that were his eyes"; and Dickinson's "Dog," in its extreme personal loyalty and its provision of domestic well-being, is a symbol of stable, common-sense identity, which is more exactly what the sea threatens. "The Brain, within its Groove / Runs evenly — and true —," begins another poem that goes on to say that the slightest "swerve" of a "Splinter" causes such a flood of the irrational as to render it easier "To put a Current back — / When Floods have slit the Hills —" (P556). The sea in this poem as in that is not merely death and not merely evil, for it promises a pearly bliss, a "sea change / Into something rich and strange" by which ecstacy is bought at the price of sanity and ordinary selfhood. In addition, the sea's male identity and his implicitly sexual assault upon the speaker in the third stanza suggest an identity with any mastering principle that might "eat me up — / As wholly as a Dew," not because it is violent but because it is all too powerfully attracting. In a letter to her future sister-in-law Susan Gilbert, Dickinson notes that their maiden lives may seem dull to a bride but they might seem highly desirable "to the *wife*, Susie, sometimes the *wife forgotten*," whom she compares to flowers satisfied with the morning dew, then with heads bowed at noon "in anguish before the mighty sun; think you these thirsty blossoms will *now* need naught but — *dew?* No, they will cry for sunlight, and pine for the burning noon, tho' it scorches them, scathers them; . . . Oh Susie, it is dangerous, and it is all too dear, these simple trusting spirits, and the spirits mightier, which we cannot resist" (L93). In this poem, water itself, the flood tide, takes the place of the sun as a mastering passion, and the self becomes a dew that will be subordinately dissolved into it. But I do not mean to argue that the poem is merely about marriage or overwhelming desire as destructive of rational selfhood, though that is one potential meaning. Rather, the sea is the symbol of all the experiential unknowns and of all the denied irrational urges. The speaker begins by visiting the shore that borders these, but these unknowns, this all-purpose id, then erupts beyond its bounds. The speaker retreats to the "Solid Town" where of course no one recognizes the Sea because the Town represents both the conventions of society that would deny the irrational and the sanctions of the sane self that protect against exposure to aspects of our internal wildness that would topple sense. In retreating, the speaker regains rational life but at the cost of the wild, which includes passion and apotheosis. And the sea withdraws "bowing — with a Mighty look" in such a way as to suggest mockingly, like the sheriff in the old Dodge commercial, "We're gonna get ya," if only via actual death and transfiguration. Desired, feared, never finally obliterated, this sea has absolutely nothing in common with any body of water anyone has ever visited, with or without canine companionship, but it has everything to do with what we humanly are and what we humanly face, for "One need not be a Chamber — to be Haunted — / . . . / The Brain has Corridors — surpassing/ Material Place — " (P670). The sea may threaten the self but is not external to it, is indeed part of an organism capable of stunning itself with bolts of melody. It is our shore, our sea, internal equipment prior to any beach and any tide in the material world.

Dickinson's symbols thus imitate her larger poetic designs in providing a kind of precise imprecision and again ask us to resist pointing or pinning down a poetry which depends on expansible meaning. Charles Rosen has commented wonderfully upon the deliberately "loose" employment of concept-words in romantic poetry to the point where, sometimes annoyingly, they "referred potentially to everything and therefore to nothing so that the processes of association were completely liberated and magnified." The romantic tendency "of stripping forms of their original significance and giving them a new sense" thus creates a "tension between the new meaning and the inevitable residue of the old," which is what Dickinson does in all of her symbolic narratives implicitly and then explicitly in her poems of definitions such as " 'Heaven' is what I cannot reach!" (16, 14). Geoffrey Hartman, writing on Wordsworth, inveighs against "pointing" because "pointing is to encapsulate something: strength, mind, life. It is to overobjectify, to overformalize," though he confesses that some pointing is necessitated by the referential nature of language itself. Yet he adds that Wordsworth "can emancipate the direction of the reference" (*Beyond* 50), and that is exactly what we see Dickinson doing, creating Emersonian circles, concentrics or spirals of meaning rather than allegorical lines and pointings.

Dickinson's scenelessness is not simply a poetic technique but something of a metaphysic. At the least it is an epistemology, an alternative way of putting together the world; and E. Miller Budick has written memorably of the argumentative nature of Dickinson's symbology, its capacity to undermine reductive systems of thought, sacramental and otherwise. It is as if the usual ways of ordering phenomena had been cross-sectioned or tipped over, revealing intricate networks otherwise unseen. The claim, in a very broad but real sense, is structuralist — but it is also, toward not only competing metaphysics but some of its own hopes that do not prove out, deconstructionist. And it should surprise no one that Dickinson was at these locales before they were commemorated by these recent coinages.

Now that we are not pointing, we may be ready for a particularly magnificent, capacious, and demanding poem, as it tempts pointing more perhaps than any other. Like "Come slowly — Eden —," it develops a single extended analogy, and it does so with a peculiar literalness that makes the temptation for allegorical assignings all the greater:

> My Life had stood — a Loaded Gun —
> In Corners — till a Day
> The Owner passed — identified —
> And carried me away —
>
> And now We roam in Sovereign Woods —
> And now We hunt the Doe —
> And every time I speak for Him —
> The Mountains straight reply —
>
> And do I smile, such cordial light
> Upon the Valley glow —
> It is as a Vesuvian face
> Had let its pleasure through —
>
> And when at Night — Our good Day done —
> I guard My Master's Head —
> 'Tis better than the Eider-Duck's
> Deep Pillow — to have shared —
>
> To foe of His — I'm deadly foe —
> None stir the second time —
> On whom I lay a Yellow Eye —
> Or an emphatic Thumb —
>
> Though I than he — may longer live —
> He longer must — than I —
> For I have but the power to kill,
> Without — the power to die — (P754)

I probably need to mention here that I spent a month with this poem two decades ago and wrote about it at length in a book on Dickinson published thereafter. My approach, which then as now required the reader to suspend the very understandable desire to identify the speaker and the owner or master in an allegorical manner, encountered some skepticism but has had a little influence, which pleases me. But my egotism is interrupted and qualified by the fact that only now, after another twenty years of reading the poem, have I come to realize not only that its greatness depends on forgoing a single identification of the relation between gun and owner/master but that the poem's very idea has to do with the destructive quality of pointing. The poem exemplifies a multiform consciousness that its speaker eschews to her destruction — or at least that is one meaning among many.

I don't mean that anything goes interpretively or that the poem is a Rorschach ink blot. I do mean that the poem gets egregiously robbed if you see the gun-to-owner relation simply as that of a believer to her god or as a lover to her adored beloved or even (and more interestingly) as language personified in relation to the poet who shoots and masters it. The poem can absorb these meanings, as usual, but it is the play among the possibilities that makes the poem, and that play occurs within a pattern that we can discern if we put aside for now any attempt to identify the speaker and the owner/master.

Instead, let us simply examine the relation. The speaker experiences herself (or himself or itself, if we are letting the gun be a gun for now) as full of potential, loaded but ignored and static, motionless, unnoticed, in corners. The capitalized Owner brings identity, time itself, motion, and purpose to the gun; and the very fact that the gun so immediately names the Owner as such suggests an overpowering recognition of finding in the Owner figure that identity and that purpose. For the next three stanzas, the relationship is celebrated, and yet we wonder at each line about the quality of experience that appears to bring joy. In the second stanza, the plural and capitalized "We" that has the freedom of roaming, so different from motionless confinement in a corner, implies an equality between gun and owner. But this claim for equality is denied not only by the nature of the analogy — a gun, after all, is the mere instrument of the marksman's will — but also by the ventriloquism of the gun speaking for the owner. The speaker is a dummy, though she does not or will not understand this (yet), for this stanza and the next emphasize a sense of power. The mountains would literally echo a gunshot, and thus the speaker experiences dominion over nature — though the mountains and the valley that follows from the mountains also get subordinated to the "cordial light" of the gun's flash, which is as if a volcano erupts. This volcanic "pleasure" of course is destructive, just as the cordial light is about as cordial as the animal diners of "As the Starved Maelstrom" — or the ruined pastoral of the preceding stanza here, where the doe is hunted.

But in this third stanza something very odd is happening. The life-gun is beginning to speak in relation to itself, for the face which "shows through" the gun must be the flash of firing, and thus the owner gets lost for a moment as if the gun can pull its own trigger. We see this even more in the fifth stanza where, after the gun mindlessly accepts the master's foes as its own (as a gun would), it far more explicitly seems to actuate itself. And yet in between those increasingly delusional mistakings occurs a stanza in which subservience is celebrated as far preferable to the loving equality of a shared pillow — and bed.

While the speaker means to be celebrating loyalty and power, the poem is warning against the delusion of achieving self-realization through subservience. As I wrote many years ago, "The speaker unwittingly creates a demonic world, a world where the only choices are purposelessness or self-negating subservience, and where the 'I' becomes an 'it'" (*Poetry* 27).[1] The poem concerns the delusions of borrowed power and the resultant despoiling of potentially harmonious and loving connections to the world outside the speaker–owner relationship — though I will go on to show how it now seems to me that even this statement needs crucial qualification. But how else to explain the sudden switch from celebration to complaint in the final stanza, unless the speaker-gun comes to understand its own error of uncritical servitude? The life-gun's kickback occurs as it projects a future which is also the enlarged sense of its present circumstance. Though the gun may live longer than the owner in the sense of mere existence — an inanimate object may indeed outlive us in that sense — the owner/master must outlive the gun in terms of a truly meaningful existence, a self-actualizing animate being, for of course a gun does not in that sense live at all. Nor — the implication goes — does anyone who gives away their own will and attempts to gain power by becoming the instrumentality of another, whether that other is another person or a mastering ideology. In a sense, the tragedy of the speaker is determined in the very first line, by the speaker's very self-definition as a gun that requires another to fire it.

Thus it becomes easily possible to read the poem as a commentary on a particular kind of love relationship. It is impossible not to be put off by the renunciation of a sexual sharing in the fourth stanza, and that abnegation is simply part and parcel of the larger refusals in the poem — of a solitary fulfillment, of an equal relationship, of a friendly relation to the world outside of the owner rather than the enraged subjugation or destruction of that outer world, of any relation but this one in which the "partners" are so absolutely unequal as to spoil any marriage and debase the human condition. From there, too, the poem can be read in the terms Cristanne Miller proposes, as "an adolescent fantasy about coming of age that breaks down before what should be its happy conclusion — powerful adulthood — revealing the flaw in its initial fiction but perhaps also the extreme limitation the speaker feels in her life choices" (*Grammar* 123). As Miller argues, the speaker adopts the masculine figure's perspective on foes; in killing the doe, Albert Gelpi very helpfully remarks, the speaker kills her own femaleness to adopt male destructiveness ("Deerslayer"), an act she repeats differently in preferring servitude to sex; and as Sharon Cameron notes, the poem is informed by a violence in which Being itself is tied to "accepting the power and the inescapable burden of doing violence" (*Lyric Time* 67) but where this itself seems to result from a rage that, as Miller adds, occurs because the speaker "has felt her (or his) potential for explosion but never expressed it" and so allows herself its expression only in the cause of another who "will 'own' the anger for her and thereby release her to express herself" (*Grammar* 125).

This is an extraordinarily trenchant feminist poem in one of its aspects, a brilliant dramatization of how a woman might be attracted by a cultural system that ultimately denies her an authentic life; it is also a psychologically rich poem for men, for men in other ways subordinate themselves to rulers and causes large and small; and yet it is either and both only within a still greater circle of meaning. The poem is also about, say, devotion to any mastering idea, including God — and there is certainly a theological feel at the edges of some of these lines. The poem is devotional in multiple ways. But if it is a poem about giving up oneself to a religious (or for that matter a political or social) ideal, its pattern of thought nonetheless remains constant: bad deal, it says, however attractive, to make oneself into Stevens's man of one idea in a world of ideas.

But let me suggest one more possibility where in fact the overall meaning of the poem may seem to change. Let's say that the poem is about language in the hands of the poet and that the speaker is a sort of speaking word. There is supporting evidence for this seemingly quixotic view. To her cousin Louise Norcross, Dickinson writes of the consequential nature of letter writing, of language itself: "An earnest letter is or should be life-warrant or death-warrant, for what is each instant but a gun, harmless because 'unloaded,' but that touched 'goes off'?" (L656). Here it is time, an instant, that is explosive, but only as tied to language. Or again, in the poem "A Word made Flesh" (which I am suggesting is what may happen in "My Life had stood"), we find a surprising gloss on the last stanza of our poem:

> A Word that breathes distinctly
> Has not the power to die
> Cohesive as the Spirit
> It may expire if He —
>
> "Made Flesh and dwelt among us"
> Could condescension be
> Like this consent of Language
> This loved Philology. (P1651)

Apply this poem to the life-gun, and the negative meanings get transformed. The life-gun is language shot off, creatively, to describe the world; the hunting of the second stanza is not to be taken literally but as a capturing of meaning, which is what language does — it hunts the doe by describing it. Dickinson often described the greatness of language and poetry in violent terms, as in her famous criteria, "If I read a book and it makes my whole body so cold no fire can ever warm me I know *that* is poetry. If I feel as if the top of my head were taken off, I know *that* is poetry. Is there any other way?" (L342a). If, in other words, the violence of the poem is really creative, then the assignations of speaker and owner that we make create not wonderfully intricate circlings of meaning but flat contradictions: in the final stanza, for instance, if it is language that lives longer than the speaker and cannot die, that is not anything terrible.

Or is it? If we look a bit closer, it seems to me that the apparent contradiction dissolves. Imagining that this is in fact a poem spoken by a word made flesh about its maker, the poet, then the poet must be a satirist, else why the talk of aiming at not just nature but foes? Dickinson's only satires, as in one I am about to quote, are directed against people or ideas that make others feel ashamed. She eschews satire, and it is a use of language that Dickinson fully condemns. She can imagine, for instance, language in the cruel mouth of a hateful woman, and there the destructive imagery means what it says:

> She dealt her pretty words like Blades —
> How glittering they shone —
> And every One unbared a Nerve
> Or wantoned with a Bone — (P479)

This is a misuse of the word's power, and in fact it takes us closer to the effects of the speaker in "My Life had stood." And the final stanza of "My Life" is actually glossed better by this poem than the earlier one:

> A Word dropped careless on a Page
> May stimulate an eye
> When folded in perpetual seam
> The Wrinkled Maker lie
>
> Infection in the sentence breeds
> We may inhale Despair
> At distances of Centuries
> From the Malaria — (P1261)

The life-gun does shoot language carelessly in "My Life had stood" by being directed by a force external to the self, and the result is a spiritual malaria replete with "Yellow Eye." In all, then, if we want to read the poem as about poetic inspiration — and it is also possible to consider the speaker as the poet and the owner as the muse in terms of an inspiriting idea — the process goes wrong and ugly here and becomes a mere simulacrum of authentic inspiration, illusory just as the life-gun's inspiriting by the owner/master is shown to be delusive in the overt development of the analogy.

And yet I have not gone on at such length merely to argue that, whatever identities we assign to gun and owner, the meaning is identical. The pattern of misused and borrowed power prevails, but there are any number of additional implications that arise as we assign differently these two identities. As the pattern absorbs each, it becomes richer with every additional hue; and there certainly are different parts of the poem that gain or lose emphases as one sees them via one subject or another. In fact, subjects finally help talk here as long as they remain plural. The intricate play among them adds to the poem's extraordinary life. And that is what I meant in saying that finally I see that this is also a poem which, if only by negation, is about why Dickinson constructs meaning as she does. Her speaker here is a monomaniac, devoted to the point of madness to a single something, whatever we decide that something is. And the result is disastrous. She lives forever only in not being truly alive at all. Dickinson, eschewing single meanings, weaving and spiraling and circling rather than pointing, compares her works to the wild and wavery Northern Lights in "Of Bronze and Blaze," concluding that

> My Splendors, are Menagerie —
> But their Competeless Show
> Will entertain the Centuries
> When I, am long ago,
> An Island in dishonored Grass —
> Whom none but Beetles — know. (P290)

Better a surrounding menagerie than a pointing gun, a consciousness than a cause. Then not we but what we make gains not the gun's not-death which is also not-life but instead Life Eternal and Everlasting, competeless, outside of power competitions and their attendant aggressions, joking at mortality. In "My Life had stood — a Loaded Gun —," Dickinson surrounds her speaker with meanings that not only betray that speaker's terrible error but allow the poem itself to contradict and cure it.

DON'T PRY MEANS you mustn't look for Dickinson's life in the poems. (You also shouldn't look for Dickinson's life in the life, but that is a different matter.) It is tempting to do so because the details of Dickinson's life are tantalizingly unclear, the mode of her living was extremely distinctive — dressing in white, speaking from hiding, all such tabloid oddities which in fact increasingly seem sane and brave once one understands that Dickinson was wonderfully and terribly unprotected psychologically so that each life occurrence, small to most of us, was easily tremendous to her — and the genre of the lyric is confessional. It won't work, of course, because the poems are not literal. Imagine the frustration my colleague who wanted the speaker and dog of "I started early" to be just a girl and her pet would face in coming upon those many death poems like "I felt a Funeral, in my Brain" (P280) or "I heard a Fly buzz — when I died — " (P465), where the speaker is ostensibly dead and thus rendered impossible. I've tried here to show that Dickinson's poems posit no specific situation apart from the language and which the language then serves merely to convey or even interpret. Instead, the poems define the essence of a whole range of experiences by the development of a versatile analogue, or several. This is not a romantic poetry of experience, where the poem's meanings develop alongside a narrative, as in Wordsworth's autobiographies. Dickinson's speaker does not proclaim, "I was there and this is what happened to me," but says "I was somewhere, or many places, exact location doesn't matter, and this poem will express the meaning of the experiences minus the claptrap of their details — but with made-up details to provide the colors, the flavors to the inner self of such experiences." That is, the poems do not lack a situational matrix, but any mimetic situation is transported to a world of analogical language that exists as a kind of crucible in relation to the world of everyday phenomena, as its definition. Dickinson's literal life will not occur in them.

A different intimacy — in fact, several kinds of intimacy — occurs instead. In fact, it is my sense that readers of Dickinson experience a sense of extraordinary closeness to the writer and then get led to the biographical fallacy by not examining the nature of this feeling carefully enough. She must be telling us about her life, they reason, because it feels so intimate. But the intimacies Dickinson offers are different and more formidable.

The primary intimacy has to do with her strategy of writing itself, for the analogical technique brings us close to a mind at active work, so close that there is a shocking aesthetic immediacy. In small, Dickinson's language calls extraordinary attention to itself in melding words that usually belong to very different realms of discourse. Time becomes space: "Beyond the March and April line — / That magical frontier / Beyond which summer hesitates / Almost too heavenly near" (P1764). Or an emotional condition is described in terms of travel over and back from another frontier, as when Dickinson writes of "The lonesome for they know not What — " as "Eastern Exiles" who "strayed beyond the Amber line" (P262). Place itself is internalized: "Gethsemane — / Is but a Province — in the Being's Centre — " (P553). Synaesthesia abounds, as in the fly's "Blue — uncertain stumbling Buzz" (P465), and causality gets refigured in the things-as-perceived phrase, "The Dust did scoop itself like Hands — / And throw away the Road — " (P824). These confusions of category do not so much claim an identity as announce a perceived resemblance, which in turn implies a perceiver, a presence. In her extreme elliptical qualities, Dickinson illustrates perhaps more strikingly than any other poet what John Lynen has called "the odd self-consciousness which makes the American abnormally aware of his symbolizing" (45).[2] And even her

syntactical and typographical habits contribute to the sense of a mind dynam-
ically at work in the writing of a poem. Dickinson's idiosyncratic capitalizations, for instance, which provide the dignity of abstraction to otherwise concrete words, award importance away from the conventionally capitalized
words of generality. And to a far greater extent, her dashes suggest a poet en
route to an idea within the poem. One of the many functions of the dashes is to
serve as a hinge, with meaning moving forward and back in a poem like a
swinging door. For example, a poem on the capacity of art to transgress the
limits of temporality exemplifies exactly that by its swinging hinge:

> The One who could repeat the Summer day
> Were greater than itself — though He
> Minutest of Mankind should be
>
> And He — could reproduce the Sun —
> At period of going down —
> The Lingering — and the Stain — I mean
>
> When Orient have been outgrown —
> And Occident — become Unknown —
> His Name — remain — (P307)

The One is of course writer or painter (or more largely anyone with a functioning mind) who is greater than nature in being able to picture it, with the
picture remaining after the event it portrays is ended—whether it is a literal
day ending in sunset (which is the primary meaning here) or a life ending in
death or a superseded world for that matter. This mind-enclosing-matter
claim, which in a sense reverses the modesty of mimesis, gets developed in
such a way that the poem itself "swings upon the Hours" (P512) in the final
stanza. There, the first two lines at first serve to expand upon the Sun's "period
of going down," for after sunset, when night falls, both east and west can be
said to be outgrown and unknown. But then of course, when we see that the
last line of the poem cannot be read without the previous two lines attached to
it, the outgrown Orient and the unknown Occident refer not merely to a day
that has ended in sunset but to this world which no longer exists for the now-
dead artist but which the artist continues to exist in ("His Name — remain —"
even postmortem) by virtue of his achievement. The artist can trick time by
commemorating a natural moment, the "Summer day," in a permanent rendering; can trick time again by the fame attaching to this rendering which
provides him with an immortality; and then Dickinson, herself "him" as an
artist, can exemplify this playing with time in the versatile diction of the last
five lines of the poem with their perfect double reference to a day and an entire
life, a sunset and a death and transcendence of death. Or again, in the second

stanza of another poem having to do with fame, since one gets it only by eschewing it,

> So let us gather — every Day —
> The Aggregate of
> Life's Bouquet
> Be Honor and not shame — (P1427)

The first three lines appear to be a sentence and remain so even after the fourth line requires that we place a faint period after the first and read the second and third with it as a different sentence.

My point in all of this is that we experience an idea coming into being, a mimesis of the mind; and that the process, in which the demands upon the reader to cooperate in sense-making are huge, is revelatory of the poet's process and relates any reader to her intensely. More largely, because an analogy is a metaphor-in-the-making, the entire analogical strategy displays her connective process and thus makes a claim not simply for how the world is but for how her mind actively puts it together. We are taken to a mental backstage to watch the play get constructed. Thought to Dickinson, as Eliot said of Donne, was an experience, a corporeal thing and sensed event. "A Thought went up my mind today —" (P701), she begins one poem, and that is where we are, right with the Thought, while the occasion for it, a distraction, is obliterated.

Thus in some of the greatest of her poems a self-correction takes place, a living revision within the very development of an idea. We saw that in the disastrous self-knowledge of the final stanza of "My Life had stood." In "Because I could not stop for Death," mortality is figured as a suitor who takes up the speaker in his carriage, accompanied by the protecting thought of Immortality as a chaperone. The carriage passes the various scenes and ages of life, and then "We passed the Setting Sun —" and, after a significant stanza break, "Or rather — He passed Us —." To pass the setting sun of course is to go beyond death to a heaven of immortality; to be passed by the sun is quite another thing, and the speaker suddenly begins to experience a coldness we can associate with the grave. Henceforth, the poem is far more ambiguous in its trust in immortality; we are left uncertain of whether the surmise that "the Horses' Heads / Were toward Eternity —" (P712) sees those heads as pointing forward to the Immortal or down, to an eternal moldering. But my emphasis here is that Dickinson suddenly, midpoem, has her thought change, pulls in the reins on her faith, and introduces a realistic doubt; and we are right there as this occurs. Or again, in a poem that begins by boasting of the mind's capacity, "The Brain — is wider than the Sky —" and "deeper than the sea" because it can contain phenomenal nature in its ken, absorbing the sea, for instance as "Sponges" can absorb "Buckets," but then the unscheduled reversal occurs:

> The Brain is just the weight of God —
> For Heft them — Pound for Pound —
> And they will differ — if they do —
> As Syllable from Sound. (P632)

At first it seems that the claim is merely being extended to the Emersonian limitlessness where Self is coequal with the All. But in fact there is a crucial difference between sound, which is invisible and weightless and God, and syllable, which is material and thus hefty and our mind. The difference is minute but absolute, the claim is bogus, and human limitation is reasserted. Dickinson celebrates her poetic powers "in Vision — and in Veto!" (P528), and sometimes, as here, her veto power refers not to the ideas of others but to her own cherished hopes as well. Here the poet is learning as she speaks, and we are right with her as it happens.

This intellectual intimacy is not merely intellectual. Dickinson shamelessly hawks the operations of her special logic and even teases our more literal expectations in a poem like "As the Starved Maelstrom" where we might expect the opening word to announce a temporal coincidence (say, as the starved maelstrom laps the navies, the sailors cry out) when in fact it announces an analogical comparison, meaning "just as this, so that." And yet Dickinson is not a *Star Trek* Spock. At each stage of the analogical process in Dickinson's best poems, the persona serves to make the word flesh, to register the consequences of the pattern her own words are evolving. Calling poetry "the Art to stun myself / With Bolts of Melody!" (P505), Dickinson is surpriser and stunned victim of surprise at once, a wounded dialectician. In considering "My Life had stood," we quoted a number of poems and statements in which Dickinson testifies to the power of language, and within her poems she is powerfully affected by her own language as well. While you never know what in particular has made the poet feel this way, there is no doubting an experiential force to the analogies. In fact, another function of the dashes is to connect the written language to a voice, dashes being the most colloquial of marks, and more particularly the voice in pause, even in a hesitation that is always overcome so that the rest of the poem may be written. If " 'tis when / A Value struggle — it exist" (P806), Dickinson's dashes announce a defeated reticence, as if the words are almost, not quite, too harrowing to be spoken, so that the poem is made to struggle for its very existence and its presence becomes a sacrifice for the poet, provided as a trust for the reader.

On one hand, then, Dickinson's emphasis on her logic is a tight-lipped pretense for an intensely subjective, even suffered relation to the word. Every time Dickinson defines and vivifies a word by implying that a felt experience informs the definition—whether " 'Hope' is the thing with feathers" (P254) or "Hope is a subtle Glutton —" (P1547)—this very naming teases a dictionary definition by insisting on the poet's livid living-out of the word. In that sense, while we never learn what happened to Dickinson to cause this or that felt thought, she is relentlessly self-exposing in describing "internal difference / Where the meanings are," that is, how it feels; and that is a second kind of intimacy. But at the same time, she can afford this disclosure because the word's abstract status also makes a claim for the poet's experience as typical, normative, shared. The self is all selves in phrases like "The Brain — is wider than the Sky —" (P632) or "The Mind lives on the Heart" (P1355), even as that latter phrase makes the very point that all thought is emotionally charged. Dickinson employs a plural "we" 542 times in nearly 300 different poems, and it usually means all of us as human beings—and in fact "us" occurs over 200 times as well. This kind of universalizing, which can drive sociological readers to a rage, is yet not at all an aristocratic ignoring of class but rather a Whitman-like notion of the democratic commonality of feelings. In fact, when there is an excluded "they" in the poems, it always refers to those who themselves inflict class inferiority on others, as with the "Brittle" lady who "dealt her pretty words like Blades," or to agents of repression as in "They shut me up in Prose — / As when a little Girl / They put me in the Closet — / Because they liked me still" (P613). Otherwise, the explicit and implicit plurals of her poetry tend to refer to intense emotional states that are also claims upon the nature of being, and this is a third kind of intimacy the poems provide. Dickinson's reader, freed from a particular subject to bring any number of her or his experiences that fit the poem's pattern to participate in the poem's meaning, experiences an intimacy without egotism, forced to perceive that others, in their own, perhaps ostensibly very different experience, have been here too. A former and very fine student who has become a psychiatrist recently wrote to me asking whether I felt Dickinson had suffered sexual abuse as a child. She based her suspicion on such poems as

> There is a pain — so utter —
> It swallows substance up —
> Then covers the Abyss with Trance —
> So memory can step
> Around — across — upon it —
> As one within a Swoon —
> Goes safely — where an open eye —
> Would drop Him — Bone by Bone (P599)

Freud of course theorizes that the sudden release of repressed materials could cause death, and this poem describes the automatic protections the self creates to guard against thinking the unthinkable. The trance — expressed in "After great pain, a formal feeling comes — " as a kind of imitation of control and rationality in which "The Feet, mechanical, go round" while "the stiff Heart" loses any sense of time and sharp memory to question "was it He, that bore / And Yesterday, or Centuries before?" (P341) — enforces forgetfulness from a pain too frightening to recall and a formality that is actually the stupor of a frozen scream. And just as Freud theorizes, the repressed thought thus retains its original force, making the passage of time, centuries or a day, meaningless. The psychiatrist, noting that her patients often express a startled sense of recognition when she shows them such poems, is of course forgivably guilty of the pointing we warned against. There are any number of kinds of pain that can create such repression, and these poems say precisely nothing about Dickinson's unique experience. But they do afford an extraordinary comfort precisely because different people can bring their trouble to them. The poems in this sense are an autobiography not of Dickinson but of the reader. And yet finally, if the reader gets into the community these poems create, that reader is re-created beyond the limits of one's personal experience, the bounds of ego.

But there is a final and far less comforting intimacy the poems provide as well, one that in fact questions the existence of the united ego. Ego identity is so deep a fiction that it seems no fiction at all in the West, where in fact thinking itself assumes an "I," as the Cartesian cogito makes plain. Yet Dickinson's generation of Americans finds ego identity no more than the object of a shaky faith. Thoreau describes himself to Harrison Blake as "A mere collection of atoms" and as a "spiritual football" (302). Whitman's all-absorbent Walt is a happily porous questioner of boundaries; Melville's protean Ishmael is a half-comic version of that; Melville's Confidence Man, who is either one person of several parts or several people too interchangeable for stable identity to occur, is a disaster to all ontologies. Emerson praises a different instability in "Circles," proclaiming "There are no fixtures to consciousness," adding "People wish to be settled; only in so far as they are unsettled is there any hope for them" (2: 189). But in his gloomy alternative phase, in "Experience," people "seem alive," yet are merely repetitive temperaments, dead allegories. "Let us treat the men and women well," he murmurs laconically, "treat them as if they are real; perhaps they are" (3: 31, 35). Nihilistic, neutral, or celebratory, Dickinson's contemporaries are busy challenging commonplace selfhood.

Never nihilistic, Dickinson anatomizes, refiguring the internal self as plural. "One need not be a Chamber — to be Haunted — / One need not be a House — " begins a poem in which "The Brain has Corridors — surpassing /

Material Place —." There is no Gothic danger so severe as "Unarmed, one's
a'self encounter — / In lonesome Place." In this poem, even the "Assassin hid
in our Apartment" is deemed "Horror's least" in comparison to "Ourself
behind ourself, concealed — " (P670). This concealed self is often a "volcano"
upon which grows disguising "Grass," making for "A meditative spot" while,
meanwhile, "How red the Fire rocks below — / How insecure the sod"
(P1677). This interiority, where the internal self becomes a battleground of
the need for sanity and the urge toward the wild, is not in itself a form of
intimacy, though it does enforce upon the reader the requirement not to
reduce oneself to something single in figuring a relation to these poems. But
more importantly, when Dickinson speaks in this dichotomizing fashion,
when for instance she hypothesizes "the Art to stun myself — / With Bolts of
Melody!" she is speaking to us from the reactive part of the self. That is, she is
speaking from the part of herself, more sane and a little worried, that is itself a
reader. We see the poet as reader in this fine four-line lyric:

> Presentiment — is that long Shadow — on the Lawn —
> Indicative that Suns go down —
> The Notice to the startled Grass
> That Darkness — is about to pass (P764)

Presentiment is the active part of the self here, anticipating an apparently
dread event. But of course it is reactive, for the event that the presentiment
foresees is never mentioned. Yet there is a third part of the self, more reactive
than presentiment, upon which presentiment records itself, and this is "the
Lawn," the "startled Grass" of that aspect of consciousness that receives the
warning. An internal function, presentiment, is treated as if it is an external
property in relation to an aspect of self still more immediately internal, the
startled nerve endings. And while such dense innerness is not a constant of all
the poems, in most the speaker is a part of the self affected by another, more
active part of the self which is affected by whatever externalities go unmen-
tioned. In that sense, Dickinson is a readerly writer, and this draws her closest
to us, for she makes us readers who almost need to write in order to complete
her elliptical meanings. Who we become with Dickinson is my final issue.

But before we engage it, a last word on Dickinsonian disclosure: I am
arguing here that we need to relocate our sense of what it means to know a
writer, even what it means to gain insight into the life. Cristanne Miller makes
the very good point that, even in her letters, Dickinson does not represent
herself fully and accurately. The letters, to varying degrees, are figured writing, works of art. Miller quotes Austin, Dickinson's brother, as saying, "Emily
definitely posed in those letters," and she herself notes that "Dickinson tells
even her closest epistolary friends remarkably little about the events of her

life" (*Grammar* 13).[3] And yet any reader of them will experience startling warmth, a sense of strong emotional presence. And Virginia Jackson, arguing against the going notion of the lyric as a private and overheard utterance to find in Dickinson's work a more transactive relation to the addressee, sees Dickinson defining the letters as more personal even than actual presence can be, in Jackson's words "more intimate than the whisper — more intimate, that is, than the metaphor of a voice, a speaking presence, would allow." She cites a letter to Susan Gilbert in which Dickinson describes her solitude of writing as "the old *king feeling*," royal in its autonomous resistance of trivial interruption, allowing for "this Sweet Sabbath of ours." The letter, Jackson argues, redefines a solitude "in which I am not alone, but 'alone with . . .'" (82, 83). I should say that I find the life, the little I can know of it, brave and unique, not crippled; but my point here is that Dickinson in her poems as in the friendships in her life, transacted more by letter than by actual presence, offers a different intimacy, a different knowing of her, to which we must adjust. When we do, we find that the absences provide more than they prevent.

Don't settle for one truth. Whoever we are to become with Dickinson, it won't be as a complaisant homesteader supine upon a field of settled belief. I have been arguing implicitly that to pry into the biographical details of Dickinson's life is not only futile but insufficiently ambitious. The Dickinson that matters most is in the poems that are at least partway open, not the life which is forever closed. But then it is certainly reasonable to ask: well, what did she believe? How do the poems tell us to live? And yet as we move from individual poems to try to make sense of them as a total body of work, again the most natural and usual questions prove to be disastrously misshapen because this is a poet who will not stop thinking. One final meaning of the dash seems to be its implication that any thought is liable "to be continued." To expect settled truth from Dickinson is to wish for a contradiction in terms. Even reviewing quickly where we already have been, we find a Dickinson delighting every bit as much as Whitman in contradiction. The same poet who could warn against the dangers of borrowed power in "My Life had stood" also can write,

> 'Twas my one Glory —
> Let it be
> Remembered
> I was owned of Thee — (P1028)

Again, neither poem is a final word, because in Dickinson there are no final words. "Immortality contented / Were Anomaly" (P1036), and the same holds true for Thought.

Thus, for instance, in one whole set of poems, Dickinson posits a self which is God-like, powerful, unlimited, her own version of a Walt. Here common-place objects and acts blaze into spiritual significance, and what she memorably called "transport" is a matter of will: "Paradise is of the option," she proclaims in one letter (L319), and in another, "Eden, always eligible, is peculiarly so this noon" (L391). One poem begins, "Forever — is composed of Nows —" (P624), and another philosophizes, "Not 'Revelation' — 'tis — that waits, / But our unfurnished eyes —" (P685). But elsewhere Dickinson will argue with equal vehemence for "the Thief ingredient," by which view of things paradise is given only to be revoked.

> Had I not seen the Sun
> I could have borne the shade
> But Light a newer Wilderness
> My wilderness has made — (P1233)

If paradise is available for the right asking in every instant, it lasts only for an instant as well, and its departure makes a newly intolerable gloom of absence. If it is only "our unfurnished eyes" that prevent constant revelation, well, what prevents us then is nothing less than the limits of being human:

> Perception of an object costs
> Precise the Object's loss —
> Perception in itself a Gain
> Replying to its Price —
> The Object Absolute — is nought —
> Perception sets it fair
> And then upbraids a Perfectness —
> That situates so far — (P1071)

In this Kantian poem, absolute reality, the capitalized Object, is never grasped by human perception. Perception, with its internal capacities and limits, reduces the Object to an object, though without such loss in the translation we would perceive nothing at all — the Object Absolute, beyond our bounds, "is nought," and we can have any experience of it only by the diminution our unfurnished eyes provide — and provide with just enough self-knowledge to allow us to complain of how little we comprehend of that absolute reality situated so far beyond our eyes' capacity to see and our capacity for experience. In fact, then, this is not really in contradiction to the poem that sees revelation as available but for the inadequacy of our eyes, and yet the differing emphases create what is as much as a contradiction.

These very different notions of what the self can do and what the world allows simply coexist in a creative tension. In Dickinson's more Emersonian moments, there is a God within us as well as abroad, hidden but explosively present in nature and always threatening within us to overrun the grooves of

sense. In her more skeptical, someway New England moments of acknowledged limitation, God is unavailable and possibly ultimately absent, a "power"
behind "the Cloud / If any Power behind it, be" (P293). And in this set of
poems, the protagonist need fear not an involuntary transport or the mind's
overflowing abundance, so destructive of common selfhood, but rather the
poverty of mortal experience and the mind's frustrating limits. Sometimes in
Dickinson life will provide Paradise if we just dare, as Reverend Ike used to say,
to be great; sometimes in Dickinson life prevents us everywhere, dangling
transcendence beyond our reach as a torture.

Not only are these senses competing, but contradictions within each world
view abound. In that more transcendental view, for instance, in one poem we
are told to grab for life's lightning ("But I would not exchange the Bolt / For
all the rest of Life — "), this "Electricity" of being that is so much more than
mere "Oxygen" (P1581). Yet elsewhere that is not even a choice. "The Lightning playeth — all the while — " but "when He singeth," then "we approach
Him — stern — / With Insulators — and a Glove — " (P630). Again, in one
poem she proudly proclaims, "I lived on Dread," terming "Other Impetus" as
"numb and Vitalless" (P770), and yet we also have reviewed those poems like
"After great pain, a formal feeling comes — " where a numbing repression is
automatic. And in still another poem, Dickinson confesses, she knows no
"man so bold" that "he dare in lonely Place / That awful stranger Consciousness / Deliberately face — " (P1323). Sometimes, then, Dickinson's persona is
all ready for revelation, where as elsewhere Dickinson evinces a healthy respect for survival, at whatever cost to thrill. And elsewhere still, as in her
encounter with the sea in "I started Early — Took my Dog —," she will give
each side its due.

Likewise, in those poems of limitation, at times she "upbraids a Perfectness
/ That situates so far"; and elsewhere she worries that though, with some false
bravado, "I know that He exists / Somewhere — in Silence —," and that it is
just preparation for a "fond Ambush," what if "the play / Prove piercing
earnest —," making God's nonappearance as final as the piercing of the eyes of
Oedipus, so that "the glee glaze / In Death's — stiff — stare — " (P338)? Yet at
other times she takes it as a matter of faith that eventually, even if postmortem,
her limits will be lifted and her quest completed: "Tho' I get home — how late
— how late / So I get home — 'twill compensate —" (P207). In still other
poems, we give thanks for the very incompleteness of the quest since "Immortality contented / Were Anomaly" (P1036). Dickinson thus praises "The service without Hope — " as "tenderest" precisely because it demands a "Dili-
gence" that "knows not an Until — " (P779) and writes the many "harebell"
poems in which privation is requisite for the high value of desire.

But the idea is that you cannot define Dickinson by what she believes but by what she keeps caring about, turning it this way and that. Roland Hagen-büchle rightly emphasizes Dickinson's key practice of "holding alternatives in dialectical tension" with a special, perhaps specially American experimental zest ("Covenant" 311). If a value must struggle to exist, she makes all valued thoughts struggle one against the other. And yet the result is something more than a blankness. The contradictions come together in complex understandings — we do sometimes get to a paradise, but as soon as we are there we find "a further,"

> As if the Sea should part
> And show a further Sea —
> And that — a further — and the Three
> But a presumption be —
>
> Of Periods of Seas —

themselves "the Verge of Seas to be" and "Eternity — is Those" (P695). We really do not want a final contentment, then, though we can hate the frustrations, because traveling is best. Our limits, which we hate, still enable the quest: "Desire's perfect goal" is by definition "Within its reach, though yet ungrasped" (P1430), and "Utmost is relative" (P1291). Or again, though repression is sometimes automatic and though Dickinson has a very healthy respect for the sane and commonplace self if only because she sees it as ever vulnerable to wreckage, nonetheless because "A *Wounded* Deer — leaps highest —" (P165) and since "Power is only Pain," best to indulge the dangerous authentic feeling: "If your Nerve, deny you — / Go above your Nerve —" (P292). In her Emersonian view, "Peril as a Possession / 'Tis Good to bear" (P1678); in her quasi-Puritan sense of limitation, "Faith is Doubt" (L912); and in both, a dynamism fired by dread is a predominating goal. The contradictions, not coalescing, yet resolve into a large and difficult sense or, though contradicted in some places, a value will struggle not only to exist but to predominate.

And yet the struggle is more valuable. The above paragraph, which names the victors in a few of Dickinson's value struggles, has the hollowness of noting the final score without experiencing the drama of the game. "The soul should always stand ajar" is something of a motto for Dickinson's endless quest, where any thought is open to revision or extension, and it needs to become her reader's motto as well. This is what I mean about prisming Dickinson. "Beauty — be not caused — It Is —" and, just as it is not caused, it is not to be captured, fixed: "Chase it, and it ceases — / Chase it not, and it abides —" (P516). So too for the beauty Dickinson provides. You will let go, spreading your fingers to gather her plural paradises. You will forswear selfish ownership to gain far greater bounty as a medium. Prisming, you will allow her her bronzes and blazes, all her colors:

> Pursuing you in your transitions,
> In other Motes —
> Of other Myths
> Your requisition be.
> The Prism never held the Hues,
> It only heard them play — (P1602)

NOTES

1. Parts of this essay recapitulate ideas from my *Emily Dickinson's Poetry*, cited here, and from my recent article, "Nobody's Business: Dickinson's Dissolving Audience" in *Emily Dickinson and Audience*. But most of this essay is new or decisively altered, and the structure of ideas is entirely new.

2. The best, most comprehensive study of the characteristics and consequences of Dickinson's elliptical language is provided by Miller in *Grammar*.

3. The quote from Austin is recorded first by Richard B. Sewall in his magisterial *Life* (2: 538).

FURTHER READING

McGann, Jerome J. *The Textual Condition*. Princeton: Princeton University Press, 1991.

GUDRUN GRABHER

Dickinson's Lyrical Self

Adventure most unto itself
The Soul condemned to be —
Attended by a single Hound
It's own identity. (P822)

$\mathcal{U}$ntil quite recently the question about the self in literature was answered rather unsystematically although certainly not unanimously. If addressed seriously, the issue has to be raised both on a metalevel and on an intrinsic level. In the postmodern age it has become a questionable task to probe into the significance and coherence of a "self" since the very term seems to have been emptied of meaning, a view which I cannot completely share.

I would argue that the self in Dickinson's poetry is no longer a romantic self that merely records its existence and experience but the modern self that creates a self enlarging and expanding both his/her own as well as the reader's experience and existence. I would therefore agree with Terence Diggory, who argues that the "view that personality is *created* distinguishes the tradition of the self from its origin in the romantic theory of artistic self-expression" (5). In his study of the "Discovery and Creation of Self in Modern Literature" Enrico Garzilli explores "the relationship of the consciousness of an individual to self, the labyrinthic patterns within and outside the self, and finally creativity and the self" (144). This describes exactly the field of self-exploration in Dickinson. The search for identity is forever unfinished; self-definition is always as yet impossible. Self-exploration turns into self-invention. "Perhaps the most significant desideratum of an identity quest is that which comes about through the possibilities that creativity reveals. Creativity meaningfully links together the various areas of self-exploration" (Garzilli 144). Paul Jay, who in his book *Being in the Text* examines the variety of self-reflexive works from the romantic to the modern period, argues along the same lines by proposing that literary self-representation is an act of self-transformation. The self created in the literary work is different from the actual psychological self (cf. Jay 45). If for Donald Thackrey Emily Dickinson is a "divine magician" in her perfection and creation of her world in poetry, she is even more magically divine in inventing and creating the self (*Approach* 62).

MANY CRITICS HOLD the view that Dickinson's self is largely autobiographical. Especially in regard to her love poems they have sought to link those elements to her personal romance. Barbara Mossberg, in her investigation of the "Anti-autobiographies" of Dickinson and Stein, attributes Dickinson's intimacy and immediacy to the autobiographical format of her writing ("Double" 239). However, Mossberg argues, this self chooses not only not to tell us everything but even to deceive us. Mossberg identifies the poet's deceit as the woman poet's necessity to create a self which seemingly conforms to tradition and at the same time invents itself according to its own ideas. The woman's trickiness is her survival mechanism. It is above all her faculties of creativity, activity, independence, and reason that woman is forced to conceal in a patriarchal society (140).

In her essay " 'A Privilege So Awful': The Poetry of Emily Dickinson" Suzanne Juhasz argued that "to command her own self is . . . the necessary condition for Dickinson to be a poet" (*Naked Forms* 20). Juhasz, however, now repudiates most of her readings in that early book and no longer argues that Dickinson's poems are autobiographical. Dickinson indulges in exercising both her forces of self-annihilation and her power of self-control. By confronting her own death she manages to dissolve her self in the pure abstractness of timelessness. Yet on the other hand she exposes her self in the matrix of her temporal existence that is marked by pain and suffering.

I will deal with the lyrical self in Dickinson's poetry along the lines of an argumentative analysis. In order to make that argument clear and coherent, I will work the various interpretations of the self in Dickinson scholarship into three major points. An introductory investigation of the "self" in literary theory will provide the framework. My investigation of the lyrical self in Emily Dickinson will therefore deal with the following three aspects:

1. Traditional (prepostmodernist) theories of the lyrical self in Dickinson's poetry on a metalevel: this involves questions about the assumed dichotomy between the lyrical and the biographical self, the constitution of a poetic world by a transcendental self, the representative self, an emphasis on the "unitary self"; the participation of the reader's self in the lyrical self; "negative identity" (Hagenbüchle); self-exploration, self-discovery, self-disdain, self-reliance; the quest for the "essential, authentic self," the finite versus the infinite self, the transcendent self.

2. Identifications of the self within the poetry: various personae, such as the self as woman, child, good/bad little girl, madwoman, performing (and ridiculing) actress, the self in love, and the question of sexual identity.
3. The postmodern dissolution of the self: the discontinuous or decentered self (Dickie), the polyvocal self (Crumbley), the split self, the dialogical self.

Investigations of the self, in one form or another and with more or less emphasis, pervade almost all Dickinson studies. Until the very concept of the "self" started to be an issue in literature and literary theory (initiated by the modernists and intensified by the postmodernists), the self was unquestioningly understood to be a unique identity. This understanding of the self has been manifest in Dickinson scholarship until only recently (the past decade). Dickinson herself, out of historical necessity, shared this traditional understanding of the self. When in a letter to Higginson Dickinson writes, "There is always one thing to be grateful for — that one is one's self & not somebody else" (quoted in the note to L405, Jan. 1874), she conceives of her self as uniquely her own, separable and distinguishable from anyone else's. However, in regard to her poetry, she also takes a clear stand on separating her "self" as Dickinson from the "self" she aesthetically creates: "When I state myself, as the Representative of the Verse — it does not mean — me — but a supposed person" (L268 to Higginson, July 1862). In his book *Emily Dickinson's Poetry: Stairway of Surprise* (1960) Charles Anderson takes precisely this quote as a warning against the critic's overemphasis on the autobiographical issue (168). Moreover, he argues that, since Dickinson found the natural world impenetrable, she sought to discover meaning in the map of her self. Her inner world thus becomes for her the major field of exploration (166). Suzanne Juhasz has dedicated a book-length study to the exploration of the "undiscovered continent," the mind in Dickinson's poetry (*The Undiscovered Continent: Emily Dickinson and the Space of the Mind*). Already in his article of 1959 on "The Conscious Self in Emily Dickinson's Poetry" Anderson argues that her main purpose in writing poetry is "to identify and define the Self" (290). It is, according to Anderson, the existential self that she explores, the self being the only reality for the poet. By using soul, mind, and consciousness interchangeably she explores the "self-behind-the-self," acknowledging that the self can never be fully comprehended. Even more impossible is it for her to penetrate another self (303). The self as "representative wo/man" in Dickinson's poetry has been an issue of investigation from the very beginning to the present. Dickinson scholars have found themselves in the dilemma between reading her lyric self as the representative self in an Emersonian way and reading her idiosyncratic handling of the self as a sign of rejecting the idea of representation as such. On the other hand, the issue of "representation" also raises the question of how the reader participates in the lyrical self.

In order to trace the three points made above I will start out with an inquiry into Dickinson's metaphysical concept of the self. I will then use my own book to introduce my concept of the self as "transcendental I" but will eventually question, though not ultimately deny, its thesis in view of the postmodern denial of the very concept of the self. In *Emily Dickinson: Das transzendentale Ich* (1981) I defined the lyrical self as a transcendental one, adopting Kant's explanation of transcendental as "the condition of the possibility to (know)." For the self to "make" sense (a phrase that in itself characterizes postmodernism, so Ihab Hassan argues) it takes, according to Kant, both the experience of an outside world and the a priori forms of perception and cognition of the human subject. This transcendental self may well be identified as a "supposed person," yet first of all only in a most general, universal sense since it is more of a modus operandi than a concrete person. However, since it is a self created by Dickinson it is also affected by her in its very identity. Here I would like to argue that Dickinson herself got trapped in the false idea that she could actually separate her real self completely from the aesthetic self created by her. I agree with Juhasz, Miller, and Smith that "poetry functions [also] as self-expression" (3). This, of course, is not identical with an encouragement to read her poems autobiographically.

The next step will then be to move from the transcendental self as the constituent of the poetic world, created by the real self of Dickinson, to the various possibilities of identifying this self within the poems. In this context it will be of importance to show how and for what purposes this self may be and has been identified in the concrete sense. What masks does the self take on; what roles does it "play"; how does the "concretization" of the self vary through circumstance, situation, society, sex, and gender. And it will be of equal importance to demonstrate how the lyrical self makes the "self" an object of inquiry in the poems. Self-exploration ("Soto! Explore thyself") is an essential theme in Dickinson. The quest for the authentic self is an existential and ontological issue (emphasized, e.g., by Kher). It manifests itself as the "seraphic self," the invisible behind the visible self, in distinction from and communication with other selves and, above all, God. The very concept of the authentic self is, however, only hypothetically constructed and needs, if at all possible, further identification. The "transcendent self" (Waggoner, "Transcendent") is the one in touch with questions about death and immortality; it is the hypothetically infinite self imagined beyond yet represented by the finite self (by means of extrapolation in the death-poems where Dickinson paradoxically identifies the self with the lack of that which ontologically characterizes the self—consciousness and the awareness of its existence in time; this is what "distinguishes the living from the dead" [Sherwood]). Self-reliance not only presupposes a sense of self in contrast to others but implies a sense of one's self as the center of the universe.

THAT THE "I" is at the very center of most of Dickinson's poetry was re-marked, among others, by Archibald MacLeish, who observed that more than 150 poems begin with the word "I," "the talker's word" (MacLeish 150).

> Self is the matrix of creation; it refers to the sense of being that envelopes man's whole existence. It is the center to which each life converges (680), the sea toward which every river runs (162). It is the ultimate of wheels (633), which governs man's destiny and forward movement. It subsumes all the dimensions of possibility (1208). "Without this — there is nought" (655): it is the source of the human imagination which gives order and form to man's chaotic perceptions; it is the secret of man's freedom. It intensifies man's experience of love and gener-ates spiritual strength to meet the challenge of death. It communicates through its essential silence; at times it seems still, but stillness is volcanic (175). It is the presence which asserts itself more by being invisible. Dickinson's poetry fully dramatizes the ontological necessity of realizing this "seraphic self" (1465), and proposes this "as a continuous adventure and a perpetual crisis," to use Glauco Cambon's expression. (Kher 229–30)[1]

The realization of the self or identity is for Kher an endless process. Dick-inson plunges into the abyss of the self, where pain, darkness, loneliness, and suffering open up the dimensions of terror and silence where the self both loses and finds itself. Here Kher is totally in keeping with Hagenbüchle, as we will see later on, when he argues:

> She shows perfect awareness of the paradox that the realization of the essential self demands the negation of self, and that the achievement of identity costs man "Precisely an existence" (1725) because "All — is the price of All" (772). Also in her aesthetics of the "I-thou" relationship, Dickinson lays stress on the creative ability to lose one's self in order to find one's self; it is only by losing one's narrow or egocentric self that one can discover the larger self. (Kher 230)

The self's search for identity is a painful task, aimed at finally grasping the "experience of existence" (Kher 233). Coping with this pain, the self is re-warded with spiritual awareness, "spiritual ripeness or transcendence over the limitations of the empirical ego, or the created self" (235). The most paradoxi-cal aspect of this quest is that it is never meant to come to an end: "One deserves identity only by constantly seeking it" (237). Kher further distin-guishes between what he calls the empirical or egocentric self as opposed to the authentic or "fundamental" self. The egocentric self needs to be over-come: "To venture upon the ontological problem of identity is to come to terms with the negation of egocentric self, to bear utter loneliness or spiritual isolation, and to undergo the experience of sacrifice and renunciation of all that one normally prizes in life" (237). Only by thrusting into one's innermost self can the human being determine his/her inner quality. The terror, the lonesomeness, and the darkness of this interior self are transformed by Dickinson into the translucence of creativity since "she associates identity or the self with the act of creation" (243). "In her quest for identity, she transmutes the dust of existence and achieves through it a firelike clarity of perception. Once she perceives the self, Dickinson consecrates herself to the vision. In this posture, she experiences the sense of power and spiritual elation" (244). Kher refuses to equate the self in Dickinson's poetry with Emerson's transcendent self or Over-Soul. Rather, he argues that "in Dickinson's poetry the self is proposed as an artistic principle" and its awareness "dominates the very creative act" (249). The creative act also involves the confirmation of the other, through which, again, the self is confirmed. Ultimately, however, the authentic self is self-sufficient. "The authentic self generates the sense of self-sufficiency within one's own being, which is reflected through one's individuality. This determines the spiritual health of the existing being" (262). Finally, Kher concludes, "the self is the all" (268).

In order for the quest for the authentic self to be fulfilled, the self must be humble. When Roy Harvey Pearce argues that Emily Dickinson's major concern is with herself at the very center of her world, it is not her egocentrism that he intends to underline but rather her "humble, tragic, pathetic, even humorous realization of limitations" (175). It is from this sense of limitations that Dickinson's self derives its strength. For Dickinson, as opposed to Emerson and Whitman, there is never — according to Pearce — the dialectic compulsion to be herself in spite of the world and yet somehow also in terms of the world (174). It is out of her consciousness of limitations that Dickinson emerges triumphant.

The self in search of its identity is the central theme of Roland Hagenbüchle's *Emily Dickinson: Wagnis der Selbstbegegnung*. He argues that the lyrical self in general not only perceives the world but constantly reflects on itself in doing so. In Dickinson, this "Quest Romance" is the main goal. Self-encounter (*Selbstbegegnung*), self-transcendence, and interior monologue are thus often combined in her poetry. But it is also in her encounter with the "You" — be it erotic, mythic, or mystic — that Dickinson looks for and constitutes her identity, as temporarily as it might be. Hagenbüchle distinguishes between poems in which the lyrical self is explicitly differentiated from the You and others in which the identification of self and You is more central. But in any case, the You is viewed as essentially constitutive for the self. Ultimately, however, it is the absolute identity of God that guarantees, if at all, the identity of the finite self (241). Thus the I–You relationship is the epistemological basis for the self's identity.

Names have always served as the label of identity. In Dickinson's poems names as well as their absence are markers of identity found, given, or missed ("He found my Being," "I'm Nobody"). A new name implies both a new identity and the loss of the old one. According to Hagenbüchle, the lyrical self in Dickinson is mainly in search of the ultimate meaning of life. Through her encounter with death the lyrical self gets in touch with the infinite and eternal and thus reaches a new dimension of meaning. The self in Dickinson is, of course, also in search of her identity as woman ("I'm wife," "Title divine — is mine"). This quest for her female identity has often been connected to Dickinson's biographical background (e.g., Anderson, *Stairway*). The poems in which the self denies herself as woman are often characterized by the paradox of simultaneous self-discovery and self-loss. Dickinson retreats into what Hagenbüchle, borrowing from Keats, calls "negative identity." Her withdrawal from a patriarchically dominated society was her silent revolt against social, religious, and literary conventions. Self-reliance, as Emerson had noted, is made impossible by a society that lives by rigid convention. This negative identity is preferably expressed metaphorically by Dickinson as the white existence. In poem 271, "A solemn thing — it was — I said — / A woman — white — to be — " is interpreted by Hagenbüchle as Dickinson's choice to leave her self totally undetermined as a reflection of the unknowable mythical You. The white existence may, on the other hand, also be seen as a renunciation of life. This goes hand in hand with Dickinson's definition of life as "life-in-death." Self-negating imperatives, as Hagenbüchle points out, indicate her will to negative identity (*Wagnis* 498). John Cody, however, sees in Dickinson's self-denial a psychotic element rather than a sign of metaphysical strength (255 ff.). Withdrawal from society is for Dickinson a necessary prerequisite for the self-encounter of the human being. Negative identity is a logical consequence ("The Soul selects her own Society").

Dickinson's rejection of society has also been put into a biographical context, for example by Anderson and Ruth F. McNaughton. Furthermore, the color white has been investigated as connoting biblical and mystical stories. In the more recent context of feminist criticism it also has to be interpreted in the sense of woman as nonidentity. Joanne Dobson, for example, in the chapter " 'Are there Any Lives of Women?': Conventions of the Female Self in Women's Writing" in *Dickinson and the Strategies of Reticence* (1989), refers to the image of the "Invisible Lady" as coined by Thomas Wentworth Higginson in *Women and the Alphabet* (1881). Higginson, whom Dobson calls Dickinson's "chosen 'preceptor' " and a feminist (56), notes that woman's voice was present but her person invisible. According to Dobson, the decorum of "invisibility" had the effect of barring female subjectivity from the public sphere. Because their unique female presence had to remain invisible, women writers had to turn to specific images in order to make themselves heard while denying their presence as a female subject. The image of the little girl, to which Dickinson frequently turned, was one of the images most popular with women writers. The voice made audible and the person invisible are most clearly expressed in Dickinson's "Nobody" poem. Dobson further argues that Dickinson chose to make use of conventional figures with which to identify — the little girl or wife/ bride image preferably — in order to distort that kind of self-representation and display her suspicion of those modes of being. The use of the little-girl persona served women in two disparate ways: it allowed them to show feminine obedience and perfection but also to express female anger and rebellion (63 f.). However, Dobson points out that Dickinson's good/bad little-girl persona shows no correlation with the little-girl convention of her contemporaries: "The most striking fact about Dickinson's good/bad little girl is that she lacks one essential feature of each aspect of the conventional child: she is neither redemptive nor is she redeemed. Pathetic, sullen, and lost she continues in a state of misery" (68). The wife image and the woman-as-corpse image likewise signified for women writers the loss of consciousness, silence, the ultimate invisibility. In the poem "I'm 'wife' — I've finished that —," for example, the self is transformed through marriage yet also made ultimately invisible. Although Dickinson chose insignificance as one mode of self-representation, she was fully conscious of her strength and power. Probing into the conventional modes of being prescribed for women she unmasked them as inadequate (Dobson 77).

At the same time, however, the color white evokes a plurality of meanings hidden behind the ungraspable whiteness. Hagenbüchle's "negative identity" would then be an appropriate label also in the sense of implying a multiple identity that does not show itself but rather hides behind the masks of whiteness. Because of the plurality that is suggested by the color white in that it represents all colors, this identity again is not to be fixed onto one point. Hagenbüchle quotes Clark Griffith, to whom the color white signifies the extent "to which she [Dickinson] could think of her life as a retreat from the mundane" (Griffith 220). White representing all colors as well as the absence of color is, of course, also reminiscent of Melville's *Moby Dick*. Hyatt H. Waggoner, in his essay "Emily Dickinson: The Transcendent Self," puts Dickinson in the tradition of Melvillean whiteness: "She herself in the end chose to wear only white, a color that contained as many ambiguities for her as it had for Melville in his explication of 'The Whiteness of the White Whale' " (298).

It is characteristic of Dickinson to avoid fixing a meaning, especially fixing the self as a static identity. The quest itself is important rather than the act of finding. It is within the framework of the *absence présente* that the search takes place, always leaving room for the unknown as the prerequisite for the human being to fully realize him/herself. It is privation that sets the soul going, that starts philosophical thought, that makes the quest fundamental. Since the self is never in search of a definite identity, the quest itself is to be understood as a constant act of self-transcendence. The poetic quest thus demands of the self that it constantly transform itself. According to Hagenbüchle, this does not contradict the self's search for a center as Dickinson states in the poem "Each Life Converges to some Centre —." The striving for the center is there; the goal, however, remains forever unattainable. Hagenbüchle also notes that Dickinson's poems hardly ever deal with the social aspects of the human being. Rather, her poems try to capture the anthropological universality that is shared by all human beings. Direct self-encounter would be self-destructive. Dickinson therefore creates protective means in her consciousness that enable her to encounter the other. It is this encounter with the other that triggers the encounter with the self.

IN MY OWN BOOK, *Emily Dickinson: Das transzendentale Ich*, I identified the self in Dickinson's poetry as the "transcendental I," which I defined from various perspectives. My approach to the lyrical "I" was mainly a philosophical one. Starting out by identifying the self in the sense of the Cartesian ego, I put Descartes's axiom "cogito ergo sum" at the center of my investigation. This dictum was altered into "credo ergo sum" in the context of American tran-scendentalism and finally into "sentio ergo sum" on the background of Zen-Buddhism and the haiku, emphasizing the emotional self as opposed to the rational self. Most important, however, is the Cartesian self in the sense of being constitutive of its world. The self in Dickinson's poetry may therefore be compared to the Cartesian ego after having performed its method of doubting or to Husserl's ego after having exercised the "epoché." This new self now ventures to discover and constitute the world according to its own experi-ences. Thus every aspect of the world gains sense and meaning only through the perception of the "I." This kind of relation of the "I" to the world has been designated as "intentionality" by Husserl. Intentionality is the connecting line between the human consciousness and the world. But the idea of a pure tran-scendental consciousness is merely fiction, both in philosophy and in litera-ture. The "I" automatically saves and maintains things and experiences from its *Lebenswelt*. This can also be seen in Dickinson's poetry, where the "I" is clearly "tainted" by common aspects of everyday life. One must therefore conclude that it is impossible to clearly differentiate among biographical I, lyrical I, and persona.

A central question that remains to be pursued is whether we are to assume and look for a unified identity beyond the various facets of "I" and persona. Robert Langbaum's statement therefore needs to be reconsidered: "The concept of persona does not change, it merely refines our understanding of the connection between the poem and the process by which the poet, and to a lesser extent the reader, establishes and maintains an identity. We are still in an area where the self is believed in" (169). In her search for meaning, it is clear to Emily Dickinson that revelation will not be granted to a passive I. Rather, the self has to participate actively in the process of world discovery. This is explicitly expressed in the lines "Not 'Revelation' — 'tis — that waits, / But our unfurnished eyes —." There is no revelation of given facts, but the self has to be ready and willing to recognize the world by endowing it with meaning. The "eyes" therefore have to be understood in the sense of the rational means of cognition. To "see" is to understand. Revelation waits in the eyes; it is from the eyes that intentional constitution emerges. Dickinson's vision is of the interior self. Trying to find meaning and sense in the world, Dickinson is concerned not with the "thing in itself" but with the way in which we may perceive and understand it. This is made clear in the poem "Perception of an object costs / Precise the Object's loss —," where "The Object Absolute — is nought —" but "Perception in itself a Gain" (Grabher 45–55).

Whereas it is one major concern of the "transcendental I" to experience, discover, and constitute the (empirical) world, it is another to place itself within the framework of transcendence. Dickinson's self seeks meaning not only in its relation to the world but also in its relation to the beyond. The transcendent questions about God, immortality, eternity, and the divine order haunted Dickinson but did not force from her any definite answers. If Dickinson defines anything in this respect, it is the framework within which she prefers to leave the answers illegible. A perfect example of a poem that merely sets the framework is "All Circumstances are the Frame," in which she frames God's portrait without even mentioning him. Likewise, Dickinson defines the self by means of the concepts of Eternity and Immortality, yet without semantically fixing either those terms or herself. In the poem "Behind — me — dips Eternity — / Before Me — Immortality" she calls her self "the Term between." The ambiguity of the "Term" leaves the self undefined. In a linguistic sense the word "term" designates the self as something abstract and undefinable, a something in-"between." But the word "term" also alludes to the temporally limited existence of the self in-between Eternity and Immortality. Dickinson knows how to let those concepts dangle in semantic indefiniteness; she knows that they can't be grasped and finalized by definition.

From a purely philosophical (transcendental) point of view, the other as the other human being presents a problem. On the one hand, it is inevitably part of the world that is constituted by the I. On the other hand, however, the other is also a human being in its own right. Dickinson thematizes the problems of bridging the gap between the I and the other, the difficulties of understanding the other and communicating with the other. Very often loneliness remains the only friend of Dickinson's self.

In the context of American transcendentalism Dickinson's lyrical self is mainly challenged to meet Emerson's requirement of self-reliance. Dickinson certainly rests on a "Columnar Self." However, I agree with Kher in that Dickinson saw no need to place her column on societal ground. The spiritual stability that was required from her columnar self allowed her to place herself in her own world, uncompromisingly living according to her own terms. The female self of the nineteenth century had to dwell in the possibility of her mind. Albert Gelpi, too, argues that since the columnar self stands alone, it needs to be self-sufficient. This self-sufficiency, however, he does not necessarily equate with Emerson's or Thoreau's self-reliance or their belief in perfection and elevation. Rather, he observes, the self is the center of circumference, the host of consciousness that absorbs experience only in order to continually modify the self (*Mind*, 94–104). But consciousness itself triggers a number of difficulties. On the one hand, it is the means to establish the relation between the self and the not-me. On the other hand, by being open to everything else, it also effects an interior division of the self. Gelpi here speaks of double consciousness, in that the self that is establishing its link to the outside world, to nature, and to the cosmos is simultaneously observing itself in its activity (101 f.).

In the third chapter of my book I undertook a comparison between Dickinson and haiku poetry against the background of Zen-Buddhism in order to demonstrate how she has the self in her poetry dissolve in the paradoxes she creates beyond which she seeks enlightenment. The haiku, which often relies on the teachings of Zen-Buddhism, lives on contradicting the laws of logic. Logical rules limit the scope of human understanding. Breaking those rules allows the mind to penetrate further into the mysteries of the universe. In Zen-Buddhism this is most often achieved by means of the koan, a riddle that must be solved beyond the boundaries of logic. Dickinson takes similar steps into the spheres of contradiction, as for example in the poems "I'm Nobody" or "Much Madness is Divinest Sense." By transcending dualistic logic, the self advances to a higher level of understanding him/herself and the world. It also succeeds in empathizing with other beings and in grasping the mystery of existence as such. Transcending its own sense of limited self it expands itself into a sense of oneness with the universe. In this context the I is not transcendental in the sense that it constitutes the world. Rather, the world is internalized by the I or, vice versa, the I is absorbed by the world. There is no more dualism between the subject and the object, between the I and the world.

Exploring the world, the self discovers him/herself; exploring him/herself, the self discovers the world. Dickinson likes to make use of the moon as a means of having her self mirrored. In "You know that Portrait in the Moon" she projects her own self onto the moon only to have her self externalized and reflected back as the self recognized. "At last, to be identified!" is therefore more than an exclamation of joy about the finding of one's identity. The passive voice here signifies a state of being that implicitly involves both the I and the world.

The label of the "transcendental I" for the self in Dickinson's poetry serves as a helpful modus operandi in coming to terms with the multiple functions of the self. It is an I in search of both its identity and its power to create that identity. It is an I in charge of the constitution of his/her world yet simultaneously at the mercy of a transcendent power by which in turn it is constituted. In its spiritual strength and power it is as solemn as a column. In its essence, however, it is as vague and whimsical as the moon. It is self-reliantly lonely but always in touch with the world. Loneliness is its ontological crutch, empathy with the mystery of the universe its ontological wing. The self vanishes into nobody when it has discovered that it is All.

FROM THIS MORE abstract, universal, and metaphysical investigation of the self it is necessary to proceed to the question of how the individual self in different poems takes on a concrete identity.

In 1973 John Emerson Todd was one of the first critics to argue that "the 'I' speaking in a Dickinson poem is not necessarily the 'I' bearing the poet's name" (x). Before that, critics had been more inclined toward reading Dickinson's poetry as a "biographical allegory" (ix). Two such sample studies are George F. Whicher's *This Was a Poet: A Critical Biography of Emily Dickinson* (1938) and Theodora Ward's *The Capsule of the Mind* (1961). Those critics who argue for Dickinson's use of the persona unanimously take Dickinson at her word, quoting her from an early letter to Higginson: "When I state myself, as the Representative of the Verse — it does not mean — me — but a supposed person" (L268). Starting with the etymological meaning of the persona, Todd demonstrates that Dickinson's poetry is highly dramatic and that the poet likes to put herself on stage. The dramatic character of Dickinson's poetry and her eager interest in performance have more recently been emphasized by Juhasz, Miller, and Smith in *Comic Power in Emily Dickinson*. The persona as the speaker of the individual poems varies in its degree of autonomy. Whereas at times Dickinson uses a persona as a means of wish-fulfilling change, at other times she turns to personae that are totally different from herself. Todd investigates the little-girl persona, the lover-wife-queen persona, personae in death and eternity, and personae involving the divided personality in order to show how Dickinson engaged the various aspects of her extraordinary personality in dialogues. He ascribes her frequent use of personae to her uncertainties in religious belief. On the other hand, however, her use of the persona also allowed her to transcend the narrow confines of the self and project herself into vaster realms.

In the chapter "Persona as Voice, Persona as Style" in his book *Emily Dickinson's Poetry* (1975), Robert Weisbuch remarks that through the multiple presence of personae in Dickinson's poetry the reader is discouraged from ever finding her final self in any one of the poems. Although Weisbuch also refers to the little-girl, the queen, or the wife persona, the point he makes is more abstract in content. He seeks to define the "Representative of the Verse" in the syntactical features of her style. He subsumes the various personae under the headings of the "impersonal bard" and the "involved sufferer," which for him "personify opposite desires: the one for order, for logic, for a clear view of things; the other for personal enunciation, for emotional catharsis, for comfort" (71). Dickinson combines both strategies to play them off against each other.

Elizabeth Phillips, in *Emily Dickinson: Personae and Performance* (1988), calls Dickinson a "biographer of souls" (5) and looks at her use of the personae as frequent transformations of episodes in the life of friends and literary or historical characters. Intriguing is her identification of the word itself as persona in the poem "My Life had stood — a Loaded Gun —" (210).

Jane Donahue Eberwein, in *Dickinson: Strategies of Limitation* (1985), links Dickinson's frequent use of the child persona with her "explicit longing for delayed maturity" (97). Due to its paradoxical powers the child is free to adopt various roles. The little-boy persona, according to Eberwein, allowed Dickinson to satisfy her longing for liberties denied to young girls. Eberwein furthermore observes that Dickinson was intrigued by the idea of transforming herself into the most unlikely aristocrats, assuming the role of queen or earl. In regard to the bride-persona poems Eberwein points to the fact that in those poems the groom is missing. This for her indicates that Dickinson is more interested in experimenting with a certain role playing than in fantasizing about a love relationship with a specific lover (103). That the bridal fantasies are much more positively depicted than the marriage fantasies is interpreted by Eberwein as a sign of Dickinson's wish for a secret bonding with the lover. In general, she sees Dickinson's role playing as a means of compensating for the inadequacies and shortcomings in her real life: "When frustrated by restrictions on girls, she played at being a boy. When mortified by her apparent nonentity, she crowned herself a queen. When consigned to probable spinsterhood, she acclaimed herself a bride" (108). Eberwein also shows that in her role playing Dickinson did not merely rely on her experience. Contemporary sentimental literature provided her with role models which she could adopt, expand, and modify. It even allowed her to present herself as a romantic heroine. Most of all, however, the various roles empowered her to grow and transcend the restrictions on her self. When dealing with psychic pain Dickinson loved to identify with Gothic victims. The presentation of her lover as death is one such Gothic version. What did Dickinson gain from assuming such a variety of personae? "Bounty, plenty, escape from limitation—these were the rewards Dickinson gained from vicarious participation in a remarkable range of human roles" (127).

In her book *Emily Dickinson* (1991) Joan Kirkby remarks on Dickinson's delight in taking on countless identities: "In the poems and letters Dickinson adopts the persona of countless 'supposed persons,' boy, wife, corpse, etc.; the 'I' in any given poem is simply the speaker of that particular poem. Her delight in assuming other selves is related to her idea that life itself is a fiction" (40). Speaking of "the grammar of the self" Kirkby argues that Dickinson's self is primarily based on language (19–41). Just as Dickinson is aware of the limitedness of language, so is she aware of the limitedness of the self. The self, which in poem 643 is referred to as a syllable, is, according to Kirkby, no autonomous, transcendent self but rather, along with modern theories of language, the point of intersection of various discourses; "language structures as well as expresses experience and self-knowledge comes not from introspection into 'an inner world of autonomous consciousness,' but from 'reflection upon the field of expressions in which one finds oneself'" (21 f.).

Indeed, if one probes into the sheer, endlessly possible manifestations of the self in Dickinson's poems, that self may seem to reveal itself as anything but a self in the traditional sense of the term. It is both everyone and nobody ("it could contain the All, be the All, displace the All" [Gelpi, *Mind* 97]). Dickinson's famous puzzling "self-identification" in "I'm Nobody" has called forth numerous interpretations. It has also been taken as a starting point for a postmodernist argument for the dissolution of the self. Joining in Dickinson's playfulness, one might even alter the line, saying "I'm no body," thus depriving the self of its concreteness. The discontinuity of the self, also in the light of what has been said above, then becomes a modus operandi with different consequences. In *Lyric Contingencies* (1991), in the chapter " 'The dazzled Soul / In her unfurnished Rooms': Dickinson and the Lyric Self," Margaret Dickie convincingly shows how Dickinson's sense of self differs from Emerson's, whose Cartesian faith "in the sovereignty of the *Cogito* as the basis of subjectivity" (15) allowed him to be equally confident in the representativeness of the self. Dickie, however, diagnoses the representative self as a repressive and unnecessary fiction. The female gender and the lyric genre made it possible for Dickinson to reject this fiction. Rather than universalize individuality

Dickinson could express it as both fragmented and excessive. Disagreeing with a psychoanalytic (e.g., Cynthia Griffin Wolff's) or the American feminist model, Dickie believes that the conscious choice of the lyric form, in which the "I" is expressed only in limited detail and lacks a narrative context, was a choice against representation. Providing an inquiry into self-representation, Dickinson defeats the illusion of a "coherent and definitive presentation of the self" (Dickie, *Lyric* 19), of the self as a "publicly knowable, organized, single entity" (18). It is therefore in vain that we seek to construct a unified identity out of the numerous occurrences of the "I" in Dickinson's poems. "No single 'errand' for her, the lyric speaker is singular, unique, isolated, changeable, not to be made into one composite person by joining poems together. The lyric 'I' is not the real-life poet or even part of her, because she will not share her beginning or end, her history. She is not a copy of that original either, because she is always and conventionally partial" (28). Precisely because this discontinuous, profligate, and excessive self obstructs narrative reading it "represents" "the nineteenth century's most revolutionary expression of individuality" (29). In her article "Dickinson's Discontinuous Lyric Self" (1988) Dickie had already suggested refraining from a narrative reading of Dickinson's poetry and offered her conception of the "discontinuous lyric self" as a new "feminist model of self-presentation" (553).

The discontinuous self closes itself to any identification as a unique entity, as a subject different from anyone else, but offers itself as a vessel of interaction. More recently, the self has been characterized as dialogic, as polyvocal. Paul Crumbley (herein), basing his argument on Bakhtin's dialogism, has pointed to the importance of recognizing the dialogic voice, especially through its connection to heteroglossia, in Dickinson's poetry. This remains a field still to be explored.

But any "dia-logic" view of the "self" renders itself impossible if it lacks the "two" (dia-logic): the self and the other. Since we cannot deny the fact that the lyrical self is stated linguistically as "I," this "I" will keep calling for identification.

NOTE

1. Glauco Cambon, *The Inclusive Flame: Studies in American Poetry* (Bloomington: Indiana University Press, 1963), 49.

FURTHER READING

Altieri, Charles. *Self and Sensibility in Contemporary American Poetry*. Cambridge: Cambridge University Press, 1984.

Grabher, Gudrun M. "Formen des lyrischen Ich im Modernismus: Subjekt-Kult und Subjekt-Absage durch die Sprachskepsis." *Geschichte und Vorgeschichte der modernen Subjektivität*. Ed. Roland Hagenbüchle and Reto Luzius Fetz. 2 vols. Berlin: Walter de Gruyter, 1998. 2: 1096–110.

Maritain, Jacques. *Creative Intuition in Art and Poetry*. New York: New American Library, 1974.

CRISTANNE MILLER

Dickinson's Experiments in Language

$\mathcal{U}$nusual features of Dickinson's language have long been a point of interest in Dickinson studies, although the focus of this interest has changed dramatically more than once in the century following the first publications of her poems. As I see it, the history of scholarly attention to Dickinson's language may be broken into roughly four periods, which might be labeled as late-nineteenth-century, early- to mid-twentieth century, post-Johnson, and post-Franklin — the last two periods following the 1955 publication of Thomas H. Johnson's three-volume variorum *Poems of Emily Dickinson* and the 1981 publication of Ralph W. Franklin's *Manuscript Books of Emily Dickinson*, respectively. The most substantial work took place following the publication of Johnson's edition, between the late 1950s and 1980s, in conjunction with the prominence of formalist, structuralist, and deconstructionist theory.

As these divisions suggest, there is more at stake in the study of Dickinson's language than objective description. Moreover, not surprisingly, the history of attention to unusual features of Dickinson's language develops in tandem with that of twentieth-century critical thought generally and the editing of Dickinson's poetry. Starting with the terminology itself, the very notion of "experiments" in language assumes that Dickinson was a writer conscious of her craft and of at least some level of design — an idea widely held at present but quite foreign to earlier perspectives on the poet and still debated. Similarly, changing critical notions of authorial intentionality have affected this study; in some ways, the question of Dickinson's intention has dominated studies of her language — first provoking readers to question whether anything irregular could be other than accidental or mistaken, then generating defensive insistence on Dickinson's fully conscious intent with regard to every aspect of her art, from grammar and meter to calligraphy. Only recently has the study of Dickinson's language led away from the question of intention altogether. The changing availability and types of editions of Dickinson's poetry have also enormously influenced studies of her language. The wide variety of editions available at different points between the 1890s and the 1990s has affected both whether critics tend to regard characteristics of Dickinson's language as a focal point of study and what they say about it. To mention only the extremes, the 1890s poems edited and regularized by Mabel Loomis Todd and Thomas W. Higginson necessarily provoked responses different from R. W. Franklin's 1981 holograph edition of Dickinson's handwritten manuscripts.

In short, the study of experimental elements of Dickinson's language has tended to be evaluative as well as descriptive. Evaluations have focused on the question of what Dickinson intended and on the degree of "success" Dickinson achieved with particular uses of meter, rhyme, grammar, and phrasing (intended or not), but also on the epistemological question of whether unconventional language use amounted to just another way of expressing familiar ideas or constituted a new statement in itself. Such questioning was in turn linked to changing concepts of what constituted the grammar of any language. Inevitably, the following analysis of late-nineteenth- and twentieth-century views on this topic will reveal my own conviction that Dickinson's language strategies are meaningful and innovative, a conviction that is currently widely shared. To conclude my analysis, I will turn to a brief reading of the elliptical "Four Trees — upon a solitary Acre — " (P742) to demonstrate some of the pleasures and rewards of analyzing "experimental" features of Dickinson's language.

EARLY REVIEWS AND essays admiring Dickinson's poetry followed Thomas Wentworth Higginson's lead in proclaiming the poems exceptional in tone, thought, or feeling but lacking "the proper control and chastening of literary expression" (1890; Blake and Wells 3).[1] The poems, Higginson comments, were "wayward and unconventional in the last degree; defiant of form, measure, rhyme, and even grammar"; they "will seem to the reader like poetry torn up by the roots, with rain and dew and earth still clinging to them" (10, 11). In 1890 Arlo Bates agrees, commenting that Dickinson combined the "insight of the civilized adult" with the "simplicity of the savage child," being "unconscious" of metrical form (Blake and Wells 16). For these readers, the unconscious artlessness of the poems was a sign of the poet's lack of skill but simultaneously of her natural insight and power (noted in metaphors like "earth," "roots," "dew," and the reference to savage or childlike qualities). Unusual features of grammar, syntax, and word choice were thus seen not as the result of experimentation but as proof of unguided inspiration and indifference to or incapacity for art as craft. As Bliss Carman wrote in 1896, "so eminent in wit, so keen in epigram, so rare and startling in phrase," Dickinson nonetheless found that "the extended laborious architecture of an impressive poetic creation was beyond her" (Blake and Wells 67).

By the late 1910s, no doubt in response to burgeoning experimentalism in all the arts, at least some critics approached Dickinson's work with a different literary taste, hence a different sense of these features. For example, in 1915 Elizabeth Shepley Sergeant described "the difficulties of [Dickinson's] syntax, the obscurities and abstractions which mark her verse" in relatively affirmative terms (Blake and Wells 93). In 1922 Robert Hillyer questioned with proclamatory rhetoric, "Who, in the presence of these amazing poems, would wish a single twisted syllable straightened to ensure the comprehension of mediocre minds or the applause of pedants?" (Blake and Wells 103). Early-twentieth-century enthusiasm for the psychological and "primitive" in all art forms may have contributed to the more laudatory reception of this aspect of Dickinson's poetry during these years. In an age that created modern psychology, when visual artists borrowed heavily from "primitive" iconography and modernist poets experimented with free verse, broken lines, and irregular grammar, the forms of Dickinson's verse that had seemed untutored to the 1890s may instead have seemed a sign of her precocious modernity.

The modernist period also produced the first formalist defenses of unusual features of Dickinson's verse. In 1925 Susan Miles argued that Dickinson's "irregularities have a definite artistic significance" in creating an "aesthetic impression of a cleft and unmatching world" (Blake and Wells 124, 129). Miles focused her argument on metrical and rhyming structures. In 1935 Grace B. Sherrer defended several of Dickinson's grammatical irregularities by demonstrating that they had well-established precedents in the work of Shakespeare and Milton. Sherrer's primary intent was to show that Dickinson's apparently ungrammatical usages — especially verb forms — were in fact old-fashioned but grammatically correct. In effect, Sherrer brought the poet's irregularity into the realm of the regular or grammatical, thus implicitly arguing against those who celebrated Dickinson's unconventionality, while showing interest in similar language features. Stanley T. Williams may be the first to have used the word "experiment" in regard to Dickinson, entitling his essay in the 1948 *Literary History of the United States:* "Experiments in Poetry: Emily Dickinson." Like Miles, but more specifically and with greater focus on language than on meter and rhyme, Williams argued that Dickinson "omitted conjunctions; used half and quarter-rhymes; played with the subjunctive mood or with legal phrases; dispensed with agreements of nouns and verbs" in order to mirror "the incongruities and frustrations of human experience" (Blake and Wells 255). Although he still saw little evidence of a "conscious plan" in her experimentation, he did acknowledge "principles" of use, thereby anticipating the studies of Dickinson's language that began to appear after the 1950s.

While such positive attention to unusual features of Dickinson's language, especially in the 1920s, marks a change in attitude from the 1890s, the majority of responses to Dickinson in the first half of the twentieth century combined high praise for the poet with extreme skepticism about her experimentation with meter, punctuation, grammar, and rhyme, and even critics who praised her irregularity tended to do so in paradoxically negative terms. One sees characteristic aspects of both this paradoxical language and the increasing appreciation of Dickinson as a poet yet simultaneous condemnation of her craft in R. P. Blackmur's 1937 essay. Blackmur caricatures Martha Dickinson Bianchi, by this time editor of several books of Dickinson's poetry, as making the extreme claim that "the slips and roughnesses, the truncated lines, false rhymes, the inconsistencies of every description which mar the majority of Emily Dickinson's poems are examples of a revolutionary master-craftsman" (Blake and Wells 203). Although neither she nor anyone else says precisely this, Blackmur's caricature indicates how unquestionably he perceives that, while Dickinson's idiosyncracies may in part be defended, criticism which celebrates every aspect of her language is open to ridicule. Blackmur's parody also accurately echoes the ambiguous language in some of these early defenses: his "inconsistencies . . . which mar" reflect Sergeant's "difficulties" and "obscurities," Hillyer's "twisted syllables," and Williams's lack of "conscious plan." Equally characteristic of this period is Conrad Aiken's skepticism about what he calls Dickinson's "disregard for accepted forms or for regularities." As he put it, "grammar, rhyme, metre — anything went by the board if it stood in the way of thought or freedom of utterance. Sometimes this arrogance was justified; sometimes not" (Blake and Wells 117). Yet in spite of what he saw as her "perversity," Aiken pronounced Dickinson "among the finest poets in the language" (117), and he published these comments on the poet in the introduction to his 1924 edition of her poems — a "selection" of most of the poems of the three 1890s editions into a single volume.

By the end of the 1930s, such a confusing array of "selected," "complete," "new," and "further" editions of Dickinson's poetry had appeared that any clear judgment of her general style and oeuvre would have been difficult. Readers had to negotiate their views of Dickinson's craft or, as Aiken saw it, "perversity" according to their access to particular, or multiple, editions of the poems. New editions, most containing at least some previously unpublished or newly edited poems, appeared in 1914, 1924, 1929, 1930, 1935, 1937, and 1945, and 1924 saw the publication of two editions of poetry (Aiken's, and Bianchi's *Complete Poems*; see Smith, herein). There was, in short, neither a clear body of work to which scholars could refer nor any sense of how the various editions of the poems reflected or revised Dickinson's manuscripts.

Such instability in the accessible body of Dickinson's poetry may have generated some of the excitement one feels in the eagerness of several well-known twentieth-century poet-critics to judge the quality of her work for themselves. It is inevitable in such circumstances, however, that the various editors' emendations, ordering, and selection would sometimes be confused with the poet's art, and this confusion may account for some of the more condemnatory aspects of those judgments. Regularized versions of the poems, for example, might make the remaining "irregularities" seem anomalous, ill fitting, rather than characteristic of the poet's style generally. Moreover, none of Dickinson's editors matched her as a poet, so it was inevitable that their changes of her meter, word choice, and rhymes should flatten the verse. Again, Blackmur can be seen as typical in his claim that Dickinson was a great poet but one who "never knew anything about the craft of verse well enough to exemplify it, let alone revolt from it" (Blake and Wells 203). Dickinson has what he repeatedly calls an "aptitude for language" but no idea that "poetry is a rational and objective art" (212, 214, 221, 223). Yvor Winters is even more extreme in his perception of Dickinson as a great poet with "innumerable beautiful lines and passages wasted in the desert of her crudities" (1938; Blake and Wells 188). In contrast, at the positive end of this period's poet-critics' responses, Marianne Moore judged Dickinson's as a poetry of "select defect," using the current language of flaw but transforming it to make a different point: "Emily Dickinson was a person of power and could have overcome, had she wished to, any less than satisfactory feature of her lines. The self-concealing pronoun . . . independence of the subjunctive, and many another select defect, are, for the select critic, attractions" (1933; *Prose* 292).[2] By marking Dickinson's stylistic "defects" as "select" "attractions," Moore ironizes the claim that they are defects at all, to the choice reader.

Following the publication of Johnson's three-volume variorum edition of the poems in 1955, features of Dickinson's language that had been attributed to primitive or impulsive artlessness, or "defect," began to be more broadly viewed as conscious experimentation. Johnson's edition transformed the possibilities for studies of Dickinson by publishing in a single edition all poems known to have been written by her, offering a tentative chronology for these poems, and providing all known versions and variations for each poem. While not claiming to establish definitive accounts of form or chronology, Johnson did provide standards for comparing early and later work with respect to punctuation, capitalization, rhyme, and word choice — including notation of variant word choices. One sees the effect of such clarity immediately. In reviewing this edition in 1957, for example, Austin Warren wrote that Johnson's chronology proved that Dickinson's "deviation" from standard rhyme and meter was purposeful; the poet proceeds both "by intuition, and by relatively conscious theorizing" (Blake and Wells 272, 273). Similarly, in 1956 John Crowe Ransom heralded Johnson's edition as ushering in "the principal literary event of these last twenty years" — the restoration of Dickinson's poetry —

and further named Dickinson as one of the two "greatest forces in American poetry in the nineteenth century" (R. Sewall, *Essays* 89, 98). Like Warren and like Johnson himself, however, Ransom assumed that later editors would and should "[straighten] out some of those informalities in the manuscripts," while, respectfully and reluctantly, future editors would rightly "feel obliged" to omit odd capitalizations and "substitute some degree of formal punctuation for the cryptic dashes which are sprinkled over the poet's lines" (89). Warren, in contrast, suggests the more modernist practice of omitting all punctuation except periods, to avoid interpretive additions to the poems through punctuating them.

Charles Anderson's 1960 *Emily Dickinson's Poetry: Stairway of Surprise* shows great sensitivity to the nuances of Dickinson's unusual language features, as edited by Johnson, but it was not until 1966, with David Porter's publication of *The Art of Emily Dickinson's Early Poetry*, that a critic made Dickinson's style the central topic of a book-length study. Clearly writing in response to the continued primacy of claims like Aiken's and Blackmur's that Dickinson was a poet of brilliant insight and flawed craft, Porter explored the poet's stylistic habits in order to locate her vocabulary of basic forms rather than focusing on the judgment of her use of such forms or examining the poet's themes. Hence, he devoted whole chapters to discussion of the poet's metrical and rhythmic variations; combination of images from seemingly disparate sources; deliberately varied uses of rhyme; and various grammatical irregularities. This latter category, for Porter, included Dickinson's use of the subjunctive mood and of eccentric verb forms echoing the subjunctive; capitalization; punctuation; substitutions of abstract for concrete terms (and vice versa); substitution of one part of speech for another — for example, having nouns function as adjectives, adjectives as nouns or adverbs; and alternation of collective and singular nouns. Like earlier critics, and despite his more descriptive focus, Porter still prominently discriminated between Dickinson's successful and unsuccessful uses of these "mannerisms," arguing that such experimentation should not "intrude on the argument" or "dominate the experience" of a poem (140). This study was tremendously influential in laying the ground for more detailed, and more affirmative, studies of Dickinson's experimentation, as well as heralding Porter's own return to these themes fifteen years later.

In 1981 Porter's second book on Dickinson, subtitled *The Modern Idiom*, modified the pathbreaking argument he himself had made in 1966. Perhaps, given the shift in critical thinking that had occurred — partly in response to his own influential early work — Porter felt it necessary in this book to downplay the element of conscious experimentation and stress instead the lack of an overall coherence in Dickinson's poems. Porter writes:

Unable to compose broad fields of ordinary experience, Dickinson's language produces a strange discourse that is full of gaps and shadows and brilliant glints of light (7). . . . a reader encounters language distorted by defects in syntax and grammar, unreasonable transpositions, extreme ellipsis and lost connectives, and many other types of contortions or excisions (38) . . . the poems formed no meaning. There was intensity but no light, sensation but no idea. The void startles us, for we have assumed . . . with our formalist assumption of inevitable coherence in any poet's makeup . . . that Emily Dickinson too might be seen to have a way of looking at the world. Not so . . . Emily Dickinson is the only major American poet without a project. (151–52)

In passages like these, Porter repeats earlier critics' emphasis on Dickinson's inability or limitation while also asserting her importance as an (early) "modern" poet.[3] Porter's two books thus both cap the long and prestigious line of studies that affirm Dickinson's genius while regretting her defects and map out primary areas of discussion in the developing field of linguistic and structural analysis of Dickinson's language.

With the rise of formalism and then structuralism in European philosophy and its merging of linguistic and literary study, European criticism took the lead in major studies of Dickinson's language — although critics in the United States, including and preeminently Porter, also moved in this direction. Although focused on vocabulary rather than structural or grammatical features, William Howard's "Emily Dickinson's Poetic Vocabulary" (1957) provided detailed word counts and tallies showing that the unusual qualities of Dickinson's language lay not in her word choice or coinages (which he claims were not unusual for the nineteenth century) but in the way she combined her words. Samuel Levin's equally brief "The Analysis of Compression in Poetry" (1971) reemphasized that extreme compression crucially characterized Dickinson's work (a primary claim of Porter's first study) and provided a vocabulary for understanding the function of particular kinds of compression. Distinguishing recoverable from nonrecoverable deletions, Levin argued that Dickinson's poetry contains multiple instances of both. The first causes no difficulties in comprehension as such deletions are a common part of English grammar: for example, "To pile like Thunder to its close / Then [ ] crumble" for "Then [to] crumble" (P1247).[4] The second, however, is partially responsible for that ambiguity or tension in meaning so characteristic of Dickinson's poetry: for example, later in the same poem, "Experience either and consume — ." Only through interpretation can the reader decide whether this is an elliptically transitive verb requiring extension — "experience either [Love or Poetry] and [you will] consume [both? either?]" or "experience either and [you will be] consume[d]" — or whether "consume" should be read intransitively, as meaning "to decay, rot, perish" — in which case the deletion is merely recoverable ([you will] consume). Perhaps because Levin's essay was published in *Foundations of Language* and addressed to a linguistic rather than a literary community — although all its examples are from Dickinson — it remained unnoticed by Dickinson scholars until the 1980s.

Brita Lindberg-Seyersted's two books of structural analysis, *The Voice of the Poet* (1968) and *Emily Dickinson's Punctuation* (1976), provide crucial descriptive categorization of Dickinson's language. Focusing the argument of the former, as her title implies, on the colloquial or spoken qualities of Dickinson's verse, Lindberg-Seyersted sets out to introduce "the new type of studies which takes account of the theories and methods of modern linguistics in analyses of literary works" to Dickinson criticism (10). Nearly one-third of this book analyzes physical aspects of rhythm or sound in the poems (meter, rhyme, and punctuation); the rest analyzes in detail Dickinson's diction, use of semantic contrasts of various kinds, syntax, patterns of rhetoric, and multiple aspects of style contributing to the overall effect of informal speech in the poems. These particular areas of emphasis are, in turn, discussed under the rubric of what Lindberg-Seyersted sees as the three primary aspects of the poems: colloquialness, slantness, and privateness or idiosyncrasy. In her preface, Lindberg-Seyersted emphasizes that she is not a linguist: "My primary concern is . . . with the *poetic effects* of the texts I am studying, and my investigation will focus on the poetic meaning of one or another feature" (10). The descriptive and linguistic terminology, however, tends to overwhelm the interpretive aspects of her study, and perhaps for this reason it appears to have had little effect on the broader terms of Dickinson criticism, while remaining an invaluable guide to Dickinson's language structures. In her equally precise and descriptive book on punctuation, Lindberg-Seyersted argues that Dickinson's punctuation functions primarily in rhythmic and rhetorical ways.

Closely following Lindberg-Seyersted's *Voice of the Poet*, Sirkka Heiskanen-Mäkelä's *In Quest of Truth: Observations on the Development of Emily Dickinson's Poetic Dialectic* (1970) provided an important complement to it. Not primarily focusing on language use, Heiskanen-Mäkelä nonetheless uses a structuralist analysis to mount what might be seen as an anticipatory counterargument to Porter's claim that Dickinson was a "poet without a project." Heiskanen-Mäkelä sees Dickinson as developing a clear and coherent poetic based on both a Wordsworthian overflow of the poet's perception onto the natural world and a more objective and rational assertiveness that pushes the poet's articulation of her perception toward extreme abstraction. Although she is more concerned with tropes than with other elements of the language, Heiskanen-Mäkelä devotes several pages each to unraveling patterns of parallelism in Dickinson's poetry (including phonetic patterning); developing a theory about the function of the quatrain — in Dickinson's verse and generally—as the "shortest *dialectical* unit of poetry" (153); exploring the economy of the poet's grammatical form; and delineating characteristic elements of the poet's "elliptical syntax" (183). This broadly interpretive analysis has, in my opinion, been undervalued by U.S. Dickinson scholars.

Also focused on structuralist analysis of Dickinson's figurative language, but widely influential, was Roland Hagenbüchle's 1974 "Precision and Indeterminacy in the Poetry of Emily Dickinson," a study of the effects and structures of metonymy in Dickinson's verse. Hagenbüchle makes explicit what Lindberg-Seyersted and Heiskanen-Mäkelä imply, by stating at the outset that he intends to counter previous assumptions that unusual features of Dickinson's language reveal "a certain intellectual deficiency in the poet" (33). He concludes that her poetry "is characterized by an element of deliberate indeterminacy, which alone can do justice to the mystery of existence" (50). She manipulates "the method of metonymy, inference and pure *deixis*" strategically (51). Dickinson's poetry constitutes an "endless quest" rather than a failed attempt to provide clear, definite answers (52).

Working from feminist and deconstructionist theory, in 1980 Margaret Homans expanded this concept of Dickinson's language ambiguities as strategic by arguing that the poet understood all dualism or binary opposition (including that between the sexes) as a fiction, and hence developed a disruptive language to dislocate Adamic or phallogocentric structures of truth, identity, and meaning. Homans's *Women Writers and Poetic Identity* argues that Dickinson's linguistic power lies in her deliberate and rebellious manipulation of words to call attention to the inherent instability or fictiveness of language itself.[5]

Without this rich and varied foreground, my own 1987 *Emily Dickinson: A Poet's Grammar* and brief 1989 "Dickinson's Language: Interpreting Truth Told Slant," which modified a part of the *Grammar*'s argument, would not have been possible. Designed to combine the strengths of Lindberg-Seyersted's and Levin's categorical and linguistic descriptions with the rich interpretive strategies of critics like Anderson, Heiskanen-Mäkelä, and Hagenbüchle, and the language-focused feminist criticism of writers like Margaret Homans, Suzanne Juhasz, and Joanne Diehl, *A Poet's Grammar* provided multiple lenses for understanding the most characteristic elements of Dickinson's language use, while avoiding primary focus on those aspects of language already frequently analyzed—namely, word choice, metaphor, and the formal elements of meter and rhyme. A lengthy "grammar" dominates this book, organized both by grouping Dickinson's characteristic usages under the broad categories of compression, disjunction, repetition, syntax, and speech and by outlining the basic interpretive functions of individual features through repeated and increasingly layered readings of five poems containing characteristic elements of her language. The intent of the "grammar" was not to dictate interpretive strategies for any poem or type of language but to provide an explanatory grid that might prove helpful in analyzing those same linguistic features in other poems or in the work of other poets; consequently, it attempted to analyze the values and assumptions underlying Dickinson's characteristic manipulations of language as much as to describe particular features themselves.

As an example of a distinctive feature of the *Grammar,* I revived Levin's recognition of the role of nonrecoverable deletion in creating the characteristic tone of Dickinson's poetry — a concept I modified in 1989 to "multiply recoverable deletion" as describing more accurately how such deletion actually functions in a poem. The *Grammar* analyzes several differing types of such deletion characteristic of Dickinson's poems. "Syntactic doubling," for example, seems to me one of Dickinson's most striking strategies of multiply recoverable deletion. "Syntactic doubling" refers to the use of a single word or phrase to cover two nonparallel syntactic contexts — as in "A Bird came down the Walk" (P328), where the line "Like one in danger, Cautious" may apply syntactically and logically to both the bird and the speaker (*Grammar* 37–39). This grammar also includes a lengthy analysis of Dickinson's paratactic syntax (with its background in biblical ellipticism and grandeur) and her unusual repetition of pronouns, and it extends previous analyses of the poet's hypotactic and inverted syntax, grammatical experiments (both nominative and predicate forms), punctuation, use of negation and contrast, and colloquial elements of diction.

Other chapters of *A Poet's Grammar* provide historical contexts for Dickinson's language use, giving particular focus to her familiarity with the Bible, Watts's hymns,[6] her 1844 Webster's *American Dictionary of the English Language,* and nineteenth-century expectations for proper women's speech. These chapters explore biographical, theoretical, and feminist understandings of why Dickinson wrote as she did, as well as the contemporary contexts encouraging such language use. Like the grammar, the more traditionally interpretive chapters of the book were designed to open multiple possibilities for interpretation rather than to assert a particular one. Such a reading of Dickinson rests on the assumption that one cannot know with certainty the personal, psychological, aesthetic, or accidental causes underlying particular manipulations of language in any of her poems. The reader must rely on the language of a poem itself, in its full idiosyncrasy, for the most important clues to its meaning(s). Hence, a reader's choice of a single interpretation for the complexity of her language use generally, or for any one language strategy, is likely to be misleading.

Also in 1987, Mutlu Blasing published *American Poetry: The Rhetoric of Its*

Forms, with a chapter on Dickinson as representing the trope of irony, through which she "deconstruct[s] the process of meaning itself" (5). According to Blasing, Dickinson's most important disruptions occur at the level of "dissections of the word" (9): "Her functional unit is the syllable, which is the borderline between articulation and disarticulation and mediates between sense and nonsense. A primary unit of sound that becomes a unit of sense as well, the syllable links and separates sound and sense, nature and spirit" (181). Such dissection, in turn, produces the characteristic tension in Dickinson's poetry between the limitations of her metrical form and syntax and the "centrifugal force of semantic expansion" (180).

Although Franklin's *Manuscript Books of Emily Dickinson* appeared in 1981, it took nearly a decade for the impact of this publication to be felt in the new fields it opened to Dickinson language studies. Since then, issues and questions previously afforded little attention have become central for some writers — for example, the extent to which Dickinson's line endings are metrically determined, and the degree of meaningful variation present in punctuation and variants to the poems. Such discussions have been led by Martha Nell Smith in *Rowing in Eden: Rereading Emily Dickinson* (1992) and by poet Susan Howe in *The Birth-mark* (1993). In addition, a Dickinson Editing Collective has taken on the enormous task of producing hypermedia and newly edited print texts of Dickinson's letters and poems, attending to the visual and material aspects of her handwritten manuscripts. Similarly, Franklin himself is reediting Dickinson's poems, in part because of what he sees as problematic or questionable in the Johnson edition. Perhaps as a result of this renewed critical uncertainty about the best edition of the poems to use, and while waiting for newer editions to appear, the focus of language-oriented critics has been primarily on material-textual rather than linguistic matters: what constitutes a line in Dickinson's poetry? How are her variant word choices to be notated and understood? Does she use more than one kind of dash?[7]

Related to although not directly reliant on these shifts in the focus of language-oriented study are the increasing number of studies focused on Dickinson's fascicles and variants (see Cameron herein) and on dialogic aspects of Dickinson's voice (see Crumbley herein) — both lines of interpretation based on close attention to Dickinson's texts although not taking the language per se as their primary focus. The latter, for example, argues that the poet deliberately creates a heteroglossia through her experiments with language, such as that later theorized by Mikhail Bakhtin and Julia Kristeva. Sabine Sielke combines deconstructionist, feminist, and dialogic analysis in her 1997 *Fashioning the Female Subject: The Intertextual Networking of Dickinson, Moore, and Rich*. Similarly to Heiskanen-Mäkelä, Sielke combines rich interpretive and theoretical analysis with extended close readings of individual poems and

precise attention to details of language. Two contemporary feminist poets —
Heather McHugh (1993) and Alice Fulton (1989) — also focus on what Mc-
Hugh calls Dickinson's avoidance of "semantic mono-determination": "Dickinson's sentences and lines often seem designed (in judicious ellipses, elisions,
contractions, puns, and dashes) to afford the greatest possible number of
simultaneous and yet mutually resistant readings" (105). Fulton compares
Dickinson's dashes to the "resonant gaps" of quantum mechanics: her "dashes
are a linguistic analogue of [Heisenberg's] probability waves" ("Moment" 29).
Four years later, Fulton argues more broadly in a brief essay on tonal qualities
of the poems, particularly their "discordant registers of diction," that "the
uncanny quality of Dickinson's work is attributable in large part to its grammatical subversions" ("Capsizals" 97–98).

Several essays and one book focusing on single aspects of Dickinson's language have appeared in the last decade as well. In 1990 Judy Jo Small published an excellent study of Dickinson's innovative rhyming practices (*Positive
as Sound: Emily Dickinson's Rhyme*). Kamilla Denman's 1993 essay "Emily
Dickinson's Volcanic Punctuation" argues that the poet's patterns of punctuation change over time but that in every period Dickinson used punctuation to
create units of words that, as units, functioned variously: to disrupt conventional patterns and meanings, to explore "the inherent dissociation and ambiguous nature of language," to heighten tone and emotional force, or to serve
other rhythmic, tonal, imagistic or aural ends (29–30). John Mulvihill's 1996
"Why Dickinson Didn't Title" points out that, historically, the "innovation of
providing titles for short poems grew out of the commercialization of poetry"
and that the poet's lack of titles for all but three of her poems strongly suggests
her lack of interest in commercial publishing (73–74). While noting Porter's,
Blasing's, and Howard's previous discussions of Dickinson's nontitling as part
of the poet's general linguistic and epistemological skepticism, Mulvihill instead focuses on the poet's dislike of commerce and "distrust of names as
knowledge" (75).

The most important recent development in language study of Dickinson
was the formation of an international "Cognitive Approaches to Dickinson"
workshop called "Translit" as an outgrowth of the International Cognitive
Linguistics Conference in Louvain in 1993. This group uses the tools of
cognitive linguistics to explain the principles of the poet's syntax and grammar.
Using linguistics not to deny the unexpectedness of Dickinson's experimentation but to help explain the regularity of its patterns, Translit represents the
linguistically trained branch of those who have been working since the 1950s
to bring linguistics and literary analysis into closer conjunction in understanding Dickinson's poetry. An outgrowth of the midcentury development of
transformational generative grammar, which, unlike traditional grammars, is

based on a comprehensive description of modern rather than classical language, cognitive linguistics provides both better descriptive tools for characterizing Dickinson's language patterns than traditional rhetorics and grammars and a different principle for understanding features that were previously marked as abnormal or ungrammatical. As Elzbieta Tabakowska puts it, cognitive linguistics "aims at pointing out tendencies and principles rather than formulating deterministic rules, and considers all values as relative and continuous rather than absolute and discrete" (16). It attempts to understand the principles organizing an individual's language use rather than to judge that use "grammatical" or not according to the rules of a prototypical grammar. The question, then, for cognitive linguists is not whether Dickinson's language is grammatical, or even, primarily, why she might have chosen to write as she does, but how best to describe and understand her basic patterns of language.

An example of the potential wealth of this direction of study is revealed in Margaret Freeman's 1996 essay "Emily Dickinson and the Discourse of Intimacy." Freeman demonstrates that the elision of Dickinson's verse resembles patterns of silence in informal discourse: such silence, she argues, creates a feeling of intimacy between speaker and audience—a useful explanation for why so many readers find Dickinson's poems difficult yet feel personally moved by them. As Freeman argues, the same syntactic structures both create the difficulty and signal intimacy. Obviously, the Cognitive Approaches workshop takes a further step in the continuing move away from notions of Dickinson's language as flawed by providing terminology that gives positive identification to the poet's grammatical strategies without making intent or particular meaning central to its focus.[8]

AT THIS POINT, let me turn to a single poem to demonstrate what I see as the kinds of questions raised and, potentially, answered by attention to the idiosyncracies of Dickinson's language.

> Four Trees — upon a solitary [/] Acre —
> Without Design
> Or Order, or Apparent [/] Action — *[signal/noticest
> Maintain —   *[Do reign
>
> The Sun — upon a Morning [/] meets them —
> The Wind —
> No nearer Neighbor — have [/] they —
> But God —
>
> The Acre gives them — [/] Place —
> They — Him — Attention of [/] Passer by —
> Of Shadow, or of Squirrel, [/] haply —
> Or Boy —

What Deed is Their's [/] unto the General Nature — [they bear
What Plan
They severally — retard — or [/] further — [promote — or hinder
Unknown — (F37, 903–4, P742)

Although the punctuation is disruptive in its several dashes, this poem proceeds relatively clearly until one reaches the (normally transitive) verb "Maintain," with its apparent lack of direct object. And here the complexity begins. If
no object exists, then one could regard this as a multiply recoverable deletion,
in which one of the reader's interpretive acts is to figure out through the
context of the rest of the poem *what* these trees "maintain." Or, if the phrase
beginning stanza 2 — "The Sun" — provides a direct object ("Four Trees . . .
Maintain — / / The Sun"), then one must both attempt to understand the
metaphysics of this claim and analyze the effect of the syntactic doubling that
makes "The Sun" both an object and a subject of the following sentence (four
trees maintain the sun; the sun meets them). Here questions of independence
inevitably come to mind: can the trees be met by that which they maintain? Is
any element of nature independent of other elements it meets? Or, one might
take Dickinson's alternate "Do reign" as suggesting that "Maintain" is similarly intransitive: the trees are lordly, sufficient unto themselves in their own
continuing existence, despite what may seem to an observer to be lack of
anything over which to "reign." In this case, one would, however, similarly
question the relation of the sun to these trees. Does it meet them as an equal in
"reigning," or as a courtier, or by chance? Lindberg-Seyersted's and Denman's
studies of punctuation would also have the reader question how the multiple
dashes, commas, and line breaks — all features that both disrupt and connect —
function in constructing this poem about an apparent lack of "Order" and
dependence in solitude.

Such questions of interdependence might then lead one to speculate about
the form of the verb "maintain": it is possible that Dickinson deletes the verb's
inflection as well as its object — making the first sentence read, "Four trees . . .
[are] maintain[ed]." This increases the interpretive possibilities. These trees
may owe their continued existence to some other individual or power that
functions without "Apparent" order, design, "signal," or action at the same
time that they may structure some plan or element of nature on their own.
Like the variants "Maintain" and "Do reign," such readings may be exclusive
or complementary.

One encounters similar ambiguity at the end of the second stanza, where
the phrase "But God" may be read doubly as completing the claim that they
have "No . . . Neighbor . . . / But God" or as beginning the following sentence, in inverted form: "But God // The Acre gives them — Place —." Here,

whether one understands God to be their neighbor or their provider, the trees seem to live in the neighborhood only of Sun, Wind, and God. At stake, then, is the question of agency—whether God gives them the acre, hence "Place," or whether the acre itself gives them place through its existence as foundation. As in the first stanza, then, the question here is to what extent the trees and other aspects of nature maintain themselves in a kind of interactive harmony, where each provides the other relatively indefinable but nonetheless identifying "Attention" or "Place" or greeting. In addition, the extreme brevity and elision of this poem may suggest that all this interaction remains unspoken, an indication of intimacy (as Freeman proposes) or of a kind of regal formality and respect. As the poem concludes, "What Deed is Their's [/] unto the General Nature" or "What Deed they bear" is "Unknown —." We know only that, at least in the poem's terms, their particular "Deed" or function appears to be less important than that they "Maintain —." The anthropomorphic verbs (maintain, reign, meet, give) may also hint that these four trees represent an interdependent yet self-sufficient element of the self or soul, as well as an element of nature.

This is not a poem about certainties, and virtually every element of the poem's language underlines the open questioning of the poem's theme, with its focus on matters of "Attention," independence, and on what it means for some element of nature to "reign" or "Maintain —" itself and/or something else. Such structural underlining occurs in the poem's lack of definite closure in punctuation (no periods), the multiple variants in word choice (none of which dramatically alters the sense of the poem but all of which contribute to its feeling of unsettledness), its free-verse form which rocks between one- or two-word and longer lines, its use of very slant rhymes (design/maintain or reign; wind/God; by/boy; plan/unknown), and its highly compressed, elliptical language. Studies of Dickinson's language indicate that all these features are common in her verse. One understands their function in this poem, then, not as unique occurrences having only to do with the theme of this poem but as general characteristics of the poet's style. At the same time, of course, each instance of these features contributes to the tone and manner, if not more directly to the meaning, of this poem, and the congruence of so many features that can suggest uncertainty of "Order" and "Action" seems particularly apt here. As I hope my reading of these structures suggests, the more clearly one understands general principles of Dickinson's use of particular language features, the more fully one may understand their appearance in individual poems, while close interpretive attention to such features in poem after poem provides the basis for arriving at a sense of those general principles.

That the language and punctuation of a poem like "Four Trees — upon a solitary Acre —" are unusual, or fall outside the bounds of a prototypical grammar, is unquestionable. Further, I would argue that in this poem such language is highly effective. Whether such language always (or some might argue, never) "succeeds" or constitutes "great" poetry remains, however, a question. Some critics take the position that whatever Dickinson has written is intended and hence "right," so that evaluative judgments based on idiosyncrasy do not come into play; others have argued that only Dickinson's most formally and grammatically regular poems may be considered great or fully successful. My sense is that critics with an interest in unusual language structures are apt to take a middle ground, leaning toward descriptive interpretation and hence evaluations of interest rather than toward categorical aesthetic judgment. Of interest for such critics is how individual language strategies function in a variety of particular contexts — semantic, aural, thematic, historical, or cultural — rather than whether they are in some objective sense "right," be it grammatically, aesthetically, or in the traditions of literary form.

This approach does leave open, however, the question of whether it is ever possible to say that the language of a poem is "unsuccessful" or to judge a poem unsuccessful on the basis of its use of unusual language features. Does an experiment in language fail if it contributes in no apparent way to the texture, feeling, or sense of a poem or, perhaps more to the point, if it detracts from what is otherwise the poem's texture, feeling, or sense? Perhaps. Yet such a line of thought inevitably opens the further question of whether the "failure" is then in the critic's interpretive capacity or in the poem itself. The history of Dickinson criticism is full of brilliant readings that have made previously little-read or disparaged poems into centerpieces of her oeuvre. Dickinson's poems indeed challenge the reader to meet her at her own level.

At the same time, I must confess that years of teaching Dickinson have convinced me that the unusual features of her work lend themselves to overinterpretation, providing eager critics with the opportunity to see every mark and syllable as individually deeply significant. Such interpretive practice can easily become exaggerated. There are then dangers, as well as benefits, to attention to Dickinson's unusual language, and the dangers are twofold: one may, through lack of sensitivity or imagination, see no significance or interest in features that another reader may prove critical to a poem; or one may, through excess of imagination or interpretive zeal, attribute exaggerated and specific significance to features that recur throughout Dickinson's work. And here we come full circle to the question of poetic intention and critical bias. Because of the particular state of Dickinson's manuscripts and her elliptical privacy in discussing her art, there can be no definitive answer as to whether she intended (for example) multiple styles of dashes, more or less capitalization, and a poetic line based on meter or on a more open and fragmented form; current critical theory insists that such an answer would not matter in any case.

On the other hand, the undeniable experimentation in the poems with grammar, rhyme, meter, and metaphor leads a reader to anticipate, and hence discover, other aspects of experimentation in the verse as well. Only one's own, and each age's collective, "good sense," textual access, and aesthetic or theoretical bias will determine what constitutes open ground for interpretive significance in a poem. In the meantime, critical descriptions of Dickinson's language will continue to illuminate distinctive general features of the poetry and hence provide basic tools of analysis for all further interpretation.

NOTES

1. See Buckingham's *Emily Dickinson's Reception in the 1890s* for a thorough review of responses to the earliest editions of Dickinson's poetry.

2. Cynthia Hogue called my attention to this phrase of Moore's in a conference paper: "The Plucked String: Emily Dickinson, Marianne Moore, and the Poetics of 'Select Defects.'" American Literature Association, Baltimore, 1995.

3. E. Miller Budick makes a similar argument in her 1985 *Emily Dickinson and the Life of Language: A Study in Symbolic Poetics*, although her descriptions of Dickinson's language are far more impressionistic than Porter's. Budick sees a "disturbing uncertainty," a "hint of disruption," "understated anxiety," or a "sense of struggle and failure" underlying the enthusiastic or "frantic" aspects of language in Dickinson's poems (4, 12).

4. When quoting an entire poem later in this essay, I use notation that includes the line breaks indicated in Dickinson's manuscripts, as published in Franklin's holograph edition. Consequently, there I give a fascicle number as well as the more familiar Johnson numbering of the poem. Here and elsewhere in reference to individual lines, for simplicity, I use the Johnson edition and numbering.

5. Joanne Diehl's essay "Ransom in a Voice: Language as Defense in Dickinson's Poetry" makes a similar argument, in the context of American rather than British romanticism (in Juhasz, *Feminist Critics*); an early essay of mine in the same volume also argues that Dickinson experimented with formal aspects of verse and grammar for gendered reasons ("How 'Low Feet' Stagger: Disruptions of Language in Dickinson's Poetry").

6. Others have also written at length about Dickinson's use of Watts' hymns or of hymn form generally in her poems. For example, see Porter, *Early Poetry* (1966) and James Davidson's "Emily Dickinson and Isaac Watts" (1954). More recently, Noel Tipton has written a play, *Amherst Sabbath*, to demonstrate his theory that Dickinson's poetry was influenced by hymn tunes as well as lyrics (first performed, June 1997).

7. This question goes back to the work of Edith Wylder in 1971. Wylder argues that Dickinson appropriates a system of rhetorical notation that she learned at the Amherst Academy in her use of dashes that slant in different directions and are of various lengths.

8. Elizabeth Perlmutter's 1977 essay on Dickinson's use of the "existential sentence" constitutes an early use of transformational generative grammar in interpreting Dickinson's poetry.

Further Reading

Borroff, Marie. *Language and the Poet: Verbal Artistry in Frost, Stevens, and Moore.* Chicago: University of Chicago Press, 1979.

Freeman, Margaret. "Reading Emily Dickinson: Studies in Cognitive Poetics" (manuscript).

Grabher, Gudrun M., and Ulrike Jessner, eds. *Semantics of Silences in Linguistics and Literature.* Heidelberg: Winter, 1996.

Hollis, Carroll C. *Language and Style in "Leaves of Grass."* Baton Rouge: Louisiana State University Press, 1983.

Margaret H. Freeman

A Cognitive Approach to Dickinson's Metaphors

Introduction

I am Judith the heroine of the Apocrypha, and you the orator of Ephesus. That's
what they call a metaphor in our country. Don't be afraid of it, sir, it won't bite. If
it were my *Carlo* now! The Dog is the noblest work of Art, sir. (L34)[1]

*E*mily Dickinson's lighthearted comment in the first of her
works to be published reveals a characteristic intrinsic to the human mind: the
ability to analogize, to create metaphors which "carry over" (from μeta +
φérein) a concept from one domain to another. After drawing attention to the
analogy she has just made ("That's what they call a metaphor"), Dickinson
promptly transforms the metaphor itself into the shape of a dog ("it won't
bite"), which then becomes a "work of Art," closing the metaphorical circle.
For metaphor has, since classical times, been associated with art, with poetry.
But Dickinson is also doing something else in this passage. She is poking fun
("Don't be afraid of it, sir") at the nineteenth century's cultural valuing of "real
life," the life of industry and commerce, of things as they are, over the life of
the imagination, of making things appear as they are not, of the "dangers" of
the analogizing mind.[2]

Nineteenth-century New England was, of course, not alone in fearing the
effects of reasoning by analogy. Analytical logic was invented to replace it, and
introduced into Puritan New England through the writings of Peter Ramus
(P. Miller). Rhetoric attempted to contain and control it by categorization and
classification, breaking it into separate, discrete components, into tropes and
figures, making them "figures of speech" rather than "figures of thought."
The seventeenth and eighteenth centuries suppressed it, in Gérard Genette's
words, "by the repressive objectivism proper to the Classical ethos, which
a priori regarded any metaphor as suspect of the excessively fantastical, and
kept the 'symbolic' imagination strictly on a leash" (120). But, like the dog, it
could not be kept down. As Emerson remarks in his essay on nature, "man is
an analogist, and studies relations in all objects." By the end of the twentieth

258

century, enough is known about the cognitive processes of the mind to explain why. Analogical thinking is what the mind does (Holyoak and Thagard). It pervades every aspect of our lives. It is the process by which human beings make sense of their world, whether it is the world of politics, law, medicine, science, commerce, art, or philosophy itself (M. Johnson, "Anniversary Issue").

Literary critics have always recognized the analogical processes of poetry, and all literary criticism engages it in one way or another. Emily Dickinson criticism is no exception. Although in one sense all readings of her poetry can be said to involve the analysis of tropes and figures, some literary critics have focused their interpretations specifically on figurative language. These works fall into three major categories: (1) the analysis of imagery in individual poems or across a cluster of poems; (2) the exploration of global figurative patterns or "themes"; (3) the development of a compositional figurative theory. The order of these categories reflects a general trend in the twentieth century (trend, not movement, since examples of each category can be found throughout the century of Dickinson criticism) toward critical theoretical approaches.[3] Thus one finds in the criticism explorations of specific images, such as "house-door-prison," bees and butterflies, hunger and thirst, or barefootedness, along with the major themes of love and death, life and immortality, nature and art.[4] After T. H. Johnson made all the known poems available in his three-volume edition in the 1950s, a minor explosion of scholarship dealing with global patterns erupted, such as Rebecca Patterson's cardinal points of Dickinson's "geography," Inder Nath Kher's "landscape of absence," Jane Donahue Eberwein's discussion of circumference, or Wendy Barker's analysis of light/dark imagery. As the second half of the century proceeded, studies were developed that located Dickinson's figurative language in the context of psychology (Cody; Pollak, *Anxiety*) or feminism (Juhasz, "Adventures"), or literary theory (Stonum). In all the critical studies that span the century, there is a paucity of explicit reference to tropes and figures, per se, reflecting the classical assumption that, as figurative language is the domain of poetry, the role of the critic is simply to use tropes and figures as tools for explication and analysis, without considering the theoretical principles on which they rest.

Several Dickinson critics have, however, dealt explicitly with metonymy, synecdoche, metaphor, and irony. In this essay, a representative sampling of criticism shows how critics have used one or more of these tropes to reveal the structure of Dickinson's poetic design and thus her poetic vision. The analysis that follows explains how two different feminist readings of Dickinson develop from traditional metaphor theory. In contrast, the theory of cognitive metaphor (D. Freeman, "According" and "Catch[ing]") illuminates the ways different interpretations of a Dickinson poem complement or conflict with each other. Finally, I present an example of a basic conceptual metaphor in everyday thought by which Dickinson constructs her conceptual universe.

DICKINSON'S "IRONIC CAW [CORE?]"

In what is perhaps the most detailed study to date on the structural use of poetic tropes in American poetry, Mutlu Konuk Blasing presents a "chart" of correspondences (6; see table below).

Trope	Poetic strategy	Relation between signifier and referent, vehicle and tenor
metonymy	allegory	consequence; expression; reduction
metaphor	analogy	resemblance; correspondence
synecdoche	anagogy	identity; isomorphism
irony	literalism	difference; dissemblance; anomaly

Blasing's thesis is that, although all poets make use of these tropes for stylistic purposes, only one dominates as a rhetorical strategy for a particular poet, thus providing a "genetic typing" of poetic structure. Because she finds in Dickinson's poetry difference, dissemblance, and anomaly, and a focus on the literal meaning of words, Blasing claims that Dickinson is overwhelmingly the poet of irony, with the consequence that "Dickinson's work presents an ironic comment on nineteenth century poetics" (173). She sees Dickinson's poetry as subversive, whether of patriarchy, Christian metaphysics, or language itself.

It is no accident that Shapiro and Shapiro identify irony as *the* deconstructionist trope. The consequences of irony's two main strategies — discovering the incoherence in arbitrary linguistic signs and reducing everything to text — mean that it can only serve as subversive commentary; it cannot of itself construct a world view. It is, Shapiro and Shapiro note, allied to the grotesque in literature (12), a point confirmed by Cristanne Miller's discussion of Dickinson's "humor of excess" as focusing attention simultaneously on the literal and the figurative in order to disrupt and subvert ("The Humor of Excess"). Irony, by its very nature, is the one trope that cannot "construct." Blasing's analysis creates ironically suggestive readings at the expense of those that reveal Dickinson's construction of a world view. Although Dickinson frequently resorts to irony, defining her poetic strategy as ironic reduces the value of her world view to aporia, to nothing, to silence.

Dickinson's "Clue divine"

Blasing's chart of correspondences is too neat, too pat. It is true that most critics recognize the elements of difference, dissemblance, and anomaly in Dickinson's poetry. But by restricting these relations to the trope of irony, Blasing is forced by her own methodology to see irony as the structural principle of Dickinson's poetic strategy. In a subtle and more philosophical approach, Roland Hagenbüchle has identified these relations as belonging also to the trope of metonymy. With its contiguous relations of cause and effect, metonymy lends itself, as Kenneth Burke has noted, to the characterization of the abstract and intangible through the concrete and tangible (*Grammar* 506). Metonymy is closely related to the cognitive strategies that transform thought into language. Its defining characteristic is associated not with the *identification* of abstract concept with concrete image but with a *reference* from one to the other, the suggestive pointing toward the intangible from the tangible. It creates, in Hagenbüchle's words, a "poetry of inference" in which "language can only be a sign, a reference to that 'syllable-less sea' which the philosophers, for want of a better name, termed 'being' " ("Precision" 48).

Robert Weisbuch also claims that Dickinson "can proceed only by inference" (*Poetry* 79).[5] He places Dickinson within the romantic tradition of "anti-allegory," antiallegory that frustrates one-to-one correspondence and substitutes instead "concentrically expanding and contracting connotations, for analogical meanings within the single word" (53). Dickinson's poetic strategy is metonymic, as his analysis of Dickinson's typology of death and his chapter on "quest fiction" show. Typology is a special case of metonymy in that it not only creates an unequal connection between terms but completes and defines the meaning of the other (79). Poetry for Dickinson, Weisbuch says, becomes "the mind's continual thrust toward the ungraspable, as questing rather than completed vision" (175).

Metonymy, then, is claimed to be the structural principle of Dickinson's poetics because, in Hagenbüchle's words, metonymy's "deliberate indeterminacy . . . alone can do justice to the mystery of existence" ("Precision" 50).[6]

Dickinson's Preference for "Dis" over "Syn"

Although metonymy and synecdoche have been considered close cousins, they are, as tropes of thought, quite different in their effects. Whereas metonymy reflects unstable, asymmetrical relations, synecdoche, as Blasing's chart shows, is the trope of anagogy, of identity and isomorphism. It projects a world which is stable, unified, and meaningful. It is the trope of transcendentalism, of ulti-

mate knowledge, informing what E. Miller Budick calls sacramental and idealist symbolism. In a detailed study of Dickinson's "symbolic poetics," and using
a vocabulary of as many as twenty "dis-" words, from "disappearance" to "dis-
unity," Budick's analysis shows why synecdoche, although it occurs as a figure
in the poems, does not fit the structural principles of Dickinson's poetics.

Budick describes how Dickinson dismantles the deceptive and false sym-
bolisms of both Puritan and transcendental thinking. Since knowledge, however, cannot exist without symbol, Budick advocates for Dickinson "a symbolism within boundaries, a measured and self-critical symbolism in which the
borders between God and nature are firmly drawn" (121). Budick goes beyond
Hagenbüchle's metonymy and Weisbuch's quest fiction, claiming that these
"material-idealism" symbols "convey an accurate portrait of cosmic reality" (187) and "can effectively put us in touch with divine truth" (188). By
claiming that the poems "strive for a mimesis so total that it can reenact a
temporal as well as geographic unfolding of cosmic processes and laws" (227–
28), Budick falls into the very synecdochic trap she was at pains to show
Dickinson escaping.

DICKINSON'S ANALOGICAL THINKING

Budick's analysis depends on the traditional "body–mind" split of Western
philosophy and the belief in a world external to the mind that the mind can
know independently of itself, a belief cognitive theorists call Objective Realism (M. Johnson, *Body*). Both the acceptance and denial of sacramental or
idealist symbolism rest on this belief (you either can or cannot know the true
nature of the external world). It is right at this point that cognitive theory
differs. Under cognitive theory, knowledge of the world is *formed* by our
experience of the world.

In *Emily Dickinson's Poetry*, Weisbuch identifies analogy as "the pattern" of
Dickinson's thought (12), thus in a way stepping "behind" symbolism and all
the tropes, since analogy's associating of one concept with another is common
to them all (for irony, it is the association of context or meaning). With this
move, Weisbuch restores the relation of similarity observed by classical dif-
ferentiations without reducing the "figures of thought" to sameness. His "analogical poetics," prefiguring cognitive metaphor, claims that "the analogical
poet displays his connective process and thus makes less of a claim for how the
world is put together than for how his mind puts it together" (14). Analogy,
under this view, is "metaphor-in-the-making, in which the associative process
calls attention to itself" (13). Dickinson's focus on analogical connection,
Weisbuch observes, explains the "scenelessness" of her poems: "Most often,

the boundary of a Dickinson poem is not a particular scene or situation but the figure of the analogy as it moves from scene to scene" (16).

Weisbuch identifies three types of analogy in Dickinson's poetry: (1) analogical collection, in which a series of analogies illustrates the major argument; (2) simple extended analogy, which is made up of two parts — the "structure of intent" or "self sufficient design of action" of the inner analogy and the "illustratory imagery" or "specific applications" of the "outer" analogy; and (3) symbolic, in that the analogies are only implied, not stated, and "its implications, its 'outer' analogies, are invariably plural and occasionally conflicting" (43). It is this third category of analogy that invites antiallegorical, quest fiction, or metonymic readings and, by doing so, relates metonymy to metaphor, the trope of Weisbuch's first two analogical types.[7]

Metaphor has been called *the* analogical trope, "*the* figure, the trope of tropes" (Jacques Sojcher, qtd. in Genette 115), a view reflected in the opening sentence of one doctoral dissertation, which "examines Emily Dickinson's metaphors, focusing on the major traditional categories of figuration: simile, metaphor, metonymy, synecdoche, paradox" (Guerra). In their treatment of metaphor in Dickinson, critics have by and large adopted the classical definition of metaphor as a figure of thought that describes one object or idea in terms of another, without exploring the nature of metaphor and how it works in cognition and language.[8] As a result, divergent readings of a Dickinson poem can result from the particular stance a critic takes toward the definition of metaphor itself. Two recent studies that exemplify this point draw very different conclusions from the same data (Homans, "Love and Death"; Juhasz, "Adventures").

Margaret Homans's definition of metaphor, though based on Lacanian subjectivity and Irigaray's theory of hierarchy, is the more traditional, in its assertion that "[o]ne thing, the word, stands for or in the place of something else, the object" ("Love and Death" 116).[9] In comparing some of the heterosexual love poems with those between two women, Homans sees metaphor as "depend[ing] on and reproduc[ing] a hierarchical power structure in which one term claims the authority to define the other term — or, in its implications for the personal, one person claims the authority to define another person" (116). As a result, since the love poems between women envision them as equal partners, this stance forces Homans into a position of claiming that Dickinson, in undermining the hierarchical view she takes in the heterosexual poems, is undermining metaphor itself.

Although Suzanne Juhasz also emphasizes the "subversive" nature of Dickinson's poems, her definition of metaphor is more psychologically oriented, following Kristeva's theory of metaphor as an agent of the semiotic and associating it with Freud's "condensation," which "allows us to represent in language a complex series of associations in relatively simple grammatical structure" ("Adventures" 151). It is in her recognition, however, that the transferring aspects of metaphor seem rather to create and highlight relationships than to suppress them, that Juhasz's own theory of metaphor insightfully illuminates the way Dickinson "employs it to say at least two things at once and, even more significantly, to create a complicated relationship between two ideas and images" (152). The ensuing analysis of Dickinson's poem, "Joy to have merited the Pain" (P788), shows how the function of metaphor in bridging two dialects (one of cultural norms and values, the other of mutually shared personal experience) effectively transcends the constraints of both to make language real, creating a "moment" of "imagined actuality — an actual figuration" (160). In this sense, Juhasz's theory of metaphor moves away from the objectivist tradition exemplified by Homans and into the domain of seeing metaphor as a cognitive construction of experience, the domain of cognitive metaphor.

A spate of new books on metaphor in the 1980s created a watershed in metaphor theory (D. Freeman, "Songs"). Lakoff, Johnson, and Turner have shown how basic conceptual metaphors enable us to understand abstract notions through our embodied experiences and to appreciate their power in constructing the way we see our world (Lakoff and Johnson; Lakoff and Turner). They challenge the notion that metaphor is restricted to the domain of literature by showing that metaphors are pervasive in human language, that we cannot think abstractions without thinking metaphorically. The cognitive basis of metaphor is analogy, which, as Holyoak and Thagard point out, we comprehend through the constraints of similarity, structure, and purpose (220). When we read a literary text, we engage in a twofold analogical exercise, applying our own analogical imaginative reasoning to a text that has already been created by the analogical imaginative reasoning of the writer. The analogical process we exercise can be shaped by any one of its three aspects of similarity, structure, and purpose. For the literary critic, this explains how multiple interpretations of a text can occur. When the critic maps on the basis of similarity or purpose, the kind of analogy Weisbuch calls "outer analogy" is created.[10] Mapping on the basis of structural or systematic design creates "inner analogy," which is thus central to any "outer analogy" readings the poem may bear.

Readings of a Dickinson poem can be considered members of a category which includes all viable interpretations of the poem. Under cognitive theory, categories form radial relationships, from the most prototypical to the least prototypical (Lakoff, *Women*; Rosch).[11] Because Weisbuch's "inner analogy" reflects the structural or systematic design of a poem, it is, I would suggest, its central or prototypical reading.

DICKINSON'S CONCEPTUAL METAPHORS

In other words, a metaphorical reading of a poem based on systematic mapping will produce a prototypical reading of that poem; metaphorical readings based on similarity or purpose will produce nonprototypical or illustrative readings. Metaphorical readings of Dickinson's poems invariably take the form of Weisbuch's "outer analogies." They account for readings of poems that may differ in their conclusions but do not directly conflict with each other. When readings do conflict, it is because they depend on a conflicting interpretation of the "inner" or systematic design of the analogy. When nonprototypical readings conflict directly with each other, it is usually because of a conflict in attribute mapping, the one-to-one correspondence between tenor and vehicle that traditional metaphorical theory produces, or because of a conflict in "purpose" — in the ideological stance that critics may take. Nonprototypical readings that conflict with the prototypical reading of the poem will be false readings; those that do not conflict will be true readings. Failure to recognize this distinction is, I believe, the reason critics argue over whether differing interpretations are valid or not. Such arguments can never be resolved until the readings are checked against the prototypical reading.[12]

To show how this works, I can do no better than explore different critical analyses of a single poem: "My Life had stood — a Loaded Gun —."

> My Life had stood — a
> Loaded Gun —
> In Corners — till a Day
> The Owner passed — identified —
> And carried Me away —
>
> And now We roam + in Sovereign Woods —
> And now We hunt the Doe —
> And every time I speak
> for Him —
> The Mountains straight reply —
>
> And do I smile, such
> cordial light
> Upon the Valley glow —
> It is as a Vesuvian face
> Had let its pleasure through —
>
> And when at Night — Our
> good Day done —
> I guard My Master's head —
> 'Tis better than the Eider —
> Duck's
> + Deep Pillow — to have shared —

To foe of His — I'm deadly
foe —
None + stir the second time —
On whom I lay a Yellow
Eye —
Or An emphatic Thumb —

Though I than He — may
longer live
He longer must — than I.
For I have but the + power
to kill,
Without — the power   to die —
+ the — + low + harm + art (F34, 825–26, P754)[13]

The adjective most frequently used to describe Dickinson's Loaded Gun poem is "notorious." Although it is one of Dickinson's most frequently analyzed poems, few if any critics have produced a reading that they themselves are satisfied with. The problem lies in reconciling the final stanza with the rest of the poem. Attempts at reconciliation seem forced. Most critics give up and conclude that the poem fails or breaks down. This situation occurs, I think, because all these critics, in adopting a traditional approach to metaphor, produce nonprototypical readings of the poem without considering its prototypical reading. Only Weisbuch's discussion of the poem distinguishes the two readings in his analysis of the inner analogy and then of the outer analogy or illustrative possibilities. His inner-analogy reading, as one would expect since it is mapping on the basis of the structure of the poem's design, matches my prototypical reading, although his is not presented from the perspective of cognitive metaphor as is mine.[14] Like Weisbuch, I will show that the final stanza, far from being an anomaly or an enigma, is the climax of a coherent progression through metaphor that has been building from the very first stanza.

To take the last first: the speaking persona of the poem — a loaded gun — is comparing itself to its owner/master. The gun realizes that it, like its owner, has the power to kill; it does not, however, as its owner does, have the power to die. In itself, since inanimate objects can be instruments of death without themselves able to experience it, this does not seem a particularly insightful observation. As Sharon Cameron has noted, "something further seems intended" (*Choosing* 66).

Something further *is* intended. A preliminary reading of this poem is straightforward and unproblematic. Its narrative is told from the perspective of a gun — more specifically a rifle — as the poet metaphorically projects the domain of human experience onto the domain of the gun as it recounts the story of its "life." In contemporary metaphor theory, the image-schematic structure of the target domain constrains which image-schematic structures from the source domain are mapped onto it (this is the invariance principle of Lakoff and Turner). In Dickinson's poem, however, a reversal takes place: it is the concrete source domain of the physical object "gun" that constrains the way we are invited to interpret the abstract domain of "life." (Failure to recognize this reversal is partly why some literary critical analyses go wrong.) Because the dominant metaphors in the poem map only those objects of the source domain *gun* that are coherent with the target domain *life*, the poem is deeply ironic. Although the gun persona attempts to project itself as a living being, it fails throughout to do so. By implicitly comparing the "life" of a gun to human life, Dickinson makes us see how impoverished and inadequate the gun's projected "life" actually is, and thus how impoverished and inadequate human life would be if it experienced only those characteristics of life expressed by the gun. From the first stanza to the last, the gun tries, but fails, to experience life as humans do. This failure can be traced in each stanza through the application of cognitive metaphor.

George Lakoff has shown how the EVENT STRUCTURE metaphor has two "versions": LOCATION and OBJECT ("Contemporary Theory").[15] The difference can be seen in the contrast between "we're coming up on Lent" (Lent as LOCATION) and "Lent is approaching" (Lent as OBJECT). In the first stanza, based on the metaphors ABSTRACTIONS ARE OBJECTS, A PERSON IS A POSSESSED OBJECT, EVENTS ARE ACTIONS, and LIFE IS A JOURNEY, the life of the gun is seen as an object that has come to a standstill, stuck in corners. Now objects in the EVENT STRUCTURE metaphor are self-moving, as in the example just given, "Lent is approaching." But the gun isn't. It must wait for its owner (who *is* self-moving) to pass, identify, and carry it away. Thus the contrast between the gun's life and its owner's life with respect to the question of self-propulsion and self-motivation is laid down in the very first stanza.

If this were a poem mainly predicated on the LIFE IS A JOURNEY metaphor as is Robert Frost's celebrated poem, "Two Roads Diverged in a Yellow Wood," it would be unproblematic. However, "My Life had stood" ranges across a series of complex metaphor systems that interact, as Zoltán Kövecses has shown, to represent abstract concepts like friendship, love, and life itself. That is to say, the JOURNEY metaphor is not the only source domain for LIFE in this poem: the COMMUNICATION, EMOTION, and BOND metaphors are also active.[16] Thus, in stanza 2, both EMOTION and COMMUNICATION metaphors are activated: AN INSTRUMENT IS A COMPANION in the first two lines (We roam, We hunt), and a LANGUAGE COMMUNICATION metaphor underlying the gun's attempt to assert independence as it "speaks for" its owner and gets a "reply" from the mountain. Nevertheless, the gun's "language" is, ironically, not the interactive pro-

ductive communicative system that characterizes human language. The sound
of the gun is merely echoed, not answered. Again the gun has failed to experience life, here as interactive communication, that humans experience.

From the attempted "companionship" of the second stanza, the gun unsuc-
cessfully attempts to ally itself with its human owner in a progressive movement through the EMOTION metaphor toward the climax of total identification
in stanza 5.[17] Briefly, EMOTION IS TEMPERATURE governs the image of cordiality
(relating to the heart). As the gun attempts to "enliven," give life to its flash by
the metaphor of a smile, it tries to ally itself with the mountains it ironically
failed to communicate with by comparing itself to Mount Vesuvius. But the
"pleasure" of seeming affection (with the AFFECTION IS WARMTH metaphor) is
undermined for the reader by the associated threatening image of a volcanic
eruption, and the actual function of a gun—death—overrides its attempt to
assert its opposite—life.

The suggestion of emotion and affection is, in stanza 4, reinforced by the
metaphor INTIMACY IS CLOSENESS, as the gun sees its function as protecting its
master. Here, the gun again fails in its attempt to attain human life, fails to
understand that the MORE SHARING THERE IS, THE GREATER THE INTIMACY, in its
almost defensive assertion that protecting is better than sharing. THE MORE
INTIMACY THERE IS, THE MORE TWO BECOME ONE. But in becoming one (stanza
5), the gun conceives its relationship to its master as one of PROTECTION in the
context of WAR (again an image more appropriate to the real function of guns
than to what this gun is trying to achieve), instead of INTIMACY IN A SEXUAL
RELATIONSHIP. The gun's self-deceptive identification with its master is complete; the yellow eye and the emphatic thumb as the sighting and cocking
activities that the owner employs on the gun's instruments is an ironically
sexually suggestive *death* image. The gun's tone by now is brash, confident, a
tone that will be totally undermined by the concessionary recognition of the
final stanza.

Here, the gun faces the truth. Although it "may" live, have the potentiality
it expressed at the beginning of the poem for a rich and fulfilling life, it cannot.
Genderless, the gun cannot experience life as humans do. Engendered human
beings experience fully the three great themes of life, love, and death. The
"scope of the metaphor," to use Kövecses' phrase, is consistent. The irony is
central to the poem's recognition of what it means to be human: to live and to
love, to experience and practice violence, to suffer, ultimately to die.

Under cognitive theory, metaphorical conceptualization is more than a
simple one-to-one mapping of attributes. In Dickinson's "Loaded Gun"
poem, several basic conceptual metaphors cohere to produce, in Weisbuch's
phrase, "the single extended analogy." These metaphors are productive in the

sense that they enable metaphorical mappings that are multiple and coherent. A reading that is based on a traditional approach to metaphor, that starts with a one-to-one correlation between, for example, gun and woman, is bound to encounter difficulties with the final stanza. It is not the case that the gun is simply a metaphor for a woman or daemon, for language or Christ, to cite just a few critical readings, or that the owner is simply a metaphor for a man or the self, for the mind or God.[18] The poem exists on a more abstract level of analogical mapping; it is "about" all these things through the image schemas that represent the various aspects of what it means to experience life, issues such as love and sex, language and power, aggression and violence. A reading that starts at a more abstract level of metaphorical mapping can generate all the insightful metaphorical interpretations critics have produced without conflicting with the poem's inner coherence.

On an even more abstract level, the different metaphorical readings of the poem raise the same ultimate questions as to the meaning and significance of human life and death. It is no wonder that Dickinson's "Loaded Gun" poem is so celebrated — it includes them all.

A cognitive metaphor reading of a literary text based on its systematic design is a prototypical reading of that text. Therefore, any literary critical analysis that construes Dickinson's poem (insightfully, I may say) as dealing with issues of power, identity, and aggression, that interprets the poem in terms of religion, male/female relations, or language, must be consistent within the scope of the cognitive metaphor reading I have given. Critics, for example, who make a direct correlation between the gun persona and a woman, and whose interpretation as a consequence inevitably founders on the last stanza, need to revise their reading to a more indirect analysis of the poem as representing a woman's role in life, a role that may be suggested in the genderless gun's view of what life is.

CONCLUSION

Although a cognitive metaphor approach can illuminate the reading of a single poem, its power lies in its ability to uncover the basic conceptual metaphors common to the poetry as a whole and which contribute to the very structure of a poet's conceptual universe. As I have shown elsewhere, at least one such conceptual metaphor forms Dickinson's thought (M. Freeman, "Metaphor"). Dickinson's LIFE IS A VOYAGE IN SPACE metaphor enables us to understand that her so-called abstract images are grounded in her physical and intellectual experience of the world and the universe around her. The constructive power of metaphor enables a poet like Dickinson to create her own individual world truth, a truth that is grounded in a physically embodied universe. Metaphors in themselves, perhaps, don't bite. But the "noblest work of Art" created by them does. It is through such conceptualizing ability that we make our world real.

NOTES

1. This excerpt is taken from a prose valentine Dickinson wrote in 1850. It was the first of her works, so far as we know, to be published, appearing in Amherst College's *Indicator* in 1850. No manuscript version has so far been found.

2. A year later, Dickinson writes to her brother: "We dont *have* very many jokes tho' *now*, it is pretty much all sobriety, and we do not have much poetry, father having made up his mind that it is pretty much all *real life*. Fathers real life and *mine* sometimes come into collision, but as yet, escape unhurt!" (L65).

3. One can see the trend in the subject indexes of Dickinson bibliographies. In Buckingham's bibliography, from 1850 to 1968, under "metaphor," the reader is directed to "imagery"; Dandurand's bibliography, from 1969 to 1985, cites sixteen entries under "metaphor."

4. Examples (among many too numerous to record) are as follows: the "house-door-prison" imagery (Schreiber); bees and butterflies (Gelpi, *Mind*; Khan); hunger and thirst (Copple); barefootedness (McGuire); love and death, life and immortality (Anderson, *Stairway*; Griffith); nature and art (De Eulis).

5. Although Weisbuch does not use the term "metonymy" his approach parallels that of Hagenbüchle, Weisbuch's "precise imprecision" (*Poetry* 53) reflecting the "precision and indeterminacy" in the title of Hagenbüchle's article.

6. Other studies dealing with metonymy can be found in Kaplan; Khan; Oakes.

7. In "Rhetoric Restrained," Genette deplores the conflation of metaphor and metonymy in Proust's habit of naming any figure of analogy "metaphor" (113). That this has become the standard term can be seen in the proliferation of books on metaphor and, in particular, in the theory of cognitive metaphor.

8. In his work on metaphor, Mark Turner discusses the role of literary critics in making important observations about literature and the need for them to better understand the tools of their trade (*Death; Reading*).

9. This definition reflects the reduction of metaphor to a figure of speech rather than a figure of thought, which occurred with the decline of rhetoric into style (Genette), and also reflects Objective Realism in its assumption that "words" can stand for "things."

10. Mapping — finding a systematic set of correspondences between the two terms of an analogy — was initially associated with Max Black's interaction theory. The term has been generally adopted in analogy research, although Black's interaction theory has not been generally accepted. See Ortony for a useful survey of recent theories.

11. Under cognitive theory, in order to be members of a category, members do not necessarily share the same features, as is true in classical classification theory. Prototypicality refers to the fact that some members may be more "central," i.e., better examples of the category than others (Lakoff, *Women*).

12. E. D. Hirsch, Jr., makes a similar point when he says that interpretation is not complete until the "structure of component meanings" and their emphases have been considered (230). My approach differs from his in positing the notion of a prototypical reading that is central to all valid readings.

13. The text of Dickinson's poem is taken from Franklin's *Manuscript Books*. Variants are marked with crosses and placed at the end of the poem, as in the original manuscript. Line breaks are left as they appear in the original manuscript to enable each reader to determine whether to consider them as new lines or runovers. Where spacing seems deliberate (as in the last line), I have tried to reflect it. Following the practice in this book, no attempt has been made to capture the difference of the slant marks or "dashes."

14. Weisbuch's lengthy discussion of the poem (in *Poetry*) seems to me absolutely correct in its analysis and conclusions. The only distinction between his reading and mine is that, in applying cognitive metaphor theory, my reading makes more explicit the conceptual basis on which Weisbuch's reading rests and shows how the poem, like all poetry, adopts the same conceptual metaphorical structures that occur in everyday language.

15. It has become customary in cognitive metaphor research to indicate the image schemas, structural metaphors, and basic conceptual metaphors in small capital letters to indicate an unanalyzed complex structure, much as the Δ is used in transformational grammar. For example, for the purposes of this discussion, I have not opened up the metaphor of AN INSTRUMENT IS A COMPANION, although instrumentality is a significant component in the poem's total metaphorical statement.

16. The unanalyzed metaphors in this section are all drawn from Kövecses' article.

17. See Weisbuch's reading of the poem, especially stanza 3. He proposes that the process of total identification is occurring faster than my analysis suggests: "Unless we see that volcanic face as the owner's (and this would disrupt the physical exactness of the poem, for the face which 'shows through' the gun must be the flash of firing, not the gun's owner and shooter), the life-gun is beginning to speak in relation to itself, as though it can pull its own trigger. Yet from the analogy we know that no such independence is possible. Instead, the life-gun has equated its purpose so thoroughly with the owner's that it is beginning to perpetuate him; another illusion of selfhood and self-expression" (*Poetry* 29).

18. The following chart outlines the metaphorical correspondences that seven representative critics have drawn for the gun and its owner:

Gun	Self	(Sharon Cameron)
Owner	World force	
Gun	Woman artist	(Albert Gelpi)
Owner	Masculine animus	
Gun	Adolescent girl	(Cristanne Miller)
Owner	"Owner/Master"	
Gun	Dickinson	(Vivian Pollak)
Owner	Male personification of her aggression	
Gun	Language	(David Porter)
Owner	Self	
Gun	Woman poet	(Adrienne Rich)
Owner	Daemon/destructive power	
Gun	Death	(Cynthia G. Wolff)
Owner	Christ/God	

All these readings are nonprototypical in that they either map on the basis of similarity (e.g., gun/woman; gun/language) or on the basis of purpose (e.g., feminist/patriarchy; psychological/struggle within the self; linguistic/poetry, language). All are uneasy readings, in the sense that the critics themselves are not entirely satisfied that their readings holistically characterize the poem, and yet all capture essential aspects of the metaphoric domains included in the poem's world.

FURTHER READING

Fauconnier, Gilles. *Mappings in Thought and Language*. Cambridge: Cambridge University Press, 1997.

Fishelov, David. *Metaphors of Genre: The Role of Analogies in Genre Theory*. University Park: Pennsylvania State University Press, 1993.

Freeman, Margaret H. "Grounded Spaces: Deictic -*Self* Anaphors in the Poetry of Emily Dickinson." *Language and Literature* 6:1 (1997): 7–28.

———. "Poetry and the Scope of Metaphor: Toward a Cognitive Theory of Literature." *Metaphor and Metonymy at the Crossroads*. Ed. Antonio Barcelona. The Hague: Mouton, forthcoming.

Lakoff, George, and Mark Johnson. *Philosophy in the Flesh*. Chicago: University of Chicago Press, forthcoming.

Turner, Mark. *The Literary Mind*. Chicago: University of Chicago Press, 1996.

Josef Raab

The Metapoetic Element in Dickinson

> "Pass in, pass in," the angels say,
> "In to the upper doors,
> Nor count compartments of the floors,
> But mount to paradise
> By the stairway of surprise."
>
> Ralph Waldo Emerson, "Merlin"

*T*wo letters written in the summer of 1862 may facilitate our understanding of Emily Dickinson's view of her role as a poet. She told Thomas Wentworth Higginson:

> Perhaps you smile at me. I could not stop for that — My Business is Circumference — An ignorance, not of Customs, but if caught with the Dawn — or the Sunset see me — Myself the only Kangaroo among the Beauty, Sir, if you please, it afflicts me, and I thought that instruction would take it away. . . .
> When I state myself, as the Representative of the Verse — it does not mean — me — but a supposed person. (L268)

And in Dickinson's letter to Dr. and Mrs. J. G. Holland we read:

> Perhaps you laugh at me! Perhaps the whole United States are laughing at me too! *I* can't stop for that! *My* business is to love. I found a bird, this morning, down — down — on a little bush at the foot of the garden, and wherefore sing, I said, since nobody *hears?*
> One sob in the throat, one flutter of bosom — "*My* business is to *sing*" — and away she rose! How do I know but cherubim, once, themselves, as patient, listened, and applauded her unnoticed hymn? (L269)

These letters show that at the height of her poetic creativity Emily Dickinson is very much aware of her outsider status in a world that may "smile" and "laugh" at and about her. She, however, has found her vocation as a poet and

273

will not be distracted from the task she has set herself. The "supposed person" which she creates in her poetry is in part a defense mechanism.[1] When she states that her "business is to love" and when she joins the bird in proclaiming "*My* business is to *sing*," Dickinson assumes the pose of the romantic poets, which is not unlike that of Walt Whitman. But hers is a different kind of poetry. While others may believe that the object of a poem can be grasped in language, Dickinson is less confident: "My Business is Circumference," she concludes, since she knows that truth or essences lie beyond human understanding; they can at best be approximated indirectly — by the mind as well as by language. As it is impossible for her to reach the center, the poet needs to circle around this center, to examine it indirectly from various perspectives and with various alternatives in mind. While this process of approximation aims at exploring the "Mystery" (P1768) of things, all it manages to do is to uncover more that is unknown or unknowable. Echoing Shelley, Dickinson explains, "I work to drive the awe away, yet awe impels the work" (L891). The awe of the ungraspable is caused by and also calls for the poetic method of circumferential approximation, as Dickinson's expression "Circumference thou Bride of Awe" (P1620) implies.[2]

This essay aims at illustrating Dickinson's attitudes toward the nature of poetry and the role of the poet. After a concise review of scholarship on this topic I will examine the various kinds of metapoetic commentary contained in Dickinson's work, particularly in her poems. Specifically, I shall address her remarks on the nature and possibilities of language, the importance of the imagination, her own poetic technique, and finally her view of the poet's task. It is hoped that those metapoetic comments will promote our understanding of Dickinson's art. But it will be impossible to reach any consensus on which exactly are to be considered her most "metapoetic poems," since, to a certain degree, all of Emily Dickinson's poetry could be read as dealing with the poet and her art.

With regard to her place in literary history, Dickinson's metapoetic comments will allow us to position her as a protomodernist. While she is often classified as a romantic poet, a closer examination of her poems on poetry reveals that, although she sometimes seems to adhere to Wordsworth's idea of poetry as the "spontaneous overflow of powerful feelings" or Coleridge's organicist thought and although she sees the role of the poet primarily in romantic terms, Dickinson is also a precursor of the modernists.[3] What she seeks to achieve in poetry is to render the indeterminate meaning of the world and of human existence. Since unambiguous truth no longer exists, language, in her opinion, cannot get to the center of objects or issues. Like the human mind, language and poetry can at best hope to approximate essences; process has to replace stasis and stability, a slanted view must take the place of direct-ness. For this reason the modernist Dickinson is convinced that the poet's realm is that of "Circumference."

REVIEW OF SCHOLARSHIP

The only in-depth treatment devoted exclusively to the metapoetic element of Emily Dickinson's work is "Emily Dickinson: Poems on Poetry and Poets" by Siegfried Baruffol, a thesis available from the University of Zürich.[4] Baruffol starts out with the awe behind Dickinson's poems and moves on to an analysis of the poet's statements on the weight of words and the evanescence of "true poems" as well as the primacy of the imagination in Dickinson's poetic cre-ations. The principal roles of the poet are considered to be those of seer, sayer, and singer. While this study is the only one specifically concerned with the metapoetic aspect of Dickinson's oeuvre, this element receives some degree of critical attention in the majority of scholarly works on Dickinson. Only a limited number of these and their various emphases can be mentioned here.

The importance of the word for Dickinson has been the focus of numerous books and essays. The pioneering work on Dickinson's language was Brita Lindberg-Seyersted's *Voice of the Poet: Aspects of Style in the Poetry of Emily Dickinson*. It deals with Dickinson's playful and serious uses of words, her colloquialisms, rhetoric, syntax, and sound, her lexical and grammatical neolo-gisms, but the book has little to say on the metapoetic element. Similarly, Charles R. Anderson writes about Dickinson's use of language with regard to its sources and effects but not primarily with regard to Dickinson's own meta-poetic comments:

> The Bible was one of her chief sources of imagery, Shakespeare her chief model in revitalizing language through new strategies. . . . Instead of surface borrow-ings she plundered them outright, stealing the secrets by which they gave life and power to words, but transvaluating them so as to create an idiom all her own. . . . Slant and surprise, the distinctive marks of her best poetry, are the result of her brilliant verbal strategy. (*Stairway* 31)

Albert J. Gelpi defends a similar point of view. He claims that Dickinson had to be a linguistic innovator in order to express her mind's experiences. "Like Ezra Pound, William Carlos Williams, Marianne Moore, and E. E. Cum-mings, Emily Dickinson sought to speak the uniqueness of her experience in a personal tongue by reconstituting and revitalizing—at the risk of eccentric-ity—the basic verbal unit" (*Mind* 147). In a later essay, "Emily Dickinson's Word: Presence as Absence, Absence as Presence," Gelpi deals primarily with what he calls Dickinson's "alternately Romantic and Modernist sense of verbal medium," that is, her responses to the question whether human language can adequately represent experience (42). Despite her frequent feelings of loss, writes Gelpi, "Dickinson affirmed language as presence against its implications of absence" ("Word" 50).

Various aspects of Dickinson's use of language and her attitude toward it have been of interest to scholars for decades. David Porter, for example, commented on the poet's linguistic economy. He wrote that, because of the brevity of Dickinson's poems, "Often for Emily Dickinson a single word must carry *all* of the meaning without the benefit of contextual help from additional and qualifying words" (*Early Poetry* 135), while Roland Hagenbüchle, in "Sign and Process: The Concept of Language in Emerson and Dickinson," convincingly illustrates Dickinson's use of language in her representations of processual experience. Margaret Dickie relates Emily Dickinson to Wallace Stevens and emphasizes "the metonymic habit of the lyric language" (*Lyric* 1), which expresses the idea that the lyric self need not be continuous or coherent, and Suzanne Juhasz analyzes the poetic language Dickinson creates in order to talk about mental experience (*Undiscovered*). Joseph C. Schöpp, in his essay " 'Amazing Sense Distilled from Ordinary Meanings': The Power of the Word in Emily Dickinson's Poems on Poetry," deals with Dickinson's use of language in general and with her comments on the power of words. Starting out from the age's strong concern with language and lexicography, Schöpp presents Dickinson as wavering between what he considers to be a (male) view of language as power and a (female) view of language as a prison house.[5] It might be more correct to say, however, that rather than seeing *language* as a prison house, Dickinson took *consciousness* to be such a confining space. Schöpp concludes that "her poetry can be read as a continuous attempt to negotiate between these two positions of a waning romantic view and a waxing modernist temper. This instability generated by the historical moment accounts for the self-reflexivity and self-referentiality in Dickinson's oeuvre." While the first part of this statement is certainly correct, the second one is debatable.

More encompassing studies of Dickinson's language are E. Miller Budick's *Emily Dickinson and the Life of Language: A Study in Symbolic Poetics*, which explores the poet's symbolism as well as the dangers which the living word holds for her, and Cristanne Miller's *Emily Dickinson: A Poet's Grammar*, which deals with Dickinson's style and diction and the enormous importance that language had for the poet. The latter study constitutes the most in-depth analysis of this aspect since Lindberg-Seyersted's.

Dickinson's metapoetic comments on language and her innovative use of linguistic material impact the communication of her poetry. This subject interested Donald E. Thackrey, who wrote:

> Emily Dickinson's attitude toward words and poetry is something of a paradox. Her intellect and intuitive imagination told her that human communication was unavailing before the greatness of the universe and the complexity of man's experience within it. But her emotional nature, her delight in a struggle, and her unlimited courage bade her make the attempt regardless of its futility. As long as her poetry could at least suggest the infiniteness and wonder of the universe, she thought the effort was justified. And if nothing else, she could vividly call attention to poetry's inadequacy for the most significant communication by, paradoxically enough, communicating that very idea as profoundly as she could to any possible reader of her poems. ("Communication" 67)

Because of the alleged inadequacy of poetry and language to express what she sought to convey, Dickinson decided to choose indeterminacy. As Robert Weisbuch has pointed out, openness and possibility are at the center of Dickinson's poetics: "In Dickinson's celebratory, Transcendentalist world, everyday events and objects are italicized into symbols, appearances rush toward essences, and possibilities never end" (*Poetry* 2). Nonetheless, Weisbuch claims, Dickinson's other side is that of a skeptical sufferer.

Other studies focus on Dickinson's poetic technique, on her muse, and on her attitude toward romanticism. To some degree, these also rely on the metapoetic element of Dickinson's work. Sharon Cameron, especially in her chapter on "Naming as History" (in *Lyric Time*), is concerned with Dickinson's strategies of naming experience, including internal insights. She concludes that Dickinson was successful "in wresting meaning from the elusive territory of the mind" (55). Jane Donahue Eberwein further examines the ways in which Dickinson achieved this wresting of meaning. Eberwein calls Dickinson's technique a "poetics of distillation" which "eliminated as much dross as possible from the verses, leaving a residue that was alive, potent, explosive" (*Strategies* 155).

More strictly concerned with the metapoetic element is Rita di Giuseppe. In her analysis of Dickinson's tropes of poetic creation, di Giuseppe makes two central points, namely "that Emily Dickinson is first and foremost a poet questing for creative autonomy who addresses a muse; and secondly, that for the woman poet the roles of muse and poet may have to be recast" (40). Examining especially what are often called Dickinson's "love poems," di Giuseppe concentrates on religious, natural, and erotic tropes of poetic creativity that are meant to show how the poet dissociates the "God/father/lover" figure from her muse and how she posits the woman poet above that muse. It remains doubtful, however, whether in the case of Dickinson "lover" and muse are in fact separable. Joanne Feit Diehl, finally, reads Dickinson against the male romantic poets, especially Wordsworth, Keats, Shelley, and Emerson. With these Dickinson shares "a faith in the sovereignty of the

imagination and a belief in its powers" (*Romantic* 183), but she is more skeptical than her male fellow poets. While the others find beauty and solace in
nature, Dickinson insists on the creation of a separate reality based upon the
powers of a single consciousness.

Although few studies concentrate solely on the metapoetic element of Emily Dickinson's work, the comments on her art which the writer makes in her
poetry and letters inform much of Dickinson scholarship. They illustrate
the poet's theoretical positions, which can then be tested against her poetic
practice.

THE POWER OF WORDS

Emily Dickinson told her friend Joseph Lyman, "We used to think, Joseph,
when I was an unsifted girl and you so scholarly that words were weak &
cheap. Now I dont [*sic*] know of anything so mighty" (qtd. in R. Sewall, *Lyman
Letters* 78). She was struck by the enormous power that words could have, even
if they were not always able to convey what the poet sought to express. The
culture into which Dickinson had been born was one that, as a consequence of
its Puritan heritage, treasured the word. This concern with language had
reached a culmination with Noah Webster's publication of his *American Dictionary of the English Language* in 1828. Dickinson used the enlarged 1847
edition, which was essential to the composition of her poetry. In 1862 she
wrote to Higginson that "for several years, my Lexicon — was my only companion" (L261). If poetry was Dickinson's religion, then the dictionary was her
Bible.

Nonetheless, language also meant a constant struggle for Emily Dickinson
because it could not adequately render the external world:

> Nature is what we know —
> Yet have no art to say —
> So impotent Our Wisdom is
> To her Simplicity. (P668)

If language cannot even express the concrete, external, then it must certainly
fail in rendering the abstract and internal. For example, Dickinson stressed the
"speechlessness" of love (L645): no words can be adequate for it. What is
significant and often awe-inspiring in the external world, for Dickinson, is
wrapped in silence and mystery: "Aloud / Is nothing that is chief, / But still"
(P662). Consequently, the choice of words, the search for the Flaubertian *mot
juste*, becomes an obsession: in 1883 Dickinson wrote, "I hesitate which word
to take, as I can take but few and each must be the chiefest" (L873). Words are
precious and powerful, but not necessarily sufficient.

Because of the inadequacy of language to convey what Dickinson sought to express, she "attempted to develop a [symbolical] shorthand system of poetic language which would combine the advantage of conciseness with the capability of connoting a rich complex of suggestions" (Baruffol 33). It is a romantic element of her work that the universe which her poetic language depicts is not an external one but one that exists only in the poet's mind: "Best Things dwell out of Sight / The Pearl — the Just — Our Thought" (P998). Dickinson therefore concentrated on her inner world, on what she called the "undiscovered continent" (P832). She sought to explore this universe through poetic language, knowing full well that (conventional) language is not up to the task: "It is the Ultimate of Talk — / The Impotence to Tell — " (P407). Thus the kind of language she decides to use is one of *absence présente*, a language that expresses more through its economy and ellipses than it could through explicitness, because to Dickinson, "Absence is condensed presence" (L587). Silence is for her a means of communication that can express more than uttered words: as she wrote to Susan Gilbert, "If you were here . . . we need not talk at all, our eyes would whisper for us, and your hand fast in mine, we would not ask for language" (L94). We are reminded of Keats here, who had written in his "Ode on a Grecian Urn": "Heard melodies are sweet, but those unheard / Are sweeter."

Nonetheless, in her poetry, words are all that Dickinson has to express what is significant. She realizes that despite its shortcomings the word can be overpowering in its immediacy: like Wordsworth and Freud she believes that "A Word is inundation, when it comes from the Sea" (L965). But language can also be violent:

> There is a word
> Which bears a sword
> Can pierce an armed man —
> It hurls its barbed syllables
> And is mute again — (P8)

The word has the terrifying might of a sword, and it can be just as harmful.[6] But once its work is done it will be "mute again." However, the result ("barbed") remains. Through her use of the eye rhyme "word/sword," the impure rhyme "man — / again —," and the absence of a rhyme for "barbed syllables" Dickinson reinforces the idea that despite its imperfections language is a mighty — even a violent — tool.

The personifying term "mute" points to another characteristic of Dickinson's understanding of language. For her, as for Coleridge (or Robert Lowell), words are living organisms; they assume a life of their own once they are uttered:

A word is dead
When it is said,
some say.
I say it just
Begins to live
That day. (P1212)

As living organisms, words have the power to perform actions and to have effects.[7] Emerson's view in "The Poet" is similar: "Words and deeds are quite indifferent modes of divine energy. Words are also actions, and actions are a kind of words" (3: 6).

According to Dickinson's metapoetic comments, language is able to perform actions because words involve much more than they seem to. They can, in fact, be overpowering:

Could mortal lip divine
The undeveloped Freight
Of a delivered syllable
'Twould crumble with the weight. (P1409)

Dickinson reduces and sharpens the word to the evocative "syllable" — a tendency through which she seems to pave the way for the modernist technique of fragmentation. She shrouds language in mystery, attributing to it weighty dimensions that are beyond human perception. The "undeveloped Freight" (reinforced through the rhyme with "weight") that words in general have implies that her poems — which are made up of such words — also carry meanings and implications that lie beyond "mortal" limits of understanding.

Another image that Dickinson uses for the "Freight" or "weight" of particular words is that of a germ. Even those words that seem inconsequential may exert an immense power on the immediate audience as well as on later readers:

A Word dropped careless on a Page
May stimulate an eye
When folded in perpetual seam
The Wrinkled Maker lie

Infection in the sentence breeds
We may inhale Despair
At distances of Centuries
From the Malaria — (P1261)

The word — as well as the poem that employs it — can animate or "stimulate," but it can also be contagious and bring doom. Once uttered or written, the word assumes a dynamics of its own; it can never be recalled by its "Wrinkled Maker" since at the moment of its use the word acquires its independence.

Dickinson seems fascinated by this concept of uncontrollable language. The allusiveness and power exerted by an individual word will be increased through its poetic context.

Dickinson agrees with Emerson that poetic language is not fixed but rather in a flux and that its goal is to uncover and thereby discover. But despite her reverence and awe, she simultaneously believes — as a protomodernist poet — that words, in their ordinary usage, cannot grasp the meaning of experience (P300). The poet's search for the *mot juste* reflects the desire to uncover complexities and thus to gain new insights:

> The Poet searched Philology
> And when about to ring
> For the suspended Candidate
> There came unsummoned in —
>
> That portion of the Vision
> The Word applied to fill
> Not unto nomination
> The Cherubim reveal — (P1126)

The poem's inspiration and message come out of language. While the word lover (*philologos*) is looking for the most fitting "Candidate" among the words at her disposition, the "Vision" or poetic revelation occurs. The rational probing of philology in the search for the right word prepares the poet for the inspiration that does not come out of philology but presents itself to the creative mind "unsummoned." Philological reflection is necessary but cannot replace inspiration. As Roland Hagenbüchle rightly pointed out, "the moment of wording appears to coincide with the moment of epiphany. The search for the word, the meaning, and the vision become one" ("Sign" 151). It is this borderline between actual experience and the expression of experience that especially concerns Dickinson. Pushing the borderline further into language allows her to reach insights into "portion[s]" of experience that would otherwise remain undetected. For Dickinson, the act of putting an experience into words is thus an act of grasping an experience more fully. Language — which is powerful and impotent at the same time — helps to explore the mysteries of existence, even if it has to fail in conveying them adequately.

IMAGINATION

The poetic word can live out its potential only if the writer allows it to do so. Whereas a conventional and direct use of language cannot elucidate any hidden mysteries, an indirect use of words coupled with the poet's indirect gaze (i.e., her imagination) may yield new insights. Beauty, for example, cannot be described, claims Dickinson; it can only be inferred through the imagination: "The Definition of Beauty is / That Definition is none" (P988). If one tried to render beauty directly or scientifically, rather than through the imagination, one would destory it: "To tell the Beauty would decrease / To state the Spell demean — " (P1700). The mystery can only be explored indirectly and imaginatively. While direct description might involve a loss of meaning, an imaginative approach can lead to an ecstatic explosion of potential: "The Possible's slow fuse is lit / By the Imagination" (P1687). Prosaic description, on the other hand, would bar the reader from the possibility of co-creation.

Since straightforward human language is inadequate for Dickinson's vision, the imagination takes a prominent position. Dickinson preferred the subjective world of her creative mind to the objective external reality, believing that a reduction of external light might involve an increase in clarity:

> By a departing light
> We see acuter, quite,
> Than by a wick that stays.
> There's something in the flight
> That clarifies the sight
> And decks the rays. (P1714)

Only when the light of the imagination takes precedence over the actual daylight can the mystery of human existence be illuminated. Nonetheless, the imaginative approach, like the search for the right word, is an eminently cognitive tool for understanding.

Imagination is therefore an indispensable prerequisite for writing a poem; in Dickinson's recipe for a poem, the external world (e.g., the "bee") is an optional ingredient, while imagination ("revery") is a sine qua non:

> To make a prairie it takes a clover and one bee,
> One clover, and a bee,
> And revery.
> The revery alone will do,
> If bees are few. (P1755)

The playful rhyme may lull the reader into thinking of an actual landscape. But this is of course an imaginary, "made" one.[8] The rhyme hints at a childlike approach which rejects scientific construction in favor of imaginative (re-)creation. This (re-)creation rests on metonymy and synecdoche; they evoke the whole picture — as long as they are accompanied by imagination, which tends to become an autogenic force. The "revery" through which the poet empathetically shapes her subject is a prerequisite for painting the mental picture and for understanding its lessons.[9] Emotional distance, on the other hand, would prevent the artistic (re-)creation.

Poetic Technique

The importance which the imagination has for her demonstrates that Dickinson's method of approaching truth is not realistic representation ("I would not paint — a picture — ") but empathetic artistic creation ("I'd rather be the One / Its bright impossibility / To dwell — delicious — on — " [P505]). Therefore, she asked Higginson whether her poetry was "alive" and "breathe[d]" (L260). Like the individual words that constitute it, the poem as a whole is also ideally meant to be like a living being. This adherence to a romantic organicist view explains that for Dickinson poetry itself is an overwhelming, stunning, mysterious power (P1247).

Poetry is meant to overcome awe, yet at the same time it is the generator of awe: "I work to drive the awe away, yet awe impels the work" (L891). The following verse reads like a commentary on the letter passage:

> Her spirit rose to such a height
> Her countenance it did inflate
> Like one that fed on awe.
> More prudent to assault the dawn
> Than merit the ethereal scorn
> That effervesced from her. (P1486)

Poetic composition and the expression of experience come out of the poet's awe of the world and of her work. She must try to grasp and render even the difficult and the evanescent, like "the dawn," or else despise herself. The fact that "her" is the first as well as the last word of this self-portrait suggests that the work of the poet is subjective, originating within herself rather than in the world around her. It is her vision and the words she finds for it rather than the external reality that determine her poetic creation. Acting upon her desire to express that vision (despite the meager chances of success in "assault[ing] the dawn") is considered preferable to inaction. A manuscript of the poem's last three lines (in the handwriting of 1880) was sent to Sue. Here "Dawn" is capitalized, thus stressing how overwhelming the poet's task is; "effervesce" takes the place of "effervesced," and the poem ends in a dash rather than a period, implying that courage is a timeless and continuing requirement of the poet.[10]

The element of awe that drives the poet's creativity should, through the poetic form, affect the reader if the work is to be considered successful. As Dickinson told Higginson on August 16, 1870 (according to Higginson's letter to his wife), "If I read a book [and] it makes my whole body so cold no fire ever can warm me I know *that* is poetry. If I feel physically as if the top of my head were taken off, I know *that* is poetry. These are the only way I know it. Is there any other way" (L342a).

The awe that impels poetry and that is to emanate from it calls for the poetic method of circumferential approximation, as Dickinson's expression "Circumference thou Bride of Awe" (P1620) implies.

> Circumference thou Bride of Awe
> Possessing thou shalt be
> Possessed by every hallowed Knight
> That dares to covet thee (P1620)

The awe of experience is linked to the circumference that is the poet's realm. "Circumference" is seen dialectically: it "possess[es]" (a link to the center), and it is "possessed" (by poets who dare write in this vein).[11] Awe is a prerequisite for gaining knowledge and translating it into poetry. As she told Higginson in 1876, Dickinson believed that "Nature is a Haunted House — but Art — a House that tries to be haunted" (L459A). The artist's task, therefore, is to re-create awe. She does so by "fit[ting] into place" experiences (P1009) and by "winnow[ing] what would fade" (P178). Those are momentary insights, which are expressed even if they may contradict conventional rationality. It is typical for Dickinson that experience takes the form of a sudden illumination, which would imply a center in which the insight originates. Since the center itself cannot be grasped, Dickinson focuses on its circumference, which expresses the eternity surrounding the center as well as the unfulfilled desire of reaching that center. Through circumference the poet partakes in a large variety of relationships and connections:[12] "Ages coil within / The minute Circumference / Of a single Brain — " (P967). Circumference is thus internal as well as external; it is at work inside the imagination ("Brain") as well as outside it. Only the Bible, wrote Dickinson, "dealt with the Centre, not with the Circumference" (L950). Since this center, namely God, is not fully accessible to her, the poet approaches it indirectly by illuminating its circumference.

She circles around the center in order to explore it from various perspectives and because the circuit is inextricably connected to the center. "Success in Circuit lies" (P1129). The circuit remains the path toward the center, the "Firmament" the path toward the "Star," even if the ultimate goal will always remain unreachable:

> No matter where the Saints abide,
> They make their Circuit fair
> Behold how great a Firmament
> Accompanies a Star. (P1541)

What "Accompanies" the center is what the poet can "Behold" and what she can re-create in language. In this respect Dickinson follows Thoreau's conviction that "around every circle another can be drawn."[13]

Since trying to represent the center or truth (insofar as it can be approximated) straightforwardly would be futile, she uses a slanted perspective that might reveal what would otherwise remain hidden:[14]

> Tell all the Truth but tell it slant —
> Success in Circuit lies
> Too bright for our infirm Delight
> The Truth's superb surprise
>
> As lightning to the Children eased
> With explanation kind
> The Truth must dazzle gradually
> Or every man be blind — (P1129)

The use of "Circuit" in this poem recalls that of "Circumference" elsewhere. As a romantic *vates*, the poet needs to use "explanation kind" in order to communicate to her audience the (limited) truth she beholds ("I . . . Went out upon Circumference — " [P378] and "Disseminating their Circumference — " [P883]; in both verses "circumference" is followed by a dash, which stresses its open, outreaching quality). But the only means she can employ to explore this truth is an approach characterized by "Circuit" and "slant." Since Dickinson, as a protomodernist, does not have the confidence of stable faith, her method cannot be based on "center" or "direct." While the center would express faith, circumference expresses doubt.

Dickinson's slanted perspective is directly related to her slanted use of imagery. Although Walt Whitman was to voice the poetic celebration of America which Emerson had demanded in "The American Scholar," it was Dickinson who explored the semantic richness of symbols of which Emerson had spoken in "The Poet": "We are far from having exhausted the significance of the few symbols we use. We can come to use them yet with a terrible simplicity. It does not need that a poem should be long. Every word was once a poem" (3: 11). Dickinson's work illustrates Emerson's point. Many of her symbols take on new dimensions of meaning through her slanted use of them. Rather than pursuing a postmodern dissolution of meaning, however, she strives for an expansion of meaning.

This same desire, coupled with the conviction that conventional language usage is inadequate to render complex experiences and insights, may explain the use of alternate words and expressions in Dickinson's manuscripts. They suggest that for Dickinson poetry is an evocative art of options and alternatives, rather than of fixed words or meanings. The manuscript versions of her poems can therefore be taken as implicitly metapoetic. Their openness finds its equivalent, for example, in Dickinson's use of ellipses and dashes. Moreover, the manuscripts illustrate her search for the right word. Her reluctance to make definitive choices among the various options — her "choosing not choosing," as Sharon Cameron calls it — reveals, on the one hand, Dickinson's desire to be encompassing. On the other, it expresses the poet's conviction that there is no *mot juste*. Consequently she puts several options down on the page, a technique that makes her poetry processual. Meaning, with this proto-modernist, is in a flux rather than resting on stable and static concepts.

Because of its reliance on options rather than fixed meanings the world of the poem is necessarily subjective and fictitious. It originates in a "vision" and develops into something as authentic as the external world which has caused that original vision.

> The Vision — pondered long —
> So plausible becomes
> That I esteem the fiction — real —
> The Real — fictitious seems — (P646)

It is no longer possible or necessary to distinguish between the "Real" and the "fictitious." Theoretically, those are different ways of exploring our existence, but in fact the "Real" is already a subjectively experienced reality so that fiction becomes itself a reality. The power of the fictitious is made explicit in the following poem:

> The Outer — from the Inner
> Derives its Magnitude —
> 'Tis Duke, or Dwarf, according
> As is the Central Mood —
> . . .
> The Inner — paints the Outer —
> . . .
> Eyes were not meant to know. (P451)

Objects and issues appear in the poem with the relative importance that the poet grants them. It is the poet's creative mind that decides on size and impor-tance. "Eyes," that is, realistic exterior vision, will not lead to knowledge, but interior re-vision will.

As they were for Keats, truth and beauty are joined together for Dickinson in the aesthetic, interior vision of poetry:

> I died for Beauty — but was scarce
> Adjusted in the Tomb
> When One who died for Truth, was lain
> In an adjoining Room — (P449)

Beauty and truth represent the "imaginative understanding" (Baruffol 12) or interior re-vision which is at the basis of art. Dickinson's link between truth and beauty may have been inspired by the final two lines of Keats's "Ode on a Grecian Urn": " 'Beauty is truth, truth beauty,' — that is all / Ye know on earth, and all ye need to know." Beauty, Dickinson believes, cannot be forced: "Beauty is not caused — It is — / Chase it, and it ceases — / Chase it not, and it abides — " (P516).

Truth and beauty need to be explored slowly and circumferentially or else they either disappear or become too overwhelming ("Too bright for our infirm Delight"): "The Truth must dazzle gradually / Or every man be blind — " (P1129). But dazzle it must if it is true poetry. In its impact, poetry is like love:

> To pile like Thunder to its close
> Then crumble grand away
> While Everything created hid
> This — would be Poetry —
>
> Or Love — the two coeval come —
> We both and neither prove —
> Experience either and consume —
> For None see God and live — (P1247)

Ultimate perception would be like seeing God. But this is impossible; the poet can only hope to catch a glimpse and record it. Love and poetry are their own proof; we cannot prove them, but we use them to explore our world. As is suggested in the word "crumble," poetic exploration is processual and transitory. In this view Dickinson surpasses the romantic poets.[15]

Because of its processual character and its sudden revelations poetry is, in Dickinson's view, evanescent. Similarly, Shelley had written in "A Defense of Poetry": "When composition begins, inspiration is already on the decline, and the most glorious poetry that has ever been communicated to the world is probably a feeble shadow of the original conception of the poet." Dickinson agrees: "To see the Summer Sky / Is Poetry, though never in a Book it lie — / True Poems flee — " (P1472). What is actually represented on the page is far less than what should be represented. Therefore the poet resigns herself to the idea that "All we secure of Beauty is its Evanescences" (L781). Poetry, like life, is "A Route of Evanescence" (P1463) to Dickinson, a transitory realm where everything is processual and evades our grasp. But on the other hand this evanescence engenders desire, which impels a new vision.[16] The joy we feel at a moment of fulfillment, however, is transitory and leaves behind a feeling of loss:

> It comes, without a consternation —
> Dissolves — the same —
> But leaves a sumptuous Destitution —
> Without a Name — (P1382)

The poet then endeavors to find a name or poetic language to render the experience. Since she cannot arrest the process, she tries to picture the moment and her excitement about it: "Take all away from me, but leave me Ecstasy, / And I am richer then than all my Fellow Men" (P1640).[17]

THE POET

Emily Dickinson thinks highly of the poet. Among the roles she attributes to this figure are those of craftsman, (almost divine) creator, and visionary. While she posits the poet above most other people, she does not forget that his or her work also involves a skill. In one poem she calls herself "a Carpenter" (evoking a Christ figure) who builds "Temples" (P488); but in another she refers to her work as "Blossom[s] of the Brain" (P945). Those can come into existence through divine inspiration which "fumbles at your Soul" and "stuns you by degrees" (P315), through the storm in the poet's soul (P362) or the fire in her heart (P638). The outcome is Dickinson's "letter to the World" (P441), which she sends no matter what the chances are of its being received, opened, or understood.

The material she uses in her craft is language. Her role as maker suggests a similarity to the divine Creator:

> A Word made Flesh is seldom
> And tremblingly partook
> Nor then perhaps reported
> But have I not mistook
> Each one of us has tasted
> With ecstasies of stealth
> The very food debated
> To our specific strength —
>
> A Word that breathes distinctly
> Has not the power to die
> Cohesive as the Spirit
> It may expire if He —
> "Made Flesh and dwelt among us"
> Could condescension be
> Like this consent of Language
> This loved Philology. (P1651)

The process of God and the divine Word becoming flesh is Dickinson's model for making her own poetic word live. Poetry becomes sacramental here. The poet and "Each one of us" have tasted in Holy Communion the flesh of which she speaks and have received "strength" by thus partaking of the divine Word. This is the divine flesh that came out of the original Word, namely, God, the

"Word" that, according to the Bible, existed "in the beginning." But it is also the word of the poet, which became a living organism when it was uttered. Like God who became Man, a "Word" that becomes "Flesh" will not die. So the poet's creation is similar to God's. Her "loved Philology" provides for her the poetic and linguistic material that comes to life with the help of the imagination. Whereas the "Word made Flesh" of the first line is the poet's inspiration, the "loved Philology" of the last line is her creation. Through her use of rhyme Dickinson further reinforces the poem's movement from the momentary to the permanent, from the separate to the permeating, from the weak to the strong: in the first octet only lines 2 and 4 contain a strong rhyme, while lines 3, 5, and 7 end in weak rhymes; in the second octet, however, the "ecstasies" (represented through the strong rhymes) become more constant (with lines 12, 14, and 16 rhyming), since the divinely inspired word "has not the power to die." Aided by the simile of line 15, "He" is connected to "Philology" — both of them rhyming with "be," which underlines the constancy of the Word " 'dwel[ling] among us' " and thus of poetic creativity.

What the poet has created will continue to exist (and live) even after her own death. The "Lamps" which she "light[s]" will continue to radiate:

> The Poets light but Lamps —
> Themselves — go out —
> The Wicks they stimulate —
> If vital Light
>
> Inhere as do the Suns —
> Each Age a Lens
> Disseminating their
> Circumference — (P883)

Now the poem itself becomes the radiating center, whose "Circumference" will affect present and future readers. The text will keep shedding light on the issues or subjects with which it deals. The various "lenses" or viewpoints of successive generations will all distill their own kind of light out of the shining poem, which implies that the poem must be open rather than closed in order to allow for such a range of meanings.

For this purpose, poetry needs to be evocative. Since formal restrictions and the stylistic expectations of her age would have prevented the ambiguity and indeterminacy which Dickinson deemed indispensable, she rejected those conventions, calling them "Prose":

> They shut me up in Prose —
> As when a little Girl
> They put me in the Closet —
> Because they liked me "still" —

> Still! Could themself have peeped —
> And seen my Brain — go round —
> They might as wise have lodged a Bird
> For Treason — in the Pound —
>
> Himself has but to will
> And easy as a Star
> Abolish his Captivity —
> And laugh — No more have I — (P613)

She will not be shut up by routine or conventional expectations. And even if her exterior liberty was to be curtailed, she would never give up the freedom of her mind and creativity. Curtailment would be demanded by and would result in commonsensical prose and stagnation, whereas poetry is the mode of expression that goes against the grain and that reflects the ecstasy of human experience and poetic creation. As she wrote to Susan Gilbert already in 1851, "for our sakes dear Susie, who please ourselves with the fancy that we are the only poets, and everyone else is *prose*, let us hope they will yet be willing to share our humble world and feed upon such aliment as *we* consent to do!" (L56). Later in her poetic career, the audience response would be of lesser importance to Dickinson. Even Higginson's criticism of her style as "spasmodic," "uncontrolled," or "odd" did not make her alter her poetic expression. She continued to emulate the "Bird" of P613, one of her favorite metaphors for artistic freedom. While she associates restrictiveness with prose, her poetry is the realm of "Possibility":[18]

> I dwell in Possibility —
> A fairer House than Prose —
> More numerous of Windows —
> Superior — for Doors — (P657)

"Windows" and "Doors" are metonyms for this openness that the poet requires; they open up possibilities of imaginative creation that straightforward prose description can never have.

Dickinson's verse cannot be controlled, because it retains the ecstasy that accompanied its creation. What the poet is ecstatic about is not the world as such but the world as transformed by her poetic vision; the liquor she tastes is not actual alcohol but "a liquor never brewed —." And rather than considering air and dew unexciting natural phenomena, she writes: "Inebriate of Air — am I — / And Debauchee of Dew —" (P214). Thus the poet's ecstasy originates more in her own attitude than in anything external. To her, because of her different mode of experience, "Much Madness is divinest Sense" (P435). She goes against simplifications and orderly arrangements because she knows that "Except the smaller size / No lives are round —" (P1067). Dickinson domesticates neither the material of her poetry nor her creative urge, which is as indomitable as a fire or a flood: "You cannot put a Fire out — / A Thing that can ignite / Can go, itself, without a Fan — / Upon the slowest Night — // You cannot fold a Flood — " (P530).

While this image of the poet as seized by forces beyond her control is genuinely romantic, it transcends the Wordsworthian kind of romanticism through its violent and explosive potential. But with regard to her conception of the poet as visionary, Dickinson can be aligned with the romantics. Objects in themselves do not have meaning, but they are given meaning by the perceiver. The oriole's tune therefore does not originate in a tree on the outside; rather, it comes from within the poet:

> To hear an Oriole sing
> May be a common thing —
> Or only a divine.
>
> . . .
>
> The "Tune is in the Tree —"
> The Skeptic — showeth me —
> "No Sir! In Thee!" (P526)

Similarly, Wallace Stevens answers the charge that "You do not play things as they are" upon the blue guitar by replying that "Things as they are / Are changed upon the blue guitar." In her role as visionary, the perceiver alters and gives new meaning to what she renders. The poet's subjectivity, the creative imagination in the act of perception, engenders meaning. What is decisive is not the external object or world but its transformation through the poet. As mentioned above, "The Outer — from the Inner / Derives its Magnitude — " (P451).

The poet is a *vates* figure because she can look behind the surfaces and explore the "mystery" of things, which she then shares with her readers:

> This was a Poet — It is That
> Distills amazing sense
> From ordinary Meanings —
> And Attar so immense
>
> From the familiar species
> That perished by the Door —
> We wonder it was not Ourselves
> Arrested it — before —
>
> Of Pictures, the Discloser —
> The Poet — it is He —
> Entitles Us — by Contrast —
> To ceaseless Poverty —

> Of Portion — so unconscious —
> The Robbing — could not harm —
> Himself — to Him — a Fortune —
> Exterior — to Time — (P448)

The uniqueness of the poet's vision makes what is perceived special and mean-ingful. As Inder Nath Kher has written, "In the creative process, the poet arrests the flux of our perishable existence. He creates pictures of immortality, and when these rich visions are disclosed to us in the form of images and metaphors, our daily world fades by contrast into ceaseless poverty" (118). The poet manages to recognize and re-create essential qualities, to "distill" meaning: the "Attar" is the expression of the rose (the precious fluid that is pressed out of it) in the same way as the poem is the expression of the poet. The rose must be destroyed in order to get the attar, and similarly the poet leaves the exterior behind in order to create/distill something new out of it.

It is no accident that in the fascicle this poem was placed next to poem 613, "They shut me up in Prose." Poetic use of language brings out (or "Distills") meanings that remain unheard in a prose use of the same word. Moreover, the "Attar" of poetry is more evocative than the rose of prose: while the rose can be seen, touched, and smelled, the attar is less concrete; it can only be smelled, and thus it invites a wider range of interpretations. It may be true that, as Cristanne Miller has pointed out, Dickinson feels "ambivalent toward this 'Poet'" of poem 448 (*Grammar* 45). Nonetheless, Dickinson would agree with the poetic technique described in "This was a Poet": "Rather than painting pictures, the poet discloses them — presumably by eliminating overlays of grime and erasing surface distractions" (Eberwein, *Strategies* 208).

Her activity of disclosing a potential and of creating imaginatively groups the poet in Dickinson's opinion with the forces that shape the universe. She even goes so far as to suggest that the poet can encompass all those forces:

> I reckon — when I count at all —
> First — Poets — Then the Sun —
> Then Summer — Then the Heaven of God —
> And then — the List is done —
>
> But, Looking back — the First so seems
> To Comprehend the Whole —
> The Others look a needless Show —
> So I write — Poets — All — (P569)

The poet thus becomes in Dickinson's view an almighty Maker, a force that subsumes in it all the other forces. No wonder she attests to this force "A nearness to Tremendousness —" (P963). Her admonition "faithful be / To Thyself, / And Mystery" refers to the "Lad of Athens" (P1768) as well as to the poet figure. Her vision, shaped through her experience and consciousness, is tantamount in the exploration of the mystery of human existence.

EMILY DICKINSON's metapoetic commentary situates her in between romanticism and a modernism that does not yet exist. She combines her romantic view of the poet's role with her modernist poetic technique and use of language as well as with a modernist epistemology. What she creates in her poetry is a circumference of meaning(s). This is the response she considers most adequate to the loss of religious faith and the shortcomings of intellect and word. One could therefore call her not an "either/or" poet but rather a "both/and" poet: instead of discarding meaning she expands it. This is the task which, as her metapoetic comments illustrate, she has set herself. She will pursue it even if "the whole United States are laughing at me too!" (L269).

In her work, Emily Dickinson has transferred to the realm of poetry the Kantian question of the relation between subject and object. How do we recognize what we recognize? What Kant calls *transzendental* (our way of recognizing and knowing) and *transzendent* (that which goes beyond the boundaries of empirical experience) were also central concerns of Dickinson.[19] As the metapoetic element of her work demonstrates, Kant's interest in epistemology is also hers. Dickinson can be said to have completed the Copernican shift in poetry, since with her the word (the poet's concept or thought) determines the object to which it refers, not vice versa—an insight which was to find its counterpart in physics with Werner Heisenberg's uncertainty principle. Dickinson's epistemological doubt and her resulting poetic indeterminacy are not projected onto her retroactively by current critical orthodoxy, but they reflect her personal doubts concerning religious faith and her age's growing uncertainty and restlessness. Doubt and desire impelled Emily Dickinson's epistemological and poetic quest rather than frustrating it: "I shall keep singing," she proclaimed (P250). And her song will continue to be heard.

NOTES

1. Inder Nath Kher has called this "supposed person" "the creative I of the poem. This creative I is the personality which the poet realizes as she creates it and realizes it persistently. This personality is not the ordinary individual; rather, it is a type which represents one's creative existence" (3).

2. Judith Farr claims that in Dickinson's writing " 'circumference' generally means either poetry itself or the significance of all that exists, on earth and in heaven. She marries it here to awe: the respectful fear or veneration that should be chief dweller in God's universe" (*Passion* 319).

3. Joanne Feit Diehl has pointed out (*Romantic*) that Dickinson's sense of a muse differs fundamentally from that of male romantics: unlike them, she is unable to sepa-

rate the "Composite Precursor" from her muse, and she wavers between expecting the Master/muse and rejecting his presence.

4. I am grateful to Roland Hagenbüchle for pointing this study out to me and to the English Department at the University of Zürich for granting me access to this thesis.

5. This view will be contested by feminist critics, for whom Dickinson's use of language *is* an act of power.

6. This poem could therefore be used to challenge Schöpp's view that language is for Dickinson also a prison house.

7. Albert J. Gelpi writes that this poem "ends up attesting to the vitality of words, to the adequacy of language for the task of rendering and sustaining the life of consciousness; but in fact, the disquieting possibility that words die upon articulation receives equal time and equal space in the verses" ("Word" 41). Nonetheless, this poem moves from words that are "dead" to words that "live."

8. Suzanne Juhasz points out that in this poem "action is set in the mind and not somewhere in Kansas, that in this recipe we are concerned with prairie-ness and not an instance of it. . . . A prairie in the world of nature cannot be composed from one clover and one bee, but the idea of prairie can" (*Undiscovered* 50).

9. As Judith Farr has written, Dickinson characteristically "trace[s] artistic inspiration to love" (*Passion* 319).

10. P1486 has received little attention in Dickinson scholarship so far. Albert Cook is one of the few critics who have commented on it. However, his contention that "The feelings engendered here enact their apocalyptic correlatives confusedly" (196) seems misguided.

11. As Albert J. Gelpi has stated, this poem unites "the themes of sexual, religious and aesthetic fulfillment in the union of the bride and the knight, Circumference and Awe" (*Mind* 126).

12. Charles R. Anderson has pointed out that in Dickinson's use of the term, "circumference" suggests not a boundary but a limitlessness: "The literal meaning of 'Circumference' as the boundary of a circle (like the disks of the lamps) has been expanded by her special meaning into a sphere like the sun, radiating its light outward to infinity" (*Stairway* 59).

13. Thoreau wrote: "This is the key to the power of the greatest men, — their spirit diffuses itself. A new quality travels by night and by day, in concentric circles from its origin. . . . We should not walk on tiptoe, but healthily expand to our full circumference on the soles of our feet. . . . Our life is an apprenticeship to the truth that around every circle another can be drawn" (qtd. in Gelpi, *Mind* 121).

14. In P1631 Dickinson reveals a similar reluctance to accept a straight path. Here she refers to a straight path into the "Future"; she is looking for a "circuit sage" that might help avoid destiny.

15. Her attitude is similar to that expressed in Emerson's "Merlin": the "trivial harp" of traditional romantic poetry is outdated. It cannot fulfill what Emerson considers to be the tasks of the poet, namely, the emotional appeal to a reader and the guidance in discovering mysteries of human existence. Both Dickinson and Emerson believe that poetry must "make the wild blood start / In its mystic springs," that it must be "Artful thunder, which conveys / Secrets of the solar track, / Sparks of the supersolar blaze."

16. On desire as the driving force behind Dickinson's poetry, cf. Roland Hagenbüchle, " 'Sumptuous Despair': The Function of Desire in Emily Dickinson's Poetry."

17. On the importance of ecstasy in Dickinson's poetic creations, see the second chapter in Hagenbüchle, *Wagnis*.

18. Margaret Homans has demonstrated how Dickinson pushed beyond the limits of dualism by undermining the concepts of opposites (*Women Writers*), and Wendy Barker analyzes Dickinson's stance of "Dwelling in Possibility." Possibility is, according to Robert Weisbuch, Emily Dickinson's synonym for poetry (*Poetry* 1).

19. On Kant and Dickinson, see Grabher 19 ff. and 61 ff. For a detailed analysis of the relationships between poet and existential reality, poet and poetic experience, poet and creative process, and poet and poem, see chap. 3 in Kher.

FURTHER READING

Baker, Dorothy Z., ed. *Poetics in the Poem: Critical Essays on American Self-Reflexive Poetry*. New York: Lang, 1997.

RECEPTION AND INFLUENCE

Marietta Messmer

Dickinson's Critical Reception

Importance of the Topic

*M*ore than twenty years ago James Woodress introduced his review of Emily Dickinson's critical reception with the remark: "[a] sizeable problem that the student or teacher of American literature today has in confronting Emily Dickinson is in keeping up with the scholarly and critical explosion" (185). How much more true this statement is now is proven by a cursory glance at the annual MLA listings: on average, there are more than fifty entries for each year (with a peak of eighty-three listings for 1986), testifying to scholarly activities around the globe (in English, Japanese, Polish, German, French, Slovenian, Russian, Spanish, Macedonian, and Portuguese, among many other languages). English-language book-length studies alone have been published at a stable rate of five to seven per year since the 1980s, and 1989 saw the foundation of the Emily Dickinson International Society, which issues the biannual *Emily Dickinson Journal* as well as the *Emily Dickinson Bulletin*.

This prolific scholarly activity has led to an increased need for bibliographic material.[1] After Willis J. Buckingham's *Emily Dickinson: An Annotated Bibliography: Writings, Scholarship, Criticism, and Ana, 1850–1968* (1970), Karen Dandurand continues with the year 1969 in *Dickinson Scholarship: An Annotated Bibliography, 1969–1985* (1988). This is followed a year later by Jeanetta Boswell's *Emily Dickinson: A Bibliography of Secondary Sources, with Selective Annotations, 1890 through 1987*; and Joseph Duchac's 1993 sequel to his *Poems of Emily Dickinson: An Annotated Guide to Commentary Published in English, 1890–1977* (1979), organized by poems, now covers the period from 1978 through 1989.[2]

Faced with what has become a formidable Dickinson industry, bibliographic studies of this writer's critical reception show an increasing tendency to concentrate on a specific time period, geographic area, or particular thematic or theoretical approach. In many ways, this essay is no exception. While I have attempted to trace the development of Dickinson's critical reception from the 1860s to 1995, my primary intention has been to reread earlier discussions of Dickinson's works in the context of current theoretical debates.

Since evaluative reviews of individual Dickinson studies published during the 1970s and early 1980s are, for the most part, readily available,[3] I have concentrated on examining how major critical works, predominantly those published in English during the last decade, have contributed to or reshaped our current understanding of the poet and letter writer.

After a brief survey of scholarship, this discussion will progress in three parts: the first part offers an examination of the politically motivated discrepancy between "private" readers' and journalistic critics' responses to Dickinson's poems from the early 1860s until approximately 1930. The second section, following earlier reception studies in its termination year 1955 — coincidental with the publication of Thomas H. Johnson's variorum edition — discusses the first twenty years of Dickinson's academic reception in a predominantly biographical and New Critical context. The last and most comprehensive part traces the ways evolving psychoanalytic, New Historicist, linguistic, and feminist perspectives have gradually transformed critical readings of central issues in Dickinson studies in the areas of (*a*) biography, (*b*) cultural-historical contextualization, and (*c*) language/textuality.

SURVEY OF SCHOLARSHIP

A study of Emily Dickinson's critical reception during the nineteenth century largely depends on the availability of source material.[4] Starting with the 1890s, two (selective but for the most part complementary) collections of reprinted review articles are Caesar R. Blake and Carlton F. Wells, *The Recognition of Emily Dickinson* (1964); and Richard B. Sewall, *Emily Dickinson: A Collection of Critical Essays* (1963). While Blake and Wells reprint sixteen essays published prior to the twentieth century and twenty-nine from 1900 to 1960, Sewall concentrates on post–1924 criticism (with an overlap of only five essays). The most comprehensive compilation of critical reviews exists for the last decade of the nineteenth century. Willis J. Buckingham's collection of 600 articles in *Emily Dickinson's Reception in the 1890s: A Documentary History* (1989) makes otherwise hard-to-come-by documents readily accessible; by including all extant materials for the 1890s, Buckingham's collection reveals the ideological bias of more selective ones against the "common reader" and allows for an analysis of divergent responses to Dickinson's poetry based on the reviewer's gender or regional/national descent, or on the power dynamics at play among specific literary magazines, journals, and newspapers. A particularly useful appendix lists diary entries and private letters which remained unpublished until the twentieth century.[5]

The most comprehensive developmental study of Dickinson's critical reception is Klaus Lubbers's *Emily Dickinson: The Critical Revolution* (1968), which covers 100 years of criticism from 1862 until 1962. Tracing the responses of private readers and journalistic as well as academic critics from a historical perspective, Lubbers's study outlines the interconnectedness of Dickinson's critical reception with "the revaluation of nineteenth-century American poetry by the twentieth, the development of modern American literary criticism and history, and the British reception of American literature" (ix). Sheila T. Clendenning's introduction to *Emily Dickinson: A Bibliography, 1850–1966* (1968) provides a complementary short summary of Dickinson's early editorial history and biographical criticism.

The most recent book-length study of Dickinson's critical reception is Mary Lynn Cooper Polk's doctoral dissertation "Emily Dickinson: A Survey of the Criticism and Selective Annotated Bibliography" (1984). Covering material from the 1890s until 1981, Polk discusses her sources in the context of their critical/theoretical approaches. James Woodress's excellent "Emily Dickinson," first published in 1971 and reprinted with an addendum in Earl N. Harbert and Robert A. Rees's *Fifteen American Authors before 1900* (1984), is still the most useful and comprehensive essay-length reception study to date. Woodress covers the period from the 1890s until 1981 and provides an annotated list of bibliographies, traces Dickinson's publication history, lists locations of manuscripts and editions of letters, and offers both a concise history of Dickinson's reception and an evaluative guide to scholarship in the field of biography and other forms of criticism.

Subsequent reviews of critical studies on Dickinson tend to be more selective in their range and scope. In her introduction to Rebecca Patterson's *Emily Dickinson's Imagery* (1979), Margaret H. Freeman discusses the contributions of biographical and, in particular, psychoanalytic, structuralist, and linguistic studies to Dickinson scholarship. Roland Hagenbüchle, in "New Developments in Dickinson Criticism" (1979), analyzes an "evaluative selection (biographical and psychological studies excepted)" of Dickinson criticism from 1960 until 1976, with a specific focus on structuralist and linguistic aspects. Paul J. Ferlazzo's essay "Emily Dickinson" (in *The Transcendentalists: A Review of Research and Criticism*, 1984) traces studies of Dickinson's relation to transcendentalism; and Judy Jo Small's introductory chapter to *Positive as Sound: Emily Dickinson's Rhyme* (1990) focuses specifically on criticism dealing with Dickinson's use of language. Recent reviews of feminist scholarship include Joan Kirkby's seventh chapter in *Emily Dickinson* (1991), and Mary Loeffelholz's introduction to *Dickinson and the Boundaries of Feminist Theory* (1991). The latter also provides a discussion of deconstructionist, New Historicist, and psychoanalytic works.

"IF FAME BELONGED TO ME": JOURNALISTIC CRITICISM FROM THE 1860S TO THE 1930S

A study of Emily Dickinson's critical reception during the nineteenth century constitutes a challenge to the very concept of "critical reception." Klaus Lubbers's historical analysis and Willis J. Buckingham's compilation of review articles both demonstrate that the first phase of primarily evaluative criticism from the 1860s to 1897[6] was characterized by a marked discrepancy between private readers' and female reviewers' widespread enthusiasm for Dickinson's poems and letters, on the one hand, and a more mixed reception by a small number of predominantly male literary journalists and writers on the other.[7] The latter group's reviews, grounded in an attempt to reinforce a genteel standard of poetic form, focused mainly on faulting Dickinson for her formal irregularities. Yet after 1890 these few — albeit highly influential — voices increasingly tended to overshadow the many positive responses and creative tributes to Dickinson from nonprofessional readers.[8]

Among the earliest surviving responses are those of Susan Gilbert Dickinson, Mabel Loomis Todd, and Helen Hunt Jackson. Although all of them comment on the "strangeness" of Dickinson's poems (Lubbers 12), they nevertheless focus in their critical assessments on the force of the writer's genius ("A damascus blade gleaming and glancing in the sun")[9] and the originality of her imagery ("full of power"),[10] thus deprivileging the aspect of form. As early as 1876, Helen Hunt Jackson had called Dickinson a "great poet" without any qualifications (L444a). Summarizing the extant responses of Dickinson's earliest readers, Lubbers thus concludes that her verses "were valued and remembered, copied and recommended" (12).

With the publication of the first and second series of *Poems* in 1890 and 1891, edited by Thomas Wentworth Higginson and Mabel Loomis Todd, however, professional journalistic critics set the tone for a more mixed reception. Both Higginson's "An Open Portfolio," published two months prior to the first edition, and his "Preface," written to prepare his audience for the unusual quality of Dickinson's verse, skillfully attempt to deemphasize the "rain and dew and earth still clinging" to the poems in favor of the "flashes of wholly original and profound insight into nature and life." His "Preface" concludes with the famous statement that, "[a]fter all, when a thought takes one's breath away, a lesson in grammar seems an impertinence" (Buckingham, *Reception* 14).[11]

Even though many of Dickinson's subsequent reviewers attempted to find a "holistic" approach to the poet by combining discussions of unusual formal elements, thematic aspects, "difficulties of understanding, aesthetic evaluation, comparisons, attempts at classification, [and] biographical speculations"

(Lubbers 22), Higginson's dichotomy between irregularity of form and originality of content exerted a profound influence. Thomas Bailey Aldrich, for
example, a representative of the prominent critical elite engaged in defining
literary standards for canon formation, is unable to overlook Dickinson's "major" violations of form. In his famous essay "*In Re* Emily Dickinson" (1892), he
chooses "a little poem" from among Dickinson's "poetical chaos,"[12] "which
needs only slight revision in the initial stanza in order to make it worthy of
ranking with some of the odd swallow flights in Heine's lyrical *intermezzo*,"
and then proceeds to perform the necessary surgery (Buckingham, *Reception*
283).[13] A review attributed to Lilian Whiting (1890), on the other hand, likewise echoes Higginson's dichotomy, yet reaches an entirely different conclusion: if the author had "learned to chip and polish the marble," Whiting
argues, "[i]t might be that such work as hers would lose in strength rather than
gain in melody" (Buckingham, *Reception* 28).[14]

In the context of this controversy, the positive evaluation by the influential writer, critic, and editor William Dean Howells (1891) assumes added significance. Even on the technical side, he emphasizes, Emily Dickinson has
reached "the perfect expression of her ideals." Howells then goes one step
further in situating Dickinson's poems within the context of her New England
environment and argues that, "in the work of Emily Dickinson, America, or
New England rather, had made a distinctive addition to the literature of the
world, and could not be left out of any record of it" (Buckingham, *Reception* 77,
78).[15] Such nationalistic pride, however, sparked hostile reactions from British
reviewers, foremost among them Andrew Lang (1891), who saw Dickinson's
use of grammar as a symptom of America's uncivilized state:

> We may be told that Democracy does not care, any more than the Emperor did,
> for grammar. But even if Democracy overleaps itself and lands in savagery again,
> I believe that our savage successors will, though unconsciously, make their
> poems grammatical. Savages do not use bad grammar in their own conversation
> or in their artless compositions. That is a fault of defective civilizations. (Buck-
> ingham, *Reception* 122)[16]

Yet this attack was countered by an American voice, again from a female
reader, and in private form; an 1892 journal entry by Alice James mockingly
states: "It is reassuring to hear the British pronouncement that Emily Dickinson is fifth-rate—they have such a capacity for missing quality" (qtd. in
Lubbers 42).

The land feud between Lavinia Dickinson and Mabel Loomis Todd
brought the latter's editorial activities to an abrupt end in 1897, which, in turn,
led to a decline of critical interest in Dickinson's poetry until Martha Dickinson Bianchi's publication of *The Single Hound* in 1914.[17] Around that time

Lubbers identifies "a radical turnabout in critical thinking" (97) linked to the founding of Harriet Monroe's magazine *Poetry*, and a concomitant shift in the reception of Dickinson's œuvre. In her review of *The Single Hound* (1914), Monroe refers to Dickinson as "an unconscious and uncatalogued *Imagiste*" (qtd. in Lubbers 104),[18] a view repeated a year later in Elizabeth Shepley Sergeant's essay "An Early Imagist."[19] These reviews start a new trend in Dickinson criticism: she is now being catalogued and classified, initially in the context of New England transcendentalism[20] and Puritanism,[21] but increasingly also within European intellectual traditions, especially in a metaphysical[22] and mystic context (Lubbers 107–9). Generally, Dickinson's place among America's major poets is now no longer under dispute; in his response to Conrad Aiken's praise of Dickinson's poetry as "perhaps the finest, by a woman, in the English language," Martin Armstrong comments in 1923: "I quarrel only with his 'perhaps' " (Blake and Wells 108).[23]

Aiken's introductory essay to his edition of *Selected Poems of Emily Dickinson* (1924) marks a shift from evaluative toward explanatory criticism, featuring theoretical approaches which have played a central role in Dickinson scholarship ever since. He provides a psychological study (Dickinson's seclusion is seen as a conscious choice) combined with a thematic approach (her death and nature poems, in particular), a treatment of the question of influences (especially transcendentalism and the writer's critique of the Puritan concept of God), and a discussion of poetic form (epigrammatic symbolism). With respect to Dickinson's form and technique, Susan Miles's essay "The Irregularities of Emily Dickinson" (1925)[24] is the first to regard the writer's "slant" rhymes as deliberate and as an organic expression of her skeptical world view. Miles thus anticipates Dickinson's reception by the New Critics and finally, as Lubbers has pointed out, transcends the form–content dualism established by Higginson.

"ALL MEN SAY 'WHAT' TO ME": ACADEMIC CRITICISM FROM 1930 TO 1955

The publication of *Further Poems of Emily Dickinson* (1929) and *Unpublished Poems of Emily Dickinson* (1935) by Martha Dickinson Bianchi and Alfred Leete Hampson consolidates the shift from journalistic evaluation to academic explication (Lubbers 149), a shift which coincides with the rise of New Criticism. According to Lubbers, New Critical readings of Dickinson focus for the most part on an explication of individual poems rather than a general assessment of the poet (176) and firmly establish Dickinson's reputation as a metaphysical poet of wit and as a mystic (146–47). One of the earliest and most famous examples of the New Critical school is Allen Tate's 1932 essay "New England Culture and Emily Dickinson,"[25] in which the poet's "fusion of sensibility and thought" (as it was formulated by T. S. Eliot, in particular) makes her a prime example of the New Critical ideal. Rejecting a biographical approach (the "incurable interest" in her possible lover), Tate roots Dickinson's poetry firmly in her native Puritan culture. Essays such as Yvor Winters's castigation of Dickinson's "silly playfullness" and "obscurantism" (Blake and Wells 188, 200)[26] testify to what academic critics regarded as the "deplorable popularity" of her poetry (Lubbers 175). No longer calling into question the poet's "greatness," these essays constitute an academic attempt at redefining Dickinson "as a quality writer who would appeal mainly to 'the few'" (Buckingham, *Reception* xviii).

Biographical criticism from the 1930s through the 1950s is predominantly interested in gathering external data about Dickinson's life in general and her elusive "lover" in particular. The idea of a secret man in her life, initially introduced by Susan Gilbert and later enshrined by Martha Dickinson Bianchi in her 1924 biography *The Life and Letters of Emily Dickinson* (in which she identifies Charles Wadsworth as the candidate), was further developed by Genevieve Taggard and Josephine Pollitt, who introduced George Gould and Major Hunt, respectively, into the field. The first reliable biography of Dickinson was published by George Frisbie Whicher in 1938. In *This Was a Poet*, Whicher discusses Dickinson in her historical context (with Puritanism and Yankee humor as the major influences) and, refusing to participate in speculations about a possible love affair, establishes Wadsworth's and Benjamin Newton's roles as intellectual advisors rather than lovers (Lubbers 166–67).

Whicher's account was followed by two other primarily biographical studies in 1951: Richard Chase's *Emily Dickinson* and Rebecca Patterson's *Riddle of Emily Dickinson*. Employing a biographical approach to explicate a selection of poems, Chase follows Whicher in situating Dickinson within her Puritan context (deemphasizing the influence of transcendentalism). Patterson, on the other hand, was the first to discuss Dickinson's possible lesbian relationships (based on a chronological analysis of love poems and recurrent geographical imagery patterns) with Susan Gilbert and Kate Scott Turner Anthon.

"MY LITTLE FORCE EXPLODES": ACADEMIC CRITICISM FROM 1955 TO 1995

The year 1955 saw the publication of Thomas H. Johnson's pioneering effort to collect all of Dickinson's poems extant to this date in *The Poems of Emily Dickinson: Including variant readings critically compared with all known manu-*

scripts, followed in 1958 by *The Letters of Emily Dickinson,* edited by Johnson and Theodora Ward. These three-volume variorum editions were the first attempt at a more accurate reproduction of Dickinson's idiosyncratic spelling and punctuation and provided a "conjectural" chronological order of the material. The availability of all of Dickinson's extant poems and letters to date led to a proliferation of Dickinson criticism during the 1960s, with a continued interest in biography and contextualization, an increased focus on her thematic range, and an intensified concern with her use of language.

While biographical and linguistic studies as well as discussions of Dickinson's relation to Puritanism, transcendentalism, and increasingly also romanticism continue during the 1970s, the most important innovations of this decade can be found in areas opened up by psychoanalytic and feminist theories. In various contexts feminist critics demonstrate that Dickinson, rather than merely contributing to or subverting a predominantly male tradition, is situated at the center of a hitherto critically neglected female literary and cultural continuum and can be regarded as "the great woman poet to serve as foremother to a dormant tradition" (Juhasz, *Naked Forms* 7). In addition to emphasizing the decisive function of gender in the creative process and in the reconstruction of literary history, feminist critics also revise theories about Dickinson's "withdrawal from the world" and point out the centrality of her poetic personae.

The 1980s show an even stronger proliferation of scholarship. Gradually shifting away from thematic studies, critical interest focuses, for the most part, on the aspect of gender in linguistic and psychoanalytic studies, on feminist reinterpretations of Dickinson's relation to Puritanism and romanticism, on attempts to read Dickinson as a "protomodernist," and on a revaluation of nineteenth-century popular American literature and culture. In addition, scholars concern themselves with the writer's letters and fascicles and with creative receptions of Dickinson.

Currently the primary critical focus lies, as Juhasz (herein) has pointed out, on the materiality of Dickinson's texts, which has led to an increased scholarly activity in the areas of fascicles, manuscripts (including variants), and the textual and sexual politics of editing. Moreover, the theorization of genre boundaries has challenged the traditional subdivision of Dickinson's canon into poetry and prose; feminist theories have revealed a gender bias in earlier psychoanalytic and linguistic analyses; a discussion of affinities between Dickinson's texts and movements in contemporary arts complements her contextualization within contemporary literature and culture; and biographical studies concentrate on the importance of female friendships for Dickinson's artistic development, thus qualifying the centrality of male figures (God, Master, a male lover) in the writer's life.

Biography

Biographical studies of Dickinson have developed in two main directions: on the one hand, critics compile data about the poet's life, her relationships to family members and to her male and (increasingly) female friends, as well as the lives of other members of the Dickinson circle. On the other hand, psychoanalytic and psychobiographical analyses attempt to chart Dickinson's psychosocial development in search of an explanation for the nature of her creativity as well as the reasons for her "withdrawal from the world." Not infrequently, these two categories overlap.

Under the first category falls Johnson's *Emily Dickinson: An Interpretive Biography*, published together with his variorum edition in 1955. Building on Whicher, Johnson focuses on the writer's family, friends, and religious environment. In addition, the book includes a study of Dickinson's prosody in the context of Isaac Watts's *Psalms, Hymns, and Spiritual Songs*. Jay Leyda's *Years and Hours of Emily Dickinson* (1960) offers a compilation of documentary source materials (letters, diary entries, newspaper clippings, sermons), arranged chronologically and without commentary, and intended as a basis for future biographies. A major contribution in the field of Dickinson biography is Richard Sewall's two-volume *Life of Emily Dickinson* (1974). Devoting a substantial part of his study to Dickinson's immediate family and friends as well as to the Todd–Dickinson affair, Sewall provides a thorough compilation of data concerning the poet's life and environment. The relationship between Austin Dickinson and Mable Loomis Todd receives full focus in Polly Longsworth's *Austin and Mabel* (1984) and Jerome Loving's *Emily Dickinson: The Poet on the Second Story* (1986). In *This Brief Tragedy: Unraveling the Todd–Dickinson Affair* (1991), John Evangelist Walsh adds his own interpretation of the events, surmising that Emily Dickinson may have committed suicide by taking strychnine.

Initial attempts at identifying Dickinson's elusive "lover" presume for the most part that he is male and concentrate primarily on the so-called Master letters. While the majority of critics have opted for Samuel Bowles (George Frisbie Whicher, David Higgins, Ruth Miller, Theodora Ward, Thomas H. Johnson, Judith Farr, and [emphasizing the impossibility of solving the mystery completely] Richard Sewall), John Evangelist Walsh (1971 and 1991), Barton Levi St. Armand (1984), and Cynthia Griffin Wolff (1986) have suggested Judge Otis Lord. Benjamin Lease (1990) relates Dickinson's crisis in the Master letters to a crisis in Wadsworth's life and argues that these letters stylistically echo passages from Wadsworth's sermons. Wadsworth had been advanced earlier by William H. Shurr (1983), whose sequential reading of the fascicles offers a marriage story complete with pregnancy and possible abortion.

Lillian Faderman (1981) and Adalaide Morris (1983) have challenged the assumption that the recipient of the Master letters is necessarily male. Morris compares and contrasts these letters with those mailed to Sue Gilbert and suggests a possible homoerotic relationship. Similarly, Paula Bennett (1986) considers Sue Gilbert the most likely addressee. Opting against a real-life person, Albert Gelpi (1975) has interpreted Dickinson's Master letters as addresses to a troubled aspect of herself, while Roland Hagenbüchle (1988) reads them as strategies of self-transcendence. Wendy Martin (1984) follows Adrienne Rich (1976) in regarding these letters as possible references to the poet's creative self. Martha Nell Smith (1992), finally, considers them as imaginative exercises, to be read as documentation of the composition process rather than as sources of autobiographical information.

Dickinson's parents have been studied by Vivian Pollak in her edition of *A Poet's Parents: The Courtship Letters of Emily Norcross and Edward Dickinson* (1988). As Pollak argues,

> [t]hese letters help to delineate the poet's maternal legacy, modify our understanding of male dominance and female submission in the Dickinson household, and show how conventional courtship patterns in the nineteenth century could be subtly undermined by an intellectually unambitious woman who was also a covert role rebel. (xxvii)

Pollak's earlier study, *Dickinson: The Anxiety of Gender* (1984), had already focused on Emily Norcross's failure in her mother role as a determinative factor in her daughter's psychosocial development. Bridging the gap between biographical and feminist approaches, Pollak applies biographical readings to the poems and regards loss and renunciation as the sources of Dickinson's creativity.

With her attempt to link Dickinson's creative output to an emotional and psychological crisis, Theodora Ward in *The Capsule of the Mind* (1961) sets the trend for subsequent psychobiographical studies. Employing a Jungian approach, Ward reads Dickinson's poems and letters as "self-revelations" (vii) which are at times "so unrelated to reality as to betray their origin in the subconscious world of dream and phantasm" (ix). In his psychoanalytic study *The Long Shadow: Emily Dickinson's Tragic Poetry* (1964), Clark Griffith characterizes Dickinson as "post-Emersonian" or "Transcendentalist-in-reverse" whose tragic outlook on the world manifests itself in angst and terror. Explaining her seclusion not as the result of a secret romance but due to personal and metaphysical causes (a cold father, a rejecting God), Griffith suggests that Dickinson's so-called psychological problems stem mainly from a rejection of her own femininity. A similar emphasis on the writer's psychological crisis can be found in John Cody's controversial *After Great Pain: The Inner Life of Emily*

Dickinson (1971). In this psychobiographical analysis, Cody interprets Dickinson's "Terror — since September" as mental collapse caused by her mother's failure to provide sufficient love and affection. This attempt to regard Dickinson's poetry as the result of a personal neurotic disposition is modified by Albert Gelpi's *Tenth Muse: The Psyche of the American Poet* (1975). Incorporating the aspect of gender into a Freudian/Jungian approach, Gelpi argues that Dickinson has internalized the psychological burden imposed on nineteenth-century women in general. Confronting the masculine Other as personification of her emotional, erotic, spiritual, and religious needs, the writer eventually achieves an androgynous selfhood by integrating her *animus* and *anima*.

Sandra Gilbert and Susan Gubar's *Madwoman in the Attic* (1979) initiates a feminist reinterpretation of Dickinson's sources of creativity as well as of the reasons for her "withdrawal from the world." In response to Harold Bloom, whose model of "anxiety of influence," based on the agonistic relationship between precursor and ephebe, they consider inadequate for a female writer due to its gendered dependence on the Oedipal family romance, Gilbert and Gubar argue that a woman's creativity is impeded by an "anxiety of authorship," since, traditionally, artistic creativity is linked to masculinity, thus rendering the expression "woman poet" a contradiction in terms. Rather than competing with her precursor, Gilbert and Gubar explain, the female writer will experience a sense of mutuality and identification with her foremother(s).

This emphasis on the importance of a female network also runs through Adrienne Rich's response to Emily Dickinson ("Vesuvius," 1976). However, in contrast to Gilbert and Gubar's notion of Dickinson as the "helpless agoraphobic" who acts out the cultural myth of the "madwoman" (87–88),[27] Rich rejects the "frustrated-spinster" approach and challenges "the traditional view of Dickinson as a victim forced into seclusion and renunciation by a failed love affair" (Erkkila, "Dickinson and Rich" 553) by interpreting the poet's withdrawal as a deliberate choice in her commitment to writing.[28] Dickinson thus emerges as a woman who "had it out on her own premises." This idea is echoed in Juhasz's claim that Dickinson "devises a life that will enable her to be a woman poet on her own terms: rejecting the life for which society had prepared her, choosing the life of the mind" (*Naked Forms* 14), a thesis which she expands on in her study *The Undiscovered Continent* (1983).

The most comprehensive feminist psychobiography to date is Cynthia Griffin Wolff's *Emily Dickinson* (1986). Wolff devotes the first quarter of her book to Dickinson's family and the environment that shaped her but argues that, "as the woman becomes Poet, biography must shift its principal focus from the person to that Voice of the verse, for it was in her poetry and not in the world that Emily Dickinson deliberately decided to 'live'" (168). Like Cody (1971), Sewall (1974), Mossberg (1982), and Pollak (1984), Wolff locates the reasons for Dickinson's reclusiveness and subsequent commitment to poetry in her mother's shortcomings: deprived of maternal eye communication as a baby, Dickinson replaces this lack of intimacy with a "fall into language." Using Jacob's wrestling match with God as the key to Dickinson's poetry, Wolff identifies the writer's struggle for power against her father and against the Puritan God (who appears as liar, betrayer, rapist, killer) as central to her work; Dickinson eventually appropriates this power through poetic language. Similarly, Budick (1985) suggests that Dickinson "decided to cut herself off from the social interactions of life in this world" and chose to withdraw into the symbolic realm of language (n.p.). Hagenbüchle (1988) interprets Dickinson's renunciation of a social self and her concomitant choice of a "negative identity" as the writer's search for an authentic self and an act of self-transcendence. Loeffelholz (1991) finally shifts the emphasis "away from biographical and generally social/historical determinations and onto more narrowly literary/textual grounds" by drawing an analogy between Dickinson's withdrawal and the "condensed difficulty of her poetry" (116).

For Paula Bennett, the woman writer's ambivalence toward her creative power, and thus toward language, becomes central. In *My Life a Loaded Gun: Female Creativity and Feminist Poetics* (1986), she argues that Dickinson had to reject the traditional New England model of female socialization (consisting in dutiful self-denial) in order to pursue the "life of self-indulgence and self-gratification" associated with writing poetry (17). This is also the reason, Bennett suggests, for Dickinson's continuous (romantic) refusal to "grow up" and accept an adult woman's role in life, which manifests itself in her ambivalent attitude toward Sue Gilbert's marriage and in the adoption of the pose of the child. This child-persona, however, later becomes a source of power for the writer.

Situating Dickinson among nineteenth-century woman poets, and modifying the image of Dickinson the recluse by pointing out that there exists no conclusive evidence that her life was unfulfilled or restrained, Bennett's *Emily Dickinson: Woman Poet* (1990) emphasizes the importance of female friendships for the writer's life: "Based on shared domestic values, especially the values of mutuality and nurturance, Dickinson's relationships with women sustained and protected her throughout her life" (14). For Dickinson, the central emotional experience, according to Bennett, was her relationship with Sue Gilbert, and an analysis of Dickinson's erotic imagery reveals that her sexual desire and imagination were homoerotic and autoerotic. What Bennett calls "clitorocentrism" is thus fundamental to Dickinson's work and explains her emphasis on littleness and her predilection for paradox (21).

Mary Loeffelholz (1991), arguing from a feminist-deconstructionist-psychoanalytic perspective, critiques the traditional feminist focus on the mother–daughter relationship as too exclusionary and rejects a definition of female creativity in terms of failure. She points out that, "[i]n light of the new psychoanalytic theories of women, Dickinson's art can be related in some ways to 'typically' female development, rather than viewed as a symptom of developmental failure" (5).

Attempts to challenge predominantly biographical readings of Dickinson's poems have been launched by Donna Dickenson and Elizabeth Phillips. In *Emily Dickinson* (1985), Dickenson points out that, even in feminist criticism "the personal has often been emphasized at the expense of the professional" (1), and intends to dispel the "myths" about Dickinson's forbidding father and her ineffectual mother. Reading the writer's use of romance in her poems as a "stock poetic theme" (25), she argues that to regard Dickinson as a poet by default (due to an abandonment) makes the professional depend entirely on the personal (21). Taking a similar stance, Phillips rejects a psychobiographical approach to Dickinson's poetry and insists on a clear separation between a writer's life and the texts she produces. In *Emily Dickinson: Personae and Performance* (1988), Phillips explores the ways in which Dickinson dramatized her own life and used her poems as performative acts rather than as sublimation of personal experiences.

Dickinson's use of roles and masks had already been examined in earlier studies. John E. Todd (1973) discusses the function of four personae, which he identifies as the little girl, the lover-wife-queen, the dead persona, and the split persona. In particular, Todd emphasizes the ironic quality of Dickinson's humility pose. Most discussions of Dickinson's "supposed persons," however, are primarily interested in the little-girl persona, which reflects the gender-inflected attributes of weakness and submission. Rich (1976) and Nina Baym (1979) present Dickinson's strategic use of the role of the child in relation to male authority figures as an attempt to conceal power (Rich) and to denounce God as insensitive father (Baym). Cristanne Miller (1987) and Cynthia Griffin Wolff (1986) highlight the subversive potential of this ambivalent pose, and Jane Donahue Eberwein (1985) considers it as a strategy of self-empowerment. Ronald Wallace (1984) comments on the paradoxical claim for power through powerlessness in the context of Dickinson's humorous stances toward God, through which she can "shine superior to an antagonist by claiming to be inferior" (78).

A different kind of "biographical" reception can be found among the vastly increasing number of creative responses to Dickinson which fictionalize, reinterpret, and/or appropriate various aspects of the writer's life. Susan Howe has published a book-length creative study of "her" Emily Dickinson (1985) in which she allows Dickinson's voice to enter into a dialogue with critics and other writers (thereby refuting Gilbert and Gubar's image of Dickinson as "madwoman" and attacking Cody's *After Great Pain* as "the rape of the great poet" [*My Emily* 24). In addition, Howe draws attention to the importance of the manuscript versions of the poems and devotes a chapter to rehabilitating Higginson, who had been maligned as the obtuse "professor" in William Luce's play *The Belle of Amherst* (1976). Jamie Fuller's *Diary of Emily Dickinson* (1993) constitutes a piece of "historical fiction" for the years 1867–68. Imaginatively chronicling Dickinson's day-to-day existence, Fuller also intersperses twenty-five "previously unknown" fictional poems and annotates the "diary" entries with comments on controversial issues in Dickinson criticism: he rejects Patterson's thesis of a love affair with Kate Scott Turner Anton, undercuts the notion of Dickinson as an early feminist, and "disproves" the thesis that all poems dated by Johnson for 1862 were actually composed in that year. Lewis Turco's *Emily Dickinson, Woman of Letters* (1993) echoes the current critical interest in Dickinson's correspondence. In the first section of his book, Turco demonstrates the close generic link between Dickinson's poetry and prose by casting passages from letters into poems; the second part includes scholarly and creative essays on Dickinson's letters.

Cultural-Historical Contextualization

Critical attempts to situate Emily Dickinson within European and American literary, cultural, and intellectual traditions (Puritanism, transcendentalism, romanticism, metaphysical poetry, mysticism, among others) have shifted in focus over the years. While an initial emphasis was on the poet's transcendence of her local environment due to her stature as a "major" author within "the great tradition" of world literature, more recent reconstructive studies emphasize the writer's "New England" perspective and show a gradual deprivileging of "high culture" and a concomitant revaluation of nineteenth-century American popular culture.

Most of the earliest contextualizations of Dickinson focus on her relation to transcendentalism and Puritanism, privileging either one or the other. Charles Anderson's *Emily Dickinson's Poetry: Stairway of Surprise* (1960) rejects Dickinson's link to transcendentalism,[29] whereas both Thomas W. Ford (1966) and Hyatt Waggoner (1968) stress Emerson's influence on the poet; yet ultimately, they claim, Dickinson redefines faith in modern existentialist terms. Albert Gelpi's discussion of *The Mind of the Poet* (1965) situates Dickinson in relation to nineteenth-century New England, transcendentalism, and romanticism. Gelpi employs the concept of the double consciousness (the "Calvinist mind turning against itself and its Maker") to explain the writer's rebellion against orthodox Puritan doctrines as an outgrowth of a general crisis in Puritanism. In *Emily Dickinson's Poetry* (1975), Robert Weisbuch regards Dickinson as emerging from her cultural heritage of Puritan Calvinism, Emersonian transcendentalism, and nineteenth-century romanticism. Gudrun Grabher's *Emily Dickinson: Das transzendentale Ich* (1981) expands the discussion by analyzing the transcendental subject constituting its own world in the context of American, German, and Japanese forms of transcendentalism, as well as Zen-Buddhism.

The most extensive early analysis of Dickinson in relation to contemporary nineteenth-century America is Karl Keller's historical, cultural, and feminist study *The Only Kangaroo among the Beauty: Emily Dickinson and America* (1979). Keller discusses Dickinson in the context of, among others, Bradstreet, Taylor, Hawthorne, Emerson, Whitman, Stowe, and Jackson and concludes that Dickinson's skepticism often results in a parody of Emerson. Keller's major achievement, as Polk has pointed out, lies in having "redefined American literary tradition in light of Emily Dickinson's contributions" (85). His study concludes with the observation that Emily Dickinson "is now strong enough as a writer in our literary history to transform our view of the culture itself. She makes *it* indigenous to *her*. We may understand much of it somewhat differently because of her" (334).

Recent feminist critics have pointed out that, in addition to the patriarchal constraints of orthodox Calvinism, certain aspects of Puritanism can also be interpreted as empowering for women. Donna Dickenson (1985) focuses on the privileging of the private space:

> Puritanism gave women an inner world to conquer, a private realm of equal or greater importance to the masculine public one. A woman was dependent on no one but herself for her own spiritual well-being, and it was by an intense spiritual striving that she was to gain her own salvation. (34)

Discussing Dickinson's self-imposed renunciation as an empowering symbolic behavior pattern, Jane Donahue Eberwein (1985) argues that for Dickinson deprivation functioned as stimulus for growth:

> Her Calvinist heritage, then, helped to instill in Emily Dickinson her sense of herself as a small, vulnerable quester — deprived of external aids to salvation and even of lasting assurance of grace; but it also provided her with a belief system that recognized limitation and deprivation as entry points to growth. (*Strategies* 84)

Wendy Martin (1984) points out that "Puritan reformation and feminist transformation are structurally similar: both envision the creation of a new world" (7).

The link between Dickinson and romanticism consists, according to Robert Weisbuch ("Veil," 1985) as well as Greg Johnson (1985), in the writer's internalization of the quest romance. Joanne Feit Diehl (*Romantic*, 1981) applies a revision of Bloom's Oedipal model to Dickinson's works and argues that the writer's most important divergence from the romantic tradition consists in her gender and thus her male-gendered muse.

Analyses of Dickinson's modern(ist) aspects tend to focus on the writer's alienation from her own time and place. Concentrating exclusively on language in his discussion of *Dickinson: The Modern Idiom* (1981), David Porter provides a "lingusitic archaeology" (3) of Dickinson's compositional methods and her nonreferential, antimimetic, elliptic language characterized by absences on the level of morpheme, work, phrase, poem, text, corpus, life. According to Porter, "[t]his unyielding remystification of signs establishes Dickinson first of all as an early member of the modern movement of poetry" (6). Ultimately, he tries to "establish the existence of an extreme, perhaps terminal, American modernism of which [Dickinson] is the first practitioner" (1). For Porter, Dickinson remains alienated from her own environment, and it is this "apartness" and "otherness" that defines her as the prototype of the modern alienated writer. Kenneth Stocks (1988) locates Dickinson's "modern" (rather than modernist) quality in her consciousness and her responses to the "abyss" of the new scientific, technological, and economic order. He considers Dickinson "a representative poet in the mainstream tradition of modern Western literature" and "a representative modern poet" (1).

A different attempt at situating Dickinson "in the mainstream tradition of modern Western literature" is undertaken by Jack L. Capps. *Emily Dickinson's Reading, 1836–1886* (1966) traces sources of Dickinson's literary allusions to the King James Bible, the metaphysical poets, Shakespeare, Burns, Emerson, and the Brownings, among others. Although he focuses on canonical texts, Capps also comments (disparagingly) on Dickinson's interest in popular contemporary literature.

This latter aspect is revalued and explored more fully by Barton Levi St. Armand in *Emily Dickinson and Her Culture: The Soul's Society* (1984) and by David S. Reynolds. For his "biography of Victorian American culture" (2), St. Armand has assembled a wide variety of materials drawn from popular culture: women's scrapbooks, journals, folk art, and landscape painting. In relating Dickinson to contemporary female authors such as Sigourney, Stowe, and Phelps, St. Armand demonstrates that she appropriates her own culture at folk, popular, and elite levels. In *Beneath the American Renaissance: The Subversive Imagination in the Age of Emerson and Melville* (1988), Reynolds analyzes the reciprocity and cross-fertilization between popular and elite culture and challenges the view of "great" writers as alienated rebels against their dominant culture. Stressing the subversive potential of nineteenth-century American "women's literature," Reynolds also rejects the traditional way of reading these documents as socially conservative texts, written merely to reinforce the cult of domesticity and to sanctify women's role as nurturing mothers.

Joanne Dobson in *Dickinson and the Strategies of Reticence: The Woman Writer in Nineteenth-Century America* (1989) disagrees with Reynolds in her discussion of Dickinson's attitude toward the nineteenth-century ideology of womanhood. In contrast to Reynolds's emphasis on subversiveness, Dobson sees Dickinson as displaying attitudes of "deviation" as well as "conformity" (xiii). While the poet opposes the didactic orientation of contemporary women's literature, Dobson argues, she nevertheless complies with the strictures of her socially defined identity by concealing her personal experiences behind "slant expressive strategies" such as irony, ambivalence, disruptions of expected sequential patterns, and "conventional feminine images" (xii–xiii). In addition, Dobson claims, Dickinson chose not to publish, "in conformity with the attitudes of her female contemporaries toward the private nature of personal lyrics" (xiv). Contrasting Dickinson's life with that of public/published women writers, Dobson concludes that Dickinson actually perfected the ethos of feminine domesticity by internalizing cultural prescriptions. Dobson also suggests that Dickinson's references to contemporary social and political issues are merely metaphorical (79).

Shira Wolosky's *Emily Dickinson: A Voice of War* (1984), on the other hand, not only situates Dickinson's work within intellectual and literary currents of her time but also, for the first time, registers an impact of concrete historical events on Dickinson's writing. Arguing that the poet's "departures from linguistic convention are a function of a growing doubt concerning traditional metaphysical sanctions for causality, teleology, and axiology" (xv), Wolosky demonstrates how this metaphysical conflict is caused and reinforced by the trauma of the Civil War and discusses how Dickinson uses political events to question religious schemata. In *The Passion of Emily Dickinson* (1992), Judith Farr attempts to read Dickinson in the context of nineteenth-century visual arts, in particular the Pre-Raphaelites and Thomas Cole. Farr also interprets Dickinson's white dress in the Marianic iconographic tradition (39).[30]

Language/Textuality

Whereas the earliest critical analyses of Dickinson's use of language were necessarily based on heavily edited texts with "regularized" spelling, punctuation, rhymes, and syntax, Johnson's variorum edition made much more accurate and specific stylistic studies possible. In *Emily Dickinson's Poetry: Stairway of Surprise* (1960), Charles Anderson discusses wit, puns, shifting grammatical categories, etymologies, asymmetries, juxtaposition of meter and speech rhythm, and rhyme in the context of a thematic study of Dickinson and art, nature, self, death, immortality. David Porter's *Art of Emily Dickinson's Early Poetry* (1966) offers the first strictly formalistic approach. Concentrating on poems written, according to Johnson's dating, before 1862, Porter examines

Dickinson's use of meter, rhyme, imagery, diction, personae, and the ironic counterpoint produced by expressing a skeptical attitude toward the world in hymn measure. Edith Wylder (1971) focuses on an interpretation of the manuscript dashes as elocutionary signs marking inflection, pause, and stress.

This argument is refuted by Ralph W. Franklin as well as Brita Lindberg-Seyersted. In *The Voice of the Poet: Aspects of Style in the Poetry of Emily Dickinson* (1968), Lindberg-Seyersted employs a lingusitic approach to identify colloquialness, slantness (indirection), and privateness (idiosyncracy) as the three governing principles of Dickinson's use of language. Slantness in particular can be regarded as a deep structure with realizations on the levels of phonology, semantics, and syntax. In addition, Lindberg-Seyersted's study concentrates on Dickinson's use of ellipses, paradoxes, negations, and word coinages, and elaborates on the contrast between Anglo-Saxon and Latin vocabulary (a contrast first identified by Tate). Sirkka Heiskanen-Mäkelä's stylistic analysis of phonetic patterns, elliptic metaphors, quatrains, and riddles in her *In Quest of Truth: Observations on the Development of Emily Dickinson's Poetic Dialectic* (1970) constitutes (in its focus on later poems) a sequel to Porter (*Early Poetry*) and attempts, as Polk has suggested, "to understand the cultural and situational influences upon the poet's use of language" (102).

One of the central aspects of Dickinson's language has been identified by Roland Hagenbüchle ("Precision," 1974; "Sign," 1979) and Inder Nath Kher (1974) as its indeterminate, nonreferential, and nonmimetic quality, which is echoed in Weisbuch's concept of "scenelessness." Both Hagenbüchle and Kher also emphasize negation and silence as important deep-structural elements with multiple surface realizations in Dickinson's poetry. As Hagenbüchle has demonstrated, the absence of an outward reality forms the prerequisite for Dickinson's poetic imagination. Regarding the poetic word as an autonomous unit, Dickinson creates meaning through context and opposition. Hagenbüchle ("Covenant," 1993) has further suggested that Dickinson employs situational and semantic rather than descriptive mimesis and privileges semantic shifts. It is this processual quality of Dickinson's poetry, Hagenbüchle argues, which makes disambiguation impossible. Similarly, Judy Jo Small comments on the fluid and dynamic quality of Dickinson's poems in the context of rhyme (1990). Viewing Dickinson's rhymes as a structural principle marking stanzaic regularity, Small nevertheless problematizes the facile association of full rhymes with stability and partial rhymes with instability.

The nonmimetic aspect of Dickinson's language has been reinterpreted in feminist terms by Margaret Homans. In *Women Writers and Poetic Identity* (1980), Homans discusses Dorothy Wordsworth, Emily Brontë, and Emily Dickinson as feminist responses to the masculine romantic tradition and argues that, because language itself embodies and enacts patriarchal assumptions, Dickinson's gender prompts her to identify with Eve, to learn from Satan not to trust the mimetic concept of God's/Adam's language, and to accept instead the dislocation of words from their referents. Cristanne Miller further develops this argument in her "grammar" of Dickinson's poetry (1987) and regards the structural and linguistic features of compression and fragmentation, indirection, nonlinearity, nonrecoverable deletions, disjunctive syntax, syntactic and semantic doubling, and transposition of grammatical classes of words as oppositions to an existing social order and as "a nineteenth-century anticipation of possibilities for an *écriture féminine*" (*Grammar* 184).

Earlier discussions of Dickinson's language of indeterminacy have recently been challenged by Paula Bennett (1990), who argues for a qualification of the concept of nonreferentiality: "By establishing the literary, social and biographical contexts for Dickinson's poetry," what initially seems fragmented and unrelated will become clearer (*Woman Poet* 23). Emphasizing the need for studying Dickinson's poems in their fascicle context, Sharon Cameron (1992) uses the term "in(ter)determinacy" to foreground a similar idea: it is a suppression of contexts which generates "that understanding of Dickinson's poems as enigmatic, isolated, culturally incomprehensible phenomena" (*Choosing* 19).

In her essay "Adventures in the World of the Symbolic: Emily Dickinson and Metaphor" (1994), Suzanne Juhasz proposes a revision of Julia Kristeva's concept of *écriture féminine*. Critiquing the fact that *écriture féminine* denies women access to the symbolic and thus to the realm of meaning-making, Juhasz proposes

> that symbolic language is not antithetical to women's gendered identity, but that it has more than one aspect — or dialect or idiom: one that inscribes cultural norms or values, which we might indeed associate with "the masculine"; another that, as it communicates a "sharing of mutually created meanings about *personal* experience," comes out of the mother-infant matrix and can thus be associated with the feminine. (143)

The fact that women have access to and need to choose between those two "dialects" creates a sense of doubleness. In this sense Dickinson's language is both symbolic and semiotic, and metaphor is used to bridge these two "idioms" to create a third alternative: "a place in language where the dichotomous constraints of culture are transcended" (144).

Recent studies of Dickinson's poetry have highlighted the importance of an audience in the process of meaning-making. Emphasizing the role of the reader in co-creating Dickinson's texts, Hagenbüchle (1993) suggests that the process of wording creates an experiential emptiness, "a semantically open interspace implying potential fullness," which, then, has to be filled by the reader ("Covenant" 20). Gary Lee Stonum (1990) comes to a similar conclusion: refuting the thesis that Dickinson's is an author-centered aesthetics, Stonum emphasizes the writer's commitment to a rhetoric of stimulus, a concept that was suggested earlier by Hagenbüchle (*Wagnis,* 1988) in the context of his discussion of Dickinson's "poetry of provocation." In their analysis of *Comic Power in Emily Dickinson* (1993), Juhasz, Miller, and Smith focus on the crucial role of the audience in Dickinson's performative poetry: her comic strategies, employed to disrupt and subvert the patriarchal authority of contemporary institutions, require an audience who translates into practice the poet's offer of "a transforming vision of the world" (1). Smith (*Rowing,* 1992) also discusses the role of the reader/editor in general (and Sue Gilbert in particular) as collaborator in the meaning-making process and thus in the production of the poems, especially in view of Dickinson's refusal to resolve variant readings and variant punctuation.

Sharon Cameron is the first to propose a deconstructionist analysis of Dickinson and the lyric genre. In her *Lyric Time: Dickinson and the Limits of Genre* (1979), Cameron explores the relationship between contextual disorder and temporal conception in Dickinson's poems. "Fragmentary lines, the refusal of syntax and diction to subordinate themselves to each other, the subsequent absence of context and progression, the resulting ambiguity and tension" (18) are directly linked to the fact that the lyric as a genre rejects the limitations of narrative and objective concepts of time. Since the lyric voice can only speak out of a single moment in time, it can represent division, conflict, and multiple points of view only by an internalization of a plurality of characters, which, in turn, leads to ambiguity and contradiction. A more recent generic approach to the lyric has been offered by Margaret Dickie in *Lyric Contingencies: Emily Dickinson and Wallace Stevens* (1991). In drawing a link between genre and gender, Dickie emphasizes the nonteleological quality of the lyric, which foregrounds the lyric speaker as processual, "changeable and duplicitous" in contrast to a centered self (9). Dickinson's lyric speaker is thus able to challenge the Emersonian concept of a continuous and coherent identity.

Due to an increased scholarly interest in the materiality of Dickinson's texts, recent criticism has returned to the fascicles, first published in a two-volume facsimile edition by Ralph W. Franklin in 1981. In *The Manuscript Books of Emily Dickinson,* Franklin relies on pin impressions and paper stains to re-create the original arrangement of Dickinson's poems (forty fascicles and fifteen unbound sets) as they had been left by the poet on her death in 1886 (before Todd restructured and renumbered them). Ruth Miller (1968) was the first to concentrate on the structure of the fascicles, identifying a narrative pattern for their groupings (from acceptance through suffering and rejection to resolution) analogous to Francis Quarles's organization of *Emblems, Divine and Moral.* This question of a possible narrative and sequential structure within and between fascicles has been of central interest ever since. Franklin himself has found no evidence for a reading of the fascicles as "careful constructs governed by theme, imagery, narrative and dramatic movement, or similar principle" ("Fascicles" 17); on the contrary, he observes, there are indications that some poems are arranged according to the space available on the page. This view is shared by Barton Levi St. Armand (1984), who can discern

> no ostensible dramatic or dynamic sequence of images, motif, or ideas. What strikes us rather is the emotional intensity of the individual fragments combined with a seemingly random patchwork pattern. . . . Poems are entered in order to use up blank spaces rather than to augment or modify a narrative. (*Culture* 9)

Rosenthal and Gall (1983), on the other hand, argue for a sequential, narrative reading of Dickinson's manuscript booklets, regarding fascicles 15 ("The Poetry of Psychic Trauma") and 16 ("A New Start") as interdependent formations of "an epic of the subjective life" (53). Dorothy Huff Oberhaus (1995) concentrates on the fortieth fascicle, in which she identifies a "deep structural and thematic unity" (3). Oberhaus considers this last fascicle as

> an architectural tour de force, a three-part meditation, a letter addressed to the reader, a garland of praise, and a conversion narrative, as well as the triumphant conclusion of the protagonist's account of her poetic and spiritual pilgrimage from renunciation to illumination to union and finally, after many conflicts, to contentment with this union. (*Fascicles* 168)

What makes this narrative account somewhat problematic, however, is the underlying assumption that Dickinson composed each poem in fascicle 40 with the architectural conception of the entire fascicle in mind.

In contrast to Oberhaus, Sharon Cameron argues against a narrative reading of Dickinson's manuscript booklets. In *Choosing Not Choosing: Dickinson's Fascicles* (1992), Cameron demonstrates that Dickinson's refusal to make choices on a textual, formal, thematic, and philosophical level calls into question the poem as discrete unit. Rather than as independent lyrics, Cameron reads the poems within each fascicle as variants of each other, thus concluding that Dickinson challenged the idea of limits or boundaries: Dickinson might have attempted "to redetermine our very understanding of how the identity of a poetic structure is to be construed" (18).

The textual and sexual politics of editing have been among the central concerns of Paula Bennett and Martha Nell Smith. Bennett (*Woman Poet*, 1990) and Smith (*Rowing*, 1992) outline how the public image of "Emily the poetess" predisposed her first editors in their choice and arrangement of poems. The interpretive and mediating function of the editor is also one of the major foci of Smith's *Rowing in Eden: Rereading Emily Dickinson*. Smith challenges the concept of Dickinson as writing in isolation and invites the reader to reconsider the concept of "publication." Highlighting Dickinson's careful distinction between "publish" and "print," Smith regards the writer's letters and fascicles as alternative forms of publication: "her chirographic 'publication' was not simply 'part of an unusual and painful strategy that signaled privacy and alienation' but was instead a consciously designed alternative mode of textual reproduction and distribution" which would guarantee Dickinson independence of the limitations imposed by mechanical modes of production on features such as calligraphy or punctuation (1–2).

Since Sue Gilbert received more poems than any other correspondent (276 in total), Smith focuses on Gilbert's role as critic, editor, and possible co-author. Moreover, Smith argues that Austin Dickinson's deletions and expurgations in the writer's letters to Gilbert "seek to expunge the record of Dickinson's affection for this woman" (*Rowing* 20–21). In her most recent article ("Hypermedia," 1995), Smith outlines future editorial projects in the context of these ongoing critical concerns: in addition to Franklin's new print edition of the poems, the Dickinson Editing Collective will establish a hypermedia archive with online reproductions of all extant documents and their publication histories, which will open up numerous new avenues for future Dickinson criticism.

NOTES

1. For a review of bibliographies published before those mentioned below, see Willis J. Buckingham's essay "The Bibliographical Study of Emily Dickinson." Buckingham discusses major descriptive and critical bibliographies until the year 1970.

2. Two additions to be mentioned here are: Joel Myerson's guide to editions of and collections containing Dickinson's writings, *Emily Dickinson: A Descriptive Bibliography* (1984); and S. P. Rosenbaum's *Concordance to the Poems of Emily Dickinson* (1964).

3. See, among others, the back issues of *Dickinson Studies* and the annual listings in *American Literary Scholarship* for these years.

4. This assumes added significance in the context of private readers' responses to Dickinson's manuscript poems and letters circulated during the writer's lifetime. Although currently no more than ten of Dickinson's poems are known to have been published in print prior to her death, Dickinson's letters, addressed to more than ninety correspondents, contain a large number of "letter-poems" enclosed with, incorporated into, or inextricably fused with their "prose" context. Most responses to these texts, however, have been lost or were destroyed by Lavinia, who, after her sister's death, burned all of Dickinson's private papers.

5. When I quote from nineteenth- and early twentieth-century reviews, I will cite these more easily accessible collections (Blake and Wells; Buckingham, *Reception*); original sources are provided in the notes to this essay.

6. When Mabel Loomis Todd resigned her editorial activities.

7. The popularity of Dickinson's poetry among private readers, as both Buckingham and Terris have pointed out, can be attributed to the fact that, in addition to portraying the New England landscape, Dickinson's poems "drew upon popular themes in female verse, such as womanhood, home, human relationships, melancholy and death" (Buckingham, *Reception* xv). In addition, the poems also fulfilled many of the common reader's religious and sentimental expectations for poetry (Buckingham, *Reception* xvi).

8. While nearly 40 percent of all nineteenth-century responses to Dickinson came from women, for example, their — almost unanimously enthusiastic — voices were frequently marginalized due to gender and generic biases: most of their reviews were published in (less influential) women's journals and religious magazines; in addition, as professional poets and fiction writers, many women responded to Dickinson's writings by publishing creative tributes rather than journalistic evaluations, which, while contributing substantially to the favorable reception of Dickinson, nevertheless failed to win their authors status among journalistic critics.

9. From Sue Gilbert Dickinson's laudatory obituary "Miss Emily Dickinson of Amherst," *Springfield Republican* 18 May 1886: 4; qtd. in Lubbers 5. Rpt. in Buckingham, *Reception*, App. A; Leyda 2: 472–74.

10. From Todd's diary entry for 8 Feb. 1882; qtd. in Lubbers 10; Leyda 2: 361.

11. Quotations are from Higginson's "Preface" to *Poems by Emily Dickinson*, ed. Mabel Loomis Todd and Thomas Wentworth Higginson (1890), [iii]–iv. Rpt. in Buckingham, *Reception* 13–14.

12. "I taste a liquor never brewed" (P214).

13. Aldrich's essay was first published in the *Atlantic Monthly* 69 (Jan. 1892): 143–44. The strong gender bias inherent in Aldrich's review is disclosed in Ellen Battelle Dietrick's spirited response: "Not content with a sweeping condemnation of Emily Dickinson's 'incoherence and formlessness' (qualities which are now supposed peculiarly to manifest genius in Walt Whitman), not content with denying her the right of poetic title, with pronouncing her thoughts 'ideas which totter and toddle,' the critic goes out of his way to accuse Col. Higginson of sentimentality in behalf of women. . . . Such a fling is more worthy of a school boy than of one who aspires to the dignity of a critic" (Buckingham, *Reception* 291).

14. This review first appeared in the *Boston Budget* (23 Nov. 1890) under the title "Literature."

15. Howells's review was first published as the "Editor's Study," *Harper's New Monthly Magazine* 82 (Jan. 1891): 318–21.

16. Lang's critique was first published as "Some American Poets," *Illustrated London News* 98 (7 Mar. 1891): 307.

17. Lubbers also mentions "Higginson's resignation as coeditor and promoter" and the general decline of poetry as additional reasons for the "lean years" in Dickinson criticism (84–85).

18. H.M. [Harriet Monroe], "The Single Hound," *Poetry* 5 (Dec. 1914): 138–40.

19. Sergeant's essay was first published in the *New Republic* 4 (14 Aug. 1914): 52–54. Rpt. in Blake and Wells 88–93.

20. By Sergeant (Blake and Wells 88–93).

21. By Robert Hillyer, in "Emily Dickinson," *Freeman* 6 (18 Oct. 1922): 129–31. Rpt. in Blake and Wells 98–104.

22. By Theodore Spencer, in "Concentration and Intensity," *New England Quarterly* 2 (July 1929): 498–501. Rpt. in Blake and Wells 131–33.

23. Armstrong's essay was first published as "The Poetry of Emily Dickinson," *Spectator* 130 (6 Jan. 1923): 22–23.

24. Miles's essay was first published in *London Mercury* 13 (Dec. 1925): 145–50, 157–58. Rpt. in Blake and Wells 123–29.

25. Tate's essay was first published in *Symposium* 3 (Apr. 1932): 206–26. Rpt. in Blake and Wells 153–67.

26. Winters's essay was first published as "Emily Dickinson and the Limits of Judgment," *Maule's Curse* (Norfolk: New Directions, 1938), 149–65. Rpt. in Blake and Wells 187–200.

27. A notion which is shared by Maryanne Garbowsky (1989), who suggests that Emily Dickinson "was reclusive due to an agoraphobic syndrome that left her in fear of the outside world" (*House* 22).

28. Juhasz comments on the phallocentricity of the "frustrated-spinster" approach which implies that: "(a) Emily Dickinson wrote poetry because she did not have a sex life or (b) the only explanation for such poetry was an active (albeit secret) sex life. Both interpretations lodge the male at the center of a woman's creativity" (*Naked Forms* 10).

29. A similar position is taken by William R. Sherwood in *Circumference and Circumstance: Stages in the Mind and Art of Emily Dickinson* (1968).

30. A second focus of the book lies on an analysis of Dickinson's erotic relationship to Sue Gilbert and Samuel Bowles as Master.

Vivian R. Pollak

American Women Poets Reading Dickinson: The Example of Helen Hunt Jackson

O n February 8, 1882, Mabel Loomis Todd, then a young woman recently arrived in Amherst, recorded in her journal that she had just paid a call on Susan Gilbert Dickinson, the poet's sister-in-law and close friend. Todd was a cultivated, ambitious, and passionate person, who prided herself on her freedom from convention. This is what she wrote: "Went in the afternoon to Mrs. Dickinson's. She read me some strange poems by Emily Dickinson. They are full of power" (Leyda 2: 361). As many people have noticed, Emily Dickinson's poems *are* strange and powerful, though the intricate relationship between their strangeness and their power has been rather continuously contested. As early as 1861, for example, Susan Dickinson had written to the poet in a poignant interchange that "Strange things always go alone,"[1] but Dickinson seems not to have agreed with her, or at least did not take her advice about the intellectually challenging poem "Safe in their Alabaster Chambers" (P216), which they were then discussing. More generally, history has proved the friend and sister-in-law wrong in her seemingly categorical judgment, for Dickinson's poems have had plenty of company, despite the fact that, as Dickinson herself once wrote to the male critic who was to become Todd's coeditor, "All men say 'What' to me, but I thought it a fashion" (L271).

From the beginning, then, women were crucial in disseminating Dickinson's letter to the world. Though her own mother did not "care for thought," in her immediate family circle there were two who listened attentively and who believed in her genius: her sister Lavinia and her sister by marriage, Sue.[2] Beyond this intimate circle, which included Mabel Loomis Todd on its perverse periphery,[3] there were more or less comprehending others: the reformer, essayist, short story writer, novelist, and poet Helen Hunt Jackson, for one, who pleaded with Dickinson to publish, who asked to be her literary executor, and whose early enthusiasm contributed to Dickinson's unexpected popularity in the 1890s. Endorsed by Jackson, Dickinson took on "taller feet" (L238), as she told Sue she hoped someday to do. Helen Hunt Jackson's unhesitating, apparently unequivocal response to Dickinson focuses a complicated critical conversation, which I should like to pursue in considerable detail.[4] Jackson did not claim to understand everything Dickinson wrote or to understand her reclusion. But, in contradistinction to such influential taste-makers as Thomas Wentworth Higginson and Josiah Gilbert Holland, she was sure that Dickinson had something of unique value to contribute to a shared vision of American life. Whereas both Higginson and Holland expressed the view that Dickinson's poems were too "delicate" to merit publication, Jackson called Emily Dickinson a "great poet" and chastised her for not singing "aloud." "What portfolios of verses you must have," she wrote. "It is a cruel wrong to your 'day & generation' that you will not give them light" (L937a). Jackson's impassioned attempts to champion a poet whose horror of personal publicity was even greater than her own nevertheless emerged out of some of the major contradictions of her own career. "Dickinson," as we shall see, became a vehicle for negotiating those contradictions. Like many of the better poets who followed her, Jackson was thus intent on using Dickinson to lend cultural authority to her own self-representation. In Dickinson's terms, her zeal was both affectionate and jealous. In short, her project was to use Dickinson to justify herself.

The chances that two women born in tiny Amherst, Massachusetts, in the fall of 1830 should each have been a Higginson protégée and that each should have been variously acclaimed as America's leading poet seem remote. Yet such was the case. As a child, Helen Maria Fiske had a nodding acquaintance with the young Emily Elizabeth Dickinson, but they were not particular friends. An "everlasting talker" who, according to her mother, was "inclined to question the authority of everything" (R. Sewall, *Life* 2: 325), Helen was boisterous and robust, whereas Dickinson, though noted for her wit, was already frailer and more self-contained. Helen was sent away to boarding school when she was eleven, and after the death of the mother she later remembered as "good and wise" as well as "loving, caressing, overflowing . . . whom the whole town loved and who herself loved the whole world," the thirteen-year-old Helen began to live with relatives on Cape Cod, since her father was unable to care for her. Her younger and more tractable sister Ann, who was a friend of Lavinia Dickinson's, was sent elsewhere. While Helen was attending Ipswich Female Seminary, her father, who had been devastated by the loss of his wife, followed the advice of his colleagues at Amherst College and took a trip to the Holy Land to restore his health. But Nathan Welby Fiske, professor of moral philosophy and metaphysics, died of dysentery in

Jerusalem and was buried on Mount Zion. Orphaned now of both parents, Helen was only sixteen.[5]

Exhibiting her usual courage and resourcefulness, she completed her education first at Ipswich, which she disliked, and then at the Abbott Institute in New York City, where she felt very much at home. (Jacob Abbott had been a close friend, coauthor, and colleague of her professorial father). This progressive school was a family affair, and all the Abbott brothers (including Helen's favorite, John) "did important pioneering in the early movements for women's better education" (Odell 40). Eventually, Jacob and John were also well-known writers.[6] Helen taught for a year at this school for the higher education of girls in 1851 (by then called Spingler Institute), fell in love with her future husband Edward Bissell Hunt while on a visit to Albany, mingled with high society, gave up thoughts of teaching, and then married her already distinguished husband when she was twenty-two. Their first son, Murray, was born in 1854, but he died in infancy. Helen tried not to blame herself for his death, and their second son, Rennie, was born in 1857. Tragedy struck again in 1863, however, when Major Hunt, a West Point–educated army engineer, accidentally blew himself up in the Brooklyn Navy Yard while working to perfect a "sea miner," an early form of submarine. Several years later, when she lost her beloved nine-year-old Rennie to diphtheria, Helen's friends feared for her life. Turning emphatically to writing to assuage her multiple griefs and to earn a living (though she had also inherited some money from her mother, Deborah Vinal Fiske, the only child of a well-to-do Boston merchant), the sociable and resourceful "H.H." moved to Newport, Rhode Island, and took up residence in Mrs. Dame's literary boardinghouse, where she met Higginson and became his protégée. She learned of Dickinson's poetry through him.[7]

A decade or so later, Jackson was considered by some the leading woman poet in America. Writing in the *Springfield Republican* on January 1, 1874, Samuel Bowles, for one, announced that "Mrs Hunt stands on the threshold of the greatest literary triumphs ever won by an American woman" (Sewall, *Life* 2: 579). That same year Emerson included five poems by "H.H." in his anthology *Parnassus*, while omitting any mention of Walt Whitman; he told Higginson that he considered her the leading *poet*, not just the leading woman poet, on the continent. Meanwhile, Higginson did everything he could to advance his friend's reputation; he edited her work and included her in his 1879 *Short Studies of American Authors*, along with Poe, Hawthorne, Thoreau, Howells, and Henry James (Jr.). But Jackson's career had been impelled by personal tragedy, and in that sense she gave voice to her experience reluctantly. She published much of her own work anonymously or pseudonymously, including her first two books of poetry, the 1870 *Verses* (Boston: Fields, Osgood) and her 1874 new and enlarged *Verses* (Boston: Roberts Brothers). According to Louise

Pound, her aversion to personal publicity was an "obsession" (542).[8] Writing to secure control over her disordered life but printing, as she once said, "for money," Jackson, particularly early in her career, mocked the more aggressive forms of nineteenth-century feminism, such as the suffrage movement, and under certain circumstances even questioned the right of women to lecture in public. Suffering from periodic and prolonged bouts of ill health following Rennie's death, she traveled widely beginning in the mid-1860s in search of healthier and less depressing places. She lived in Europe in 1868–70, moved to Colorado Springs in 1872, where she met her second husband, and returned to Europe without him for five months in 1880. Meanwhile, she had heard a lecture that changed her life. Listening to Chief Standing Bear, the leader of a group of starving Ponca Indians who had been tragically and mistakenly dispossessed from their tribal home in the Dakota Territory and then removed against their wishes to Indian Territory (present-day Oklahoma), Helen Hunt Jackson found the cause for which she felt she had been destined. At the deepest level, she identified with Standing Bear's tragic story of exile and bereavement—he had watched helplessly "as over one hundred of his tribe died, including his son" (Mathes, Foreword to Jackson, *Century* ix). Ruth Odell notes that "Her sudden and consuming interest is the more remarkable by reason of the fact that Helen had always shrunk from the idea of a woman with a hobby" (155).

As an Indian rights advocate, Jackson was praised by the *New York Times* for her "ripe scholarship" and "facile pen," but also for exhibiting "an enthusiasm and a sympathy with the wronged which none but a tender-hearted and just woman can possess" (Mathes, in Jackson, *Century* xiv).[9] (She adored children, and it is said that her eyes misted whenever she heard the name of her lost son, Rennie). Provoking both praise and controversy, Jackson worked herself into states of nervous exhaustion, fleeing to Europe on May 29, 1880, after completing a *Century of Dishonor.* (Higginson was to read proof in her absence.) In May 1884 her physician, fearing a "general nervous breakdown," urged her to stay out of Colorado for two years and to abstain from "brain work" (Banning 205). Unable to take his advice, she returned briefly to Colorado and then moved on to California, where she remained intellectually active until the final days of her life, penning an appeal on behalf of the Indians to President Grover Cleveland shortly before morphine was administered to ease the stomach cancer from which she died in San Francisco on August 12, 1885. Terribly shocked by the news of her friend and supporter's imminent death, which was widely reported in the national press, Emily Dickinson wrote immediately to Higginson on August 6 (L1007). Several weeks later, she wrote a condolence note to Jackson's widower and asked for information about the final days (L1009). In late September, she exclaimed to the clergyman Forrest F. Emer-

son, apparently their mutual friend, "Oh had that Keats a Severn!" (L1018).
But no Severn has emerged to write Helen Hunt Jackson's life, and we are
greatly in need of a new biography, especially one which will make fuller use of
her letters and fiction. Such a biography would need to read her most enduring work, *Ramona*, not merely as a sentimental romance masquerading as an
Indian rights novel but also as a study in female agency, colluding and colliding
with a racist culture.

More particularly, a fuller recuperation of Jackson's life would need to
account for the destructive power of Ramona's foil, the widowed Señora
Moreno, who comes close to ruining Ramona's life. Identified always as a
member of a powerful family, the Spanish-born Señora dominates her only
son and rules her ranch with a will of iron. More often than not, we see her as a
psychotically controlling mother, determined to preserve the purity of her
family and of her race. (Her son Felipe is always on the verge of falling in love
with Ramona, his foster sister and childhood sweetheart.) Thus, just as the
cultural work performed by Harriet Beecher Stowe's antislavery novel *Uncle
Tom's Cabin* depends crucially on its idealization of family ties, so too the
cultural work performed by *Ramona* emerges from Jackson's narrative of maternal rejection, which constitutes an indirect appeal to happier paradigms of
continuous family life. Eventually, Ramona leaves her childhood home to
marry for love, but she is disempowered as the wife of an Indian, even a clearly
superior being such as her husband Alessandro. Having been schooled in
hardship by her disastrous childhood, she suffers many wrongs stoically and,
under the circumstances, cheerfully. Eventually she is widowed, deeply impoverished, and on the verge of death. Fortunately, she is rescued by Felipe
Moreno, who, after his despicable mother's death, is freed to search effectively
for the woman he loves. Consequently, Ramona returns to the scene of her
childhood humiliation only after the Señora's death and later marries Felipe,
an amiable but weak man who had been incapable of protecting her while his
mother was still alive. This second marriage enables Ramona to recoup her
rightful inheritance, an inheritance that the Señora had willfully withheld. But
Jackson suggests that Ramona's sufferings as the Señora's illegitimate ward and
as an Indian wife have numbed her for life. The novel's ending, which necessi-
tates a move to Mexico, is only qualifiedly happy.

Jackson's new biographer would need to attend to her sense of having been
expelled from childhood "Paradise" following the death of her parents, an
expulsion begun (with the advantage of hindsight) when she was eleven and
sent away to boarding school, in part to tame her down. Survivor's guilt would
eventually emerge as a dominant factor in her literary career, and in her desire
to influence the future through Dickinson (as, on a small scale, she has done).
Both *Ramona* and *A Century of Dishonor* were written at white heat, under the

force of a great compulsion. Consider, for example, the following description of the publication history of *Century*, written by Valerie Sherer Mathes:

> In early January 1881, Jackson received a "wet copy" of *A Century of Dishonor* from Harper and Brothers, who had guaranteed her ten percent of the royalties in the May 21, 1880, contract. This was the first work that openly carried her name, and she read it fondly, "but with some terror," she noted to [Charles Dudley] Warner. "I don't know what they'll do to me." Jackson sent copies of her book, bound in blood-red cloth, to each congressman at personal expense. Embossed on the cover were the words of Benjamin Franklin: "Look upon your hands! They are stained with the blood of your relations." (Jackson, *Century* xiii)

On her deathbed, she wrote to Higginson, "My 'Century of Dishonor' and 'Ramona' are the only things I have done of which I am glad. . . . They will live, and . . . will bear fruit." Haunted, I speculate, by a sense of having been stained with the blood of her relations (mother, father, child, husband, child), Jackson turned to the writing of these later works driven by terrible internal pressures and as to a "lover"; she couldn't keep away from them, she explained, and was almost frightened by her own intensity. Similarly, in her desire to help Dickinson, she was impelled by a combination of forces. In perpetuating herself through her friend, she was returning to the happier scene of her unstained, though cruelly severed past. And in aligning herself with the future, she hoped that her "criminal" self might be tamed, the imperfectly repressed stain of her relations' blood wiped clean at last. But whatever the fuller truth of Jackson's inner life, which might include the anger and guilt that she felt toward her second husband, whom she had to all intents and purposes deserted in order to pursue her independent writing career,[10] several facts emerge clearly enough. Because of her Amherst origins, her star-crossed history, and her well-known aversion to personal publicity, Jackson was exceptionally well positioned to challenge the inevitability of the reclusion on which Dickinson's writing life depended. A commanding presence, she sought to shape Dickinson, as she herself had been shaped, by some notion, however vague, of writing not merely autotherapeutically but for the greater good. Fearing engulfment, Dickinson was wary.

LET'S RETURN NOW to Jackson's bold letter of September 1884 (L937a), in which she asked to be Dickinson's literary executor and accused her former schoolmate of perpetrating a "cruel wrong." Without responding directly to this heated language — the earlier "wrong" (L444a) has become "a cruel wrong" — Dickinson deftly deflected her correspondent's request. Whereas Jackson had called her "stingy" in 1876, metaphorically and elliptically Dickinson now suggested that hoarding (or self-control) has its virtues. Figuring the release of poetic power as a strike against the status quo, assaultive in its intensity, she justified her thrifty logic with a witty quatrain in which she problematized the poet's "natural" cultural work as follows:

> And then he lifted up his Throat
> And squandered such a Note —
> A Universe that overheard
> Is stricken by it yet — (L937)

Gendering poetic power as profligate and male, Dickinson in effect cautioned Jackson against typecasting her as just another cheering and pleasing poetess. The idea that language might wound as well as soothe was not of course new. Jackson herself had demonstrated as much in "A Woman's Death-Wound," one of her *Masque of Poets* contributions, a sonnet in which someone, presumably an insensitive husband, tortures someone, presumably his loving wife, with "but a word. A blow had been less base."[11] Whereas in Jackson's poem the wielder of the fatal word is condemned as a murderer, Dickinson revels in power alone, troping the effect of sound on an eavesdropping universe as cataclysmic: possibly awe-inspiring, possibly sublime, but ever and always uncontrollable. The delicious sensuous pleasure of self-expression emerges as its own reason for being, indifferent to audience.

Here as elsewhere, Dickinson's language leads in many different directions. Consequently, this provocative and rich correspondence — like the quatrain, which is excerpted from a longer poem (P1600), like the letter, like the relationship between poem and letter, among poem, letter, and literary occasion — can be read in many different ways. For example, in my reading, Dickinson is writing her own autobiography. But since the convalescent bird may be either herself or Jackson or both, depending on historical and narrative context, on another level she offered the minipoem quoted above as a compliment to her injured friend, reminding Jackson that *Jackson's* power of language remained intact. (In 1884 both Dickinson and Jackson had taken their summers "in a Chair," Dickinson from " 'Nervous prostration,' " Jackson from a severely broken leg, which despite her progress from "crutch to cane" was never to heal. Jackson was now weakened for life.) Yet on another level, more is at stake in Dickinson's highly allusive consolation tropes than the desire to compliment her ailing friend. "Mrs Hunt's Poems are stronger than any written by Women since Mrs — Browning, with the exception of Mrs Lewes [George Eliot]," she had explained to Higginson in 1871. And then again in December 1879, after considering his published opinion that Helen Hunt Jackson was America's greatest woman poet: "Mrs Jackson soars to your estimate as lawfully as a bird, but of Howells and James — one hesitates" (L622). Given that Dickinson often prided herself on her identification with lawlessness, such praise is perhaps less wholehearted than it might at first appear.

Several years later, in writing to Jackson herself, Dickinson's stance is even more tantalizingly ambiguous.

> I infer from your Note you have "taken Captivity Captive," and rejoice that martial Verse has been verified. He who is "slain and smiles, steals something from the" Sword, but you have stolen the Sword itself, which is far better—I hope you may be harmed no more—I shall watch your passage from Crutch to Cane with jealous affection. (L937)

Masculinizing Jackson and endowing her with a castrating sword, Dickinson flirts with her friend, who herself flirted with the pleasures of cross-dressing in her orientalizing narrative poem "The Story of Boon," which was set in a *King and I* Siamese harem. Joyful criminals together, Dickinson and Jackson escape both nervous prostration and weakened bodies. They also escape from Higginson's normalizing literary standards, which cause him to prefer Jackson over herself. Drawing together these various motifs and determined to preserve an honest record of their friendship, Dickinson responds "with jealous affection." Appropriating the Bible (Judges 5:12) and Shakespeare's *Othello* (1.3.208), she swiftly transforms Jackson's language into her own idiom.[12] "With jealous affection": in effect, these words reverberate throughout Dickinson's correspondence with Jackson; they may serve to focus subsequent readings of a complicated and underexplored subject, namely Dickinson's influence on women poets in the twentieth century. In the next sections of this essay, I want to look further at Dickinson's ambivalence toward the women poets who were her contemporaries, especially Jackson, whose vociferously successful public career was in many ways a countertype to Dickinson's private vocation. Then I want to look further at the production of "Dickinson" as an exemplary and cautionary figure: evidently much admired by other women poets but also much rebuffed.

Though characteristically angered by requests for poems from strangers,[13] Dickinson was not wholly immune to Jackson's appeals. She had met both Helen Hunt and her first husband at the Dickinson family's annual Commencement Tea in August 1860; Major Hunt found Dickinson "uncanny" and is reported to have disliked her (Pound 542). And she had been corresponding with "Mrs. Helen Hunt" since at least 1868 when the now widowed "H.H.," whose other pseudonyms included "Marah" and "Rip Van Winkle," spent the summer in Amherst.[14] On the basis of the experience of her Norcross cousins, Dickinson recommended a boardinghouse there "as being one with no dampness perceptible; indeed her two cousins had stayed in it and 'they were timid themselves'" (Odell 129). In the fall of 1876, Jackson, remarried the previous year to William Sharpless Jackson, a Colorado Springs banker with whom she had comparatively little in common, returned to Amherst, though her hus-band remained at home. Following a third visit in 1878, Jackson, now accom-panied by William, implored Dickinson to authorize publication of the poem "Success," which she had memorized and which may have been one of the sources of her own poem "Coronation," published by the *Atlantic Monthly* in 1869.[15] Thus Dickinson was represented in *A Masque of Poets*, which was part of the "No Name" series published by the prestigious Boston firm of Roberts Brothers; authorial anonymity was guaranteed. And thus Thomas Niles of Roberts Brothers, the firm that eventually agreed to publish the 1890 *Poems* edited by Todd and Higginson, began to correspond with Dickinson and to express interest in publishing a volume of her verses, on the basis of Helen Hunt Jackson's enthusiastic endorsement of their literary merit. Again, Dick-inson was not wholly immune to his appeals. By 1884, however, when Jackson penned her "cruel wrong" letter and Dickinson her emulous, jealously affec-tionate response, it was too late for either poet to pursue this partly affection-ate, partly rivalrous collaboration further. There had already been speculation in the local press that Dickinson was the author or the subject of stories written by her friend (Wells 274); the fated cultural typology of the reclusive writing spinster strongly pointed her way. Though "Success" was edited by Niles, who approved five changes, two of them perhaps made by Jackson, Dickinson made no protest.[16] The entire poem was reprinted in the influential *Literary World* on December 10, 1878, preceded by the comment, "If anything in the volume was contributed by Emerson, we should consider these lines upon 'Success' most probably his." And Dickinson continued to correspond with Jackson, who on at least one occasion functioned specifically as her muse.[17] Ironically, both women, whose careers so fortuitously intersected, died in their midfifties, Jackson in 1885, Dickinson a year later. In fact, Dickin-son never appointed a literary executor but trusted instead, it seems, to her slightly younger and much more "practical" sister Lavinia to find a way. And so Lavinia, after several false starts, famously did.

Jackson's late-nineteenth-century rhetoric of scandal, pointed toward the poet as criminal, has not prevailed. Though a version of her criminally "cruel" Dickinson has recently resurfaced in the melodramatic critical imagination of Camille Paglia,[18] throughout most of the twentieth century Dickinson the in-flicter of wrongs has interested poets and critics alike less than Dickinson the victim of Victorian convention (in Amy Lowell's terms), or Dickinson the nonnotorious and wholesome (in Marianne Moore's terms), or Dickinson the poet of "enormous emotional vitality" whose "enjoyment in living" and "satisfaction . . . in her work" was "perfectly real" (in Elizabeth Bishop's terms), or Dickinson the courageous (in Adrienne Rich's terms), choosing to have her identity battle out at last, but on her "own premises." Literary history has produced many other more or less scandalous Dickinsons, including Dickinson the merely spacy: supposedly immune to the great social, political, and economic issues of her day. Yet as we move into the twenty-first century, there is remarkably little consensus among poets or biographers or literary scholars about the course Dickinson chose: about what motivated her strange and powerful career, about the constancy of her determination not to publish, about her understanding of the poet's public role, and about her vision of her own place in future literary histories. Criticism of Dickinson has been, at best, partial. Though for many years the attempt to see her steadily and as a whole was frustrated by the piecemeal publication of her manuscripts, by the mid-1920s, when Marianne Moore was editing *The Dial* and carving out for herself the iconic public career that Dickinson never had, Dickinson had nevertheless emerged as *the* touchstone of female literary genius produced by "the" American experience. Ironically, she had come to occupy precisely the dominant cultural role she had seemingly mocked and trivialized with such (by now) well-known disclaimers as the following:

> I'm Nobody! Who are you?
> Are you — Nobody — Too?
> Then there's a pair of us!
> Don't tell! they'd advertise — you know!
>
> How dreary — to be — Somebody!
> How public — like a Frog —
> To tell your name — the livelong June —
> To an admiring Bog! (P288)[19]

Commodified as a genius, Dickinson has been disseminated in many guises. Mainly, however, poets who identified with her courage, with her pain, with her pleasure, and with her artistry have also used "Dickinson" to justify and, in some instances, to clarify their own creative projects. Jackson, for example, was a social missionary who hoped to arouse the conscience of Christian America and to do for the Indian what her predecessor Harriet Beecher Stowe had done for the slave. Generous to other writers, Jackson nevertheless needed a poet who was weakest where she was strongest. And so she produced a poet without a social conscience, an antitype to herself.[20]

In the 1890s, other people who had known Dickinson, or known those close to her, sought to explain both her reclusion and her public silence in ways that were generally complementary to themselves. Emily Fowler Ford, for example, another of Dickinson's Amherst schoolmates, published a sonnet entitled "Eheu! Emily Dickinson!" in the *Springfield Sunday Republican* on January 3, 1891, in which she expressed pity for the person behind the poems.

"Social with bird and bee," she wrote, "You shun the eye, the voice, and shy elude / The loving souls that dare not to intrude / Upon your chosen silence."

> Friend, you thought
>   No life so sweet and fair as hiding brought,
> And beauty is your song, with interlude
> Of outer life which to your soul seems crude,
>   Thoughtless, unfeeling, idle, scant of grace;
> Nor will you touch a hand, or greet a face, —
> But common daily strife to you is rude,
>   And, shrinking, you in shadow lonely stay
>   Invisible to all, howe'er we pray. (Buckingham, *Reception* 99)

Social herself and determined to be visible, Ford was a granddaughter of Noah Webster and, like Jackson, the daughter of an Amherst college professor. She left the town in which she was a reigning "belle" in 1853 to become the wife of Gordon Lester Ford, then a promising New York attorney and later a successful business executive. He was a noted book collector, and Dickinson apparently sent him a copy of her "robin chorister" ("Some keep the Sabbath going to Church"). Mother of eight, including two (at one time) well-known writers, Paul Leicester and Worthington Chauncey Ford, author of stories and essays, Emily Fowler Ford was also the author of *My Recreations* (1872), which she sent to Dickinson in 1882. But Dickinson was not interested in rekindling this early friendship. Though she was gracious in their minimal correspondence and told her that "The little Book will be subtly cherished" (December 1882), she had refused to see her in Amherst that summer (Leyda 2: 372). Nor did she accept the almost comical invitation "to Emily and Vinnie" to visit her "sometime" in Brooklyn, extended through Austin and Sue shortly after the death of their son Gilbert in 1883 (Leyda 2: 412). Ford later explained to Mabel Loomis Todd, "I only wish the interest and delight her poems have aroused could have come early enough in her career to have kept her social and communicative, and at one with her friends" (R. Sewall, *Life* 2: 378). Ironically, however, sometime after Josiah Gilbert Holland founded *Scribner's Monthly* in 1870 and before his death in 1881, Ford had concurred with his opinion that the poems were too ethereal for publication. As she explained to Mabel Loomis Todd,

> Once I met Dr. Holland, the Editor then of *Scribner's Monthly*, who said, "You know Emily Dickinson, I have some poems of hers under consideration for publication — but they really are not suitable — they are too ethereal." I said, "They are beautiful, so concentrated, but they remind me of orchids, air-plants that have no roots in earth." He said, "That is true, — a perfect description. I dare not use them"; and I think these lyrical ejaculations, these breathed out projectiles sharp as lances, would at that time have fallen into idle ears. (Sewall, *Life* 2: 377)

We will never know what would have happened had Dickinson herself determined to publish more (or some) poems *and* had she been able to exert some control over their form in print. Presumably the latter condition would have been a precondition for the former. She felt strongly about every detail of (mis)representation, down to the last comma, and on that score alone the publication history of "Success" must have been a cautionary example. Praised in print, it was also changed: by Jackson, perhaps by Niles, the series editor, perhaps by Hawthorne's son-in-law George Parsons Lathrop, the editor of the volume in which it appeared. Nevertheless, Dickinson went on to correspond intermittently with Jackson's publisher Thomas Niles, whom she probably held responsible for the changes in her poem. In March 1883, for example, she sent him a "very rare" copy of poems by "Currer, Ellis, and Acton Bell" (the Brontë sisters), which he returned, stating that the book was too precious for him to keep and that he already owned a modern, more inclusive version, but that "If I may presume to say so, I will take instead a M.S. collection of your poems, that is, if you want to give them to the world through the medium of a publisher" (L813b). Though Dickinson was also sending Niles poems of her own, such as "My Cricket and the Snow" ("Further in Summer than the Birds" and "It sifts from Leaden Sieves"), and though he sent her a presentation copy of Mathilde Blind's *Life of George Eliot*, we will never know what would have happened had Dickinson been willing to go to market. Or what would have happened had she been in a position, psychologically and financially, to have a volume of poems privately printed and selectively distributed. (We know very little about Dickinson's access to money of her own and about whether, following her father's death in 1874, she would have needed Austin Dickinson's approval for such a venture.)[21]

We *do* know that, after some hesitation, Austin Dickinson supported publication during the 1890s through Mabel Loomis Todd but that Todd felt the need to emphasize Emily Dickinson's personal normality, as did Susan Gilbert Dickinson. Each attempted to account for Dickinson's introversion and in some measure to deny it. She was not an invalid, they wrote, nor had she suffered any love disappointment; these themes were constant. Meanwhile, in private, Lavinia Dickinson was taking a different tack, telling tales of forbidden love and thereby recapitulating romantic elements of her own history. Lavinia's accounts, however, were inconsistent. Previously she had suggested that her sister's reclusion was "only a happen" (Sewall, *Life* 1: 153), an appealingly vague idea she never dropped, but in 1895 she also wrote to the critic Mary J. Reid that "Helen Hunt Jackson was a brilliant, dashing woman of the world, fearless and brave, while Emily was timid and refined, always shrinking from publicity" (Bingham, *Ancestors'* 320). Jackson's "cruel wrong" motif is here softened into the somewhat different trope of excessive diffidence, marked by laudable refinements of gender and class. Some such vocabulary was evidently needed to explain why Dickinson was different from and superior to other people without suggesting that her path in life should be emulated. Thus, just as Walt Whitman was eventually surrounded by a group of "hot little prophets" who believed that he could do no wrong, Dickinson's early supporters closed ranks around her, as a wide-eyed Mabel Loomis Todd had already begun to do when she first came to Amherst in 1881. Shortly thereafter, she wrote to her parents:

> I must tell you about the *character* of Amherst. It is a lady whom the people call the *Myth*. She is a sister of Mr. Dickinson, & seems to be the climax of all the family oddity. She has not been outside of her own house in fifteen years, except once to see a new church, when she crept out at night, & viewed it by moonlight. No one who calls upon her mother & sister ever see her, but she allows little children once in a great while, & one at a time, to come in, when she gives them cake or candy, or some nicety, for she is very fond of little ones. But more often she lets down the sweetmeat by a string, out of a window, to them. She dresses wholly in white, & her mind is said to be perfectly wonderful. She writes finely, but no one *ever* sees her. Her sister, who was at Mrs. Dickinson's party, invited me to come & sing to her mother sometime . . . People tell me that the *myth* will hear every note—she will be near, but unseen . . . Isn't that like a book? So interesting. (Leyda 2: 357)

Perhaps taking her cue from Susan Dickinson's elegantly crafted *Springfield Republican* obituary ("Not disappointed with the world, not an invalid until within the past two years, not from any lack of sympathy, not because she was insufficient for any mental work or social career—her endowments being so exceptional" [qtd. in Buckingham, *Reception* 551]), Todd sought to naturalize Dickinson's reclusion in her preface to the 1891 *Poems* by stating that "She had tried society and the world, and found them lacking. She was not an invalid, and she lived in seclusion from no love-disappointment. Her life was the normal blossoming of a nature introspective to a high degree, whose best thought could not exist in pretence" (*Poems*, Second Series 8). Yet these attempts to explain the inexplicable—"for some shy reason," Lavinia Dickinson noted (qtd. in Bingham, *Ancestors'* 320)—contributed to Dickinson's appeal in the 1890s as a frankly experimental poet who had led a life of unprecedented originality and who, in selecting her own society, had refused, in Amy Lowell's terms, to be patterned.

By the time, then, that Marianne Moore was encountering Dickinson the ironist in Miss Georgiana Goddard King's English class at Bryn Mawr in 1909, the production of Dickinson's poetry, of her letters, and of her biography was helping to legitimate the cultural authority of the woman writer. Though Moore herself turned away from the subjective first-person lyric to pursue a densely allusive, perspectival, and mainly impersonal style, at the beginning of her career Dickinson seemed to her an ally in her quest for the right kind of voice: pointed, yet not sour; powerful, yet not masculinized; moral, yet not didactic. Reading Bacon, Hooker, Fulke Greville, Raleigh, Jeremy Taylor, Burton, Milton, and Clarendon in this course, which was intriguingly titled "Imitative Prose Writing," Moore noted that "in Irony the pt. is to keep your temper and not fall into invective." Emily Dickinson, Swinburne, and James, though not part of the official curriculum, were discussed as "observers of civility and decency of order," even though they had all been accused of being, according to Moore's notes, "carnally minded and earthly minded" (Stapleton 57). Dickinson is the only woman in this catalogue, as well as the only American who, like Moore, stayed home. Though Moore never explicitly acknowledged Dickinson as an influence in the years that followed, twenty-four years later, in 1933, she did choose to review the new and enlarged edition of the *Letters of Emily Dickinson*, edited by none other than Mable Loomis Todd. "Comparing omissions with inclusions," Moore wrote, "one notes reticence: a determination to cover from the voracity of the wolfish, a seclusive, wholly non-notorious personality; an absence of legend; and care lest philistine interest in what is fine be injudiciously taxed." The carnally minded and earthly minded trope of the 1909 Bryn Mawr lecture had remained in her mind; Marianne Moore, with her deep interest in strategies of resistance against the merely prurient, was still determined to combat it.

As we move into the twenty-first century, the strange power of Dickinson's multiply charged language is no longer at issue, but few of the many books and articles on her life and work, including my own, have had much to say about her possible stylistic influence on other (American women) poets.[22] In 1982, however, Cheryl Walker boldly resisted the critical tradition that viewed Dickinson as too original to follow, when she suggested that "What Emily Dickinson did for later women poets, like Amy Lowell who wanted to write her biography, was remarkable; she gave them dignity. No other aspect of her influence was so important. After Emily Dickinson's work became known, women poets in America could take their work seriously. She redeemed the poetess for them, and made her a genuine poet" (*Burden* 116). Though Walker is vague about the historical institutions that enabled this redemption, she remains one of the few critics who have been willing to thematize Dickinson's influence on the poetry subsequently written by American women and to theorize her effect on the cultural typology of the woman poet in the twentieth century. But the "dignity" issue is not quite as simple as Walker believed it to be in 1982, when she published *The Nightingale's Burden: Women Poets and American Culture before 1900*, from which this provocative quote is taken.[23] "Dignity" remains an ongoing concern for women poets who still must earn the right to be heard, each, as Adrienne Rich would have it, on her own "premises," but also now as part of a female tradition for which the name "Dickinson" necessarily functions as a multivalent signal. One fact is clear, however. It is no longer possible to banish Dickinson to the attic of the house of poetry as Amy Lowell attempted to do in her by now well-known poem "The Sisters" (1922), in which she floats the image of Emily Dickinson as a freak: brilliant, but a freak nonetheless. As we write fuller histories of women's poetry in the twentieth century, Dickinson's jealous efforts of affection, as well as the jealous efforts of affection she has inspired, will command further attention. Her interaction with Helen Hunt Jackson provides a model for such inquiry, not least because Jackson herself recognized that her own poetry was not likely to last, unlike that of her friend, in whose perdurability she had wisely come to believe.

Emily Dickinson detested moral cant. And to the end, it seems, she who had been stricken by "words like Blades" (P479), words deployed not only by men but also by women, refused to romanticize the healing power of her art or to gender virtue. Yet in the 1890s many women who had never seen Emily Dickinson face to face were curiously drawn by the emerging narrative of a fabulously reclusive poet whose fine mind would not be shut up in prose and who, dreading silence, found "Ransom in a Voice" (P1251), especially her own. Early explanations of her private vocation emerged out of a genteel tradition of gendered reserve. Dickinson was represented as one of the last flowers of the pure old New England stock: a lady through and through, content with her home life, content with private audiences. We now know that Dickinson's decision not to publish was fraught with creative ambivalence; no simple binary of the "she did or did not want an audience" will suffice to explain Dickinson's "No," which was surely one of the most complex "No"s in the history of American letters.

Though responses to Dickinson living cannot be organized along a simple gender binary, especially since early advocates such as Jackson and Mabel Loomis Todd were influenced by the fact that, in Todd's hyperbolic words, "all the literary men are after her to have her writings published" (Leyda 2: 361), in this essay I have suggested that originary responses such as Helen Hunt Jackson's inaugurated a larger critical conversation in which women like Jackson who challenged gender binaries and who sought to deessentialize women's "nature" participated with particular urgency. Dickinson formed part of her interpretive community, and she would not let her go. This conversation extends well into the late twentieth century and includes such contemporary women poets as Gwendolyn Brooks, Lucille Clifton, Rita Dove, Alice Fulton, Lynn Emanuel, Heather McHugh, Sharon Bryan, Joy Harjo, Adrienne Rich, Susan Howe, and Lucie Brock-Broido: all writing women for whom personal and poetic dignity remains, in the "nature" of things, very much at issue.

NOTES

1. Susan Gilbert Dickinson is quoted in Johnson and Ward, *Letters* 2: 380. See also her obituary for Dickinson, reprinted in Leyda 2: 472–74. By this time, however, she was praising the poems not only for their "startling picturesqueness" but also for their "simplicity," "profundity," and "homeliness." For the historical context of this obituary, see Lubbers 5.

2. For Dickinson and her mother, especially her mother as resolutely reluctant reader and writer, see Pollak, *Parents*. On Dickinson and Lavinia and Sue, see Pollak, *Anxiety* chaps. 2, 5. For Sue as sympathetic reader, see Smith, *Rowing* chaps. 4, 5, 6.

3. On Todd as Austin Dickinson's lover, see R. Sewall, *Life;* Longsworth, *Austin and Mabel;* and Gay. On Todd as editor, see Bingham, *Ancestors'*.

4. I use the phrase "critical conversation" rather than the more formal "critical tradition" advisedly. We are just beginning to formulate ways to think about Dickinson's influence on both women and men. As Alice Fulton points out in "Her Moment of Brocade: The Reconstruction of Emily Dickinson," "Essays and reviews of twentieth-century poets frequently point to Whitman as influence or forebear. . . . Yet it's hard to think of any criticism that places a man poet within a primarily Dickinsonian orbit, although she's often mentioned in passing. . . . Perhaps the resistance to a Dickinsonian linkage or lineage has its basis in the patriarchal assumptions and cultural insecurities surrounding gender" (10–11). Fulton further contends that when *female* poets are compared to Dickinson, "the comparison serves to underscore eccentricity rather than brilliance" (11).

5. Helen's father died on May 27, 1844. Apparently he had begun to recover from the tuberculosis and depression of spirits which had plagued him since the death of his wife, but he then succumbed to dysentery in the house of a British medical missionary. According to Odell, "He bore his suffering as another evidence of the will of God, who had appointed as a final test that he should suffer and die far from home and friends and relatives" (34). On the early life of Helen Maria Fiske Hunt Jackson, see Odell and Banning. Odell, though comparatively thorough, is dated; Banning's scholarship is often slipshod. For discussion of the need to reconstruct a fuller life of Jackson, see below.

6. Edward Dickinson owned John's *History of the Civil War in America* (Leyda 2: 75), as well as *The Mother at Home*, the latter the subject of extensive discussion in John Cody's psychobiography, *After Great Pain: The Inner Life of Emily Dickinson* (1971), where it is viewed as contributing to the Dickinson's dysfunctional family life.

7. On Jackson and Higginson, see Wells. But Wells pushes the view that Jackson was in love with Higginson, which seems unlikely. See Jackson's 1866 letter to the writer Kate Field in which she mocks Higginson's effeminacy (Leyda 2: 111–12).

8. According to Pound, so intense was this obsession that much of Jackson's prose work may never be identified and "she liked to mystify her readers" (542).

9. Theodore Roosevelt, on the other hand, later described her *Century of Dishonor* as "thoroughly untrustworthy from cover to cover." In *The Winning of the West* (1889),

Roosevelt attacked her as one of a group of "purely sentimental historians." Though he credited her with a "pure and noble life" and with good intentions, he condemned her "polemic" for "hysterical indifference to facts" (vol. 10 of *Works* [New York: Scribner's, 1924], 93–94).

10. Jackson's marital relations, however, may have involved desertion on both sides. And it remains unclear how William Sharpless Jackson's attachment to Jackson's niece, Helen, might fit into this larger psychological history of Jackson's career I am proposing. Did Helen Jackson, for example, encourage their mutually beneficial friendship? Valerie Sherer Mathes notes that "In one of her last letters to her husband, 'Will,' a gravely ill Helen Hunt Jackson bid him goodbye while her mind was still clear. Fully aware that she had failed to be the kind of wife she had 'longed & hoped to be,' she reminded him that she loved him 'as few men are ever loved in this world. . . . *Nobody* will ever love you so well,' she concluded. She encouraged him not to 'live the life of a homeless, tieless man' but to remarry soon and have children" (Jackson, *Century* vii).

11. Jackson's success in extorting Dickinson's poem "Success" (P67) for the Roberts Brothers anthology *A Masque of Poets* is one of the more poignant and comical episodes in their interaction (see below). Jackson appears to have submitted the poem without Dickinson's approval and then to have coerced Dickinson into agreeing to its publication. As I have already suggested, Jackson encountered what we would now call "boundary issues" with Dickinson.

12. Dickinson also uses the *Othello* quote in L478 to her aunt Catherine Sweetser, when she writes that "He that is robbed and smiles, steals something from the thief."

13. In 1872 she wrote angrily to her cousin Louise Norcross: "Of Miss P — I know but this, dear. She wrote me in October, requesting me to aid the world by my chirrup more. Perhaps she stated it as my duty, I don't distinctly remember, and always burn such letters, so I cannot obtain it now. I replied declining. She did not write to me again — she might have been offended, or perhaps is extricating humanity from some hopeless ditch" (L380). "Miss P" is sometimes identified as the popular author Elizabeth Stuart Phelps.

14. Based on Leyda's record, Jackson was also in Amherst in December 1860 when she saw the Austin Dickinsons, January 1861, July 1868, and winter 1868. The pen-name "Marah" is taken from the Book of Ruth, where it is associated with bitterness. "Rip Van Winkle" has many associations, including New York State, where Jackson first met Edward Hunt.

15. Jackson knew "Success" through Higginson. Emily Dickinson had sent him the poem in July 1862, together with "Your Riches — taught me — Poverty," "Some keep the Sabbath going to Church," and "Of Tribulation, these are They." "Coronation" pivots on the contrast between a dissatisfied king, who is weighed down by the burdens of office, and a beggar, who soon grasps that men do not "Fare better, being kings." Unlike "Success," "Coronation" moves toward an unproblematized happy ending, as king and beggar exit hand in hand.

16. Johnson suggests not only that Jackson had already submitted the poem for publication but that it was probably too late for her to withdraw it. Erkkila accepts this speculation as fact and describes Jackson as participating actively with Niles in editing the text. She calls her "willful and overbearing" and contends that, "Although these changes were no doubt made in the interest of clarity and conventional taste, the total effect was to mutilate and efface Dickinson's own poetic signature" (*Wicked* 91–92).

Though I agree with her larger point that there was tension in the Dickinson–Jackson relationship on both sides, Erkkila's account of the history of the editing of "Success" introduces a note of desperation into Jackson's voice that I do not hear. And I am less sure that it was already too late for the volume to appear without Dickinson's contribution. Niles's letter to Dickinson does, however, suggest the possibility that if there had been more time he would have sent the proof to her for approval (L573d). Niles's letter is consistent with the possibility that Dickinson wrote him protesting these changes, but the editor of the volume was Hawthorne's son-in-law George Parsons Lathrop, whereas Niles was the series editor. So exactly who did what to whom remains unclear, though it is clear that in one way or another Jackson effectively persuaded Dickinson into print and that there was an element of coercion in her plotting.

17. Erkkila provides one of the strongest modern accounts of Jackson's influence on Dickinson. She suggests that, "As Dickinson's most attentive audience after their meeting in 1876, Jackson was the recipient, source, and inspiration for several poems, including 'Spurn the temerity —,' 'Before you thought of Spring,' 'One of the ones that Midas touched,' 'A Route of Evanescence,' 'Upon his Saddle sprung a Bird,' 'Pursuing you in your transitions,' 'Take all away from me, but leave me Ecstasy,' and 'Of God we ask one favor' " (*Wicked* 93). In a longer version of this essay, I would like to distinguish more finely between Jackson as recipient and Jackson as source or inspiration. On at least one occasion, however, she specifically commissioned a poem. See L601a, in which Jackson asked for an "oriole," and Dickinson's "hummingbird" response (L602).

18. Paglia identifies instances of heavily gendered erotic sadism throughout Dickinson's poetry. While Paglia uses Dickinson to justify her own (perhaps) deliberately scandalous critical performance, Clark Griffith, too, was fascinated by Dickinson's imagination of sexual violence, tending to see her as neurotically intimidated by the powerful mark of the male.

19. Two of the poets in Sharon Bryan's anthology (*Where We Stand*) cite this poem approvingly. See Martha Collins (31) and Joy Harjo (72).

20. Versions of this critique persist. Dobson, for one, suggests that "Whereas other women writers forged satisfactory social and professional lives for themselves, often courageously flouting convention to do so, Dickinson retreated into the home and eschewed — as a refined woman was taught to do — the jostling and strife of the world. In marked contrast with the groundbreaking activities of her contemporaries, this behavior appears conservative, indeed, strongly acquiescent to cultural demands" (48).

21. In *The Anxiety of Gender*, I developed the argument that Dickinson's strained relations with her father inhibited her desire to reach a larger audience and compete in the literary marketplace. See also Wolff on Edward Dickinson's hostility toward literary women (*Dickinson*, chap. 4).

22. Among the most influential theories of female influence are those of Sandra Gilbert and Susan Gubar. See Gilbert and Gubar, "Affiliation Complex," and Gilbert, "Daughteronomy." There have been a number of valuable studies linking Dickinson with individual modernist, postmodernist, and contemporary American women writers, but we are as yet lacking a theory sufficient to account for the historical particulars of Dickinson's career as it extends into the twentieth century and beyond.

23. I discuss these issues at greater length in my unpublished conference paper "Dickinson, Bishop, and Sororophobia: A Lost Connection," delivered at the American Literature Association Women Writers Symposium, San Antonio, Texas, October 1993.

FURTHER READING

Bogan, Louise. "A Mystical Poet." *Emily Dickinson: Three Views.* By Richard Wilbur, Louise Bogan, and Archibald MacLeish. Amherst: Amherst College Press, 1960. Rpt. in *Emily Dickinson: A Collection of Critical Essays.* Ed. Richard B. Sewall. Englewood Cliffs, N.J.: Prentice-Hall, 1963. 137–43.

Brock-Broido, Lucie. *The Master Letters.* New York: Knopf, 1995.

Emanuel, Lynn. "Homage to Dickinson." *The Dig and Hotel Fiesta.* Urbana: University of Illinois Press, 1995. 68.

McHugh, Heather. "Interpretive Insecurity and Poetic Truth: Dickinson's Equivocation." *American Poetry Review* 17 (1988): 49–54.

Melhem, D. H. "Gwendolyn Brooks and Emily Dickinson." *Emily Dickinson International Society Bulletin* 7(May/June 1995): 14–15, 17.

Rukeyser, Muriel. "Backgrounds and Sources." *The Life of Poetry.* New York: Wyn, 1949. 61–87.

Sarton, May. "My Sisters, O My Sisters." *The Women's Tradition in Literature.* Ed. Sandra M. Gilbert and Susan Gubar. New York: Norton, 1985. 1772–75.

MARGARET DICKIE

Feminist Conceptions of Dickinson

$\mathcal{F}$eminist conceptions of Dickinson and Dickinson's conception of feminism: it has been a two-way process. If feminist studies of Dickinson have shifted and shaped our understanding of the poet for the last twenty years, no less important has been the impact of Dickinson's poetry on the development of feminist criticism. As the greatest American woman poet of all time, she has been central to feminist criticism in all stages of its development. Her prominence has demanded a feminist criticism responsive to it even as her poetry has cast up a formidable resistance to such explication. In turn, feminist critics have answered the poetry with an energy and imagination of their own that has spilled into every approach to the poet. Taking over biographical, psychoanalytic, and linguistic, textual, cultural studies, feminist approaches seem, like Dickinson's notion of poets, "To Comprehend the Whole —" (P569). It is not that "The Others look a needless Show" (P569), but rather, for the last twenty years, the whole show has been largely feminist.

Feminist conceptions of Emily Dickinson began developing in the first wave of new feminist criticism. Although concentrating generally on women novelists where the plots for women are most evident, even early studies of the woman writer, such as Gilbert and Gubar's *Madwoman in the Attic: The Woman Writer and the Nineteenth-Century Literary Imagination* (1979), made a place in their discussions for Dickinson. And, as feminist criticism has developed and matured, Dickinson has remained at its center, the figure against which it has been able to test its insights, its theories, and its ambitions.

As a poet, Dickinson encouraged the move of feminist criticism from narrative explanations of women writers into stylistic analyses of their work, opening new areas of study informed by linguistic and psychoanalytic theories and intensifying a feminist focus on language, rhetoric, and grammar. From this work, critics went on to reconsider the woman writer's relationship to her culture and to less-well-known women writers among her contemporaries, to examine her interest in the social and political issues of her time, and to

342

explore the whole question of her intimate bonding with other women. Finally, because she left her manuscripts unpublished and thus in the care of women relatives, Dickinson has inspired a feminist interest in questions of textual editing, and in how her editors have determined what constitutes a poem and who constitutes it.

If conceptions of Dickinson have directed the development of feminist criticism, no less certainly have feminist conceptions of Dickinson come to dominate our understanding of the poet. Vivian Pollak's major study, *Dickinson: The Anxiety of Gender* (1984), established definitively the importance of gender in Dickinson's life and in her career. From this groundbreaking study to the most recent work by Martha Nell Smith and Susan Howe on Dickinson's manuscripts, feminist critics have both broadened and deepened awareness of Dickinson's work and, at the same time, fixed her importance in literary history as a major writer.

As the field of feminist criticism has grown, transforming itself almost completely every decade, so have its conceptions of Dickinson. A survey of this work starts in the late 1970s with the focus on Dickinson's place in a literary world largely dominated by male writers; it shifts in the 1980s to linguistic and psychoanalytic approaches to her poetry and her life, inspired variously by Freud, Lacan, and the French feminist theorists; and it concludes in the 1990s with explorations of her lesbian identity and her relationship with Susan Gilbert, which have led to renewed interest in the study of her manuscripts. In this decade, cultural historians have also made efforts to place Dickinson once again in the context of her times.

Through all these changing approaches to the poet, feminist critics have almost always been divided between those who want to place Dickinson firmly in the context of nineteenth-century literature and culture and those who want to claim her as a poet for all times or, in less flattering terms, as a modernist poet. As a nineteenth-century poet, Dickinson can be placed in the context of less-well-known American women poets over whom she obviously towers or in the context of male figures from both English and American romanticism where, discussed as a woman writer by feminist critics, she will obviously have more trouble finding a place. As a modernist or poet for all times, she will display whatever traits are most interesting to a particular critical approach: for example, rage for the revolutionary feminist, a disjunctive style for the linguist interested in French feminist theories of *l'écriture féminine*, compression for the Freudians, condensation for the Lacanians, conservative politics for the cultural historian. Neither romantic nor modernist, Dickinson, the poet, escapes all efforts to contain her. After all, she is the one who wrote, "Good to hide, and hear 'em hunt!" although she could also agree:

Good to know, and not tell,
Best, to know and tell,
Can one find the rare Ear
Not too dull — (P842)

In her feminist readers, Dickinson has found the "rare Ear" that has caught something of her art's secrecy.

THE WOMAN POET AS AN ENRAGED AND SUBVERSIVE POWER

Perhaps nowhere in literary history is there an example quite like Adrienne Rich's reading of Emily Dickinson in her talk and later published essay, "Vesuvius at Home: The Power of Emily Dickinson" (1976). Pointing out how Dickinson regards herself as imperious energy and her poetic creation as a form of aggression, Rich revolutionized understanding of Dickinson and of poetic power in women. She created the enraged Dickinson of the first feminist conceptions of the poet. Moreover, she turned attention to the complicated, perplexing, and little-read poem, "My Life had stood — a Loaded Gun —", that was to become the centerpiece of feminist criticism of Dickinson. Admitting that she had mused over this poem for a long time and taken it into herself, Rich argued that it is a central poem for understanding Dickinson and the condition of the woman artist because it indicates how dangerous the medium of poetry could feel for a woman. Experiencing herself as a loaded gun, Dickinson felt the lethal power of poetry for women, Rich argued.

Rich's Dickinson is the poet Sandra Gilbert and Susan Gubar place at the summit of their monumental study of the woman writer and the nineteenth-century literary imagination, as they draw attention to "the magnitude of the poetic self-creation Emily Dickinson achieved through working in a genre that has been traditionally the most Satanically assertive, daring, and therefore precarious of literary modes for women: lyric poetry" (*Madwoman* 582). Enraged and assertive, the Dickinson they describe exemplifies the split in the nineteenth-century woman writer between her conventional role in society and her creativity, between the Angel in the House and the madwoman in the attic. While the women novelists simply wrote about madwomen, Gilbert and Gubar claim that Dickinson actually became one, both ironically in her deliberate impersonations and truly in her retreat into her father's house.

The enraged Dickinson is also the poet Sharon Cameron describes in *Lyric Time: Dickinson and the Limits of Genre* (1979). Although this study is not specifically feminist, its exploration of how Dickinson displaced speech and time from a definitive context and thus pushed to extreme limits the lyric genre has been influential in turning study of the poet in the direction that feminist critics were to take. Certainly, Cameron, Gilbert and Gubar, as well as Rich, enlivened Dickinson studies; but perhaps, in their enthusiasm for the powerful and enraged poet, they overcorrected the conventional image of the reclusive and eccentric woman who was easily discouraged from publishing.

Moderating the image of the enraged Dickinson into that of the duplicitous poet in this early stage of feminist studies, Margaret Homans explores her conflicted relationship to the literary tradition of the romantic age when women were identified with nature and men with language in *Women Writers and Poetic Identity: Dorothy Wordsworth, Emily Brontë, and Emily Dickinson* (1980).[1] While Dorothy Wordsworth and Emily Brontë succumbed to the difficulties of such an identification, Dickinson escaped, according to Homans, by aligning herself with the subversive Eve and with Eve's understanding of the duplicity of language. Discovering language's fictiveness, Dickinson was also able to identify the fictionality of nature's traditional sexual identification, so that her "undoing of rhetorical dualism becomes a model for a revised pattern of relations between the sexes" (201), according to Homans. Another effort to fit Dickinson into British romanticism is Joanne Feit Diehl's *Dickinson and the Romantic Imagination* (1981), which again pictures the poet as subverting the tradition of Wordsworth, Shelley, Keats, as well as Emerson — a tradition from which she was excluded as a woman. Revising Harold Bloom's theory of the anxiety of influence, Feit Diehl shows how Dickinson used her sense of exclusion and estrangement as a source of power.

Emily Stipes Watts and Cheryl Walker also provide early feminist readings of a poet more moderate in her ambitions and achievements than Rich's enraged Dickinson. Watts places Dickinson in her history of American women's poetry from 1632 to 1945 by connecting the themes, metaphors, and prosodic qualities of her verse to what she calls the "female realism" of that history. Walker seeks to see Dickinson's work as more than an extension of the themes evident in her contemporaries among women poets who took up the "nightingale's burden" to sing of secret sorrow and forbidden love. Looking for historical trends and cultural patterns, these critics are less interested in readings of the poetry, more concerned with contexts, and, as such, they prepared the way for the next development of feminist criticism.

THE POET IN CONTEXT

The models of the woman writer that dominated early feminist criticism fit Dickinson poorly for two reasons: first (with the exception of the works of Watts and Walker), these models were drawn chiefly from women novelists and from English literature of the romantic period; and second, they were efforts to find a general explanation of the woman writer rather than a detailed

account of a particular distinguished writer. The next stage of feminist conceptions of Dickinson focused directly on her life and culture in an attempt to
provide a more subtle and accurate assessment of her work. The enraged and
subversive Dickinson gave way in these studies to a more complicated and
interesting figure.

Vivian Pollak's study is the most important and lasting book in this new
stage of feminist conceptions of Dickinson. Combining a sympathetic handling of biographical details and a sensitive reading of the poetry, Pollak illuminates a figure of the poet, divided between her awareness of the conventional role for women and her drive to write poetry, who became, Pollak
claims, "the laureate of sexual despair" (*Anxiety* 9). Reading from the details of
Dickinson's own life, her conflicted relationship with her family, her efforts to
find in other women and in an inaccessible "Master" the close relationships
she missed in her family, Pollak discovers a poet whose inner experiences were
split between two selves: the "conventional woman dependent on the power
structure which had in some measure nurtured her, unconventional poet ham-
mering away at its most cherished texts" (31). Pollak too has her reading of
"My Life had stood — a Loaded Gun"; but she sets it against a more submis-
sive image of woman in Dickinson's poetry, suggesting that the rift between
these two images was never bridged. In a series of compelling readings of
Dickinson's poems of sisterhood, of heterosexual love, of what she calls "Dickinson's death marriage" (190), Pollak places the poetry in the context of the life
with such care and exactitude that they seem inevitably connected.

Unlike so many studies that were to follow hers, Pollak does not choose
between the two Dickinsons she discovers. Wisely, she suggests that she has
never been able to decide whether, as Gilbert and Gubar argue, Dickinson's
art would have been better if she had written under less constraining circumstances or whether, as the poet herself contended, under such circumstances
she would never have written at all. Nor does Pollak decide whether, had
Dickinson's temperament been more flexible, these circumstances might have
seemed to her "ampler, more various" (*Anxiety* 31). This tact and wisdom
distinguish Pollak's work and attest to its achievement.

The split Dickinson is also the subject of Barbara Antonina Clarke Mossberg's examination of the poet in *Emily Dickinson: When a Writer Is a Daughter*
(1982), which reads the poetry more narrowly as a response to the poet's
relationship with her parents. Moving outside Dickinson's family in efforts to
place the poet in the context of her culture, Shira Wolosky in *Emily Dickinson:
A Voice of War* (1984) and Barton Levi St. Armand in *Emily Dickinson and Her
Culture: The Soul's Society* (1984) make no effort to relate their inquiries to
those of feminist critics, yet they too have provided raw material for the
ampler feminist conceptions of the poet. Leaving to later feminist critics the

task of understanding the problematic relationship of a woman writer to her culture, these studies have nonetheless confirmed the feminist understanding of the poet that finds her — far from the isolated and eccentric figure of conventional literary history — a woman whose creative imagination was inspired by events in the world around her.

Cynthia Griffin Wolff's monumental critical biography of the poet moves the poet to the center of her culture by taking literally Dickinson's statement to Higginson that "When I state myself, as the Representative of the Verse — it does not mean — me — but a supposed person" (*Dickinson* 141). Griffin Wolff reads this statement as invoking Emerson's description of the poet as "representative of *man*, in virtue of being the largest power to receive and to impart" (141). Thus Griffin Wolff can claim of Dickinson's poetry:

> The poetry is not offered as a record of individual introspection, however intelligent and sensitive that might be: Dickinson does not intend to speak for herself, uniquely fashioned; she intends to speak of the general condition and for all men and women. (142)

This view places Dickinson's poetry at the center of the religious anxieties of her time, or rather it places her religious anxieties at the center of her culture in what might be another overcorrection of the view of the poet as a recluse and isolated figure. A different approach to the importance of religious tradition in Dickinson's poetry is Beth Maclay Doriani's *Emily Dickinson, Daughter of Prophecy* (1996). Drawing on the stance, style, and structures of the biblical prophets and of contemporary sermons, Dickinson assumed an important prophetic voice and continued a tradition of American female prophecy.

Language is another context in which Dickinson, as a poet, has demanded to be considered. As the work of French feminist theorists such as Julia Kristeva and Hélène Cixous moved feminist criticism in the direction of language study, so feminist conceptions of Dickinson began to form around studies of what Cristanne Miller calls, in the subtitle of her book, *A Poet's Grammar* (1987). For example, Miller, Homans, Diehl, and Adalaide Morris write on feminist conceptions of Dickinson's language in Suzanne Juhasz's 1983 collection, *Feminist Critics Read Emily Dickinson*. Some of this work was anticipated by Roland Hagenbüchle's two early and influential articles, which have been important to feminist conceptions of the poet. In the first, "Precision and Indeterminacy" (1974), he identified the difficulties of Dickinson's language as stemming from her reliance on metonymy rather than metaphor, and in the second, "Sign and Process" (1979), he described her differences from Emerson by demonstrating how she was a lover of the word, connecting man (*sic*) to the eternal through words rather than through nature, as Emerson had done.

Cristanne Miller picks up these insights and develops them in a major reading of Dickinson's unusual use of language in *Emily Dickinson: A Poet's Grammar*. She studies strategies of compression, disjunction, repetition, interrupted syntax, and feminine speech, which she then applies to readings of four poems, including "My Life had stood — a Loaded Gun —." Refusing the biographical reading of this poem, Miller sees it as "an adolescent fantasy about coming of age that breaks down before what should be its happy conclusion — powerful adulthood" and perhaps also as "a terrible fantasy of adult womanhood — that condition which allows none of the privileges of childhood but few of the privileges of male adulthood in their place" (123). In a concluding chapter, connecting the defining figures of Dickinson's language with French and American feminist theories of women's writing, Miller argues convincingly that "Gender is the cohering factor of influence in the development of her poems' compressed, disruptive, doubling style" (185).

Moving from language to a study of Dickinson's "strategies," her images or her poses, a series of feminist critics turn feminist criticism to an exploration of the themes of the poetry. These critics, including Suzanne Juhasz in *The Undiscovered Continent: Emily Dickinson and the Space of the Mind* (1983), Jane Eberwein in *Dickinson: Strategies of Limitation* (1985), and Joanne Dobson in *Dickinson and the Strategies of Reticence* (1989), find Dickinson's strength in her diminished modes. Examining the ways in which Dickinson evaded or negotiated the limitations that her culture imposed upon her, these critics retreat from the earliest feminist image of the enraged and powerful poet into a new feminist conception of a writer who, herself, retreated into language, usurping there for her own subversive purposes the very strategies by which she felt herself limited in her culture.

This view of Dickinson places her once more in her culture and, in Dobson's study, in a newly recovered range and tradition of nineteenth-century women writers. Here again, draped in general terms appropriate to cultural studies, is the divided Dickinson writing in "a community of feminine expression where women's articulation was seen as potentially incendiary and women's reticence perceived as a prudent virtue" (127). But, in that particular community, the distinction and distinctiveness of the poet are lost, and Dickinson seems again a writer who made eccentric, unusual, and unnecessary choices both in her life and in her work.

The Poet in the Lesbian Context

Although the recent development of gay and lesbian studies has moved feminist conceptions of Dickinson toward a more elaborate exploration of the homoerotic elements of her life and work, in fact, interest in this aspect of her poetry goes back to Rebecca Patterson's *Riddle of Emily Dickinson* (1951) and *Emily Dickinson's Imagery* (1979) and to the work of Lillian Faderman in her 1977 and 1978 articles on Dickinson's homoerotic poetry and her letters to Sue Gilbert. Pollak also treats the issue of Dickinson's relationship to Sue Gilbert, agreeing that the materials for considering the poet a suppressed lesbian are there but arguing convincingly that "carnality" was not the major focus of her relationship with her sister-in-law (*Anxiety* 79).

The critic who has pushed the interpretation of Dickinson's poetry as homoerotic most relentlessly recently is Paula Bennett in *My Life a Loaded Gun: Female Creativity and Feminist Poetics* (1986) and *Emily Dickinson: Woman Poet* (1990). As the title of her first book suggests, Bennett wants to return to the earliest feminist view of the poet as a figure of power and rage, although, for Bennett, Dickinson could only claim that power once she had worked through and written out her rage against her culture and against her own erotic attachments. Deriving Dickinson's power from her lesbian identity, Bennett argues, along lines by now familiar in the study of the poet, that Dickinson's "clitorocentrism may well explain, therefore, certain fundamental and yet anomalous features in Dickinson's work, in particular, her consistent paradoxicality, her insistence on autonomy and her emphasis on 'little/bigness' in image, form and word as well as theme" (*Woman Poet* 184). As this survey reveals, however, "clitorocentrism" is not the only explanation that has been offered for some of these same themes, and, to make her point, Bennett has had to stretch several points.

Because the case for Dickinson's identity as a lesbian must rest on her relationship with Susan Gilbert, critics have begun to look with extreme care at the letters and poems exchanged between the poet and her sister-in-law. The most interesting work on this subject is being done by Martha Nell Smith. Her work has involved both close readings of the poems and an examination of what the letters reveal about the relationship, work which has brought her to consider the problems involved in deciphering the letters in manuscript. Reading the poetry and letters and deciphering the manuscripts are two quite distinct and separate enterprises, and it is testimony to Smith's perspicacity that she has attempted to do both.

Separating these two issues simply to suggest the different and varied opportunities they provide for feminist conceptions of Dickinson, I want to acknowledge, first, Smith's *Rowing in Eden: Rereading Emily Dickinson* (1992) as a major advance in our understanding of the importance to her poetry of Dickinson's relationship to Susan Gilbert. While Bennett, for example, ties her conclusions about this relationship to a dramatic narrative that relies heavily on the dating of the poems by Thomas Johnson in his presumed definitive (although now largely challenged) edition, Smith goes directly to the manuscripts to study the interchange of letters and poems between the two women. Attempting to correct the critical interest lavished on Dickinson's three letters to the unidentified "Master" by a careful study of the lengthy correspondence with her sister-in-law, Smith demonstrates Susan Gilbert's important role as reader and editor of the poems Dickinson sent to her. Like H.D., who claimed that she could not write without the love and support of her friend Bryher, "Dickinson unequivocally acknowledges that her relationship with Sue is important to her creative insight and sensibilities," according to Smith (140). The importance of sexual identity to literary creativity becomes central, then, to an understanding of the poems which, Smith demonstrates, will be read one way in a heterosexual context, another way in a homosexual context.

Further, Smith re-creates the atmosphere of the poetry workshop in which she imagines this exchange took place, and she surveys Susan Gilbert's actions and attitudes toward the poetry after Dickinson's death. Finally, Smith suggests that, if we place this relationship at the center of Dickinson's life and consider her love as lesbian desire, it can

> clarify and enhance our reading so that her cross-dressing characters and speakers, her impassioned rhetoric to Sue, "Austin's" responses to those inflamed expressions, and the rhetoric of similarity in many of her love poems make a new sense. (*Rowing* 33–34)

The second issue that concerns Smith is the editing of Dickinson's poems and letters, partly because this issue is central to any reading of the heavily edited, censored, and mutilated letters that she wrote to Susan Gilbert; but partly, too, because issues of sexual identity are important here. First, the censorship of these letters, attributed to Austin Dickinson by Mabel Loomis Todd but perhaps made by someone else, was certainly gender-related. But also, Thomas Johnson and other editors have reformulated Dickinson's writing to conform to foreordained genres, identifying some late letter-poems simply as letters, a practice, in Smith's view, which has tended to blur Susan Gilbert's importance to Dickinson as a primary audience and to limit our own reading of the poet's literary project.

THE EDITED POET: A FEMINIST ISSUE

With the publication of R. W. Franklin's two-volume edition of *The Manuscript Books of Emily Dickinson* (1981) and *The Master Letters of Emily Dickinson* (1986), critical interest has been directed to the way Dickinson has been edited. Alongside Smith's work on Dickinson's manuscripts is that of the poet

Susan Howe (see *Birth-mark*). In a 1990 interview reprinted in *The Birth-mark*, Howe has commented:

> Editing of her poems and letters has been controlled by gentlemen of the old school and by Harvard University Press since the 1950s. Franklin's edition of *The Manuscript Books* and now *The Master Letters* should have radically changed all readings of her work. . . . But they haven't. This is a feminist issue. It takes a woman to see clearly the condescending tone of these male editors when they talk about their work on the texts. But on this subject there is silence so far. And this is a revolutionary way for women to go in Dickinson criticism. (170)

Access to the original manuscripts is now difficult to obtain, however necessary it is to an understanding of this poet who refused the printed text. Howe herself admits to having seen only the originals of two manuscript books, but they have convinced her of the importance of the quirks of Dickinson's writing — its line breaks, dashes, marks in various hands on the manuscripts, odd punctuations, even the ways she crosses her t's — to the interpretation of her poems. But Howe has cast doubt on any interpretation of the poems through the fascicles because, she has argued, their original order was broken by Dickinson's friends and first editors so that even Franklin — the only scholar apart from the curator of the manuscripts who has been allowed unlimited access to the originals at Harvard University's Houghton Library — can be sure only of a particular series order for poems on a single folded sheet of stationery. "Maybe the poems in a packet were copied down in random order, and the size of letter paper dictated a series; maybe not," she concludes sensibly (*Birth-mark* 144). At the same time, Howe argues for the importance of these manuscript books which, she claims, represent the poet's "letter to the world." Not only did they galvanize Lavinia Dickinson into action when she discovered them, but they also provided a publishable collection of poems, whereas, Howe argues, it is doubtful that Dickinson's various correspondents would have bothered to collect and then publish her poem-letters.

Following Howe, Jerome McGann in *Black Riders: The Visible Language of Modernism* (1993) argues that, "Whatever explanations we favor for Dickinson's refusal of print, we must not let them obscure the deep interest she took in the visual aspects of her writing" (26). Claiming that "Johnson's edition goes astray — misrepresents Dickinson's writing — because it has approached her work as if it aspired to a typographical existence," McGann states that Dickinson's poetry was not written *for* a print medium, and "When we come to edit her work for bookish presentation, therefore, we must accommodate our typographical conventions to her work, not the other way round" (38). While McGann is no feminist, nonetheless his work also adds to a feminist conception of Dickinson's creative habits as a woman writing outside the largely male-dominated conventions of editing and publishing.

While feminist critics must wait for a new generation of scholars to pursue the insights of Howe and McGann (and some, such as Ellen Louise Hart and Marta Werner, are already beginning work), Sharon Cameron has returned to Dickinson studies to examine the fascicles in *Choosing Not Choosing: Dickinson's Fascicles* (1992). Stalwartly nonfeminist, Cameron looks at three representative fascicles to argue for the unboundedness of Dickinson's conception of a poem, claiming that reading Dickinson's poems in the context of the fascicles brings up the question of what constitutes the identity of the poem. The variants in the fascicles reveal, Cameron writes, that "Dickinson sets up a situation that seems exclusionary, and that she then refuses choices which she presents as inevitable. Thus in Dickinson's poetry the apparent need to choose is countered by the refusal to choose" (21). This conclusion too provides useful insights for feminist conceptions of Dickinson's poetry that a future generation of critics and perhaps the new Dickinson Editing Collective organized by Smith will have to pursue.

New Directions in Feminist Conceptions of Dickinson

Clearly, editing is only one of the directions that new feminist conceptions of Dickinson will take. Another will be the effort to set Dickinson in the context of all those twentieth-century women poets who have been empowered by her. Although she has only begun to present this work in conference papers, Pollak promises a new major study of this subject. Betsy Erkkila has changed her own views on this subject since she first discussed it in "Dickinson and Rich: Toward a Theory of Female Poetic Influence" (1984), where she used a model based on the object-relations theory of female development to explain Adrienne Rich's changing relationship with Dickinson. More recently, in *The Wicked Sisters: Women Poets, Literary History, and Discord* (1992), Erkkila has been anxious to see the difficulties and struggles in women's literary relationships, theorizing now not on a psychoanalytic model but on a cultural and historical pattern. Arguing against what she calls popular feminist views (but which are actually her own early published ones) that maternalized and sentimentalized the interrelations between women writers, Erkkila now wants to place Dickinson in the context of her race, class, and ethnic environment. There, in the "gap between Dickinson's revolutionary poetics and the revolutionary struggles of blacks, women, and workers that marked her time," Erkkila finds that "her radical poetics was conjoined with an essentially conservative and in some sense reactionary and Know-Nothing politics" (*Wicked* 52–53). Erkkila's interest in politics takes her far from the poetry, and, when she does bend toward it in her reference to "I'm ceded — I've stopped being Their's —," for example, as evidence that Dickinson deploys "the politically charged language of secession" (51), she is mistaken. Clearly, feminist critics need to do more work in this area.

Taking Dickinson out of the context of the Emersonian tradition in which she is so often placed, my *Lyric Contingencies: Emily Dickinson and Wallace Stevens* (1991) examines Dickinson's sense of the discontinuous self, of the interactional nature of language, and of the audience she both craved and feared, as formed by her gender and by the reconception of the lyric genre that she undertook. Freed from the need to be Emerson's representative self (and Griffin Wolff's conception of Dickinson as representative), Dickinson's lyric speakers represent a sense of the changeable, contingent, and aleatory self that looks forward to the modernist poetry of Wallace Stevens and to feminist conceptions of the decentered self.

Using the insights of both deconstruction and psychoanalytic theories in her efforts to set Dickinson in a tradition of women writers, Mary Loeffelholz has begun this work in *Dickinson and the Boundaries of Feminist Theory* (1991). Hers is a complex and responsive reading of the poems that does not neglect the importance of Dickinson's cultural context. Discussing again Rich's relationship to Dickinson, Loeffelholz also acknowledges the need for feminists to develop a nonidealizing model of a countertradition in women's writing, one that, like Erkkila's, will acknowledge difference and dissent but will also respond to the actual complexity of women's texts and women as subjects. Both a sophisticated reader of poetry and a feminist theorist, Loeffelholz works at the boundaries of feminist theory which the poetry of women is constantly informing and revising. At these boundaries, Dickinson is and will remain central.

Fitting Dickinson into a tradition of women writers in *Women Poets and the American Sublime* (1990), Feit Diehl makes the ingenious argument that for Dickinson the Sublime must incorporate a defense against its own radical discontinuities, a defense that takes the form of "denying need, privileging the process of doing without such an implosion of power, and converting renunciation of that power into a force of equal grandeur — into a counter-Sublime" (26). Following this counter-Sublime through the work of Marianne Moore, Elizabeth Bishop, Sylvia Plath, and Adrienne Rich, Feit Diehl ranges through a variety of detailed and elaborate readings to show how "Dickinson's consciousness of competition falls away before Rich's hope of mutuality, as Rich's 'plaine style' emerges from the complexities of Dickinson's encoded poetics" (167–68). Concentrating on Dickinson and the Sublime outside a feminist countertradition, Gary Lee Stonum's *Dickinson Sublime* (1990) offers a more detailed and comprehensive examination of Dickinson's fascination with the power that the Sublime provides. Making no claims to be a feminist, Stonum nonetheless draws a complex and subtle portrait of the powerful poet with which many feminists would agree.

The future of feminist conceptions of Dickinson will continue to be informed by the poetry itself. At least two major routes appear open for further investigation: the manuscripts and literary history. As work on the manuscripts continues, the feminist issues that editing problematizes will begin to explode received notions of what constitutes a poem, the editing of a poem, and the establishment of a text. At the same time as this close study of the poet goes on, critics will also have to begin looking at the larger field of literary history where Dickinson has still not found her commanding place. Until a new *American Renaissance: Art and Expression in the Age of Emerson and Whitman* is written with Dickinson not only in the title but in center place, the task of feminist criticism of Dickinson will not be complete.

NOTE

1. Although Homans's book was published in 1980, a year after *The Madwoman in the Attic*, Homans's introduction is dated 1978 and carries with it an acknowledgment that her book was completed before the work of Gilbert and Gubar was published. Thus Homans's reading of Dickinson is not a reaction to their book but a refinement to it.

FURTHER READING

Bennett, Paula. "The Pea That Duty Locks: Lesbian and Feminist-Heterosexual Readings of Emily Dickinson's Poetry." *Lesbian Texts and Contexts: Radical Revisions.* Ed. Karla Jay and Joanne Glasgow. New York: New York University Press, 1990. 104–25.

Bzowski, Frances. "Emily Dickinson's Use of Traditional Female Archetypes." *ESQ: A Journal of the American Renaissance* 29.3 (1983): 154–69.

Edelstein, Tilden G. "Emily Dickinson and Her Mentor in Feminist Perspective." *Nineteenth-Century Women Writers of the English Speaking World.* Ed. Rhoda B. Nathan. New York: Greenwood, 1986. 37–43.

Ferlazzo, Paul J., ed. *Critical Essays on Emily Dickinson.* Boston: Hall, 1984.

Fetterley, Judith. *The Resisting Reader: A Feminist Approach to American Fiction.* Bloomington: Indiana University Press, 1978.

Foster, Thomas. "Homelessness at Home: Placing Emily Dickinson in (Women's) History." *Engendering Men: The Question of Male and Feminist Criticism.* Ed. Joseph A. Boone and Michael Cadden. New York: Routledge, 1990. 239–53.

Galperin, William H. "Emily Dickinson's Marriage Hearse." *Denver Quarterly* 18.4 (1984): 62–73.

Gilmore, Leigh. "The Gaze of the Other Woman: Beholding and Begetting in Dickinson, Moore, and Rich." *Engendering the Word: Feminist Essays in Psychosexual Poetics.* Ed. Temma Berg et al. Urbana: University of Illinois Press, 1989. 81–102.

Hart, Ellen Louise. "'Syllables of Velvet': Dickinson, Rossetti, and the Rhetorics of Sexuality." *Feminist Studies* 11.3 (1985): 569–93.

Hughes, Getrude Reif. "Subverting the Cult of Domesticity: Emily Dickinson's Critique of Women's Work." *Legacy* 3.1 (1986): 17–28.

Juhasz, Suzanne. "Writing Doubly: Emily Dickinson and Female Experience." *Legacy* 3.1 (1986): 5–15.

Keller, Lynn, and Cristanne Miller. "Emily Dickinson, Elizabeth Bishop, and the Rewards of Indirection." *New England Quarterly* 57.4 (1984): 533–53.

Martin, Wendy. "Emily Dickinson." *Columbia Literary History of the United States.* Ed. Emory Elliott et al. New York: Columbia University Press, 1988. 609–26.

Michelson, Bruce. "The Refeminization of Dickinson." *Review* 14 (1992): 135–42.

Smith, Martha Nell. "To Fill a Gap." *San Jose Studies* 13.3 (1987): 3–25.

———. "Gender Issues in Textual Editing of Emily Dickinson." *Women's Studies Quarterly* 19.3–4 (1991): 78–111.

Walker, Cheryl. "A Feminist Critic Responds to Recurring Student Questions about Dickinson." *Approaches to Teaching Dickinson's Poetry.* Ed. Robin Riley Fast and Christine Mack Gordon. New York: MLA, 1989. 142–47.

Walker, Nancy. "'Wider than the Sky': Public Presence and Private Self in Dickinson, James, and Woolf." *The Private Self: Theory and Practice of Women's Autobiographical Writings.* Ed. Shari Benstock. Chapel Hill: University of North Carolina Press, 1988. 272–303.

Wolff, Cynthia Griffin. "Emily Dickinson, Elizabeth Cady Stanton, and the Task of Discovering a Usable Past." *Massachusetts Review* 30.4 (1989): 629–44.

Roland Hagenbüchle

Dickinson and Literary Theory

Introduction

*T*his essay sets out to assess the impact of critical thought on Dickinson studies by demarcating both the range and the limitation of individual theories in their application to the poet's oeuvre.[1] The following questions will be central to my argument:

1. What larger issues does a particular literary theory help to raise?
2. Which literary aspects (hitherto overlooked) does a given method throw into relief, and which (new) elements of the text does it help to elucidate?
3. What have the several approaches contributed to our overall understanding of Dickinson's work, and (conversely) which are their respective blind spots?

It is of course quite outside the scope of this essay to present a full picture of the different critical movements.[2] Nor is it my ambition to push individual scholars into a Procrustean bed of theoretical schools. If I try to point out in their diverse approaches what I consider to be flaws or gaps, it is with the avowed intention of evaluating the critical theories underlying their work rather than the scholarly work itself. This will not deter me from giving praise where I feel it is due. Nor can I quite withhold my critical preferences — a shortcoming for which I apologize. In an effort to provide a common denominator, I shall focus throughout this essay on "My Life had stood — a Loaded Gun — " (P754), using the poem whenever possible as a test case.

Finally, I would like to point out that the approach used in this essay, covering the major critical phases, inevitably entails a degree of overlap with some of the other contributions gathered in this volume. Whenever this is the case, I will refer the reader to the respective essay in which the matter at hand (albeit from a different angle) is given fuller scope.

Impressionistic Beginnings

Before the advent of New Criticism there is no full-fledged theory of criticism in the modern sense, although the list of critics who have set forth their critical principles is a long and impressive one.[3] At least since Samuel Johnson, but based on time-honored precedent going back to antiquity, it has been accepted as a critical commonplace that poets must mirror "nature" (including human nature) and "life," that they must both teach and delight the reader, and that it is the critic's task to assess the writer's merits and faults according to the "rules" of literature and in keeping with an accepted sense of proportion and decorum. Johnson is among the first to set writers in their wider context, judging them in relation to their epoch, their biography, their learning, their social position, and — not least — their sources.[4]

Among the most important elements that S. T. Coleridge added to critical theory (besides his concept of the symbol) was his claim that, contrary to Plato's views, there is no antagonism between poetry and philosophy, that a "great poet" must also be a "profound philosopher" — a premise that Emerson and Aiken were to share but that Eliot fiercely attacked. Both Johnson's contextual approach and Coleridge's biographical interest came to play a significant role in early Dickinson criticism. Coleridge's assumption that poetry and philosophy are next of kin was later adopted by critics like Winters, Blackmur, and Tate, all of whom felt justified in disparaging Dickinson's seeming lack of philosophical ideas and her allegedly muddled thought.[5] Although a poet of sorts, they argued, she certainly was not a thinker. The ideological (gender-specific) bias behind such censures needs no further comment here. The misjudgment was eventually set right by Gudrun Grabher, who demonstrated in her perceptive study *Emily Dickinson: Das transzendentale Ich* (1981) that the poet achieved in the field of art what Kant had brought about in the realm of philosophy, namely, an epistemological revolution in thought and perception, by shifting the emphasis from the outside world onto the constructive potential of the human mind.

Emerson once called his age "the age of the first person singular" (S. Whicher 135). The claim holds true for Whitman as well as for Dickinson, but nobody seems at first to have deemed this fact worthy of notice. The most distinguished American critic at the end of the nineteenth century, Edmund Clarence Stedman, sturdily clung to Victorian norms in singling out Tennyson as the model of perfect workmanship. Despite Stedman's call for scientific criticism, his terminology as set down in *The Nature and Elements of Poetry* (1892) proved of little help to critics, and his own interpretations remained idiosyncratic and impressionistic (Bischoff 55–69; Lubbers, s. v. "Stedman"). One might have suspected that the rivalry between subjective or romantic poetry on the one hand (which Stedman favored) and objective or realistic poetry on the other (which Howells advocated) would have made an impact on Dickinson criticism, but this does not seem to have been the case. Nor did Stedman's support for an indigenous American literature (in the wake of the

Young America movement) prove to be of interest to readers of Dickinson. Stedman's call for dramatic impersonality (modern as it now seems in view of Eliot's poetic manifesto) went unheeded. It was, if anything, detrimental to an appreciation of Dickinson's work since many of her poems were actually written in the subjective first-person singular. Nevertheless, Stedman's inclusion of Dickinson in his *American Anthology* (1900) along with his admiration for her experimental style marked a breakthrough and may have fired Amy Lowell's interest in the New England poet's "modern" style (qtd. in Lubbers 111).

The most insightful criticism composed in the nineties by Martha Shackford, Samuel G. Ward, and William Dean Howells is not grounded in some critical theory at all (Lubbers 43–45, 98–100). What it still holds of interest for us is quite simply the result of close and intelligent reading. This should warn us from the start that good criticism need not necessarily have a theoretical armature to it.

In 1912 Ezra Pound asked Harriet Monroe: "Are you for American poetry or for poetry?" He himself was of the opinion that "the latter is more important" (qtd. in Paige 43). After tearing her to pieces, Monroe proclaimed Dickinson an imagist *avant la lettre* and (like Amy Lowell) praised her art as "modern" (qtd. in Lubbers 115). However, the marked change in the critical climate had surprisingly little influence at the time. It was not until Conrad Aiken that twentieth-century modernism began to make itself felt in Dickinson studies (Lubbers 110–11, 114, 121–22). Being situated between late Victorianism and early modernism, Aiken had a special flair for the premodern qualities of this poet. Three assumptions enabled him to appraise Dickinson's originality more adequately than most other critics before him: (1) literature as heightened consciousness, (2) form as the expression of mind, and (3) the assumption that the critic has to adopt a scientific method based on (Freudian) psychology, history, and anthropology. Unfortunately, the psychological aspect dominated all the others. Although Aiken's rediscovery of Dickinson must be acknowledged as a pioneering act, his critical essays on this poet have not survived the test of time. In view of Aiken's intense interest in Dickinson, the complete absence of any reference to Dickinson from the criticism of his friend T. S. Eliot is the more surprising. Eliot, one suspects, must have sensed Dickinson's powerful protomodernist style as a danger to his own modernist program and therefore preferred to avoid her.

New Criticism

Despite its many detractors, the effects of the New Critical movement, dominating the forties and fifties, can still be felt today. Both its affirmative and its prohibitive tenets turned out to be of special relevance to Dickinson scholarship. Although the two principal "fallacies," the affective fallacy and the intentional fallacy, could not deflect critical attention from an immoderate curiosity about the poet's private life, the New Critical interest in paradox, tension, and irony moved these aspects of Dickinson's style into center place. Charles Anderson's *Emily Dickinson's Poetry: Stairway of Surprise* (1960), the finest interpretive study up to that time, is strongly indebted to New Critical practice.[6] Using close textual analysis ("staring holes in the text"), Anderson focuses on a selected number of poems, paying critical attention to paradox, irony, and metaphoric tension but also to shifting grammatical categories, to the poet's use of puns and her exploitation of etymology. He stresses the asymmetries created by metrical counterpoint and by suspended rhyme, interpreting the formal dissonances as symptoms of a "fractured universe." While closely following New Critical precepts, Anderson's impressive exegesis is just as often the result of patient and intelligent reading.

Anderson's interpretation of "My Life had stood — a Loaded Gun —" is a major example of New Critical practice (*Stairway* 172–76).[7] Even though he concludes that the poem's welding of different form types (folk ballad, courtly love lyric, tall tale, metaphysical and aphoristic verse) does not quite come off, he tackles the verse with great gusto. He stresses the tension between the inanimate gun and vital life, and he explains the paradoxical reversal of gender roles (adored but passive master versus active servant) as a characteristic of "frontier conditions." Remarking on the self's loyalty and sheltering function, Anderson appears to be puzzled by the nonfulfillment of physical love in these lines, wondering whether the poem might be on "the limitations of earthly love." In an attempt to solve the paradox of the concluding stanza, Anderson sets the mortal "I" off against the immortal "He," hinting at a "suicidal wish" on the part of the poetic self.

All in all, it is an impressive interpretation, throwing into relief the poem's intriguing paradoxes but leaving important facets of the text unexplored. Like other New Critics, Anderson neglects the possibility that the verse might also reflect an individual or/and cultural situation. Though generally interested in Dickinson's language, he is unaware of the poem's metapoetic quality. Nor does he pay attention to the power relation holding between the poem's male and female personae in terms of ideological or gender conflict, a blind spot characteristic of his New Critical approach. Although propagating the principle of tension, the New Critical claim that all literary works display an inherent "organic unity" encouraged the search for an underlying matrix and hindered critics from fully recognizing the conflicting sociocultural voices inscribed in Dickinson's oeuvre. Studies like those by Ruth Miller or, more recently, by Dorothy Huff Oberhaus, both of whom try to uncover an ultimate explanatory principle in Dickinson's fascicles (Quarles and the Bible, respectively), reflect the spirit of New Criticism. Although Miller's biographical assumptions may at times be questioned, she was the first to detect in the poems a distinct metafictional element expressive of the poet's frustrated desire for publication.

Though an easy enough target for ridicule, it cannot be denied that the New Critical movement has been an ongoing success story. All serious studies have since to rely on close textual analysis to gain critical approval. Even the most progressive deconstructive and historicist readings rely on tension, paradox, and contradiction, albeit for reasons beyond the grasp of New Criticism.

STRUCTURALISM

Structuralism had its roots in structural linguistics, in Russian formalism, and in structural anthropology.[8] Unlike the movement of New Criticism, structuralism — having its heyday in the 1960s and early seventies — is a strictly functional method. What it shares with New Criticism is its insistence on close reading. Curiously enough, the structuralist focus on binary oppositions, deep structure, and cultural sign systems had at first no visible influence on Dickinson criticism, although these tools (with Jakobson's and Lotman's interpretations as models) might have lent themselves ideally to Dickinson's oeuvre. What did make a marked impact, if only in the long run, was Jakobson's redefinition of metaphor and metonymy. In my essay "Precision and Indeterminacy in the Poetry of Emily Dickinson," I have applied Jakobson's terms to Dickinson's oeuvre. The discovery that this poet preferred metonymy over metaphor not only helped to solve some of the most vexing interpretive cruxes but also established the poet firmly as an important precursor of modernism. From a different viewpoint, and drawing on the insights of Worringer, Pongs, and Wheelwright, Heiskanen-Mäkelä perceptively analyzed Dickinson's "diaphoric [metonymic] style," noting her use of "elliptic metaphor" (173).[9]

One important side effect of the structuralist movement was the growing interest in linguistic and rhetorical devices. Brita Lindberg-Seyersted's *Voice of the Poet* (1968) was the first extended study dealing with the verbal features of Dickinson's work on all levels of language (vocabulary, imagery, syntax, meter, and rhyme).[10] Lindberg-Seyersted substantiated in elaborate detail what so far had only been impressionistic suggestions. She demonstrated the "spokenness" (colloquialness) of Dickinson's language, stressing the importance of dramatic monologue and the doubled self. Most importantly, she traced the poet's use of counterpoint between different verbal registers (first noted by Allen Tate). Lindberg-Seyersted also examined stylistic devices like metrical and prosodic innovations (the uneven line arrangement and unorthodox rhyme scheme), the gradually increasing tendency for ellipsis, the use of non-finite forms, the pervasive element of "slantness" (asymmetry), the growing tendency toward abstraction, the poet's predilection for paradox, and her astonishingly frequent use of negation. Lindberg-Seyersted's lucid interpretation of "Further in Summer than the Birds —" (P1068) is a masterpiece of linguistic and rhetorical analysis that leaves little to be desired. The very choice of a nature poem as a test case demonstrates, however, that the author did not want to engage in questions of gender, ideology, or cultural criticism — all of them issues largely outside the concerns of the structuralist school.

Lindberg-Seyersted's groundbreaking work has been extended and refined by Cristanne Miller. In *A Poet's Grammar* (1987) Miller reexamines Dickinson's language and style with the latest linguistic apparatus at her disposal. Registering the "breathless" syntax ("a nineteenth-century anticipation" of "écriture féminine" [184]), and noticing in precise detail how "words talk to words" (24, 90–98), Miller investigates the complex semantic effects of Dickinson's most distinctive feature: compression. She scrutinizes the poet's non-recoverable deletions, ponders the indeterminacy of reference, and evaluates the lack of a signifying center along with the blurred margins of meaning. Miller's reading of "The Angle of a Landscape —" (P375) offers a brief but exquisitely sophisticated example of her interpretive technique. After carefully analyzing the poem's syntactical structure, she shrewdly uncovers the semantic implicature, noting how the poem's "self-embedding creates the artful suspense of hidden object or cause later mastered by Henry James" (93). In dealing with "My Life had stood — a Loaded Gun —" Miller throws into relief the element of "power" as the poem's underlying theme (34–37, 71–72, 122–26). Enriching her rhetorical approach with a distinctly feminist stance, she demonstrates how this theme unfolds into the perplexing ambivalence of feminine subjectivity, at once powerless and powerful — an aspect that had hitherto been overlooked or slighted by most male critics. Assuming a wide literary and cultural perspective, Miller competently manages to transcend the limitations of a narrowly structuralist approach.

In retrospect, the movement of structuralism no doubt intensified the critical concern with the formal aspects of Dickinson's poetry, but in its methodical tendency to isolate a set of binary concepts as timeless fundamentals of human nature/culture, it neglected important issues like cultural history, the question of ideology, or the problem of gender. Because of its predilection for strictly logical argument, structuralism remained largely insensitive to the elements of ambiguity, ambivalence, and plurisemantic implicature generally, and it tended to disregard the conflictual qualities of texts and their sociocultural heteroglossia.

Archetypal and Myth Criticism

Archetypal and myth criticism in the wake of Northrop Frye's *Anatomy of Criticism* (1957) has so far had little effect on Dickinson scholarship. This is to be deplored since Frye's theory combines close hermeneutic interpretation with a fascinating model of literary history. For Frye (as Todorov has noticed), every text is a palimpsest, and all texts are intertexts. In addition to his four generic types, Frye's model of literary modes (myth, romance, high and low mimetic, irony), in both their anthropological and historical aspects, could usefully be drawn upon to characterize Dickinson's style and to place the poet in her cultural milieu. Similarly, his redefinition of the symbol (as sign, motif, image, archetype, and monad) might be of invaluable help in analyzing the poetry's complex imagery. Frye insists that all criticism ought to be written with a specific vision of the world in mind, an assertion essential to the practice of criticism whose relevance ultimately depends on a utopian horizon of values. The ideal synthesis, Frye claims, never comes into existence; the tension of opposites is the only form in which a society may finally exist. In his eyes, literature as a self-contained universe attempts to incorporate an alien and indifferent world into archetypal patterns that serve to satisfy enduring human needs and desires (120–28). Clearly, Dickinson scholarship would have much to learn from Frye's approach. His last publication was aptly called "The Double Vision."

In contrast to Frye's theory, the Jungian school of archetypal myth criticism has found a number of followers among Dickinson critics. In his magisterial work, *The Tenth Muse: The Psyche of the American Poet* (1975), Albert Gelpi argues that it is the poetry of Dickinson and Whitman that works out most compellingly "the lifelong contention of eros and psyche," bringing about "their reconciliation" (xii). In applying C. G. Jung's depth psychology, Gelpi is at his best in reading poems that center on the motif of the mystic marriage, and he explores the blurring of sexual roles in relation to the self's *rite de passage*. In Gelpi's view, the I–Thou structure of many of Dickinson's poems is in reality an I–Me relationship, an interior dialectics that in part explains the poet's frequent role inversions (249–55, 266–67). From a Jungian perspective, Gelpi throws into relief Dickinson's enormous need for conscious (Apollonian) control of her animus, whereas Whitman in a truly Dionysian fashion could entrust himself to the fluidity of his anima. Why this should be so is never fully explained, however.

Gelpi has repeatedly called attention to the ambiguous nature of Dickinson's animus figure. This figure appears at once as God, lover, demon, and death, "the masculine 'other' filling what her female nature" both "lacked and feared" (*Muse* 251). And he quotes approvingly Adrienne Rich's claim that "to a lesser or greater extent, every woman writer has written for men." Gelpi describes the poet's search for androgynous wholeness (Jung's mature psychic state) as a "dying" into a transfigured self (264). He refers approvingly to Erikson's concept of inner space understood as a specific quality of the feminine psyche: "In female experience an inner space is at the center of despair even as it is at the very center of potential fulfillment" (271). In his reading of "Circumference thou Bride of Awe" (P1620) Gelpi brings his admirable knowledge of Jungian myth criticism to bear on the *hieros gamos* as it is enacted in Dickinson's verse. He concludes: "Dickinson preferred to be Kore, the maiden-bride more than Demeter the mother or Persephone the wife" (281). The chapter on Dickinson is valid not least because Gelpi is fully aware of the poet as a woman author writing in the context of a patriarchal society. Although myth criticism, in its search for archetypal images shared by all individuals in all cultures, has an inherent tendency to focus on ahistorical patterns of imagination and is therefore likely to miss the culture-specific dimension of literature, Gelpi's early work on Dickinson's Puritan roots helped him to balance this potential defect.

A remarkable example of myth criticism, based this time on Freudian psychology, has been offered by Marcello Pagnini in his essay " 'I never told the buried gold': Un esempio di semiosi pluriisotopica" (1976). Unlike Gelpi, Pagnini sees the Oedipal model at work in this poem, with the Freudian interdiction of the father and the accompanying pain of death, should the secret be revealed. Pagnini's approach yields rich results on all levels: the psychological, the folkloristic, and the mythological. What is typically missing in this interpretation is a historical framing of Dickinson's text. This shortcoming has recently been remedied by Loeffelholz in her revisionary discussion of the poem's "male arche-plot" (14).

Myth criticism of the Jungian type has proved amazingly fruitful in the comparatist study of literary motifs. With the advent of ideological criticism (based on cultural history), however, it has begun to recede into the background. Being premised on anthropological fundamentals, it lacks two interpretive features indispensable to literary analysis: intertextuality (in Kristeva's definition) and historical perspective.

PSYCHOANALYTICAL CRITICISM

From the start, biography has been a favorite way of approaching Dickinson's work and, spliced with psychoanalysis, it has enjoyed a recurrent vogue in Dickinson criticism. In some cases the results were dubious. Martha Dickinson Bianchi's creation of a biographical legend is an early example. More recently, William H. Shurr's alleged discovery of the poet's secret marriage and abortion has enjoyed a veritable *succès de scandale*. Shurr praises Gelpi's interpretation of "My Life had stood — a Loaded Gun —" and finds it corroborated in the marriage context of the fascicles (*Marriage* 110–11).[11] He reads the various stanzas as a process of "sexual awakening" by the Master, accompanied as it is by "a sense of pleasure." But Shurr also notes "the lack of sexual intimacy" (because forbidden), and he acknowledges the self's "fierce loyalty" to the beloved. He eventually risks an explanation for the perplexing paradox found in the poem's final lines. The concluding stanza "begins with a plea that lover and beloved not be separated by the death of one of them." The gun, Shurr reasons, "can kill but not die or destroy itself, and the same is true in several senses for the immortal human being." In Shurr's "conservative reading," the image of the gun "serves to focus much in Dickinson's mind regarding her [actual] marriage and its aftermath." He points to the loneliness and "adventurousness of her enterprise," notes the self's passionate devotion to the husband (though "without the licence to share his bed"), and concludes by interpreting the love relation as "a link to be fulfilled in death but which is at the same time threatened by the death of one of the lovers." Shurr's reading highlights the potential dangers of the biographical method, namely, a super-imposition of real-life assumptions onto the poems (and letters) along with an unwillingness to let the text have its own say.

Dickinson's suspected love affair has always had its attractions for the biographer. Rebecca Patterson was among the first to posit a lesbian love relation between Susan and Emily Dickinson, and some sort of love affair there certainly was, however frustrated in the end. Judith Farr, discussing the "Master" figure in the gun poem, settles on the editor Samuel Bowles, and the passages she draws on from poems and letters powerfully support her conclusion. Dickinson's note to Maria Whitney after Bowles's death is especially revealing: "I fear we shall care very little for the technical resurrection, when to behold the one face that to us comprised it" (*Passion* 244). Although Bowles is certainly a legitimate choice for the poem's biographical model (if there is to be one), the letter's overall significance far surpasses the realm of biography. What it throws into relief is Dickinson's revolutionary world view that holds reality and fiction, immanence and transcendence, world and afterworld in a precarious (dialectical) balance. Choosing not choosing (to use Cameron's felicitous title) is among Dickinson's crucial tactics; but at the same time, as I have argued in "Emily Dickinson's Poetic Covenant," the poet also risks making final choices, the lines "I've known her . . . Choose One —" (P303) being a powerful example. Once the choice has been taken, Dickinson abides by it with absolute faith and loyalty.

Biographical studies provide much of the background indispensable to the critic, but they rarely manage to elucidate the poetic text. Aiken's warning still ought to be heeded: The biographical method permits valid results only if placed within a larger historical context. That is precisely why John Cody's psychobiography, trying to get at Dickinson's mind through a Freudian reading of her poetry, tends to sound reductive at times. Cody is relatively uninterested in the formal artistry of Dickinson's work, but his findings are by no means negligible; in fact, many of his interpretations are highly attractive. His reading of "My Life had stood — a Loaded Gun —" is a case in point. Directed against Anderson's exegesis (which, like Thomas Johnson's, he finds inconsistent), it is Cody's most sustained analysis (399–415). His argument relies on three thematic elements: (1) the destructiveness of sexuality, (2) the Oedipal constellation, and (3) the poet's adaptation of masculine aspects of her personality. What Johnson and Anderson have in common, in Cody's view, is their emphasis on the poem's libidinal symbolism: "[A] wish to love, to be sexual, to be creative, is mated to its opposite—a furious propensity to destroy" (403). Whence this pent-up aggression? Dickinson's psychotic breakdown and her subsequent depression, Cody speculates, made the poet aware that aggressive and libidinal drives might get out of control—hence the need for an ordering principle. He interprets the identifying "Owner" as an aspect of the author's own (divided) self that has unexpectedly become accessible to her.

Some of Cody's most insightful discoveries in explaining the gun-poem reach beyond the narrower bounds of psychoanalysis. "Sovereign Woods" is metapoetically understood by him as the habitat of fiction and of ideal love, and he persuasively interprets the "Doe" as a symbol of poetry—hunted but not shot (406–7). He also shrewdly unravels the implications packed into the "Eider-Duck's Deep Pillow." That Cody himself plays down these insights as negligible ("On a more superficial level the 'Doe' stands for the poetry itself") is the direct result of his unswervingly clinical analysis. Sticking to Freud's Oedipal family narrative, he eventually identifies "Doe" and "Owner" with mother and father, respectively. In this way, he limits the poem's richness to a specific psychoanalytic pattern, giving away much of what might be truly enlightening in his reading. Cody's suspicion that the self's assumption of male attributes reveals a "rejection of femininity" (409) makes sense from a Freudian point of view, but he largely neglects the possibility that this might also be understood as an act of self-empowerment. Alternative readings of this kind are all too often repressed by Cody's psychoanalytical perspective.

True to his Freudian model, Cody interprets the "emphatic Thumb" as the phallic woman (409). To a non-Freudian this remains ingenious speculation, and so does Cody's suggestion of the poem's "thinly disguised death-wish" for "Austin and Father" (406). Although young Emily's anger at her brother is well documented (as Cody himself remarks at the outset), the poem itself hardly authorizes such conclusion. The reason why Cody's psychoanalytic terminology all too often marginalizes the trouvailles found in his study seems to derive from two facts: (1) The univocal and technical discourse of psychoanalysis cannot do justice to the multisemantic discourse of art, and (2) the search of the biographer for real-life referents (with life as the primary text) truncates the richness of poetic language that raises personal experience onto a transpersonal and intersubjective level. In trying to interpret a literary text, psychoanalytic terminology is decidedly inferior to the critical discourse that embeds a work of art in its wider literary and sociocultural context, letting the network of meanings unfold through the different layers of theme and form.

Biography in Context

The magnificent studies by Richard B. Sewall (1974) and Cynthia Griffin Wolff (1986) are invaluable because they both situate the poet's life within its literary and cultural background. In Wolff's vivacious and richly informative *Emily Dickinson*, the poet's life becomes intensely alive to the reader. The work achieves a balance among cultural history, biography, psychology, and literary craft rarely met with in biographical studies. Sewall is extremely careful in using biographical facts to "explain" lyric texts (or the other way round). Wolff is more audacious in her critical judgments, and through her biographical lens Dickinson emerges as a daunting rebel defining herself against her time and culture. Wolff's reading of "My Life had stood — a Loaded Gun —" strikingly documents her approach (443–46).[12]

Wolff bases her reading of the poem's final paradox on a psalm text (8:6) and on St. Paul's venerable observations on death (1 Cor.). In asking the question: "Who am 'I' and who is 'He'?" an Amherst audience (Wolff suggests) would no doubt have responded: death and Christ. Christ must live longer to raise the dead from the graves. In Wolff's reading, by contrast, "Dickinson's poem bitterly exploits the *opposite* paradox." Christ the God-man is also "the Father, the Destroyer and Avenger." "And, most terrible of all, death [as Christ's agent] *enjoys* his job." To Wolff, then, death is the speaker, and God is the Master. She refers the reader to the "Angel of Death" on New England headstones that (until "identified" by God) has to wait like "a Loaded Gun / In Corners." The "Sovereign Woods" (the king's hunting preserve) is taken to be God's hunting ground, the world. The place of the "crudely bragging backwoods ballad" is claimed by Wolff to be Trinitarian Amherst itself, "a town set among hills and mountains." Shooting the "Doe," Wolff reminds us, is used in Elizabethan songs and madrigals as a synonym for seduction. The "violence of this trope angrily captures the lascivious obscenity of a Christian tradition that accepts all the notions implicit in a bride-of-Christ fable." The Puritan New England God is "motivated principally by phallic rage." Nevertheless, "the hero-poet possesses her own immense retaliatory power," as many other poems testify. With Dickinson's "Trinitarian culture" passing "into desuetude" (and with New England Puritanism losing its "transcendent valence"), "the central meaning of the verse was all but lost." Not sufficiently accessible anymore, the poem appears to Wolff (and, she suspects, to many others as well) a fascinating "failure."

Although the several influences — especially the religious background and the medieval intertext — are carefully taken into consideration, something jars in Wolff's interpretation. She certainly has a point in suggesting that Dickinson rebels against the orthodox Christian tradition of the bride-of-Christ, and she is also right in stressing the poet's anger at God's emissary, death. Nor can it be denied that Dickinson was indeed "able to see through the falsities of her own time." However, to read the poem centrally as an attack on the blood-lust of a Puritan Godhead plays it false. The poem's "Master" is not simply the revengeful and sadistic Jehovah that Wolff discovers in this verse, nor is the "I" bluntly identical with the figure of death. Wolff effectively draws attention to the sexual undertone and the quality of violence, but she neglects the ecstatic awakening expressed in this verse, nor is she interested in the mutual relationship of the two personae. In accordance with her biographical stance, Wolff understands "My Life had stood — a Loaded Gun —" primarily as a text of cultural rebellion, a text protesting in anger against the sadistic God of Puritanism and the beguiling bride-of-Christ motif. The conclusion seems inevitable that — in this case at least — the bold single-mindedness of Wolff's analysis cannot do full justice to this rich and sophisticated poem.

CULTURAL CRITICISM

The significance of cultural studies for literary interpretation was, from a theoretical point of view, first set forth in the 1970s. Its scope was much extended by the recent movement of New Historicism (spearheaded by Greenblatt). Although direct influences are hard to trace, the frequent appearance in recent Dickinson studies of terms like "negotiation," "self-fashioning," "circulation," and "exchange" — all of them referring to cultural processes — clearly reveals the impact of New Historicist writing on Dickinson criticism. Unquestionably, the New Historicist concern with authority, power, ideology, and social relations has become a commonplace in contemporary scholarship.

From early on, the poet's cultural heritage has been of crucial interest to critics. After Gelpi's (somewhat misnamed) *Emily Dickinson: The Mind of the Poet* (1965), critics began to focus increasingly on Dickinson's place within the wider cultural tradition. The late Karl Keller's *The Only Kangaroo among the Beauty: Emily Dickinson and America* (1979) puts Dickinson's work squarely in its American literary context. But Keller's tactics do not always work well. In appraising his interpretation of "My Life had stood — a Loaded Gun —," one is led to observe an unfortunate narrowing down of the text's significance to the Puritan marriage code. In this "justly famous but much over-psychoanalyzed poem," Keller argues, "she is the [Puritan] woman fulfilled in her wifely devotion to the man" (26). In addition, Keller limits the poem's overall meaning to an "American Erotic," suggesting that in this verse "Sex is for a woman, ludicrously, a waiting for the power to 'die' — that is, to have sex" (268). A more reductive reading is hardly imaginable. Fortunately, this is a rare kind of slip. In his comparison of Dickinson and Frost, Keller persuasively sketches the intertextual links, underscoring the mischievous spirit and the teasing playfulness shared by the two New England writers.

Other critics like Inder Nath Kher have widened the horizon. Kher's fine study *The Landscape of Absence* (1974), the first to tackle the poet's complete work, is strong on three aspects: (1) thematic motif clusters, (2) poetic "Perception" (a superbly argued chapter), and (3) the poet's quest for self-identity. The thematic chapters, dealing with motifs like Sea, Love, Death, and Self, manage to show the intricate semantic network visible throughout Dickinson's oeuvre, but they suffer (as all motif studies do) from a methodological problem, that of tautological reasoning. All too often, poems are quoted in order to illuminate other poems. Kher's laudable effort to pay full attention to "the larger [i.e., universal] structure of the imagination" (Frye), which makes Dickinson's work available to readers of other cultures, has its price; it lacks a sociohistorical context. The gain is no less remarkable, however. Dickinson's existential aesthetics — her "Aesthetics of Terror," as Kher calls it (7) — has for the first time found its rationale here, enabling the reader to connect Dickinson's stance to Kierkegaard as well as to Aurobindo, Berdyaev, or Buber.

Other critics have read Dickinson in the context of British, German, and French writers (Hopkins, Hölderlin, Droste-Hülshoff, Baudelaire, and Mallarmé,[13] among them), and quite a few have explored Dickinson's possible links with Russian, Indian, and Japanese authors. This broadening of perspective goes hand in hand with the ongoing effort to translate Dickinson's poems into other languages, thus rendering her work globally available.

In his superbly documented study *Emily Dickinson and Her Culture: The Soul's Society* (1984), Barton Levi St. Armand (expanding his earlier work done in collaboration with Monteiro) has collected a profusion of cultural materials such as women's scrapbooks, journals, folk art, landscape painting, and emblems in order to present a true "biography of American Victorian culture" (2). His admirable effort at reconstruction on the basis of — as he puts it — "no set methodology" (2) is not unproblematic, however. Small wonder that St. Armand has been taken to task, most trenchantly perhaps by Mary Loeffelholz

(1–3). What also becomes (almost embarrassingly) plain from this study is the qualitative gap between the gathered material and the transformation these sources undergo in Dickinson's work — a real quantum leap. Such reservations appear small-minded, however, in view of St. Armand's magnificent achievement. Indeed, this rich quarry provides a context absolutely indispensable to the Dickinson critic, and it helps to unravel some of the most intractable cruxes. In approaching "My Life had stood — a Loaded Gun —," St. Armand sturdily maintains that the poem had not become an indisputable part of the Dickinson canon until the rise of feminism, a surprising and factually misleading statement that allows him to disregard the poem altogether.

Judith Farr has recently expanded the scope of St. Armand's groundbreaking work by including literary as well as painterly sources from Europe and America. Farr's detailed comparison of Dickinson's use of light imagery with the painterly technique of the luminist school stands out from her many fascinating trouvailles. Although the similarity has been noted before, it has so far lacked full documentation. What Farr provides in her study is a "thick" context for embedding Dickinson's work in her American and European culture. The book has tremendously enriched our knowledge of the poet, but it also proves — as the author herself admits — that the meaning of Dickinson's poems cannot be reduced to their (frequently speculative) sources. Sources may clarify problems, but they cannot solve them. Commenting on "My Life had stood — a Loaded Gun — " (according to Farr one of the most-discussed but neither the best nor an especially characteristic poem in the Dickinson canon), she refers the reader to American hunting pictures and to landscape scenes. More importantly, Farr understands the poem's "Master" as an avatar of "Dickinson's redeemer" (*Passion* 244), and, as noted before, suggests Bowles as a model for this mysterious figure. Regrettably, the poem's interpretive cruxes are left unattended to.

In "The Poet as Cartoonist," Martha Nell Smith (building on Monteiro and St. Armand) has taken a close look at some of Dickinson's iconotexts (visual, verbal, and ekphrastic),[14] using the poet's snippets of newspaper drawings, cartoons, etchings, and the like. As Smith notes, Dickinson's cutouts do not necessarily show disrespect, but they certainly undercut single-minded textual, poetic, and cultural expectations (68–69, 77, 100–102). Most importantly, Dickinson's humorous mode destabilizes established semantic meanings as well as fixed mental and rhetorical conventions. The engravings attached to "A poor torn Heart — a tattered Heart" (P78), for instance, turn the seemingly sentimental poem into a veritable parody of angelic transcendence. In both the cuttings and the poems humor privileges questions over answers, freedom of choice over choice. Humor, then, is part of the poet's unsettling "compound vision," which leaves the reader dangling between high seriousness and witty playfulness. In setting Dickinson's cutout picture of slanting tombstones (sent to John Graves) against her verse that exhorts the reader "to lean against the grave" (P262) when in extremity, we are struck by the poet's sly ekphrastic joke creating far-reaching existential and cultural implications.

Smith has recently announced the project of a complete hypertext library. In order to provide the critic with all available resources so as to achieve maximum cultural "thickness," she plans to gather not only manuscript material and critical writings but also the larger background including nontextual sources such as paintings, music, photographs, and so on. This library promises to become the Dickinson encyclopedia of the future. Infinitely expandable and instantaneously updatable, it ought to be accessible worldwide to all students interested in Dickinson's work.

FEMINIST CRITICISM

Feminist theory, starting in the late 1960s, has come to display a variety of critical perspectives: psychoanalytic, Marxist, poststructuralist, and deconstructive.[15] They all have exerted a decisive influence on the study of literary subjectivity in general and on gender studies in particular. Strangely enough, Kenneth Burke's concept of (poetic) language as "symbolic action" has so far been of little interest to feminist critics. In Burke's view, there is a close relationship between rhetorical structures and the structures of human relations (with synecdoche as a kind of master trope). This neglect of Burke's theory is the more surprising as he has tried hard to enlarge the act of close reading into the field of psychological, sociological, and cultural analysis — all of them issues that are at the heart of the feminist movement.

Among the critical tools used by feminists, special mention must be made of three concepts: Lacan's definition of the decentered subject as a "desiring subject," Derrida's notion of *différance*, and Foucault's concern with the modes of human discourse and their related power and disciplinary structures. In *Dickinson and the Boundaries of Feminist Theory* (1991), Mary Loeffelholz underscores the close relation among feminism, deconstruction, and psychoanalysis (3–6). Because of their central interest in concrete sociohistorical conditions, feminists will find Derrida's deconstructive move in undermining hierarchical oppositions extremely useful (though his method might at the same time serve as a cautionary signal to radical feminists). Paul de Man's project, by contrast, of uncovering the aporias inherent in all verbal representation is only marginally helpful (a reservation I shall revert to later on). Within the feminist camp, therefore, deconstruction serves primarily as a method of laying bare the various power structures hidden behind traditional gender relations.

The link between feminism and psychology, as Loeffelholz points out, raises problems of a different kind. What is at stake here is the ongoing rivalry between Lacan's revisionary Freudian model and the object-relations theory, pioneered by Nancy Chodorow, who foregrounds the mother–daughter relationship responsible for an incipient *écriture féminine* (Loeffelholz 4–6, 85–89).[16] Julia Kristeva, from a different angle, describes a pre-Oedipal ("semiotic") signifying process, centered on the mother. Although later repressed by the "symbolic" logic of the father, it tends to break through in the disruptive style of experimental and avant-garde poetry.[17] We ought to bear in mind, however, that the Oedipal model is now largely fallen into disrepute. Neither clinical research nor the foundational Greek myth lends support to Freud's assumptions. The writings of Victor Frankl, Jean-Joseph Goux's *Oedipus, Philosopher* (1993), and the criticism of Paul Ricoeur have done much to undermine the Freudian family saga as a reliable explanatory tool in the fields of both psychoanalysis and literary hermeneutics.

The feminist concern with the position of the female subject in particular and with gendered power relations in general has found an ideal testing ground in Dickinson's work. It is hardly surprising, therefore, that women critics have from the start been extremely sensitive to Dickinson's rebellious stance vis-à-vis her traditional Puritan and Victorian heritage in terms of gender, religion, and aesthetics. Following the lead of Elaine Showalter, of Sandra Gilbert and Susan Gubar, as well as of French critics like Hélène Cixous and Luce Irigaray, a substantial body of feminist writing has recently dealt with Dickinson as a woman author. The justly famous study *The Madwoman in the Attic* (1979) by Gilbert and Gubar is a landmark of feminist scholarship. In their final chapter, "A Woman — White," the authors demonstrate Dickinson's subtle tactics in avoiding and subverting the limiting boundaries of her patriarchal culture. The reader is made aware that poems like "I gave myself to Him — / And took Himself, for pay" (P580) radically subvert the hierarchy of traditional gender roles by signaling the mutuality of the risk entailed. The question "[W]ho is the master and who the slave?" becomes undecidable (P607). Redefined in feminist terms, Lévi-Strauss's concept of woman as the basic exchange value in a patriarchal order makes astounding sense in interpreting Dickinson's recurrent motif of reciprocal transaction.

Although male critics of Dickinson's work have occasionally mentioned the predicament of the woman writer in nineteenth-century Victorian America, it was feminist critics like Homans, Juhasz, Loeffelholz, Mossberg, Pollak, and Smith who finally moved the problem to center stage. Martha Nell Smith has put the case with laconic conciseness: Dickinson "was privileged by class but disenfranchised by gender" (*Rowing* 14). To counter the sociocultural pressures exerted on the woman writer by "the law of the Father," the mythic

Other in Dickinson's work, as Loeffelholz contends, comes to assume all the desired qualities denied women in Dickinson's patriarchal culture (30). In discussing "My Life had stood — a Loaded Gun —" and quoting Rich (who had invoked the gun-poem as early as 1965), Loeffelholz notes that this poem has become the favorite "locus of discussion for feminist critics," concerned as they are with Dickinson's anger and aggressiveness as a woman writer. What has sometimes been interpreted in myth criticism (especially by followers of Jung) as Dickinson's timeless engagement with the animus, or in philosophical terms as the equally timeless Hegelian encounter of *Self* and *Other* in the act of self-reflection, can now be reinterpreted in the light of feminist scholarship as historically engendered cultural attitudes and power relations cast in psycho-social terms.

Martha Nell Smith's *Rowing in Eden: Rereading Emily Dickinson* (1992) has thrown into relief the importance of Susan (Huntington Gilbert) Dickinson "as a participatory reader of Dickinson's works" (220, 158–206). Smith explores the intense bond between the two women on both the emotional and the professional level, thereby correcting the partial view of Emily and Sue as alienated friends. Superseding R. Jackson Wilson's discussion of the same subject, Smith places Dickinson squarely in the literary marketplace. Most importantly, she draws attention to the poet's self-empowerment. In fascicle 21 (describing the career of a "poet of the portfolio"), for example, "[T]he female speaker of the final poem" champions "her power"; and in the verse "It was given to me / by the Gods," the speaker totally overthrows the "monotheistic, patriarchal culture" of her time (90–91).[18] Smith also points out that the term "man" (beyond its generic sense) assumes a highly polemical meaning in Dickinson's poetry. "All men say 'What' to me" is as familiar to readers as is the poet's daunting claim: "No man instructed me" (P326). What Dickinson voices here, according to Smith, is not only an expression of proud self-reliance; it is ultimately a statement about the self's rejection of the male literary tradition with the poet slyly implying her preference for a female countertradition (91).

Although Dickinson frequently appears to take over the conventional notion of femininity (the little-girl persona, the wife persona, etc.), her verse — as Gilbert, Gubar, and other feminists have emphasized — actually exploits, tests, criticizes, subverts, and often angrily attacks these clichés. Margaret Homans has even suggested that "Dickinson's greatest originality lies in her breaking out of the terms of gender altogether" (qtd. in Smith, *Rowing* 116). Smith in turn has laid emphasis on Dickinson's "cross-dressing," a practice that manages to invert (and subvert) conventional gender roles. Whether the Master letters should also be interpreted as an act of "elaborate cross-dressing" (116) may be questioned, but the argument certainly holds for the poem "My Life had stood — a Loaded Gun —" in which female passivity and male activity appear to trade places. Smith quotes a passage from *The Madwoman in the Attic* where Gilbert and Gubar (drawing on Northrop Frye's "The Orc cycle") link this poem to the "Master" myth in Dickinson's oeuvre. In the gun-poem, as they contend, Dickinson "turns on that passive and suffering doe in herself and hunts her down" (611), thereby transforming passivity into deadly activity. What comes to the fore here is the angry woman poet. As a result, Gilbert and Gubar conclude "that the Gun and not the Master, the poet and not her muse . . . will have the last word" (609).

In their collection *Shakespeare's Sisters*, the editors approvingly include Gelpi's essay "Emily Dickinson and the Deerslayer." Gelpi celebrates Dickinson for grasping her situation in terms of the major myth of the American experience: the pioneer life of the West. Following closely Adrienne Rich's seminal essay "Vesuvius at Home: Emily Dickinson's Power," Gelpi claims that the poem is "a powerful symbolic enactment of the psychological dilemma facing the intelligent and aware woman, and particularly the woman artist, in patriarchal America" (122). What should be added here is the all-important truth that Dickinson's use of the myth reflects the ur-American quest for self-identity to which the West stands as symbol. Gelpi himself speaks of "the universal hero myth [à la Campbell] indigenous to our specific historical circumstances," which remains even today "the mythic main story of American individualism" (124).

In review, we may conclude that feminist studies have redirected critical attention away from value-free readings of Dickinson's work and toward the poet's gender-bound sociocultural place in mid-nineteenth-century patriarchal culture. Feminist criticism, intent on questions of ideology and power, occasionally tends to underrate Dickinson's superb craft as a poet. There is no doubt, however, that — with Dickinson's oeuvre as a paradigm — the feminist concern with the conflictual structure of traditional gender relations has brought issues to the fore that will continue to be of central importance to the history of literary criticism and of Western society in general.

DIALOGIC CRITICISM

Mikhail Bakhtin first gained attention when his studies on Dostoevsky, Rabelais, and the novel (written in the twenties and thirties) were translated in the 1980s. From the start, Bakhtin moved beyond a narrow preoccupation with literature to an engagement with wider sociocultural issues. Indeed, Bakhtin's criticism is cultural criticism at its best, focusing on the plurality of warring and mutually qualifying sociocultural voices that disrupt the author's single voice and thus allow for no resolution into monologic truth.[19] If the distinguished collection *Comic Power in Emily Dickinson*, coauthored by Suzanne Juhasz, Cristanne Miller, and Martha Nell Smith, leaves anything to be desired at all, it is the omission of the Bakhtinian concept of the carnivalesque, unquestionably an important feature of the poet's humor. What the carnivalesque attempts is a subversive critique of the reigning cultural order by playfully turning existing value systems upside down.

A lasting enrichment to Dickinson scholarship is provided by Bakhtin's theory of dialogic poetics, a conceptual model first taken up by Kristeva and eagerly appropriated by other critics. According to Bakhtin, the word of the other (the listener) — in the presence of an authoritative word (the speaker) — is being silenced. It is only through dialogue, through responsive exchange, that the democratic heteroglossia of voices can be preserved. By extending Bakhtinian dialogism to the interaction of artistic works, aesthetic systems, and cultural phenomena in general, the critic is given a handle for studying the intertextual dimension of literary works. Intertextual studies differ from source studies in that they trace the way in which textual elements are being transformed through the processes of historical transmission, an approach that invites critical comparisons between the varying usages found in different cultural periods and discourses.

Dialogic poetics radically questions the single-voice utterance of a given hegemonic culture and its institutions, thus opening the fields of law, religion, economics, and their encoded cultural practices for rival claims. What also tends to disappear behind these several voices is the voice of the author as an authoritative voice (clearly, Bakhtin's author as ventriloquist and Roland Barthes's "death of the author" have much in common). The model of poetic dialogics might be enhanced by adding Foucault's more sophisticated concept of discourse, which allows us to examine the various power relations holding between the different voices. In applying Bakhtinian dialogics to Dickinson's poetry, as has recently been done by Paul Crumbley in his perceptive study *Inflections of the Pen: Dash and Voice in Emily Dickinson*, readers of Dickinson are not only led to recognize the poet's multiple heritage as competing norms; they also become aware of the different cultural discourses as distinct — and infighting — voices in her oeuvre. Dialogic criticism is a relatively new approach and in no way exhausted. To the Dickinson scholar, it offers a promising field of research.

READER RESPONSE THEORY

As the example of Thomas Wentworth Higginson graphically demonstrates, readers of Dickinson's verse were from the start disoriented by the formal and thematic "oddities" of her style. And it soon became clear that the poet's innovative strategies required a new mode of reading. Linguistic analyses, by focusing on the poet's verbal art, helped to acclimatize the reader to Dickinson's verse. Among literary critics, Robert Weisbuch was the first to work out a structural model, (1) demonstrating the poet's use of the analogical chain as a basic pattern, and (2) noting the quality of scenelessness and of semantic openendedness as important poetic tactics. Weisbuch and Martin Orzeck have recently published an essay collection entitled *Emily Dickinson and Audience.*

Building on Wolfgang Iser's influential studies *Der implizite Leser* (1972) and *The Act of Reading* (1978), both indebted to Roman Ingarden, David Porter's *Dickinson: The Modern Idiom* (1981) offers the reader a kind of primer for disentangling the poet's "writerly" style. Among Iser's central tenets is the assumption that the text (implicitly or explicitly) provides a set of instructions so that its meaning is offered to the reader as something to be constructed and assembled. Porter shares with Iser an emphasis on textual gaps (the famed *Leerstellen*). From what appears to be a rather disjointed or even defective surface text, Porter attempts to reconstruct the underlying matrix in order to bring out what has been lost (or deleted) in the process of form-giving. Though it is true (as Suzanne Juhasz has argued) that the fill-in method runs the risk of eliminating the poetry's deliberate ambiguities, the reader is nonetheless intensely involved in a process to which the text is both question and response. Reading as co-creation not only helps one to understand more fully the underlying experience embodied in the text, it also compels the reader to respond to the situation both imaginatively and concretely. Reading thus becomes a social act in its own right. As Peter Brooks has superbly phrased it, the meaning of a text is neither the exclusive result of the author nor that of the reader, but of their collaborative (and also corrective) interaction in that both work on a text that simultaneously works on them.

Porter signals out "otherness" (*Idiom* 1) as the defining quality of Dickinson's modernity. He suggests that the poet's language begins with a void, arguing that the poems not only are a stay against confusion but often "take part in confusion itself" (6), a statement that some critics would quarrel with. He closely inspects the compositional method, pointing out the syntactical ellipses, the deleted referents, and the suppressed inflections. But he also draws attention to the visual irregularities of the manuscripts as meaning-carrying marks that are all too often smoothed out in print by editorial decisions. Disregarding Dickinson's sensitive hand, print tends to replace the modulation of her writing by regularized spaces, capital or small letters, dashes, and other — often unwarranted — punctuation marks (an aspect that has now been studied in sophisticated detail by Smith and Crumbley).

"My Life had stood — a Loaded Gun —" is understood by Porter as the key utterance of Dickinson's existential condition, displaying the poet's principal features of "autism and opacity." Dealing with "the dilemma of instrument and purpose," with "destructive" power "without coherent design," the poem underscores Dickinson's artistic paradox: the "gun-language" (*Idiom* 209). Porter pursues the destructive potential of words within Dickinson's work, he emphasizes the "unquenchable 'spirit'" (213) of poetic language in her oeuvre, and he finally raises the question of authority that might confer identity to the poet. Porter contends that language cannot find its purpose in this poem, that it lacks the (practical) world, thus revealing Dickinson's existential plight, namely her "autogenous . . . self-concern" (226). The lyric self, Porter concludes, deceives itself by claiming a master that it does not really have. What we discover, then, in this "allegorical verse" are "failures to organize" along with the dire lack of concrete experience and the fruitless self-reflexivity of a language vainly searching for "the body of the world" (216). It is the void, the lack, the missing center, and the nonfulfillment that are at the center of Porter's interpretation. In what appears to be a defensive gesture against feminist pressure, he vigorously refuses to see this lack as resulting from cultural conditions. Although Porter quotes Adrienne Rich to the effect that the poem can be understood as the condition of the woman artist in the nineteenth century, he insists that Dickinson's fate "is deeper than cultural behavior," that it reaches into "the authentic realm of individual tragedy" (216).

Martha Nell Smith (invoking Jauß) and Paul Crumbley have recently reopened the question of how to transcribe and interpret the manuscripts. Sharing Porter's caveat, Smith warns that reproductions in print tend "to erase" the poet's "significant textual experimentation directed toward prospective readers" (*Rowing* 13). Recovery of Dickinson's original design is therefore vital to the act of reading. Quoting Susan Howe, Smith points out the iconic shape of Dickinson's handwriting, from the overall style down to individual letters: "[H]er pencil or pen was her printing press and her calligraphic orthography her typeface" (16). Smith astutely demonstrates how biographical preconceptions are bound to influence (male) editing practices that in turn predetermine the reader's act of reception. After criticizing the ideological distortion in technical reproductions of Dickinson's poetry as finished text, Smith refers the reader back to the manuscripts. Only the powerful resonances of handwritten individual letters, dashes, and other notations allow us to experience in full the quality and meaning of the verse. Despite the technically superb edition of the fascicles by Franklin, a complete facsimile edition is still sadly lacking.

The theory of reception has been supplemented by what is now known as the history of response (termed by Hans Robert Jauß *Wirkungsgeschichte*). *Wirkungsgeschichte* is to be distinguished from a history of Dickinson criticism proper as presented in Klaus Lubbers's seminal *Emily Dickinson: The Critical Revolution* (1968). Dickinson's *Wirkungsgeschichte* has not yet been written, though it is sorely needed. Karl Keller was among the first to trace systematically Dickinson's impact on subsequent writers. Among the important figures in the male tradition we must count William Carlos Williams, Hart Crane, Randall Jarrell, and Theodore Roethke. Regarding the female tradition, we ought to give pride of place to Adrienne Rich as Dickinson's most passionate interlocutor. In her challenging essay "Vesuvius at Home" (1976), Rich pays tribute to "My Life had stood — a Loaded Gun —" (a poem that she had brooded over and "taken into [herself] over many years") as the "only begetter" of her liaison with Dickinson (qtd. in Loeffelholz 83). In "The Spirit of Place" Rich attacks academic scholarship for its empty admiration and its pious legends (qtd. in Loeffelholz 167). Instead of offering self-important celebratory gestures, a *Wirkungsgeschichte* of this poet might help to bring to light what has so far been largely hidden or felt to be an underground female countertradition. Clearly, a history of women poets might go a long way toward realizing the Jaußean project of "Literary History as Provocation."

PHENOMENOLOGY

The phenomenological method derives originally from Husserl's analysis of human consciousness as it is embedded in a concretely lived world—the two realms being interinvolved and reciprocally implicative. A work that may rightly be claimed to belong in the phenomenological camp is Sharon Cameron's impressive *Lyric Time* (1979). What links Cameron's resolutely deconstructive study with phenomenology is its persistent emphasis on temporality. The lyric genre (especially since the romantics) is preoccupied with the lyric self and its experience, but also with the limitations of language to give this experience form. Irony and paradox are thus from the start built into the genre. Experience can meaningfully be known only if expressed in language, but the act of form-giving, in an effort to contain experience, ineluctably destroys the quality of immediacy. Memory is "Murder" precisely because it replaces "presence" by representation (144).[20] The word, as the poet came to recognize, both vivifies and kills. Dickinson, Cameron claims, is our "great rhetorician of loss" (69).

In her chapter "The Dialectic of Rage," Cameron pays close attention to "My Life had stood — a Loaded Gun —," arguing that the poem "makes sense neither as religious allegory" nor "as the depiction of an erotic relationship" (*Lyric Time* 66). Its central trope, she notes, is imbued with violence and rage. Coming to life involves accepting the power and the burden of doing violence as well as of suffering violence. The ultimate signum of such violence is death. To guard herself against it, the speaker tries to deny death by imagining herself immortal. Cameron admits that her interpretation sounds extreme, but she finds it justified by the final stanza. Since "any reading will prove inadequate," she maintains, the verse "draws our attention away from explanation toward something else" (68). Metaphor and allegory collapse and give way to the inescapable reality of death. The poem's deeper story, then, is the assertion "that human life gains its identity [only] when it encounters death." Deriving identity from otherness, "the meaning of the speaker's experience remains hidden in the future of its defeat" (74). The poem cannot have an ending because death, lurking "in the underlying rhythm of all action" (74), defeats completion.

A problematic aspect of this interpretation is its exclusive focus on death, violence, and rage. True enough, we do violent battle with the world (or otherness), and the mind helplessly rages against the shattering fact that human identity and meaningful existence are ineluctably coupled with death. What is largely neglected in such an analysis, however, is a cultural investigation of the poem's "I"–"Master" relationship. Cameron is not concerned primarily with gender relations, nor is she centrally interested in situating the poem in its historical context. The phenomenological approach, used here on a high level of abstraction, attempts to uncover fundamental problems inherent in the lyrical genre: the fight against temporality, the dilemma of verbal representation, and the (in)significance of human finitude. On this level, the study brilliantly succeeds.

Cameron convincingly argues that the poem's final paradox offers no meaningful solution. What come to light instead are the unsolvable contradictions among life, identity, violence, and death, contradictions that the paradox — in an evasive act — tries to overcome through an optative gesture of desire ("He longer must — than I —"). Dickinson's maneuvers against time, as Cameron demonstrates, are only partially successful. The deeper reason is, in a large measure, a generic one. Although the lyric genre is profoundly concerned with the experiential moment, its presentation in language, as Cameron works out in elaborate detail, falls into story, sequence, temporality, ignorance, death — hence the element of rage and grief in Dickinson's poetry. In her reading of the poem "There is a pain — so utter —" (P599), Cameron underscores the relation between pain and self-reflexiveness, concluding that the self absorbs and devours itself, "hollowing itself out to the shape of an 'Abyss' " (*Lyric Time* 159). However, the self's rage has other (individual and cultural) reasons as well. It would have enriched the study to place Dickinson's anger more deliberately within the poet's sociohistorical context. Admittedly, neither deconstruction (in de Man's sense) nor phenomenology is vitally interested in these issues. Although phenomenologists are by no means uninterested in what Georges Poulet has called "period-consciousness," the focalization on individual consciousness (as an existential given) pushes historical considerations into the background.[21]

In Cameron's study Dickinson criticism has reached a level of subtlety to which future research will have to measure up. However, her language also raises the question of critical discourse as no other work has done before. Cameron's critical style, though admirably precise, occasionally overtaxes the reader by translating Dickinson's complex language into a critical language of similar (or at times even higher) complexity. Critical discourse, it should be remembered, like poetic discourse has its genre-specific laws and its genre-specific boundaries that cannot be overruled with impunity.

DECONSTRUCTION

In pointing out the tension within Dickinson's poetry between a background of patriarchal forces and the poet's resistance to those forces, feminists (as noted earlier) not infrequently attempt to join deconstructive methods to New Historicist techniques. In *Dickinson and the Boundaries of Feminist Theory* (1991) Loeffelholz tries to combine such an approach with a revisionary psychoanalytic theory based on Lacanian principles, although — in part — she also argues against Lacan.

There has been no attempt so far to study Dickinson's oeuvre from a strictly deconstructive vantage point (à la de Man). This is the more surprising as her poetry is in many ways deeply conflictual. According to Barbara Johnson, it is the declared aim of deconstructive criticism to discover specific "differences" within a text that subvert its claim to an organic unity or a unitary meaning. Deconstruction is defined by her as "the careful teasing out of warring forces of signification within the text itself" (5). What a text expresses on the argumentative level, as de Man proclaims, is invariably being questioned on the rhetorical level. As a result, de Man concludes, all language necessarily runs into aporias. Literary texts in particular, he asserts, are self-destructive, and it is (in J. Hillis Miller's words) the critic's task to discover the "loose stone which will pull down the whole building" (qtd. in Harris 60).

One might wonder whether there is a specific rationale for the deconstructive neglect of Emily Dickinson's work. Apart from the fact that few critics share the assumption that all language at all times necessarily falls into aporias, deconstructive techniques fail to yield substantial results for the simple reason that, with Dickinson, the deconstructive act has already been performed by the poems themselves. Joining Paul de Man (and Derrida), J. Hillis Miller observes that "Deconstruction is not a dismantling of the structure of a text but a demonstration that it has already dismantled itself" (126). No doubt, Dickinson's paradoxical text, in conflict with itself, is invariably ahead of the critic. Deconstructive criticism only throws into relief what the poet has already done in full awareness of the issues in question. It is the critic's demanding task to set forth how Dickinson is ahead. Cameron's study has gone a long way toward achieving this goal. In order to throw Dickinson's astounding arsenal of deconstructive features into full relief, it would be requisite to examine, in detail, how the poetry's (ant)agonistic elements are brought into play on all levels: stylistic, rhetorical, aesthetic, and sociocultural.

The Hermeneutic Basis

Although deconstruction derives mostly from the work of Derrida (with Nietzsche as axial precursor), one ought to remember that Derrida in turn has "gone to school" with Husserl and Heidegger. And it is from Heidegger that Gadamer and Ricoeur have taken over what may justly be called the grounding method of the humanities: hermeneutics. None of the theories mentioned so far has any claim to validity without a sound hermeneutic basis. Whereas older hermeneutics in the romantic tradition of Schleiermacher and Dilthey still assumed that one might in principle recover a text's meaning, dialectical hermeneutics, as developed and practiced by Gadamer and Ricoeur, has recognized this aim as illusory.[22] What dialectical hermeneutics, vitally concerned with the tensions within and among texts, puts at its center is the element of temporality. Both text and reader, as well as the tools employed by the critic, are radically subject to time. From this perspective, there is no original or ideal meaning to a text that can be reconstructed. Most importantly, there is no universal human nature to which the critic may have recourse. In consequence, Ricoeur and Habermas aptly speak of a "hermeneutics of suspicion,"[23] suggesting that it is part of the hermeneutic endeavor to uncover "false consciousness" (Marx, Althusser) and *mauvaise foi* (Sartre). From this perspective, the conflictual elements within Dickinson's text may be seen as projections of the culture at large. The poet reveals in her oeuvre what is systematically "false" in her society and time. "False consciousness" and *mauvaise foi* — not least with regard to the reduced position of woman — have been systematically examined from a feminist point of view. To extend the ideological analysis (ideology being used here in a positive sense) of gender problems to other spheres of nineteenth-century cultural life will allow us to recognize the structural tensions in Dickinson's poetry and the value conflicts in her culture as mutually dependent.

A Summary and a Caveat

In view of the continuous (and often daunting) growth of theories, the approach to Dickinson's work through a study of her sources, themes, and motifs might appear quite old-fashioned. This is a crass misunderstanding. Source studies, thematic and motif studies, have proved to be of invaluable help to the critic and have immensely enriched our understanding of this poet. But none of these approaches can now eschew the critical demand for embedding Dickinson's work in a "thick" context of her time and culture.

In reviewing the impact of literary theory on Dickinson, one notes that the poet's work yields equally rich results no matter whether one approaches the poems through time-honored literary methods (Judy Jo Small's *Positive as Sound: Emily Dickinson's Rhyme* is an outstanding example) or through the rigorous lenses of more recent theories. As Loeffelholz (quoting Helen McNeil and Jonathan Arac) has remarked: "Dickinson's language speaks back to all theories" (6). However, no critical study of importance — as reviewed in this essay — has relied on one specific theory alone. In fact, critics are notorious *bricoleurs*. They tend to select from the theoretical arsenal whatever comes in handy for the text in question and for the specific work to be done. Each text offers its own possibilities and makes its own demands, and no single theory is applicable to every text. If used unreflectively, theories may even turn into intellectual blinkers. Krieger's dictum, "[N]o critical theory is likely to make any of us a good critic" (ix–xiv), is true as far as it goes, but textual criticism that is totally unaware of its own premises looks suspiciously naive.

The crucial function of theories is their critical power to uncover blind spots in the sociocultural fabric by analyzing the different modes of self-presentation. Our academic discourse is itself part of this cultural self-fashioning. Theories help to raise questions, they clarify problems, but they cannot provide answers. As T. S. Eliot pointed out long ago: "[T]here is no method except to be very intelligent."[29]

Taking stock of the enormous critical effort at elucidating "My Life had stood — a Loaded Gun —," one might conclude that almost all has been said — at least for the present. And yet, the central crux — "Who is the Master?" and "What function precisely does he fulfill in relation to the gun and its instrumental character?" — still largely eludes us. No biographical suggestion, no theory — whether formalist, feminist, psychological, or cultural — is capable of offering the reader a fully satisfactory answer. One might wonder, after all, whether the question is a legitimate one. If Farr is correct in claiming that the "Master" is at the same time "Dickinson's redeemer" (*Passion* 244), it ought to be. In her chapter "Love after Death," Loeffelholz has neatly juxtaposed some of the poems turning on Dickinson's concern with the "Other," the "Master." Arraying all the theoretical tools at one's command and bearing in mind (as best one can) the impressive range of interpretations, to read these poems in context is still a baffling experience.

What has been clarified through such painstaking exegesis is the span of alternatives, but such clarification has only deepened the problem, if anything.

Is the "Master" a biographical person? And if so, who is it? Is it really the same person in each of these poems? Or is it perhaps the soul's "Oversoul"? The mind's male animus? The self's creative alter ego? Is it (in some sense) Christ or Dickinson's appropriation of Christ? The looked for and always desired but infinitely deferred "Other"? A messenger of Eros or of Thanatos — or both? All we can safely say is that the "Master" stands for what the lyric self lacks, desires, and fears. Biographical, psychological, cultural, and existential aspects converge in this evasive figure.

Ultimately, we remain unsure whether Dickinson's focus is on a beloved person, a historical or divine "Other," an exteriorized part of the psyche, or a mythopoetic muse. What we cannot ignore, however, is the fact that the lyric self yearns to bind this Eros/Thanatos figure to itself either by submission or by an act of overpowering. Throughout her oeuvre, we perceive the poet's ceaseless effort to sustain this "Master" by her own power, while simultaneously trusting in this fictive (or figurative) "Other" to transcend, redeem, and hopefully complete her wanting selfhood.[25] One may ground this curiously de/con-structive dialectics of desire in private or sociocultural conditions or in the *conditio humana* as such, but it invariably remains a phenomenon whose exact nature eludes us. In fronting the figure of the Master/Other in Dickinson's poetry, we face no less than our own yearned-for (individual and cultural) identity, our feared alterity, the ungraspable center — or void — of our own finite and desiring self. Whether (as some critics claim) Dickinson was herself uncertain how her poems should be read or whether her slantwise style generates meanings it cannot master are issues that appear largely irrelevant to me. What is at stake in Dickinson's poetic language is her tireless effort to grasp "Something" (P122) that is ultimately beyond the direct reach of words. If the author in her stupendous oeuvre could not fully come to terms with the "Master" of the gun-poem, how should the critic as host presume to identify this figure? To acknowledge the range of existential and cultural possibilities is the most we can achieve as readers; not in helpless puzzlement, however, but imbued with rich — if teasingly uncertain — meanings. What we are finally left with, then, is a sense of humility, admiration, and wonder.

NOTES

I am gratefully indebted to Marietta Messmer for her stimulating suggestions; without her encouragement this essay would not have come into existence. To Gudrun Dreher and to Josef Raab I owe thanks for their discriminating criticism of the final draft.

1. A specialized study evaluating the influence of theory on Dickinson scholarship does not yet exist. However, the wide-ranging and richly varied collection of essays *Approaches to Teaching Dickinson's Poetry*, ed. R. R. Fast and C. M. Gordon (1989), gives

an excellent idea of the many options available to the student of Emily Dickinson's work.

2. For a comprehensive survey dealing with the tensive relation between theory and literary criticism, see Hagenbüchle, "Literaturwissenschaft."

3. For a knowledgeable discussion of the critical reception, see the contribution by Marietta Messmer in this volume.

4. For an excellent presentation of the critical principles of Johnson and Coleridge (as referred to in this and the subsequent paragraphs), see *The Johns Hopkins Guide to Literary Theory and Criticism*, s.v. "Johnson" and "Coleridge."

5. For an early rebuttal of the charges leveled against Dickinson by Winters, Blackmur, and Tate, see Hagenbüchle, "Precision" 33, n. 2.

6. For a more detailed estimate of Anderson's achievement, see Hagenbüchle, "New Developments." All the quotes in this paragraph are taken from this review article.

7. The following quotes are all taken from Anderson's discussion of the gun-poem (*Stairway* 172–76).

8. For a splendid example of the structuralist method (enriched by a feminist stance), see the contribution by Cristanne Miller in this volume.

9. See also Heiskanen-Mäkelä's chapter "The Physics and Metaphysics of Metaphor."

10. The following discussion relies on my review article "New Developments," 456–57, and on my recent "Homage to Brita Lindberg-Seyersted."

11. All the subsequent quotes are taken from Shurr's discussion of the gun-poem (*Marriage* 110–11).

12. All the subsequent quotes are taken from Wolff's discussion of the gun-poem (*Dickinson* 443–46).

13. Mallarmé in particular raises the long-standing question of Dickinson's symbolist techniques and at the same time signals out her oeuvre as a full-fledged precursor to the European symbolist movement.

14. For an authoritative definition of the terms "ekphrasis," "iconotexts," "intermediality," see Peter Wagner's magisterial Introduction to *Icons — Texts — Iconotexts* (Berlin: Walter de Gruyter, 1996).

15. For a masterly discussion of feminist concerns, see the contribution by Margaret Dickie in this volume.

16. For a discussion of the mother–child relationship, see also the authoritative studies by D. W. Winnicott on child development.

17. For a critical evaluation, see *Feminism and Psychoanalysis: A Critical Dictionary*, ed. Elizabeth Wright (Oxford: Blackwell, 1992), s.v. "Chodorow" and "Kristeva."

18. A reference to Emerson's equally irreverent plural (itself echoing romantic usage) would have been useful.

19. For an expert discussion of dialogic criticism, see the contribution by Paul Crumbley in this volume.

20. See also Cameron, *Lyric Time*, Index, s.v. "Presence" and "Loss."

21. See *Hopkins Guide*, s.v. "Poulet."

22. For an outline of dialectical hermeneutics, see Hagenbüchle, "Literaturwissenschaft."

23. For a concise definition, see *Encyclopedia of Contemporary Literary Theory*, s.v. "Hermeneutics."

24. Eliot, "The Perfect Critic." *Selected Prose of T. S. Eliot,* ed. Frank Kermode (London: Faber and Faber, 1975), 55. See also Eliot's essay, "The Use of Poetry and the Use of Criticism."

25. For a detailed discussion of these issues, see Hagenbüchle, "Desire."

FURTHER READING

Guerin, Wilfred L. et al. *A Handbook of Critical Approaches to Literature.* New York: Oxford University Press, 1992.

Murfin, Ross C., ed. *Joseph Conrad's "Heart of Darkness": A Case Study in Contemporary Criticism.* New York: St. Martin's, 1989.

Roughley, Alan. *James Joyce and Critical Theory: An Introduction.* Ann Arbor: University of Michigan Press, 1992.

JONNIE GUERRA

Dickinson Adaptations in the Arts and the Theater

*A*daptations of Emily Dickinson's life and poetry in drama, dance, the visual arts, and music have been widespread in the United States throughout the twentieth century and are becoming so abroad. They open an important new avenue to a full understanding of Dickinson's reception and influence — to date one most scholars have bypassed in their studies. Yet Dickinson herself makes a convincing case for this approach. Both in her writings and in biographical accounts, the poet emerges as one keenly aware of the relation between composing poetry and creating other kinds of art or being audience to the work of other artists. The Dickinson corpus includes numerous poems in which metaphors connect writing poetry to artistic endeavors like ballet dancing, painting, and playing musical instruments. Moreover, to create a poem as witness to her appreciation for another artist was, for Dickinson, a common response — be it to reading Elizabeth Barrett Browning whose poetry "enchanted" her (P593) or to listening surreptitiously from the hallway as Mabel Loomis Todd sang and played the piano in the Homestead parlor. In fact, recent commentators argue provocatively that Dickinson's poetry records her frequent and subtle inspiration from art and literature she enjoyed.[1]

Contributing to the subject's significance are two additional facts: first, the variety of the creative projects Dickinson and her poems have inspired; and, second, that some of this century's most distinguished artists — for example, Aaron Copland, Joseph Cornell, Martha Graham, and Julie Harris — have produced or performed in memorable, internationally renowned works in tribute to Dickinson. The personal testimonies of these artists about the poet's influence and the art works themselves constitute a rich source to be mined by current and future Dickinson specialists.

Klaus Lubbers's study, *Emily Dickinson: The Critical Revolution* (1968), stands as the first evidence of scholarly attention to adaptations of Dickinson's life and poetry into other art forms. Although his analysis focused on the poet's critical and literary reception in the United States and England from 1862 to

1962, Lubbers dedicated a few pages of the appendix to commentary and a bibliography on dedicatory verse honoring Dickinson, musical settings of her poems, and novels and plays about her life. Such works, he argued, established "the non-critical acceptance" of Dickinson and her oeuvre by audiences other than academicians and journalists and should not be "underestimated" (217).

Lubbers deserves credit for preserving early adaptations from obscurity, but his discussion needs reevaluation in light of its overall brevity and statements that contradict fact. For instance, my own research on Susan Glaspell's *Alison's House*, a 1930 drama loosely based on Dickinson's biography, uncovered the error of Lubbers's conclusion that the play received the Pulitzer Prize as a mark of its success. In truth, *Alison's House* never achieved popularity with either audiences or critics, and the Pulitzer jury was criticized for its selection and even charged by one reviewer with "publishing its ignorance" (Atkinson 1).

Lubbers's insight that artistic adaptations deserve recognition as an important measure of Dickinson's influence and reception apparently failed to awaken other scholars to the subject's potential. Thus a challenge to researchers who wish to pursue this topic is the scarcity of bibliographical information. There exists no complete catalogue of the dramatic literature, choreography, or visual art created in response to Dickinson's life and poetry. Only the poet's influence on the musical world has been charted in detail, thanks to Carlton Lowenberg.

Lowenberg's *Musicians Wrestle Everywhere: Emily Dickinson and Music* (1992) presents a list of over 1,600 musical settings of Dickinson letters and poems by 276 composers. Each annotation covers publication and performance history as well as recording availability. The entries also include quotations from Lowenberg's personal correspondence and other sources to document Dickinson's influence on and meaning to individual composers. Worthy of more notice than it has received, *Musicians Wrestle Everywhere* not only removes a gap in Dickinson bibliography but also provides a model for future inventories of Dickinson-inspired art.

Until such tools appear, the *Emily Dickinson International Society Bulletin* may be the primary vehicle for disseminating information about artistic adaptations of the poet's life and work. Especially under the editorial leadership of Georgiana Strickland, brief essays on this topic, including interviews and performance reviews, have been a staple of the biannual publication. Features have included essays on the visual art of Will Barnet, Joseph Cornell, Lesley Dill, and Roni Horn; an analysis of the poet's influence on Jane Campion's film *The Piano;* and testimonies of contemporary poets to their share in the Dickinson legacy. Additionally, the *Bulletin's* coverage of Dickinson projects in Denmark and Great Britain not only confirms the success of Dickinson's voyage out of New England but also makes evident that the adaptation of the poet's life and work into other art forms has evolved to an international phenomenon.[2]

Scholars investigating Dickinson's reception by other artists will find enlightening commentary in primary and secondary source materials by and about well-known figures like Martha Graham and Aaron Copland. Less predictable to study are the adaptations of artists with local rather than national or international reputations, especially those by artists outside the United States. Many recent works are unavailable in published form or in easily accessible exhibitions and productions. Correspondence and interviews with the artists themselves have proved to be the most reliable sources for locating biographical information about Dickinson's contemporary adapters and reviews of their work.

The remainder of this essay will survey adaptations of Dickinson's life and poetry within drama, dance, the visual arts, and music. Each section will examine several works inspired by Dickinson, including some that have earned local rather than national or international recognition, and also will highlight traditions unique to the individual art forms. To balance the independent histories, a few comments about general trends seem in order first.

One trend is that adaptations of Dickinson's life and poetry signal a collaborative effort. This collaboration occurs between the dead poet and the living artist as well as between their "texts" and often also involves biographers, other artists, and/or performers. In some instances, artists come by their interest in Dickinson indirectly: encountering an art work she previously influenced leads them to seek out a biography or her poems and then to create their own tributes, sometimes in a different art form.

Second, testimonies of the creators foreground their strong personal identification with Dickinson. Some describe their attraction to the poet in terms of her "Americanness," whereas others identify specifically with Dickinson's New England heritage. They also may cite an affinity with aspects of her personality or life style. Especially for women artists, regardless of field, Dickinson is memorialized as an inspiring role model. Often, too, women artists express their identification with Dickinson as a symbol not simply of female creativity but also of the female struggle to create.

Third, adaptations in the arts and theater have continued to reflect the views of her early biographers, editors, and critics. Thus the trend has been to reinforce what contemporary scholars tell us are misconceptions about Dickinson, especially the powerful romantic legends that have shaped the poet's reception at home and abroad. Artistic adaptations also have been influenced by the thematic categories proposed for the poems in the 1890s and remaining, for much of the twentieth century, a key factor in critical and editorial

approaches to Dickinson's work. The sophisticated readings that have radically revised and enriched the scholarly community's understanding of Dickinson and her poetry may take decades to filter down into popular conception,
and their impact on the poet's future reception by other artists is open to
speculation. It may be that the simplification of her life and work will prove
necessary to the creative collaboration between Dickinson and her adapters.

Fourth, individual Dickinson poems are often a featured part of the artistic
adaptations. Impersonating Dickinson, actresses perform her poems and letters within the context of dramatic works. Choreographers combine the voice
of a narrator with movements that enact the meaning of the words being
spoken. Musical settings and visual art adaptations act as frames within which
an audience experiences the language of individual poems in innovative ways.[3]
Despite such value, the focus on single poems rather than the entire corpus
may contribute to the simplified conceptions of Dickinson that dominate this
area of her reception.

Finally, although adaptations of Dickinson generally do not portray the
complexities of her life and poetry, many individual works — for example, Martha Graham's *Letter to the World* and Aaron Copland's *Twelve Poems of Emily
Dickinson* — have won acclaim as exemplars of particular artistic forms and
techniques. If some works related to Dickinson have earned presentation primarily to intellectuals and connoisseurs in the world's elite concert halls, theaters, and museums, others have been widely displayed or performed for the
public at large in local settings: quilt shows, community theaters, and high-
school auditoriums, to name a few. Taken as a whole, the vast array of creative
responses to her life and writings demonstrates Dickinson's broad appeal
to diverse audiences in terms of age, gender, class, country of origin, and
artistic taste.

DRAMA

Plays about Emily Dickinson made their debut on the Broadway stage in the
1930s. Joseph Mersand associated this decade with a "sudden vogue for biographical plays" (93), a trend that coincided with the appearance of several
critical as well as theatrical biographies devoted to Dickinson. Indeed, plays
about the poet have tended to follow on the heels of significant publication
events in Dickinson studies and to adapt academic theories into dramatic
formats. For example, reading Genevieve Taggard's *Life and Mind of Emily
Dickinson* (1930) is thought to have inspired Susan Glaspell to write *Alison's
House*. *Brittle Heaven* (1935), jointly authored by Vincent York and Frederick
Pohl, was indebted to Josephine Pollitt's *Emily Dickinson: The Human Background of Her Poetry* (1930).[4] A decade later, Dorothy Gardner's *Eastward in*

Eden: The Love Story of Emily Dickinson (1949) had its source in George Frisbie Whicher's *This Was a Poet: A Critical Biography of Emily Dickinson* (1938). All three plays perpetuate the speculation of Dickinson biographies about the identity of the man with whom the poet allegedly experienced a thwarted love relationship and make this romantic loss the central incident of her life. All also construct views of Dickinson's creativity that espouse its compensatory role when she failed to marry and sustained disappointments in other life arenas.

Despite the limitations of such portrayals, the plays merit contemporary scrutiny for what they reveal about Dickinson's early reception. If critics have identified Taggard's biography as the springboard for Glaspell's invention of the character of Alison Stanhope in *Alison's House*, they have ignored or failed to recognize the playwright's skepticism about Taggard's speculations.[5] Although the poet's family refused Glaspell permission either to use the Dickinson name or to quote from the poetry, stock traits of the Dickinson myth characterize Alison, and recognizable allusions to Dickinson's poems and poetic ideas also appear. Perhaps as a result of Glaspell's failure to gain the cooperation of Dickinson's family for her dramatic project, the main plot line develops the conflicts among family members and between the family and representatives of "the world" over who should control the story of Alison's life and the publication of her work. Notably, Glaspell sets the play after Alison's death and capitalizes on her absence from the stage.[6] At one time or another, all of the characters — the cast includes a scholar and a poet-journalist as well as family members — assert their authority as interpreters of Alison's life and the destiny she would have desired for her poems. Their interpretations are self-serving, partial, and conflicting. Alison eludes them as Dickinson does her biographers and readers. Ultimately, Glaspell's play insists, such attempts to derive the meaning of Alison's (and by extension Dickinson's) life and creative identity from a failed romance are unreliable.

Like *Alison's House*, *Brittle Heaven* and *Eastward in Eden* are family dramas. In both, lines from actual poems and letters are used, and the Dickinson character appears on stage, spotlighted within a romantic plot that culminates with the melodramatic spectacle of her emotional devastation. As the final curtain falls in *Brittle Heaven*, Dickinson lies on the floor, her collapse prompted by the news of Major Edward Hunt's death. According to Pollitt's theory, Dickinson had renounced her love for Hunt in deference to his wife, her childhood friend — Helen Fiske Hunt (later Jackson). *Eastward in Eden* similarly climaxes when a messenger arrives and announces the death of Dickinson's "beloved." Gardner, however, adopted Whicher's theory and presented the Reverend Charles Wadsworth as the person Dickinson loved. Unlike *Alison's House*, neither play questions the validity of the biographical view it showcases. Gardner's play does establish some slight dramaturgical originality with a dream scene that recalls a common motif of Dickinson's love poetry, the imagined union between herself and an unnamed "other" in Immortality. Certainly, the image of Dickinson as a woman whose intellectual gifts magnetically attract strong men, which each play foregrounds, contrasts sharply with critics' portrayal of the poet as a writer whose intellectual deficiencies marred her literary accomplishment. Dickinson scholars also should be interested to assess the treatments of the poet's family members, of her interaction with them, and of blatant departures from fact such as Austin's portrayal as a Civil War veteran in *Brittle Heaven.*[7]

The most significant play about Dickinson to be written and produced in the twentieth century is William Luce's *Belle of Amherst,* which premiered in 1976, two years after the publication of Richard Sewall's biography. The play has been credited, probably justly, with having "had more impact on public awareness of the poet than anything since the original publication of the poems" (Strickland 1).[8] Undoubtedly, Julie Harris, Emily Dickinson, and Luce's construct, "the Belle of Amherst," *have* become conflated in the public mind. This may be due less to the impressive Broadway run—a total of 117 performances and an unprecedented fifth Tony award for Harris—than to the subsequent presentation of *The Belle of Amherst,* in edited version, again starring Harris, as a public television special. Additionally, Luce's play—in the original English as well as in translation—has enjoyed tremendous popularity with actresses and audiences in amateur and professional theaters around the world.

That reputation alone justifies some serious charges against the work's biographical representation of Dickinson. The monodrama offers a circumscribed view of the poet's life, narrowing the spectator's attention to focus on a "Dickinson" defined exclusively within domestic space. What is problematic in the script is that Luce chose to emphasize Dickinson's homemaking talents like baking, perhaps to compensate for the eccentricities of her story: her reclusiveness, unmarried status, and unwomanly ambition to write poetry.

Equally troubling are the number and type of personal failures from which Luce weaves together his view. Although the play does not employ a strictly chronological format, the sequence of episodes establishes a linearity within which cause–effect relations are unavoidably implied. Thus, as in its dramatic predecessors, *The Belle of Amherst* connects the fact that Dickinson became a poet to her "failure" within the courtship-marriage plot conventionally used to narrate women's lives. On stage, Luce's "Dickinson" worries about her attractiveness to men, speaks apologetically and wistfully about why she did not marry, defensively assures the audience that she *did* have suitors, and enacts with wrenching emotion her final meeting with Wadsworth, whom this interpretation, like *Eastward in Eden*, posits as the person she addressed as "Master."

The episodes that shift the dramatic focus from the woman to the poet also are vexing, for they deny Dickinson control over her life as a writer. A case in point is Luce's portrayal of Dickinson's 1870 meeting with Thomas Wentworth Higginson. The scene of encounter bears little resemblance to the one described in Higginson's well-known letter to his wife but is the playwright's fabrication to substantiate his personal view that Dickinson was eager to be published and courted Higginson through correspondence for that purpose. Perhaps Luce meant to jar the audience with the elaborate irony, given her twentieth-century fame, of Higginson's "failure" to appreciate Dickinson's poetic style. But what is actually witnessed on stage — Harris/Dickinson's devastation, the squelching of a female author's ambition — leaves a more powerful impression on spectators than any implied condemnation of Higginson's taste. This effect is especially strong in the television drama, in which Higginson's judgment is not tempered, as it was in the original script, by juxtaposing it with the poet's revelation, in an aside to the audience, that Helen Hunt Jackson respected her literary gifts and encouraged Dickinson to share her poetry with the world. While most Dickinson scholars recognize the limitations of Luce's dramatization, the general public has accepted the distorted presentation as a fact of literary history.

A final concern about Luce's work arises from his use of the poems themselves. Reviews of the original production unanimously praised Harris for her performance of Dickinson's poetry. For example, a New York theater critic wrote that, as Harris began "Because I could not stop for Death" (P712) in the production he attended, a woman seated near him "made a sound that was half gasp, half sighing approval" (Kerr 5). Yet the reductive understanding that results from linking the poems to specific events in Dickinson's life is disturbing. If the play offers a misleading and too simplistic explanation for the poet's enigmatic existence, it also diminishes the poetry, promoting biographical meanings that are unsubstantiated.

Whatever its flaws, *The Belle of Amherst* has succeeded in making Dickinson familiar to audiences who otherwise never might have been engaged by her life and poetry. For example, a translated version of *The Belle of Amherst* was the centerpiece of an interdisciplinary project, *Emily Dickinson Live*, which toured Denmark in 1991.[9] Reflecting on her impersonation of Dickinson within the Luce vehicle, an American actress shared that "[r]epeatedly audience members have told me after seeing the play that they felt they knew Emily personally, that they wanted to read more of Emily's poetry, that they felt as if they had peeked into her brilliant mind or spent an evening in her parlor" (Loeschke 128). *The Belle of Amherst* also has been the impetus for a series of one-woman performance pieces about the poet. Today, quite literally, actresses portray Dickinson in cities and towns from coast to coast in the United States and in at least one European country.[10]

DANCE

Dance is an artistic arena in which adaptations of Emily Dickinson's life and poetry have been rare. Yet that Martha Graham, grande dame of twentieth-century dance, choreographed and then performed in a major work dedicated in the poet's honor has secured the importance of the medium for consideration. In Graham's own career, the 1940 work, *Letter to the World*, represented a turning point. Convinced that modern dancers had alienated their audiences "through grimness of theme and a nontheatrical approach" (qtd. in McDonagh 148), Graham used the occasion of *Letter*'s New York premiere to announce a new theatrical direction for her choreography.

Lauded for its dramatic intensity and innovative movement, *Letter to the World* stands as one of Graham's signature pieces. When Graham died in 1991, newspaper memorials regularly reprinted *Kick* (1940), the most famous of Barbara Morgan's photographs of Graham performing as Dickinson in *Letter*.[11] Morgan captured Graham, costumed in the white dress of Dickinson legend, in a movement emblematic of the extraordinary strength, control, and balance demanded by her revolutionary technique. Graham leans forward from a standing position, her right leg as fulcrum, her left leg extended and elevated behind her in a sickle shape. Added theatricality and emotional quality result from the positioning of Graham's arms and face. Her left arm is raised parallel to her torso, the hand tense and cupped; her right bends at the elbow, the hand flexed forward supporting her head. Graham's hair is drawn back, calling attention to her chiseled features and consciously lengthened throat. In its dynamic stillness, its sculpted poise, the image of Graham as Dickinson remains hauntingly memorable.

In *Letter to the World*, Graham reached beyond realism to express the spirit and meaning of Emily Dickinson's life and poetry. Using the poet's own words to provide "narrative continuity" (McDonagh 147), *Letter* interprets Dickinson's multifaceted interior life and struggle to reconcile the competing demands of her world and her art. Graham conceived the role of Dickinson to be played by two women, a dancing Emily and a speaking Emily. Other major characters included the Lover, who symbolized all the world's attractions rather than a specific person; March, Graham's personification of "Dickinson's frolicsome wit" (de Mille 242); and the Ancestress, seen as representative "of Puritan conscience, of Emily's austere heritage, of the 'postponeless creature,' Death" (*Harper's Bazaar*, April 1941, 81). The ballet follows the two Emilys

from youthful frolic through a series of worldly temptations, losses, and renunciations to the climax when the dancing Emily embraces her solitary fate
to be a poet.

Graham's choice of Dickinson as the subject of a major work reflects her
interest in and commitment to American themes. In *Blood Memory*, her autobiography, Graham also implies a strong personal attachment to the poet: she
alludes to the poems and letters with the kind of easy familiarity that suggests
a long, congenial acquaintance with Dickinson.[12] The poet may have represented a creative foremother for Graham — someone, like herself, whose
independent spirit had a transforming effect on the art form within which
she worked. Or it may be, as Agnes de Mille argues somewhat romantically,
that *Letter* expresses Graham's identification with Dickinson because of her
own growing personal belief in the "artist as self-immolater who gives up
everything in ordinary life to find the lonely goals which are the essence of
truth" (243).

Although it is possible to recover the basic plot of the ballet from accounts
by Graham's biographers, the single existing film of *Letter* made in 1973 is
unavailable to the general public because of Graham Company and union
restrictions (Brooks 62). The original version danced by Graham herself has
been partially preserved in photographs. In one section of *Martha Graham:
Sixteen Dances in Photographs* (1941), Barbara Morgan has arranged a series of
images, together with excerpts from Dickinson's poetry, to distill the essence
of *Letter* (see 113–25).[13] Although Morgan's photographs magnificently highlight specific moments from the production of *Letter*, they cannot repli-
cate fully the dynamic performance by Graham that witnesses of the dance
recollect. For example, Agnes de Mille's memory of Graham as Dickinson remained so vivid that she claimed the experience, even in retrospect,
"flood[s] . . . the heart" (245).

That Graham's work was acclaimed as a masterpiece may have discouraged
other choreographers from selecting Dickinson as a subject, for only a few
other dance pieces connected to the poet have come to light. For the Royal
Danish Ballet Company, Warren Spears choreographed a ballet called *Rowing
in Eden* (1987), in which the second and third movements are based on Dickinson poems (P249 and P829). Another contemporary choreographer credited
with a Dickinson work is Heinz Poll, artistic director of the Ohio Ballet and
creator of *Called Back. — Emily* (1984). Poll explores Dickinson's enigmatic
final message to her Norcross cousins in a work that combines spoken poetry
and movement, as did Graham's, to portray the personal turmoil that preceded
Dickinson's discovery of freedom and beauty in solitude. Poll's choreography
similarly seems derivative of Graham's in its use of two Emilys — one to recite
the poems and one to interpret them in dance — and in supporting characters

that resemble the Lover and the Ancestress of *Letter.* Whatever the limits of its originality, the ballet earned favorable reviews for both its Ohio premiere and subsequent performance as part of the Jacob's Pillow Summer Dance Festival in Massachusetts. Critics praised its "emotional resonance" (Rosenberg B5) as well as Poll's success "in evoking a literary figure through dance" (Christman 1). More recently, in the Department of Dance at Randolph-Macon Woman's College in Virginia, Dickinson's poetry has provided an inspirational source for the choreographic experiments of student majors. Seven original works based on individual Dickinson poems premiered there in December 1995.[14]

VISUAL ARTS

Adaptations of Emily Dickinson in the visual arts have been numerous and fascinatingly diverse. During the latter half of the twentieth century alone, the poet has inspired painters, sculptors, and folk artists — primarily Americans — to undertake projects in her homage.[15] The tributes range from paintings of the Homestead and portraits of Dickinson based on the existing daguerreotype to illustrated editions of the poetry and monuments in several media that create analogues to Dickinson's life or poems. The most innovative adaptations, a representative sampling of which were showcased in the 1997 exhibition, "Language as Object: Emily Dickinson and Contemporary Art," at the Mead Art Museum at Amherst College, involve collaboration between the artist's visual images and Dickinson's words.[16] In technique, they invite comparisons with her figural strategies.

The pictorial features and emotional content of Dickinson's poems have been a stimulus for illustrators. Two examples will suffice to suggest the styles of book illustration that have been produced.[17] In *For Love of Her* (1974), Walter Stein presents thirty-two Dickinson poems in conjunction with drawings that, in his words, function as "visual metaphors" (Dickinson, *For Love* 10). The drawings are either in black and white or in color, and Stein's purpose is to complement the poems with images that "add dimension and variety, familiarity and surprise to the reader's experience [of Dickinson]" (11). In subject, they underscore the artist's interpretation of the poet's attachment to the natural world and its small, homely glories. Notable for their simplicity and precision, Stein's drawings seem intentionally to emulate Dickinson's "manner of distillation after long contemplation" (11).

In contrast to Stein's coffee-table book is Margaret Taylor's *From Amherst to Cashmere* (1986), published in an exclusive edition of fifty copies, signed and numbered by the artist, and offered at $1,600 each. An Amherst-based painter, Taylor was drawn to the passion in Dickinson's work, especially in the poet's color and landscape imagery. Taylor first spent three years "walking and looking [in Amherst and the surrounding countryside] and sketching . . . drafting . . . proofing and reworking [her images]" (Wright 24) and then two more years printing and collaborating with other artists on the book's design and craft-based production process. The end result is a silk-bound volume, hand-painted on German paper, and designed to open in the accordian-like fashion of many Chinese or Japanese books.

Taylor's collection features twelve Dickinson poems and ten exquisite color etchings, each a miniature of about two by three inches. The etchings and poems are ordered to portray the cycle of the year. In both, the interplay of color and light predominates as the defining characteristic of the progression of seasons. For example, the fifth poem, "A something in a summer's Day" (P122), records Dickinson's awestruck memory of brilliant summer noons with these lines: "A depth — an Azure — a perfume / Transcending exstasy [*sic*]." The illustrative etching—a view from the Hadley fields near Northampton, the Holyoke Range on the right and Amherst beyond—represents Taylor's visual rendering to "capture this description—the clear light, the blue shadows of summer" ("Painting Emily Dickinson's Poetry" 68). In every case, Taylor's etchings highlight and reinforce the emotional resonances of the Dickinson poems they accompany. Taken together, the poems and etchings vividly chronicle the changing beauty of the natural world and, at the same time, paradoxically impress on the spectator the reality of its evanescence. Primarily a collector's item, *From Amherst to Cashmere* has earned Taylor local acclaim and special acknowledgment among Dickinson scholars in both the United States and Japan.[18]

Most renowned among twentieth-century visual artists for whom Dickinson has been an inspirational figure is the American assemblage artist, Joseph Cornell. Cornell celebrated Dickinson in works he described as "box sculptures" or "box constructions." Using collage, painted interiors, grids, and arrangements of small objects or props, Cornell constructed the complex symbolic settings that give his boxes their distinguishing signature. Art historians already have examined Dickinson's significance as a source for Cornell's work, with varying interpretations of the nature and extent of her influence.

Dore Ashton, for example, has written about Cornell's strong identification with Dickinson and demonstrated their many affinities, ranging from their mutual love of nature and gardens to their similarly reclusive life styles and secretive work habits. Ashton uses the fact that Cornell collected books by and about Dickinson to support the speculation that the artist "very probably knew the poems by heart" (39). Some boxes like *Toward the "Blue Peninsula" (for Emily Dickinson)* (1953) and *An Image for 2 Emilies* (1954) obviously allude to the poet by name, but Ashton proposes that others, like *Deserted Perch* (1949), also should be recognized as possible "visual analogues" (43) to Dickinson works. In particular, Ashton links Cornell's persistent iconography of absence to Dickinson's verbal preoccupation with the theme and generalizes that the artist's constructions, like those of the poet in language, are "cryptic" and "never quite graspable" (43).

Carter Ratcliff and Dickran Tashjian also have explored Cornell's relationship to Dickinson and the boxes he dedicated to her. To date, Tashjian's work, *Joseph Cornell: Gifts of Desire* (1992), offers the most comprehensive treatment of the artist's collaboration with the poet and is noteworthy for its meticulous research of Cornell's diaries and of the marginalia found in books housed in his personal library. According to Tashjian, Cornell studied with scholarly care nearly a dozen biographical and critical works about the poet during the course of completing his two explicit Dickinson projects. Tashjian quotes, from the artist's diary, Cornell's reflections about this reading and its influence on his creation of "gifts" to Dickinson. For example, in the diary, Cornell reveals the impact that Rebecca Patterson's *Riddle of Emily Dickinson* (1951) had on his understanding of the poet. In fact, diary entries indicate that the visual motifs of *Toward the "Blue Peninsula"* and *An Image for 2 Emilies* may encode Cornell's sympathetic reaction to Patterson's theory about Dickinson's sexuality and unrequited passion for Kate Scott Anthon. As Tashjian shows persuasively, the meaning of the iconography within the boxes (the abandoned aviary setting of the former and the grid structure of the latter—with a blue glass marble centered inside a chimney lamp in each of the twelve cubicles) is enriched when the images are traced to Cornell's intimate knowledge of passages in Dickinson's letters and poetry.

No one has yet compiled a definitive list of Cornell works influenced by the poet, and the artist's practice of duplicating his boxes may produce confusion and dating difficulties that will exacerbate this task for scholars.[19] If Cornell specialists have contributed most analyses of the collaboration to date, essays by Maryanne Garbowsky and David Porter promise that Dickinson scholars have fresh insight to add to the discussion.

A more recent example of Dickinson's inspirational power and collaborative reach across time and artistic form can be found in the work of New York–based artist Lesley Dill. In 1989 Dill began creating works she called "poem sculptures," many of which made enlarged body parts and uninhabited clothing their main imagery. Dill's original Dickinson project generated both freestanding sculpture and relief. Her materials included wire, paper, wood, cloth, thread, rice paper, tea, ink, horsehair, silk, copper, gold leaf, paint, charcoal, and silver print. Most important, all incorporated lines or the complete text of a Dickinson poem. As Dill explains, "In each of my sculptures, I tried to knit the poem into the emotional metaphor of their separate personae" (*Lesley Dill* n.p.).

Interestingly, Dill completed *Black Suit* (1989–90), the first sculpture in the series, before she ever encountered Dickinson's work. Receiving a volume of Dickinson's poetry as a gift convinced Dill that the poet's words were exactly what she needed to infuse the suit with human emotion and led her to embed "I many times thought Peace had come" (P739) into the "being" of the sculpture. Since then, Dill has developed more than a hundred art works in collaboration with Dickinson. In addition to sculptures, she now produces prints and cloth banners as well as performance pieces. Dill's reliance on the poet's words "for their embodiment of psychological states of despair and euphoria" (*Lesley Dill*) continues, but the images of her recent works also challenge viewers to explore issues of sexuality, gender, and race.

Dill has expressed her special interest in specific Dickinson texts by producing multiple works of art that invite viewers to consider several responses to a single poem. For example, for the 1994 DaDa Ball, Dill created a three-tiered paper wedding dress on which she hand-stamped the complete text of "The Soul has Bandaged Moments" (P512).[20] The same poem provided inspiration for several performance pieces, including *Speaking Dress* (1996). In this fourteen-minute work, mysterious figures — presumably Dill's interpretation of the poet's "Ghastly Fright" — chant Dickinson's poem as they approach a female and then ritualistically strip off her paper dress. Poem 512 also inspired a series of photolithographs. In one titled *Word Made Flesh* (1994), Dill's subject is a seated naked woman, photographed from behind. Written vertically down her spine is the poem's opening line.[21]

Dickinson's poem 351 similarly has been the catalyst for several Dill treatments. *Poem Hands* (1994) is a powerful relief: from two wooden hands hang cloth letters strung together in a semicircle to spell out the opening two lines "I felt my life with both my hands / To see if it was there —." A later work titled *Poem Hands (Double), "Palpe mi vida, con dos mi manos"* (1995) features the same lines and imagery of hands — this time on side-by-side cloth banners that cascade from ceiling to floor. On each, Dill has imprinted Dickinson's words directly on the fingers and palms of the down-stretched hands. Below the fingers, the two-line Dickinson excerpt is repeated, but Dill suggests new meanings with her Spanish translation of the text.[22]

Although the number of Dill's Dickinson-inspired works makes a summary impossible, a few additional examples should confirm their range and variety. *Blue Circulatory System* (1994), constructed from wire and paper, resembles both a human form in metamorphosis and the intricate branchwork of a tree. Into this sculpture Dill has incorporated the incantatory first stanza of "To be alive — is Power" (P677). A free-standing wooden sculpture, *Poem Tree* (1994), appears spindly and barren, an ironic visual contrast to the optimistic spirit of the carved message that rises on its trunk: "I think To Live — may be a Bliss / To those who dare to try — " (P646). Dill's *Copper Poem Dress* (1994), a relief, is made of copper letters stitched to form a female figure wearing a very full dress. Her preposterously long arms end in hands, noticeably different in size, that dangle unevenly below her hemline. The letters themselves lack uniformity in size and shape, a technique with which Dill "physically captures the compression, reserve and sudden propulsion of Dickinson's phrasing" (Koplos 137). Once spectators decipher the sculpture, they are able to read the complete text of "This World is not Conclusion" (P501). Experiencing the poem within Dill's humorous context offers viewers a heightened appreciation of its playful observations on the question of immortality.[23]

Overall, Dill's art has much in common with Dickinson's poems in theme and technique. Like Dickinson's, Dill's work probes the boundaries between inner and outer, spirit and flesh, through figural strategies and tremendous wit. In particular, like Dickinson, Dill often adeptly uses synecdoche: an isolated body part comes to stand for the whole and, in that way, to intensify the viewer's experience of human fragility and vulnerability. Certainly, too, Dill's representations of empty clothing resonate with the white dress that, for Dickinson lovers, is the poet's quintessential sign.

Dickinson has attracted practitioners not only in the so-called high arts but also in what traditionally are regarded as women's crafts — china painting and textile art such as sewing, embroidery, and quilting. The most well-known as well as controversial craft project with a connection to Dickinson is Judy Chicago's *Dinner Party*, first exhibited in San Francisco in 1979 and subsequently seen around the world by more than a million viewers. Conceived as "a proud affirmation of the female presence in Western civilization" (Chicago 1), the work required five years and the collaboration of hundreds of artisans to complete. At regular intervals on each of the forty-eight-foot sides of a triangular table are positioned thirteen custom-made place settings. As Chicago's catalog essay explains, "each of the thirty-nine women [invited to dinner] is symbolized by a specially designed and painted porcelain plate which is placed on a decorated fabric runner representing the woman's cultural and historic period" (3). The names of an additional 999 women are inscribed on the tile floor on which the table sits.

Chicago chose Emily Dickinson to embody "women's struggle to find their own voice" (8), and, at the dinner party, the poet is seated as the representative for twenty-six other American and European women writers, social reformers, and educational pioneers. For Dickinson's place setting, Chicago sought imagery that would express the poet's incongruous situation as a creative genius living during a historical period whose conventions were stifling to female power and creativity.[24] Chicago designed the commemorative Dickinson plate with a strong, carved, vulva-like center surrounded by raised "layers of immobile lace" (91). The selection of lace as a dominant motif reflects that, when Chicago thought of the Victorian expectation for women to contain their passions and curtail their ambitions, she "envisioned lace: lace collars and cuffs on . . . dresses, lace doilies on all the chairs, lace cloths on the tables, and lace edgings on . . . demure nightgowns" (91). Heightening the sense of the repressive cultural milieu in which the poet lived and wrote is the antique lace runner decorated with elaborate ribbon embroidery on which the Dickinson place setting is presented. On the other hand, by painting the plate in fleshy pink tones, Chicago intended to invest Dickinson with "a sensuality that nineteenth-century women were not supposed to have" (91). The iconography, like that of all the plates, evokes the butterfly form, a favorite image of both Dickinson and Chicago and one they similarly associated with self-expression and freedom.[25]

Although less well-known than *The Dinner Party*, the art quilts of Ann Kowaleski offer an equally unusual and dramatic tribute to Dickinson. A Michigan textile artist whose quilts have achieved regional and national recognition in gallery shows, competitions, and publications, Kowaleski developed an interest in Dickinson through the roundabout route of another artist's creative production. A lifelong love of dance led Kowaleski first to the discovery of Martha Graham's affinity with the poet and then to a strong personal identification with Dickinson. For Kowaleski, Dickinson's solitary existence "was a source of knowing that this is what one must do to do the work one loves" (17 Oct. 1994, personal communication).

Since 1984 when Kowaleski began a series of pictorial "dancing" and "performing" quilts — also designated by the artist as "stage scenes" — she has made images of Dickinson and/or the poet's words narrative features of three quilts. The largest, most arresting work, titled *The Spirit: Graham, Dickinson, and O'Keeffe* (1990), functions as a visual diary to honor women Kowaleski respects "as strong American artists and inspirational people [who did] things out of the 'normal' realm of expectation" (17 Oct. 1994, personal communication; see Lemmon 4). The quilt measures forty-five by ninety-eight inches and exhibits colorful mixed fabrics, embellishments, and a variety of quilting techniques. In representing the women, Kowaleski uses dancing as a powerful metaphor for the genius that animated their creative work and linked their lives. Dickinson is placed in the middle of the triptych to show her influence on both Graham and O'Keeffe. Kowaleski's visual rendering purposefully makes the poet "look different from any way she ever looked in her life" (26 Sept. 1994, phone interview). Attired in a full-body leotard made of a multicolored flowered fabric, Dickinson appears to be dancing wildly as pages of her poems fly or float around her.[26] For the representation of Graham, who is portrayed on Dickinson's left, Kowaleski was more conventional, choosing to reproduce the pose captured by Morgan in *Kick* and described earlier in this essay. Flanking Dickinson on the opposite side, Kowaleski's depiction of Georgia O'Keeffe is based on a photograph taken by Alfred Stieglitz and emphasizes the painter's "youth and strength that persisted throughout her life" (26 July 1995, phone interview). O'Keeffe balances on one foot as her right arm hugs an enlarged jack-in-the-pulpit and the other lifts a skull and antlers over her head and against the background of a blue sky. Collectively, Kowaleski's images foreground the solitary nature of the individual creative life and, at the same time, the possibility for comradeship and solidarity that exists among artists across time and discipline because they share in "the spirit."

Music

In music, adaptations of Emily Dickinson have proliferated, beginning with the 1896 publication of Etta Parker's *Three Songs*, one of which sets to music the text of "Have you got a Brook in your little heart" (P136). The excellent introduction to musical adaptations that Lowenberg provides in *Musicians Wrestle Everywhere* validates composer Alan Leichtling's view that Dickinson's poems "have been an important literary staple of the musical world [without which] a sizable amount of American vocal music would not exist" (Leichtling letter of 22 Dec. 1990, qtd. in Lowenberg 66). Among those influenced by Dickinson, Lowenberg identifies American, European, and Asian composers of both genders, including four Pulitzer Prize winners — Ernst Bacon, Aaron Copland, Leon Kirchner, and George Perle — as well as a number of composers whose settings have achieved performance but not publication or recording.[27] Moreover, Lowenberg's research demonstrates a steady increase in interest in the poet. As his bibliography documents, "what [began] as a trickle of Dickinson settings throughout the 1920s became a stream in the 1930s and 1940s [and then] a flood after 1950" (xxvi).

The musical works inspired by Dickinson are astonishing not only for their quantity but also for the variations in performance medium they encompass. Although the most typical settings are those composed for piano and solo voice, even within that category the type of voice ranges from male to female and from highest to lowest. Other works call for multiple solo voices or a chorus. Although some settings are purely instrumental pieces, most employ both vocal and instrumental components. Lowenberg has located settings that feature unusual individual instruments like the electric keyboard, the marimba, and the viola da gamba, as well as some that are intended for performance by instrumental ensembles or even a full orchestra. Many composers have created settings for a selection of Dickinson poems and then arranged them into a song cycle or other type of collective work. In addition, some have used Dickinson poems as the basis for ballet scores (Hunter Johnson), operas (Vivian Fine and Jan Meyerowitz), incidental music for dramatic works (Andre Singer), and rock music (Gerhard Pilz). Finally, on occasions of both public and private grief ranging from John F. Kennedy's assassination and the AIDS epidemic to the death of a child or a parent, composers have searched the Dickinson canon for the words to create songs of mourning and consolation.

Lowenberg has gathered illuminating material about what attracted individual composers to Dickinson. The commonly cited reasons reflect more often an appreciation for the poetry itself than a fascination with Dickinson's biography and its puzzles. Composers remark on her poems for their compactness, emotional urgency, challenging rhythms, vivid and sometimes fanciful imagery, and experimentation with consonant and vowel sounds. In explanation of the specific poems they have set to music, some composers also admit to being thematically driven in their selection. There are song cycles in which all poems relate to a single theme like death or love and, together, display the protean quality of the poet's attitude toward the subject. Poems that portray nature also have had appeal to composers, perhaps because Dickinson's delineation of nature's "voice" — the sounds of wind, storm, birds, bees, and sea — provides unusually rich opportunities for word painting.[28] Although choices by composers indicate clear favorites among the Dickinson canon, Lowenberg lists settings for 621 of Dickinson's poems and 33 of her letters. Moreover, as Lowenberg points out, "some composers have returned to Dickinson's works repeatedly — among them Ernst Bacon, Gloria Coates, Robert Convery, Arthur Farwell, Richard Hoyt, Ken Langer, and Leo Smit" (*Musicians* xxvi). Smit, whose Dickinson songs numbered eighty in 1991, claims that, since 1988 when he bought the *Complete Poems*, Dickinson "has been running [his] life" (letter of 24 May 1989, qtd. in Lowenberg 89). Although Smit has composed settings for several individual poems, most of his songs have been conceived as part of an ambitious series of five cycles collected under the manuscript title, *The Ecstatic Pilgrimage*.

The best-known work within the category of musical adaptations is Aaron Copland's *Twelve Poems of Emily Dickinson* (1951), composed for medium-high voice and piano and widely known as the *Dickinson Songs*.[29] In his autobiography, Copland discusses the creation of the song cycle between March 1949 and March 1950; its first performance on May 18, 1950, as part of the Sixth Annual Festival of Contemporary Music at Columbia University; and his later decision to orchestrate eight of the songs, an endeavor that occupied him from 1958 to 1970. Although several composers, including Ernst Bacon and Arthur Farwell, had been working on settings of Dickinson poems since early in the twentieth century, their works are not cited as an inspiring force by Copland, who even may have been unaware of their existence. It is possible, though nowhere documented, that Copland's decision to compose the Dickinson cy-cle was influenced by Graham, for their collaboration on the ballet *Appalachian Spring* (1944) occurred after her triumph with *Letter to the World* and before Copland embarked on his songs. In fact, Copland chose to set to music several of the same poems that Graham earlier had choreographed.

Even though the *Dickinson Songs* were not an immediate popular success, Copland's work has contributed to and perhaps even created interest in the poet. In the case of later American composers like Leo Smit and Anthony Iannaccone, a direct line of succession from Copland can be traced. On the international scene, the 1976 Danish publication of Copland's settings in translation may have sparked interest in Dickinson among Danish composers. Since then, both Erik Hojsgaard and Bent Sorensen have published Dickinson songs, and in 1994 the Reverend Niels Kjær presented an original church play, *Alting Har En Tid* [For Everything There Is a Season], that included some new musical settings of Dickinson poems by Martin Strange.

An avid poetry reader, Copland was drawn to Dickinson because there was "something about her personality and use of language that was fresh, precise, utterly unique — and very American" (Copland and Perlis 158). The *Dickinson Songs* began when he "fell in love" (158) with and set to music "Because I could not stop for Death" (P712).[30] As Copland continued to read Dickinson, set-tings for the song cycle "accumulated gradually" (158), and in no order, until he had completed a dozen. Then, he reports, "they all seemed to run to their right places" (158).[31] Although Copland chose to relate only two songs musi-cally and to forgo a title that would emphasize a theme, he was satisfied that the order of poems gave the twenty-eight-minute cycle a "cumulative effect" (159). Despite Copland's expressed preference to have the settings performed as a cycle, each song is written "to be complete in itself" (159). Frequently, in fact, singers have found the cycle's vocal range too demanding for their voices and elected to perform the settings individually or in smaller groupings than the original twelve.[32]

Copland's songs may well be the musical pieces best known and most be-loved among Dickinson enthusiasts, but, even so, little critical attention has been accorded them by scholars of the poet's work. Yet the settings that Cop-land and other composers have created constitute significant interpretive acts from which Dickinson's readers have much to learn. George Perle explains their value thus: "Out of all the possible ways of reading and interpreting a poem, the musical setting fixes just one. . . . Not only must it seem right, and seem so at once without seeming coercive and demanding, but it must go beyond this and elucidate the words" (Bialosky 862). Another composer, Joseph Jones, makes a more daring claim: "When we add music to verse, we see the poet's achievement in a new perspective. . . . [W]e are ready to explore the qualities in a poem that neither silent reading nor reading aloud will quite bring out. We now hear the poem . . . as never before" (qtd. in Lowenberg, *Musicians* xxviii). Copland's settings are remarkable for exactly this reason: they offer listeners the opportunity to hear the poet's words anew by framing them in musical contexts that heighten and refresh their dramatic and emotional power. In my own case, attending a Washington, D.C., performance of the *Dickinson Songs* enhanced my appreciation for "Nature — the Gentlest Mother is" (P790) and "Dear March — Come in — " (P1320), poems that Copland showed me were more richly nuanced and less sentimental than I had ever found them on my own. Nor have I read "Going to Heaven!" (P79) since without hearing the melisma that Copland used in setting that poem.

For Copland and a few other American composers, an analysis of their Dickinson settings has been the focus of a master's thesis or a doctoral dissertation, but almost no such commentary has found its way into print. It still remains to be seen what impact Lowenberg's *Musicians Wrestle Everywhere* will have on Dickinson scholarship. Thus far, there have been no comparative or evaluative studies of musical settings — either targeting the songs of several composers or considering different versions of a single poem.

CONCLUSION

Emily Dickinson predicted that, for poets whose work was lasting, the range of their reach and influence would be limitless: "Each Age a Lens / Disseminating their / Circumference — " (P883). The preceding overview of adaptations of Dickinson's life and poetry into drama, dance, the visual arts, and music demonstrates how aptly she characterized her own twentieth-century reception and influence among artists in many fields. Although Klaus Lubbers recommended as long ago as 1968 that Dickinson scholars regard artistic adaptations as an important gauge of the poet's reputation, until now this area of Dickinson studies has been almost totally neglected. As this survey also shows, Lubbers's inventory of adaptations no longer accurately reflects the reality of the poet's recognition outside of the academy, which has greatly expanded, as far as the number of artists for whom Dickinson has been an influence, the range of fields in which adaptations have been produced, and the evolution of artistic tributes from a national to an international phenomenon.

Among the contributions to Dickinson studies that would be especially valuable are bibliographies listing works created in the areas of drama, dance, and the visual arts and documenting performances and source materials available for further exploration. Other helpful projects would include interview essays with artists who have come under Dickinson's influence and more annotated catalogues of visual art works inspired by the poet similar to the one

Susan Danly produced to accompany the exhibition "Language as Object: Emily Dickinson and Contemporary Art." An interdisciplinary study of continuity and change in stage or visual art portrayals of Dickinson as a female author also might lead to a provocative essay or monograph. So many works in tribute to Dickinson have been collaborative ventures that further research on the people involved in their production and performance might turn up new testimony or insights about their creation. Finally, the role of artistic adaptations in enhancing Dickinson's international stature might be given a thorough assessment.

NOTES

1. See, in particular, Barton Levi St. Armand's *Emily Dickinson and Her Culture* (1984) and Judith Farr's *Passion of Emily Dickinson* (1992) for discussions of Dickinson's use of tropes from the art and literature of her day.

2. Dickinson plays written or adapted for production in Denmark are covered in the May/June 1991, May/June 1994, and May/June 1997 issues of the *EDIS Bulletin*. For a report on a multidisciplinary Dickinson festival in Plymouth, England, see the *EDIS Bulletin* for Nov./Dec. 1993.

3. Some contemporary artists purposely disrupt or complicate the viewer's ability to read the poetic texts incorporated into their art works. Through the use of three-dimensional form, color, contrasts in the size of letters within individual words, and/or the removal of line breaks or punctuation, these artists have focused attention on the physicality of Dickinson's words as objects in and of themselves.

4. Josephine Pollitt was married to Frederick Pohl.

5. Taggard's biography shared the 1930 limelight with that of Pollitt's, which proposed a different version of Dickinson's life and alleged failed romance. No doubt Glaspell was aware of the other biography and its conflicting interpretation as well as of the fact that Taggard's own speculations were based on the testimony of people who insisted on remaining anonymous. One subplot of *Alison's House* that has been virtually ignored in Glaspell criticism concerns Alison's nephew Ted and his Harvard English professor aptly surnamed "Styles." When Ted arrives on stage, his mission is to find out and provide Styles with intimate details about his aunt's life in exchange for a passing grade in an English course. When Ted's queries to family members produce no interesting gossip about Alison, he invents answers to include in his letter to Styles. On the one hand, Glaspell's subplot pokes fun at the academic profession, offering an astute critique of scholars who become obsessed with their subjects. At the same time, because the audience witnesses Ted as he commits lies about Alison to a written document that will legitimate their public repetition, Glaspell draws attention to the way distortions in literary history occur.

6. For another view of Alison Stanhope's absence from stage, see Helle 198–99.

7. In *Eastward in Eden*, Dickinson's mother is not on stage during the play, nor is she ever mentioned by the characters who do appear. Especially interesting to compare are the portrayals of the poet's relationships with her father, Susan Gilbert Dickinson, and Helen Hunt Jackson.

8. The success of *The Belle of Amherst* nationally and internationally argues for a

decided shift in the response to Dickinson by nonacademic audiences during the course of the century. Compare my comments here to Mersand's statement about the failure of *Brittle Heaven*: "A writer's works may be immortal yet his life on stage may be insufferably dull. Besides, there is the sad confession that the hundreds of thousands of spectators who are necessary to make a play successful are usually not the poetry-reading kind. Emily Dickinson's life ran for twenty-three performances, which probably exhausted the number of those who ever heard of her poetry" (114–15).

9. For my information about Dickinson's reception by artists in Denmark, I am indebted to the Reverend Niels Kjær. In a letter dated 12 Oct. 1994, he provided an annotated list of adaptations in the arts and theater to appear between 1985 and 1995.

10. The "Emily Dickinsons" present at the 1992 EDIS conference in Washington, D.C., were Agneta Bjorn (Odense, Denmark); Maravene Loeschke (Timonium, Md.); Ruth McRee (Seattle); Caroline Ryburn (New York); Camille Webb (Elgin, Ill.); and Belinda Heckler West (Belmont, Mass.). McRee, Ryburn, and West have developed one-woman performance pieces, drawing on Dickinson's poems and letters to dramatize and interpret her life. Given the popularity of *The Belle of Amherst*, I expect other "Emily Dickinsons" to be discovered both in the United States and in countries abroad. The Reverend Niels Kjær, for example, has written a one-woman play, *Brev Til Verden* [*Letter to the World*], that premiered in 1995. Inspired by John Burdett Payne's poem "Emily and Walt, Walt and Emily," it portrays "what actually happened that night Emily showed her face at [the] open poetry reading [imagined by Payne]" (12 Oct. 1994, personal communication). Additionally, the character of Emily Dickinson has made cameo appearances in two recent plays by United States authors. In Susan Sontag's *Alice in Bed*—a dramatic fantasy based on the life of Alice James—Dickinson and Margaret Fuller visit Alice for a tea party reminiscent of the "Mad Hatter's Tea Party" in Lewis Carroll's *Alice in Wonderland*. In Amy Freed's darkly comic *Psychic Life of Savages*, the character of Dickinson returns from the dead in search of a soulmate from among the coterie of American confessional poets—including Sylvia Plath and Robert Lowell—on whom the play focuses.

11. See Morgan 123, or plate 13 in Danly (89).

12. In 1981, some four decades after *Letter*, Graham drew the title for another dance, *Acts of Light*, from a letter Emily Dickinson wrote to Mrs. John Howard Sweetser in 1884: "Thank you for all the Acts of Light which beautified a summer now past to it's reward" (L951).

13. According to Morgan's son Lloyd, there exists a "substantial file of images" of *Letter to the World*, including additional photographs rejected for the book, in the Willard and Barbara Morgan Archives in Dobbs Ferry, N.Y. In a December 1995 phone conversation, Mr. Morgan described his mother as a "spiritual sister with Martha Graham" and stressed the collaborative nature of *Sixteen Dances in Photographs*. He also attributed Morgan's facile coordination of Dickinson's words with Graham's imagery to the fact that his mother was herself a poet and a "very literary person." For another attempt to capture the essence of Graham's *Letter to the World*, see Charlotte Trowbridge's drawings in *Dance Drawings of Martha Graham* (1945).

14. Since its founding, the Department of Dance at Randolph-Macon Woman's College has enjoyed strong ties with Martha Graham. A succession of former Graham Company members—Eleanor Struppa, Helen McGehee (who performed as one of the children in *Letter*), and, presently, Pamela Risenhoover—have headed the department and promoted Graham-based instructional techniques. Students with choreographic

settings of Dickinson poems to their credit include Faydra Breinig, 1996 (P666); Julie Fleming, 1996 (P928 and P1035); Laura McManamy, 1997 (P230); Mary Beth Resler, 1996 (P764 and P1304); and Jennifer Uzzi, 1996 (P303).

15. Frank Hammershoj of Denmark and Mariko Hagiwara of Japan are notable exceptions. As part of the 1991 interdisciplinary project, *Emily Dickinson Live*, Hammershoj created fourteen oil paintings in response to individual Dickinson poems. These became an integral part of the stage setting for the Danish production of *The Belle of Amherst*, which premiered in Odense and then toured throughout Denmark. Hagiwara describes her abstract expressionist paintings as "inspired by Emily Dickinson's poems" but clarifies that "they are *not* illustrations" (Sept. 1995, personal communication). Since 1992, her works regularly have been selected by the Modern Art Association for exhibition at the Tokyo Metropolitan Art Museum. Hagiwara has won awards for two 1995 paintings; one was created in response to P1158; the other, to P1620.

16. See Danly, *Language as Object: Emily Dickinson and Contemporary Art*, the catalogue created to accompany the Mead Art Museum exhibition by the same name. Curated by Susan Danly, the show was devoted exclusively to Dickinson-inspired art and ran from March 28 to June 1, 1997. Featured were paintings, photographs, sculptures, mixed media installations, and popular culture memorabilia catalyzed by specific Dickinson texts as well as Dickinson's personality and other artists' perceptions of her. Artists included Will Barnet, Judy Chicago, Joseph Cornell, Robert Cumming, Lesley Dill, Mary Frank, Roni Horn, Carla Rae Johnson, Paul Katz, Barbara Morgan, Aife Murray, Barbara Penn, and Linda Schwalen. The catalogue presents an annotated art portfolio with selected color photographs as well as essays by Karen Sanchez-Eppler, Polly Longsworth, and Christopher Benfey.

17. See Garbowsky, "Will Barnet Meets Emily Dickinson," for a discussion of another illustration project.

18. See Tamaaki Yamakawa's "Emily Dickinson and Paintings: Margaret Taylor and Her Etchings for Dickinson's Poems."

19. For example, between 1951 and 1953 Cornell created two box constructions with the same title, *Toward the "Blue Peninsula" (for Emily Dickinson)*. The boxes are slightly different in both size and iconography. Compare plate 27 in McShine with fig. 24 in Tashjian (82–83).

20. See a photograph of Dill's "wedding dress' in *New York Times* 9 Oct. 1994: Styles 55. Sketches of the dress also appeared in the Oct. 1994 issues of *Elle* and *Vogue*.

21. See fig. 9 in Danly (27).

22. See a photograph of *Poem Hands* (1994) in *Lesley Dill*. See Dill's 1995 work, *Poem Hands (Double)*, in plate 8 (Danly 79).

23. See photographs of these Dill works in *Lesley Dill*.

24. Barbara Penn is another contemporary woman artist who uses Dickinson's life and writings as a means to explore the related issues of female creativity, domesticity, and nineteenth-century Victorian protocols for women. In her assemblage art, Penn employs nontraditional materials and painterly techniques in the creation of sculptural landscapes. These symbolic settings are reminiscent of those presented in Joseph Cornell's box constructions but are uncontained and much larger in scale. See frontispiece, figs. 4 and 5, and plate 15 in Danly for examples. See Danly 92 for a short analysis of Dickinson as an inspirational figure for Penn.

25. See plate 5 in Danly (71).

26. Kowaleski embroidered each of five Dickinson poems onto cloth patches and arranged them around the dancing figure. The poems selected for the quilt (running clockwise from the upper left) are P162, P84, P441, P288, and P254 (see Lemmon 4).

27. Lowenberg's inventory names composers from Austria, Denmark, Italy, Japan, the Netherlands, Russia, and Spain.

28. Interestingly, among the Dickinson settings of all four Pulitzer winners is one for the poem "There came a Wind like a Bugle — " (P1593). In each case, the setting is part of a cycle with several thematic threads, although the title of Bacon's grouping calls attention to nature as its focus.

29. In his song cycle, Copland used the following poems, given here in the order of their final arrangement: P790, P1593, P248, P715, P47, P1320, P13, P1080, P280, P183, P79, and P712.

30. As Copland remembers, "The idea of this completely unknown girl in Massachusetts seeing herself riding off into immortality with death himself seemed like such an incredible idea! I was very struck with that" (Copland and Perlis 158).

31. Vivian Perlis points out that among the poems Copland "considered and rejected" were "A Bird came down the Walk" (P328) and "Only a Shrine, but Mine — " (P918). The drafts are among the Copland Papers housed at the Library of Congress in Washington, D.C. (Copland and Perlis 438, see n. 21).

32. Copland invited Alice Howland to sing the cycle in its premiere performance. See the testimonies of both Howland and Phyllis Curtin about their experiences of performing the *Dickinson Songs*, in Copland and Perlis 160–61, 163–66. Of particular interest are the singers' comments about how performing the song cycle affected their attitudes about Emily Dickinson.

FURTHER READING

Lesley Dill: In Black & White. Exhibition Catalogue. New York: George Adams Gallery, 1997.

Sontag, Susan. *Alice in Bed.* New York: Farrar, Straus and Giroux, 1993.

KERSTIN BEHNKE

Dickinson's Poetry in Translation: The Example of Paul Celan

For Elizabeth Petuchowski

Contemporary discussions of cultural difference, alterity, and otherness have bestowed a new emphasis on the idea and practice of translation, as it brings different languages and cultures into contact and thus defines a particular mode of cross-cultural relations. Translating is always also interpreting. Beyond its relevance for comparative, cultural, and linguistic studies in the broadest sense, literary translation therefore also affords a unique interpretive perspective on and an enlarged understanding of the texts selected for translation. A study of Emily Dickinson's verse in translation must thus address a set of issues whose assumptions and conceptions, which are subject to historical and cultural change, require specific investigation. The need for interpretation has often led to an inquiry of what distinguishes Dickinson and her work, and it has initiated the search for a defining core and for essential traits in the poet and her poetry. Such a preunderstanding, shifting as it does over time, usually influences individual modes of translation. It helps explain what specific images of Dickinson herself — which, in German, for example, range from inspired dilettante to poetic genius, from simply "Emily" to eccentric New England spinster, from worldly saint to the "Nonne [nun] von Amherst" — are projected into the text and its translation. It also determines both whether, and what kind of, emphasis is given to style, voice, sound, diction, meter, poetic technique, thematic issues, and so on, and therefore reflects, and contributes to, the reception history of Dickinson's writing.

In this essay, examples will be drawn from the German translation history of Dickinson's poetry, whose range and diversity (including several book-length translations) have already been researched to some extent.[1] Currently, the main foreign interest in Dickinson translations seems to have shifted away from the European countries toward Japan, where multiple translations of individual poems are published; interest in Dickinson translations has also risen in Latin America. For information on the past and present scope of the international translation activity regarding Dickinson's work, Cynthia Hallen at Brigham Young University (hallenc@jkhbhrc.byu.edu) can be contacted regarding the International Bibliographical project, a compilation of "all known translations and scholarly ED materials written in other languages."[2]

Beginning in the 1890s, the history of Dickinson poems in (German) translation is almost as old as their publication history and the history of their criticism in English (Buckingham, *Reception*). Documenting Dickinson's changing reception over time and thus coinciding with her reception history, the history of Dickinson in translation could in part be written as a response to dates in the publication history of her work, especially Thomas H. Johnson's critical three-volume edition of *The Poems of Emily Dickinson* in 1955, and to critical impulses derived from research. General historical developments such as the two world wars, the growing cultural relations between the United States and the European countries between the wars and after 1945 (when, for instance, Germany experienced another phase of Americanization of its culture), the 1960s (an emotionally reticent decade in Germany which declared the death of poetry), the emancipation of women, and, with a burgeoning feminism since the 1970s, a growing interest in literature by women — all influenced the critical reception of Dickinson's texts in (German) translation.

Aside from the differing perceptions of the poet and her poetry over time, a study of Dickinson in foreign languages has to take into consideration the conceptions that guide the translator's understanding of poetry and of translation in general. At stake is the question of *literary* translation, that is, the difficulty of translating poetry, rather than prose or nonfiction, as well as different and changing notions of the nature, purpose, and value of poetry, and, finally, the understanding of translation and its function and the very notion of translatability itself. What, for instance, does it mean to translate poetry as poetry and into poetry? Does the translator have to be "the poet of the poet" (Novalis)? If translating means preserving or re-creating, by means of "creative transpositions" (Roman Jakobson), the poetic character of the text, what is this poetic quality thought to be? For instance, a translator for whom Dickinson's poetry is primarily distinguished by its quality and structure of sound will emphasize acoustic references over semantic aspects and thus be forced to forgo the precision of individual expressions for their vocalic richness. Do the translator's personal style and his or her own poetic principles and affinities coincide with the conventions of his or her time and culture? Is the translator a poet — rather than a professional translator — who might assimilate the foreign modes of meaning into his or her own ways of saying?

Does the translator have a specific theory of translation or favor a distinct mode of translation? Should the foreignness of the text be felt; should it be made "strange" in the target culture or appear to be "at home" in it? Should the translation therefore read as a translation or be like a text already familiar in the target language? Or does the translation rather constitute a third realm, as it is situated between the two languages and cultures? Is it thus no longer mimetic, faithful, and self-effacing but a hybrid text which resists assimilation to either sphere? How, then, is the relation between the original and the translation viewed? Is the translation secondary and subservient to the original text, which it may at best elucidate in a very imperfect fashion, or is it its equal, a work of art in its own right? Is the translation intended to be a free poetic rendering, or is the utmost philological accuracy the declared goal?

Individual translations may become obsolete due to the changes of and within the target language. The conceptions that guide and legitimate these translations may likewise lose their currency. In a time when the idea of identity as the ruling paradigm has given way to the concept of difference, we must therefore ask—without allowing such contemporary insights to become the universal measure of all, and especially older, translations—whether the ideal of all translation is still captured in the striving toward (near) sameness with the original. Likewise, is the translator's golden rule, to find equivalents, still normative and binding? The notion of textual equivalents is problematic not least because of its very vagueness. On what level are they to be sought? What is the unit of meaning—a word, a combination of words, syntactic phrases, or whole sentences? What, however, if the meaning is primarily conveyed not through such lingusitic *units* but rather through a constellation of otherwise unconnected words, through a logic of images which only offer up their sense as a configuration, in a syntax that transcends grammar—in short, as a differential *relation?* In other words, what is expressed *in* language, through words and concepts, may be complemented by what is created *by* or *through* language, by way of relations between words, which are also bound by language, yet in a different way. Finally, there is that which is unnamable and can only be referred to by indirection but is nevertheless "present" in the text. These considerations raise the question of how textual meaning is constituted at all. If meaning is bound to structures that are unique to one language, then the translation might seek to re-create their effect rather than those structures themselves. All the meaning-producing elements in a poem—words and their length, order, and position, syntactical constructions and connections, connotations, etymological overtones, metaphors, images, rhetorical figures, proverbial phrases, quotations, enjambments, meter, rhythm, rhyme and other sound qualities, punctuation, irony, and so on—interrelate in multiple ways, yet their list and their configurations can never be exhausted and thus not mimetically transposed into the target language.

Since complete transmission of the source texts is impossible, the view on Dickinson in other languages is first of all determined by the selection offered.

Which poems from which available textual corpus are chosen for translation? Why are some poems being preferred over others? The choice may be influenced by specific thematic affinities of certain poems with texts from the target culture which makes them more accessible than others and allows them to be categorized more easily (thematic headings for Dickinson's poetry in German translation have included "Western" [*abendländisch*], "Anglo-Saxon," "Christian," and "Women's Poetry"). Poems that are already famous and widely anthologized in the original language might offer themselves more readily for translation, especially if they are no longer under copyright but have become part of the public domain. Furthermore, what does the translator add, change, or omit to be faithful? In other words, what—within the texts—is being translated (and what not)? And how or in what way is it done? Finally, why is a translation done in a certain fashion (rather than another), and to what effect?

These initial questions need to be unfolded into a more differentiated set of considerations which go beyond the scope of issues already mentioned. The difficulty that every translation encounters is difference—the difference and differences in the literary tradition, the language, and the culture between any two linguistic communities. Following this threefold orientation, translation studies can be said to branch out into three different fields: theoretical and practical investigations of the poetic quality or "das Dichterische" (Walter Benjamin, Paul Celan) in poetic translations, approaches informed by cognitive linguistics, and studies that contribute to the project of a cultural history of translation.

The history of translation studies is itself shaped by changing critical concerns which account for shifts in emphasis. While cognitive linguistics is a relatively new field, the question of "das Dichterische," which is tied to theories of language and of representation, has occupied poets and thinkers devoted to translation for a long time. A cultural history of translation is perhaps the broadest approach to translation, since it also addresses poetic and linguistic peculiarities and their translatability. A cultural history of translation would also take into consideration differences emerging from the factual belatedness of the translation, which often belongs to a different time period than the original, and differences resulting from the personal style of the translator. Furthermore, cultural, temporal, and historical differences are of importance when we ask whether a poem has been translated into a time and context (e.g., a romantic one) that do not coincide with the time of the translation (e.g., the 1970s). In German, Dickinson has thus been stylized as the American Droste (the poet Annette von Droste-Hülshoff, 1797–1848), who precedes her by a generation. If the time evoked by the translation thus differs from the time during which it was written, such a practice of situating the translation within a certain literary tradition, such historicizing, in other words, adds a double temporal tension to the existing difference between the date of the poem and the date of its translation. The translation may also merely allude to the target literature and culture by borrowing quotations and cultural symbols from it. In addition, a cultural history of translation would seek to explain why, for instance, a translation neutralizes aspects of gender or why it strengthens religious overtones or philosophical implications by drawing on detailed cultural-historical studies from a feminist, religious, or philosophical perspective.

The search for categories that conceptualize the style and effect(s) of a translation, however, must also investigate the assumptions and intentions that inform them. Any label reflects the function and purpose of what it defines. A translation might thus be said to "deviate" (rather than simply differ) from the original or from a projected ideal version. Such a statement, while apparently drawing on the authority of universal validity, is in fact an implied value judgment which derives from cultural norms and expectations, that is, ultimately subjective criteria which have come to reveal themselves as time-bound and stand in need of periodic reevaluation. If Dickinson's language is seen to be "deviating" from normative usage, a translation that wishes to be a faithful rendering might be expected to do so as well. In following Dickinson's eccentric style, the translator must determine whether it is to be valued as a dilettantish aberration or a mark of high art.

Given all these considerations, we need to ask again: to what extent is Dickinson's already very elusive voice transmissible at all? What becomes of her poetic vision and style when they are mediated, or filtered, by another's and through another language? What in her poetry resists translation? How is this American poet presented to another culture?

The differences created by the translations which arise in relation to the poetic, linguistic, and cultural conventions of a target culture cannot be traced in detail in this essay. What individual translations preserve, however, can be inferred from a study of multiple translations of one poem into the same foreign language. The analysis of several such series also allows for comparisons and provides insights into the peculiar style and method of individual translators. A history of diverse attempts at translating Dickinson could begin with a statistical assessment of a large collection of material and its detailed description, from which a set of outstanding traits could be derived and perhaps a methodology be deduced. I, however, will follow the individual transformations that Dickinson's poetry undergoes in one particular translation and offer an exemplary study of the rendering of one of Dickinson's most famous poems, "Because I could not stop for Death,"[3] into only one foreign language, namely German (both texts may be found at the end of this essay). The translator is Paul Celan, one of the foremost European poets and translators in the twentieth century, whose poetic sensibility is most congenial to Dickinson's own.

Before the analysis can begin, the textual basis of the translation needs to be determined, which presents a difficulty already familiar from Dickinson studies in English. (The question of how the form, format, and context of publication determine the reception of the translation, also of importance, can only be mentioned here.) The sheer number of different editions and individual textual differences that stem from creative editing and other editorial emendations has produced a wealth of variant readings of Dickinson's poetry, which add to her own versions of her texts. Many translators did not have access to the definitive texts. In addition, if original and translation do not appear together in print and no bibliographical references are provided, as in the case of the first publications of Celan's ten Dickinson translations, the complex editorial history of the fascicles makes it almost impossible to assign the actual source text to the translation.

The documents relating to Dickinson in Celan's posthumous papers in Paris contain a reference to "The Complete Poems of E.D., / Edited by Thomas Johnson, / Little, Brown and Co., / Boston, Toronto [n.d.]"— Johnson's one-volume reader's edition, which was first published in 1960. The editors of Celan's *Gesammelte Werke* of 1983, on the other hand, chose Johnson's—not always reliable—critical edition of 1955 for their source texts. One critic surmises that Celan used *The Complete Poems of Emily Dickinson*, edited by Martha Dickinson Bianchi (Boston, 1924) "and/or" *Further Poems of Emily Dickinson*, edited by Bianchi and Alfred Leete Hampson (Boston, 1929) (Olschner 288), and he concludes that Celan's choice of source texts cannot be clearly determined. Contrary to this opinion, the texts in question can be reconstructed by comparing the arrangement, the specific variant reading, and the textual and typographical form of Celan's ten published translations when they first came out with the American editions of Dickinson's poetry which were available at the time of those first publications (between 1959 and 1962).

Celan must have used altogether three different editions: Johnson's reader's edition mentioned in the posthumous papers and two others. The bilingual French and English editions of Dickinson poems published in 1956 and 1957—two of them in Paris, where Celan lived since 1948—contain only two or three, respectively, of the ten texts selected by Celan and were therefore probably not consulted by him. Johnson's reader's edition of 1960 cannot have provided the source text for Celan's translation of "Because I could not stop for Death," for this translation first appeared in the fall of 1959. It is also not the source for Celan's additional translation of "Eight Poems" ("Acht Gedichte"), which reached his publishing house, S. Fischer Verlag, between

January and April of 1961; *The Complete Poems of Emily Dickinson*, on the other hand, came out on October 26, 1960, in the United States and most probably only some time after that date in Europe, which would not have allowed Celan much time for the translations. Johnson's 1960 edition might, however, have provided the textual basis for the fourteen other — unpublished — Dickinson translations by Celan still in his posthumous papers and/or perhaps for "Um halb vier," his rendering into German of "At half-past three, a single bird," published in 1962.

There are also textual arguments that speak against Johnson's 1960 edition as a source text, for it offers only the main variant readings of the 1955 edition, and these versions do not always coincide with the variant readings translated by Celan. Instead of "Father, I bring thee not myself," on which Celan bases his "Ich bring dir, Vater, nicht mich selbst," the 1955 edition prints "Savior! I've no one else to tell" (the second variant of P217). Likewise, Celan certainly did not work from Johnson's 1955 variorum edition, for his German translation of "Because I could not stop for Death" leaves out the third stanza, which has only been known since the publication of that edition, where it forms part of the main text. Furthermore, Celan does not keep Johnson's chronological arrangement of the poems — according to Johnson's numbering system, Celan's sequence of his "Eight Poems" reads as follows: P1732, P891, P756, P217, P1052, P301, P1065, P742.

In English, the first seven of these eight poems first appeared in the three series of *Poems* between 1890 and 1896, where the texts are arranged thematically into four groups: I. Life, II. Love, III. Nature, IV. Time and Eternity. Martha Dickinson Bianchi, Dickinson's niece, acquired the copyright for these poems and published them, together with 146 other Dickinson poems from an earlier collection called *The Single Hound* (1914), as *The Complete Poems of Emily Dickinson* (1924). Adding "The Single Hound" as "Part Five," Bianchi took over the thematic arrangement of the *Poems*, but she reversed the order of the second ("Love") and third ("Nature") group of poems. This altered arrangement matches the sequence in which Celan published his "Eight Poems," as the page numbers of the English texts in *The Complete Poems of Emily Dickinson* (52, 131–32, 167–68, 172, 188–89, 192, 201) document. This sequence is not even interrupted by the translation of "Four Trees — upon a solitary Acre," which follows a different edition and was placed at the end of the "Eight Poems." The American text was only published in 1945 in *Bolts of Melody: New Poems of Emily Dickinson*, edited by Millicent Todd Bingham and Mabel Loomis Todd. Celan must have used this edition, for he translates "wem bahnt er den Weg und wem / steht er entgegen," which more closely echoes the variant "promote or hinder" printed in *Bolts of Melody* than Johnson's main 1955 (and 1960) version, "retard — or further."

Bianchi and Hampson's *Poems of Emily Dickinson* (1937), finally, combines more recently published Dickinson poems (from 1929 and 1937) with *The Complete Poems of Emily Dickinson* of 1924. The edition of 1937 probably did not serve as Celan's source text, for it contains a longer version of the poem "Father, I bring thee not myself," which is titled "Savior! I've no one else to tell." It is unlikely that Celan would have translated the shorter version of the poem (as he did) if he had also known the longer one. Furthermore, Celan did not choose any poem from those parts of *Poems* which complement the selection of *The Complete Poems of Emily Dickinson.*

In addition to the arrangement of the poems, which identify Bianchi's edition of *The Complete Poems of Emily Dickinson* as the source text for all but the last of Celan's published translations, the titles that Celan gave to his "Eight Poems" also point to this edition. Celan prefaced each of these poems, which are without titles in the original, with its first line in English, thus quoting his reference, and the spelling and punctuation he uses coincide with that in *The Complete Poems of Emily Dickinson.* Further indications are striking similarities in typography, variant readings, spelling, and punctuation of the texts. Thus Celan reproduces the indentations of the even lines of "My life closed twice before its close," "To my quick ear the leaves conferred," and "Father, I bring thee not myself" that only Bianchi's edition (and the three series of *Poems by Emily Dickinson* on which it is based) shows, while he maintains — in accordance with Bianchi's arrangement — the flush setting in the other texts.

Celan thus translated from conventionalized Dickinson editions that lack some of the typical "Dickinsonian" features such as ungrammatical forms, unusual capitalization, dashes, uneven rhymes and meter, the underlining of important words, quotation marks, localisms, and "sensible metaphors."

A case study — a close analysis of Celan's translation of "Because I could not stop for Death" — will now indicate what, despite Dickinson's particular linguistic idiosyncrasies, can, in principle, be retained in translation. Dickinson's famous poem begins as follows (in Bianchi's rendering):

> Because I could not stop for Death,
> He kindly stopped for me;

Celan translates:

> Der Tod, da ich nicht halten konnt,
> hielt an, war gern bereit.

"[D]a ich nicht halten konnt" reproduces "Because I could not stop," and "halten konnt"/"hielt an" retains Dickinson's word play with the verb "stop." All the words carrying a semantic content recur in the translation: "Because"/"da," "I"/"ich," "could"/"konnt," "not"/"nicht," "stop"/"halten,"

"Death"/"Tod," "kindly"/"gern," "stopped"/"hielt an." The translation omits the functional word "for," mentioned twice, and its objects, "me" and "Death" (or rather "He," for Celan chose "Der Tod"—instead of "er"/ "He"—as the grammatical subject), and it adds a "war [. . .] bereit." Celan further retains the syntactical division into main clause and subordinate clause of these two lines.

Dickinson and Celan both use a negation ("could not stop"), followed by an affirmation ("stopped"). Dickinson expresses this antithesis by a semantic chiasm: taken together, the relations of "I" and "Death" to their respective pronouns form a(n imaginary) cross:

$$I \qquad Death$$
$$He \qquad me$$

Celan transforms this figure into a hyperbaton, which breaks up the syntactical order established by Dickinson. In his rendering, the main clause with "Der Tod" at the top of the sentence encloses the subordinate clause, which is inserted in it but syntactically unrelated to it. This parenthesis separates the elements of the main clause from each other and emphasizes the presence of "Tod" at the beginning. Dickinson's smooth syntax mirrors the logic of cause and effect in that the subordinate clause precedes the main clause, just as it provides the explanation for the action in that clause. Celan, on the other hand, interrupts this sequence—he interrupts the main clause, makes it stop (after the enjambment at the end of the first line, which is another kind of trans-lation or *Über-setzung*): "Der Tod [. . .] / hielt an," while he allows the subordinate clause to proceed without a break: "da ich nicht halten konnt." The constative and the performative aspects of this clause coincide, and they are explained by the statement itself: "da ich nicht halten konnt." Celan's hyperbaton here borrows the Latinate syntax typical of constructions with the so-called *cum causale*, a Latinism which has a correspondence in Dickinson's preference for classical Latin prosody and rhetoric.

Celan appears to have given up the double causal connection between "I" and "Death" ("I [. . .] for Death" and "He [. . .] for me"), for his translation does not retain the prepositional phrases "for Death" and "for me." Celan thus seems to give no reason why the "I" of the poem is unable to stop; instead, he says of Death that he is ready ("bereit"). In the German tradition of literature on the dance of death, Death frequently figures as a travel companion to the dying, whom he typically addresses with the words, "Drum sei bereit [. . .] zu gehen" ("Be ready [or, prepared] to go"). In Celan's translation, however, it is Death who is ready. In its negation, the statement, however, also applies to the dying "I"—by implication, for the emphasis of the topical position in the first line suggests that *Death* was ready but not the "I." The "I" was not ready *for*

Death, that is. Without directly translating the prepositional phrases "for Death" and "for me," Celan is thus still able to convey their meaning, however indirectly. In German, Death's action ("stopped for me") is explained by the causative subordinate clause beginning with "da," an explanation which is also suggested syntactically by its position immediately after "Tod."

What Death is ready for remains (syntactically) ambiguous in the German text; he only "hielt an, war gern bereit." While "hielt an" indicates that Death is ready to stop, the expression "bereit," which etymologically derives from *reiten* ("to ride," "to go"), suggests otherwise — the word already announces the journey with Death, which is only mentioned later in Dickinson's poem. This last journey, however, a euphemism for dying, is also captured by "stopped"/"hielt an." In translating "kindly stopped" by "hielt an, war gern bereit," Celan redoubles the predicate. While "anhalten" designates the end of a movement, "bereit" signals the willingness to act. Celan thus points out the two aspects of "stop," namely, "to stop doing something" and "to stop (in order) to do something." He also divides Dickinson's syntactical unit of adverb and verb into separate elements and thus forms a syntactical chiasm between his translation and the original ("kindly stopped" — "hielt an, [. . .] gern [. . .]").

The example of the first two lines of "Because I could not stop for Death" in its German translation already demonstrates several traits of Celan's theory and practice of translation, which can be brought out in more detail by a wider range of examples. Celan's texts reflect their relation to the originals from their viewpoints as translations, thus indicating their own status as translated texts. The changed perspective of the translations also affects the structures that constitute meaning, especially syntactical connections and other formal configurations. Thus Celan's translation sometimes enacts what is only stated in the original. The first results of the analysis of "Because I could not stop for Death" in Celan's translation can be summarized as follows: Celan makes the explicit meanings of the prepositional phrases "for Death" (in the subordinate clause) and "for me" (in the main clause) implicit by shifting each meaning into the other clause, while his translation emphasizes otherwise covert meanings in the original. The signification of "for Death" is thus expressed by "bereit" (in the main clause) in German, and "for me" is rendered by the entire subordinate clause in Celan's text. The subordinate clause in the translation has been shortened by one element, while the main clause, in countersymmetrical fashion, has been expanded by one. Where Dickinson puts a grammatical object, Celan omits it (and vice versa). The repetition of "Death" by the pronoun "He" has not been reproduced in the translation; "stopped" in the second line, however, has been doubled into "hielt an" and "war [. . .] bereit."

Lines 3 and 4 of Dickinson's poem —

> The carriage held but just ourselves
> And Immortality.

— have been translated by Celan as

> Im Fuhrwerk saß nun er und ich
> und die Unsterblichkeit.

The translation is marked by a syntactical change of perspective, which is also the change from the original to the translation. The aspect from which the situation is viewed has shifted from the standpoint of the carriage to that of the travelers, just as it is now Celan (and no longer Dickinson) who is creating the scene for the reader. This transformation is effected by a change of (grammatical) subject and object and entails an inverted word order in the German text — the translation displays itself as a "version" or turning of the source text. By enacting such a version, it also demonstrates the principle of translation.

Another change of aspect can be found in line 9, where Celan translates "We passed the school where [. . .]" as "Ein Schulhof kam mit [. . .]." The movement of "passed" has been transferred to "kam" ("came"). The direction has likewise changed from a passing by to a coming closer. A similar alteration occurs in the translation of "We passed the fields of gazing grain" (line 11) as "Es hat das Korn uns nachgeäugt."

If the word "Immortality" in line 4 contains both "I" and "Death" — read as "I-m-*mortal*-ity" or "I-in-*mortality*," which reverses the meaning of the word — the German "Unsterblichkeit" likewise encloses both "I" and "Death" but in a different order, for it does so by repeating "er" and "ich": "Unst-*er*-bl-*ich*-keit" (and the preceding "nun" which turns into the prefix "Un-"). While this echo accounts for the splitting of "ourselves" in line 3 into "er und ich," the pairing of Death and the "I" in this form also responds to Dickinson's use of personal pronouns in lines 1 and 2, which Celan did not reproduce in the first lines of his text.

Celan often employs deictic spatial or temporal expressions such as "da" or "nun," which have no equivalent in Dickinson's English text. The word "nun" ("now," line 3) anticipates "der Nu" (line 18), Celan's translation of "the day." Celan, however, not only marks a time within the translation but also marks the time of the translation. The fate of the translation is its belatedness vis-à-vis the original, yet the translation — unlike its source text — is also part of the present. Within the text, Dickinson views the perspective into the future from the past ("were"), while Celan appears to speak in the present ("sagt" — the elided "e" at the end of the word would actually identify it as past tense — and "halten [. . .] / auf [. . .] zu"). Dickinson's last stanza refers to

> the day
> I first surmised the horses' heads
> Were toward eternity.

which Celan turns into

> der Nu,
> da ich mir sagt: Wir halten ja
> auf Ewigkeiten zu!

Covering the space in between, the translation enacts the transition from "nun" in the third line, the past present of the reported incident in the carriage ("saß nun"), to "Ewigkeiten" at the very end of the poem, thereby illustrating the biblical phrase "von nun an bis in alle Ewigkeit" ("from now on into eternity"). The earlier "*saß nun*" is echoed in reverse, as it were, in "der *Nu* / da ich mir *sagt.*" The "nun," the time of the now, actually ties together both "Nu" and "Un-" (of "Unsterblichkeit"); comprising both, it compresses the span of time that extends between "nun" and "Ewigkeit" into one moment, the "Nu" of the "nun," which is both, temporal and eternal (because immortal).

In the same passage of Celan's text, another development across the space of the poem reaches its performative power in conjunction with a double transformation of time into space. First, in the transition captured in "der Nu / da," time ("Nu") becomes space ("da"): "da" acts as a pivot, its temporal sense ("when") turns into a spatial meaning ("there"). This movement is arrested in "Wir halten ja" — which would, in an interlinear version, mean "we stop yes," or rather, "we are actually stopping." Here, Celan is (literally) articulating the expression "auf etwas zuhalten," "to head straight for a s.th."; retranslated into English, it reveals the whereabouts of the horses' "heads": they or, more precisely, the noun signifying them have been turned into a verb and thus been saved in the translation, albeit indirectly. Secondly, time, or even that which exceeds time, ultimately remains subject to spatiality which embraces it: "auf [. . .] zu," or open and shut — space swallows the "Ewigkeiten" in between. Dickinson, on the other hand, reserves the space of the last word for "eternity," thus opening up the poem toward infinity. This trajectory is already indicated in Dickinson's formulation "the day / [. . .] first" with its direction "toward eternity." This phrase — an inversion of the expression "the first day," also echoed in "day / I" (if read as "day one") — marks the (imaginary) starting point, not at the beginning but late in the poem, and thus upsets the seemingly linear straightforwardness of the journey. If Celan contains the eternities within space, he splits the "I" into two personae, "ich" and "mir," as if separating body and soul in death. This experience, although physically taking place earlier, is pondered now from beyond the grave. "I" and "me" are then merged again into a "we," exclusive of Death, who is not being addressed in this interior dialogue, just as there is no mention of him in the last stanza of Dickinson's poem, which indicates a space on the other side of death.

Just as Celan "translates" the above-mentioned biblical formula "von nun an bis in alle Ewigkeit" into his own text by splitting it into two parts, he also utilizes idiomatic German expressions for his "versions" — by inverting their meaning. Thus, when Dickinson writes in line 5, "We slowly drove, he knew no haste," Celan responds with the antithetical phrase, "Ihm gings auch langsam schnell genug." This line derives from the clichéd expression, "Es konnte ihm nicht schnell genug gehen," which characterizes a person who is hasty and likes to rush things. As with "bereit," Celan again negates the meaning of this fixed expression in his translation: for Death, slowness is fast enough. He also contracts into one sentence what Dickinson expresses in two. In short, Celan transforms structures of the original or idiomatic German coinages into their formal negative or opposite, thus complementing the source text. It is therefore not primarily the structural correspondence between the two languages or the idiomatic character of individual expressions and phrases which might require that, for example, a verbal construction in English be reexpressed as a noun in German. Rather, individual structures of meaning are converted into their symmetrical other in order to preserve the text's overall meaning *and* in order to indicate the status of the translation as a translation. It is in this double sense of translation that Celan's ingenious principle of translation reveals itself. Thus complex syntactical forms in the original are divided into a sequence of smaller units of meaning in the translation, while simple forms are condensed into a more complex structure. Dickinson's lines 9 and 10, for example,

> We passed the school where children played
> At wrestling in a ring;

are rendered as

> Ein Schulhof kam mit kleinem Volk,
> das miteinander rang . . .

Two individual actions ("We passed," "children played") appear to have been contracted into a single one ("Ein Schulhof kam") in line 9, and the caesura effected by the enjambment has been transformed into a syntactical break, which counters the circular movement of wrestling and seems to restrict it to line 10 only. The children's playful pugnacity in Dickinson's poem is conveyed more indirectly by Celan — through the etymology of German "Volk," which originally designated a band of warriors. Repetitions in the source text (such as "wrestling" and "ring," which indicate circularity) are usually not reproduced, yet what is only mentioned once in the English text may occur twice in the German version. The meaning of the English word "ring," for example, is echoed in "-hof," which, in Anglo-Saxon, also denotes "circle," "area," or "temple." The root meaning of "Hof" —*Anhöhe* ("hill"), a dry site (for building), which is safe from attacks — also anticipates the grave site alluded to in "A swelling of the ground"/"emporgewelltes Land" in line 14. Thus some textual meaning does not recur in the same line in the translation but may have been displaced into an earlier or later stanza. For instance, the information conveyed by "drove" in line 5, whose direct German equivalent would be "fuhr," is already contained in the noun "Fuhrwerk" in line 3 of Celan's text.

The translation expresses its own belatedness in relation to its original: the "ring" in line 10 of Dickinson's text is turned into a "rang" by Celan. Read together, these two words form a sequence which describes the dying away of a sound ("ring") which, perceived from a future present, turns into a mere echo in the past (English "rang"), thus indicating the temporal distance between Dickinson's and Celan's texts (and reversing the relation between past and present mentioned earlier). Although the acoustic sense is not the primary meaning of "ring" and "rang," this reading is strengthened by Celan's choice of punctuation: the three dots after "rang" in the German text visualize how the sound fades away. The belatedness of the translation is also indicated in "nachgeäugt" in line 11, which captures the mutuality of "passed" and "gazing" in "We passed the fields of gazing grain." While "passed" indicates the moment of going by, in "nachgeäugt" ("gazed after") this moment has already passed. The idea of past-ness is also addressed in Celan's "wir sahn: die Sonne sank" (line 12) for "We passed the setting sun." While Dickinson paraphrases the act of dying in her use of the topos of the setting sun, which describes the transition into the realm of Death, Celan utilizes this reference also in a more specific way. "[W]ir sahn: die Sonne sank" recalls a line from another famous poem about a journey, in a carriage, from life to death, Goethe's "An Schwager Chronos," experienced and written "In der Postchaise," where the exclamation "Sieh, die Sonne sinkt" announces the impending entrance into the underworld. Again, Celan seems to echo in the past tense what once was present. Dickinson captures the moment of dying by a double movement: the course of the setting sun and the journey of the travelers who, crossing its path, disappear behind the sun. Dickinson's text performs what it states: not only does the "I" pass the sun but it also passes, that is, dies. Celan's words often enact their meaning, as Dickinson demonstrates here with "passing," but his translations do not reproduce her poetic techniques in the places where they occur in the original; rather, Celan seems to match Dickinson's rich representation of the act of dying by his intertextual allusion to Goethe's poem. It is only a few lines later that Celan again lets the words perform what they denote. In line 15, Dickinson writes, "The roof was scarcely visible," which in Celan's version becomes "Das Dach — kaum daß es sichtbar war." Instead of faithfully reproducing Dickinson's smooth syntax, the flow of words in the translation is interrupted by a dash and then by an anakoluthic construction, which dissolve the syntactic order so that it is hardly visible ("sichtbar") itself. Moreover, and more ingeniously even, Celan structurally mimics the statement of this line in several ways. To begin, the expression "sichtbar," the only word with two syllables, visibly ("sichtbar") — or rather audibly — stands out from the other monosyllabic words, thus producing a slight elevation, as it were. The sound structure in this line, in both its alliterative and its vocalic quality, likewise describes a low roof: the internal rhyme of "*das Da*ch" at the beginning is continued in "daß," which forms an identical rhyme with the first "das." This vocalic and consonantal rhyme has a symmetrical correspondence in the "-ar" of "-bar war," at the end of both the words and the line:

$$das — Da — \ldots — daß — \ldots — \ldots — bar — war.$$

The assonances form a vocalic continuum,

$$a — a — \ldots — a — \ldots — a — a,$$

which, however, is interrupted by "kaum," whose diphthong appears as if in relief from this acoustic sequence. Yet the negating force of "kaum" ("scarcely") makes the roof, having hardly been mentioned, recede again, and the "a" in "au" also seems to pull the diphthong down into the stream of other "a's." The roof's prominence, however slight, is alluded to by the vocalic structure and its semantic correspondence, which follow the displacement introduced by "kaum." Prepared by the "e" in "es," the "i" in "sicht-" is projected out from the series of "a's." Thus the vocalic sequence in this line has its peak in the "i" — a sound which, (literally) visualizing what the word "sichtbar" expresses verbally, finally lets the roof appear — but only to make it disappear again in the final assonance of "a's":

$$a — a — au — a — e — i — a — a.$$

If visualized, the structural mimesis between acoustic and semantic elements in this line reveals further aspects. In German, the place of formation of the five vowels in the mouth and the palate as their common site are symbolized by the so-called vocalic triangle,

With the exception of the "u," which has been transposed from its place at the end, Celan's rendering of line 15 reproduces this spatial schema. Just as the "i" is produced in the center at the top of the palate (i.e., the roof of the mouth), it is also positioned at the apex (and in the middle) of the vocalic sequence in the translation, where it symbolizes the — hardly visible — roof. In addition, the structure shared by the linguistic model and the poem also represents a specific acoustic quality of the "i": it occupies the peak of this pyramid and, being the vowel with the highest pitch, indicates the shape of the roof.

The analysis of "Because I could not stop for Death" and its German translation by Paul Celan has not been exhausted with these observations. Suffice it to say, by way of a conclusion, that Celan's Dickinson translations reflect the German poet's understanding of the nature of translation as a "version" — a "trope" or turning, which is also a displacement, through which the translations reveal their relation to the original. This emphasis on the act of translation as a version, in which the original undergoes turns and shifts, calls attention not only to the translation's belatedness and spatial displacement vis-à-vis the source texts but also to the presence of its own time and place in the text. Measured against the original, the translation may appear slanted, yet the truth of the original text is preserved in Celan's version, as patterns of meaning in Dickinson's poem are turned into their structural other. Due to this structural reciprocity, meaning is not lost in the translation but reproduced by other means — through formal, instead of merely semantic, equivalents. With the mark of translation thus inscribed in it, Celan's texts complement, rather than emulate or imitate, Dickinson's poetry in a truly artistic way.

As Margaret Freeman (freemamh@smtplink.laccd.edu) reports, more recent work was presented at the 1992 conference of the Emily Dickinson International Society (EDIS) in Washington, D.C., on "Translating Emily Dickinson in Language, Culture, and the Arts." The collaboration of an Emily Dickinson translation project in the wake of this conference was published in 1997 as a special issue of the *Emily Dickinson Journal*, titled "Swearing by the Cuckoo: Translators on Translating Emily Dickinson's Poetry" and coedited by Margaret Freeman, Gudrun M. Grabher, and Roland Hagenbüchle. The August 1995 newsletter of TRANSLIT, a research network for interdisciplinary studies in cognitive linguistics, literature, and translation, addressed the question of translating P1088, and a future newsletter will publish responses to that issue. Also, a dissertation on Dickinson and translation is being prepared by Marianne Erickson (mtceriks@artsci.wustl.edu).

Because I could not stop for Death,	Der Tod, da ich nicht halten konnt,
He kindly stopped for me;	hielt an, war gern bereit.

The carriage held but just ourselves
And Immortality.

We slowly drove, he knew no haste,
And I had put away
My labor, and my leisure too,
For his civility.

We passed the school where children played
At wrestling in a ring;
We passed the fields of gazing grain,
We passed the setting sun.

We paused before a house that seemed
A swelling of the ground;
The roof was scarcely visible,
The cornice but a mound.

Since then 't is centuries; but each
Feels shorter than the day
I first surmised the horses' heads
Were toward eternity.

Im Fuhrwerk saß nun er und ich
und die Unsterblichkeit.

Ihm gings auch langsam schnell genug,
und ich hatt fortgetan
das Fronen und das Müßiggehn,
so freundlich war der Mann.

Ein Schulhof kam mit kleinem Volk,
das miteinander rang . . .
Es hat das Korn uns nachgeäugt,
wir sahn: die Sonne sank.

Dann hielten wir, da stand ein Haus:
emporgewelltes Land.
Das Dach — kaum daß es sichtbar war,
Das Sims — ein Hügelrand.

Jahrhunderte seither, doch keins
war länger als der Nu,
da ich mir sagt: Wir halten ja
auf Ewigkeiten zu!

Notes

1. For further bibliographical references see my master's thesis, on which this essay is based in part. The thesis emerged from my participation in a special research project on "Literary Translation" at Georg-August-Universität, Göttingen, chaired by Armin Paul Frank and funded by the German Research Council (DFG).

2. Information provided by Margaret Freeman. It would be impossible to gather such information by tracing the history of authorized translations in the records of Dickinson's publishers, not only because unauthorized translations or translations of poems in the public domain would not be registered there but also because the number of short-term grants of permission to translate selected poems only (rather than the whole oeuvre) cannot be summarized adequately, a problem complicated by the fact that the administration of the rights to Dickinson's poetry is in several hands (Harvard University Press; Little, Brown; and Houghton Mifflin). My thanks to Claudia Buckholts of Harvard University Press, who answered my request for information.

3. In this essay, the spelling of Dickinson's poems and their titles is rendered according to Celan's actual source texts.

New Directions in Dickinson Scholarship

SUZANNE JUHASZ

Materiality and the Poet

*T*his essay concludes a volume which provides ample evidence of the range of recent Dickinson scholarship and the issues addressed by it. More like a postscript, then, my essay offers a particular perspective on recent critical practice: that much of it is characterized by a concern for the materiality of Dickinson's work and life. By materiality I mean the physicalness or corporeality of her writing. In the 1990s, we have been struck by certain material facts about Dickinson as a writer: that her writing exists almost entirely in manuscript; that she regularly suggested alternative words or phrases to her poems and produced alternative versions of her poems; that she wrote letters with poems attached to them, embedded in them; that her writing forms possess such fluidity that we cannot precisely say what is prose and what is poetry. As a consequence, the way she wrote, the materiality of her writing, has everything to do with what and how we read when we are "reading Dickinson." This concern has been emphatically addressed from the perspectives of both editing and reading theory, enterprises which seem to me to be integrally related. Further, the rise in cultural studies on Dickinson—situating these texts and the woman writing them in a social context—has much to do with how an acknowledgment of writerly materiality is related to social and historical materiality. Thus recent studies of the poems' publishing history, of their author's circumstances in relation to her particular moment and place in culture, of her relationships with others—relationships familial, companionate, romantic, and literary—help represent material contexts that surround and define the poet Dickinson and her writing.

I write as well from another perspective, that of editor of the *Emily Dickinson Journal*. This position gives me access to work by many Dickinson scholars, providing me with a keen sense of what interests both people initiating their study of Dickinson and also those engaged in ongoing research. In this essay I am going to call primarily upon this body of recent criticism to aid me in my discussion of the material Dickinson.

What *is* a Dickinson poem? What are the genres of her literature? Are the terms "poems" and "letters" adequate or sufficient to describe her writing? What counts as "literature" in the Dickinson canon, and how should that literature be presented to her vast and varied audiences? These are some of our current questions. They are questions about editing, and they are also questions about reading. Reading means encountering her words, of course; but it means as well contextualizing those words as the expression of a particular woman writing in and against a particular world. Our cognizance of her materiality both raises these issues and, I would suggest, helps us to contend with them.

What is a Dickinson poem? We now know that to teach or write about a poem that appears in Johnson's one-volume *Complete Poems of Emily Dickinson* is to employ Johnson's version of something that Emily Dickinson wrote. This poem was probably not published in the poet's lifetime and originally existed in some manuscript version. It may have been copied by Dickinson into one of the fascicle booklets that she sewed together to bind; it may have been carefully penned on a sheet of paper; or it may have been written on a brown paper bag, an envelope, or the back of a recipe. It may have been embedded in or attached to a letter. It may have come with alternative words or phrases, neatly copied above the line or below the lines of verse. (Johnson's variorum gives us these "other" words but not their shape; Ralph Franklin's edition of the fascicle manuscripts shows us where and how they were placed.) As teachers and scholars, we find ourselves with a problem and a responsibility. What qualifies, then, as a Dickinson poem? And how can we take responsibility for the text we are using?

The current explosion of new editing has been one way to approach the dilemma. Presently, the texts available to most readers, the writing that is *in print* — the three-volume Johnson, the one-volume Johnson, and the Franklin manuscript edition of the fascicles — does not give us access to all of her writing in the form in which she wrote it. Many scholars are working to remedy this situation. Ralph Franklin's new variorum of the poems is forthcoming; Marta Werner discusses the late "scraps" in *Emily Dickinson's Open Folios: Scenes of Reading, Surfaces of Writing* (1995); Susan Howe writes on Dickinson's visual intentionalities and manuscript art in *The Birth-mark* (1993); Jerome McGann, working with Jeanne Holland, Marta Werner, and Martha Nell Smith, plans an edition of Dickinson's correspondence with Thomas Higginson; and Ellen Louise Hart and Martha Nell Smith are completing an edition of the poems, letters, and letter-poems sent to Susan Dickinson, Emily's most frequently addressed correspondent. Hart and Smith reedit Dickinson by taking into account her method of publication. Instead of organizing her works according to genre and debatable chronologies, they believe that Dickinson editions should be organized according to the audience to whom the bodies of her literature were addressed. The Dickinson Editing Collective, comprising numerous scholars working with the Dickinson manuscripts, plans to edit the many "books" Dickinson published to various correspondents. The Collective is also developing a hypermedia archive of her writings which will include photographic reproductions and publication histories of all Dickinson documents. This electronic reproduction will make facsimiles of all Dickinson manuscripts much more widely available.

Yet many readers will not be able to afford expensive facsimile or electronic editions. The best way to help readers, suggests Ellen Louise Hart in "The Elizabeth Whitney Putnam Manuscripts and New Strategies for Editing Emily Dickinson's Letters," is through " 'diplomatic transcriptions': line for line print translations of poems and letters that attempt to represent the manuscripts as accurately as possible, with a detailed apparatus describing features that do not translate into print." I think this is a good idea and look forward to such an edition.

Unquestionably, making Dickinson's writing more readily available in the forms in which she wrote it will be a wonderful asset. But it is not the only "answer" to the "problem," if only because pieces of writing exist in more than one version, whether we are thinking of the alternative words possible for a given poem or for the alternative contexts for the same words. Johnson spent a lot of time considering which was the final or finished version of a poem, whereas recent critics, such as Sharon Cameron in *Choosing Not Choosing*, have focused on the *in*conclusivity of a poem. Cameron argues that the fascicles call into question the limit of a "poem," so that whole poems can begin to seem like variants of one another. Alternates or variants of diverse magnitude and forms are a significant material fact of Dickinson's writing, which we should take into account (be responsible for) when we read her work.

Cameron's central argument about variants, which also calls attention to the ways in which they foreground materiality — "the material placement of the poem is essential to discovering its identity" (*Choosing* 6) — is that they create an irresolvable readerly tension between being asked to choose and being denied the possibility of choice. "The presumption that choosing is necessary is contested by the representation of not choosing, for in the poems the choice of particular words implied by the lyric frame to be imperative is rather shown to be impossible" (23). We could argue that there are therefore as many poems as variants, but Cameron says that this is not how words work in poems. "The variants exert pressure against each other in a *particular* poem and at particular places *within* that poem. Since one cannot read the variants simultaneously, with respect to the variants, noted as non-exclusive alternatives, Dickinson is unread because Dickinson is unreadable" (42).

I want to read the variants, and Dickinson, differently. I think that alternative words, whatever their relationship to one another, be it causal, conflicting, symptomatic, or associative, if taken together form a grid or context for meaning, which is then situated among the points of connotation and denotation that the words furnish. Alternatives, I would suggest, function in Dickinson's writing as a powerful counterweight to other of her writerly tendencies — elision, ellipsis, "unrecoverable deletions," and missing referents: impulses that result in the obscuring or repression of meaning. The materiality of her words provides one kind of context where, frequently, other contexts are lacking. Thus Dickinson shows us not her inability to choose as much as a largesse, a way to create meaning that is more full and ample than conventional poetics generally affords.

Let us look, for an example, at the final stanza of poem 508, "I'm ceded — I've stopped being Their's —," where there are a series of alternate words.

> My second Rank — too small the first —
> Crowned — Crowing [whimpering / dangling] — on my Father's breast —
> A half [too] unconscious Queen [An insufficient Queen] —
> But this time — Adequate — Erect,
> With Will [power] to choose, or to reject,
> And I choose, just a Crown [Throne] — [1]

In this well-known poem Dickinson contrasts her first and second "baptism": the first without, the second with, "choice." The final stanza describes the second, "supremest," naming. While stanzas 1 and 2 focus on the first event, and stanza 3 on the later one, the final stanza highlights the contrast itself by balancing the two "Ranks" within its lines. The first time found her on her father's breast — crowned, crowing — or whimpering or dangling. The alternates are especially useful for thinking about "Crowing." Crowned, yes, by the father (a literal and/or spiritual figure) but subservient and uncomfortable with it. Thus "Crowing," which *could* be read as "proud" and, in concert with "Crowned," suggests that this position in conjunction with the father is just fine, seems instead a kind of bleating, a halfhearted or inadequate gesture toward self-identity (whimpering, or worse, dangling there). Queen, yes, according to the terms of this particular master. Half-unconscious *and* insufficient. Insufficient for what? The description of the new or second state makes the "what" clear. The will or power that she now possesses enables self-determination: to choose or to reject. This crown or throne is different from the first one, because rather than being crowned (named, identified, controlled by him) she does the choosing and naming. Because her kind of choosing requires variants — compound and complex meanings — it stands in stylistic as well as philosophical and ideological contrast to the first kind of naming that she experienced.

When we go on to another of her habits, using the same words in more than one context, we see once again how materiality — that is, the physical contexts themselves — helps us read when more conceptual contexts have been elided.

Johnson's poem 323, "As if I asked a common Alms," for example, exists in three versions. The first was written in approximately 1858 and copied into fascicle 1; the second was incorporated into a letter written to T. W. Higginson in 1862; the third was written in 1884 in a letter to an unknown recipient. This is a style of Dickinson poem with which we are familiar: in the format of an analogy — "as if" — it refers away from itself to a circumstance or event that prompts the comparison. However, that experience is never named, never explained. I would argue that the opportunity to see the poem in more than one context — in this case, one fascicle and two letters — suggests to the reader something about the nature of the "missing" referent.

> As if I asked a common Alms,
> And in my wondering hand
> A Stranger pressed a Kingdom,
> And I, bewildered, stand —
>
> As if I asked the Orient
> Had it for me a Morn —
> And it should lift its purple Dikes,
> And shatter me with Dawn! (P323)[2]

The first version functions as a "poem" in the conventional sense. Copied neatly into Dickinson's first fascicle, without even a title to contextualize it, it communicates as a discrete act. Or perhaps not. Studies of the fascicles frequently look for themes or narrative strands that yoke the poems in a given fascicle — that is, contextualize them. John Gerlach's essay, "Reading Dickinson: Bolts, Hounds, the Variorum, and Fascicle 39," shows, more convincingly to me, that while it is problematic to read the fascicles as mininarratives, with plots and stories, there are verbal resonances — key words that are repeated or synonyms — that echo and contrast across the poems. In fascicle 1 words about losing and finding occur in a general context which emphasizes the necessity of death and loss and hopes for a possible finding, or heaven. "As if I asked a common Alms" sits on a page which also includes the conclusion to "There is a morn by men unseen — " and the whole of "She slept beneath a tree — ." The former describes a magical otherworldly May Day celebration; the latter, either a person in a grave or a flower before it blooms — or both. The May Day poem ends with these lines: "I wait thy far, fantastic bells — / Announcing me in other dells — / Unto the different dawn!" This is the only other poem in the fascicle in which the word "dawn" occurs, and this idea of an extraordinary other place or time or future has some resonance with "As if I asked a common Alms." In general, however, the poem doesn't seem to participate directly in the thematics or image structure of the fascicle at large.

In this instance the tendency to read it discretely, which is what we do when we encounter it in the Johnson edition, is strong. In such a case, we work to use the poem as its own context. To create such a context we note and arrange its linguistic ingredients. There is an "I" who is speaking, using two quite different vocabularies — first, words having to do with money and power; second, words from nature. The speaker is describing a general situation in which she asks for something — something that is little, or perhaps ordinary. In return she gets something extraordinary, out of the context of everyday experience. But the poem itself operates as an analogy for the situation in question, not a literal description of it. "It was" — as if. *What* was? The poem never says. The beggar seeking alms and getting a kingdom, the early riser seeking a nice day and getting "flooded" or, in the second version, "shattered" with color and light, are analogues for what "really" happened.

But since we're never told what really happened, we understand the poem in terms of what we *are* told. In the first sequence, it was as if the speaker, in a beggarly posture, asks for alms. A common alms implies both an ordinary sum and an ordinary act — as in "I'm used to asking." But this time, in return, an unidentified donor puts into that outstretched hand "a Kingdom." A huge amount of money, as in that old TV show where a man showed up every week on somebody's doorstep and announced that person had become a millionaire? Or a gift of something that turned a pauper into a prince? Her response is bewilderment, speechlessness. What sort of situation might this be?

The poem then provides another example, another comparison, another analogous situation. This time "it" is as if she had asked the Orient (a common word in Dickinson's parlance for the East) for morning. The ordinariness of the request casts a certain "light" on the act of asking for alms (the two acts are paralleled in the structure of the poem) — that, too, in her life, might well seem ordinary, everyday. The kind of response she gets this one special time is also parallel: something extraordinary — and accordingly overwhelming. It's an extraordinary image, too: the darkness lifting from purple to bright, like dikes opening on a river, so that the watcher is flooded, or shattered, with the sight and feel and experience that is dawn. Those verbs of being taken over, overwhelmed, overpowered, overcome, up the ante of "bewildered" in the first stanza, casting an interesting light on that bewildered standing which seems such a contrast to the initial asking. Maybe the "gift" is not only much but a little too much. The implication is there, certainly, if we think of the poem as having to do with using language, that is, asking (and then getting — or not getting, as the case may be).

There are suggestions here for which we find echoes in other of Dickinson's poems, poems not in fascicle 1, reminding us that Dickinson's tendency to echo herself is canonwide as well as fascicle-frequent, reminding us that all the poems together provide context, or circumference, for any given poem. For example, poem 315, "He fumbles at your Soul," in which the experience of receiving "full Music" from some outside agent is described as an "Etherial Blow" that "scalps your naked Soul." Such a vocabulary, juxtaposing "Etherial" and "Blow," or "full Music" and "scalps," intimates that there is danger as well as thrill in getting more than you ask for.

Getting rather than losing places this poem at odds with the fascicle (albeit that this set of poems is also tinged with the hope that these losses are *not* forever: "To lose — if one can find again — / To miss — if one shall meet —" [P22]). "As if I asked a common Alms" may well be the exception that proves the rule, or in this case, undoes it. But in the undoing, it also hints at difficulties unimagined by speakers in the other poems who more simply try to deal with the pain of loss. The poem raises many questions, not only about why its speaker isn't used to getting what she wants, why she casts herself as a beggar or a postulant, and why she asks, but about the profound implications of getting so *much*.

In 1862 Dickinson used these lines in a letter, her third, to the editor T. W. Higginson (L265). As we know, he had written an article, "Letter to a Young Contributor," in the *Atlantic Monthly*, offering advice to beginning writers, which is probably why Dickinson wrote to him in April of 1862 to ask if her verse were "alive." (She also asked if he were "too deeply occupied." He was, after all, a stranger and someone she considered a powerful public figure.) She enclosed four poems with that letter and her name on a card in its own envelope. In the second letter she mentions his "surgery" on her first offerings, sends two more poems, and gives him a rather fictitious biography of herself.

Her third letter to Higginson provides a context for "As if I asked a common Alms," though the poem has not been written specifically for this occasion. In it she thanks him for praise, praise which has followed upon the surgery that she received first. She has, she says, had few pleasures so deep as his opinion — although, she notes, it didn't totally overwhelm her, as in, make her drunken — because that had happened to her before (when?). Still, if she really were to thank him, she wouldn't be able to speak ("tears would block my tongue"), a situation she might not especially enjoy. She goes on to rehearse the history of his blame as well as praise, and she actually spends more time defending herself against the blame than appreciating the praise. "You think my gait 'spasmodic' — I am in danger — Sir —." "You think me 'uncontrolled' — I have no Tribunal." She notes as well that although his criticism is "True" — it is "justice"; she cannot drop the "Bells whose jingling cool[s] [her] Tramp." She observes in infamous lines that if fame belonged to her she could not escape it, a comment which certainly modifies the previous remark that publishing is as foreign to her thought as "Firmament to Fin."

The letter, in fact, is fascinating in its seesaw motion, as she alternates between pride in herself and obsequiousness to him: "I have a little shape — it would not crowd your Desk — nor make much racket as the Mouse, that dents your Galleries — ." Each tone or attitude shadows the other, glossing it. What *does* she want from him? "Control," she says. "The Sailor cannot see the North — but knows the Needle can — ." Of the two figures in the analogy, the sailor is the active human agent, the needle an instrument, a tool. And yet it would be impolitic at the very least for a young woman from the provinces to talk to a respected gentleman editor as if she wanted to *use* him. So she prevaricates a little, flatters a lot — she veils her criticism in praise — she also undercuts her praise. It is a masterly performance, which concludes, almost, with the poem.

The reference for "as if" can now be read as her act of sending him the poems and receiving his praise for them. As in, "I didn't expect much" (after all, she tells him in the second letter that she has made "no verse — but one or two — until this winter — Sir — ," when actually she had written literally hundreds of poems by that period in her life) "and look what I got!" And yet, the bewildering Kingdom in the palm, the flooding, shattering Dawn, are analogies which might just as readily refer to his "surgery," his bleeding her. As in, "I asked you just to respond to the poems, and I got in return this excessive attack." In either case, her inability to *speak* after his response becomes more ominous than in our first reading of the lines. Clearly, she needs all her wiles — feminine wiles, verbal wiles — to protect herself from that fate. The epistolary act which surrounds the poem this time, the letter to Higginson, as devious a performance as one is likely to encounter ("Candor," wrote Dickinson, "is the only wile"), is her best defense against the dawn's shattering. "But will you be my Preceptor, Mr. Higginson?"

Finally, the lines reappear one more time, in a letter written in 1884, one year before her death, discovered on two drafts among her papers. The epistolary context is much more ambiguous.

> Dear friend —
>
> But of what shall I first speak — the beautiful Child, or it's deep Possessor, or the little "Book" it is famine to read till I have obtained it —
> Thank you for the grave — empty and full — too —
> As if I asked a common Alms and in my wondering Hand A Stranger pressed a Kingdom, and I bewildered stand. As if I asked the Orient had it for me a Morn, And it should lift it's Purple Dikes, and shatter me with Dawn —
> Your Letter much impressed me — Your every suggestion is Dimension
> Thought is the Knock which[3]

Dickinson refers to a child, a book, and a grave. That is about all I can say with any certainty. (Johnson suggests that she has received a photo of a mother and child, though that isn't apparent to me from her words.) These words preface our "poem," now arranged no differently from the other words on the page, with the exception of her starting a new line after "Morn" and "Dawn" (Johnson prints the poem in four lines, but he alters the manuscript form to do so [L964; *Letters* 857–58]).

Here the opening words are even more opaque in their referents than the poem, so that in this instance the "poem" sheds light, a little, on the "prose" rather than vice versa. Something about the situation at hand — the relationship of death to life? — is like getting more than you had originally expected or asked for, even if the getting is itself ambiguous in its powerful effect. Whatever the case, the words of the poem seem to Dickinson suited to and suitable for the sentiment she is expressing in her letter. They fit the situation, whatever the situation may be.

It's interesting that, even when on two occasions a context from "real life" is provided for this "sceneless" poem, that situation is itself expressed ambiguously, mysteriously, not at all *literally* (rather like a poem), and the "as if" of the poem does *not* get subsumed into the actual event, becoming as it were a simple analogy. The poem not only maintains its own life or experientiality but seems to me more immediate, more compelling, than the event or events that function as its referent. Further, we cannot ignore the fact that these events in real life are plural, not singular, and that the poem was written before either of them.

Seeing the poem in alternative contexts suggests to me — and here I differ with the Editing Collective's idea that the particularity of the intended audience or recipient determines the identity of a poem or body of writing — that the "absent referent" in many Dickinson poems is less absent than it is "archaic" or "primary." The external contexts or referents or recipients can vary, because they are not the originary occasion for these lines of poetry; they are, rather, stimuli and echo. These words seem to me to be expressive of a psychodynamic situation indigenous to Dickinson's interior or mental life. Thus it is not an event in the world that motivates the poem so much as that the poem motivates events in the world — by which I mean that the poem articulates a psychological template which influences how Dickinson interprets experience. Many occurrences seem to her to have to do with needing to ask, with getting a response out of proportion to the request, a response which could be gift or curse or both in some interrelated fashion. But the originary "event" to which the poem refers (what was as if) cannot be readily named because, I believe, it comes from a very early period in her life when she did not have words, or when what happened was never spoken about. The repetitive insistence upon finding some kind of words — an "as if" — for the event, a repetition that occurs within the very fabric of the poem itself, which tries twice for language about it, points to both its significance for the writer *and* its lack of a verbal home in her consciousness. With words she seeks repeatedly to give it a materiality: that is one of the functions of her writing.

By CALLING attention to the various materialities of her writing, I am trying to show how emphasis upon this materiality aids us in our reading of Dickinson's work that involves editing practices and goes beyond them, too. A look at the essays published in the *Emily Dickinson Journal*, a locus for what is most current in Dickinson studies, reveals a series of papers that relate to Dickinson's writing practices and their impact on the editing of her work.[4] These include "Corresponding Worlds: The Art of Emily Dickinson's Letters" by Sarah Wider (1992), " 'By a Mouth That Cannot Speak': Spectral Presence in Dickinson's Letters" by Paula Bennett (1992), "Emily Dickinson's Visible Language" by Jerome McGann (1993), and "Re-reading the Poems: Editing Opportunities in Variant Versions" by Marget Sands (1996). In fact, a Special Issue was published in 1995 on editing and the letters. It contains Ralph Franklin's "Emily Dickinson to Abiah Root: Ten Reconstructed Letters," Ellen Louise Hart's "The Elizabeth Whitney Putnam Manuscripts and New Strategies for Editing Emily Dickinson's Letters," Martha Nell Smith's "The Importance of a Hypermedia Archive of Dickinson's Creative Work," and William Shurr's "Editing the *New Poems of Emily Dickinson*," all directly focused on editing. Also included are Lewis Putnam Turco's "Iron Pyrites in the Dickinson Mine," a discussion of Dickinson's prosody and how it informs her letters, and Erika Scheurer's " 'Near, but remote': Emily Dickinson's Epistolary Voice," which examines the nature of the epistolary voice that Dickinson uses to create both intimacy and distance with the reader. Scheurer's essay is as much about how we read the letters as about how the letters are written, because more often than not, as I have been suggesting, these are overlapping concerns.

Indeed, reading Dickinson has been an important concern for contributors to the *Journal*. Such essays include "No Frame of Reference: The Absence of Context in Emily Dickinson's Poetry" by Lynn Shakinovsky (1994), "Reading Dickinson: Bolts, Hounds, the Variorum, and Fascicle 39" by John Gerlach (1994), and my own and Cristanne Miller's conference presentation, "Comic Power: A Performance" (1996). As well, we have published a series of papers by international translators of Dickinson, such as "A Perspective on Reading Dickinson in Japan" by Yoko Shimazaki (1993) and "Emily Dickinson in Polish: Recent Translations" by Agnieszka Salska (1996) in a special issue on translating Dickinson (1997).

Attention to materiality expands as well into exploration of cultural issues — for example, study of the complex publishing history of Dickinson's poetry, focused both on Thomas H. Johnson's 1955 editing of the complete poems, as in Jo-Anne Cappeluti's "Fading Ratios: Johnson's Variorum Edition of Emily Dickinson's Poetry" (1992), and on the women who *first* edited her and wrote her story: Mabel Loomis Todd, her daughter Millicent Todd Bingham, and Susan Dickinson's daughter Martha Dickinson Bianchi. That interweave of competition, anger, admiration, ambition, and dedication is a fascinating story. These papers include "Editorial Policy in *The Poems of Emily Dickinson, Third Series*" by Caroline C. Maun (1994) on Mabel Loomis Todd's editing practices, and "To Market: The Dickinson Copyright Wars" (1996) by Elizabeth Horan on the publishing battles between Martha Dickinson Bianchi and Millicent Todd Bingham. There are as well many studies of the lived experience of women in her time—including the pressures, privileges, and ramifications of class, race, and sexual orientation and how they impact writing, such as Judith Pascoe's " 'The House Encore Me So': Emily Dickinson and Jenny Lind" (1992), "Emily Dickinson, *Harper's*, and Femininity" by Mark Bauerlein (1996), and "Emily Dickinson: Reading a Spinster" by Esther Loehndorf (1996).

Thinking of Dickinson's gendered position as a woman writing leads scholars to consider her in literary as well as social contexts: for example, " 'Goblin with a Gauge': Dickinson's Readerly Gothic" by Daneen Wardrop (1992), "Emily Dickinson's Circumference: Figuring a Blind Spot in the Romantic Tradition" by Laura Gribbin (1993), "[Im]pertinent Constructions of Body and Self: Dickinson's Use of the Romantic Grotesque" by Cynthia Griffin Wolff (1993), "Dickinson's Sentimental Explorations of 'The Ecstasy of Parting' " by Marianne Noble (1996), and " 'A Letter is a Joy of Earth': Emily Dickinson's Letters and Victorian Epistolary Conventions" by Stephanie A. Tingley (1996).

Scholars are interested in exploring Dickinson's personal relationships with women, including girlhood friends and particularly her best friend and sister-in-law, Susan Gilbert Dickinson. Aífe Murray writes on Dickinson and her maid, Margaret Maher, in "Kitchen Table Poetics" (1996), and Martha Ackmann writes on Dickinson and her maternal lineage, the Norcross family, in " 'I'm Glad I Finally Surfaced': A Norcross Descendant Remembers Emily Dickinson" (1996). Scholars look as well at Dickinson's relationships, in her mind, with other women writers: American writers of her time, as does Katharine Rodier in " 'What Is Inspiration?': Emily Dickinson, T. W. Higginson, and Maria White Lowell" (1995); the British novelists George Eliot and the Brontë sisters and the poet Elizabeth Barrett Browning, whom she adored and who were vivid presences in her imagination, as Karen Richardson Gee shows in "Dickinson's Readings of Women Writers' Biographies" (1994).

Many essays situate Dickinson in her culture at large. The range of these concerns is indicated by the following: "Disclosing Pictures: Emily Dickinson's Quotations from the Paintings of Thomas Cole, Frederic Church, and Holman Hunt" by Judith Farr (1993), "Emily Dickinson and 'The Indicator': A Transcendental Frolic" by Barton Levi St. Armand (1993), "Emily Dickinson and the Limit of War" by Tyler B. Hoffman (1994), " 'This World is not Conclusion': Dickinson, Amherst, and 'the local conditions of the soul' " by Benjamin Lease (1994), "Law, Property, and Provincialism in Dickinson's Poems and Letters to Judge Otis Phillips Lord" by James Guthrie (1996), "Dickinson Reading" by Joan Kirkby (1996), and "Some of the Things We Mean When We Say 'New England' " by Jonathan Morse (1996).

There has been particular attention to her religious cultural heritage, so vital in the Connecticut Valley of her day, and its relation to her own structures of belief. Frequently, although not always, gender becomes an important element to consider here. These essays include Roseanne Hoefel's "Emily Dickinson Fleshing Out a New Word" (1992), Claudia Yukman's "Breaking the Eschatological Framework: Dickinson's Narrative Acts" (1992), Beth Maclay Doriani's "Emily Dickinson, Homilectics, and Prophetic Power" (1992), Rowena Revis Jones's "A Taste of 'Poison': Dickinson's Departure from Orthodoxy" (1993), Joanna Yin's " 'Arguments of Pearl': Dickinson's Response to Puritan Semiology" (1993), Alicia Ostriker's "Replaying the Bible: My Emily Dickinson" (1993), and Diane Gabrielsen Scholl's "From Aaron 'Drest' to Dickinson's 'Queen': Protestant Typology in Herbert and Dickinson" (1994).

Looking through the *Emily Dickinson Journal* and thinking about the material Dickinson, I am struck as well by other essays, those that focus not on the physical situation of Dickinson's writing but on its language: on, for example, punctuation, figuration, poetic structure, and lexical senses. Among these are Paul Crumbley's "Dickinson's Dashes and the Limits of Discourse" (1992), Cynthia Hogue's " 'I Did'nt Be—Myself': Emily Dickinson's Semiotics of Presence" (1992), Kamilla Denman's "Emily Dickinson's Volcanic Punctuation" (1993), Roland Hagenbüchle's "Emily Dickinson's Poetic Covenant" (1993), Cynthia Hallen and Laura Harvey's "Translation and the Emily Dickinson Lexicon" (1993), Jay Ladin's "Breaking the Line: Emily Dickinson and William Carlos Williams" (1994), Shirley Sharon-Zisser's " 'To See—Comparatively': Emily Dickinson's Use of Simile" (1994), and John Mulvihill's "Why Dickinson Didn't Title" (1996).

At first glance this kind of study seems another tack altogether: more of a "New Critical" approach, perhaps, if we think of that perspective as viewing the poem as distinct from and not needing any other context. And yet, because this is Dickinson, we might remember that she herself consistently emphasized the materiality of language—asking if her "Verse is alive" (265) or noting how "Infection in the sentence breeds" (P1261)—and that she is the poet of whom it is now quite commonplace to say that she "lived in language." For Dickinson language was definitely a "world," a context as important to *her* as Amherst, Massachusetts. And so I think that these essays are indicative of the range of what is "material" about Dickinson. They remind us that, while attention to the physical arrangement of Dickinson's words on the page, or to her physical presence in her culture, is crucial for reading her, so, too, do we need to apprehend the interior architecture of Dickinson's world of language. For language does not only point away from itself, to ideas, emotions, associations. It is a presence, an actuality; it has a material existence that provokes scholarly exploration. In conclusion, then, I would suggest that in the nineties the concept of materiality, with its manifold and complex implications, opens the way to exciting new directions for Dickinson studies.

Notes

1. Johnson (1955) 2: 389–90. Johnson places the variant words after the poem, as does Dickinson in her manuscript (see Franklin, *Manuscript Books*, 1: 363–64); I have positioned them in the line to which she refers with a cross mark so as to read them as part of the poem.

2. Franklin, *Manuscript Books*, 1: 10. In Johnson's text, however, this poem is placed far from the other poems of fascicle 1, which are all at the very beginning of his edition.

3. Manuscript 845, Amherst College Archives and Special Collections.

4. I should point out that there are many essays in the *Emily Dickinson Journal* that take other lines of critical inquiry from the one that I am identifying here as "material." There are, for example, papers that are more philosophical, psychoanalytic, or textually oriented in their focus. Nor are the essays that I cite in the following pages all of the materially based studies. I have chosen these as representative of key concerns from this perspective.

Further Reading

Morris, Timothy. *Becoming Canonical in American Poetry*, Chicago: University of Chicago Press, 1995.

Smith, Robert McClure. *The Seductions of Emily Dickinson*. Tuscaloosa: University of Alabama Press, 1996.

Wardrop, Daneen. *Emily Dickinson's Gothic: Goblin with a Gauge*. Iowa City: University of Iowa Press, 1996.

Works Cited

ABBREVIATIONS

EDIS: The Emily Dickinson International Society
EDJ: *The Emily Dickinson Journal*
ESQ: *Emerson Society Quarterly*

Ackmann, Martha. "'I'm Glad I Finally Surfaced': A Norcross Descendant Remembers Emily Dickinson." *EDJ* 5.2 (1996): 120–26.
Aiken, Conrad. "The Dickinson Myth." *Yale Review* 20 (1931): 393–96.
———. "Emily Dickinson." Blake and Wells 110–17.
———, ed. *Selected Poems of Emily Dickinson.* London: Cape, 1924.
Al-Bedrani, Fatima Falih Ahmed. "The Themes and Motifs of Emily Dickinson's Poetry." Article in ms., May 1995.
Anderson, Charles R. "The Conscious Self in Emily Dickinson's Poetry." *American Literature* 31.3 (1959): 290–308.
———. *Emily Dickinson's Poetry: Stairway of Surprise.* New York: Holt, Rinehart and Winston, 1960.
Ashton, Dore. *A Joseph Cornell Album.* New York: Viking, 1974.
Atkinson, J. Brooks. Review of *Alison's House,* by Susan Glaspell. *New York Times* 10 May 1931: 8:1.
Avery, Kevin J. "*The Heart of the Andes* Exhibited: Frederic E. Church's Window of the Equatorial World." *American Art Journal* 18.1 (1986): 52–72.
Bakhtin, Mikhail. *The Dialogic Imagination: Four Essays by M. M. Bakhtin.* Ed. and trans. Caryl Emerson and Michael Holquist. Austin: University of Texas Press, 1981.
———. *Speech Genres and Other Late Essays.* Trans. Vern W. McGee. Ed. Caryl Emerson and Michael Holquist. Austin: University of Texas Press, 1986.
Banning, Evelyn I. *Helen Hunt Jackson.* New York: Vanguard, 1971.
Banzer, Judith. "'Compound Manner': Emily Dickinson and the Metaphysical Poets." *American Literature* 23 (1961): 417–33.
Barker, Wendy. *Lunacy of Light: Emily Dickinson and the Experience of Metaphor.* Carbondale: Southern Illinois University Press, 1987.
Baruffol, Siegfried. "Emily Dickinson: Poems on Poetry and Poets." Licentiate thesis. University of Zürich, 1975.
Bates, Arlo. "Miss Dickinson's Poems." Blake and Wells 12–18.
Bauerlein, Mark. "Emily Dickinson, *Harper's,* and Femininity." *EDJ* 5.2 (1996): 72–77.
Baym, Nina. "God, Father, and Lover in Emily Dickinson's Poetry." *PMLA* 164 (1979): 193–209.

——. *Novels, Readers, and Reviewers: Responses to Fiction in Antebellum America*. Ithaca: Cornell University Press, 1984.

Beese, Henriette. *Nachdichtung als Erinnerung: Allegorische Lektüre einiger Gedichte von Paul Celan*. Darmstadt: Agora-Verlag, 1976.

Behnke, Kerstin. "Emily Dickinson in deutschen Übersetzungen unter besonderer Berücksichtigung von Paul Celans Übertragungen aus dem Englischen." Master's thesis. Göttingen, 1987.

Bennett, Fordyce R. *A Reference Guide to the Bible in Emily Dickinson's Poetry*. Lanham, Md.: Scarecrow, 1977.

Bennett, Paula. "By a Mouth That Cannot Speak: Spectral Presence in Dickinson's Letters." *EDJ* 1.2 (1992): 76–99.

——. *Emily Dickinson: Woman Poet*. Iowa City: University of Iowa Press, 1990.

——. *My Life a Loaded Gun: Female Creativity and Feminist Poetics*. Boston: Beacon, 1986.

——. " 'The Orient is in the West': Emily Dickinson's Reading of *Antony and Cleopatra*." *Women's Revisions of Shakespeare: On the Responses of Woolf, Rich, H. D., George Eliot, and Others*. Ed. Marianne Novy. Urbana: University of Illinois Press, 1990. 108–22.

Bercovitch, Sacvan. *The American Jeremiad*. Madison: University of Wisconsin Press, 1978.

Bernhard, Mary Elizabeth Kromer. "Portrait of a Family: Emily Dickinson's Norcross Connection." *New England Quarterly* 60 (1987): 363–81.

——. "Response to 'Eyes Be Blind, Heart Be Still.' " *New England Quarterly* 55 (1982): 112–14.

Bialosky, Marshall. Review of *The Twilight Stood: Song Cycle for Soprano and Piano*, by Leon Kirchner; text by Emily Dickinson. *Notes* 45 (1989): 861–63.

Bianchi, Martha Dickinson, ed. *The Complete Poems of Emily Dickinson*. Boston: Little, Brown, 1924.

——. *Emily Dickinson Face to Face: Unpublished Letters with Notes and Reminiscences*. Boston: Houghton Mifflin, 1932.

——, ed. *The Life and Letters of Emily Dickinson*. Boston: Houghton Mifflin, 1924.

Bianchi, Martha Dickinson and Alfred Leete Hampson, eds. *Further Poems of Emily Dickinson*. Boston: Little, Brown, 1929.

——, eds. *Unpublished Poems of Emily Dickinson*. Boston: Little, Brown, 1935.

Bingham, Millicent Todd. *Ancestors' Brocades: The Literary Debut of Emily Dickinson*. New York: Harper, 1945.

——, ed. *Emily Dickinson's Home: Letters of Edward Dickinson and His Family*. New York: Harper, 1955.

Bingham, Millicent Todd, and Mabel Loomis Todd, eds. *Bolts of Melody: New Poems of Emily Dickinson*. New York: Harper, 1945.

Bischoff, Volker. "Edmund Clarence Stedman's Aesthetics." *American Poetry between Tradition and Modernism, 1865–1914*. Ed. Roland Hagenbüchle. Regensburg: Friedrich Pustet, 1984. 55–69.

Bishop, Elizabeth. "Unseemly Deductions." *New Republic* 127 (1952): 20.

Black, Max. *Models and Metaphors*. Ithaca: Cornell University Press, 1962.

Blackmur, R. P. "Emily Dickinson: Notes on Prejudice and Fact." Blake and Wells 201–23.

Blake, Caesar R., and Carlton F. Wells, eds. *The Recognition of Emily Dickinson.* Ann Arbor: University of Michigan Press, 1964.

Blasing, Mutlu Konuk. *American Poetry: The Rhetoric of Its Forms.* New Haven: Yale University Press, 1987.

Bloom, Harold. *The Western Canon: The Books and School of the Ages.* New York: Harcourt Brace, 1994.

Bolger, Doreen, and Kathleen Motes Bennewitz. "Thomas Cole's *Garden of Eden.*" *Magazine Antiques* 137 (1990): 104–11.

Boswell, Jeanetta. *Emily Dickinson: A Bibliography of Secondary Sources, with Selective Annotations, 1890 through 1987.* Jefferson, N.C.: McFarland, 1989.

Bowles, Samuel. Papers. Houghton Library, Harvard University, Cambridge.

Boyle, Richard J. *American Impressionism.* Boston: Little, Brown, 1974.

Bryan, Sharon, ed. *Where We Stand: Women Poets on Literary Tradition.* New York: Norton, 1993.

Brooks, Virginia. "Martha on Film." *Dance Magazine* July 1991: 62–63. Special Issue on Martha Graham.

Buckingham, Willis J. "The Bibliographical Study of Emily Dickinson." *Resources for American Literary Study* 4 (1974): 57–71.

——. *Emily Dickinson: An Annotated Bibliography: Writings, Scholarship, Criticism, and Ana, 1850–1968.* Bloomington: Indiana University Press, 1970.

——. "Emily Dickinson's Dictionary." *Harvard Literary Bulletin* 25 (1977): 489–91.

——, ed. *Emily Dickinson's Reception in the 1890s: A Documentary History.* Pittsburgh: University of Pittsburgh Press, 1989.

——. "Poetry Readers and Reading in the 1890s: Emily Dickinson's First Reception." *Readers in History: Nineteenth-Century American Literature and the Context of Response.* Ed. James L. Machor. Baltimore: Johns Hopkins University Press, 1993.

Budick, E. Miller. *Emily Dickinson and the Life of Language: A Study in Symbolic Poetics.* Baton Rouge: Louisiana State University Press, 1985.

Buell, Lawrence. *New England Literary Culture: From Revolution through Renaissance.* Cambridge: Cambridge University Press, 1986.

Burbick, Joan. "Emily Dickinson and the Economics of Desire." *American Literature* 58 (1986): 361–78.

——. "'One Unbroken Company': Religion and Emily Dickinson." *New England Quarterly* 53 (1980): 62–75.

Burke, Kenneth. *A Grammar of Motives and A Rhetoric of Motives.* Cleveland: Meridian Books, World, 1962.

——. *Language as Symbolic Action: Essays on Life, Literature, and Method.* Berkeley: University of California Press, 1966.

Cameron, Sharon. *Choosing Not Choosing: Dickinson's Fascicles.* Chicago: University of Chicago Press, 1992.

——. *Lyric Time: Dickinson and the Limits of Genre.* Baltimore: Johns Hopkins University Press, 1979.

Capps, Jack L. *Emily Dickinson's Reading, 1836–1886.* Cambridge: Harvard University Press, 1966.

——. *The Life of Emily Dickinson.* New York: Farrar, Straus and Giroux, 1974.

Cappeluti, Jo-Anne. "Fading Ratios: Johnson's Variorum Edition of Emily Dickinson's Poetry." *EDJ* 1.2 (1992): 100–120.

Carman, Bliss. "A Note on Emily Dickinson." Blake and Wells 61–68.

Carton, Evan. *The Rhetoric of American Romance: Dialectic and Identity in Emerson, Dickinson, Poe, and Hawthorne.* Baltimore: Johns Hopkins University Press, 1985.

Celan, Paul, *Gesammelte Werke.* Ed. Beda Allemann and Stefan Reichert. Frankfurt/Main: Suhrkamp, 1983.

———. "Der Tod, da ich nicht halten konnt." *Almanach S. Fischer* 73 (1959): 59.

Chase, Richard. *Emily Dickinson.* American Men of Letters Series. New York: Sloane, 1951.

Chicago, Judy. *The Dinner Party: A Symbol of Our Heritage.* New York: Anchor/Doubleday, 1979.

Chilvers, Ian, ed. *The Concise Oxford Dictionary of Art and Artists.* Oxford: Oxford University Press, 1990.

Christman, Kelly. "Ballet Recreates Emily Dickinson." *Springfield (Mass.) Morning Union* 26 July 1984: 1.

Cikovsky, Nicolai, Jr. "Modern and National." *Winslow Homer.* Ed. Cikovsky and Franklin Kelly. New Haven: National Gallery of Art and Yale University Press, 1995.

Clendenning, Sheila T. *Emily Dickinson: A Bibliography, 1850–1966.* Kent, Ohio: Kent State University Press, 1968.

Cody, John. *After Great Pain: The Inner Life of Emily Dickinson.* Cambridge: Harvard University Press, 1971.

Cole, Thomas. "Essay on American Scenery." *American Art, 1700–1960.* Ed. John W. McCoubrey. Englewood Cliffs, N.J.: Prentice-Hall, 1965.

Colton, A. M. *The Old Meeting House and Vacation Papers, Humorous and Other.* New York: Worthington, 1890.

Concord Enterprise. 5 March 1896. Concord Free Public Library, Concord, Mass.

Concord Freeman. 11 Jan. 1894. Concord Free Public Library. Concord, Mass.

Cook, Albert. *Thresholds: Studies in the Romantic Experience.* Madison: University of Wisconsin Press, 1985.

Copland, Aaron, comp. *Twelve Poems of Emily Dickinson.* New York: Boosey, 1951. Columbia M30375.

Copland, Aaron, and Vivian Perlis. *Copland since 1945.* New York: St. Martin's, 1989.

Copple, Lee Biggerstaff. "Three Related Themes of Hunger and Thirst, Homelessness, and Obscurity as Symbols of Privation, Renunciation, and Compensation in the Poems of Emily Dickinson." Ph.D. diss. University of Michigan, 1954.

Crumbley, Paul. "Dickinson's Dashes and the Limits of Discourse." *EDJ* 1.2 (1992): 8–29.

———. *Inflections of the Pen: Dash and Voice in Emily Dickinson.* Lexington: University Press of Kentucky, 1997.

Damon, S. Foster. *Amy Lowell: A Chronicle.* Boston: Houghton Mifflin, 1935.

Dandurand, Karen. "Another Dickinson Poem Published in Her Lifetime." *American Literature* 54 (1982): 434–37.

———. "Dickinson and the Public." Orzeck and Weisbuch 255–77.

———, ed. *Dickinson Scholarship: An Annotated Bibliography, 1969–1985.* New York: Garland, 1988.

———. "New Dickinson Civil War Publications." *American Literature* 56 (1984): 17–27.

Danly, Susan, ed. *Language as Object: Emily Dickinson and Contemporary Art.* Amherst: University of Massachusetts Press, 1997.

Davidson, James. "Emily Dickinson and Isaac Watts." *Boston Public Library Quarterly* 1954: 141–49.

Decker, William Merrill. "A Letter Always Seems to Me Like Immortality: The Correspondence of Emily Dickinson." *ESQ* 39 (1993): 77–104.

De Eulis, Marilyn Davis. "Whitman's 'The First Dandelion' and Emily Dickinson's 'The Dandelion's Pallid Tube.'" *Walt Whitman Review* 25 (1979): 29–32.

De Jong, Mary. "'With my burden I begin': The (Im)personal 'I' of Nineteenth-Century Hymnody." *Studies in Puritan American Spirituality* 4 (1993): 185–223.

de Mille, Agnes. *Martha: The Life and Work of Martha Graham.* New York: Random House, 1991.

Denman, Kamilla. "Emily Dickinson's Volcanic Punctuation." *EDJ* 2.1 (1993): 22–46.

Dickenson, Donna. *Emily Dickinson.* Leamington Spa: Berg, 1985.

Dickie, Margaret. "Dickinson's Discontinuous Lyric Self." *American Literature* 60.4 (1988): 537–53.

——. *Lyric Contingencies: Emily Dickinson and Wallace Stevens.* Philadelphia: University of Pennsylvania Press, 1991.

Dickinson Editing Collective. *Dickinson Electronic Archives.* Available http://jefferson village.virginia.edu/dickinson/.

Dickinson, Edward. Papers. Emily Dickinson Collection. Houghton Library. Harvard University. Cambridge.

Dickinson, Emily. *Bolts of Melody: New Poems of Emily Dickinson.* Ed. Millicent Todd Bingham and Mabel Loomis Todd. New York: Harper, 1945.

——. *Collected Poems.* Ed. Peter Siegenthaler. Philadelphia: Courage Books, 1991.

——. *The Complete Poems of Emily Dickinson.* Ed. Martha Dickinson Bianchi. Boston: Little, Brown, 1924.

——. *The Complete Poems of Emily Dickinson.* Ed. Thomas H. Johnson. Boston: Little, Brown, 1960.

——. *Emily Dickinson's Home: Letters of Edward Dickinson and His Family.* Ed. Millicent Todd Bingham. New York: Harper, 1955.

——. *For Love of Her: Poems by Emily Dickinson.* With drawings by Walter Stein. New York: Potter, 1974.

——. *From Amherst to Cashmere: Selected Poems of Emily Dickinson.* With ten color etchings by Margaret Taylor. Amherst: Tiamat, 1986.

——. *Further Poems of Emily Dickinson.* Ed. Martha Dickinson Bianchi and Alfred Leete Hampson. Boston: Little, Brown, 1929.

——. *The Letters of Emily Dickinson.* Ed. Thomas H. Johnson and Theodora Ward. 3 vols. Cambridge: Harvard University Press, 1958.

——. *The Life and Letters of Emily Dickinson.* Ed. Martha Dickinson Bianchi. Boston: Houghton Mifflin, 1924.

——. *New Poems of Emily Dickinson.* Ed. William H. Shurr. Chapel Hill: University of North Carolina Press, 1993.

——. *Poems by Emily Dickinson.* Ed. Thomas Wentworth Higginson and Mabel Loomis Todd. Second Series. Boston: Roberts Brothers, 1891.

——. *Poems by Emily Dickinson.* Ed. Mabel Loomis Todd and Thomas Wentworth Higginson. Boston: Roberts Brothers, 1890.

——. *The Poems of Emily Dickinson*. Ed. Thomas H. Johnson. Cambridge: Harvard University Press, 1951.

——. *The Poems of Emily Dickinson*. Ed. Thomas H. Johnson. 3 vols. Cambridge: Harvard University Press, 1955.

——. *Selected Poems of Emily Dickinson*. Ed. Conrad Aiken. London: Cape, 1924.

——. *The Single Hound: Poems of a Lifetime by Emily Dickinson*. Ed. Martha Dickinson Bianchi. Boston: Little, Brown, 1914.

——. *Twelve Poems of Emily Dickinson*. Comp. Aaron Copland. New York: Boosey, 1951. Columbia M30375.

——. *Unpublished Poems of Emily Dickinson*. Ed. Martha Dickinson Bianchi and Alfred Leete Hampson. Boston: Little, Brown, 1935.

Dickinson, Susan Gilbert. "Miss Emily Dickinson of Amherst." Buckingham *Reception*, App. A; Leyda 2: 472–74.

Diehl, Joanne Feit. " 'Come Slowly—Eden': An Exploration of Women Poets and Their Muse." *Signs* 3.3 (1978): 527–87.

——. *Dickinson and the Romantic Imagination*. Princeton: Princeton University Press, 1981.

——. "Ransom in a Voice: Language as Defense in Dickinson's Poetry." Juhasz, *Feminist Critics* 156–76.

——. *Women Poets and the American Sublime*. Bloomington: Indiana University Press, 1990.

Diggory, Terence. *Yeats and American Poetry: The Tradition of the Self.* Princeton: Princeton University Press, 1983.

di Giuseppe, Rita. "The Maiden and the Music: Dickinson's Tropes of Poetic Creation." *Quaderni di Lingue e Letterature* 12 (1987): 39–56.

Dijkstra, Bram. *Idols of Perversity*. New York: Oxford University Press, 1986.

Dobson, Joanne. *Dickinson and the Strategies of Reticence: The Woman Writer in Nineteenth-Century America*. Bloomington: Indiana University Press, 1989.

Doriani, Beth Maclay. *Emily Dickinson, Daughter of Prophecy*. Amherst: University of Massachusetts Press, 1996.

——. "Emily Dickinson, Homilectics, and Prophetic Power." *EDJ* 1.2 (1992): 54–75.

Duchac, Joseph. *The Poems of Emily Dickinson: An Annotated Guide to Commentary Published in English, 1890–1989*. Boston: Hall, 1979 (vol. 1) and 1993 (vol. 2).

Eberwein, Jane Donahue. *Dickinson: Strategies of Limitation*. Amherst: University of Massachusetts Press, 1985.

——. "Doing Without: Dickinson as Yankee Woman Poet." *Critical Essays on Emily Dickinson*. Ed. Paul J. Ferlazzo. Boston: Hall, 1984. 205–23.

——. " 'Graphicer for Grace': Emily Dickinson's Calvinist Language." *Studies in Puritan American Spirituality* 1 (1990): 170–201.

Emerson, Ralph Waldo. *The Collected Works*. Ed. Alfred R. Ferguson and Jean Ferguson Carr. 5 vols. Cambridge: Harvard University Press, 1979.

England, Martha Winburn. "Emily Dickinson and Isaac Watts: Puritan Hymnodists." *Bulletin of the New York Public Library* 59 (1965): 83–116.

Erkkila, Betsy. "Dickinson and Rich: Toward a Theory of Female Poetic Influence." *American Literature* 56.4 (1984): 541–59.

——. "Emily Dickinson and Class." *American Literary History* 4 (1992): 1–27.

——. "Emily Dickinson on Her Own Terms." *Wilson Quarterly* 9.11 (1982): 98–109.

——. *The Wicked Sisters: Women Poets, Literary History, and Discord.* New York: Oxford University Press, 1992.

Faderman, Lillian. "Emily Dickinson's Homoerotic Poetry." *Higginson Journal* 18 (1978): 19–27.

——. "Emily Dickinson's Letters to Sue Gilbert." *Massachusetts Review* 18.2 (1977): 197–225.

——. *Surpassing the Love of Men: Romantic Friendship and Love between Women from the Renaissance to the Present.* New York: Morrow, 1981.

Farr, Judith [Banzer]. " 'Compound Manner': Emily Dickinson and the Metaphysical Poets." *American Literature* 32 (1961): 417–33.

——. "Disclosing Pictures: Emily Dickinson's Quotations from the Paintings of Thomas Cole, Frederic Church, and Holman Hunt." *EDJ* 2.2 (1993): 66–77.

——, ed. *Emily Dickinson: A Collection of Critical Essays.* Englewood Cliffs, N.J.: Prentice-Hall, 1995.

——. "Emily Dickinson's 'Engulfing' Play: *Antony and Cleopatra.*" *Tulsa Studies in Women's Literature* 9.2 (1990): 231–50.

——. *The Passion of Emily Dickinson.* Cambridge: Harvard University Press, 1992.

Fast, Robin Riley, and Christine Mack Gordon, eds. *Approaches to Teaching Dickinson's Poetry.* New York: MLA, 1989.

Ferber, Linda. "Luminist Drawings." Wilmerding 237–65.

Ferber, Linda, and William H. Gerdts. *The New Path.* New York: Brooklyn Museum, 1985.

Ferlazzo, Paul J. "Emily Dickinson." *The Transcendentalists: A Review of Research and Criticism.* Ed. Joel Myerson. New York: MLA, 1984.

First Church, Amherst, Mass. *The Articles of Faith and Government.* Amherst, 1834.

——. *Manual of the First Congregational Church.* Amherst, 1880.

Ford, Thomas W. *Heaven Beguiles the Tired: Death in the Poetry of Emily Dickinson.* Tuscaloosa: University of Alabama Press, 1966.

Franklin, Ralph W. *The Editing of Emily Dickinson.* Madison: University of Wisconsin Press, 1967.

——. "The Emily Dickinson Fascicles." *Studies in Bibliography* 36 (1983): 1–20.

——. "Emily Dickinson to Abiah Root: Ten Reconstructed Letters." *EDJ* 4.1 (1995): 1–43.

——, ed. *The Manuscript Books of Emily Dickinson.* 2 vols. Cambridge: Harvard University Press, 1981.

——, ed. *The Master Letters of Emily Dickinson.* Amherst: Amherst College Press, 1986.

Freedman, Jonathan. "An Aestheticism of Our Own: Women Writers and the Aesthetic Movement." *In Pursuit of Beauty, Americans and the Aesthetic Movement.* New York: Metropolitan Museum of Art/Rizzoli, 1987.

Freeman, Donald C. " 'According to My Bond': *King Lear* and Re-Cognition." *Language and Literature* 2.1 (1993): 1–18.

——. " 'Catch[ing] the Nearest Way': Macbeth and Cognitive Metaphor." *Journal of Pragmatics* 24 (1995): 689–708.

——. "Songs of Experience: New Books on Metaphor." *Poetics Today* 12.1 (1991): 145–64.

Freeman, Margaret H. "Emily Dickinson and the Discourse of Intimacy." *Semantics of Silences in Linguistics and Literature.* Ed. Gudrun M. Grabher and Ulrike Jessner. Heidelberg: Carl Winter Universitätsverlag, 1996. 191–210.

——, ed. Introduction. *Emily Dickinson's Imagery*. By Rebecca Patterson. Amherst: University of Massachusetts Press, 1979.

——. "Metaphor Making Meaning: Emily Dickinson's Conceptual Universe." *Journal of Pragmatics* 24 (1995): 643–66.

Frey, Hans-Jost. "Die Beziehung zwischen Übersetzung und Original als Text." *Colloquium Helveticum* 3 (1986): 35–43.

Frye, Northrop. *Anatomy of Criticism*. Princeton: Princeton University Press, 1957.

Fuller, Jamie. *The Diary of Emily Dickinson*. San Francisco: Mercury House, 1993.

Fulton, Alice. "Her Moment of Brocade: The Reconstruction of Emily Dickinson." *Parnassus* 15.1 (1989): 9–44.

——. "Outlandish Powers: Dickinson's Capsizals of Genre and Tone." *EDJ* 2.2 (1993): 97–103.

Fussell, Paul. *Poetic Meter and Poetic Form*. New York: Random House, 1965.

Galinsky, Hans. *Wegbereiter moderner amerikanischer Lyrik: Interpretations- und Rezeptionsstudien zu Emily Dickinson und William Carlos Williams*. Heidelberg: Winter, 1986.

Garbowsky, Maryanne M. *The House without the Door: A Study of Emily Dickinson and the Illness of Agoraphobia*. Rutherford, N.J.: Associated University Presses, 1989.

——. "Joseph Cornell Meets Emily Dickinson." *EDIS Bulletin* 5.2 (1993): 6–7, 15.

——. "Will Barnet Meets Emily Dickinson." *EDIS Bulletin* 6.2 (1994): 8–9, 18.

Gardner, Dorothy. *Eastward in Eden: The Love Story of Emily Dickinson*. New York: Longmans, Green, 1949.

Garzilli, Enrico. *Circles without Center: Paths to the Discovery and Creation of Self in Modern Literature*. Cambridge: Harvard University Press, 1972.

Gay, Peter. *The Bourgeois Experience, Victoria to Freud: Education of the Senses*. New York: Oxford University Press, 1984.

Gee, Karen Richardson. "Dickinson's Readings of Women Writers' Biographies." *EDJ* 3.1 (1994): 24–40.

Gelpi, Albert J. *Emily Dickinson: The Mind of the Poet*. Cambridge: Harvard University Press, 1965.

——. "Emily Dickinson and the Deerslayer: The Dilemma of the Woman Poet in America." *Shakespeare's Sisters: Feminist Essays on Women Poets*. Ed. Sandra M. Gilbert and Susan Gubar. Bloomington: Indiana University Press, 1979. 122–34.

——. "Emily Dickinson's Word: Presence as Absence, Absence as Presence." *American Poetry* 4.2 (1987): 41–50.

——. *The Tenth Muse: The Psyche of the American Poet*. Cambridge: Harvard University Press, 1975.

Genette, Gérard. *Figures of Literary Discourse*. Trans. Alan Sheridan. New York: Columbia University Press, 1982.

Gerdts, William H. "Through a Glass Brightly: The American Pre-Raphaelites and Their Still Lifes and Nature Studies." Ferber and Gerdts 39–77.

Gerlach, John. "Reading Dickinson: Bolts, Hounds, the Variorum, and Fascicle 39." *EDJ* 3.2 (1994): 77–99.

Gilbert, Sandra. " 'Life's Empty Pack': Notes toward a Literary Daughteronomy." *Critical Inquiry* 11 (1985): 355–83.

Gilbert, Sandra M., and Susan Gubar. " 'Forward into the Past': The Female Affiliation Complex." *Historical Studies and Literary Criticism*. Ed. Jerome J. McGann. Madison: University of Wisconsin Press, 1985. 240–65.

——. *The Madwoman in the Attic: The Woman Writer and the Nineteenth-Century Literary Imagination.* New Haven: Yale University Press, 1979.

Glaspell, Susan. *Alison's House.* London: Samuel French, 1930.

Goethe, Johann Wolfgang von. *Werke. Hamburger Ausgabe in 14 Bänden.* Ed. Erich Trunz. Vol. 1. Munich: Deutscher Taschenbuch Verlag, 1982.

Gordon, Susan Phelps. *John Ruskin and the Victorian Eye.* Phoenix: Phoenix Art Museum, 1993.

Gould, Stephen Jay. "Church, Humboldt, and Darwin: The Tension and Harmony of Art and Science." Kelly 94–107.

Goux, Jean-Joseph. *Oedipus, Philosopher.* Trans. C. Porter. Palo Alto: Stanford University Press, 1993.

Grabher, Gudrun. *Emily Dickinson: Das transzendentale Ich.* Heidelberg: Carl Winter Universitätsverlag, 1981.

Graham, Martha. *Blood Memory.* New York: Doubleday, 1991.

Grahn, Judy. *The Highest Apple: Sappho and the Lesbian Poetic Tradition.* San Francisco: Spinster's, 1985.

Green, Elsa. "Emily Dickinson Was a Poetess." *College English* 34 (1972): 63–70.

Gribbin, Laura. "Emily Dickinson's Circumference: Figuring a Blind Spot in the Romantic Tradition." *EDJ* 2.1 (1993): 1–21.

Griffith, Clark. *The Long Shadow: Emily Dickinson's Tragic Poetry.* Princeton: Princeton University Press, 1964.

Groden, M., and M. Kreiswirth, eds. *The Johns Hopkins Guide to Literary Theory and Criticism.* Baltimore: Johns Hopkins University Press, 1993.

Guerra, Jonnie Gay. "Emily Dickinson's Metaphoric Art." Ph.D. diss., Purdue University, 1982.

Guthrie, James R. " 'Before I got my eye put out': Dickinson's Illness and Its Effects on Her Poetry." *Dickinson Studies* 42.1 (1982): 16–25.

——. *Emily Dickinson's Vision: Illness and Identity in Her Poetry.* Gainesville, Fla.: University Press of Florida, 1998.

——. "Law, Property, and Provincialism in Dickinson's Poems and Letters to Judge Otis Phillips Lord." *EDJ* 5.1 (1996): 27–44.

Habenstein, Ernst, and Herbert Zimmerman. *Lateinische Sprachlehre.* Stuttgart: Klett, 1971.

Hagenbüchle, Roland. *Emily Dickinson: Wagnis der Selbstbegegnung.* Tübingen: Stauffenburg, 1988.

——. "Emily Dickinson's Poetic Covenant." *EDJ* 2.2 (1993): 14–39; expanded version: *Anglia* 112.3–4 (1994): 309–40.

——. "Homage to Brita Lindberg-Seyersted." *EDIS Bulletin* 6.1 (1994): 12–13.

——. "Literaturwissenschaft und Methode: ein Grundsatzbeitrag." *Anglistik* 6.1 (1995): 73–95.

——. "New Developments in Dickinson Criticism." *Anglia* 97 (1979): 452–74.

——. "Precision and Indeterminacy in the Poetry of Emily Dickinson." *ESQ* 20.2 (1974): 33–56.

——. "Sign and Process: The Concept of Language in Emerson and Dickinson." *ESQ* 25.3 (1979): 137–55.

——. " 'Sumptuous Despair': "The Function of Desire in Emily Dickinson's Poetry." *Amerikastudien* 41.4 (1996): 603–21.

——. "Visualization and Vision in Emily Dickinson's Poetry." *Poetry and the Fine*

Arts. Ed. Roland Hagenbüchle and Jacqueline Ollier. Regensburg: Pustet, 1989. 61–71.

Hagstrum, Jean H. *The Sister Arts.* Chicago: University of Chicago Press, 1958.

Hallen, Cynthia L., and Laura M. Harvey. "Translation and the Emily Dickinson Lexicon." *EDJ* 2.2 (1993): 130–46.

Harris, Wendell V. *Dictionary of Concepts in Literary Criticism and Theory.* New York: Greenwood, 1992.

Hart, Ellen Louise. "The Elizabeth Whitney Putnam Manuscripts and New Strategies for Editing Emily Dickinson's Letters." *EDJ* 4.1 (1995): 44–74.

———. "The Encoding of Homoerotic Desire: Emily Dickinson's Letters and Poems to Susan Dickinson, 1850–1886." *Tulsa Studies in Women's Literature* 9.2 (1990): 251–72.

Hartman, Geoffrey. *Beyond Formalism: Literary Essays, 1958–1970.* New Haven: Yale University Press, 1970.

———. *Criticism in the Wilderness: The Study of Literature.* New Haven: Yale University Press, 1980.

Heiskanen-Mäkelä, Sirkka. *In Quest of Truth: Observations on the Development of Emily Dickinson's Poetic Dialectic.* Jyväskylä: Jyväskylän Yliopisto, 1970.

Helle, Anita Plath. "Re-presenting Women Writers Onstage: A Retrospective to the Present." *Making a Spectacle: Feminist Essays on Contemporary Women's Theater.* Ed. Lynda Hart. Ann Arbor: University of Michigan Press, 1989. 195–208.

Higgins, David. *Portrait of Emily Dickinson: The Poet and Her Prose.* New Brunswick: Rutgers University Press, 1967.

Higginson, Thomas Wentworth. *Contemporaries.* Boston: Houghton Mifflin, 1900. 142–67.

———. "Emily Dickinson's Letters." *Atlantic Monthly* 68 (1891): 444–56.

———. "An Open Portfolio" and "Preface to Poems by Emily Dickinson." Blake and Wells 3–10, 10–12.

———. Preface. *Collected Poems.* Ed. Peter Siegenthaler. Philadelphia: Courage Books, 1991. 13–15.

———. *Short Studies of American Authors.* Boston: Lee and Shepard, 1879.

Higginson, Thomas Wentworth, and Henry Walcott Boynton, eds. "New England Period." *A Reader's History of American Literature.* Boston: Houghton Mifflin, 1903. 108–33.

Higginson, Thomas Wentworth, and Mabel Loomis Todd, eds. *Poems by Emily Dickinson.* Second Series. Boston: Roberts Brothers, 1891.

Hillyer, Robert. "Emily Dickinson." Blake and Wells 98–104.

Hilton, Timothy. *The Pre-Raphaelites.* London: Thames and Hudson, 1970, 1987.

Hirsch, E. D., Jr. *Validity in Interpretation.* New Haven: Yale University Press, 1967.

Hirschhorn, Norbert, and Polly Longsworth. " 'Medicine Posthumous': A New Look at Emily Dickinson's Medical Conditions." *New England Quarterly* 69.2 (1996): 299–316.

Hoefel, Roseanne. "Emily Dickinson Fleshing Out a New Word." *EDJ* 1.1 (1992): 54–75.

Hoffman, Tyler B. "Emily Dickinson and the Limit of War." *EDJ* 3.2 (1994): 1–18.

Hogue, Cynthia. " 'I Did'nt Be — Myself': Emily Dickinson's Semiotics of Presence." *EDJ* 1.2 (1992): 30–53.

——. "The Plucked String: Emily Dickinson, Marianne Moore, and the Poetics of 'Select Defects.'" *EDJ* 7.1 (1998): 89–109.

Holland, Jeanne. "Scraps, Stamps, and Cutouts: Emily Dickinson's Domestic Technologies of Publication." *Cultural Artifacts and the Production of Meaning: The Page, the Image, the Body.* Ed. Margaret J. M. Ezell and Katherine O'Brien O'Keeffe. Ann Arbor: University of Michigan Press, 1994. 139–82.

Hollander, John. "Versions, Interpretations, and Performances." *On Translation.* Ed. Reuben A. Brower. Cambridge: Harvard University Press, 1959.

Holyoak, Keith J., and Paul Thagard. *Mental Leaps: Analogy in Creative Thought.* Cambridge: MIT Press/Bradford Books, 1995.

Homans, Margaret. *Bearing the Word: Language and Female Experience in Nineteenth-Century Women's Writing.* Chicago: University of Chicago Press, 1986.

——. "'Oh, Vision of Language!': Dickinson's Poems of Love and Death." Juhasz, *Feminist Critics* 114–33.

——. *Women Writers and Poetic Identity: Dorothy Wordsworth, Emily Brontë, and Emily Dickinson.* Princeton: Princeton University Press, 1980.

Honan, Park. *Authors' Lives: On Literary Biography and the Arts of Language.* New York: St. Martin's, 1990.

Horan, Elizabeth. "To Market: The Dickinson Copyright Wars." *EDJ* 5.1 (1996): 88–120.

Howard, William. "Emily Dickinson's Poetic Vocabulary." *PMLA* 72 (1957): 225–48.

Howe, Susan. *The Birth-mark: Unsettling the Wilderness in American Literary History.* Hanover, N.H.: Wesleyan University Press, 1993.

——. *My Emily Dickinson.* Berkeley: North Atlantic Books, 1985.

Huntington, David C. "Church and Luminism: Light for America's Elect." Wilmerding 155–90.

Iser, Wolfgang. *The Act of Reading: A Theory of Aesthetic Response.* Baltimore: Johns Hopkins University Press, 1978.

——. *Der implizite Leser.* Munich: Wilhelm Fink, 1972.

Jackson, Helen Hunt. *A Century of Dishonor: A Sketch of the United States Government's Dealings with Some of the Indian Tribes.* Foreword by Valerie Sherer Mathes. Norman: University of Oklahoma Press, 1995.

——. *Poems.* Boston: Roberts Brothers, 1895.

——. *Ramona.* New York: Avon, 1970.

——. [H.H.]. *Verses.* Boston: Fields, Osgood, 1870. New and enlarged edition, Boston: 1874.

Jackson, Virginia. "Dickinson's Figure of Address." Orzeck and Weisbuch 77–103.

Jakobson, Roman. "Closing Statement: Linguistics and Poetics." *Style in Language.* Ed. T. A. Sebeok. Cambridge: MIT Press, 1960. 350–77.

——. *Selected Writings II.* The Hague; Paris: Mouton, 1971.

Jauß, Hans Robert. *Literaturgeschichte als Provokation.* Frankfurt/Main: Suhrkamp, 1970.

Jay, Paul. *Being in the Text: Self-Representation from Wordsworth to Roland Barthes.* Ithaca: Cornell University Press, 1984.

Johnson, Barbara. *The Critical Difference.* Baltimore: Johns Hopkins University Press, 1980.

Johnson, Greg. *Emily Dickinson: Perception and the Poet's Quest.* Tuscaloosa: University of Alabama Press, 1985.

Johnson, Mark. *The Body in the Mind: The Bodily Basis of Meaning, Imagination, and Reason.* Chicago: University of Chicago Press, 1987.

——, ed. "10th Anniversary Special Issue: Metaphor and Philosophy." *Metaphor and Symbolic Activity* 10.3 (1995): 157–245.

Johnson, Thomas H., ed. *The Complete Poems of Emily Dickinson.* Boston: Little, Brown, 1960.

——. *Emily Dickinson: An Interpretive Biography.* Cambridge: Harvard University Press, 1955.

——, ed. *The Poems of Emily Dickinson.* 1 vol. Cambridge: Harvard University Press, 1951.

——, ed. *The Poems of Emily Dickinson.* 3 vols. Cambridge: Harvard University Press, 1955.

Johnson, Thomas H., and Theodora Ward, eds. *The Letters of Emily Dickinson.* 3 vols. Cambridge: Harvard University Press, 1958.

Jones, Rowena Revis. "The Preparation of a Poet: Puritan Directions in Emily Dickinson's Education." *Studies in the American Renaissance* (1982): 285–324.

——. "A Taste For 'Poison': Dickinson's Departure from Orthodoxy." *EDJ* 2.1 (1993): 47–64.

Juhasz, Suzanne. "Adventures in the World of the Symbolic: Emily Dickinson and Metaphor." *Feminist Measures: Soundings in Poetry and Theory.* Ed. Lynn Keller and Cristanne Miller. Ann Arbor: University of Michigan Press, 1994. 139–62.

——, ed. *Feminist Critics Read Emily Dickinson.* Bloomington: Indiana University Press, 1983.

——. "From the Editor." *EDJ* 4.1 (1995): vii.

——. *Naked and Fiery Forms: Modern American Poetry by Women: A New Tradition.* New York: Harper and Row, 1976.

——. "Reading Emily Dickinson's Letters." *ESQ* 30 (1984): 170–94.

——. *The Undiscovered Continent: Emily Dickinson and the Space of the Mind.* Bloomington: Indiana University Press, 1983.

Juhasz, Suzanne, and Cristanne Miller. "Comic Power: A Performance." *EDJ* 5.2 (1996): 85–92.

Juhasz, Suzanne, Cristanne Miller, and Martha Nell Smith. *Comic Power in Emily Dickinson.* Austin: University of Texas Press, 1993.

Kaplan, Cora. "The Indefinite Disclosed: Christina Rossetti and Emily Dickinson." *Women Writing and Writing about Women.* Ed. Mary Jacobus. New York: Barnes and Noble, 1979. 61–79.

Kazin, Alfred. *An American Procession.* New York: Knopf, 1984.

Keller, Karl. *The Only Kangaroo among the Beauty: Emily Dickinson and America.* Baltimore: Johns Hopkins University Press, 1979.

Kelly, Franklin, ed. *Frederic Edwin Church.* Washington, D.C.: National Gallery of Art and Smithsonian Institution, 1989.

Kerr, Walter. "Musicals That Don't Sing and a Performance That Does." Review. *New York Times* 9 May 1976, sec. 2: 5.

Khan, M. M. "Dickinson's Phenomenology of Evolution and Imperfection and the Butterfly Symbolism." *Panjab University Bulletin* 14.1 (1983): 55.

Kher, Inder Nath. *The Landscape of Absence: Emily Dickinson's Poetry.* New Haven: Yale University Press, 1974.

Kirkby, Joan. "'Big My Secret': Emily Dickinson and *The Piano*." *EDIS Bulletin* 6.1 (1994): 6–7.

———. "Dickinson Reading." *EDJ* 5.2 (1996): 247–54.

———. *Emily Dickinson*. Women Writers Series. London: Macmillan, 1991.

Kluge, Friedrich. *Etymologisches Wörterbuch der deutschen Sprache*. Berlin: de Gruyter, 1975.

Koplos, Janet. "Lesley Dill at Gracie Mansion." *Art in America* Oct. 1994: 137.

Koppenfels, Werner von. "Intertextualität und Sprachwechsel: Die literarische Übersetzung." *Intertextualität*. Ed. Ulrich Broich and Manfred Pfister. Tübingen: Niemeyer, 1985.

Kövecses, Zoltán. "American Friendship and the Scope of Metaphor." *Cognitive Linguistics* 6.4 (1995): 315–46.

Krieger, Murray. *Theory of Criticism: A Tradition and Its System*. Baltimore: Johns Hopkins University Press, 1976.

Ladin, Jay. "Breaking the Line: Emily Dickinson and William Carlos Williams." *EDJ* 2.1 (1994): 41–58.

Lakoff, George. "The Contemporary Theory of Metaphor." Ortony 202–51.

———. *Women, Fire, and Dangerous Things: What Categories Reveal about the Mind*. Chicago: University of Chicago Press, 1987.

Lakoff, George, and Mark Johnson. *Metaphors We Live By*. Chicago: University of Chicago Press, 1980.

Lakoff, George and Mark Turner. *More Than Cool Reason: A Field Guide to Poetic Metaphor*. Chicago: University of Chicago Press, 1989.

Lambert, Robert Graham, Jr. *A Critical Study of Emily Dickinson's Letters: The Prose of a Poet*. Lewiston, N.Y.: Mellen University Press, 1996.

Langbaum, Robert. *The Modern Spirit. Essays on the Continuity of Nineteenth and Twentieth Century Literature*. New York: Oxford University Press, 1970.

Lausberg, Heinrich. *Elemente der literarischen Rhetorik*. Munich: Hueber, 1982.

Lease, Benjamin. *Emily Dickinson's Readings of Men and Books: Sacred Soundings*. New York: St. Martin's, 1990.

———. " 'This World is not Conclusion': Dickinson, Amherst, and 'the local conditions of the soul.' " *EDJ* 3.2 (1994): 38–55.

Leder, Sharon, and Andrea Abbott. *The Language of Exclusion: The Poetry of Emily Dickinson and Christina Rossetti*. New York: Greenwood, 1987.

Lemmon, Marilyn, ed. *Connections in Time and Place: New and Old Quilts from Ohio and Its Neighbors*. Canton: Canton Art Institute, 1993.

Lesley Dill. Exhibition Catalog. New Orleans: Arthur Roger Gallery, 1994.

Levin, Samuel. "The Analysis of Compression in Poetry." *Foundations of Language* 7 (1971): 38–55.

Levine, George, and William Madden, eds. *The Art of Victorian Prose*. Oxford: Oxford University Press, 1968.

Leyda, Jay. *The Years and Hours of Emily Dickinson*. 2 vols. New Haven: Yale University Press, 1960.

Lilliedahl, Ann Martha. *Emily Dickinson in Europe: Her Literary Reputation in Selected Countries*. Washington, D.C.: University of America, 1981.

Lindberg-Seyersted, Brita. *Emily Dickinson's Punctuation*. Oslo: University of Oslo, 1976.

——. *The Voice of the Poet: Aspects of Style in the Poetry of Emily Dickinson*. Cambridge: Harvard University Press, 1968; Uppsala: Almquist and Wiksells, 1968.

Loeffelholz, Mary. *Dickinson and the Boundaries of Feminist Theory*. Urbana: University of Illinois Press, 1991.

Loehndorf, Esther. "Emily Dickinson: Reading a Spinster." *EDJ* 5.2 (1996): 113–19.

Loeschke, Maravene. "Challenges of Portraying Emily Dickinson in William Luce's Play *The Belle of Amherst*." *EDJ* 2.2 (1993): 124–29.

Lombardo, Daniel. *A Hedge Away: The "Other" Side of Emily Dickinson's Amherst*. Northampton: Daily Hampshire Gazette, 1997.

Longsworth, Polly. *Austin and Mabel: The Amherst Affair and Love Letters of Austin Dickinson and Mabel Loomis Todd*. New York: Farrar, Straus and Giroux, 1984.

——. *The World of Emily Dickinson*. New York: Norton, 1990.

Lotman, Jurij. M. *Die Struktur literarischer Texte*. Munich: Wilhelm Fink, 1972.

Loving, Jerome. *Emily Dickinson: The Poet on the Second Story*. Cambridge: Cambridge University Press, 1986.

Lowell, Amy. *Poetry and Poets*. Boston: Houghton Mifflin, 1930. 88–108.

——. "The Sisters." *Literature by Women: The Tradition in English*. Ed. Sandra Gilbert and Susan Gubar. New York: Norton, 1985. 1300–1304.

Lowenberg, Carlton. *Emily Dickinson's Textbooks*. Lafayette, Calif., 1986.

——. *Musicians Wrestle Everywhere: Emily Dickinson and Music*. Berkeley: Fallen Leaf, 1992.

Lubbers, Klaus. *Emily Dickinson: The Critical Revolution*. Ann Arbor: University of Michigan Press, 1968.

Luce, William. *The Belle of Amherst: A Play Based on the Life of Emily Dickinson*. Boston: Houghton Mifflin, 1976. PBS broadcast, dir. Charles Dubin, perf. Julie Harris. 1976.

Lynen, John. *The Design of the Present: Essays on Time and Form in American Literature*. New Haven: Yale University Press, 1969.

MacLeish, Archibald. "The Private World: Poems of Emily Dickinson." R. Sewall, *Essays* 150–61.

Makaryk, Irena R., ed. *Encyclopedia of Contemporary Literary Theory: Approaches, Scholars, Terms*. Toronto: University of Toronto Press, 1993.

Martens, Klaus. "Dickinson's 'Much Madness is Divinest Sense.'" Qtd. in Armin Paul Frank et al., "Towards a Cultural History of Literary Translation: An Exploration of Issues and Problems in Researching the Translational Exchange between the USA and Germany." *REAL: The Yearbook of Research in English and American Literature* 4 (1986): 359–73.

"Martha Graham Dances the Life of a Poet." *Harper's Bazaar* Apr. 1941: 80–81.

Martin, Wendy. *An American Triptych: Anne Bradstreet, Emily Dickinson, Adrienne Rich*. Chapel Hill: University of North Carolina Press, 1984.

Martz, Louis. *The Poem of the Mind*. New York: Oxford University Press, 1966.

Matthiessen, F. O. *American Renaissance: Art and Expression in the Age of Emerson and Whitman*. London: Oxford University Press, 1941.

Maun, Caroline C. "Editorial Policy in *The Poems of Emily Dickinson, Third Series*." *EDJ* 3.2 (1994): 56–77.

McDonagh, Don. *Martha Graham: A Biography*. New York: Praeger, 1973.

McGann, Jerome. *Black Riders: The Visible Language of Modernism*. Princeton: Princeton University Press, 1993.

——. "Emily Dickinson's Visible Language." *EDJ* 2.2 (1993): 40–51.

McGill, Frederick T., Jr. *Channing of Concord*. New Brunswick: Rutgers University Press, 1967.

McGuire, Mary Ann C. "A Metaphorical Pattern in Emily Dickinson." *American Transcendental Quarterly* 29 (1976): 83–85.

McHugh, Heather. *Broken English: Poetry and Partiality*. Hanover, N.H.: Wesleyan University Press, 1993.

McNeil, Helen. *Emily Dickinson*. London: Virago, 1986.

McShine, Kynaston, ed. *Joseph Cornell*. New York: MOMA, 1980.

Mersand, Joseph. *The American Drama, 1930–1940: Essays on Playwrights and Plays*. New York: Modern Chapbooks, 1941.

Miles, Susan. "The Irregularities of Emily Dickinson." Blake and Wells 123–29.

Miller, Cristanne. "Dickinson's Language: Interpreting Truth Told Slant." Fast and Gordon 78–84.

——. *Emily Dickinson: A Poet's Grammar*. Cambridge: Harvard University Press, 1987.

——. "How 'Low Feet' Stagger: Disruptions of Language in Dickinson's Poetry." Juhasz, *Feminist Critics* 134–55.

——. "The Humor of Excess." Juhasz, Miller, and Smith 103–36.

——. " 'A Letter is a Joy of Earth': Dickinson's Communications with the World." *Legacy* 3 (1986): 29–39.

Miller, J. Hillis. *Theory Now and Then*. New York: Harvester Wheatsheaf, 1991.

Miller, Perry. *The New England Mind*. Cambridge: Harvard University Press, 1953.

Miller, Ruth. *The Poetry of Emily Dickinson*. Middletown, Conn.: Wesleyan University Press, 1968.

Monson Academy Catalogue, 1819. Wilbraham-Monson Academy Library, Wilbraham, Mass.

Monteiro, George. *The Presence of Camoes: Influence on the Literature of England, America, and Southern Africa*. Lexington: University Press of Kentucky, 1996.

Moore, Marianne. *Complete Poems*. New York: Viking, 1981.

——. "Emily Dickinson." *The Complete Prose of Marianne Moore*. Ed. Patricia C. Willis. New York: Viking, 1987. 290–93.

Morgan, Barbara. *Martha Graham: Sixteen Dances in Photographs*. New York: Duell, Sloan, and Pearce, 1941.

Morris, Adalaide K. " 'The Love of Thee — a Prism Be': Men and Women in the Love Poetry of Emily Dickinson." Juhasz, *Feminist Critics* 98–113.

——. " 'Two Sisters Have I': Emily Dickinson's Vinnie and Susan." *Massachusetts Review* 22.2 (1981): 323–32.

Morse, Jonathan. "Some of the Things We Mean When We Say 'New England.' " *EDJ* 5.2 (1996): 209–14.

Mossberg, Barbara Antonina Clarke. "Double Exposures: Emily Dickinson's and Gertrude Stein's Anti-autobiographies." *Emily Dickinson: A Celebration for Readers*. Ed. Suzanne Juhasz and Cristanne Miller. New York: Gordon and Breach, 1989. 239–50.

——. *Emily Dickinson: When A Writer Is a Daughter*. Bloomington: Indiana University Press, 1982.

Mudge, Jean McClure. *Emily Dickinson and the Image of Home*. Amherst: University of Massachusetts Press, 1975.

Mulvihill, John. "Why Dickinson Didn't Title." *EDJ* 5.1 (1996): 71–87.

Murray, Aífe. "Kitchen Table Poetics: Maid Margaret Maher and Her Poet Emily Dickinson." *EDJ* 5.2 (1996): 285–92.

Myerson, Joel. *Emily Dickinson. A Descriptive Bibliography.* Pittsburgh: University of Pittsburgh Press, 1984.

Nettleton, Asahel. *Village Hymns for Social Worship.* New York, 1842.

Newall, Christopher. *John Ruskin and the Victorian Eye.* Phoenix: Phoenix Art Museum, 1993.

Noble, Marianne. "Dickinson's Sentimental Explorations of 'The Ecstasy of Parting.'" *EDJ* 5.2 (1996): 280–84.

Norcross Family Papers. Emily Dickinson Collection. Houghton Library. Harvard University. Cambridge.

Novak, Barbara. *American Painting of the Nineteenth Century: Realism, Idealism, and the American Experience.* New York: Praeger, 1969.

———. *Nature and Culture: American Landscape and Painting.* New York: Oxford University Press, 1978.

Oakes, Karen. "Welcome and Beware: The Reader and Emily Dickinson's Figurative Language." *ESQ* 34 (1988): 181–206.

Oberhaus, Dorothy Huff. "Emily Dickinson's Books." *EDJ* 2.2 (1993): 58–65.

———. *Emily Dickinson's Fascicles: Method and Meaning.* University Park: Pennsylvania State University Press, 1995.

———. "In Defense of Sue." *Dickinson Studies* 48 (1983): 1–25.

Odell, Ruth. *Helen Hunt Jackson [H.H.].* New York: Appleton, 1939.

Oliver, Virginia H. *Apocalypse of Green: A Study of Emily Dickinson's Eschatology.* New York: Lang, 1989.

Olschner, Leonard. *Der feste Buchstab: Erläuterungen zu Paul Celans Gedichtübertragungen.* Göttingen: Vandenhoek and Ruprecht, 1985.

Ortony, Andrew, ed. *Metaphor and Thought.* 2nd ed. Cambridge: Cambridge University Press, 1993.

Orzeck, Martin, and Robert Weisbuch, eds. *Dickinson and Audience.* Ann Arbor: University of Michigan Press, 1996.

Ostriker, Alicia. "Replaying the Bible: My Emily Dickinson." *EDJ* 2.2 (1993): 160–71.

———. *Stealing the Language: The Emergence of Women's Poetry in America.* Boston: Beacon, 1986.

Paglia, Camille. *Sexual Personae: Art and Decadence from Nefertiti to Emily Dickinson.* New Haven: Yale University Press, 1990.

Paige, D. D., ed. *The Letters of Ezra Pound, 1907–1941.* London: Faber and Faber, 1951.

"Painting Emily Dickinson's Poetry." *Mount Holyoke Alumnae Quarterly* Summer 1985: 68.

Park, Edwards A., Austin Phelps, and Lowell Mason. *The Sabbath Hymn Book for the Service of Song in the House of the Lord.* New York, 1858.

Pascoe, Judith. "'The House Encore Me So': Emily Dickinson and Jenny Lind." *EDJ* 1.1 (1992): 1–18.

Patterson, Rebecca. "Emily Dickinson's Debt to Gunderode." *Midwest Quarterly* 8 (1967): 331–54.

———. *Emily Dickinson's Imagery.* Ed. Margaret H. Freeman. Amherst: University of Massachusetts Press, 1979.

———. *The Riddle of Emily Dickinson.* Boston: Houghton Mifflin, 1951.

Pearce, Roy Harvey. *The Continuity of American Poetry.* Princeton: Princeton University Press, 1961.

Perlmutter, Elizabeth F. "Hide and Seek: Emily Dickinson's Use of the Existential Sentence." *Language and Style* 10.2 (1977): 109–19.

Pessen, Edward. *Jacksonian America: Society, Personality, and Politics.* Rev. ed. Homewood, Ill.: Dorsey, 1978.

Phillips, Elizabeth. *Emily Dickinson: Personae and Performance.* University Park: Pennsylvania State University Press, 1988.

Polk, Mary Lynn Cooper. "Emily Dickinson: A Survey of the Criticism and Selective Annotated Bibliography." Ph.D. diss. University of North Carolina, 1984.

Pollak, Vivian R. *Dickinson: The Anxiety of Gender.* Ithaca: Cornell University Press, 1984.

——. "Emily Dickinson's Literary Allusions." *Essays in Literature* 1 (1974): 54–68.

——, ed. *A Poet's Parents: The Courtship Letters of Emily Norcross and Edward Dickinson.* Chapel Hill: University of North Carolina Press, 1988.

Pollitt, Josephine. *Emily Dickinson: The Human Background of Her Poetry.* New York: Harper, 1930.

Porte, Joel, ed. *Ralph Waldo Emerson: Essays and Lectures.* New York: Library of America, 1983.

Porter, David T. *The Art of Emily Dickinson's Early Poetry.* Cambridge: Harvard University Press, 1966.

——. "Assembling a Poet and Her Poems: Convergent Limit-Works of Joseph Cornell and Emily Dickinson." *Word & Image* 10.3 (1994): 199–221.

——. *Dickinson: The Modern Idiom.* Cambridge: Harvard University Press, 1981.

——. Review of *New Poems of Emily Dickinson*, ed. William H. Shurr. *EDJ* 4.1 (1995): 126–28.

Porter, Ebenezer. *The Rhetorical Reader; Consisting of Instructions for Regulating the Voice with a Rhetorical Notation . . .* New York: Dayton and Newman, 1842.

Poulet, Georges. *Studies in Human Time.* Trans. Elliott Coleman. Baltimore: Johns Hopkins University Press, 1956.

Pound, Louise. "Helen Maria Fiske Hunt." *Dictionary of American Biography.* Ed. Dumas Malone. New York: Scribner's, 1932. 9: 541–53.

Quarles, Francis. *Emblems, Divine and Moral.* London, 1824.

Ransom, John Crowe. "A Poet Restored." R. Sewall, *Essays* 88–100.

Ratcliff, Carter. "Joseph Cornell: Mechanic of the Ineffable." McShine 43–67.

Reitmayer, Sabine. "Emily Dickinson in deutscher Übertragung: Studien zur Übersetzungskunst anhand einiger Beispiele eigener Wahl." Staatsexamensarbeit Mainz, 1966.

Reynolds, David S. *Beneath the American Renaissance: The Subversive Imagination in the Age of Emerson and Melville.* New York: Knopf, 1988.

Rich, Adrienne. "I am in Danger — Sir —." *Adrienne Rich's Poetry.* Ed. Barbara Charlesworth Gelpi and Albert Gelpi. New York: Norton, 1975. 30–31.

——. "'Vesuvius at Home': The Power of Emily Dickinson." *Parnassus* 5(1976): 49–74.

Rich, Susanna. "Skin of Words: Lesley Dill's Poem Sculptures." *EDIS Bulletin* 5.2 (1993): 4–5, 15.

Ricks, Christopher. *The Force of Poetry.* Oxford: Oxford University Press/Clarendon Press, 1984.

Rodier, Katharine. "'What Is Inspiration?': Emily Dickinson, T. W. Higginson, and Maria White Lowell." *EDJ* 4.2 (1995): 20–43.

Roque, Oswaldo Rodriguez. *American Paradise: The World of the Hudson River School.* New York: Abrams, 1988.

Rosch, Eleanor. "Human Categorization." *Advances in Cross-Cultural Psychology.* Ed. N. Warren. New York: Academic, 1977.

Rosen, Charles. "Isn't It Romantic?" *New York Review of Books* 20.10 (14 June 1973): 14, 16.

Rosenbaum, S. P. *A Concordance to the Poems of Emily Dickinson.* Ithaca: Cornell University Press, 1964.

Rosenberg, Donald. "Emotional Resonance Fills Poll's Poetic Ballet." *Akron Beacon Journal* 4 May 1984: B5.

Rosenthal, M. L., and Sally M. Gall. *The Modern Poetic Sequence.* Oxford: Oxford University Press, 1983.

Rukeyser, Muriel. *The Life of Poetry.* New York: Wyn, 1949.

Ruskin, John. *The Complete Works.* Ed. E. T. Cook and Alexander Wedderburn. London: Allen, 1904.

Salska, Agnieszka. "Emily Dickinson in Polish: Recent Translations." *EDJ* 5.2 (1996): 215–20.

——. "The Place of Letters in Dickinson's Opus." *Emily Dickinson.* Ed. Antoine Cazé. *Profils Americains* 8 (1996): 27–40.

——. "Emily Dickinson's Letters: The Making of a Poetics." *Crossing Borders: American Literature and Other Artistic Media.* Ed. Jadwiga Maszewska. Warsaw: PWN, 1992.

Sanchez-Eppler, Karen. *Touching Liberty: Abolition, Feminism, and the Politics of the Body.* Berkeley: University of California Press, 1993.

Sands, Marget. "Re-reading the Poems: Editing Opportunities in Variant Versions." *EDJ* 5.2 (1996): 139–48.

Saturday Club Files. Concord Free Public Library. Concord, Mass.

Scharnhorst, Gary. "A Glimpse of Dickinson at Work." *American Literature* 57.3 (1985): 483–85.

Scheurer, Erika. " 'Near, but remote': Emily Dickinson's Epistolary Voice." *EDJ* 4.1 (1995): 86–107.

Scholl, Diane Gabrielsen. "From Aaron 'Drest' to Dickinson's 'Queen': Protestant Typology in Herbert and Dickinson." *EDJ* 3.1 (1994): 1–23.

Schöpp, Joseph C. " 'Amazing Sense Distilled from Ordinary Meanings': The Power of the Word in Emily Dickinson's Poems on Poetry." *Poetics in the Poem: Critical Essays on American Self-Reflexive Poetry.* Ed. Dorothy Z. Baker. New York: Lang, 1997. 90–103.

Schreiber, Flora Rheta. "Emily Is in the House: Emily Dickinson as Revealed through Her Imagery." *Poet Lore* 46 (Spring 1940): 76–82.

Sergeant, Elizabeth Shepley. "An Early Imagist." Blake and Wells 88–93.

Sewall, Richard B., ed. *Emily Dickinson: A Collection of Critical Essays.* Englewood Cliffs, N.J.: Prentice-Hall, 1963.

——. *The Life of Emily Dickinson.* 2 vols. New York: Farrar, Straus and Giroux, 1974.

——, ed. *The Lyman Letters: New Light on Emily Dickinson and Her Family.* Amherst: University of Massachusetts Press, 1965.

——. "Teaching Dickinson: Testimony of a Veteran." Fast and Gordon 30–38.

Sewell, Darrel. "Thomas Cole: *The Voyage of Life.*" *A New World: Masterpieces of American Painting, 1760–1910.* Ed. Theodore E. Stebbins, Jr. London: Mansell, 1983. 225–28.

Shakinovsky, Lynn J. "Hidden Listeners: Dialogism in the Poetry of Emily Dickinson." *Discours social/Social Discourse* 3.1–2 (1990): 199–215.

———. "No Frame of Reference: The Absence of Context in Emily Dickinson's Poetry." *EDJ* 3.2 (1994): 19–37.

Shapiro, Michael, and Marianne Shapiro. *Figuration in Verbal Art*. Princeton: Princeton University Press, 1988.

Sharon-Zisser, Shirley. " 'To See — Comparatively': Emily Dickinson's Use of Simile." *EDJ* 3.1 (1994): 59–84.

Sherrer, Grace B. "A Study of Unusual Verb Construction in the Poems of Emily Dickinson." *American Literature* 7 (1935): 37–46.

Sherwood, William R. *Circumference and Circumstance: Stages in the Mind and Art of Emily Dickinson*. New York: Columbia University Press, 1968.

Shimazaki, Yoko. "A Perspective on Reading Dickinson in Japan." *EDJ* 2.2 (1993): 153–59.

Shurr, William H. "Editing the *New Poems of Emily Dickinson*." *EDJ* 4.1 (1995): 118–25.

———. *The Marriage of Emily Dickinson: A Study of the Fascicles*. Lexington: University Press of Kentucky, 1983.

———, ed. *New Poems of Emily Dickinson*. Chapel Hill: University of North Carolina Press, 1993.

Siegfried, Regina. "Bibliographic Essay: Selected Criticism for Emily Dickinson's Religious Background." *Dickinson Studies* 52.2 (1984): 32–53.

Sielke, Sabine. *Fashioning the Female Subject: The Intertextual Networking of Dickinson, Moore, and Rich*. Ann Arbor: University of Michigan Press, 1997.

Small, Judy Jo. *Positive as Sound: Emily Dickinson's Rhyme*. Athens: University of Georgia Press, 1990.

Smith, Martha Nell. "The Importance of a Hypermedia Archive of Dickinson's Creative Work." *EDJ* 4.1 (1995): 75–85.

———. "The Poet as Cartoonist." Juhasz, Miller, and Smith 63–102.

———. *Rowing in Eden: Rereading Emily Dickinson*. Austin: University of Texas Press, 1992.

St. Armand, Barton Levi. *Emily Dickinson and Her Culture: The Soul's Society*. Cambridge: Cambridge University Press, 1984.

———. "Emily Dickinson and 'The Indicator': A Transcendental Frolic." *EDJ* 2.2 (1993): 78–96.

———. "Emily Dickinson's Garden." *EDIS Bulletin* 2.2 (1990): 1–2.

———. "Veiled Ladies: Dickinson, Bettine, and Transcendental Meditation." *Studies in the American Renaissance* 1 (1987): 1–51.

Stapleton, Laurence. *Marianne Moore: The Poet's Advance*. Princeton: Princeton University Press, 1978.

Steiner, George. *After Babel: Aspects of Language and Translation*. Oxford: Oxford University Press, 1975.

Stocks, Kenneth. *Emily Dickinson and the Modern Consciousness*. London: Macmillan, 1988.

Stonum, Gary Lee. *The Dickinson Sublime*. Madison: University of Wisconsin Press, 1990.

Strickland, Georgiana. " 'Thunderstruck!': A Conversation with Julie Harris." *EDIS Bulletin* 3.1 (1991): 1–2, 11.

Szondi, Peter. "Poetry of Constancy—Poetik der Beständigkeit: Celans Übertragung von Shakespeares Sonett 105." *Sprache im technischen Zeitalter* 1971: 9–25.

Tabakowska, Elzbieta. *Cognitive Linguistics and the Politics of Translation.* Tübingen: Guntar Narr Verlag, 1993.

Taggard, Genevieve. *The Life and Mind of Emily Dickinson.* New York: Knopf, 1930.

Takeda, Masako. *Love Poetry of Emily Dickinson.* Hachi-shobo, 1988.

Tashjian, Dickran. *Joseph Cornell: Gifts of Desire.* Miami Beach: Grassfield, 1992.

Terris, Virginia. "Emily Dickinson and the Genteel Critics." Ph.D. diss. New York University, 1973.

Thackrey, Donald E. "The Communication of the Word." R. Sewall, *Essays* 51–69.

———. *Emily Dickinson's Approach to Poetry.* Lincoln: University of Nebraska Printing Division, 1978.

Thoreau, Henry David. *The Correspondence.* Ed. Walter Harding and Carl Bode. New York: New York University Press, 1958.

Tingley, Stephanie A. "'A Letter is a Joy of Earth': Emily Dickinson's Letters and Victorian Epistolary Conventions." *EDJ* 5.2 (1996): 202–8.

Tipton, Noel. *Amherst Sabbath.* First performed at Cape Cod Community College, Hyannis, Mass. June 1997.

Todd, John E. *Emily Dickinson's Use of the Persona.* The Hague: Mouton, 1973.

Todd, Mabel Loomis, ed. *Letters of Emily Dickinson.* 2 vols. Boston: Roberts Brothers, 1894; new and enlarged ed., New York: Harper, 1931.

———. Preface. Higginson and Todd, *Poems by Emily Dickinson,* Second Series.

Todd, Mabel Loomis, and Thomas Wentworth Higginson, eds. *Poems by Emily Dickinson.* Boston: Roberts Brothers, 1890.

Trowbridge, Charlotte. *Dance Drawings of Martha Graham.* New York: Dance Observer, 1945.

Truettner, William H., and Alan Wallach, eds. *Thomas Cole: Landscape into History.* New Haven: Yale University Press, 1994.

Turco, Lewis Putnam, ed. *Emily Dickinson, Woman of Letters.* Albany: State University of New York Press, 1993.

———. "Iron Pyrites in the Dickinson Mine." *EDJ* 4.1 (1995): 108–17.

Turner, Mark. *Death Is the Mother of Beauty: Mind, Metaphor, Criticism.* Chicago: University of Chicago Press, 1987.

———. *Reading Minds: The Study of English in the Age of Cognitive Science.* Princeton: Princeton University Press, 1991.

Van Doren, Mark. Introduction. *Letters of Emily Dickinson.* Ed. Mabel Loomis Todd. New York: World, 1951.

Vendler, Helen. "The Unsociable Soul." *New Republic* 3 Aug. 1992: 34–37.

Voorsanger, Catherine Hoover. "Dictionary of Architects, Artisans, Artists, and Manufacturers." *In Pursuit of Beauty: Americans and the Aesthetic Movement.* New York: Metropolitan Museum of Art/Rizzoli, 1987.

Waggoner, Hyatt H. *American Poets from the Puritans to the Present.* Boston: Houghton Mifflin, 1968.

———. "Emily Dickinson: The Transcendent Self." *Criticism* 7.4 (1965): 297–334.

Walker, Cheryl, ed. *American Women Poets of the Nineteenth Century.* New Brunswick: Rutgers University Press, 1982.

———. *The Nightingale's Burden: Women Poets and American Culture before 1900.* Bloomington: Indiana University Press, 1982.

Wallace, Ronald. *God Be with the Clown: Humor in American Poetry*. Columbia: University of Missouri Press, 1984.

Walsh, John Evangelist. *The Hidden Life of Emily Dickinson*. New York: Simon and Schuster, 1971.

———. *This Brief Tragedy: Unraveling the Todd–Dickinson Affair*. New York: Grove Weidenfeld, 1991.

Wand, Martin, and Richard B. Sewall. "'Eyes Be Blind, Heart Be Still': A New Perspective on Emily Dickinson's Eye Problems." *New England Quarterly* 52 (1979): 400–406.

Ward, Theodora. *The Capsule of the Mind: Chapters in the Life of Emily Dickinson*. Cambridge: Harvard University Press, 1961.

Wardrop, Daneen. "'Goblin with a Gauge': Dickinson's Readerly Gothic." *EDJ* 1.1 (1992): 39–53.

Warren, Austin. "Emily Dickinson." Blake and Wells 268–86.

Watts, Emily Stipes. *The Poetry of American Women from 1632 to 1945*. Austin: University of Texas Press, 1977.

Watts, Isaac. *The Psalms, Hymns, and Spiritual Songs of the Rev. Isaac Watts, D.D.* Ed. Samuel N. Worcester. Boston: Crocker and Brewster, 1834.

Webster, Noah. *An American Dictionary of the English Language*. 2 vols. New York: Converse, 1828; Amherst, 1844.

Weisbuch, Robert. *Emily Dickinson's Poetry*. Chicago: University of Chicago Press, 1975.

———. "The Necessary Veil: A Quest Fiction." *Modern Critical Views: Emily Dickinson*. Ed. Harold Bloom. New York: Chelsea House, 1985. 81–98.

———. "Nobody's Business: Dickinson's Dissolving Audience." Orzeck and Weisbuch 57–76.

Wells, Anna Mary. *Dear Preceptor: The Life and Times of Thomas Wentworth Higginson*. Boston: Houghton Mifflin, 1963.

Werner, Marta. *Emily Dickinson's Open Folios: Scenes of Reading, Surfaces of Writing*. Ann Arbor: University of Michigan Press, 1995.

Whicher, George Frisbie. *This Was a Poet: A Critical Biography of Emily Dickinson*. New York: Scribner's, 1938.

Whicher, Stephen E., ed. *Selections from Ralph Waldo Emerson*. Boston: Houghton Mifflin, 1960.

White, Fred D. "'Sweet Skepticism of the Heart': Science in the Poetry of Emily Dickinson." *College Literature* 19 (1992): 121–28.

Wider, Sarah. "Corresponding Worlds: The Art of Emily Dickinson's Letters." *EDJ* 1.1 (1992): 10–38.

Williams, Stanley T. "Experiments In Poetry: Emily Dickinson." Blake and Wells 251–60.

Wilmerding, John, ed. *American Light: The Luminist Movement, 1850–1875*. Princeton: Princeton University Press and National Gallery of Art, 1989.

Winters, Yvor. "Emily Dickinson and the Limits of Judgment." Blake and Wells 187–200.

Wolff, Cynthia Griffin. *Emily Dickinson*. New York: Knopf, 1986.

———. "[Im]pertinent Constructions of Body and Self: Dickinson's Use of the Romantic Grotesque." *EDJ* 2.2 (1993): 109–23.

Wolosky, Shira. *Emily Dickinson: A Voice of War*. New Haven: Yale University Press, 1984.

Woodmansee, Martha. *The Author, the Art, and the Market: Rereading the History of Aesthetics.* New York: Columbia University Press, 1994.

Woodress, James. "Emily Dickinson." *Fifteen American Authors before 1900: Bibliographical Essays on Research and Criticism.* Ed. Earl N. Harbert and Robert A. Rees. Madison: University of Wisconsin Press, 1984. 185–229.

Wright, Patricia. "Looking into Emily Dickinson." *Daily Hampshire Gazette* (Northampton, Mass.) 15 May 1985: 24.

Wylder, Edith. *The Last Face: Emily Dickinson's Manuscripts.* Albuquerque: University of New Mexico Press, 1971.

Yamakawa, Tamaaki. "Emily Dickinson and Paintings: Margaret Taylor and Her Etchings for Dickinson's Poems." *English Literature Review* 32 (1988): 73–98.

Yin, Joanna. " 'Arguments of Pearl': Dickinson's Response to Puritan Semiology." *EDJ* 2.1 (1993): 65–83.

York, Vincent, and Frederick Pohl. *Brittle Heaven: A Drama in Three Acts.* New York: French, 1935.

Yukman, Claudia. "Breaking the Eschatological Framework: Dickinson's Narrative Acts." *EDJ* 1.1 (1992): 76–94.

Notes on Contributors

MARTHA ACKMANN. Assistant professor of women's studies at Mount Holyoke College. Author of essays on Dickinson and coordinator of the Emily Dickinson International Society (EDIS) 1999 conference, "Dickinson at Home," at Mount Holyoke College. Cofounder and advisory editor of *LEGACY: A Journal of American Women Writers*. Her forthcoming book is on Dickinson's matrilineage.

KERSTIN BEHNKE. Assistant professor of German and comparative literature at Northwestern University. Author of "Emily Dickinson in deutschen Übersetzungen unter besonderer Berücksichtigung von Paul Celans Übertragungen aus dem Englischen" (M.A. thesis, Göttingen, 1987).

SHARON CAMERON. Professor of English at Johns Hopkins University. Author of *Choosing Not Choosing: Dickinson's Fascicles* (University of Chicago Press, 1992) and *Lyric Time: Dickinson and the Limits of Genre* (Johns Hopkins University Press, 1979).

PAUL CRUMBLEY. Assistant professor of English at Utah State University. Author of *Inflections of the Pen: Dash and Voice in Emily Dickinson* (University Press of Kentucky, 1997).

MARGARET DICKIE. Professor of English at the University of Georgia, Athens. Author of *Lyric Contingencies: Emily Dickinson and Wallace Stevens* (University of Pennsylvania Press, 1991).

JANE DONAHUE EBERWEIN. Professor of English at Oakland University. Author of *Dickinson: Strategies of Limitation* (University of Massachusetts Press, 1985). Editor of *An Emily Dickinson Encyclopedia* (Greenwood Press, 1998).

JUDITH FARR. Professor of English at Georgetown University. Author of *The Passion of Emily Dickinson* (Harvard University Press, 1992) and *I Never Came to You in White* (Houghton Mifflin, 1996). Editor of *Emily Dickinson: A Collection of Critical Essays* (Prentice-Hall, 1995).

MARGARET H. FREEMAN. Professor of English at Los Angeles Valley College. Author of several essays on Dickinson's poetry and a book-length manuscript entitled *Reading Emily Dickinson: Studies in Cognitive Poetics*.

GUDRUN GRABHER. Professor of American studies at the University of Innsbruck, Austria. Author of *Emily Dickinson: Das transzendentale Ich* (Carl Winter Universitätsverlag, 1981).

JONNIE GUERRA. Dean of the college and professor of English at Randolph-Macon Woman's College. Director of the first EDIS conference, Washington, D.C., 1992, "Translating Emily Dickinson into Language, Culture, and the Arts." Editor of the Poet to Poet Series for the *EDIS Bulletin*. At work on a study of Dickinson on stage.

ROLAND HAGENBÜCHLE. Professor emeritus of American studies at the Catholic University of Eichstätt, Germany. Author of *Emily Dickinson: Wagnis der Selbstbegegnung* (Stauffenburg, 1988).

SUZANNE JUHASZ. Professor of English at the University of Colorado, Boulder. Author of *The Undiscovered Continent: Emily Dickinson and the Space of the Mind* (Indiana University Press, 1983). Editor of *Feminist Critics Read Emily Dickinson* (Indiana University Press, 1983). Coauthor of *Comic Power in Emily Dickinson* (University of Texas Press, 1993). Editor of the *Emily Dickinson Journal*.

MARIETTA MESSMER. Assistant professor at the University of Göttingen, Germany. Author of "Reconstructing Dickinson's Epistolary Subject Positions" (Ph.D. diss., University of Toronto, 1997).

CRISTANNE MILLER. William M. Keck Distinguished Service Professor and professor of English at Pomona College. Author of *Emily Dickinson: A Poet's Grammar* (Harvard University Press, 1987). Coauthor of *Comic Power in Emily Dickinson* (University of Texas Press, 1993).

VIVIAN R. POLLAK. Professor of English at Washington University, St. Louis. Author of *Dickinson: The Anxiety of Gender* (Cornell University Press, 1984). Editor of *A Poet's Parents: The Courtship Letters of Emily Norcross and Edward Dickinson* (University of North Carolina Press, 1988).

DAVID PORTER. Professor emeritus of English at the University of Massachusetts, Amherst. Author of *The Art of Emily Dickinson's Early Poetry* (Harvard University Press, 1966) and *Dickinson: The Modern Idiom* (Harvard University Press, 1981).

JOSEF RAAB. Assistant professor of American studies at the Catholic University of Eichstätt, Germany. Author of "Elizabeth Bishop's Hemisphere" (Ph.D. dissertation, University of Southern California, 1993).

AGNIESZKA SALSKA. Professor of English at the University of Lodz, Poland. Author of *Walt Whitman and Emily Dickinson: Poetry of the Central Consciousness* (University of Pennsylvania Press, 1985).

RICHARD SEWALL. Professor emeritus of English at Yale University. Author of *The Life of Emily Dickinson* (Farrar, Straus and Giroux, 1974). Editor of *The Lyman Letters: New Light on Emily Dickinson and Her Family* (University of Massachusetts Press, 1965) and *Emily Dickinson: A Collection of Critical Essays* (Prentice-Hall, 1963).

MARTHA NELL SMITH. Professor of English at the University of Maryland, College Park. Author of *Rowing in Eden: Rereading Emily Dickinson* (University of Texas Press,

1992). Coauthor of *Comic Power in Emily Dickinson* (University of Texas Press, 1993) and *Open Me Carefully: Emily Dickinson's Intimate Letters to Susan Huntington Gilbert* (Paris, 1998). Coordinator of the Dickinson Electronic Archives Project. Currently completing *Life Before Last: Reminiscences of a Country Girl* (coedited autobiography of Martha Dickinson Bianchi).

GARY LEE STONUM. Professor of English at Case Western Reserve University. Author of *The Dickinson Sublime* (University of Wisconsin Press, 1990).

ROBERT WEISBUCH. President of the Woodrow Wilson National Fellowship Foundation and professor of English at the University of Michigan. Author of *Emily Dickinson's Poetry* (University of Chicago Press, 1975). Coeditor of *Emily Dickinson and Audience* (University of Michigan Press, 1997).

General Index

The titles of the works of the authors are abbreviated. See Works Cited for full indications.

Index of Poems

Poetry discussed is listed here by first line and number. In those cases where the text discusses poems without using their first line, a short phrase follows the page reference to link it to the text. An asterisk marks pages where a poem is quoted in full or discussed in detail.